DIRECT, DIGITAL & DATA-DRIVEN MARKETING

Lisa Spiller

DIRECT, DIGITAL & DATA-DRIVEN MARKETING

5th Edition

Los Angeles | London | New Delhi
Singapore | Washington DC | Melbourne

Los Angeles | London | New Delhi
Singapore | Washington DC | Melbourne

SAGE Publications Ltd
1 Oliver's Yard
55 City Road
London EC1Y 1SP

SAGE Publications Inc.
2455 Teller Road
Thousand Oaks, California 91320

SAGE Publications India Pvt Ltd
B 1/I 1 Mohan Cooperative Industrial Area
Mathura Road
New Delhi 110 044

SAGE Publications Asia-Pacific Pte Ltd
3 Church Street
#10-04 Samsung Hub
Singapore 049483

Editor: Matthew Waters
Assistant editor: Jasleen Kaur
Assistant editor, digital: Sunita Patel
Production editor: Nicola Carrier
Copyeditor: Sharon Cawood
Proofreader: Leigh C. Smithson
Indexer: Silvia Benvenuto
Marketing manager: Lucia Sweet
Cover design: Francis Kenney
Typeset by: C&M Digitals (P) Ltd, Chennai, India
Printed in the UK

First published as *Contemporary Direct Marketing* by Prentice Hall
in 2004. Second edition published in 2010. Third edition published
as *Contemporary Direct and Interactive Marketing* by Racom
Communications in 2012. Fourth edition published in 2018.

Library of Congress Control Number: 2019955360

British Library Cataloguing in Publication data

A catalogue record for this book is available from the British Library

ISBN 978-1-5297-0818-9
ISBN 978-1-5297-0817-2 (pbk)

At SAGE we take sustainability seriously. Most of our products are printed in the UK using responsibly sourced papers and
boards. When we print overseas we ensure sustainable papers are used as measured by the PREPS grading system. We
undertake an annual audit to monitor our sustainability.

DEDICATION

Martin Baier

Martin Baier, 1999

Direct marketing legend Martin Baier died on June 30, 2016. He was 93 years old. Martin was truly one of the founding fathers of the direct marketing field, and a staunch supporter and active contributor to direct marketing education nearly his entire professional life. His keen intellect and business vision, combined with his many significant intellectual contributions, will live on forever in our marketing discipline.

Martin helped define direct marketing and was a key figure in developing and expanding the direct marketing industry. He was known as the 'Father of Zip Code Marketing' after writing an article in 1967 for the *Harvard Business Review* entitled 'Zip Code: New Tool for Market Segmentation.'

Martin Baier authored or coauthored many seminal books on direct marketing during his lifetime. His *Elements of Direct Marketing*, published in 1983 by McGraw-Hill, was the first academic textbook on direct marketing. A Japanese edition of this text was published by Nikkei in Tokyo in 1985, and an international student edition was published in Singapore in 1986. Martin's *How to Find and Cultivate Customers through Direct Marketing* was published by NTC Business Books in 1996. *Contemporary Database Marketing: Concepts and Applications*, an interactive college textbook and CD, coauthored with Kurtis Ruf and Goutam Chakraborty, was published by Racom Books in 2001. Martin coauthored with Lisa Spiller the first edition of *Contemporary Direct Marketing*, released in 2004, and the second edition, *Contemporary Direct and Interactive Marketing*, released in 2009, both published by Prentice-Hall. Their third edition was published in 2012 by Racom Books.

Martin was recognized by his peers and received many awards for his achievements and contributions to the field. The Direct Marketing Educational Foundation, now known as Marketing EDGE, presented him its Ed Mayer Award, and the Direct Marketing Insurance Council named him Direct Marketing Insurance Executive of the Year, both in 1983. Martin was inducted into the Direct Marketing Association (DMA) Hall of Fame in 1989. The Mail Advertising Service Association honored him with its Miles Kimball Award in 1990. The Ed Sisk Award for Direct Marketing Vision was presented to him by the Direct Marketing Association of Washington Educational Foundation in 1994. The 1995 Andi Emerson Award for contribution of outstanding service to the direct marketing creative community was awarded to him by the Direct Marketing Creative Guild and the John Caples Awards Board. In 1995, he was elected International Fellow of the Institute of Direct Marketing (U.K.) in recognition of exceptional services to the profession. The New England Direct Marketing Association honored him with a Lifetime Achievement Award in 1996.

Martin was with Old American Insurance Company as Senior Executive and Vice President of Marketing for more than 25 years. After retiring in 1987 as executive vice president of the marketing group, he was a direct marketing consultant and educator. He founded the Center for Direct Marketing Education and Research in the Henry Bloch School of Business and Public Administration of the University of Missouri—Kansas City (UMKC), where he served for 25 years as adjunct professor. He created and taught a Professional Direct Marketer certification program at UMKC and traveled the world speaking at direct marketing conferences.

Martin consulted with a variety of organizations involved in adopting the discipline of direct marketing. He was affiliated with many professional organizations and is listed in *Who's Who in Finance and Industry* and *Who's Who in Advertising*. He taught direct marketing at many universities and conducted numerous seminars throughout the United States as well as in Europe, Australia, New Zealand, and Asia.

Martin's education included an MA in economics (1970), a BA in business administration (1943), and a BS in economics (1943)—all from UMKC.

Martin was an active and passionate member of both the Direct Marketing Association (now known as the Data & Marketing Association) and the Kansas City Direct Marketing Association. His passion for direct marketing was second only to his love for his family—his devoted wife Dorothy Baier; his daughter, Donna Baier Stein; his grandson, Jonathan Baier Stein; and granddaughter, Sarah Rachel Stein.

This book, *Direct, Digital & Data-Driven Marketing*, in both its fourth edition and the present edition, has been written with Martin Baier in my heart and on my mind. I hereby dedicate this text to him.

CONTENTS IN BRIEF

CONTENTS

PREFACE

Welcome to *Direct, Digital & Data-Driven Marketing*, the fifth edition of the book formerly titled *Contemporary Direct and Interactive Marketing*. Called '3D Marketing' for short, this new title is well suited to its contents as the book overviews the historical foundations of direct marketing, explores the present and future transformation of marketing relative to the explosion of digital marketing formats, and details the constant and consistent use of data to drive marketing strategies and activities. In essence, this book presents modern marketing concepts, strategies, tactics, formats, and activities, which have blossomed from the implementation of direct marketing methods.

The updated title is also consistent with other recent name changes in the direct marketing industry. In October 2016, the DMA rebranded itself by replacing 'direct' with 'data' in its name. DMA now stands for the Data & Marketing Association. This rebranding strategy showcases the fact that relevant customer data has always been the driver behind targeted marketing and customer relationship enhancement. Another name change occurred a few years earlier when the Direct Marketing Educational Foundation (DMEF) changed its name in 2013 to Marketing EDGE. EDGE is an acronym that represents the nonprofit organization's mission: to Educate, Develop, Grow, and Employ college students in the field of marketing. Thus, the new title of this book, *Direct, Digital & Data-Driven Marketing* ('3D Marketing'), appropriately reflects the multi-dimensional aspects of this dynamic field as it continues to transform and becomes increasingly relevant in today's modern business world. Direct marketing is truly multi-faceted and three-dimensional, given the many mediums and channels used to engage with consumers today.

Just as with previous editions, this book was written to help you understand the theories behind modern '3D marketing' and to learn how to apply these theories in your classes and in your career. In other courses, you may have studied psychology and human behavior, the basics of advertising, communications theory, and practice, and even accounting. In this book, you will see how these, and many more disciplines, converge in the field of direct marketing to form a discipline that changes with time but is always creative, useful, and even fun! When reading the following chapters, I hope you will be able to apply many concepts you have already studied and learn how they are essential to successful marketing. I also hope that, as you consider your career, whether in marketing or a related field, you will have found it helpful to understand how so many activities we all undertake daily are affected by direct, digital, and data-driven marketing. In some sense, we are all marketers and consumers, and we all become involved in the techniques of modern marketing. Decades ago, direct marketers gathered customer names and addresses, created mailing lists, established relationships with customers, and sold goods and services on a one-on-one basis to customers via mail and telephone. Today, modern marketers are still concerned with gathering information and creating relationships with each customer in order to maximize customer value and personalize the customer experience, but customer databases and digital, social, mobile, and text message media have dramatically changed the speed and effectiveness of these activities. More and more companies and organizations are using the concepts of direct, digital, and data-driven marketing as their primary methods for business transactions.

This fifth edition recognizes the growth of various digital marketing formats as the newest interactive channels for conducting modern marketing today. Although digital, mobile, and social media marketing channels are similar to direct mail in that they target messages on a personal one-on-one basis with great precision and effectiveness, they do so with much greater speed of transmission and enable both immediate customer response and excellent measurability and analysis. Today's consumers desire both the speed and the control that the digital, social, and mobile media formats provide. Marketers must include these important mediums in their marketing campaigns. Direct marketing has always been accountable and measurable. Now, with the various digital media formats and computer technology, it is more interactive and precise than ever before. The fifth edition builds on the traditional foundations of direct marketing that are still applicable today, and it extends into the future where constant digital innovations continue to transform the marketing landscape. The new media of yesterday have become mainstream media today. We cannot begin to envision what changes are ahead. But one thing is certain: traditional direct and data-driven marketing principles will still apply. This latest edition builds on these traditional foundations, captures the new media and methods, and explores the future innovations of modern marketing.

USING THIS BOOK

This fifth edition of *Direct, Digital & Data-Driven Marketing* contains the following four major sections:

1. Build, Develop, and Measure Direct Marketing Strategies
2. Create and Place Direct Marketing Campaigns
3. Serve and Adapt to Customers and Markets
4. Applications, Examples, and Careers in Direct Marketing

Individual chapters within these major sections deal with such subjects as database marketing and customer relationship management; developing lists and profiling customers; testing, measuring, and analyzing campaigns; planning value propositions; creating compelling message and media strategies; fulfilling the offer; serving the customer; understanding environmental, ethical, and legal issues; exploring international strategies; and applying direct marketing. Each chapter includes a chapter outline, key terms, end-of-chapter summaries, review questions, exercises, readings and resources and cases. The material does not progress from easy to difficult, but it does progress logically from introduction to application. To be successful in any course, you must read each chapter carefully and outline key concepts along the way. The chapter spotlight for each chapter will give you a real-world example that provides a sense of what that chapter will address. Read the chapter spotlight prior to the chapter. Each chapter also contains state-of-the-art modern marketing content, many photos and images, and numerous applications and examples to drive home important concepts. The discussion questions at the end of each chapter will assist you in reviewing the important concepts and the mini exercises will enable you to critically think about and apply the chapter's content. Be sure to explore the four appendices that are designed to contribute to your marketing education and help you during your college years and beyond. Keep your eyes and ears open to the marketing world around you and you will be able to easily understand and apply the concepts, strategies, tools, and techniques of direct marketing that have become mainstream marketing in today's world.

ACKNOWLEDGMENTS

Lisa Spiller & Martin Baier, 1999

As the author, I am personally responsible for this comprehensive text; however, I must acknowledge the valuable input and assistance from many individuals. I am especially grateful to the following people who surrounded me, motivated me, put up with me, and contributed very valuable information to select chapters of this textbook:

Huge thanks to Dr. Matt Sauber and David Marold, both of Eastern Michigan University, for coauthoring the business-to-business chapter with me and for updating their 'Domino's Pizza: Growing Sales with Technology' comprehensive case. Extra thanks to Dave Marold for coauthoring the new Direct and Digital Marketing Campaign Proposal Guide featured in Appendix D.

Sincere gratitude goes to Dr. Carol Scovotti, University of Wisconsin–Whitewater, for coauthoring the international chapter with me. In addition, much appreciation to Freddy Rosales, Universidad de CEMA, Argentina, for contributing the 'Coca-Cola in Peru' case for the International chapter.

A great deal of thanks to Dr. Dae-Hee Kim, Christopher Newport University, for his many valuable contributions to the Marketing Analytics chapter, and for his insight and advice on other chapters as well. Also, special thanks to Susan Jones, Ferris State University, for contributing the new and expanded catalog section in the Print Media chapter.

Genuine appreciation to Dr. Tracy Tuten, University of Michigan, for her inspiration and support, very valuable insight and assistance regarding much of the revision content for this current edition, coauthoring the new Appendix C on Branded Digital Marketing Certification Programs, and her contribution of many of the new Readings and Resources provided at the end of each chapter.

I am sincerely indebted to the many business professionals who kindly assisted in providing valuable input, case and spotlight information and textbook examples for this fifth edition. These include:

- Tyler Baesman, Jeff Sopko, Evan Magliocca, and Brian Garner, Baesman Group, Inc.
- Breeze Holmgren, Bloomin
- Nadine Drath, Doctors Without Borders/Médecins Sans Frontières (MSF)
- Debbie McNeil and Wendy Werner, DuPont
- Yumi Lawlor, Instacart
- Rick Pallen, Johnson Controls Security Solutions
- Mike Lasher, Siegmund Brundl, Roberto Gallegos, Mike Luksatich and Bente Hughes, Mike's Bike Tours
- Joe Psych, NextMark
- Russ and Rebekah Tinsley, Oozlefinch Craft Brewery
- Liz Lacey and Bella Nguyen, Pandora

- Lori Barnett and Kristina Pontillo, PepsiCo
- Carrie Schweikart, Quad
- TJ Blease, Uber

Many of the valuable contributions of business professionals to previous editions of the text have continued to enhance the fifth edition. Those contributors included: Dan Caro and Faith Albers, both of Whereoware, for their excellent work on each of their client features (Evergreen, Interlude, Sullivans, and Mud Pie), and for their valuable contributions to the Careers Appendix. To Dan Dipiazzo and Andrew Scogna, formerly of Busch Gardens/Water Country USA, for their many outstanding real-world examples that appear in several chapters throughout the textbook.

Special appreciation to Elizabeth Baumann, Lids; Will Blanton, Snow Companies; Senny Boone, Data & Marketing Association (DMA); LaRhonda Burley, The Washington Redskins; Corrina Ferguson, Greater Williamsburg Chamber & Tourism Alliance; Amy Hart, Hauser's Jewelers; Nicole Hoadley, Snow Companies; Michael Kimball, Williamsburg Winery; Bill Leber, Swisslog Logistics; Muriel Millar, Fear 2 Freedom; Herbie Morewitz, ChirpXM; Leslie Sink, Hi-Ho Silver; Rosemary Trible, Fear 2 Freedom; Judy Triska, Virginia Living Museum; and Sylvia Weinstein, *Oyster Pointer*.

I remain grateful to Dr. Elizabeth Young, who coauthored the 'Testing, Measuring, and Analyzing Customers and Campaigns' chapter; Dave Marold of Eastern Michigan University for his networking assistance and his contributions in coauthoring several of the end-of-chapter cases; Dr. Matt Sauber of Eastern Michigan University for his contributions to several end-of-chapter cases and select chapter material; Charles George for his contributions to the 'Mobile, Text, and Telephone' and 'Digital and Social Media' chapters; and the talented and dedicated people at The Martin Agency for the agency feature in Appendix A, for their contributions to and assistance with Appendix B and several opening vignettes and cases featuring their clients.

I continue to appreciate the contributions of Chuck Applebach, formerly of the Virginia Beach Convention & Visitors Bureau; Greg Ward and Justine Thompson of BCF Boom Your Brand; Kurt Ruf, Ruf Strategic Solutions; Joe Pych, NextMark; Ruthie Keefe, BlueSky Creative, Inc.; Florence Camenzind and Mark Honeyball, Chevrolet Europe; Mary Eckenrode and Denise Meine-Graham, Cheryl's; Michael Sparling, 1-800-FLOWERS.com; Mike Simmons and Ken Gammage, Directed Electronics; Vicki Rowland, formerly of the Peninsula SPCA; Janel Mootrey and Lisa Mihalcik, Zappos.com, Inc.; Amber Nettles, *The Daily Press*; Elizabeth Baran, DICK's Sporting Goods, Inc.; Jenelle Allemon, Domino's Pizza; Ted Ward, GEICO; Jody Wagner and Anne Walsh, Jody's Popcorn; Deanna Williams, Macy's Inc.; Karen Rice Gardiner, formerly of the National Geographic Society; Carrie Schweikart, QuadDirect; David Noonan, Mountain Gear; Jessica Wharton, Newport News/ Williamsburg International Airport (PHF); Peter Samuel, PING; Sandra Jarvis, Peace Frogs, Inc.; Chris Mainz, Southwest Airlines; Roger Phelps and Cama Poffenberger, STIHL, Inc.; Matt White, White & Partners; and Wendy Weber, Crandall Associates.

I am truly grateful for the outstanding professional communication assistance, administrative support, and close friendship of Clare Maliniak, the ongoing secretarial support of Teresa Tornari, and the valuable media assistance and contributions of Johnnie Gray, all of Christopher Newport University (CNU).

I also recognize and appreciate the research assistance of several former CNU students: Raegan Hasty and Zachary Smith, for their valuable research work on many of the chapter updates for this fifth edition text. In addition, thanks to Alexa Hladlick for her case research work.

I would like to continue to recognize former CNU students who assisted with previous textbook editions, as much of their work remains relevant in the current edition. Thanks to Dana Nissel, Morgan Garner, Kacie Melton, Sarah Wallace, Kate Earle, and Samantha Rabinek. Also, my continued thanks to my niece, Amanda Lee, for her work on the fourth edition as well.

I am so sincerely blessed to have two of my family members, daughter Suzanne, and son Jack, pitch in and provide thoughtful reviews and contributions to this textbook edition, and, of course, to have an amazing and compassionate husband throughout the entire book revision process.

I extend genuine gratitude to the wonderful and supportive people at SAGE Publishing, including Matthew Waters (Senior Commissioning Editor), Jasleen Kaur (Assistant Editor), Sunita Patel (Assistant Editor, Digital), Nicola Carrier (Production Editor), Sharon Cawood (Copyeditor) and Leigh Smithson (Proofreader).

I am extremely grateful to the following colleagues for their thoughtful reviews and recommendations regarding the fifth edition content and structure:

- Dae-Hee Kim, Christopher Newport University
- Susan Jones, Ferris State University
- Dina Vees, California Polytechnic State University
- Dr Ofer Dekel Dachs, de Montford University
- Raymond Yang, British Columbia Institute of Technology

Many reviewers at various institutions provided valuable comments and suggestions for this and the previous editions. I am grateful to the following colleagues for their thoughtful inputs and recommendations:

Fourth Edition Reviewers

- Susan Jones, Ferris State University
- Dae-Hee Kim, Christopher Newport University
- Harvey Markovitz, Pace University
- Dave Marold, Eastern Michigan University
- Matt Sauber, Eastern Michigan University
- Carol Scovotti, University of Wisconsin–Whitewater

Third Edition Reviewers

- Janel Bell, Alabama State University
- Shawn Grain Carter, Fashion Institute of Technology
- John Cronin, Western Connecticut State University
- Susan Jones, Ferris State University
- Eric Larson, Villanova University
- Harvey Markovitz, Pace University
- Dave Marold, Eastern Michigan University

- Henry Greene, Central Connecticut University
- Jack Mandel, Nassau Community College

Second Edition Reviewers

- Robert M. Cosenza, University of Mississippi
- Dale Lewison, University of Akron
- Mark A. Neckes, Johnson and Wales University
- Carol Scovotti, University of Wisconsin–Whitewater

First Edition Reviewers

- Dennis B. Arnett, Texas Tech University
- Bruce C. Bailey, Otterbein College
- Dave Blackmore, University of Pittsburgh at Bradford
- Deborah Y. Cohn, Yeshiva University
- John J. Cronin, Western Connecticut State University
- Wenyu Dou, University of Nevada–Las Vegas
- F. Robert Dwyer, University of Cincinnati
- James S. Gould, Pace University
- Richard A. Hamilton, University of Missouri–Kansas City
- Susan K. Harmon, Middle Tennessee State University
- Sreedhar Kavil, St. John's University
- Barry Langford, Florida Gulf Coast University
- Marilyn Lavin, University of Wisconsin–Whitewater
- Paula M. Saunders, Wright State University
- Donald Self, Auburn University–Montgomery
- Carmen Sunda, University of New Orleans
- William Trombetta, St. Joseph's University
- Ugur Yucelt, Penn State Harrisburg

Finally, I am humbled to recognize the dramatic influence and impact the legendary direct marketing guru Martin Baier, coauthor of the first three editions of this textbook, has had on my writing both the fourth and current editions. In 1984, Martin and I met at the University of Missouri–Kansas City, where he taught the graduate direct marketing classes and I taught the undergraduate direct marketing classes. The rest is history ... and our years of teaching experience and knowledge of direct marketing have been captured in earlier versions of this text. Our friendship lasted decades and I am forever grateful to him for believing in me and asking me to coauthor the first edition of this textbook with him back in 1999. We made a synergistic team right from the start, as the photo from 1999 portrays. This fifth edition textbook stems from my deep passion for higher education in marketing, and especially in direct, digital, and data-driven marketing, which was first sparked when I met Martin Baier.

Lisa Spiller

ABOUT THE AUTHOR

Lisa D. Spiller, PhD

Dr. Lisa Spiller is distinguished professor of marketing in the Joseph W. Luter III School of Business at Christopher Newport University (CNU) in Newport News, Virginia. She has been teaching marketing courses to undergraduate business students for more than 30 years and has helped her university pioneer a major in direct marketing. Dr. Spiller's marketing students won the coveted Collegiate Gold ECHO Award from the Direct Marketing Association (DMA), now known as the Data & Marketing Association, in 2003, 2005, 2007 and 2011; they won the Collegiate Silver ECHO Award in 2002. Her students also received the Gold Collegiate Marketing Award for Excellence and Innovation (MAXI) from the Direct Marketing Association of Washington Educational Foundation (DMAW-EF) in 2004, 2005, 2006, 2007, 2009, 2011 and 2014; the Collegiate Silver MAXI Award in 2002, 2003, 2010 and 2017; and the Guy Yolton Creative Direct Mail Award in 2002, 2004, 2005, 2007 and 2009.

Dr. Spiller was named the Robert B. Clark Outstanding Direct Marketing Educator in 2005 by the Direct Marketing Educational Foundation (DMEF), now known as Marketing EDGE. She was the inaugural recipient of the DMAW-EF O'Hara Leadership Award for Direct Marketing Education in 2008. Professor Spiller has received numerous awards for her teaching, including the inaugural CNU Alumni Society Faculty Award for Excellence in Teaching and Mentoring in 2007; Faculty Advisor Leader Awards from the Direct Marketing Educational Foundation (DMEF) in 2002, 2003, 2005, 2007 and 2011; a Distinguished Teaching Award in 1997 from the DMEF; and the Elmer P. Pierson Outstanding Teacher Award in 1987 from the University of Missouri–Kansas City. Her research studies, the majority of which have been related to some aspect of direct, digital, and database marketing, have been published in numerous journals. Dr. Spiller served on the Abstract Editorial Board of the *Journal of Interactive Marketing* for ten years, was an Academic Representative on the DMEF Board of Trustees for two years, and was a member of the Academic Advisory Board of the DMAW-EF for more than a decade.

Dr. Spiller received her B.S.B.A. and M.B.A. degrees from Gannon University and her Ph.D. from the University of Missouri–Kansas City. Prior to joining academia, she held positions as a marketing director with an international company and an account executive with an advertising agency. Through the years, she has served as a marketing consultant to many organizations. Dr. Spiller possesses a true passion for teaching and has been a strong advocate of direct marketing education throughout her entire academic career.

Dr. Spiller resides in Newport News, Virginia, with her husband of 30 years, James Spiller. Together they have three children, Suzanne, Chad, and Jack; a daughter-in-law, Kailey; and two adorable grandchildren, Jaxson and Harper.

ONLINE RESOURCES

Direct, Digital & Data-Driven Marketing 5e is supported by a wealth of online resources for both students and lecturers to help support learning and teaching. These resources are available at: **https://study.sagepub.com/spiller5e**

FOR LECTURERS

- **Support** your teaching each week by using **PowerPoint slides** prepared by the author for each chapter.
- **Encourage discussion** in class by making use of the comprehensive **case study teaching notes** provided.
- **Test understanding** with the **essay questions** that accompany each chapter.
- Help students **apply their knowledge** by using the Appendix D **marketing campaign samples** to aid in the creation of their own marketing strategies.

FOR STUDENTS

- **Revise** everything you've learnt with the **multiple-choice questions** provided for each chapter.

PART 1

Build, Develop, and Measure Direct Marketing Strategies

1

PROCESSES AND APPLICATIONS OF DIRECT MARKETING

CHAPTER CONTENTS

CHAPTER SPOTLIGHT

PEACE FROGS

Like most college students, Catesby Jones needed some extra cash, so he decided to create beach volleyball shorts to sell around campus at the University of Virginia. He wanted an unusual design that would appeal to his target market, so he arranged an eye-catching assortment of national flags all over the boxer shorts. To put flair into his design, Catesby added a frog holding two digits in the air, forming a peace sign. After receiving numerous orders, he began manufacturing and selling the unique shorts from his dorm room. Soon, he began selling other items featuring the creative peace-signing frog, such as the T-shirt featured in Figure 1.1.

Figure 1.1   Peace Frogs Hope T-shirt. Used with permission of Peace Frogs, Inc.

Catesby saw the potential in his creation, so he and a few buddies decided to place a $15,000 direct marketing advertisement in *Rolling Stone* magazine. The advertisement generated a total of 1,000 orders. By the time Catesby had finished his degree in international relations, he was already four years into what would become his passion and a very successful business.

Peace Frogs began to dispense products through multichannel distribution, using a mail-order catalog, retail stores–company-owned and licensed (from wholesale to department stores and specialty retailers)–and on the Internet at www.peacefrogs.com (see Figure 1.2). These channels allowed the company to distribute its products to a vast number of consumers and save resources through cross-marketing. They also helped create brand recognition and loyalty because the consumer could see the merchandise at many different outlets.

Figure 1.2   Peace Frogs Web page. Used with permission of Peace Frogs, Inc.

Now a million-dollar company, Peace Frogs operates a 37,000-square-foot distribution center at its home office in Gloucester, Virginia. This multipurpose facility houses Peace Frogs's merchandise, ordering systems, and a retail store. The 25 employees who work in the distribution center try to ensure that customers are completely satisfied.

The company not only has unique clothing, it has also found a distinctive way to distribute merchandise–by psychedelically painted VW vans driving the roads and highways of the United States. Peace Frogs chose this vehicle, shown in Figure 1.3, both as a means of transportation and as a marketing statement, a representation of 'reliability and freedom.' As it did with its products, the company has taken something ordinary and transformed it into a unique message that leaves a distinct impression and has a positive impact on its customers. The peace frog and its related 'positively peaceful thinking' message have become a significant symbol to which many can relate.

PEACE FROGS VW VAN STORE

Van Size:
Length - 16'
Width - 7'
Height - 6'5"

Peace Frogs uses customized VW vans from the late 1960s and early 1970s as retail merchandising units to sell its line of distinctive sportswear and accessories. This award-winning marketing concept has been placed in major amusement parks, malls and retail stores.

1-800-44-PEACE

Visit our Homepage @ www.peacefrogs.com

P.O. Box 137
White Marsh, Virginia 23183

Figure 1.3 Peace Frogs van. Used with permission of Peace Frogs, Inc.

The company's line now includes T-shirts, sweatshirts, hats, boxer shorts, lounge pants, jewelry, accessories, and school supplies. In the process of building a business through direct marketing, Catesby Jones showed that with dedication and hard work, and by daring to be a little different, people can make an impact.

THE SCOPE OF DIRECT MARKETING

Find us on Facebook! Send us a Tweet!

Follow us on Snapchat! View our Instagrams! Pin this now!

Connect with us on LinkedIn! Watch us on YouTube!

Check out what's trending!

Figure 1.4   Social media logos and icons

Note: The logos and icons shown in this figure are owned by the following companies: Facebook Inc., Twitter, Inc., Snap Inc., LinkedIn Corporation, Google, Inc., and Pinterest, Inc.

Visit our website! Click here! Text this number now! Call this toll-free number! Complete the bottom portion of this mailer and return it in the enclosed postage-paid envelope! Clip this coupon and visit our store! The use of direct marketing in today's business world is booming! Direct marketing is now at the center of the communications revolution and is being used by businesses, organizations, associations, and individuals across the world with great fervor.

Long ago, Roland Rust and Richard Oliver foretold the rise of direct marketing at the expense of traditional advertising. They claimed:

> Mass media advertising as we know it today is on its deathbed. Advertising . . . agencies are restructuring to accommodate a harsher advertising reality, direct marketing is stealing business away from traditional advertising, and the growth of sales promotion and integrated marketing communications both come at the expense of traditional advertising.[1]

Practitioners and scholars suggest that a paradigm shift in marketing, fueled by the growth in the use of direct marketing techniques, is under way. New digital and social media marketing developments are dramatically changing how marketers create and communicate customer value. Today's marketers must know how to leverage new information, communication, and distribution technologies to connect more effectively with customers in this digital age.[2] For many companies, direct marketing—especially in its most recent transformation, digital marketing, including mobile and social networking—constitutes a complete business model. This new direct model is quickly changing the way companies think about building relationships with customers.[3]

Direct marketing has literally transformed the way marketers engage with consumers today and the manner by which people purchase products and services. New digital technologies have put nearly everything at the tip of consumers' fingers. With a few taps on their digital devices, they can do almost anything! Need groceries? Tap. Want to order flowers for your mother? Tap. Want to vote on your favorite brand? Tap. Want to enjoy a certain type of music? Tap. Want to check on an order that you recently placed? Tap. Etc.! Direct marketing has enabled consumers to enjoy a plethora of modern conveniences and the trend is bound to continue in the future.

Today, direct marketing is a fundamental marketing tool in a growing variety of businesses. Direct marketing grew faster than almost every other marketing activity in the latter part of the twentieth century.[4] Total U.S. spending on digital advertising in 2018 was $39.1 billion.[5] Future predictions indicate that digital advertisement spending will continue to steadily increase over the coming years, and digital ads are expected to comprise two-thirds of all advertisement spending by 2023.[6] These statistics strongly suggest that direct marketing is becoming an integral element in the marketing manager's arsenal worldwide. The economic impact of direct marketing is simply mind-boggling! With this much emphasis being placed on direct marketing, it is important to understand what it is and how it is used.

CHARACTERISTICS AND GROWTH OF DIRECT MARKETING

Despite its growth, there is no universal agreement about exactly what direct marketing is. Both practitioners and academicians grapple with a contemporary conceptual definition. Unquestionably, the concept known as direct marketing continues to evolve. However, its definition provides a framework from which we can improve our understanding and determine the critical elements of its process. The definition you are about to read is the result of years of scholarly research involving a content analysis of direct marketing definitions published in direct marketing, principles of marketing, integrated marketing communication, and advertising textbooks.[7]

Definition and Description

Direct marketing is a database-driven interactive process of directly communicating with targeted customers or prospects using any medium to obtain a measurable response or transaction via one or multiple channels. This definition identifies database, interactivity, direct communications, target customers, measurable response, and one or multiple channels as key dimensions in direct marketing activities. Two concepts commonly used to describe forms of direct marketing are interactive marketing and digital marketing. **Interactive marketing** implies two-way communications between the marketer and the prospective customer. Interactive marketing employs one-on-one communication tactics to enhance personal customer relationships. Marketers focus on adapting to the needs and wants of consumers when implementing interactive marketing. **Digital marketing** is the process of using technology and its full capabilities to communicate seamlessly with consumers through the Internet and technological devices. Direct marketing possesses unique characteristics, including each of the following:

- customer/prospect databases that make one-to-one targeting possible
- a view of customers as assets with lifetime value
- ongoing relationships and affinity with customers
- data-based market segmentation
- research and precise experimentation (testing)
- benefit-oriented direct-response advertising
- measurement of results and accountability for costs
- interactivity with customers on a personalized, individualized basis
- multimedia direct-response communication
- multichannel fulfillment and distribution.

Direct marketing is *database-driven* marketing. It is a process, a discipline, a strategy, a philosophy, an attitude, a collection of tools and techniques. In summary, its goal is to *create* and *cultivate* customers, regardless of whether these customers are themselves consumers, buyers for industrial organizations, or potential donors or voters. It is a way to market a for-profit business or a not-for-profit organization. Its principles apply to marketing activities targeting both business consumers, business-to-business (B2B) and final consumers, business-to-consumer (B2C). Today, direct marketing is being used by many traditional brand advertisers, and many experts believe that all marketing is converging.

The Convergence of Direct and Brand Marketing

Historically, direct marketing and traditional brand marketing were two separate disciplines. **Brand marketing** was mass marketing, and direct marketing was niche marketing. Brand marketers primarily used newspapers and broadcast media (television and radio) to get products or services recognized and preferred by masses of consumers. Direct marketers, in contrast, predominantly used direct mail and catalogs with customized offers designed for individual customers to motivate a specific response that could be tracked and measured to determine its effectiveness and resulting sales. Table 1.1 outlines the inherent differences between these two disciplines.

The clear distinction between direct marketing and brand marketing has blurred with the digital revolution. Most companies now have a virtual storefront in the form of a website. Companies have the ability to store, track, and target information about consumers like never before. Direct marketing strategies, such as displaying URLs, toll-free numbers, e-mail addresses, and calls to action, have found their way into TV and radio spots, print ads, mobile ads, as well as text messages, websites, e-mails, blogs, social networks, online video games, and almost every other type of media. Direct marketing's versatility, measurability, and undeniable return on investment

Table 1.1   Differences between direct marketing and traditional brand marketing

Direct marketing	Traditional marketing
Direct selling to individuals with customers identifiable by name, address, and purchase behavior	Mass selling with buyers identified as broad groups sharing common demographic and psychographic characteristics
Products have the added value of distribution direct to the customer, an important benefit	Product benefits do not typically include distribution to the customer's door
The medium is the marketplace	The retail outlet is the marketplace
Marketing controls the product all the way through delivery	The marketer typically loses control as the product enters the distribution channel
Advertising is used to generate an immediate transaction, an inquiry, or an order	Advertising is used for cumulative effect over time for building image, awareness, loyalty, and benefit recall; purchase action is deferred
Repetition of offers, promotional messages, toll-free numbers, and Web addresses is used within the advertisement	Repetition of offers and promotional messages is used over a period of time
Customer feels a high perceived risk–product bought unseen and recourse is distant	Customer feels less risk–has direct contact with the product and direct recourse

have gradually garnered the respect of even the most traditional brand advertisers and agencies.[8] Direct marketers are also recognizing the importance of creating and reinforcing brand strategies at the individual level. Therefore, direct marketing and brand strategies are now viewed as complementary, and when applied correctly, they can create a synergistic marketing effect. Although these two disciplines have come from vastly different origins, they are indeed converging, with many companies recognizing the value of their combined marketing strategies.

Today, direct marketing is used by virtually every organization in every sector, including political, governmental, nonprofit, and sports. Its history is rich, and its future is seemingly unlimited!

Factors Affecting the Growth of Direct Marketing

The first mail-order catalogs are said to have appeared in Europe in the mid-fifteenth century, soon after Johann Gutenberg's invention of movable type.[9] There is record of a gardening catalog, the predecessor of today's colorful seed and nursery catalogs, issued by William Lucas, an English gardener, in 1667. From these beginnings there followed a proliferation of catalogs during the post-Civil War period when agrarian unrest, through the National Grange (the oldest American agricultural advocacy group), fueled the popular slogan 'eliminate the middleman.' Then, as now, mail-order catalogs reflected social and economic change.

While mail-order merchandise catalogs were becoming more accepted, new cultural, social, and economic phenomena were breeding another form of mail order, via standalone direct mail pieces. Further enhancing the growth of direct marketing, during the 1960s and to this day, has been the increasing availability of advertising media (other than direct mail) suitable for direct-response advertising, especially those geared to highly defined market segments. The same evolution has been occurring in the broadcast media, television, and radio, through special cable programming geared to market segments, along with the convenience of toll-free telephone calling. The phone itself has become another major medium for direct marketers, enhanced by cellular and wireless technologies. The Internet has surely changed the way most consumers make purchases and the way most companies conduct business today. Virtually all companies and organizations not only have a website, but are actively employing interactive digital marketing strategies, including blogging, search engine marketing (SEM), online social networking, and mobile and text marketing.

The social and economic changes that have given impetus to the burgeoning rise of direct marketing since the mid-twentieth century have been coupled with equally impressive advances in the technology used in various elements of direct marketing. A few of these technological and social advances are worth mentioning.

Printing Technology

The versatility of laser printing, personalization of inkjet printing, advances in press technology, and computerized typesetting are important examples of how the printing process is becoming more conducive to the demassification of the printed word. Desk-top publishing enables businesses to create newsletters, brochures, and other print materials that can have a highly professional look at a fraction of former costs. Graphic capabilities have also taken major strides. Compare, for example, the carnival cover design of the 1976 Oriental Trading Company catalog with its 2008 carnival catalog cover design, shown in Figure 1.5. Indeed, much has changed!

Credit Cards

Since the advent of credit cards during the 1950s, there has been enormous growth of mail order as a selling method. Credit cards greatly enhanced and expedited transactions, which up to that time had been mainly cash or check with order. The ready availability of worldwide credit systems, together with rapid electronic funds transfer, has contributed to the feasibility and viability of direct marketing by simultaneously offering convenience and security.

Personal Computers

Personal computers have made possible the record-keeping, work operation, and model building that are so much a part of the art and science of direct marketing. The complex maintenance of lists and the retrieval of data associated with them are just two examples of the computer's contribution. Of course, the use of highly sophisticated analysis can mean the difference between direct marketing success and failure.

Figure 1.5 Oriental Trading catalog covers. Used with permission of Oriental Trading Company.

Changing Consumer Lifestyles

As travel becomes more expensive and communication becomes less expensive, there is further impetus to the use of mail, telephone, and Internet. Mailed catalogs, websites, and toll-free telephone numbers provide the convenience of shopping from home. Furthermore, as more women have entered the workforce, families are placing a greater emphasis on time utilization. Once a leisurely pastime, shopping has become more of a chore, especially for the majority of households in which both spouses work. The advent of mail order and the Web has made anytime day-or-night shopping even more convenient for these working spouses.

Negative Aspects of Retailing

Many consumers enjoy shopping in traditional retail stores. However, there is a strong belief that traditional retail shopping has a number of negative aspects associated with it. Some of these include inadequate parking facilities; concerns about safety; long walking distances; uninformed sales clerks; difficulties in locating retail sales personnel; long waiting lines at check-out; in-store congestion; difficulty in locating certain sizes, styles, or colors of products; and the hassle of juggling packages out of the retail stores. For these consumers, direct marketing, with all of its modern methods and conveniences, has been a welcome alternative.

The foregoing social and technological factors have served not only to popularize the use of direct marketing over the years, but also to affect the way direct marketing activities are carried out today. If the logic of direct marketing has become the logic of all marketing, its process must be explored and mastered. Let's investigate the process involved in conducting direct marketing.

THE PROCESSES OF DIRECT MARKETING

Direct marketing guru Edward Nash once said:

> Direct marketing is somewhat like laser surgery: a powerful, precise, and very effective tool in the hands of professionals, but a potential disaster in the hands of amateurs. We must approach it as if we are surgeons, not butchers, as if we are cabinetmakers, not carpenters.[10]

The process of direct marketing is presented in the model shown in Figure 1.6. This model is parallel to the definition of direct marketing provided earlier in this chapter. The model recognizes the importance of responses that are measurable and the value of customer data in driving direct marketing strategies. It also encompasses the strategic use of multiple channels—a topic that is of emerging importance to direct marketers.

First and foremost, direct marketing activities are based on their historical foundations. Inherent to the effectiveness of the direct marketing process is the constant focus on customers. Customers are the lifeblood of an organization.[11] Enterprise thrives on customers. They are the reason for its existence. The creation and cultivation of customers is what direct marketing is all about. Much has been written in recent times about **customer relationship management (CRM)**. We examine *interactive customer relationships* as well as the related subjects of customer affinity and loyalty, pointing to the need for determining the lifetime value of a customer in greater detail in Chapters 2, 4 and 12.

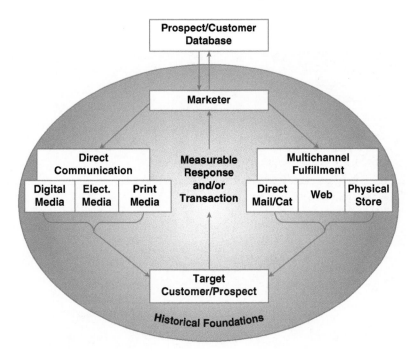

Figure 1.6 Direct marketing model

Source: Model created by Lisa Spiller and Carol Scovotti. Used with permission.

Although new media like the Internet change the mechanism by which direct marketing activities are performed, its cornerstone—database-driven direct-response communications—remains in effect today. In addition, the quality of the targeted list or database segment is critical to direct marketing success. That success is determined by measuring response rates. The formula for success remains constant—reaching the *right* people with the *right* offer using the *right* creative approach. Now let's detail the process of direct marketing.

Here is a brief overview of the direct marketing process. The marketer sends out a customized direct-response communication via any type of medium to customers or prospective customers on the basis of the information the marketer has about that customer or prospect. In the case of prospecting efforts, because customer data do not yet exist in the company's database, the company often rents a list of prospective customers based on specific selection criteria. The targeted customer or prospect receives that communication and responds directly to the company or organization via multiple channel options. The customer response, which could take many different forms (inquiry, transaction, donation, visit, vote, etc.), is entered into the company database and is processed. Once processed, the customer's response is fulfilled and delivery of the requested product, service, or information is provided directly to that customer. Then, the entire process begins again with the direct marketer using the data contained in its database to distribute more customized messages to select recipients and the process continues. Let's examine each component of the process in greater detail.

Figure 1.7   BlueSky personalized advertisement. Used with permission of BlueSky Creative, Inc.

Direct Communication 1:1

The goal of direct marketers is to interact with customers on a one-to-one basis, with reference to the information obtained and stored about each customer in the customer database. Direct marketers then provide the customer with information and product/service offers that are relevant to each customer's needs and wants. This, too, is different from the activities of traditional marketers, who normally attempt to communicate with customers on a mass or segmented basis but not normally on a personal, individual basis. Direct marketers actively seek out and identify those target customers to whom they will connect and send a catalog or some follow-up correspondence. An example of the personalization in direct marketing can be seen in the advertisement featured in Figure 1.7.

Given the rise of digital, social, mobile and text marketing, communicating with customers on an individual basis is common these days. One of the latest technological innovations to enable interactive communication on a one-to-one basis with customers and/or potential customers is the geo-tag or geo-location identifier. Geo-tagging basically implies that your physical location is registered from your mobile device's GPS or your computer's IP address. With geo-tags, marketers are able to target relevant communications to customers based on geographic location. For example, let's say you are driving in your car and you are nearing a mall where one of your favorite shoe stores is located. All of a sudden that shoe store pings you through its mobile app with a special sale offer on a specific brand of shoes that you just so happen to have purchased in the past. That's the power of marketing via geo-tagging.

In addition to geo-tagging, NFC mobile marketing is another relatively new avenue for marketers to enable their brands to connect with targeted customers. NFC stands for near field communications, which are communications via short-range wireless technology that makes use of interacting electromagnetic radio fields. NFC tags or chips have the power to convert all forms of print media, including posters, business cards, retail displays, signs, product packaging, direct mail, etc., into interactive and measureable marketing tools. Marketers are able to print NFC tags or place NFC stickers on any promotional marketing collateral. Once in place, the NFC tag will also effectively track analytics and generate valuable data for enhancing a company's customer database. More will be discussed on both geo-tags and NFC technology later, in Chapter 9 (on the use of mobile, text, and telephone for marketing), as these communication platforms are used primarily with mobile devices.

Multiple Media

While direct mail and direct-response advertising are items within the historical foundations, direct marketing is not dependent on any one medium. In fact, it demonstrates that many media may be used to directly communicate with prospects and customers. Thus, media are basically placed into three categories: high-tech, electronic, and print. High-tech media include Internet, e-mail, search engines, blogs, online social networking, mobile marketing, text messaging, and whatever new digital formats emerge in the future. This dimension stresses the importance of interactivity and acknowledges that direct marketing will continue to evolve with technological advances. In addition to the Internet, practitioners also consider electronic media like telemarketing and direct-response television to be powerful vehicles for directly communicating with customers. Print media, such as newspapers, magazines, brochures, flyers, catalogs, and mail order, are media options for direct marketing practitioners.

Measurable Response

The single most notable differentiating feature of direct marketing is that it always seeks to generate a *measurable response*. This response can take the form of an order, an inquiry about the product or service, or traffic driven to a website or brought into a store. The activities of direct marketing are *measurable*, and the direct marketer must be *accountable*, always relating results to costs. Unlike most of the activities of traditional brand advertising—creating awareness for a product, service, or organization, or enhancing the image of a product, brand, or company—direct marketing activities can always be measured by the response of targeted customers and/or prospects. Most direct-response ads today include a strong call to action, along with a URL encouraging consumers to visit a website, as the advertisement for the City of Virginia Beach in Figure 1.8 illustrates.

Figure 1.8 Virginia Beach 'Be Yourself' advertisement. Used with permission of the City of Virginia Beach Convention & Visitors Bureau.

Database

The key technological tool that enables the building and maintenance of long-term relationships is the database. One of the most important tasks of direct marketing is capturing these customer responses and storing them in a database. This includes data capturing of customer responses at different stages of the consumer buying process—from awareness, through interest, desire, intention, to ultimate action. In addition to customer response data, the reality of today's modern digital world offers a ubiquity of data collection, processing availability, accessibility, and action-ability. Customer data has never been more available and robust than it is today—which bodes well for the development of invaluable marketing databases.

The creation of a database enables direct marketers to target their best prospects and best customers, build customer relationships, and maintain long-term customer loyalty—the hallmarks of CRM. Thus, the goal of direct marketers is not just to make a sale but to *create a customer!* Although traditional marketers have a long history of building relationships with customers, their activities and interactions with them are not normally measurable, accountable, or captured and recorded in a database.

Customer Relationships

Successful direct marketing relies on building strong customer relationships. While relationship building is referred to in many different ways (e.g., relationship marketing, one-to-one marketing, permission marketing, and CRM), the end result is the same—mutually beneficial long-term bonds between buyer and seller. The success of that relationship is measured in terms of lifetime customer value. Successful relationships also require respect for and protection of personal information shared by customers. Customer bonds with the seller strengthen when he or she trusts that the information shared is protected. Direct marketers have long known the long-term value of customers and have exercised CRM strategies to retain them.

Multichannel Fulfillment

Direct-response communication is intended to generate a measurable action (such as an order, inquiry, charitable donation, or vote for a candidate) via multiple channels. Of course, each customer response generates information that is stored in the organization's database and is used by the direct marketer in future marketing activities. The customer selects the desired channel, such as a visit to a website or store, or a phone call. Direct marketers must process or fulfill each customer's response, regardless of whether it is an inquiry or an order. These are the customer service and fulfillment activities, which are often called 'back-end' marketing. They include delivery of information or order shipment directly to the target customer. Multichannel fulfillment is also called **multichannel distribution** because it refers to a marketer using several (two or more) competing channels of distribution to reach the same target consumer. By practicing multichannel distribution, direct marketers may incur greater expense, but normally achieve greater customer satisfaction by enabling customers to select their preferred shopping channels. Some customers prefer product delivery to their doorstep, and others won't purchase the product without careful personal examination of it, including trying it on for size and style decisions.

For example, Victoria's Secret, the well-known marketer of women's fashions and lingerie, uses three competing channels of distribution. First, its catalogs are mailed to its database of customers and prospective customers and contain both its toll-free number and Web address for consumers to place direct orders; second, its website permits consumers to shop online at www.VictoriasSecret.com; and third, its retail stores are located in most major shopping malls, enabling consumers to come into the store to browse and purchase the merchandise in person. These three channels of distribution may compete with one another for the same target customer's order, yet if the company didn't offer all of these options, it might lose potential customers to other marketers. Multichannel fulfillment, or distribution, offers multiple options for today's increasingly demanding consumer. The bottom line: consumers want choices! Multichannel fulfillment gives them exactly that.

Now that we have examined the process of direct marketing, you might be wondering: how does the marketer carry out these processes for each individual customer on a one-to-one basis? The answer lies in precise measurement and analysis, and proper targeting. The marketer follows each direct marketing campaign with a response analysis that examines the results for effectiveness. He or she can then initiate future communication designed specifically for each target customer by using the customer information stored in the database. The process begins again: each direct-response communication builds on the relationship the direct marketer has with each individual customer and reinforces that customer's loyalty to the company or organization. We'll expand on each of these characteristics of direct marketing in subsequent chapters in this textbook. For now, it is important to keep in mind that *all direct marketing is database-driven marketing!* Today's direct marketing activities are centered on providing consumers with an 'omni-channel marketing' experience. Let's explore this important concept.

Omni-Channel Marketing[12]

Today's marketers and consumers have access to more channels than ever before. New channels continue to emerge while traditional channels remain relevant. Today's consumers now engage with a company in a variety of ways, such as through a physical store, online website, mobile app, printed catalog, or social media. All channels work from the same database of products, prices, and promotions to enable consumers to experience the brand. All products, services and promotions must be consistent across all channels. This concentrated, seamless approach to delivering a consistent brand experience across all available channels and devices a customer uses to interact with a company or an organization and its brands is called **omni-channel marketing**. Simply put, omni-channel marketing is concerned with managing the overall consumer experience through all available shopping channels in order to maximize customer satisfaction. For example, DICK'S Sporting Goods, Inc. is a leading omni-channel sporting goods retailer. DICK'S offers an extensive assortment of authentic, high-quality sports equipment, apparel, footwear, and accessories through a content-rich eCommerce platform that is integrated with its physical retail store network and provides customers with the convenience and expertise of a 24-hour storefront.

Another example of an omni-channel marketer is that of a luxury apparel brand[13] that is sold in retail stores around the world, as well as in its own retail stores. The company's marketing team was searching for strategies to drive direct-to-consumer growth and build brand image as it launched its online business to complement its wholesale strategy. In addition, the team wanted to better understand its customer's behavior. They needed to analyze the transactional behavior of their customers to identify data-driven strategies for ecommerce. Baesman Group of Columbus, Ohio, helped the company tackle this marketing challenge, starting with a customer relationship management (CRM) program designed to database customers through omnichannel strategies to understand consumer path to purchase. Baesman produced a customer profile, providing a comprehensive transactional analysis of the brand's consumer. The company's customer profile was the foundation driving increased sales, new customers, and reactivating lapsed customers through direct mail. The result was a 15 percent campaign increase in customer acquisition, with a 50 percent increase in customer data capture. Analyzing customer data to better serve customers is paramount to omni-channel marketers.

With a marketing database, customer offers can be customized and personalized. Customer data should drive all marketing activities and should be based on all relevant customer interactions via purchase patterns, social networks, apps, website visits, direct mail response, e-direct marketing response, loyalty programs, and data-mining. In omni-channel marketing, it is critical that the customer's needs, desires, and time are respected and are at the focal point of the entire marketing process.

Given developments in technology and big data, companies must develop omni-channel marketing strategies that truly put the consumer first. The term 'omni-channel' may be a marketing buzzword, but it refers to a significant shift in today's marketing world. Basically, it describes how people shop and engage with a company's brand, given the plethora of options available to them.

Why don't all companies and organizations implement omni-channel marketing? This concentrated, seamless approach is easier said than effectively delivered. Lack of budget, marketing skills, and senior-level buy-in are real challenges that today's marketers are facing. The marketing challenge, therefore, lies in creating and delivering that seamless customer experience, regardless of the channel or device. Creating a synergy where all of the channels work together to provide the best experience for the customer is the marketer's goal. Now, let's talk about who uses direct marketing to provide omni-channel marketing experiences for consumers.

APPLICATIONS OF DIRECT MARKETING

You can immediately recognize a direct-response advertisement, regardless of the medium used, by noting whether the reader, listener, or viewer is requested to take an immediate action: visit a website, text a given number, reply to an e-mail, mail an order form, call a phone number, come to a store or an event, redeem a coupon, ask for a salesperson to call, send a contribution, vote for a particular candidate, attend a meeting, and so on. If there is a request for an immediate, measurable action, it is an example of direct marketing.

Users of Direct Marketing

At some time or another, virtually every business and every organization—charitable, political, educational, cultural, and civic—and every individual has used and uses direct-response advertising and, indeed, has a database for doing so. As individuals, we use e-mail or direct mail whenever we send greeting cards, wedding invitations, and birth or graduation announcements. Job hunters find that websites and social media networks are excellent ways to get their résumés to prospective employers. Businesses, especially small businesses, use a variety of media for direct-response advertising and employ many of the other elements of direct marketing. This is true of giant corporations as well as small retailers and industrial service organizations.

Figure 1.9 Busch Gardens Spring Vacations New York advertisement. Used with the consent of Busch Gardens/Water Country USA. All Rights Reserved.

Today, most companies are realizing the great value direct marketing brings. Nearly all companies have increased their online marketing activities, particularly the use of e-mail and social media platforms, to take advantage of the customization, personalization, selectivity, and cost savings each presents. See Figure 1.9 for an example of a geographically targeted e-mail from Busch Gardens.

Let's look at a sampling of the many applications of the tools and techniques of database-driven direct marketing in use.

Figure 1.10   Doctors Without Borders/Médecins Sans Frontières (MSF). ©Doctors Without Borders.

Nonprofit Organizations

Direct marketing is ideal for nonprofit organizations because it is measurable, accountable, targeted, cost-effective, and requires a direct response—qualities that are all of particular importance to organizations that exist to support and advance a cause. Nonprofit organizations serve as a forum for the creation and distribution of new ideas. These organizations, like hospitals and universities, may deliver services. The American Cancer Society and the March of Dimes actively support advancing medical research in an attempt to find a cure for diseases. Mothers Against Drunk Driving (MADD) focuses on safety issues. What they all have in common is that they want people to know about their cause and respond to their pleas for support. This response could be in the form of a donation to a charitable organization or help to achieve any number of an organization's communication objectives. Any nonprofit organization can effectively use direct marketing to achieve its communication objectives.

Figure 1.10 provides an excellent example of nonprofit direct marketing by Doctors Without Borders/Médecins Sans Frontières (MSF). MSF is an independent, global movement providing medical aid where it's needed most. MSF works in conflict zones, after natural disasters, during epidemics, in long-term care settings, and more.

Which nonprofit organizations employ direct marketing strategies to achieve their goals and objectives? The answer is probably *every* organization. Most health-concerned organizations, such as the American Cancer Society, the American Heart Association, the American Diabetes Association, and the American Lung Association, avidly practice direct marketing to obtain donations to support research for their worthy causes. Organizations concerned with protecting the environment, such as the World Wildlife Fund, the Nature Conservancy, and the Rails-to-Trails Conservancy, use direct marketing.

Educational institutions have long relied on direct marketing to obtain student enrollments, offer continuing education courses, raise funds, garner political support, and communicate with alumni and the larger community. Other nonprofit organizations include those concerned with helping our youth, such as Big Brothers Big Sisters, Boys & Girls Club of America, and the Rappahannock River Rats Youth Hockey Association. Nonprofit organizations also exist to protect women, such as the Miles Foundation and Battered Women's Organization, whereas others exist to provide support to minorities, such as An Achievable Dream. In summary, nonprofit organizations use a variety of media and direct marketing tactics to generate awareness of their causes and to obtain volunteers, donors, and friends. The next section explores how political organizations are using direct marketing to promote both their cause and their candidates.

Political Organizations

Do you want to be elected president, governor, or mayor? Do you want to be elected to a school board? Do you want to build support or raise funds for the National Women's Political Caucus or Planned Parenthood? Do you want to overcome objections of legislatures to the conversion of railroad rights of way to Rails-to-Trails? Do you want to garner political and financial support for environmental causes like the Nature Conservancy, World Wildlife Fund, American Rivers, and starving elk? If you answered 'yes' to any of these questions, you will rely on direct marketing activities to obtain votes and financial support!

The Internet is a valuable tool used by political parties and candidates to raise funds, secure campaign volunteers, and win votes. However, political direct marketing activities are not always aimed at raising money. The Internet also permits the parties to send customized messages to specific groups and individuals, and to use online discussions and instant messaging in support of their candidates. In today's sophisticated world, political organizations use unique analytical tools, such as micro-targeting, to create specific offers designed to woo voters.

Political micro-targeting, also referred to as *narrowcasting*, is aggregating groups of voters based on data about them, available in databases and on the Internet—to target them with tailor-made messages.[14] Political parties gather personal information about voters to deliver narrowly targeted messages calculated to influence their votes. Micro-targeting goes beyond traditional segmentation bases to gather data at the individual level. This information can include magazine subscriptions, real estate records, consumer transaction data, demographics, lifestyle data, geography, psychographics, voter history, and survey response data. Micro-targeting can add great value to political marketing activities.

Political micro-targeting is used by political parties to determine which voters care about specific campaign issues. For example, research has shown that all people who regularly attend church are not alike. Political micro-targeting can be used to identify those churchgoers who would be more interested in hearing a Democratic message of social justice.[15] Given that direct marketing messages can be personalized and delivered to individuals on a one-to-one basis, micro-targeting is seen as a powerful tool for directing appropriate messages to voters. For example, in 2008, the Obama presidential campaign employed micro-targeting techniques to its e-mail strategy and created hyper-segmented e-mails that provided readers with customized messaging.[16] Barack Obama's techniques started a trend in the political marketing arena. German parties attempted to translate door-to-door canvassing into the German electoral setting with the goal to earn votes from the 'typical undecided.' In conclusion, political micro-targeting helps campaigns deliver more effective messages to specific individuals and households by tracking and analyzing information on a person-by-person basis.

Political organizations are not the only public administrative bodies to narrowly target select groups of individuals. A wide variety of governmental organizations regularly apply direct marketing strategies as well. This is the topic of our next section.

(Continued)

Figure 1.11 (Continued)

Department of the Navy
Navy Recruiting Command
P.O. Box 2981
Warminster, PA 18974

OFFICIAL BUSINESS

NO POSTAGE
NECESSARY
IF MAILED
IN THE
UNITED STATES

BUSINESS REPLY MAIL
FIRST-CLASS MAIL   PERMIT NO. 9280   MILLINGTON TN

POSTAGE WILL BE PAID BY ADDRESSEE

DEPARTMENT OF THE NAVY
PO BOX 2981
WARMINSTER PA 18974-9858

■ **Yes**, I would like more information.

Please print clearly.

Email Address: (optional) _____

Date of Birth:* _____

Phone: (_____)_____ Best Time to Call: ___   ☐ a.m. or ☐ p.m.

Current Year in High School:*
☐ Freshman (08)   ☐ Sophomore (09)   ☐ Junior (10)   ☐ Senior (11)   ☐ Graduate (12)

Year of High School Graduation: _____

Current Year in College:
☐ Freshman (12)   ☐ Sophomore (13)   ☐ Junior (14)   ☐ Senior (15)   ☐ Post-Graduate (16)

Year of College Graduation: _____   GPA:* ☐ 2.0 – 2.6   ☐ 2.7 – 2.9   ☐ 3.0 – 4.0

U.S. Citizen:* ☐ Yes ☐ No

*Required fields.

Navy. Accelerate your life.™

Now's the time for a wake-up call.

Alarm sounds. Another day. Another dollar. Then reality sinks in: There's got to be a better way.

There is. The prospect of a more **promising career.** A more **fulfilling life.** A more **exciting routine.**

In today's Navy, you can wake up to something new and meaningful every day. Pursue a line of work that's about **making the most of your skills.** For your benefit. And for that of those around you.

Take pride in what you do for a living.

Step into any of over 60 high-tech fields. Explore your interests and sense of adventure. Expand your job description. Protecting freedom. Supporting global relief missions.

All while **earning impressive benefits** along the way, including good pay. Comprehensive health care. **College credit** for on-the-job training. Plus **potentially over $70,000 to use toward school.**

Enjoying your work. Securing your future. Serving your country and humanity. Now that's something to get out of bed for.

Being defined by your work.
See how satisfying that can be.

Want to do great things in your world? Then spend some time in ours. Learn more about careers. Educational assistance. And the benefits waiting. In the Navy. Simply fill out and mail the attached reply card, call us at **(XXX) XXX-XXXX** or email **recruiter@localxxxxxxxxxxx.com** for more details. There's no pressure. No obligation. Just an exciting opportunity to do something extraordinary in life.

GES6

Figure 1.11 U.S. Navy direct mailers. Use of the Department of the Navy's Accelerate Your Life® mark is granted with permission of the Department of the Navy and does not constitute an endorsement of any author, publisher or product thereof, by the Department of the Navy or the Department of Defense.

Governmental Organizations

The government has relied on direct marketing for many of its public interactions. The U.S. Postal Service (USPS) distributes direct mail to both end users and organizational consumers to promote its many products and services. Direct mailers encourage final consumers to purchase uniquely designed stamps and online postage services as well as to schedule convenient and time-saving pick-up and delivery services.

All branches of the military use direct marketing for targeted recruiting to high school juniors and seniors. Figure 1.11 presents some of the direct mail pieces being used by the U.S. Department of the Navy in its recruiting activities. Note the variety of motivational headlines it uses:

'How many people can put world traveler on their resume?' 'No sense hiding from the hero you were born to be.' 'Now's the time for a wake-up call.'

The copy of each direct mail piece is compelling, promoting the benefits—world travel, the exposure to cutting-edge technology, the opportunity for a college education, respect, and the ability to make a difference—associated with joining the military.

Beyond the U.S. military, many other governmental entities use direct marketing on a regular basis. Just think about the travel and tourism industry, where most destination marketing organizations and convention and visitor bureaus fund their promotional efforts through local and state tax dollars. Most state and local tourism organizations use direct marketing because it produces campaign results that are measurable and attributable to specific media, like media sourcing, response rates, conversion rates, and sales revenue generated from visiting tourists. For example, the Williamsburg Area Destination Marketing Campaign promotes the Historic Triangle area of Virginia (which includes all of the City of Williamsburg, James City County, and York County) as an overnight travel and tourism destination. Direct marketing strategies are regularly used in promoting the Greater Williamsburg area. Featured in Figure 1.12 is one of Williamsburg Tourism's outbound e-mails promoting the area as a great place for families to come and have fun in the summer. Often, hand in hand with travel and tourism marketing is sports marketing, because the direct response that both of these marketers are often seeking is in the form of visitation. Let's now explore how sports organizations utilize direct marketing activities.

Sports Organizations

A variety of direct marketing strategies and tactics are frequently used by sports organizations to help them achieve their objectives. Virtually all sports team marketers share the common objective of filling the seats of their stadium, arena, park, or rink with loyal fans cheering them on to victory. Of course, sports marketers would prefer if these fans purchased season tickets and supported the home team for the entire season and not just one game. Sports marketers may also be interested in obtaining corporate sponsors or hosting fundraising events. These are additional areas where direct marketing can be applied in an especially effective manner. However, before you begin to think about the glamour and fun associated with sports marketing, you should be aware of its unique challenges.

Things to Do • Places to Stay • Dining • Deals & Packages • Events

Can a vacation in Greater Williamsburg really give you the freedom to have fun, relax and satisfy your curiosity? Two real families put us to the test. Watch their adventures and plan your own at VisitWilliamsburg.com.

Visit Williamsburg.

Williamsburg is fun. How fun? More fun than the Fay family could have even imagined. Don't miss a second.	What good is a vacation without a little R&R? Even thrill-seekers need to kick up their feet and recharge.	Don't think Williamsburg can satisfy your curiosity? Neither did the Settle family. Find out what changed their minds.
WHAT'S NEW	EVENT CALENDAR	BOOK NOW

Figure 1.12 Williamsburg Tourism Summer Freedom e-mail. Published with the consent of Greater Williamsburg Chamber & Tourism Alliance. All rights reserved.

29

One uncontrollable variable that often presents a challenge to direct marketing to gain attendance for an upcoming game is the record and reputation of the visiting team. When the home team plays against a big contender or rival, or a team with an excellent winning record, securing attendance is much easier. When the contender doesn't have a good reputation or record, it is much more difficult to fill the seats. Similarly, the record of the home team is an important component of sports marketing. A winning team is easily marketed. Everyone wants to support a winning team! But when the team is not performing well, the task of selling season tickets becomes quite a challenge.

Promoting special events to regular season ticket holders is another common communication objective. Often, sports organizations will partner with nonprofit organizations to hold special events to raise funds for a specific cause. For example, the Norfolk Admirals hockey team supported a breast cancer cause by creatively painting the ice pink! The Admirals donated a portion of ticket sales to the cause, auctioned off pink hockey sticks and autographed jerseys, held a pre-game Women's Hockey 101 Clinic, and provided educational materials.

Of course, sports marketers also use direct marketing activities to prospect for new fans by offering group discounts. It is also common for sports marketers to promote attendance at select games that might not naturally garner a high attendance.

So far, we've discussed how sports marketers use direct marketing activities targeting final consumers (B2C). However, equally important are their efforts to market to business consumers (B2B). Most sports marketers actively promote to business consumers to obtain sponsorship support for their team. Many of these activities entail direct marketing strategies and tactics.

Figure 1.13 Washington Redskins fans with signs. Published with the consent of the Washington Redskins. All rights reserved.

Figure 1.14 The Washington Redskins Charitable Foundation logo. Published with consent of the Washington Redskins. All Rights Reserved.

The Washington Redskins professional football team utilizes a wide array of media, including print, digital, social, signage, and transit, as well as a variety of marketing activities, including public relations, partnerships, and special events. The organization offers season ticket sales, along with sponsorship packages. In addition to providing its fans (see Figure 1.13) with outstanding football games to enjoy, the sports organization gives back to the community via The Washington Redskins Charitable Foundation.

The Washington Redskins Charitable Foundation (Figure 1.14) is ever-present in the community, constantly working to achieve the mission to make a positive and measurable impact in the lives of children who need it most. Since Redskins owners Dan and Tanya Snyder created the Washington Redskins Charitable Foundation in 2000, the organization has given back nearly $20 million to the community, and currently provides support and services for more than 190,000 individuals (mostly children) annually. The foundation focuses on education, children's health and wellness, and preparing children for their future (see Figure 1.15).

Figure 1.15 The Washington Redskins Charitable Foundation event. Published with the consent of the Washington Redskins. All rights reserved.

SUMMARY

Direct marketing is a database-driven interactive process of directly communicating with targeted customers or prospects using any medium to obtain a measurable response or transaction via one or multiple channels. Almost all types of business can and do conduct direct marketing activities, including organizations and individuals whose goal it is to establish long-term relationships with their customers. Direct marketing uses many different types of media and formats, including direct mail, catalogs, newspaper, magazine, radio, television, phone, Internet, handheld devices, and mobile. The industry has a long history and has experienced rapid growth primarily due to credit cards, computers, advances in the printing industry, the changing lifestyles of consumers, and the negative aspects of in-store retailing.

Customers are at the heart of the direct marketing process. The main goal of the direct marketing process is to develop and strengthen long-term relationships with customers.

KEY TERMS

brand marketing

customer relationship management (CRM)

digital marketing

direct marketing

geo-tagging

interactive marketing

multichannel distribution/multichannel fulfillment

near field communications (NFC)

omni-channel marketing

political micro-targeting

REVIEW QUESTIONS

1. Name and elaborate on the characteristics that distinguish *direct* from *traditional* brand marketing.
2. What is meant by measurability of and accountability for marketing decisions?
3. What is the difference between a list and a database? How important is a database for conducting direct marketing activities today?
4. Write an overview of the components of the direct marketing process and model. How does 'omni-channel' marketing relate to the process?
5. 'Direct marketing is an aspect of marketing characterized by *measurability* and *accountability* with reliance on *databases*.' Explain this statement.
6. Discuss the historical roots and the emergence of direct marketing. How has it been influenced by technological, economic, and social change?

7. Compare and elaborate on the changes in graphic design between the 1976 and 2008 catalog covers of the Oriental Trading Company shown in Figure 1.5.
8. Explain how geo-tagging and NFC are used by marketers. What is the benefit of these new technological innovations for consumers?
9. What is direct-response advertising and how does it relate to direct mail as well as print, broadcast, and websites?
10. Describe the use of direct marketing by nonprofit, sports, and political organizations. How are the marketing activities of these different types of organization similar? How are they different?

EXERCISE

Congratulations! You've just started your new entrepreneurial business venture, a gourmet foods store specializing in unique and healthy culinary delights and savory snacks. Although you are about to sign a lease for a retail store in a prime location, you have an even bigger vision–national and global distribution! You envision millennial consumers to be your primary target market. How will you reach and engage them? What will your multi-channel marketing strategies entail? How will you maximize customer relationships and truly become a sought-after omni-channel marketer?

CRITICAL THINKING EXERCISE

You have just decided to run for mayor of your town. Think about the political campaign you want to conduct and identify the various direct marketing strategies you will utilize in your campaign. From a direct marketing perspective, what can and should you do to uniquely position yourself to be perceived as the better candidate and win votes? What steps will you take in creating your campaign? How will you connect with voters in your town? What mediums will you select to communicate your message?

READINGS AND RESOURCES

- Marketing EDGE: www.marketingedge.org
- Digital trends: www.smartinsights.com/managing-digital-marketing/marketing-innovation/business-critical-digital-marketing-trends
- MARTEC: https://martechtoday.com
- Stackie Awards: https://chiefmartec.com/2017/05/57-marketing-stacks-21-essays-shared-2017-stackies-hackies
- Marketing technology landscape: https://chiefmartec.com/2018/04/marketing-technology-landscape-supergraphic-2018
- Digital transformation: www2.deloitte.com/insights/us/en/focus/industry-4-0/overview.html

CASE: FEAR 2 FREEDOM

Figure 1.16 Fear 2 Freedom logo. Published with the consent of Fear 2 Freedom. All rights reserved.

Every two minutes, someone is sexually assaulted in the United States. More than 17.7 million women and 2.8 million men nationwide are victims of sexual assault. Sexual violence is especially prevalent in college communities. In fact, nationwide 1 in 5 female and 1 in 19 male students will experience sexual assault during their four years in college.

Fear 2 Freedom (F2F) is a global 501(c)3 nonprofit organization formed in 2011 to combat sexual assault on college campuses nationwide. If you haven't heard of Fear 2 Freedom, you are not alone. Until now, it hasn't done much marketing. However, with your help, that will change. Visit www.Fear2Freedom.org to learn more.

Figure 1.17 Rosemary Trible, president and founder, Fear 2 Freedom. Published with the consent of Fear 2 Freedom. All rights reserved.

Rosemary Trible, seen in Figure 1.17, is the wife of a former U.S. senator and current university president. Rosemary was violently raped at gunpoint when she was 25 years old. In an instant, Rosemary's life was turned upside down. Left with mental and physical scars, her life became filled with fear, pain, and embarrassment. For 40 years, Rosemary waged a silent, internal war. Rosemary heeded the call to dedicate her life to being a voice for the voiceless. In 2011, she launched F2F.

F2F's mission is to redeem and restore the lives of those hurt by sexual assault, bringing them hope and healing. It also seeks to empower college students to 'Be the Change' and 'Restore the Joy' on their campuses and in their communities. F2F focuses its efforts primarily on college and university campuses. Laws pertaining to campus sexual assault violations have intensified and changes to Title IX of the Education Amendments of 1972 and the Clery Act are dramatically affecting the legal policies on college campuses nationwide. The new regulations help to create awareness, interest, and ultimately participation for nonprofit organizational causes like F2F.

F2F Combats College Sexual Violence

Beyond educational videos, F2F offers two unique events for college campuses: the shadow event and the celebration event. The shadow event is a unique, transformational university experience to highlight the personal testimonies of sexual assault victims and their journey of restoration and healing. It allows survivors of sexual assault (women and men) to anonymously share their stories with their peers. Students hear from their fellow students about their experience of abuse from behind a screen in a safe and confidential environment. Those attending the event have an opportunity to express their personal support and compassion to the survivors by writing a note to them. See Figure 1.18 for a shadow event photo.

Figure 1.18   F2F shadow event. Published with the consent of Fear 2 Freedom. All rights reserved.

The celebration event follows the shadow event. It gives students, community partners, and hospitals the opportunity to join forces to combat sexual assault and assemble after-care kits. Students hear from university administrators, survivors, and forensic nurses in this 90-minute interactive program. See Figure 1.19 for celebration event photos.

Why assemble after-care kits? When someone seeks medical attention after sexual violence, the victim's clothes are often kept as evidence. Too often, the victim has to leave the hospital in paper scrubs. A fresh change of clothes in the right size, some toiletries, and a comforting Freedom Bear stuffed animal make a world of difference. A primary function of F2F is to assemble and distribute after-care kits like the one shown in Figure 1.20.

Figure 1.19 F2F celebration event. Published with the consent of Fear 2 Freedom. All rights reserved.

Figure 1.20 F2F after-care kit. Published with the consent of Fear 2 Freedom. All rights reserved.

Volunteers and students assemble kits at celebration events held on college campuses. After assembly, kits are transported to a local hospital or community partner. The kits are then given to victims when they seek medical attention after the trauma of sexual assault. The majority of the hospitals cover the cost of the kits.

Target Markets

F2F must make college and university administrators aware of F2F programs. Its ultimate objective is to secure formal partnership agreement for one of its university programs.

To be successful, F2F must effectively target both organizational (B2B) and final or college student (B2C) prospects. Colleges and universities across the U.S. are its primary target market. However, no single administrator is responsible for making decisions. F2F must communicate with multiple targets involved in the decision. These typically include: university presidents/chancellors, Title IX coordinators/officers, deans of students, and Student Life offices. F2F must rely on precise direct marketing to effectively reach each target market.

As a relatively new nonprofit organization, Rosemary recently distributed the first national campaign e-mail blast to a targeted audience. F2F compiled a list of presidents, Title IX coordinators, and heads of counseling for each of the schools in the 26 states in Phase 1 of the F2F strategic plan. A total of 559 outbound e-mails were sent to launch the F2F national campaign. The e-mail blast, shown in Figure 1.21, was distributed via constant contact. The content included sexual assault statistics, a quote from Rosemary, an invitation to contact F2F to learn more, links to view the 'Be the Change' film trailer, as well as links to contact F2F via its website and social media networks.

Dear Scott,

A shocking fact: The latest national statistics report **1 in 5 females and 1 in 16 male students** will experience **sexual assault** during their four years in college. Fear 2 Freedom can help you address this startling issue on your campus.

As an administrator, your challenge is to combat this threatening issue and foster a cultural change that supports **intervention and prevention** among your university students. Our **Be the Change National Campaign** meets the requirements of **Title IX and the Clery Act** regulations as we join together to combat sexual assault.

Included in the campaign is a **90-minute prevention program** that features a comprehensive educational film, "Be the Change." The film raises awareness and is an effective tool that empowers students to be the solution in a **positive and impactful** event.

The Title IX Programming and Resource Tool Kit Includes:

- Educational Film: "Be the Change"
- Event Discussion Panel - Instructions & Information
- Title IX and Clery Act criteria
- Programming for Intervention and Prevention
- Sexual Assault and F2F Resources
- Empowering and Positive Messaging

WATCH "BE THE CHANGE" EDUCATIONAL FILM TRAILER

To purchase or schedule a consultation and learn about the introductory pricing options, contact us or learn more at:

As the wife of a university President, I founded the global 501(c)3 non-profit Fear 2 Freedom (F2F) with the mission to change the cultural understanding surrounding this issue on college campuses and empower champions to "Be the Change."

Since 2012, Fear 2 Freedom has supported more than 12,000 survivors in their healing and restoration from sexual assault.

We look forward to a positive partnership with you to engage your students and foster a safe and positive campus community.

Kindest regards,

Rosemary

Rosemary Trible
Fear 2 Freedom
Founder and President

Figure 1.21 F2F national campaign e-mail blast. Published with the consent of Fear 2 Freedom. All rights reserved.

Conclusion

Rosemary and the F2F staff realize that their marketing efforts to date have been reactive to opportunities and locally based. If the organization is to grow nationally, it needs a scalable marketing approach that effectively persuades university administrators, area hospitals, community partners, and students. F2F faces several marketing challenges for which direct marketing strategies and tactics can be employed. F2F needs a marketing plan that effectively reaches both its B2B and B2C target markets. It must make each target aware of its services, stimulate interest, and convert prospects into partners. Each target has distinctive interests and needs, making this marketing challenge especially difficult.

This case demonstrates how nonprofit organizations use direct marketing in the operation of their business to gain awareness, friends, funds, and support for their worthy cause. In addition, these marketing activities typically include special event planning and promotion as well as volunteer recruitment and management.

Case Discussion Questions

1. What media and messages should be communicated to each target market? Is a social media marketing campaign the most effective way to generate buzz among college students? Why do you think this would be effective?
2. Technology and smartphones now impact safety efforts on college campuses. Recently, more college campuses have adopted mobile apps to help combat sexual assault. These apps provide access resources for sexual assault victims. Should F2F partner with one of the existing mobile apps that address sexual assault on college campuses? If F2F partners with an existing mobile app, how should it be promoted on campus? Should the parents of college students be targeted as well?
3. F2F needs to better organize its fundraising efforts. The fundraising plan may include any methods you think are appropriate for the organization. What fundraising events and/or activities would you recommend? Why do you think these would be effective for F2F?

NOTES

1. Roland T. Rust and Richard W. Oliver (1994) 'The Death of Advertising,' *Journal of Advertising*, 23(4), 71–77; quote from p. 71.
2. Philip Kotler and Gary Armstrong (2008) *Principles of Marketing*, 12th ed. (Englewood Cliffs, NJ: Prentice Hall).
3. Gary Armstrong and Philip Kotler (2007) *Marketing: An Introduction*, 8th ed. (Englewood Cliffs, NJ: Prentice Hall).
4. Herbert Katzenstein and William S. Sachs (1992) *Direct Marketing*, 2nd ed. (New York: Macmillan).
5. The *DMA Statistical Fact Book* (2016) (New York: The Direct Marketing Association), pp. 3–4.

6. Ibid.

7. Carol Scovotti and Lisa D. Spiller (2006) 'Revisiting the Conceptual Definition of Direct Marketing: Perspectives from Practitioners and Scholars,' *Marketing Management Journal*, 16(2), 188–202.

8. Direct Marketing Association (2007) *The Integration of DM & Brand* (New York: Direct Marketing Association), p. xxiii.

9. Many of the early historical references contained in this section are based on documentation prepared by Nat Ross for the Direct Marketing Association.

10. Edward L. Nash (1993) *Database Marketing: The Ultimate Marketing Tool* (New York: McGraw-Hill); quote from p. 1.

11. Martin Baier (1996) *How to Find and Cultivate Customers through Direct Marketing* (Lincolnwood, IL: NTC Business Books), p. 3ff.

12. Much of the material in this section has been adapted from Mike Stocker's article 'The Definition of Omni-Channel Marketing,' blog.marketo.com, April 2014, retrieved on July 16, 2016.

13. This example is based on a case study by Baesman Group, the company's marketing agency. Used with permission.

14. 'Political Microtargeting,' SourceWatch, 2008, retrieved on May 19, 2008, https://www.sourcewatch.org/index.php/Political_microtargeting.

15. 'The 2008 Tools Campaign: Microtargeting,' New Politics Institute, retrieved on April 29, 2008, www.newpolitics.net/content_areas/new_tools_campaign/microtargeting.

16. Rahaf Harfoush (2009) *Yes We Did: An Inside Look at How Social Media Built the Obama Brand* (Berkeley, CA: New Riders), p. 48.

2

DATABASE MARKETING AND CUSTOMER RELATIONSHIP MARKETING

CHAPTER CONTENTS

CHAPTER SPOTLIGHT

DICK'S SPORTING GOODS SCORECARD® REWARDS PROGRAM

Figure 2.1 DICK's Sporting Goods ScoreCard® rewards program card. Used with permission of DICK's Sporting Goods, Inc.

He shops. He scores! DICK's Sporting Goods ScoreCard® rewards program enables its customers to earn rewards while making purchases at any of its stores or online. Customers may register for the ScoreCard® rewards program for free. Once registered, members earn points each time they shop at DICK's Sporting Goods and are awarded a $10 reward certificate for every 300 points they earn. Program members may also receive exclusive deals, new product alerts, and insider access via its direct marketing programs.

So, you don't like basketball? Are you a runner or a golfer? Might you enjoy water sports? If so, what kind of water sports do you prefer–motorized or paddle sports? Members of the DICK's Sporting Goods ScoreCard® rewards program also receive specialized direct marketing catalogs and programs based upon their sports preferences and past purchase history. Therefore, if you are a ScoreCard® rewards program member and you are a runner who has purchased running shoes at DICK's Sporting Goods, you will likely know that the month of May is National Runner's Month. How will you know? Because you would have received the DICK's Sporting Goods *Runner's Gear Guide* containing exclusive offers for ScoreCard® rewards program members.

The *Runner's Gear Guide* presents a wide variety of merchandise associated with running, such as running shoes, clothes, watches, water bottles, and other accessories. This year's *Runner's Gear Guide* also contained 14 inspirational stories of why people run, coupons to score bonus points with the purchase of a pair of athletic shoes or athletic apparel, and a special offer to go to NationalRunnersMonth.com to register to win a DICK's Sporting Goods shopping spree! The *Runner's Gear Guide* also encourages you to go to the DICK's Sporting Goods Facebook page to share your own running story with the company.

Let's say you are a ScoreCard® rewards program member who enjoys water sports and has recently purchased a canoe from DICK's Sporting Goods. You will likely receive DICK's Sporting Goods *Paddle Sports Gear Guide*. Similar to the *Runner's Gear Guide*, it features special offers on a wide variety of kayaks, canoes, paddles, storage racks, accessories, and water apparel. In addition, it presents short stories about topics related to paddle sports, such as how to choose the right kayak and water safety rules. The *Paddle Sports Gear Guide* also contains coupons for discounts on purchases related to paddle sports, along with special bonus point offers.

Today, DICK's Sporting Goods rewards go beyond earning points for purchases. Through its mobile app, users are rewarded for being active. The 'Move' feature of the DICK's Sporting Goods app allows users to connect to fitness tracking applications, such as MapMyRun and Fitbit®, to earn ScoreCard® points for achieving activity goals.[i] In addition, DICK's Sporting Goods, Golf Galaxy, Field & Stream, and Synchrony Bank have teamed up to offer customers two great credit options: the ScoreRewards Credit Card and the ScoreRewards Mastercard. ScoreRewards credit cardholders are able to take their loyalty program membership to a higher 'Gold' level. Approved members may make in-store purchases with their ScoreRewards credit card or ScoreRewards Mastercard at any DICK'S Sporting Goods, Golf Galaxy, or Field & Stream store location. They may also use their ScoreRewards Mastercard online and anywhere else Mastercard is accepted. The ScoreRewards credit card is for use only in DICK'S Sporting Goods, Golf Galaxy, and Field & Stream (not accepted at in-store kiosks, online, or for out-of-store purchases). The ScoreRewards Mastercard is for use anywhere Mastercard is accepted. Subject to credit approval, both cards automatically enroll users in the ScoreCard Gold program, where they will earn three times the points on qualified in-store purchases the day the account is opened. After that, they will earn two times the points every day on qualified in-store purchases. With the ScoreRewards Mastercard, consumers will also earn one point for every $3 spent anywhere else Mastercard is accepted.[ii] Talk about scoring points!

In conclusion, DICK's Sporting Goods makes shopping fun and easy while it creates value for its customers. With its ScoreCard® rewards program, the company is able to connect with its customers on a personalized basis uniquely tailored to each customer's lifestyle and activities. DICK's Sporting Goods illustrates the value of using its customer rewards program to build and enhance its customer database and initiate and maintain customer relationships, the topic of this chapter.

NOTES

i See www.prnewswire.com/news-releases/dicks-sporting-goods-enhances-mobile-app-to-reward-customers-for-an-active-lifestyle-300171394.html

ii See https://www.dickssportinggoods.com/s/credit-card-faqs

All direct marketers seek to maximize the profits of their business. Two ways to achieve this are by attracting new customers and by encouraging your current customers to buy more from you. However, it is very well established that a new customer acquisition program may *not* be as profitable as a customer retention program. Did you know that it costs (on average) about eight to ten times more money to acquire a new customer than it does to keep a current one?[1] Thus, direct marketers may be better served by directing their marketing efforts toward retaining the customers they already have. This is the concept behind database-driven direct marketing, which is the focus of this chapter. We also discuss what a customer database is, its importance in developing customer loyalty, and how to build, maintain, secure, and use a customer database. In addition, this chapter discusses database enhancement and database analytics. Finally, we discuss the importance of customer relationship management (CRM) and partner relationship management (PRM).

CUSTOMER DATABASE

A customer database is a list of customer names to which the marketer has added additional information in a systematic fashion. Just as a house list contains active as well as inactive customers, inquirers, and referrals, so too does an organization's customer database. Thus, we can think of a customer database as a computerized house list that contains more than merely a listing of customer names.

A customer database is the key to developing strong customer relationships and retaining current customers. It is the vehicle through which a company documents comprehensive information about each customer. This information could include the consumer's past purchases (buying patterns), demographics (age, birthday, income, marital status, etc.), psychographics (activities, interests, and opinions), and much more. Marketers use this information to direct all future marketing activities with each customer on an individual basis. For example, the customer database is used for such purposes as lead generation, lead qualification, sale of a product or service, and promotional activities. Armed with this information, marketers are able to develop a closer relationship with each customer on a personalized basis. The stronger the relationship with each customer, the more likely that customer will continue purchasing from the company. That is why current customers, with whom the direct marketer already has an established relationship, are more likely to be retained as future customers.

How does a company retain its customers? By keeping the customer satisfied and happy. Highly satisfied customers tend to be loyal customers, and loyal customers generate greater profits for an organization over their lifetime of patronage. This is due to the following reasons:

1. Loyal customers tend to increase their spending over time. These customers are better to have and more profitable than other customers.[2]
2. Loyal customers cost less to serve than new customers. Repeat customers have greater familiarity with an organization's processes and procedures, and therefore are more quickly and easily served.
3. Loyal customers are normally happy customers who tell others about the organization, commonly referred to as word-of-mouth advertising, which in turn generates additional business.

4. Loyal customers are less price-sensitive than are new customers. They see value in their relationship with the organization and may spend more freely because of their high level of satisfaction with the company.

In addition, according to Frederick Reichheld, author of *The Loyalty Effect*, a 5 percentage point increase in customer retention in a typical company will increase profits by more than 25 percent—and growth by more than 100 percent.[3] The task of creating and maintaining loyal customers is what CRM is all about. In an attempt to retain current customers, marketers invest in programs and activities to create and enhance customer loyalty. The development of a customer database is the first step in this process.

DATABASE DEVELOPMENT

Developing a customer database for marketing purposes is an ordered process. It begins with obtaining basic data about customers. This is followed by the task of converting that data into relevant information for the company. Then the company uses that information to produce knowledge about its customers and their preferences. Armed with that knowledge, a company can develop strategies to better communicate with and serve its customers. Finally, customer interaction will likely yield additional valuable customer data for the company. Figure 2.2 provides a flowchart of the process.

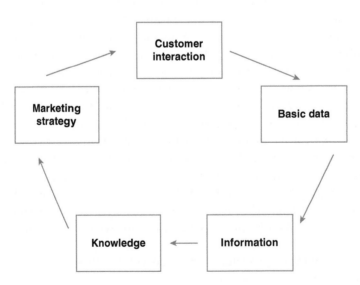

Figure 2.2 Database development process

As mentioned in Chapter 1, customer data can be obtained via many different sources, methods, and platforms at different stages in the customer buying process. Marketers often use a data management platform (DMP) to handle and organize all of the data. A **data management** platform is a centralized computing system that collects, integrates, and manages large sets of data (structured and unstructured) from disparate sources. In simple terms, DMP is a data warehouse system that stores and sorts data and converts it into useable information for marketers. Data dictates decision-making in today's marketing world. DMP ensures that marketers have the precise data they need on which to make solid marketing decisions. That said, all companies do not need the same type of data as they have different uses for data.

Thus, in building a customer database, the management must first determine the company's primary goals. For example, an organization might want to get to know its customers better to develop more effective future promotional activities. Other objectives may include selling them different products/services, thanking them for their patronage, encouraging referral business, introducing a new product or service, distributing information about an upcoming event or sale, or introducing a new staff member or employee . . . the list goes on! Customer loyalty programs are commonly used in the process of creating a customer database.

Customer Loyalty Programs

Customer loyalty programs are programs sponsored by an organization or company to encourage customer repeat purchases through program enrollment processes and the distribution of awards and/or benefits. Airlines, hotels, cruise lines, retail stores, and many other organizations have rewarded customer loyalty through structured programs for years.

Organizations primarily offer customer loyalty programs to strengthen customer relationships. Loyalty programs are also used to develop or provide additional information to a company's customer database. The beauty of customer loyalty programs is that you can obtain information about customers on a direct basis and use this information to more effectively target customers' future needs and wants.

Examples of Loyalty Programs

Southwest Airlines fosters a customer-driven approach to generating loyalty through its *Rapid Rewards* frequent flyer program (see Figure 2.3). The program, which began in 1987, was recently redesigned and its features were refined with insights gathered from its customers. The program offers three tiers or levels to provide added incentives for customers.

Figure 2.3 Southwest Airlines Rapid Rewards logo. Courtesy Southwest Airlines.

Figure 2.4 Airport sign, napkin, and peanuts. Photograph by Adam Baker, used with permission.

Figure 2.5 Rapid Rewards kiosk. Photograph by Adam Baker, used with permission.

Figure 2.6 Rapid Rewards card. Courtesy Southwest Airlines.

Members of the *Rapid Rewards* program earn points for every dollar they spend with Southwest and a number of designated partner companies. Customers may redeem these points for award travel with unlimited availability and freedom from blackout dates. Points do not expire as long as a member's account stays active within a 24-month period. As can be seen in Figure 2.4, Southwest Airlines embraces nearly every opportunity, including signage throughout airport terminals and promotional messages printed on its napkins and bags of peanuts, to advertise its Rapid Rewards program and drive customers to its website to enroll.

Customers may even sign up for a Rapid Rewards credit card that allows them to earn points after every purchase (see Figure 2.6). Southwest's most frequent customers, who fly 25 or more one-way flights or earn 35,000 points in a calendar year, also earn 'A-List' status. This preferred status carries many perks, such as priority boarding, priority check-in, and bonus Rapid Rewards points. Southwest's Rapid Rewards program is an excellent example of how companies strengthen relationships with customers and reward valuable customers for their loyalty. Establishing a customer loyalty program is not only a great way to reward customers, but it is also an excellent mechanism for collecting data from customers.

Uber[4] encourages long-term customer relationships with its loyalty program, *Uber Rewards*. The program was launched in 2018, offering free membership to consumers. Uber Rewards consists of four tiers: Blue, Gold, Platinum, and Diamond. The tiers are used to categorize users with a point system based on how much money they spent on Uber rides and Uber Eats. Customers with fewer than 500 points are enrolled at the Blue tier, while those who have accumulated between 500 and 2,499 points are at the Gold level, and people with points between 2,500 and 7,499 are enrolled as Platinum members. Finally, customers with a whopping number of 7,500 points or more achieve the Diamond level. Customers earn a point for every eligible dollar spent on Uber rides and Uber Eats. Then, for every 500 points earned, customers receive $5 Uber Cash. As an added bonus with Uber Rewards, customers obtain double the points on UberX and three times the points for Uber Black rides. The program benefits incentivize customers to continue using Uber services, while enhancing brand loyalty.

A final example of a customer loyalty program is that of one of the nation's largest retail footwear chains,[5] with more than 404 stores across the U.S. and in Puerto Rico. Along with the retailer's strong brick-and-mortar presence, its website serves as a shopping destination for shoe fans in the U.S. The company wanted to capitalize on its brand presence and increase the popularity of its customer loyalty program, so it partnered with Baesman Group to enhance its loyalty program and provide a seamless experience for all loyalty members. Baesman overhauled the customer loyalty program's member database, revamped the program's benefits, and established an online portal where members can access their account information. Since the partnership's inception, the customer loyalty program has exploded to more than 6.1 million members. In one year alone, active buyers increased 138 percent and the program's e-mail file grew by more than 270 percent. And all that growth has resulted in increased sales as loyalty program members typically spend nearly 30 percent more than non-members. This example is proof of the value that customer loyalty programs provide both to customers and to the companies that offer them.

Source Data

The information contained in a customer database is called source data. Each direct marketer must determine the particular source data needed for the organization's customer database—which often varies based on the specific products or services or the competitive situation of the direct marketer. Collecting data that will not be used simply drives up the organization's marketing costs. There are two different types of customer data: *structured* and *unstructured data*. Structured data is made up of clearly defined data types whose pattern makes them easily detectable, such as transaction data. Unstructured data is comprised of data that is typically not as defined, including formats like audio, video, and social media postings.[6] Within their house records, direct marketers usually capture certain key data, such as product preferences or credit experience, if relevant. Many companies today collect much of their customer data through online registration forms and even automatic online data collection methods. An important piece of data that many companies record is the source code of each customer. The source code indicates the media, media vehicle, or means by which the person has responded in order to become a customer. These codes should be very specific and may include sources such as participation at a specific event, referral from another customer, or referral from an employee.

Many companies, such as Amazon.com, automatically collect information, such as Internet Protocol (IP) addresses, item searches, browsing activity, and purchase history, from the viewers of its website. Through the use of cookies, in which Amazon.com stores specific identifying information on customer computers, the company can offer personalized features, including 'Recommended for You' items, relevant advertisements on other websites, and item storage in the company's online shopping cart. Amazon.com discloses this automatic data collection through its privacy policy, accessible online.[7]

Some of the basic data marketers should collect for a customer database are the customer's name and address, including ZIP code, telephone number, and e-mail address. Many direct marketers document how the customer first learned about the product or service. Additional data called transactional data include what products each customer has purchased, how recently (recency) and how often (frequency), and how much the customer spends (monetary). This information provides an avenue to analyze each customer through some variation of the recency/frequency/monetary (R/F/M) assessment. By carrying the date and volume of purchases in the master list record over a period of time, marketers can determine the transaction record of each customer in a given period, which helps determine the future potential of that customer.

Recency/Frequency/Monetary Assessment

The exact R/F/M formulation for each direct marketer naturally varies according to the importance given to each of the variables in relation to each other. For some promotions, marketers might need to manipulate their calculations by weighting one of the factors, so that, for example, the results will show those customers who purchased most recently. More sophisticated direct marketers use multivariate statistical techniques to mathematically determine the R/F/M weights and use them with greater reliability.

Table 2.1 shows how to evaluate customers on a mailing list according to the combined R/F/M values of their transactions over time. For purposes of this example, the following weights are assigned to the variables: recency ($\times$ 5), frequency ($\times$ 3), and monetary ($\times$ 2). In the example, three customers (identified as A, B, and C) have a purchase history calculated over a 24-month period. We assigned numerical points to each transaction, according to the derived R/F/M formula, and further weighted these points. The resulting cumulative point calculations—202 for A, 79 for B, and 280 for C—indicate a potential preference for Customer C. Customer C's R/F/M history, and perhaps A's as well, justify spending more promotion dollars. Customer B might be a risky investment for the company's promotional dollars. To apply R/F/M assessments, marketers must keep the customer database—especially the transaction data—current by means of continuous database maintenance.

DATABASE MAINTENANCE

A database is a perishable commodity that needs constant oversight and maintenance. Direct marketers must establish maintenance schedules and adhere to them rigorously. An initial requirement for proper list maintenance is that the list be compiled and developed in a uniform manner. Only when such uniformity exists within a computerized list is it possible to use match codes with any assurance of control.

Database maintenance activities include identifying and eliminating any duplicate records, identifying consumer names that appear on a number of different direct marketing response lists, and keeping the customer records current. Let's look more closely at each of these activities.

Match Codes and Merge-Purge

A serious and often cumbersome problem in compiling and maintaining lists is the potential for duplicating the same individual or organization, not only within house lists but also within and between response and compiled lists, and even between these lists and house lists. Given that most lists are computerized, marketers can extract from a name/address record abbreviated information about this record. This abbreviation is called a match code, and it is constructed so that each individual record can be matched with every other record. Because such matching requires a tremendous amount of computer memory, the match code is abbreviated to minimize the need for such storage. The match code abbreviation should be designed so that it addresses each area where errors are likely to occur within key parts of a record, such as transposition within a street address number as shown in the following example.

Table 2.1 R/F/M values

Assumptions

Recency of Transaction:
20 points if within past 3 months
10 points if within past 6 months
5 points if within past 9 months
3 points if within past 12 months
1 point if within past 24 months

Frequency of Transaction: Number of purchases within 24 months times 4 points each (Maximum: 20 points)

Monetary Value of Transaction: Gross dollar volume of purchases within 24 months times 10% (Maximum: 20 points)

Weighing Assumption:
Recency = 5
Frequency = 3
Monetary = 2

Example: Cust.	Purchase#	Recency	Assigned points	(x5) wght. points	Frequency	Assigned points	(x3) wght. points	Monetary	Assigned points	(x2) wght. points	Total wght. points	Cum. points
A	#1	3 mths	20	100	1	4	12	$30	3	6	118	118
A	#2	9 mths	5	25	1	4	12	$100	10	20	57	175
A	#3	24 mths	1	5	1	4	12	$50	5	10	27	202
B	#1	12 mths	3	15	2	8	24	$500	20	40	79	79
C	#1	3 mths	20	100	1	4	12	$100	10	20	132	132
C	#2	6 mths	10	50	1	4	12	$60	6	12	74	206
C	#3	12 mths	3	15	2	8	24	$70	7	14	53	259
C	#4	24 mths	1	5	1	4	12	$20	2	4	21	280

Ann Stafford	Ann Stafford
9330 West Arlington Road	3930 West Arlington Road
Alexandria, VA 22301	Alexandria, VA 22301

An example of a simple 18-digit match code derived from the name/address is shown in Table 2.2. Quite often, direct marketers add other data to the match code, such as a unique identification number or an expiration date for a magazine subscription. Mailing labels for catalogs or periodicals often demonstrate match codes of this type. An example is the ten-digit customer number used by the Newport News catalog of Spiegel Brands. This unique customer number reveals information about the particular market segment to which each customer belongs, their credit card status, whether they are a member of the Newport News Discount Club, and more.

An alternative to match codes is a unique identification number, such as a Social Security number, which identifies only one individual, but the customer or prospect has to provide this number for the marketer to be able to use it. Today, many consumers are not willing to provide their Social Security numbers due to privacy protection considerations.

Using the abbreviated match codes, the computerized merge-purge process identifies and deletes duplicate names/addresses within house lists. It can also eliminate names on house lists from outside response or compiled lists the marketer is using for new customer solicitation. Thus, the organization's own house list will not be duplicated within that promotion effort to prospects. The merge-purge process can eliminate duplication between these outside response and compiled lists as well.

Merge-purge is a highly sophisticated and complex process, but essentially it generates a match code for each name/address on each list, and these match codes, potentially many millions of them at a time, are matched with every other name on the list in sequence. Duplications are identified for special handling (which we discuss later).

It is doubtful that a 'perfect' match code could be developed, one that would compensate for all the idiosyncrasies and potential errors inherent in a name/address record. However, the one shown in Table 2.2 has a pretty good track record.

Table 2.2 Match codes

Position	Item	Description
1	State	A unique alpha-numeric code assigned to each state
2–5	Zip code	Last four numbers of 5-digit ZIP code
6–8	Surname	1st, 3rd , and 4th alpha characters of surname or business name
9–12	Address	House or business number
13–15	Address	1st, 3rd, and 4th alpha characters of street name
16	Surname	Alpha-numeric count of characters in surname
17	Given name	Alpha initial of first name
18	Given name	Alpha-numeric count of characters in first name

```
┌─────────────────────────────────────────────────┐
│ EXAMPLE ADDRESS                                   │
│ Ann Stafford                                      │
│ 9330 West Arlington Road                          │
│ Alexandria, VA 22301                              │
├───────────────────────────────────────────────── │
│ DERIVED MATCH CODE                                │
│ 8 2 3 0 1 S A F 9 3  3  0  A  L  I  8  A  3       │
│ 1 2 3 4 5 6 7 8 9 10 11 12 13 14 15 16 17 18      │
└─────────────────────────────────────────────────┘
```

Table 2.3 Economic value of merge-purge

% Duplication (or multi-buyers)	Total number of names/addresses merged					
	100,000	500,000	1,000,000	2,500,000	5,000,000	10,000,000
5%	$1,000	$5,000	$10,000	$25,000	$50,000	$100,000
10%	$2,000	$10,000	$20,000	$50,000	$100,000	$200,000
15%	$3,000	$15,000	$30,000	$75,000	$150,000	$300,000
20%	$4,000	$20,000	$40,000	$100,000	$200,000	$400,000
25%	$5,000	$25,000	$50,000	$125,000	$250,000	$500,000
30%	$6,000	$30,000	$60,000	$150,000	$300,000	$600,000

Note: Assumption: Mailing cost is $200 per thousand names mailed (or not mailed).

As demonstrated in the direct mail example shown in Table 2.3, even a 5 percent 'hit' rate, eliminating the need to mail 5 percent duplications, can result in substantial savings. This is especially true when several million name/address records are merged and purged. Thus, identifying a duplication of 15 percent of the names, when one million names on various lists are merged and purged, would eliminate 150,000 pieces of unnecessary mail. At an assumed cost of $200 per thousand names mailed, this would result in a saving of $30,000. Against this saving, of course, would be the cost of the merge-purge itself, possibly as much as $10 per thousand names examined or $10,000 for a one-million name/address input.

The merge-purge process can also effectively remove names of individuals who have expressed a desire not to receive solicitation as well as those who are poor credit risks or otherwise undesirable customers. Table 2.4, adapted from an actual merge-purge procedure, displays the manner of showing duplicate names/addresses on two or more lists. Both name and address variations are shown. All names and addresses are fictitious.

Table 2.4 Duplicate records

Name	Address	City	State	Zip
Samantha Fox	12353 N. Oak Drive	Arlington	VA	22301
Samantha Fox	12353 N. Oak Drive	Arlington	VA	22301
Christina Smith	250 Elders Drive	Arlington	VA	22301

Name	Address	City	State	Zip
C Smith	250 Elders Drive	Arlington	VA	22301
Jerry Matthis	9372 Nasaw St	Arlington	VA	22301
Jerry Matthis	9372 Nasaw St	Arlington	VA	22301
Dale Armstrong	700 Mosac Ln	Arlington	VA	22301
Nancy Armstrong	700 Mosac Ln	Arlington	VA	22301
Steven Samson	3662 S 11th St	Arlington	VA	22301
Steve Samson	3662 S 11th St	Arlington	VA	22301
Regina Jones	251 12th Ave	Arlington	VA	22301
Regina Jones	251 12th Ave	Arlington	VA	22301
Elaine Lowell	261 N. Second St	Arlington	VA	22301
Claire Lowell	261 N 2nd St	Arlington	VA	22301
Carson Snyder	690 42nd St	Arlington	VA	22301
Carson Snyder	690 42nd St	Arlington	VA	22301
Catherine Marlin	Apt 963 561 N 5th St	Arlington	VA	22301
Catherine Marlin	561 N 5th St	Arlington	VA	22301
Elizabeth Parks	68 Waverly Lane	Arlington	VA	22301
Elizabeth Parks	68 Waverly Ln	Arlington	VA	22301
Elizabeth Parks	68 Waverly Ln N	Arlington	VA	22301
Elizabeth Parks	68 Waverly Ln N	Arlington	VA	22301

Multibuyers

Eliminating duplicate names/addresses, saving costs, and minimizing irritation to those receiving duplicate mailings all are obvious advantages of the merge-purge process. But there is another, possibly even greater, advantage. If the same name/address is found on two or more response lists simultaneously, that individual may be a better prospect for a direct marketing offer because he or she is a **multibuyer**. Experimentation has shown, in fact, that those whose names appear on three lists have a higher response rate than those appearing on two lists. Likewise, names appearing on four lists are even more responsive.

In addition to identifying multibuyers, direct marketers perform database maintenance activities to keep their customer records current and accurate. These activities are discussed in the next section.

Keeping Records Current

If incorrect addresses or phone numbers result in misdirected advertising promotions, the cost is twofold: (1) the wasted contact and (2) the sacrifice of potential response. That is what is at stake if the direct marketer does not keep records current. In an effort to keep customer records current and accurate, direct marketers regularly perform change of address investigations, nixie removal, and record status updates. Let's examine each of these activities in greater detail.

Whenever possible, direct marketers request address corrections through the postal service. The U.S. Postal Service assures that mail prepaid with first-class postage is automatically returned if undeliverable or else forwarded without charge if the new address is known. In the latter instance, for a fee, the change of address notification can be sent back to the direct marketer. In the case of advertising mail, the use of the 'address correction requested' legend on the mailing envelope guarantees prepayment of any return postage and service fees. There are many variations of this particular list correction service relative to either individual mail or catalog mail, concerning forwarding or return postage guarantees.

Additionally, direct marketers encourage the recipient of mail to inform them of any change of address or phone number. If available, customers are encouraged to reference a unique account code when requesting changes. If the account number is unavailable, customers are asked to provide both the old and new address—the former for entering into the system and removing the old record, and the latter for future addressing.

Using the 'address correction requested' service on each and every customer mailing is not necessary; once or twice a year should suffice to clean the database. Using the legend more frequently, because of lags in handling times, could result in duplication of returned mail and unnecessary duplication of costs. The term **nixie** refers to mail that has been returned by the U.S. Postal Service because it is undeliverable as addressed, often due to a simple error in the street address or the ZIP code. Possibly, the person to whom the piece is addressed is deceased or has moved and left no forwarding address. The marketer will remove such names from the mailing list; unless the list owner can obtain updated information, they cannot be reinstated. According to the U.S. Census Bureau, about 12 percent of Americans move each year.[8]

Perhaps this is why e-mail addresses are quickly becoming the preferred address—because they do not necessarily change each time the person moves to a new geographical location. However, some Internet service providers are local, and if you move to a new location, you have to change your e-mail address. Also, keep in mind that many consumers may switch Internet providers due to personal preferences, change their e-mail user names, and/or use several different e-mail accounts.

The U.S. Postal Service, for a nominal handling fee, will provide direct marketers with correct address information, if available. Often, however, mail addressed to a deceased person will go to the surviving spouse. Business mail to an individual who has changed position or even left an organization will go to the replacement in that position. Although the U.S. Postal Service will not send notifications in such instances, some direct marketers correct their lists in other ways. Special notices might periodically be sent with mailings requesting list correction. Additionally, sales representatives may request consumer information changes each time he or she contacts a customer. In some cases, the mail recipient sends such notice directly. Other ways list owners can update their lists include news items, periodic updates from telephone and other directories, and public records such as birth and death notices and marriage and divorce proceedings.

Changes in telephone numbers should be made periodically to house lists that are used to access customers by telephone. Customers who have changed to unlisted numbers should be contacted by mail or an effort should be made to obtain these numbers.

It is important to perform database maintenance not only from the perspective of nixie and otherwise undeliverable mail, but also to keep the record status of customers up to date. List owners should enter new orders from customers into the database promptly because they have a major impact on the R/F/M formulation described earlier. Such prompt recordkeeping also avoids unnecessary mailings, telephone calls, or e-mails to customers who already have what the direct marketer is offering.

DATABASE SECURITY

Customer databases are assets, much the same as buildings, equipment, and inventories. Because their value is intangible, however, databases are not easily insurable (except for replacement or duplication costs), even if we can determine their future value. Unlike other assets, they're portable, especially when an entire database can be placed on a single computer disk.

For these reasons, marketers must take special precautions to prevent theft, loss, or unauthorized use of the database and to guarantee the information privacy rights of all consumers.

Information Privacy

As will be addressed in greater detail later in Chapter 13, organizations that maintain a customer database also have a responsibility to safeguard the personal information contained in it. The dramatic growth of online marketing has also led to new challenges for protecting the privacy of customer information. Online consumer databases contain a wide variety of personal identification information, and if security is breached, this information may be accessible by those with intentions of identity theft and scamming. For example, a 2018 customer database breach involving mobile telecommunication company T-Mobile impacted roughly two million of its customers. T-Mobile reported that the customers' names, billing zip codes, phone numbers, e-mail addresses, and account numbers were exposed.[9] Access to these types of information could lead to e-mail 'phishing,' in which individuals receive realistic but unauthorized e-mails that seek to obtain more personal information, such as Social Security numbers and passwords. Though the unauthorized access in T-Mobile's case likely only affected less than 3% of the company's 76 million subscribers, the incident placed T-Mobile at risk of tarnishing its reputation in the market.[10]

Direct marketers must use the information only in a highly ethical manner and honor any consumer requests to have their personal information kept confidential—which means not sharing it with other direct marketers. Therefore, regular database maintenance should include activities to protect the information privacy rights of consumers as well as to ensure that the information in each database record is accurate and kept up to date.

Proper Database Storage

A logical first step in database security is the provision of adequate storage. Usually, such storage protects against natural hazards of fire and water damage as well as theft or unauthorized use. To discourage theft, marketers should limit and control access to database files at all times. This often involves certain passwords used to protect the database. Additionally, only select individuals should be permitted access to the information stored in the database. Should records become lost, adequate backup should be available in the form of duplicate records at a remote location.

List Seeding

Direct marketers have developed a variety of marking techniques to ensure that their customer lists are not misappropriated or misused, especially when rented to outside parties. One commonly used technique is called salting or seeding a list. Seeding (salting) a list is when the direct marketer places decoys, which are either incorrect spellings or fictitious names that appear nowhere else, on the customer list so as to track and identify any misuse. Although a seeded list may reveal such misuse, it may not lead to the guilty person. Marketers should construct identification programs like seeding so that the decoy names will not be removed through match coding. Of course, the decoy names should be confidential and access to them limited.

Direct marketers discourage list theft by placing seeds on lists. Direct marketers must communicate their use of list seeds to all parties involved in the list industry. By fully disclosing the actions to protect their lists, direct marketers may discourage list theft.

DATABASE USES AND APPLICATIONS

Once we have captured and stored data, we can convert it into real information to better serve customers and maximize profitability. The uses of a customer database are virtually endless; we discuss some of the more common ones in this chapter. Keep in mind that the real beauty of a customer database is that it enables direct marketers to communicate with small market segments or individual customers without other customers knowing. This kind of communication secrecy, also called stealth marketing, enables direct marketers to extend different types of offers to individual customers on the basis of their customer information.

For example, Harris Teeter, a regional grocery store, sends elaborate gifts on a regular basis to its *very best* customers. These customers also receive a $10 Harris Teeter gift card at Thanksgiving along with a personally signed thank you letter from the store manager. Gifts of lesser value and thank you letters not containing the gift card may be sent to those regular customers who are *not as valuable* to Harris Teeter, based on the amount spent. Furthermore, Harris Teeter may send other direct mail letters containing coupons to encourage other customers (those even less valuable) to shop more often at Harris Teeter. This kind of one-on-one communication is made possible by analyzing the source data contained in a customer database. This is critical to successful direct marketing because building customer relationships is most effectively carried out on a one-to-one basis. The ability to know one's customers and communicate with them individually is the basic premise of a customer database for direct marketers.

Using a Customer Database

Though there are a million ways to use a database, let's explore eight of the more common ones:

1. *Profile customers.* By developing a geographic, demographic, social, psychological, and behavioral profile of their customers, direct marketers can better understand the various consumer market segments they serve. For example, Carnival Cruise Line has 10 brands and serves 11.5 million passengers per year.[11] Imagine all of the information its database has on its customers' prior travel habits and interests, and how the company may use this data to profile its customers. Carnival collects information regarding passenger anniversaries and birthdays, what cruises passengers took, what they paid, their sailing dates, how many people traveled in their party, and whether they traveled with children. This information enables the company to better understand the needs of their typical customers.

2. *Retain the best customers.* According to the well-known 80/20 principle, approximately 80 percent of an organization's business is generated by 20 percent of its customers. Thus, it is critical that direct marketers analyze their customer database to determine who their best customers are and to spend more effort (and promotional dollars) in keeping these customers satisfied and coming back for more! Just think of the Harris Teeter example. Harris Teeter can afford to spend more money in terms of promotional dollars to keep those customers who spend more money in groceries satisfied and to keep them coming back on a regular basis. Harris Teeter cannot justify sending its occasional shoppers gifts and personally signed thank you notes from the store manager.

3. *Thank customers for their patronage.* All customers deserve to be recognized and thanked for their decision to purchase from a given organization. This is especially true when the direct marketer has a number of competitors from whom the customer could have purchased. Customers expect to be satisfied with their purchase decisions; however, follow-up activities can often provide an avenue for future dialogue with each customer to ensure that satisfaction. Thanking customers is also an effective way to both reinforce purchase decisions and promote future purchases. An example is the thank you letter containing a bumper sticker that is mailed to an individual who makes a donation to a state or local police association. Donors take pride in displaying those bumper stickers, which state 'I Am a Proud Supporter of the Virginia State Police.'

4. *Capitalize on cross-selling and continuity selling opportunities.* Cross-selling refers to selling your current customers products and services that are related (and even unrelated) to the products/services they currently purchase from your organization. By analyzing the products and services your customers have purchased from you, you can identify and capitalize on numerous cross-selling opportunities. **Continuity selling** has also been referred to as 'club offers'; here consumers purchase on a regular basis—either weekly, monthly, quarterly, or annually. *Time* magazine, for example, cross-sells its other publications—*People, Sports Illustrated, Fortune*—to certain current subscribers.

5. *Develop a customer communication program.* As mentioned earlier, the real beauty and power of a customer database is that it enables the direct marketer to communicate on a one-to-one basis with each customer. Thus, the company can segment its promotional strategies based on the customer group and individual with whom it is communicating. For example, newer customers could receive 'welcome' letters, while established customers might receive 'thank you for your loyalty' letters. Of course, each customer does not know what is being communicated to other customers. Unlike general advertising, a customer database also enables customized marketing communications to occur between the company and its customers

without the competition knowing. This is another powerful use of the customer database. As Figure 2.7 reveals, customer communication plans or programs are targeted, tailored, and timed communications with select members or segments of the customer population. These are planned communications and most models depict a 12-month communication program.

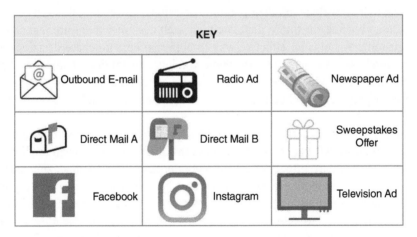

COMMUNICATION PLAN												
	Jan	Feb	March	April	May	June	July	Aug	Sep	Oct	Nov	Dec
Wealthy Seniors		Radio		Newspaper		Radio		E-mail			Newspaper	
Baby Boomers	E-mail			Direct Mail B		Direct Mail B				Television		Radio
Young Adults			Direct Mail A		Direct Mail A		Facebook		Sweepstakes		Instagram	

KEY					
Outbound E-mail		Radio Ad		Newspaper Ad	
Direct Mail A		Direct Mail B		Sweepstakes Offer	
Facebook		Instagram		Television Ad	

Figure 2.7   Communication plan

Many companies, such as Smithfield Foods featured in Figure 2.8, send e-newsletters to their customers. In the e-newsletter, Smithfield encourages its customers to 'Tail-gate with Smithfield' and offers its customers a sampling of great new recipes to try out for grilling at the game or at home.

Finally, a customer communication program implies two-way communication. Direct marketers use customer feedback to revise and improve their marketing activities to better serve the customer and maximize profitability. Examples of customer communication programs are

Figure 2.8   Smithfield Foods e-newsletter. Used with permission of Smithfield Foods.

numerous. Hotels, airlines, grocery stores, nonprofit organizations, magazines, and just about every direct marketer creates and uses one to guide its customer and prospect communications. If you purchase a new car, chances are likely that you will receive a variety of follow-up communications from the automobile manufacturer. Say you purchased a Honda Civic. The first message you receive should be a 'thank you' for your purchase. Next might be a mini-survey to assess the quality of your Honda shopping experience. After that, you might receive a number of updates about what is new at Honda and regular reminder notices about when you should bring your Civic back to the dealer for servicing. Of course, at some point in time, Honda will suggest that it is time to trade your Civic in for a new one!

6. *Perform marketing research.* The database is a natural arena for direct marketers to conduct marketing research in order to better understand the current and future needs and wants of their customers. Marketing research gathers, classifies, and analyzes information about customers. This information is normally 'problem-specific' or 'purpose-specific.' For example, if the direct marketer is thinking of bringing a new product or service to the market, investigating the potential response from current customers is a natural application of marketing research. Marketing research activities can include customer satisfaction surveys, new product research, customer needs assessments, brand preference studies, media preference research, and much more.

For example, many hotels send surveys via e-mail following customer stays. Hilton and Marriott and their associated brands are consistent with this approach, asking how expectations have been met, and even sending reminders to complete surveys that have not yet been completed and returned.

Here's another example. At the end of every core season, Busch Gardens surveys its Pass Members via e-mail and in the park in an effort to continue to improve and evolve its membership program. In 2015, the survey revealed that an overwhelming number of Pass Members listed free friend tickets as the number one desired perk. The park listened to its loyal Pass Members and implemented a new system in 2016 that provided every active Pass Member with one free friend ticket per season—spring, summer, and fall. The park saw an increase in Pass Member renewals, Pass Member satisfaction, and new pass sales, directly as a result of the appointed tickets. The survey has also been responsible for in-park facility renovations, new culinary additions, and a continued development of customer service. That demonstrates the value of using a database for marketing research and customer feedback.

7. *Generate new customers.* We've seen that analyzing the customer database enables the direct marketer to develop profiles of its average customers and its best customers. Armed with this information, direct marketers can seek out new customers who may have needs and wants similar to those of their current customers. This also enables direct marketers to rent response or compiled lists of prospects that match the profile of their best customers and target them with promotional offers to attract new customers. This is a much more effective and efficient way to generate new customers than merely blanketing the mass audience with advertisements in the hope that someone with a need or desire for the product/service will respond.

Figure 2.9   Busch Gardens Best Spring Ever postcard. Used with the consent of Busch Gardens/Water Country USA.

Another very effective way to generate new customers is via referrals. Current customers can be sent offers to encourage their relatives and friends to become customers as well. Many companies provide a 'forward to friend' option in their e-mail communications with customers. Here's an example of how a company has both thanked its customers and generated referrals at the same time. One benefit that a Busch Gardens Pass Member has is the ability to purchase discounted tickets for friends and family. Based on the level of the pass, the discount is either $12 or $15 off a single-day ticket. As shown in Figure 2.9, as a way of offering a bigger discount and to drive spring visitation prior to the launch of a new ride, Busch Gardens mailed postcards to all annual Pass Members, offering a 50 percent discount on single-day tickets good for up to six tickets. The park received a 2.2 percent response rate and gained new customers.

8. *Send customized offers.* We've seen that analyzing the customer database enables a direct marketer to develop a profile of consumer needs and wants. It also enables direct marketers to create customized offers to individuals or market segments within the customer database. Customized offers often are sent via direct mail or outbound e-mail. E-mail is generally more cost-effective and it enables companies to easily target customers who are members of a company's loyalty program. Of course, all companies provide the opportunity for customers to opt out of receiving such e-mail communication. An excellent example of a company that sends valuable customized offers to its loyalty program members is Barnes & Noble. Its members receive weekly communication about new book titles and special offers for extra discounts on these featured book titles. Various offers encourage the sale of DVDs or used books, and sometimes these offers are limited to online shopping. As Figure 2.10 shows, occasionally members receive free gift offers, like a free book light, when they spend a specified amount, or special limited time offers to obtain an extra discount on their in-store or online purchases.

Figure 2.10   Barnes & Noble offer. Used with permission of Barnes & Noble Inc.

These are examples of how a company communicates regularly with its customers by sending customized offers. Keep in mind that the more data a direct marketer has about its customers, the more specific and customized the offers can be. For that reason, most direct marketers regularly update customer records and, whenever possible, incorporate new information into their customer records. This process is called *database enhancement*, and it is discussed later in this chapter. However, every direct marketer will regularly analyze the data contained in its customer database to learn more about its customers to more effectively serve them. This process is called database analytics, and it is the key to effectively using a customer database for all purposes. Let's discuss *database analytics* in greater detail.

Performing Database Analytics

Database analytics is where the direct marketer analyzes customer information housed within the customer database to draw inferences about an individual customer's needs. This relies on customer profiling, modeling, and data mining. **Data mining** uses statistical and mathematical techniques to extract knowledge from data contained within a database. It is the process of using software tools to find relevant information from large amounts of data, typically an enterprise data warehouse, and using the results for strategic business decision-making.

A variety of database tools permit the assessment of single-variable information. However, the multivariable patterns can allow for the assessment of causes and effects in the business process. The true value of the integrated data warehouse can be found by leveraging decision support tools, such as online analytical processing (OLAP), to mine the data for hidden patterns. OLAP has long been the domain of business analysts and statisticians. Today, sophisticated new tools enable business analysis capabilities via the data warehouse throughout the entire organization. Previous tools provided only static reports, offering little flexibility in terms of what a user could glean or screen from the warehouse. With OLAP, users can slice and dice the data from a summary level down into the detail of the data record. Marketers can obtain information on customers by region or by revenue and do it all from their desktop. An example might be a direct mail transaction database in which responders are evaluated by different demographic characteristics. The analysis could allow the marketing team to select specific prospects from large compiled files that fit common customer profiles.

Let's take a look at another example. Teradata, a division of NCR, analyzed the sales data of a well-known retailer and found some interesting correlations. Based on the analysis, Teradata found a direct relationship between the purchases of beer and diapers in the evening hours.[12] On investigation, the retailer found that this was occurring because husbands were being sent out on Saturday night to buy diapers and subsequently purchased beer as an impulse item. Thus, retailers and merchandisers wanting to predict and model future consumer behavior use information like the beer and diapers relationship in their attempts to maximize the effectiveness of their marketing efforts. This example points to the fact that data analytics are only valuable if the new knowledge gained enables the users of the information to make actionable decisions. Yes, beer and diapers were found to be positively correlated, but most retailers would not rearrange their stores to stock these items side by side.

The secret to database analytics is for marketers to be able to identify their most and least valuable customers and clarify demographic and behavioral statistics that apply to each population. Then they must be able to clearly identify the differences between the two groups. Marketers use data analytics to make strategic business decisions to retain current customers and attract new ones. Think of it this way: if you can clearly identify specific differences between your 'best' or most valuable customer and your least valuable customer, then you will know how to 'mine' the most likely best customers from prospect lists and databases. Although this seems like common sense, many businesses do not take the time to analyze, evaluate, and act on this critical knowledge.

Analyzing customer data can produce powerful results. For example, an industry-leading craft retailer[13] wanted to better understand its customer base and target audience. Quad, a worldwide marketing solutions company, performed a deep data analysis on its customer database and revealed that the retailer's campaigns needed to be broadened to include an overlooked audience segment. The retailer assumed that its target audience was women and thus promotional campaigns were geared toward them, when, in fact, most of its active customer base was men. Quad revamped an existing poor-performing campaign with a new data-driven strategy and replaced discounts with multichannel engagement tactics. The new campaign included a national art contest, an in-store discount reveal, and a color quiz. The new campaign was executed across all of the relevant channels, including in-store, e-mail, direct mail, website, landing pages, and retail inserts. The results showed that integrated marketing drove sales by 4.9 percent, e-mail sign-ups increased by 58 percent, and contest entries increased by 138 percent.

The drivers to using analytical data revolve around cost, value, and accuracy: cost of the analysis, long-term value (or lifetime value) of a current or prospective customer, and accuracy of the data to be used in strategic decision-making. There is a plethora of data available to marketers, at a wide range of costs and details. The key is in obtaining the most current, relevant, and accurate data to add to your existing customer database. The process of adding data to a customer database is the topic of the next section.

DATABASE ENHANCEMENT

Database enhancement is adding and overlaying information to customer records to better describe and understand the customer. Direct marketers also call it 'appending' the database. It is a means to an end, not an end in and of itself. There are at least three specific reasons to enhance a customer database:

1. To learn more about the customer.
2. To increase the effectiveness of future promotional activities targeted to current customers.
3. To better prospect for new customers who are similar to current customers.

The kinds of information that enhance a database in this way include geographic, demographic, social, and psychological data. We can obtain the data either *internally* or *externally*.

Internal Data Enhancement

Direct marketers can obtain information internally when they conduct marketing research activities with their existing customers. Of course, each customer must be willing to furnish the given data. Examples of information that direct marketers, such as Carnival Cruise Lines, Dell Computers, or Hallmark Cards, can collect internally from their customers include:

- age
- gender
- income
- marital status
- family composition
- street address
- e-mail address
- length of time at current residence
- size of household
- type of housing
- telephone number
- preferred contact method
- do not mail (preference)
- lifestyle data.

Direct marketers cannot gather all enhancement data internally; therefore, they must rely on some external sources as well. For example, when applying for a JC Penney credit card, the company must obtain some historical information about your credit rating prior to approving your application and establishing the limit of your line of credit.

External Data Enhancement

Direct marketers purchase external data from many different sources. They purchase data compiled by companies like Experian, Equifax, R. L. Polk, and Claritas, and electronically overlay this information onto their customer databases. The data are usually demographic, although some companies compile consumer lifestyle and leisure activity data. Claritas offers several products designed to assist direct marketers with customer database enhancement. Claritas Market Place File Enhancement helps direct marketers gain a better understanding of their customers and prospects. The behavioral profiles associated with this enhancement service include a variety of consumer-buying behaviors, either from syndicated data or Claritas's own audits. Customer addresses can be standardized, geocoded, and appended with segmentation information in a matter of minutes. Claritas Consumer Point, customer targeting and strategic market planning software, connects a direct marketer's customer file with market data to expose hidden gaps in existing and untapped markets. Consumer Point's Internet-based data access provides insights into the most up-to-date segment distribution, behavioral profiles, and demographic/consumer demand data for targeting profitable customers and strategic market planning.

Examples of the data that direct marketers may obtain to enhance their customer database externally include:

- geographic address
- telephone number
- gender of head of household
- length of time of residence
- number of adults at residence
- number of children at residence
- income
- occupation
- marital status
- make of automobile(s) owned.

Companies like Equifax, Experian, Ruf Strategic Solutions, and Claritas purchase census data from the government, sometimes for small geographic areas known as census tracts. Direct marketers can purchase the data from these intermediary firms for a fee. Census data can help identify:

- specific age segments (e.g., adults aged 18 to 24)
- one-person households
- households with children
- households with specified income levels
- households with homes greater than specified values
- adults with some college education
- adults in college
- adults with specified occupations.

Finally, firms can purchase external data about businesses, rather than final consumers. Companies such as Dun & Bradstreet and Experian collect data on businesses and make it available to direct marketers for a fee. Such data may include:

- company name/address/telephone number
- industrial classification code
- number of employees
- gross sales
- primary products produced
- branch locations
- name/title of key employees.

In summary, direct marketers enhance their customer database in an effort to better serve the future needs and wants of their customers. This should result in a stronger relationship with each customer. While each customer is valuable to the direct marketer, all customers are not of equal value. Let's examine how direct marketers manage relationships with their customers.

CUSTOMER RELATIONSHIP MANAGEMENT

Market share has shifted to customer share, competition to collaboration, and mass marketing to integrated interactive relationship marketing. Technology has shifted also. Interactivity, spurred by the digital transformation, now allows marketers to engage with customers as individuals, gather and remember their responses, and reduce the amount of time necessary to make strategic decisions about how customers make purchase decisions. The marketer's tool kit has also been enhanced by the convergence of technologies such as high-speed computing, expanding communication bandwidth, massive national databases, enhanced statistical decision-support tools and campaign management. This convergence has allowed for the development of **customer relationship management** (CRM), an integrated system that delivers a single-source transactional database of up-to-date customer information throughout an entire organization, maximizes the total value of the customer relationship, and organizes the outbound communication driven by database marketing. Adobe, Oracle, and SAP are among the many vendors that provide CRM services and support for direct marketers.

Within all of this innovation, however, many companies have lost sight of the foundations of experimentation that have been the cornerstone of database marketing in the past. CRM provides a variety of sales, marketing, and service functions that allow interaction with prospects or customers across the organization and multiple media channels. The main benefit is that all information—from prospect communication to sales close to service history—is tracked and used in the management of treatment for that customer and future prospects based on patterns that emerge with analytics.

Direct marketers create and utilize customer journey maps to organize customer data. A **customer journey map** is a visual depiction of every interaction and experience a customer has with a company or an organization. Each customer's experience begins at the moment of discovery (or brand recognition) and extends through the lifetime of the customer relationship. Customer journey maps are powerful tools that produce great insight for the entire company. As the example provided in Figure 2.11 shows, customer journey maps can visually tell stories about customers and enable the company to understand how customers move through the sales funnel. This knowledge, once distributed throughout the organization to those business units that interact with the customer, will enable the company to provide an enhanced customer experience. Indeed, customers generate mounds of data about their experiences with a company every single day; however, this data is only valuable if it is captured, organized, analyzed, and shared to deliver effective engagement and improved customer satisfaction from the customer's perspective. The bottom line is that customer journey maps should help all stakeholders deepen their understanding of their customers' behaviors, thoughts, and feelings across touchpoints in their journey, and they should be actionable.[14] (See Readings and Resources at the end of the chapter for more detail on customer journey maps.)

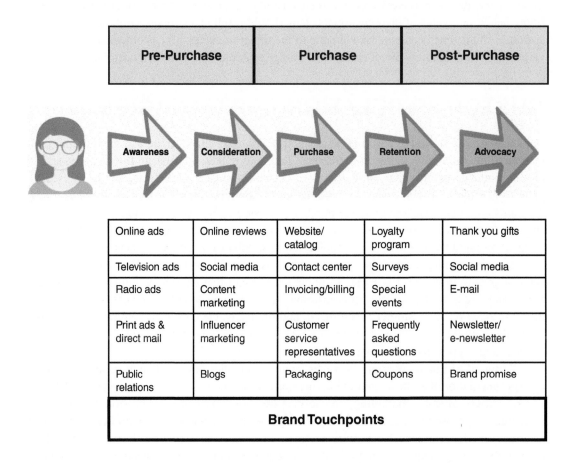

Pre-Purchase		Purchase	Post-Purchase	

Awareness — Consideration — Purchase — Retention — Advocacy

Online ads	Online reviews	Website/ catalog	Loyalty program	Thank you gifts
Television ads	Social media	Contact center	Surveys	Social media
Radio ads	Content marketing	Invoicing/billing	Special events	E-mail
Print ads & direct mail	Influencer marketing	Customer service representatives	Frequently asked questions	Newsletter/ e-newsletter
Public relations	Blogs	Packaging	Coupons	Brand promise
Brand Touchpoints				

Figure 2.11   Customer journey map example. Used with permission of Johnnie Gray.

As will be discussed in greater detail in Chapter 4, companies use predictive analytics to improve customer relationship management. Direct marketers use predictive analytics to determine individuals' future decisions based on their past actions. Statistical algorithms and machine learning techniques give direct marketers the ability to perform such predictive analyses. The power of predictive analytics is dynamic. Not only does predictive analytics optimize the success of marketing campaigns, but it also helps detect fraud in customer databases, improve overall business operations, and reduce potential risks. In the digital tech-savvy twenty-first century, more and more businesses are investing in predictive analytics software and technology. The growing usage of predictive analytics is due to increasing amounts of data, more efficient computers, user-friendly software, and a desire for a competitive advantage. Business intelligence software companies, such as Sisense, IBM, and SAS, to name a few, are vendors who offer predictive analytics solutions for direct marketers.[15]

Customer relationship management tools should be employed to track all of the outbound media touch points from a company, including e-mail, direct mail, SMS text messaging, banner ad marketing, direct-response TV, and traditional channels such as radio, newspaper, and magazine ads. A new form of CRM that has analytic tools embedded into the media planning and measurement modules allows for the scoring of response touch point data in real-time so a marketer can modify and customize their campaigns to target lists or media channels that are delivering higher value return on investment. Ruf Strategic Solutions was one of the first vendors to offer Intelligent CRM, or I-CRM, in its product called Navigator. This product allows the marketer to immediately access the marketing results through an online dashboard linked to the marketing database. Campaign management, forecasting trends, media analysis, and data-mining capabilities are connected to enable timely, results-oriented decisions for successful customer relationships. An I-CRM tool typically contains the following:

1. Multichannel marketing: Communicate with your customers across all touch points through a fully integrated data warehouse and sharpen your targeting skills to maximize response rates and reduce waste.
2. Marketing automation: Simplify complex processes, obtain instant access to key performance indicators, and compare results from different periods or campaigns in order to gauge business trends.
3. Campaign management: Manage and measure every campaign from list selection, based upon any combination of variables from your database, through results tracking and campaign return on investment (ROI).
4. E-mail marketing: Effortlessly deliver high volumes of e-mails, create customized and personalized messages, and obtain detailed response reports.
5. Analytical tools: Gain actionable intelligence with powerful tools such as OLAP, which can quickly identify the reasons behind customer actions, and Web Analytics, which can enhance your Web visitors' experiences.
6. Data services: Enhance, consolidate, and standardize all of your data into one comprehensive database.

In summary, I-CRM tools give marketers the real-time intelligence needed to be successful in modifying marketing spending and tracking market changes in a timely fashion. The goal of CRM is to allow the entire organization to be cohesive in how it communicates with each customer and to manage that customer experience as if it had distinct knowledge of needs and prior support issues. This is a 'closed-loop' process, as shown in Figure 2.12.

Full-circle marketing, which is based on the fact that not all customers are created equal, is an innovative marketing strategy that brings database marketing to a new level. Because customers change over time, marketers' communication with them must follow these changes if they are to maintain optimum lifetime value. The framework for this full-circle approach includes four dimensions that are at the heart of the experimental technique: (1) planning, (2) research, (3) testing, and (4) validation; and then repeating the steps in a never-ending feedback loop.

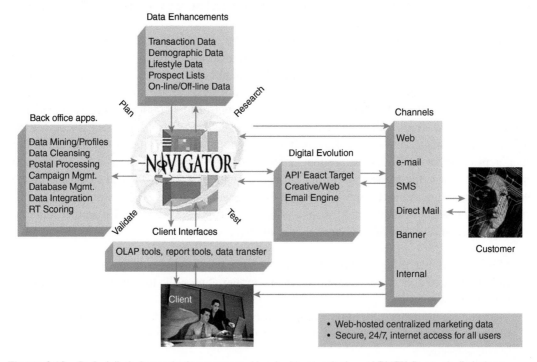

Figure 2.12 Ruf's full-circle marketing process. Used with permission of RUF™ Strategic Solutions.

CRM has been evolving over the years. With proper assessment of the organization process and readiness to adapt to a data- and customer-centric strategy, it can lead to significant business competitive advantage.

By focusing on CRM at the initial point of contact, the company has a far better chance of nurturing a long-term relationship that generates satisfaction for the customer and revenue or value for the company. Understanding customer value is a necessary element in the development of effective marketing strategies.

Customer Value

All customers are not of equal value to a company or organization. We can categorize customers according to the strength of their relationship to our company or organization. As Figure 2.13 reveals, customers can be placed in a hierarchy with the least valuable at the bottom and the most valuable at the top. *Suspects* are those prospective consumers who you think may have a need or want for your company's product or service. *Prospects* are qualified 'hand-raisers' who have identified themselves as having an interest in your company or organization. Prospects may have visited your website or dialed your toll-free number. Your *customers* have placed an order with your company. They could be called 'single buyers' as you do not know whether they will return for a repeat purchase. *Clients* are multibuyers. These are repeat customers with whom you have an established relationship. At the top of the customer hierarchy are your *advocates*. These are your most valuable customers. They generate the most revenue for your company.

Figure 2.13 Customer hierarchy. Used with permission of Johnnie Gray.

For example, a major U.S. sporting goods retailer,[16] with more than 1,000 stores across the country, was able to move customers to higher customer value segments of the customer hierarchy via data analytics and targeted marketing provided by Baesman Group. The sporting goods retailer had a mature loyalty program with millions of enrolled members, yet the company saw an opportunity to increase engagement, member value, and purchase behaviors. Baesman helped the company identify methods to improve loyalty program incrementality and ROI via the following four steps:

Step 1. Analyzed years of transactional history, producing insights into customer behavior.

Step 2. Redesigned its customer loyalty program based on customer insights and financial modeling aligned with business objectives.

Step 3. Maximized customer potential since the loyalty program had a large member base, but it was not increasing customer numbers.

Step 4. Used ghost control methodology to identify historical trends that matched back to current loyalty members. The result was proven incremental gains in revenue and engagement.

The results were outstanding. The sporting goods retailer saw an increase in sales of 57 percent from its loyalty program members; a 27 percent average increase in loyalty member migration to top value deciles; and a 16 percent growth in member purchase frequency.

In direct marketing, the emphasis is on discerning between one-time buyers versus multibuyers. A customer who has purchased twice is a proven repeat buyer and is far more likely to purchase again than a one-timer. Thus, marketing strategies are tailored to convert one-time buyers into multibuyers and to expend fewer resources on multibuyers as they age. Additionally, for companies that are multichannel (direct mail, Web, retail), those customers who purchase from more than one channel tend to be more valuable in the long run than those who purchase from a single channel. This has to be carefully evaluated to factor out the fact that a multichannel buyer is, ipso facto, a multibuyer. Thus, companies must determine what, if any, additional value for being a multichannel buyer comes above the multibuyer status.

Marketers must keep in mind that customers who buy once and never buy again have a one-time value. Prospective customers who never make a purchase usually cost the company in unrequited advertising and possibly service dollars. However, customers who buy frequently have a maximized or enhanced value to the company. Why? It's simple. As we mentioned earlier in this chapter, a company's best customers are loyal to the company, require less customer service and assistance, spend more per transaction, and generate valuable referrals. This combination adds up to greater value for the company. That is precisely why most companies have a customer-centric focus. Therefore, a company's CRM strategies that focus on customers' wants and needs at the earliest possible touch point, and make their experience long-lasting and sustainable, prove their worth in value. As with all direct and interactive marketing, what is measurable is what translates into knowing what defines value. Although all facets of measurability are important to the direct model, a company that knows the economic worth or value of its customers is the most defining. The value of customers over their lifetime allows a company to claim these customers as assets on its balance sheet, hence the importance of customer lifetime value.

Customer Lifetime Value (CLTV)

The **customer lifetime value (CLTV)** can be calculated as the discounted stream of net revenues that a customer will generate over the period of his or her lifetime of patronage with a company.[17] The information for calculating CLTV is derived from the transactions recorded in an organization's database.

Whenever we gain or retain a customer as a result of good customer relations, we earn not only the revenue generated in one month or one year, but also the *present value* of the *future profits* generated for as long as the customer remains active as a customer.[18] Just think . . . if a business were to be totally consumed in a fire, its tangible assets such as buildings, equipment, and inventory could be rebuilt in time, and each of these tangible assets is likely to be covered by insurance. The business would continue. However, if an organization lost its database of customers, an intangible but very valuable asset, the business likely could not continue. Without customers, there is no business! You might argue, well, the business would simply have to go out and get new customers. That may be true, but it would require much greater effort and cost than most companies could sustain.

Direct marketers spend a major portion of their time, effort, and money developing lists of customers and qualified prospects. In fact, many in direct marketing believe that such lists, along with descriptive databases, are in fact the key ingredients that differentiate *direct* marketing from general marketing. Therefore, direct marketers especially should view their customers as assets, as investments. They are the lifeblood of a direct marketing organization from which future sales accrue at a cost that is generally significantly lower than that attributed to the first sale.

It follows that if a marketing expenditure can result in the acquisition of *new* customers who will generate value over future time, then that action is desirable even though the initial cost to obtain those customers might be greater than the short-term return on that investment. Some might call this long-term return on investment, long-term value (LTV), the cost of goodwill. Savvy direct marketers call it 'the value of a customer.'

Naturally, when a new customer is acquired, the direct marketer does not know whether that customer will make only a single purchase or become an ongoing customer. The direct marketer cannot determine whether that customer will purchase only low-margin products that have limited profitability or purchase without paying attention to price at all. However, direct marketers know that, in most cases, the cost of acquiring customers will yield a positive return on the investment. In Chapter 4, we explain how to calculate customer LTV and explore the implications of this important metric.

One-on-One Personalized Marketing

Segmentation analysis allows the company or organization to treat the customer with one-to-one personalization and customization. Just as the corner grocer of the past could anticipate his customers' exact needs, current modeled propensities can project likely results from variable treatment of millions of respondents. Everything from the offer, price, and graphic design can be changed, customized, and personalized for a single customer in a nanosecond with information on who is entering your website or responding at your fulfillment center. This marketing customization is achieved by converting user preference data from a customer database into information and insight via intelligent machine-learning algorithms. These algorithms determine customer interests and trends to forecast the current and future needs of the customer.[19] Many travel destinations use response scores to modify the fulfillment kit that will be delivered to the inquirer. For example, a senior with an affinity for art will be sent the museum tour piece, and the middle-aged household with highly active lifestyles will get the adventure kit. This type of customization and personalization is the result of detailed market segmentation made possible by customer and prospect database analysis.

The concept of micro-targeting has become a hot topic in marketing today, as we mentioned earlier in Chapter 1. **Micro-targeting** is one-on-one personalized marketing, based on advanced, precise psychographic and lifestyle data. One of the benefits of one-on-one marketing is that you are able to deliver your message to a select customer or prospect (or group of them) without others knowing about it. Earlier in this chapter we presented that concept of stealth marketing.

This type of communication flies below the radar and can be thought of as the opposite of mass marketing. Micro-targeting abandons the concept of the big idea for an advertising campaign because those ideas included standardized offers and mass media communications. As more companies shift promotional budget allocations to more targeted media (such as e-mail, direct mail, special events, and trade shows), micro-targeting will continue to grow in both usage and applications.

In summary, as consumers' lives become more fragmented and their interests become more specialized, micro-targeting and customized communications will continue to be a growing area for marketers.

Partner Relationship Management (PRM)

Earlier in this chapter we discussed the important concept of CRM. Now we'll discuss **partner relationship management (PRM)**. PRM is where companies work closely with partners in other companies or departments to generate greater value to customers. In today's busy world, companies are networking with other companies and relying on partnerships to more effectively and efficiently serve the needs of their customers. Marketers cultivate relationships with prospective partners just as they cultivate relationships with their customers.

Often, companies and organizations engage in relationships with multiple partners to support a cause of a nonprofit organization. In this instance, the partners share a common goal or objective in that they want to promote and support a worthy cause. That is why these types of partnership strategies are often called **cause-related marketing**.

For example, the Williamsburg Winery announced its partnership with Farm Fresh Supermarkets, Reba Art and Photography, and the Virginia Aquarium & Marine Science Center to launch its new Sensible Red and Sensible White wines. These delicious, limited-edition blends became available for sale at Farm Fresh Supermarkets on October 1, 2019. For each customer purchase of these wines, The Williamsburg Winery and Farm Fresh will make a charitable donation to the Virginia Aquarium's Sensible Seafood™ program, which combats environmentally destructive and irresponsible fishing practices by promoting ocean-friendly seafood from local and sustainable sources. The beautiful wine label artwork, featured in Figure 2.14, was designed by renowned local artist, Reba McConnell of Reba Arts.[20]

Selecting the right partner is one of the most important decisions in PRM. Critical to a successful PRM program is the identification of a partner or partners who can benefit from reaching your desired target audience. Those PRM programs that are mutually beneficial to all partners will yield great success. Let's explore an example of another mutually beneficial direct marketing partnership. *The Washington Post* and XM Radio teamed up to acquire new subscribers. As Figure 2.15 presents, these partners executed a direct mail campaign targeting urban young professionals with a contest that enabled responding new *Post* subscribers to automatically be entered to win an XM2go portable receiver and three months of XM Radio service. *The Washington Post* was responsible for this promotion and the majority of associated costs. XM Radio provided, at no charge to *The Washington Post*, products and services for contest winners, plus paid for 25 percent of total program costs. Basically, XM Radio was able to reach the target market for less than the cost of Standard A postage. This shows that partner relationships can provide cost-effective marketing venues.

Figure 2.14 Williamsburg Winery Sensible Wines

Source: Published with the consent of The Williamsburg Winery. All rights reserved.

Figure 2.15 *The Washington Post* and XM Radio. Used with permission of The Washington Post and MindZoo, LLC.

Source: Photo by Jim Kirby, www.jimkirbyphoto.com.

SUMMARY

A customer is the company's most important asset. Customer retention is more beneficial to most companies than is new customer acquisition. A customer database is a tool used to retain customers. It enables a company to establish and strengthen relationships with customers by allowing them to interact with each customer on a personalized basis. The information captured and stored in a database provides the company with knowledge about the particular needs, wants, and interests of each customer. Armed with this knowledge, marketers are better able to develop products and services that will satisfy each customer's needs and wants. In addition, the information housed in the customer database may assist the marketer in more effectively communicating with each customer. The end result is this: a highly satisfied customer, a loyal customer!

Database marketing employs a number of activities designed to acquire, store, and use customer information. Database marketing activities commonly include customer loyalty programs, such as the many airline, hotel, and grocery programs. In addition, direct marketers regularly assess the value of their customers. This may include applying the recency/frequency/monetary assessment and calculating the CLTV over a period of time. Of course, direct marketers must keep their customer database current and accurate for it to be of value. Direct marketers perform common database maintenance activities, such as applying match codes and a merge-purge process to identify and delete duplicate customer records, identifying multibuyers, and performing status updates to keep each record current. Direct marketers also carry out a variety of activities designed to safeguard their database against improper use or theft. Some of these activities include salting or seeding their customer lists, applying access passwords, and ensuring information privacy protection for their customers. Each of these database marketing activities is critical in maintaining strong customer relationships, which, in turn, leads to the retention of customers. Database analytics, including data mining, are enabling marketers to better understand their current customers and target key prospects. CRM programs are highly valuable and are growing in popularity. PRM enables companies to pool their databases and achieve synergies to attract new customers.

KEY TERMS

cause-related marketing

continuity selling

cross-selling

customer database

customer journey map

customer lifetime value (CLTV)

customer loyalty programs

customer relationship management (CRM)

data management platform

data mining

database analytics

database enhancement

match code

merge-purge process

micro-targeting

multibuyer

nixie

partner relationship management (PRM)

recency/frequency/monetary (R/F/M)

salting   stealth marketing
seeding   structured data
source code   transactional data
source data   unstructured data

REVIEW QUESTIONS

1. What is a *customer loyalty program*? Identify three customer loyalty programs with which you are familiar. What are the benefits to each of the organizations sponsoring these loyalty programs?
2. When building a customer database, what must an organization first determine? What must they first identify?
3. What is a *match code*? Explain its importance for database development and maintenance.
4. Describe the activities required to maintain a customer database. How often do you think database maintenance should be performed?
5. What is the purpose of the merge-purge process? How does it work?
6. If incorrect addresses or phone numbers result in misdirected advertising promotions, what is the cost to the organization? How can this be avoided?
7. Explain the value of applying the recency/frequency/monetary assessment to an organization's customer database. Is it possible to determine when an organization should place more weight on one of the three variables over the others? If so, explain why. If not, explain why not.
8. Describe the value of database analytics. Provide examples of what can be learned via data mining.
9. Explain what is meant by the term *customer lifetime value (CLTV)*. Why is it important?
10. Imagine that you have recently started a new business venture and that you already have a database of 10,000 customers. You are going to a financial institution to obtain a loan to expand your business. The financial officer asks you, 'What is the biggest asset of your business?' How will you respond? Provide support for your answer using the information presented in this chapter.

EXERCISE

Congratulations! You have just been hired as the marketing director for a local grocery store chain. They have just launched a customer loyalty program and one of your main responsibilities will be to oversee it. What strategies and tactics will you employ in promoting the program to entice customers to become members? Also, how do you plan on generating real value for program members? Finally, what source data will you gather, and how do you intend to use the source data contained in the database?

CRITICAL THINKING EXERCISE

Research a few customer loyalty/rewards programs that utilize either a mobile device, e-mail address, or consumer website account. Do you think these programs are successful? What could or should be altered about each program to make it more customer-focused? Which program do you think is most successful? Why?

READINGS AND RESOURCES

- CRM: eWeekly@news.destinationcrm.com
- Customer loyalty programs: www.shopify.com/blog/loyalty-program
- Digital trends: www.smartinsights.com/digital-marketing-strategy/10-marketing-trends
- Attribution models: https://marketing.adobe.com/resources/help/en_US/analytics/analysis-workspace/attribution.html
- Customer journey maps: https://boagworld.com/audio/customer-journey-mapping
- Customer journey maps: www.tandemseven.com/journey-mapping/5-essentials-for-customer-journey-maps

CASE: NEVADA TOURISM

Building, maintaining, analyzing, and using customer databases for marketing purposes is what this chapter is all about. That is precisely what this case focuses on. The customers are tourists and the vacation destination is Nevada.

Nevada

When many people think about tourism in the state of Nevada, images come to mind of flashing lights adorning tall buildings and crowds of people bustling around from restaurants to shows and from casino to casino. The words that might be associated with Las Vegas, Nevada, are 'thrilling' and 'exciting' and 'alive.' But this is only part of what the great state has to offer tourists, as there is so much more to be discovered beyond Las Vegas.

Nevada's vast public lands, coupled with its plentiful sunshine (more than 300 days of sunshine a year), provide a plethora of outdoor recreational opportunities, such as hiking, biking, golfing, fishing, and hunting. Nevada offers many historic landmarks and cultural experiences as well as some of the finest resort spas for its tourists to enjoy. Nevada offers its guests year-round activities, including a winter wonderland of skiing, snowboarding, and snowmobiling fun. Promoting Nevada's many tourist attractions is the primary purpose of the Nevada Commission on Tourism.

Tourism Marketing Objectives

The Nevada Commission on Tourism (NCOT) needed a cost-effective solution to generate high-quality, electronic leads, dubbed 'eLeads,' for travel to the state. NCOT was interested in a more focused approach to actually engaging customer interactions and lead creation versus traditional awareness-building campaigns that do not optimize marketing ROI. The objective was to drive new prospective travelers to the NCOT website to share travel information and capture their contact information for future marketing campaigns.

With the strategic knowledge and technological ingenuity of Ruf Strategic Solutions (a database marketing and business intelligence company located in Olathe, Kansas), an eLead Generation and Customer Relationship Management (CRM) program was developed and implemented for NCOT. Ruf's Performance-Based Marketing solution was able to electronically deliver qualified leads to NCOT's CRM system (Navigator), while validating, verifying, and enhancing lead data. The Performance-Based Marketing solution also recalibrated lead generation settings to ensure increased returns for NCOT. Let's explore how this lead generation program worked, and how well it worked to deliver high-quality leads (prospective Nevada tourists) to NCOT.

The eLead Generation and CRM Program

Creative yet simple advertisements, as shown in Figure 2.16, promoting vacationing in the state of Nevada, were placed throughout hundreds of publisher sites to entice interested tourists to respond in order to obtain their free Nevada Visitors Guide. Once the prospective

(Continued)

Figure 2.16 (Continued)

Figure 2.16 Nevada tourist ads. Used with permission of Ruf™ Strategic Solutions.

tourists responded, Ruf's database system would go to work verifying and validating each response or 'lead' to the national compiled household database in its data center. Ruf's system also enhanced each lead record by appending rich demographic and psychographic information. These qualified and enhanced leads were then automatically added to Nevada's CRM database and sent the requested Nevada Visitors Guide. Based on any expressed individual preferences, as well as enhancement data analytics, select prospective tourists would also receive content-specific e-mails tailored to their lifestyle and other follow-up marketing communication to strengthen the relationship.

How did NCOT determine which prospects should receive follow-up communications beyond responding to the prospects' initial requests for tourist information? How did NCOT determine which leads should not be proactively followed up beyond the initial reply? And how did NCOT's CRM system know what type of follow-up information to send prospects along with the format of such communication? The answer: data analytics. Each lead was not only verified, validated, and enhanced, it was also analyzed for its quality and weighed for follow-up.

Program Analytics

While there are many different criteria that may be used to assess the quality of a lead, Ruf and NCOT decided that there were three main factors that should be used to determine the quality of a lead for Nevada. These factors are:

1. Are they engaged? Did they click on links in Nevada e-mails sent after the lead was acquired? If so, this action provided valuable data that were entered into NCOT's CRM database.
2. Can they be reached? What was the percentage of e-mail addresses retained over time and what was the e-mail delivery rate?
3. Do they resemble rural Nevada visitors? How many leads were similar to the top quintile of the Nevada (excluding Las Vegas) tourist profile and do they live in a state that has a high propensity to visit Nevada?

NCOT's CRM strategy was determined based on an analysis of the above three factors. The first two factors required analysis of the metrics provided regarding each prospect's interaction with Nevada's marketing communication outreach. The third factor required both analytics and predictive modeling. The leads were analyzed and compared with the current NCOT customer database to determine whether each lead had the propensity of becoming a valuable Nevada tourist in the future. Thus, database analysis was used to track, measure, and shape NCOT's marketing activities.

Program Results and Analysis

This eLead program was not only tailored, targeted, and well timed to respond to the varied interests of prospective Nevada tourists, but it was also a cost-effective marketing program for NCOT. According to David Peterson of NCOT, 'Ruf Strategic Solutions has made this lead generation program so easy for us! It has become one of the most cost-effective ways for us to generate leads who are interested in traveling to Nevada. We pay for exactly what

Table 2.5 Scoring report table. Used with permission of Ruf™ Strategic Solutions.

FY10 Scoring Report	Lead count	% of leads	Ever clicked	E-mails retained	E-mail delivery	Like NV visitors	Campaign providing largest # of leads
Pay-for-Performance Internet initiatives (Ruf campaigns)	68,167	66.74%	7.0%	59.5%	91.4%	47.6%	Ruf eNetwork, eMiles* 33% of the leads were just acquired in April. Not yet clicked
Broadcast/Print/Misc. Internet	16,290	15.95%	22.9%	44.5%	96.9%	15.3%	Google organic search
General print campaign	12,640	12.37%	26.1%	55.0%.	93.9%	22.9%	Endless Vacation, Sunset, Nat'l Geographic Traveler
NCOT collateral materials	1,841	1.80%	24.8%	52.8%	95.7%	15.8%	Adventure Guide, Visitors Guide, Nevada State Parks
Outbound eNewsletter communications	1,112	1.09%	90.8%	81.5%	93.8%	22.6%	eNewsletter
Co-ops (TV, print, Internet)	792	0.78%	19.5%	65.1%	96.4%	17.9%	Ski Lake Tahoe
Syndication, local cable, Time Warner, local broadcast	658	0.64%	17.4%	68.2%	97.0%	57.2%	KCBS website FOX KVVU Vegas
Paid search campaigns	227	0.22%	20.1%	54.3%	96.3%	36.5%	Google paid search
Direct-response nat'l cable TV	221	0.22%	10.6%	71.4%	95.8%	28.3%	Discovery Channel, CNN, Travel Channel, Weather Channel
Local broadcast TV	128	0.13%	33.3%	35.0%	97.5%	52.1%	NBC affiliates
Golf Direct and eMarketing	36	0.04%	88.6%	80.0%	91.4%	35.3%	eNewsletter
Ski Direct and eMarketing	31	0.03%	85.2%	70.4%	93.3%	34.6%	Ski e-mail eNewsletter
Totals/Averages*	**102,143**	**100%**	**26.6%**	**61.4%**	**95.2%**	**29.3%**	

Note: * not including outbound e-mails
Key:

| Best | Average | Worst | Internal eNewsletter excluded |

we get with no waste and the qualified leads automatically appear in Navigator, our online CRM system, with dashboard gauges to show optimum lead sources and thus, streamlines our fulfillment process.' Analysis of the metrics, as presented in Table 2.5, proved that the eLead Generation and CRM program was highly efficient and effective for NCOT.

During the first year in which the program was conducted, the eLead program used only 15 percent of NCOT's marketing budget and produced nearly 67 percent of all NCOT leads, with 62 percent of collateral requests being attributed to eLeads as well. Similarly, the program was responsible for acquiring more new e-mail addresses than any other Nevada program. Moreover, database analysis showed that prospects acquired via eLeads opted in for and were receptive to ongoing NCOT messaging at a higher rate than other NCOT marketing programs.

Further analysis revealed that people who responded to eLead campaigns greatly resembled visitors of rural Nevada, with 45 percent of the leads falling into the top quintile (20 percent) of the most valuable Nevada tourist profiles. The cost per lead was significantly less for eLead campaigns than for other prospecting sources (average $7 for eLead campaigns compared to $79 for other sources.) Finally, 100 percent of eLeads had an e-mail address compared with 69 percent for other prospecting campaign sources.

Conclusion

This case is an excellent example of a highly effective lead generation and CRM program. It also demonstrates the use and effectiveness of e-mail as a lead-generating and relationship-building medium with prospects. The leads generated by the eLead program described in this case were 100 percent accountable and measurable. Many eLead programs can be targeted to a specific geographic area and can target niche markets, such as ski and golf prospects. Such targeting can lead to more effective relationship marketing.

Building and strengthening relationships with prospects and customers is what database marketing and CRM are all about. In this case, Ruf's performance-based marketing program has enabled NCOT to effectively and inexpensively engage with highly qualified prospective travelers to the state of Nevada.

Case Discussion Questions

1. Explain why generating high-quality electronic leads, 'eLeads,' is superior to traditional awareness-building campaigns in maximizing marketing ROI.
2. Discuss the data collection methods–e.g., e-mail, telephone, online chat–that the Nevada Commission on Tourism (NCOT) uses to obtain high-quality, electronic leads, 'eLeads,' in response to NCOT advertisements. What is the mechanism to capture and extract these data and add them to Ruf's database system?
3. What role would you suggest for social media in promoting Nevada Tourism? Suggest at least three social media channels (Facebook, Twitter, Instagram, LinkedIn, etc.).
4. Visit Ruf Strategic Solutions' website, www.ruf.com, and click on TRAVELYTICS–marketing solutions built for the tourism industry. Explain how Ruf's marketing analytics help travel and tourism organizations to discover, reach, and acquire tourists. Now brainstorm to identify other industries, beyond travel and tourism, where TRAVELYTICS might be applied to provide valuable insight and marketing ingenuity.

NOTES

1. *Knowledge @ Wharton* (2007) 'Love Those Loyalty Programs: But Who Reaps the Real Rewards?', Marketing, April 4, knowledge.wharton.upenn.edu/article.cfm?articleid=1700, retrieved January 28, 2008; Ron Shevlin (2007) 'The Cost of Acquisition versus the Cost of Retention,' August 1, marketingroi.wordpress.com/2007/08/01/debunking-marketing-myths-the-cost-of-acquisition-versus-the-cost-of-retention, retrieved January 28, 2008.

2. Arthur Middleton Hughes (n.d.) 'How to Retain Customers,' www.crm2day.com/editorial/EEEZpkplyyYXurvQw1.php, retrieved February 8, 2008.

3. Frederick F. Reichheld (1996) *The Loyalty Effect: The Hidden Force behind Growth, Profits and Lasting Value* (Cambridge, MA: Harvard Business School Press).

4. The views expressed here may not necessarily reflect those of Uber. Uber was not involved in the writing of this chapter feature and has not approved this content.

5. This example is based on a case study by Baesman Group, the company's marketing agency. Used with permission.

6. www.datamation.com/big-data/structured-vs-unstructured-data.html, retrieved April 28, 2019.

7. www.amazon.com/gp/help/customer/display.html?ie=UTF8&nodeId=468496, www.amazon.com/gp/help/customer/display.html?ie=UTF8&nodeId=468496#cookies, retrieved May 6, 2011.

8. www.census.gov/newsroom/press-releases/2015/cb15-47.html, U.S. Census Bureau Research, retrieved July 31, 2016.

9. www.forbes.com/sites/leemathews/2018/08/24/t-mobile-hackers-swipe-data-on-2-million-subscribers/#665260357a52, retrieved April 28, 2019.

10. Ibid.

11. Melanie Trottman (2017) 'C-Suite Strategies (A Special Report): Cruise Lines Woo the Never-Cruisers: Arnold Donald, CEO of Carnival, says the answer is technology and exceeding expectations,' *The Wall Street Journal*, Eastern edition, February 4.

12. 'Taking Data Mining beyond Beer and Diapers' (2002) *iStart: New Zealand's e-Business Portal*, August; retrieved from www.istart.co.nz/index/HM20/PCO/PV21906/EX224/CS22580.

13. The discussion of this feature is based on case studies by Quad. Used with permission.

14. www.tandemseven.com/journey-mapping/5-essentials-for-customer-journey-maps, retrieved May 23, 2019.

15. www.sas.com/en_us/insights/analytics/predictive-analytics.html, retrieved April 22, 2019.

16. This example is based on a case study by Baesman Group, the company's marketing agency. Used with permission.

17. Martin Baier, Kurtis M. Ruf, and Goutam Chakraborty (2002) *Contemporary Database Marketing: Concepts and Applications* (Evanston, IL: Racom Communications), p. 151.

18. Adapted from Jon Anton and Natalie L. Petouhoff (2002) *Customer Relationship Management: The Bottom Line to Optimizing Your ROI* (Upper Saddle River, NJ: Prentice Hall), p. 138.

19. www.informs.org/ORMS-Today/Public-Articles/October-Volume-40-Number-5/Big-data-analytics-in-marketing, retrieved April 27, 2019.

20. Adapted from 'Limited Edition Sensible Wines,' www.williamsburgwinery.com. Used with permission.

3

LISTS AND MARKET SEGMENTS

CHAPTER CONTENTS

CHAPTER SPOTLIGHT

NEXTMARK

Finding new customers is an important activity for all businesses and organizations. Therefore, effective customer prospecting is considered a highly valuable task in enabling a company or an organization to grow. But how do direct marketers identify and locate the 'right' prospects? The answer: they rent lists. A list is a specifically defined group of organizations or individuals that possess common characteristics. There are lists available for almost anything and everything. Just name it, and there's a list for it! Unfortunately, many marketing professionals don't realize how many highly targeted prospect lists are available to them because they do not have the right tools. The challenge for most direct marketers is to locate appropriate lists that will enable them to communicate with prospects that are likely to have a need or desire for their products or services. Fortunately, this task has become much easier due to the advances in technology, the availability of lists, and companies like NextMark. NextMark, headquartered in Hanover, New Hampshire, is a leading provider of list commerce technology (see Figure 3.1).

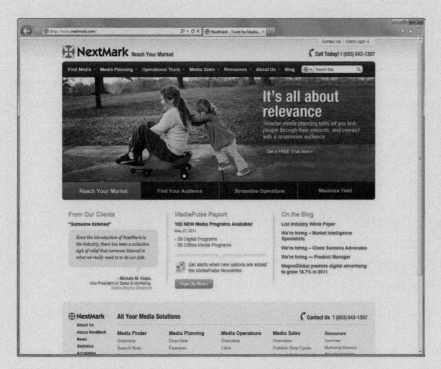

Figure 3.1   NextMark home page. Used with permission of Joe Pych, NextMark.

Joe Pych founded NextMark in 1999 with the vision of streamlining the direct marketing process, particularly the mailing list procurement process. The company has quickly risen to the top of its industry, serving marketing professionals, list brokers, and list managers.

NextMark's innovations include being the first to apply modern search technologies to the problem of finding mailing lists; the first to syndicate access to mailing list information through websites such as Direct Magazine and Multichannel Merchant, and the Direct Marketing Association; and the first to build the biggest and most up-to-date index of mailing lists in the world. More than 5,000 users from 1,500 companies can attest to the value of NextMark's services.

In 2005, NextMark unveiled a free list finder service to provide access to insider information on virtually every list on the market–which totals more than 60,000 lists! As revealed in Figure 3.2, a simple click on the Find Lists tab on NextMark's website will take you to the list finder. Simply type in the keyword for the kind of list that you wish to locate, and voilà!

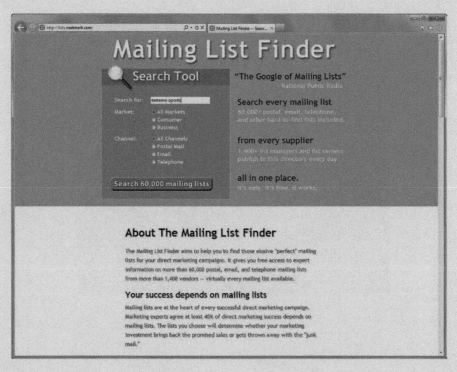

Figure 3.2   NextMark online mailing list finder service. Used with permission of Joe Pych, NextMark.

An entire page of lists pertaining to your keyword is likely to appear! What happened? The NextMark's list finder search engine identified the most relevant and popular lists based on your keyword. Each of these lists will have an associated rank–which indicates the 'relevance' or fit of the data card to the specific set of search criteria used, and, in addition, the type of channel for which the list is available, such as postal mail, e-mail, telephone, insert, or stuffer. Next, click on the list that you want to further explore and, in seconds, a data card appears for that particular list. Each data card includes detailed information about the list along with buttons to request additional information and to place orders.

NextMark does not own or manage any of the lists found on its website. Instead, it works with more than 1,400 suppliers–the list managers–to promote their lists through the list finder. According to Joe Pych, 'The main purpose of NextMark's new list finder service is to raise awareness of the excellent specialized lists that are available and to make them more accessible.' Many companies are partnering with NextMark to make this service even more valuable. In some ways, NextMark is building the technology to help eliminate the administrative headaches associated with developing lists and discovering markets. So, if you want to effectively prospect for new customers, visit NextMark at www.nextmark. com and explore its list finder. You will be pleasantly surprised at how easy prospecting can be with highly targeted lists.

Developing lists and discovering markets is the topic of this chapter. We explore the different types of lists, identify the key players in the list industry, and explain how to evaluate lists. Then we'll discuss how to use lists and market segmentation to effectively develop new markets and prospect for new customers.

93

LISTS AS MARKET SEGMENTS

Lists and data are at the very core of direct marketing. Lists identify prospects as well as customers who have something in common. Perhaps these individuals made a response to or transaction with the direct marketer. Perhaps the prospects on a list are all females who enjoy surfing as a hobby. Or a different list could identify all of the customers who purchased a surfboard from a certain sporting goods store within a given year. Yet another list could possess the names and addresses of males between the ages of 20 and 25 who are independently wealthy and own a horse! Therefore, lists cannot be thought of as mere mailing lists, because customers and potential customers on marketing lists are often reachable through media other than direct mail, such as e-mail, mobile, text, telephone, the Internet, magazines, newspaper, television, and radio. Lists are the marketplace, the 'place' of the four Ps of marketing (product, place, price, and promotion). A list denotes a market segment. Therefore, it follows that the direct marketer needs to accumulate data about the customers and prospects on its list(s). Marketers must identify relevant geographic, demographic, social, psychological, and behavioral information, using what they discover about their customers to identify prospects with similar characteristics. In the case of customer lists, the direct marketer needs to record activity in terms of responses or transactions. What direct-response medium triggered the activity? Did the person buy, inquire, or take some other action? What product was involved? Did the customer pay by credit card? Direct marketers also want to know how frequently the activity occurs, how recently it last occurred, and the dollar amount of the transaction.

A Perishable Commodity

A list is a perishable commodity. Not only does the degree of activity (or inactivity) fluctuate, which means a list could be less valuable tomorrow than it is today, but the people and organizations on lists are far from static. They move. They marry. They divorce. They die. Their attitudes change. In 12 months, for example, as many as 25 percent of the addresses on an average customer list could change.

The direct marketer must not only be aware of the condition of lists acquired from others, but also be assured that the maintenance of the house list is current and adequate. Otherwise, part of the communication with an out-of-date list will be undeliverable and result in cost without potential benefit. List maintenance involves not only name and address correction, but also continual updating of the data within the customer's record.

Data about a list are also perishable. No direct marketer wants to distribute messages indiscriminately. He wants to make sure not only that the message is delivered, but also that it is delivered to the right prospect. Direct marketers are particularly sensitive to the downside of indiscriminate mass communication, not only in terms of the waste of resources, but also in terms of the possible antagonism sparked among non-prospects.

Technology has dramatically improved the manner by which direct marketers create, store, rent or acquire, and use lists. Today, the lists of almost all direct marketers are computerized and sophisticated. However, most direct marketing lists originated long before the computer age—and were housed on simple index cards. With computerization came the ability to research, rent, and test various lists and conduct precise market segmentation of house lists. Your objective in reading this chapter is to better understand how lists are developed, tested, segmented, used, and analyzed.

Types of Lists

There are three basic types of lists. In descending order of importance to the direct marketer, these are:

1. House lists
2. Response lists
3. Compiled lists.

House Lists

House lists are lists of an organization's own customers, *active* as well as inactive. Because of the very special relationship that an organization enjoys with its own customers, sometimes called goodwill, house lists are the most productive mailing lists available in terms of future response. Of lower potential (in terms of future response), but probably still more productive than lists from sources outside the organization, are the names of customers who have become *inactive*, who have *inquired* but not purchased, and who have been *referred* or recommended by present customers of the firm.

These four segments of a house list may be among an organization's most valuable assets, inasmuch as they generate future business at a cost much less than that of acquiring responses from outside lists. It is not uncommon for a house list to be four times or even ten times as productive as an outside list with which there is no existing customer relationship.

The kind and degree of customer activity is also relevant in terms of products purchased as well as the recency, frequency, and dollar value of such purchases. The source of the customer as well as the promotional strategy the marketer used to acquire that customer is information that can also help determine future response. The original list source and whether this source was direct mail, space advertising, broadcast media, the Internet, or even a salesperson have a bearing on future productivity. With inquiries, there is only an expression of interest rather than an actual purchase. Although this information is important, inquiries do not have equal value compared with customer purchase information. With referrals, the recommendation by a customer of the organization could offer an advantage, especially when the name of the present customer can be used in the promotional effort sent to the referred prospect.

Prior to developing a house list, the direct marketer must first determine what useful data, other than accurate names and addresses, it needs to qualify individual members of the list, how to collect and record it, and in what form. Consider, too, just what purpose the data will serve in the future. Keep in mind that collection of information costs money and must therefore produce benefits commensurate with its cost. How will the data be used, and can they be analyzed and evaluated properly?

Response Lists

Response lists are the house lists of other organizations. In terms of future productivity, these lists rate right behind house lists. Obviously, the lists of those direct marketers offering similar products and services will yield the greater potential for response to a similar or even directly competitive offer. A customer who has subscribed to a news magazine, *USA Today*, for example, could be an ideal prospect for a competitive news magazine, such as *Newsweek*. Similarly, a consumer who has purchased fitness equipment online could be an ideal prospect for a sporting goods store such as the Sports Authority. The first important qualification is that the name on a list from an outside source has a history of response to direct marketed offers. The second and possibly equally important characteristic would be an indication of response to a similar direct marketed offer. Beyond this could be a history of purchase of related items. Those who have purchased gourmet meat products, for example, might be good prospects for gourmet fruit products, specialty chocolates or unique *Povitica*, a Croatian bread.

Lists of directly competitive firms, if available, are obvious choices. On the other hand, one of the real challenges to direct marketers is to determine *why* the purchaser of an online foreign language program, for example, might be a particularly good prospect for a book club.

Like an organization's house lists, other response lists should be looked at in terms of geographics, demographics, and social and psychological factors. They should also be segmented by type of response and/or ultimate transaction or purchase. Direct marketers should consider response lists in terms of source as well as the promotional strategy that caused them to be responsive in the first place.

When researching lists in NextMark, the source of the list is provided on the data card for each list to enable you to better understand how the list was created. Figure 3.3 shows a data card from Duluth Trading Company, a catalog company serving outdoor enthusiasts. The source of this list is stated as '100% Direct Mail' so it is clearly a response list. Response lists represent buyers of a given product or service.

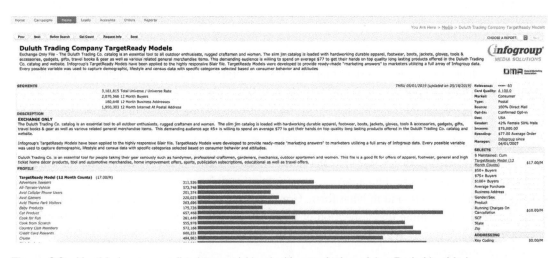

Figure 3.3   NextMark response list data card. Used with permission of Joe Pych, NextMark.

Compiled Lists

Usually falling behind both house lists and response lists in expectations are compiled lists. Compiled lists are lists generated by a third party or market research firm. Individuals on compiled lists do *not* have a response history. Examples of such lists include directory listings; automobile and driver's license registrations; the newly married and the newly born; high school and college student rosters; public records, such as property tax rolls and voter lists; rating services, such as Dun & Bradstreet; and a multitude of rosters, such as those for service and civic organizations. Other potential sources of compiled lists include manufacturer warranty cards and coupon redemptions.

Figure 3.4 shows a data card from a compiled list. Note that the source of the names contained on this data card is compiled lists, likely gathered via market research. While all of the individuals on this compiled list are sports fans, they do not possess shared purchase behavior with one another. This list, however, enables marketers to rent specific segments of it to zero in on fans of select types of sports activities, such as adventure seekers or avid gamers.

Figure 3.4 NextMark compiled list data card. Used with permission of Joe Pych, NextMark.

Although compiled lists typically do not have a response qualification built into them, market segmentation techniques coupled with sophisticated computer systems for duplication identification make possible selection of the best prospects (those most likely to effect a response or transaction) from very large compiled lists. Modern technology can also cross-identify characteristics of compiled lists, such as phone or automobile registration lists, with known response and thus further improve response potential. Combining a response list with an automobile registration list and further identifying those on the response list who own a minivan, for example, is a way of identifying responsive households with children. Direct marketers use compiled lists in market segmentation and in further qualifying response and house lists.

Let's take a look at an example of how direct marketers can effectively use compiled lists. *The Wall Street Journal* wanted to promote to one of its most challenging segments—college students. With their limited financial resources, college students have historically been a very difficult sale. *The Wall Street Journal* used a customized student segmentation strategy based on a profile of its current college student subscribers to determine high-probability prospect student responders for its nationwide direct mail campaign, shown in Figure 3.5. This profile data—major, class year, and most responsive geographical school locations— served as select criteria for obtaining student prospect data from a variety of compiled lists and data sources. The campaign was highly effective, with overall response rates three times greater than those of previous direct mail campaigns that targeted the college student market segment. Compiled lists can be extremely valuable when direct marketers want to reach a well-defined audience. Although response lists yield greater potential for consumer response since those individuals have clearly expressed a need or desire based on their actual response behavior, at the same time, direct marketers may miss out on opportunities with people who have an interest, but have not taken action to express that interest yet. With compiled lists, direct marketers may cater to individuals' needs or problems before they identify the solution for themselves.

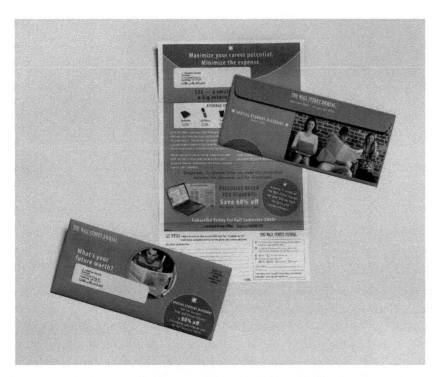

Figure 3.5 *The Wall Street Journal* program. Used with permission of *The Wall Street Journal* and MindZoo, LLC.

Source: Photo by Jim Kirby, www.jimkirbyphoto.com.

THE LIST INDUSTRY

List owners and list users often come together through the efforts of list brokers, list managers, list compilers, and even service bureaus. Typically, marketers rent response lists under an arrangement allowing them to make a specific use of the data. Sometimes they buy compiled lists outright; there is no limit on the number of times mailings may be sent to these names. List owners usually maintain rented response lists, so these lists often have better deliverability than compiled lists that have not been updated regularly. Figure 3.6 shows the relationship between the various members in the list industry. Service bureaus interact with all members of the list industry, providing expertise in the areas of data processing and analytics. List intermediaries, including list brokers, list managers, and list compilers, as well as service bureaus cater to direct marketers' needs and provide value-added services. These intermediaries assist list users to efficiently and effectively locate and rent the most relevant lists based on the direct marketer's specifications. NextMark provides a digital space where all of these intermediaries may come together to search for and locate relevant lists. Check out www.fastlist.com and www.alistnow.com for more information on list building.

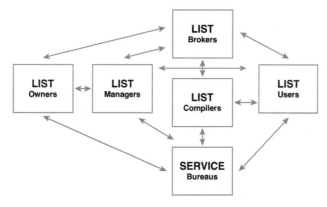

Figure 3.6 The list industry

List Users

Virtually every direct marketer uses lists. For example, Victoria's Secret, L. L. Bean, Lands' End, Eddie Bauer, Cabela's, and Macy's all use lists. There are literally thousands of response and compiled lists available from which to choose, and the starting point is usually the direct marketer's own list.

A direct marketer using lists must obviously know its own customer profile to match it against available lists. Sometimes the marketer will use only segments of these lists, selecting them according to geographic, demographic, social, psychological, or behavioral characteristics. Matching one's house list against potential response and compiled lists is in itself a stimulating exercise. It often provides the direct marketer with basic knowledge of the marketplace, which the marketer can use to develop new products and determine successful promotional strategies.

List Owners

List owners are those who describe and acquire prospects who show potential for becoming customers of the list user. A key attribute of direct marketing, aside from its measurability and accountability, is the acquisition of lists and data about the individuals or organizations on these lists. Every direct marketer is a list owner. The lists that the marketer compiles during new business acquisition activities are described as house lists.

Although the primary reason for acquiring house lists is to build and perpetuate an organization through contact with its customers, many direct marketers view their house lists as profit centers in their own right. Firms rent their house lists to other direct marketers, under specified conditions, and this activity becomes an important source of added revenue. Nearly all credit card companies participate in list rental activities. Also, if you subscribe to any major magazines, your name appears on the magazine's house list.

All respondents to a renter's offer become additions to the renter's own house list. Under the usual rental arrangement, the rented list may be mailed only one time, and the list owner must approve the offer in advance. Directly competitive offers may not be approved, except in an *exchange* that occurs when two competitive list owners provide each other with comparable numbers of their respective house lists or lists of active or inactive buyers. If you look closely at the data card of Duluth Trading Company, featured back in Figure 3.3, you'll notice that under the description it states 'Exchange Only', which means this list is not available for standard list rental, but is available in barter situations where data (from another list owner's house list) is exchanged.

An obvious advantage of renting a list rather than purchasing it outright (as is sometimes done with compiled lists) is that the list owner maintains the list, keeping it current and accurate. Another obvious advantage is that the names on such lists have a history of responding to direct marketing activity; thus they are termed 'response' lists. A history of prior response, whether by mail, phone, or the Internet, is another important advantage for direct marketers.

Owners of response lists or compiled lists provide descriptions of them in a standard format, such as the example shown in Figure 3.7. The information on a list card normally includes list quantities, market segments available, pricing, general description of the list, demographic profile, including available list selections (such as age, gender, ZIP code, state, marital status, products purchased) as well as mechanical considerations, such as the type of addressing and ordering instructions. Lists are priced on a cost-per-thousand (CPM) basis. The costs of lists can range from less than $10 per thousand names for large quantities of broad-based compiled lists to more than $100 per thousand for highly selective, up-scale response lists. The average list rental charge of approximately $40 to $50 per thousand for one-time use usually includes provision of these names on either labels or disks for computer processing. List selections (also called 'selects') normally carry a fee of $5 to $25 per thousand depending on the list, with the majority priced at $10 per thousand. These list selections enable direct marketers to narrow the list and properly choose specific narrowed segments of prospects contained within each list population. The process of choosing list selections from a given list is a form of precise market segmentation, which we discuss in detail later in this chapter. Each list is a segment, and by applying list selections to a list, direct marketers can pinpoint certain prospects with a high degree of selectivity and accuracy.

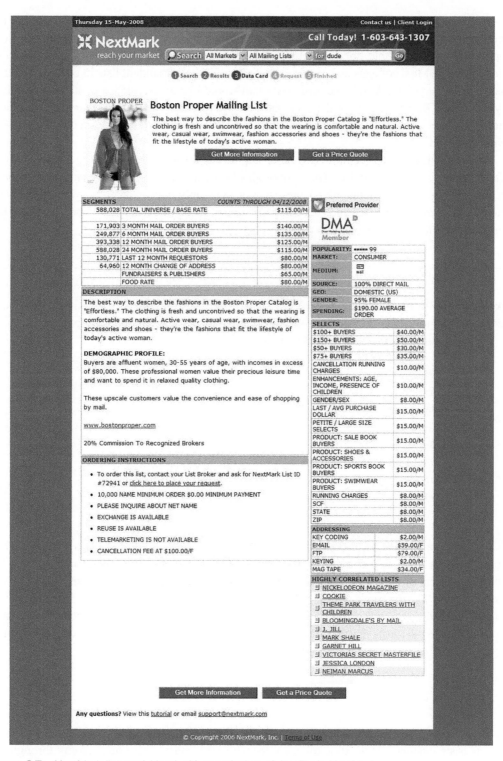

Figure 3.7 NextMark list card. Used with permission of Joe Pych, NextMark.

101

Not all direct marketers make their house lists available for use by others. Perhaps the list contains proprietary information or the list owner wishes to safeguard a very valuable asset from improper use. For example, some nonprofit organizations never rent their donor lists, in order to ensure privacy. Most colleges and universities do not allow their student lists to be used by other businesses. Can you think of some businesses that would like to rent the list of students enrolled at your school? Some list owners also feel that there is a tendency for a list to wear itself out. Even offers that do not directly compete can vie with each other for discretionary spending, these list owners contend.

The counterargument is that it is virtually impossible for individuals and organizations to be left off response or compiled lists. Thus, although a list owner has a proprietary interest in a house list, individuals and organizations on the list will inevitably appear on lists owned by others. Another counterargument contends that the more opportunities individuals and organizations are provided, the more likely they are to respond.

List Brokers

Like real estate brokers or stockbrokers, **list brokers** serve as intermediaries who bring list users and list owners together. They do not actually own lists but serve as middlemen in the industry. In so doing, they perform the following functions:

- find new lists
- verify information
- report on performance
- check instructions
- clear offers
- check mechanics
- clear mailing date
- work out timing
- ensure delivery date.

List brokers are specialists in the process of bringing list owners and list users together. They should have a very clear picture of the products of the list owner as well as the needs of the list user. List brokers usually work on a commission basis, which is paid by the list owner. Since the costs of marketing communications, such as direct mail, are high, it is critical for direct marketers to reach the right audience with promotional materials. Therefore, direct marketers should take advantage of the services that list brokers offer. List brokers will help you reach your desired target audience to achieve a desirable return on advertising investment.

List Managers

Although list rental can be an attractive profit center, direct marketers usually run it as a by-product of their basic business. Thus, they often try to maximize returns from this activity through list managers. **List managers** represent the interests of list owners and assume the responsibility, on behalf of list owners, of keeping in contact with list brokers and list users. They perform the advertising and sales functions and often maintain the lists they manage in their own facility. Like list brokers, list managers receive a commission from the list owner.

List Compilers

Organizations that develop lists and data about them, often serving as their own list managers and list brokers, are called **list compilers**. The form of list compilation they do is different from what direct marketers do in developing their own house lists through the generation of responses and/ or transactions.

List compilers usually develop their lists from public records (such as drivers' licenses or motor vehicle registrations), newspaper clippings, directories, warranty cards, and trade show registrations. In fact, the compiler owns such lists and then resells them, rather than renting them for one-time use. Instead of regularly maintaining such lists, compilers usually recompile periodically. Names and addresses in phone directories, for example, are compiled regularly, at least annually, on issuance of newly published volumes.

Service Bureaus

Service bureaus provide data processing, data mining, outsourcing, online analytical processing (OLAP), and other services to support the interchange of lists and database information within the direct marketing industry. Some of the larger direct marketing companies have their own service departments that perform this function on a regular basis.

LIST RESEARCH AND ANALYSIS

Renting lists and using them to prospect for new customers, clients, donors, members, voters, or whatever the marketer needs can be a critical element in the execution of a successful direct marketing campaign. But before you can rent a list, you must first determine the type of list you need for your campaign—business or consumer lists, postal, e-mail, or telephone lists—and the lists that are available to be rented. That requires list research. Then, once you have rented the list (or lists) and have used it to implement your marketing campaign, you will want to evaluate how well that list worked in producing new customers. That requires list measurement and analysis. Let's explore these two important activities. We will begin by walking through the online list research process available at NextMark.com. NextMark is a great 'go-to' source for information about available data and marketing lists.

List Research

The list research process begins with having precise knowledge about your customers in order to pinpoint the most likely prospective customers. We will discuss in greater detail the specific data that can be used to segment consumers later in this chapter. As was explained in Chapter 2, your customer database can and should be used as a starting point to better understand your customers. First, using your customer database, you should analyze and develop a profile of your current customers. You will also want to determine your most valuable customers. Know that your most likely prospective customers will normally resemble your current customers. Thus, you will want to find and rent those lists of prospects that resemble your current customers—especially the profile of your *best* (most valuable) customers.

Here's an example. Let's say your customers are 25 to 34 years old with sports interests, both conventional and extreme. Not only do they enjoy football and basketball, but they also are into hang gliding, surfing, skateboarding, winter sports, robot wars, and so on. Your *best* customers are interested in extreme sports that have speed, height, danger, and a high level of physical exertion associated with them. You go to www.NextMark.com and you key 'Extreme Sports' into its media list finder, as shown in Figure 3.8, and hit enter to begin the list search. The NextMark search engine will run your query against all data cards in the set you selected and display the results.

Within a few seconds, you will be able to view the 'extreme sports results.' As presented in Figure 3.9, this is a listing of all lists associated with extreme sports that are available for list rental along with each list's rank, title, and size. All search results are sorted by rank. Rank is based on the 'responsiveness' of a list to the specific set of search criteria. Each data card will receive a different rank each time a new search is conducted via the NextMark list media finder.

Now you may begin to browse through all of the lists to find those that best match your desired prospect. In order to do so, you will need to determine which of these lists have buyer profiles similar to your *best* customer profile. With a simple click on any of the lists, you can access each list's data card, which will provide the details you need to review to determine which list (or lists) might best suit your needs. As shown in Figure 3.10, each data card is arranged in two columns. The wider, left column includes the list title, summary, description information, and list segments. The right column contains availability and ordering information as well as list details such as universe, provider or source, and *selects*. List selects detail the various geographic, demographic, and lifestyle variables that are available for that particular list.

The decision of 'which list or lists might work best' for a given marketing campaign should be based on an evaluation of the descriptions, market segments, and *selections* available for each list. Each data card reveals the source of the list, the minimum quantity that can be rented, the types of lists available (postal mail, e-mail, telephone), along with other information. In addition, each list card will display its popularity score, which is based on how often the list has been rented. Once you have concluded your evaluation, you may select your lists and place your order to rent the list(s). However, if the 'extreme sports results' did not provide you with the lists you are seeking, then you may refine your search by entering different key terms into the list media finder and begin a new search. For example, perhaps you want to narrow your extreme sports search to find only those lists associated with 'snow sports.' You may do so and the search engine will continue to narrow its search and display results for each search conducted.

Figure 3.8 NextMark Find Media screen page. Used with permission of Joe Pych, NextMark.

Figure 3.9 NextMark 'Extreme Sports' results screen page. Used with permission of Joe Pych, NextMark.

Figure 3.10   NextMark 'Extreme Sports' list card. Used with permission of Joe Pych, NextMark.

List Measurement and Analysis

Recordkeeping is essential to properly evaluate the profitability of response lists as well as compiled lists. Recordkeeping includes accurate measurement of results and evaluation of response differences. Evaluating the productivity of a list you have rented and used for a marketing campaign begins with selecting and using a **key code**, a unique identifier placed on the response device or order form *prior* to sending a promotional piece to prospective customers. Key codes can be simple preprinted numbers identifying the source of the list, or they can be so complex as to incorporate not just the source but the category of list, type of product offered by the list owner, or even the degree of prior direct marketing activity. Unique tracking codes can also be created for e-mail lists, mobile, and text messaging campaigns.

Direct marketers structure key codes so that they can accumulate information across several individual lists by different categories. Thus, the direct marketer can tabulate responses not only by individual lists but also by sources of list, product lines, geographic location (ZIP code), and a variety of other broad qualifiers. The marketer then groups individual lists into such categories and makes assumptions about the overall efficiency of certain list sources, particular ZIP codes, or specific product lines.

Marketers should keep ongoing records of lists and monitor them even if they frequently contact the names on the list. The character and nature of lists change over time, just as the character and nature of the list owner's business may change. Many direct marketers have achieved the highest response rate when they have used so-called hotline names. Hotline names (also called 'hotline buyers') are those most recently acquired, but there is no consensus in the industry about what chronological period 'recent' describes. Many lists specify 'three-month hotline' or 'six-month hotline' to detail the name categories by recency.

Response differences can occur as a result of timing alone. Certain exogenous factors over which the direct marketer can exert no control (beyond the quality of the list itself), such as economic conditions or climate variations, can have a profound effect on results when lists are developed over a period of time. Other uncontrollable factors include major events or even catastrophes that divert public attention from the everyday.

Certain offers, such as a catalog of Christmas gifts, are timely and target seasonal differences in consumer buying habits. Some offers can be affected by the income tax season or by the vacation season. Some direct marketers try to time their promotional efforts so as to avoid arrival during any type of holiday event, especially those that take people outdoors. For example, if Lands' End were to send consumers a catalog offering winter sweaters in the early portion of summer, when most consumers are enjoying wearing light summer clothing, the response to their offer may be affected by the season. In addition, offers with expiration dates may need to be lengthened during the summer months due to the fact that many consumers take summer vacations and are not at home to receive their mail.

Even for non-seasonal offers, however, an apparent month-to-month cycle affects direct-response advertising. All other factors being equal, many direct marketers have noted these ebbs and flows. For example, LA Fitness and other fitness centers probably receive a greater response to their direct marketing efforts during the months of January and February, although they are open for business 12 months a year. Each direct marketer should develop an index of monthly responses and determine which month generates the highest relative response. Noting monthly variances is useful to the direct marketer who is testing lists on an ongoing basis. It makes it possible to consider the variable of timing in comparing one list with another when these are released during different months of the year. In summary, marketers rely on list analysis to predict future response from lists, or segments of lists, and to determine future list strategies.

Many companies experience peaks and valleys in response rates based on the products and services they offer. In addition, an organization's customer database is also likely to be segmented, because not all customers have the same needs, wants, or interests. Thus, direct marketers must apply the principles of market segmentation prior to interacting with customers on a personalized basis. Customers can be served best by organizations that know their characteristics. The concept and theory of market segmentation and its special relevance in both consumer and business direct marketing are the subjects of the next section.

THE NATURE OF MARKET SEGMENTATION

Because all buyers are not alike, marketers have developed ways to place them into groups, or market segments, according to geographic, demographic, social, psychological, or behavioral factors. These market segments are the focal points of product differentiation and positioning. Direct marketers have been using market segmentation strategies in their efforts to effectively promote and distribute products and services to consumers for many years. Think of a sports magazine. Its readers are probably interested in many different sports. It could easily identify its golf enthusiast consumers and offer them golf products and services. Likewise, it could offer its tennis-playing readers tennis equipment and clothing.

Market segmentation is a strategy devised to attract and meet the needs of a specific sub-market. These subgroups are referred to as market segments. A company may direct marketing strategies at several market segments. Each segment should be homogeneous (that is, its members should be similar to one another), heterogeneous (meaning its members should all be different from the members of other segments), and substantial in size (so as to be profitable).

Product Differentiation

Marketers target products and services to select market segments, rather than the total market, unless the product or service is unique and appeals equally to everyone. Many times it is necessary to *differentiate* products for particular market segments and *position* these products so that they will have special appeal to the intended market. Product differentiation is a strategy that uses innovative design, packaging, and positioning to make a clear distinction between products and services serving the same market segment. Product differentiation, like market segmentation, is an alternative to price competition. The difference might be real or simply an advertised difference. For example, a brand of toothpaste that contains fluoride is intrinsically different from one that does not. An airline may call its Boeing 777 aircraft a Star-Stream Jet without making it any different from the planes of its competitors. Product differentiation can distinguish a product from that of its competitors.

Product Positioning

Product positioning is the way the product is defined by consumers on important attributes. It enables consumers to rank products or services according to perceived differences between competing products or brands within a single product category.

Marketers can position products based on quality, size, color, distribution method, time of day the product is used, time of year, and price. Examples include Nike: 'Just do it'; M&M's: 'Melts in your mouth, not in your hand'; Taco Bell: 'Think outside the bun'; BMW: 'The ultimate driving machine.' Most big-ticket marketers, such as the manufacturers of Rolex watches and Mercedes-Benz automobiles, thrive by positioning their products as exclusive, high-quality items. So too do the well-known direct marketers of specialty products like Harry and David, Brookstone, and Victoria's Secret.

THE BASES FOR MARKET SEGMENTATION

The needs, wants, or interests of the consumers belonging to various market segments differ. However, it would be almost impossible to conduct marketing research for every product and service that could determine which market segment each consumer would best fit into. Marketers therefore use other, more general indicators for segmenting markets. These indicators include geographic, demographic, social, psychological, and behavioral factors. A brief overview is provided here.

Geographic Segmentation

Potential geographic subdivisions range in size from the country as a whole down through census divisions and Federal Reserve districts to states, counties, trading areas, cities, towns, census tracts, neighborhoods, and even individual city blocks.

In addition, there are numerical codes such as ZIP codes, geocodes, telephone area codes, computer 'match' codes, and territory and route numbers. Once upon a time, census tract numbers were the best means of geographical segmentation. Do you know which census tract you live in? Most people probably do not. However, our ZIP code number *is* meaningful, and everyone knows that number.

An important form of geographic market segmentation is that which recognizes inherent differences among those buyers who reside in central cities and suburban, urban fringe, and rural areas. Geographic location can also affect the future purchase activity of consumers. For example, the level of consumer interest in purchasing nursery plants or snow blowers is often related to the climate of the geographic area in which the consumer lives.

Let's examine an example of geographic segmentation. Busch Gardens targets most of its communication at consumers geographically, accounting for different vacation interests, ticket offers, and other communication points that vary by market. Some of these efforts are overt in appealing to residents of a particular region, such as in the park's Virginia Beach advertisement seen in Figure 3.11. More often, the communication is more subtle, with elements tailored slightly to highlight particular offers or events of greater interest to a specific geographical market.

Population changes within geographic areas, such as the decreasing population of a specific geographic area or the high mobility of the population in another, have significance for the marketer. Census data is invaluable for research regarding the changing geographic and demographic profile of the American population. The recent Census CD Neighborhood Change Database (NCDB) is a powerful product that presents decades of census tract series data. Additional information about this product is available at www.geolytics.com.

Another geographic segmentation tool, the Global Positioning System (GPS), associates latitude and longitude coordinates with street addresses. Direct marketers use this system to identify geographic locations, establish business sites, locate competition, measure distance, and generate data about the demographics of a business location. Given this information, combined with the technological mapping capabilities of most businesses, a direct marketer can better determine the business penetration and market potential in certain geographical areas.

Today, computer systems are capable of analyzing Geographic Information Systems (GIS) to help better understand data related to geographic areas. A GIS is a computer system that analyzes and displays geographically referenced information. It uses data that is attached to a unique location.[1] A GIS can help you answer questions and solve problems by looking at your data in a way that is quickly understood and easily shared.[2] The GIS software leader is ESRI, which has experts in geographic science, software development, and data analytics from 73 countries.[3]

Figure 3.11 Busch Gardens Virginia Beach ad. Used with the consent of Busch Gardens/Water Country USA. All Rights Reserved.

Demographic Segmentation

Demographics are identifiable and measurable statistics that describe the consumer population. The primary unit of observation in demography is the individual; the family unit and household are secondary concerns. Common demographic variables include age, gender, education level, income level, occupation, and type of housing. College students represent a demographic market segment based on the similarities they have in their needs and wants. Marketers can create ads specifically targeting demographic groups, such as the Busch Gardens ad featured in Figure 3.12.

There are three main sources for such data: (1) population enumeration, as in a census; (2) registration on the occurrence of some event, such as birth, marriage, or death; and (3) sample surveys or tabulation of special groups. The data obtained in these ways are generally available for marketing and other uses from governmental sources, especially the Census Bureau.

It is often wise to tabulate the effect of the interaction of many demographic variables at the same time. For example, it is highly valuable for a direct marketer to know the marital status of a certain 25-year-old male consumer. Just think of two male consumers, both aged 25; one might be married with two children and the other single with no children. These two consumers probably belong in totally different market segments based on their market needs. In this case, the more demographic data you can collect, the better. Often, a single demographic statistic can be misleading.

Figure 3.12 Busch Gardens student ad. Used with the consent of Busch Gardens/Water Country USA. All Rights Reserved.

Marketers know that currency is the key to accuracy and validity of demographic data. *Changes* in demography, such as when someone marries or has a baby, have significant marketing implications.

Social Factor Segmentation

Social factors include a person's culture, subculture, social class rank, peer group references, and reference individual(s). Social factors demonstrate the impact that other people in our society have on our decision-making process and consumption activities.

Society may well have an impact on our behavior beyond our control. For example, **reference groups** (also called 'peer groups') are the people a consumer turns to for reinforcement. This reinforcement normally comes after the consumer makes a purchase decision. Reference groups may have a direct and powerful influence on the consumption behavior of adolescents and teenagers. A **reference individual** is a person a consumer turns to for advice. This person (or persons) will influence the consumer *before* he or she makes a purchase decision. Therefore, reference individuals normally have a stronger impact on consumer decision-making than do reference groups.

Psychographic Segmentation

Psychographics is the study of lifestyles, habits, attitudes, beliefs, and value systems of individuals. Even though buyers may have common geographic, demographic, and social characteristics, they often have different buying characteristics. Psychographic segmentation divides consumers into different groups based on lifestyle and personality variables. Individual buyer behavior is influenced not only by geographic, demographic, and social factors, but also by variables that are more difficult to define, such as environment, self-perception, and lifestyles. When marketers can identify and measure these influences, they can use them effectively in segmenting consumer markets.

For example, a beverage company could offer two or more competing brands of the same beverage, such as bottled water. One of its brands might be premium-priced purified bottled water that is pH balanced with electrolytes, to serve the growing segment of millennial consumers interested in healthier beverages, while the other brand might be lower-priced natural spring water which suits consumers who are not interested in spending additional money to buy a bottle of water. This example of psychographic segmentation is being driven heavily by millennials and their lifestyles and interests. Millennial consumers are willing to pay more to purchase products that fit their worldview and marketers respond by offering brands to satisfy their unique preferences and desires.

Direct marketers have the ability to identify psychographic market segments and thus predict potential consumer response by recognizing and evaluating the simultaneous appearance of a prospect's name on a variety of lists. For example, a registered owner of a particular type of automobile, such as a Lexus, might also appear on the subscriber list of *The Wall Street Journal*, as well as the customer lists of upscale catalogs such as Neiman Marcus and Bloomingdales. This same prospect might even be a contributor to charity: water and a member of the National Geographic Society. When merged, such multiple list identifiers can describe the psychographics of consumers (activities, interests, and opinions) more specifically than consumer surveys.

Another means of psychographic identification of specific prospects is a comprehensive data file developed by Equifax under the registered name 'Lifestyle Selector.' According to Equifax:

The Lifestyle Selector is the direct marketing industry's largest and most comprehensive database of self-reported consumer information. More than 500 response segments cover all aspects of how consumers live, what they spend their money on, and what interests they possess. This file is primarily derived from two sources: responses to consumer surveys and product registration cards filled out voluntarily by consumers after they have completed a product purchase.[4]

Included for each of the 47 million consumer names and addresses are a variety of demographic characteristics and activities or hobbies. It is possible for a consumer direct marketer to develop a psychographic and demographic profile of his or her company's house lists by matching the lists with the Lifestyle Selector, and to extend his or her prospect base by adding other names from the data file.

Thus, measurement of environmental influences within geographic units, combined with demographic and psychographic indicators derived from list cross-referencing and other expressions of activities, interests, and opinions, all interact to enable the direct marketer to reach individual consumers within market segments. Such list selection is obviously more efficient and can be more effective than directing pinpointed messages to the total marketplace.

Behavioral Market Segmentation

The actions taken by consumers are certainly a viable base for market segmentation. The specific types of products and services consumers have purchased, the time the transactions took place, the method or location of their purchases, and the method of payment they chose can all reveal similarities among consumers. Each behavioral factor can indicate a consumer preference that may be shared by other consumers, consequently identifying a market segment.

Behavioral segmentation data can also be valuable in targeting specific consumer groups, such as teenagers. There are about 25 million teenagers in the U.S. This group is also part of the larger Generation Z demographic—those born between 1996 and 2015.[5] In most households, teenagers are the primary influencers in household spending decisions, including food and beverages, household goods, electronics, and family vacation destinations.[6] However, teenagers are a difficult group to reach. Research shows that listening to music is a common behavior and passion among teens, with 95 percent of them spending over 34.5 hours per week listening to their favorite music.[7] That's why marketers and advertisers interested in reaching teenagers often turn to Pandora (Figure 3.13). Pandora, a subsidiary of SiriusXM, is the leading music and podcast discovery platform that effectively reaches influential teenagers and inspires lifetime customer loyalty.

Behavioral market segmentation data may also be generated via 'cookies,' which provide marketers with the ability to segment consumers according to their online activity. A cookie is an electronic tag or identifier that is placed on a personal computer. Cookies are a tool for recognizing Web users again after they have interacted with a marketer's website in some capacity. The process is quite simple: whenever a website visitor makes a request to a Web server, that server has the opportunity to set a cookie on the personal computer that made the request. The website host can then use the cookie for tracking beyond the initial click to determine how often that visitor returns to the website, the length of time of each visit, and the particular Web pages visited, which can often detail the specific products or services in which the visitor is interested. Cookies provide valuable insight into consumer behavior.

Figure 3.13 Pandora. Used with permission of Pandora.

Cookies also enable **retargeting**, which is the act of serving previously tagged website visitors display ads when they are recognized in designated online ad networks. For instance, you may be scrolling through your Instagram feed and come across an advertisement for a particular type of shoe that you've been Googling for months. Instagram 'read your [digital] mind' and presented you with in-app options to purchase the shoe from a brand that has engaged in digital retargeting. You may even be able to buy this shoe without ever leaving the Instagram app.

To better understand how retargeting works, let's explore the successful online digital fundraising campaign of Doctors Without Borders/Médecins Sans Frontières (MSF). MSF used retargeting by placing a pixel (a string of code that drops a 'cookie' on a visitor and is stored in the visitor's browser) on its website; it was then able to promote a fundraising request ad to visitors who did not make donations after they left the organization's website. These 'ads' appeared on news sites, social-networking sites, and even online games. Donors were omitted from these retargeting efforts through the use of exclusion pixels.[8]

Here's one last example. For its digital advertising and direct marketing, Busch Gardens Williamsburg segments audiences in various ways based on behavior and attitudes, including:

- **Digital retargeting**—Based on the shopping behavior of its website visitors, Busch Gardens retargets visitors who leave the site without a purchase by serving ads to them on other sites. As shown in Figure 3.14, the specific ad the user sees depends on the products he viewed on the Busch Gardens site. For instance, someone who looked at an annual membership will receive ads tailored to membership, while someone who viewed one-day tickets would be exposed to ads offering a discount on a single day. By segmenting these consumers based on their observed behavior (which ticket type they viewed), and tailoring the message accordingly, Busch Gardens has increased the return on its advertising expenditures.

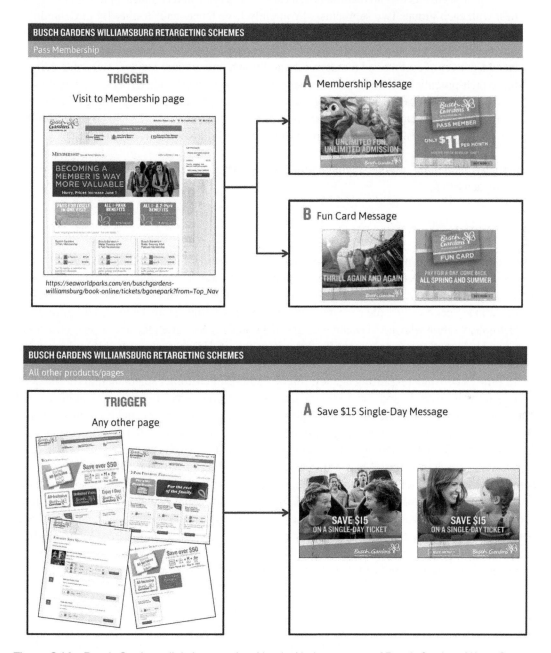

Figure 3.14 Busch Gardens digital retargeting. Used with the consent of Busch Gardens/Water Country USA. All Rights Reserved.

- **Consumer segmentation**—Through a combination of proprietary research and appended third-party data, Busch Gardens created a consumer segmentation to help the park better target prospective guests. The segmentation focused on theme park visitation, other leisure activities, and family composition. Attitudinal traits helped draw a more robust profile of each of the four segments to help marketers determine messaging and channels that would resonate best with each group. Two segments—'You Only Live Once' and 'Rather Be in Orlando'— were identified as the top targets based on their affinity for theme parks, overall leisure spending, and priority given to family activities. The consumers in these market segments received an added layer of customized direct mail in addition to advertising that was refined to address these high-potential prospects. Another segment, 'Local Entertainment Seekers,' became the focus for communication surrounding seasonal events and other park happenings. The fourth segment, 'Making Others Happy,' identified reluctant park visitors who would only attend if obligated by family or friends; this group did not receive direct marketing support.

In summary, behavioral market segmentation can be extremely valuable in customizing direct marketing activities.

Cohort Analysis

Direct marketers perform cohort analyses as a form of market segmentation based on specific groups of individuals. A **cohort** is a group of people who have in common a specific experience or characteristic. Cohorts are different from general demographics that are often used for market segmentation. Specifically, cohorts categorize individuals within their demographic groupings. For example, women who are between the ages of 18 and 22, who attended a four-year university course and belonged to a certain sorority, represent a cohort. Cohorts are a valuable tool for direct marketers to execute targeted marketing campaigns.

Equifax, a consumer reporting agency, offers methods of customer segmentation for financial services firms in order to understand their customers and prospects.[9] Equifax uses financial and economic cohorts for precise customer segmentation solutions. The financial cohorts classify individuals based on their financial potential, consisting of their financial profiles, behaviors, characteristics, as well as demographics, age, and urbanicity. Equifax has grouped the financial cohorts into three asset tiers: Mass Market, Mass Affluent, and Affluent.[10] Within each of the three tiers there are a vast number of sub-group segments. The economic cohorts use household economic information for valuable segmentation. Household economic information includes total income, total discretionary spending, credit capacity, along with demographic, behavioral, and lifestyle characteristics. Equifax has four key clusters of economic cohorts: Low Income, Moderate Income, High Income, and Elite Income.[11] In summary, cohort analysis reveals consumer groups that have unique bonds, thus they are a unified market segment.

Using Multiple Segmentation Bases

Relying on a single base for segmenting markets and selecting customers is rarely effective. Most direct marketers use multiple segmentation bases—such as combining geographic data with behavioral data. Thus, within a single ZIP code area, several smaller segments may exist on the basis of behavioral differences, like products purchased. A good example of multivariable segmentation is 'geodemographic' segmentation. Several companies, including Claritas, Experian, Acxiom, and MapInfo, combine U.S. census data with consumer lifestyle patterns to profile customers by geographic areas. These services enable marketers to choose segments wisely based on multivariable segmentation data.

Claritas, featured in Figure 3.15, began geodemographic segmentation back in 1976 by analyzing data, isolating key factors, and developing a clustering system. This clustering system began with two key drivers: age and income. But as Claritas quickly discovered, there was more than just age and income that needed to be evaluated. The statisticians who created PRIZM realized the importance of creating segments based on the demographics that correlate directly with consumer *behavior*, and made enhancements to the system to enable marketers to shift from a five-digit ZIP code to Census Tract to Block Group to ZIP+4, all the way down to household level—all within a set of 14 social groups.

Figure 3.15   Claritas PRIZM advertisement. Used with permission of Nielsen Claritas, a Nielsen company.

Google Analytics, a Web analytics service offered by Google, uses multiple segmentation bases too. The Web analytics service tracks and reports website traffic. From the detailed analyses in Google Analytics, direct marketers are able to examine their website traffic through in-depth customer segmentation. The system allows segmentation based on age, gender, affinity categories, and in-market segments. Affinity categories represent individuals' overall interest and lifestyle attributes, while in-market segments represent individuals who are actively searching and have indicated an interest in a product or service. Direct marketers use Google Analytics's customer segmentation system to determine the rationale for their website sessions, bounce rate, transactions, and revenue.

Google Analytics gathers customer data from three key sources: Third-party DoubleClick cookie, Android Advertising ID, and iOS Identifier for Advertisers (IDFA). Third-party DoubleClick cookies apply to Web-browser activity only, whereas Android Advertising ID and iOS IDGA apply to app activity only. Each of the three sources uses cookies and tracking codes in mobile applications to gather customer data for segmentation.

Each social group contains creatively named segments that tend to cluster together. For example, the 'Urban Uptown' group contains the nation's wealthiest urban consumers and has the following five segments: 'Young Digerati,' 'Money and Brains,' 'Bohemian Mix,' 'The Cosmopolitans,' and 'American Dreams.' Although this group is diverse in terms of housing styles and family sizes, residents share an upscale perspective that is reflected in their marketplace selections. Figure 3.16 shows some examples of the unique segments from a variety of social groups that Claritas created based on geodemographic analysis.

Claritas also provides an online service, MyBestSegments.com, which can help guide marketing campaigns and media strategies for specific market segments. Customer segmentation profiling information included in MyBestSegments encompasses PRIZM and a variety of categories about consumer markets, including travel, eating out, shopping, auto purchases, and more.

Close-In Couples: Predominantly African-American couples, 55-year-old plus, that live in older homes in urban neighborhoods, high school educated, empty nesting, enjoying secure and comfortable retirements.

Winners Circle: A collection of mostly 35- to 54-year-old couples with large families in new-money subdivisions. Surrounding their homes are the signs of upscale living: recreational parks, golf courses, and upscale malls surround their homes. With a median income of over $100,000, these residents are big spenders who like to travel, ski, go out to eat, and shop at clothing boutiques.

Home Sweet Home: Mostly under 55, these residents tend to be upper-middle-class married couples living in mid-size homes with few children, they have attended college and hold professional and white-collar jobs, they have fashioned comfortable lifestyles, filling their homes with toys, TVs and pets.

Up-and-Comers: Mostly in their twenties, single, many are recent college graduates who are into athletic activities, the latest technology and nightlife entertainment.

Shotguns & Pickups: These Americans tend to be young, working-class couples with large families, most have two or more kids, they live in small homes and manufactured housing, nearly a third of the residents live in mobile homes and many own hunting rifles and pickup trucks.

Figure 3.16 Examples of Claritas PRIZM segment narratives. Used with permission of Claritas, a Nielsen company.

Source: PRIZM Segment Narratives. Reprinted with permission from Nielsen Claritas, a Nielsen company, April 2008.

Demographic data are also available. Plus, these data are continually updated to be in sync with Claritas's Market Place suite of products for additional consumer behavior data. Visit MyBestSegments (https://claritas360.claritas.com/mybestsegments/?ID=64&menuOption=learnmore#seg Details) to explore the 'ZIP Code Look-Up' feature of this system, which allows you to plug in your ZIP code to obtain a profile of your neighborhood's top five segments, along with some descriptive detail about each segment's lifestyle traits. While visiting the MyBestSegment site, you may also want to investigate the 'Segment Look-Up' feature, which provides detailed descriptions of each of its 68 unique market segments. The three lifestages and 11 lifestage groups that make up the 68 unique market segments depict strong images of target customers.[12] As Figure 3.17 shows, direct marketers that subscribe to Claritas can quickly and easily obtain details about the best segments to target for a specific offer, along with additional customer profiling information.

ZIP CODE AREAS AS MARKET SEGMENTS

ZIP code areas, although originally conceived and developed by the U.S. Postal Service for the purpose of sorting and distributing mail, have become a convenient and logical method of geographic segmentation, especially in direct marketing. ZIP code areas have become a key basis

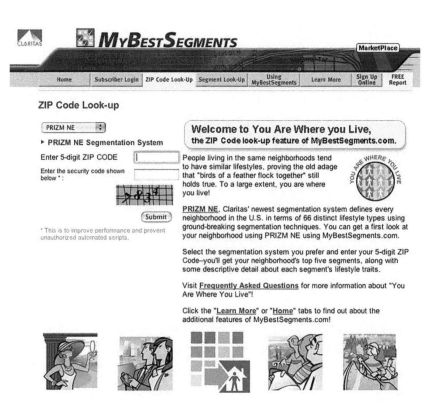

(Continued)

Figure 3.17 (Continued)

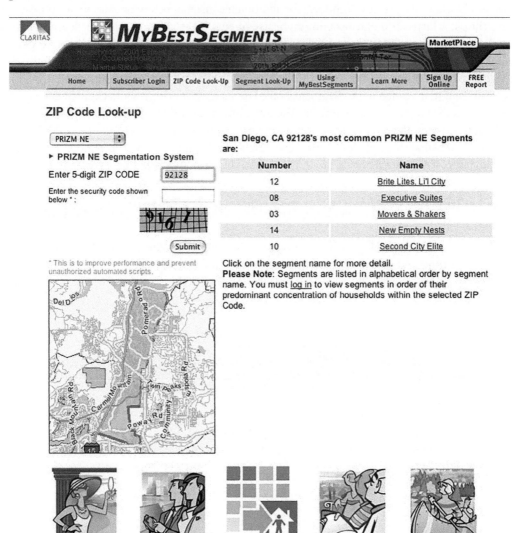

Figure 3.17 MyBestSegments.com Web pages. Used with permission of Nielsen Claritas, a Nielsen company.

for market segmentation in direct marketing, combining the characteristics of geographic, demographic, social, psychological, and behavioral factors. The value of ZIP codes for marketers is based on the simple fact that the codes tend to enclose homogeneous neighborhoods and geographical boundaries.

The old saying 'birds of a feather flock together,' explains why ZIP code areas constitute market segments. Because people with like interests tend to cluster and because their purchase decisions are frequently influenced by their desire to emulate their friends, neighbors, and community innovators, ZIP code areas provide the means to *identify* clusters of households that have a high degree of homogeneity. This homogeneity is inherent in the manner in which ZIP code areas have been constructed and relies on accepted principles of reference group theory as well as the concept of environmental influences on buyer behavior.

Marketers can use ZIP code areas in many specific ways; some of these are outlined in the following list:

- Establish and define market segments, including sales potentials based on environmental data about the unit.
- Evaluate direct marketing results performance, based on a measurement of actual penetration against the projected potential, and realign market segments as such analysis warrants.
- Process inquiries and orders more efficiently and effectively without the need for reference to a map, since the address immediately identifies the sales territory.
- Forecast more accurately based on objective analysis of the marketplace rather than on a collection of individual opinions about it.
- Pinpoint market segments in relation to profits.
- Increase regional and national advertising effectiveness when direct mail, magazines, or newspapers are used.
- Determine optimum distribution centers.
- Set up a territorial rating system for credit evaluation and perform continuing analysis of accounts receivable.
- Conduct market research, especially if demographic cross-sections or probability sampling are called for.
- Develop differentiated products that have special interest to specific market segments that can be defined by ZIP code areas, certain educational levels, or target occupation groups, for example.
- Analyze the penetration of present customers according to specific ZIP code area characteristics to more effectively direct and control marketing efforts.
- Identify growth areas, with updated demographics.
- Direct new product sampling more effectively.
- Control inventories according to historical territorial patterns.
- Coordinate data processing and information systems through use of the ZIP code as part of the computerized 'match code.'
- Distribute seasonal and climate-oriented products and information on a chronological schedule by ZIP code area.

Geographic Structure

The socioeconomic usefulness of these units, especially from a direct marketing perspective, results from the three criteria the U.S. Postal Service used in establishing each ZIP code:

1. A hub city is at the center of each cluster of ZIP code areas (termed a sectional center) that is the natural center of local transportation.
2. An average of 40–75 individual post offices lies within each sectional center, resulting in units with a fairly consistent population density.
3. Each natural transportation hub is about two to three hours' driving time away from the farthest post office in the sectional center.

An obvious convenience of these geographic units, which sets them apart from commonly used divisions such as counties, is that each household and business within the unit is readily identifiable by a five-digit number assigned to it as a part of its street address. In dissecting the ZIP code, you will find that the first digit of the five-digit code identifies one of ten (0 through 9) geographic areas of the nation, with the digit ascending from east to west. The next two digits of the five-digit number identify a major city or major distribution point (sectional center) within a state. The last two digits of the five-digit ZIP code fall into two geographic categories: (1) key post offices in each area, which normally have stations and branches in the city's neighborhoods; and (2) a series of associated small town or rural post offices served by the sectional center transportation hub, or a specific neighborhood or delivery unit within a city. Visit www.unitedstateszipcodes.org to better understand the assignment of ZIP codes.

ZIP+4

Figure 3.18 summarizes what the five-digit ZIP code designations represent. The U.S. Postal Service has added a four-digit extension to the original five-digit code. The sixth and seventh digits denote a sector and the last two denote a *segment* within a sector. These additional four digits permit mail to be sorted to carrier delivery routes. An example of the meaning of the additional four digits is as follows:

*   Digits 6 and 7—could denote the location of a specific organization, like a university.
*   Digits 8 and 9—could represent a specific segment or department within the university, perhaps the office of admissions.

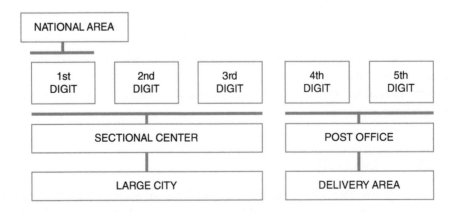

Figure 3.18 ZIP code digit designations

Clustering Areas to Segments

A key advantage of ZIP code areas is that they can be combined like building blocks to suit the individual need of the direct marketer relative to product differentiation or promotional strategy.

A ZIP code-based marketing information system enables direct marketers to know more about their markets and organize them according to local transportation patterns. Many major coupon distributors segment their markets on the basis of ZIP code areas. These companies also know which ZIP code areas possess a heavy concentration of residential households and coupon users.

Availability of Statistical Data

During the past few decades, increasing amounts of data for ZIP code areas have become available. Some of these include organizations' own records along with consumer survey data compiled by the Census Bureau, the Market Research Institute (MRI), and Simmons Market Research Bureau.

ZIP Code Business Patterns is a service published by the U.S. Census Bureau. It presents data on the total number of establishments, employment, and payroll for more than 40,000 five-digit ZIP code areas nationwide.[13] ZIP Code Business Patterns provides segmentation information that is invaluable for direct marketers.

SUMMARY

Most direct marketers conduct market segmentation to serve consumer needs and wants in an optimal way. Lists are important market segmentation tools. There are three basic types of lists: house, response, and compiled. Each list is of value for direct marketers, although house lists are considered the most valuable. The list industry is composed of list owners, list users, list brokers, list managers, list compilers, and service bureaus. Each member plays an important role in the list-rental activities of direct marketers. Direct marketers strive to keep lists current and accurate. House lists normally hold a customer's name, address, and pertinent contact information. In addition, most direct marketers rent lists in an attempt to prospect for new customers. List-rental strategies are made simple today due to computerized database services with search techniques, such as NextMark's list services. List selections afford direct marketers the opportunity to further segment a list using a variety of segmentation variables. Direct marketers segment final consumers according to geographic, demographic, social, psychological, and behavioral characteristics. Oftentimes, multiple variables are used to segment markets, such as geodemographic segmentation. Direct marketers consider ZIP code areas to be geographic market segments that provide important customer information.

KEY TERMS

cohort
compiled lists
cookie
demographics
Geographic Information Systems (GIS)
Global Positioning System (GPS)
hotline names
house lists
key code
list brokers
list compilers
list managers

list owners
market segmentation
market segments
product differentiation
product positioning
psychographics
reference groups
reference individual
response lists
retargeting
service bureaus

REVIEW QUESTIONS

1. What type of list is most important to an organization? Why?
2. Explain the difference between a *list user* and a *list owner*. How do they interact with one another?
3. What are list brokers, list managers, and list compilers each responsible for?
4. Explain the process for conducting list research via the NextMark List Research System. What is the starting point for the process?
5. What is a *key code*? How is it used in list measurement and analysis?
6. What is *market segmentation*? Explain the bases or factors used to segment consumer markets.
7. What are *psychographics*? In what way are they useful to direct marketers?
8. In the four-digit extension of an original five-digit ZIP code, what does each of the numbers stand for?
9. How can ZIP codes help achieve product differentiation or be used in executing promotional strategies?
10. Why is using multiple market segmentation data important as opposed to relying on one type of data? How does the Claritas PRIZM system integrate multiple types of data?

EXERCISE

As a Nike employee, it is your responsibility to create a house list for the company. Create a list and include all the important characteristics about customers that would be beneficial to making the company most profitable. Keep in mind that Nike sells many different types of products, so you would want the organization of your house list to be segmented accordingly. If you were to rent lists to augment your house list, where would you go to find appropriate lists? What other types of companies would have lists that would interest you?

CRITICAL THINKING EXERCISE

Identify a list of which you are a member. How did you become a member of this list? What is the profile of the other members of this list? How are you similar? Describe a few companies and organizations that might be interested in renting this list. What is your level of receptiveness to the offers these companies might present to you?

READINGS AND RESOURCES

- NextMark: https://lists.nextmark.com
- Personalization: https://yougov.co.uk/topics/consumer/articles-reports/2018/03/26/targeting-personalised-ads-right-audience
- Personas: www.roymorgan.com/findings/7752-the-next-generation-of-helix-personas-has-arrived-201809270915
- Market segmentation: www.dssresearch.com/services/strategy-research/market-segmentation
- Segment migration: www.marketingprofs.com/articles/2010/3403/segment-migration-where-your-customers-were-where-they-went-and-why
- Cohort analysis: https://medium.com/analytics-for-humans/a-beginners-guide-to-cohort-analysis-the-most-actionable-and-underrated-report-on-google-c0797d826bf4

CASE: VIRGINIA BEACH TOURISM

Do you like to travel? Do you enjoy taking a vacation? If so, you are among the millions or billions or perhaps zillions of people who do! Tourism is a powerful industry that affects many different businesses, including hotels, restaurants, retail outlets, attractions, transportation providers, and meeting facilities. Virginia Beach travel and tourism (Figure 3.19) is big business. Tourism is also an industry made up of many different types of consumers with vastly different needs, wants, and desires to which tourism marketers must strategically appeal.

This case is designed to help you to better understand how a vacation destination is able to segment its market to attract a wide variety of prospective tourists. The vacation destination is Virginia Beach, Virginia, a place that literally has something for everyone. However, in order to be effective in marketing to a diverse leisure traveler population, its marketing strategies must be customized and targeted to cater to each consumer group's interests and desires. Before we discuss Virginia Beach's marketing strategies, let's take a stroll down its beautiful boardwalk and take a glance at Virginia Beach as a vacation destination.

Figure 3.19 Virginia Beach coastline. Used with permission of the City of Virginia Beach Convention & Visitors Bureau.

Why Visit Virginia Beach?

A tourist favorite, the Virginia Beach resort area features a three-mile long, nationally acclaimed boardwalk along the Atlantic Ocean with a separate bike path–a combination perfect for strolling, running, biking, roller blading, renting a surrey, or just taking in the sights and sounds of the beach scene. Hotels, restaurants, unique shops, a fishing pier, and even playgrounds for the kids are all wrapped up in a park-like atmosphere that goes on for miles. Live musical and family-friendly entertainment is offered nightly during the summer months along Atlantic Avenue and at four oceanfront stages. Parasailing, jet ski rental, ocean kayaking, boat tours, and charter fishing trips are all available to tourists. Virginia Beach offers numerous venues to engage tourists. For example, the 800,000-gallon Virginia Aquarium & Marine Science Center is one of the best aquariums and live animal habitats in the country, featuring river otters, harbor seals, loggerhead sea turtles, stingrays, and sharks as well as hundreds of hands-on exhibits, an outdoor aviary and nature trail, and a 3D IMAX® theater.

Who's the Target Market?

The primary target market for overnight visitation to Virginia Beach can be divided into two categories–final consumers and organizational consumers–each with its own subset of defined market segments. These include:

- leisure travelers (such as families, singles without children, sports enthusiasts, and the mature market)
- meeting planners/event planners/sports planners (including social, military, educational, religious, and fraternal organizations, and more).

The secondary market includes group tour operators, motor coach operators, and group tour planners. This case focuses on how Virginia Beach targets various prospective leisure travelers.

Geographically, Virginia Beach concentrates its direct marketing efforts on prospective tourists in the Northeast region of the United States. This geographic region is important because the city's convenient location makes it only a day's drive for two-thirds of the nation's population. Therefore, the top geographic target markets include the following:

- Washington, DC
- Richmond/Petersburg, VA
- Roanoke/Lynchburg, VA
- Philadelphia, PA
- New York, NY
- Pittsburgh, PA
- Cleveland, OH
- Baltimore, MD
- Hampton Roads, VA
- Harrisburg, PA
- Raleigh, NC.

Now that you know what geographical markets are targeted by Virginia Beach, let's explore how it customizes its marketing and media strategies to attract specific demographic and behavioral segments of tourists.

Virginia Beach's Marketing and Media Strategy

Virginia Beach employs a multi-media marketing strategy, including magazines, inter-active/online, broadcast television and radio, as well as select newspapers. Its market-ing strategy is designed to achieve two objectives: (1) to generate awareness of Virginia Beach as a quality, year-round destination; and (2) to drive traffic to its tourism websites, VisitVirginiaBeach.com and LiveTheLife.com. Virginia Beach marketers have used list-rental strategies to identify e-mail lists that might prove to be useful in connecting with prospective tourists. They have recently run a dedicated Virginia Beach e-mail campaign with lists from WeatherBug, eTarget Media, iExplore, Orbitz, Sherman's Travel, Daily Candy, *The New York Times*, *The Washington Post*, *The News & Observer* (Raleigh, NC), eBrains, and *The Baltimore Sun*.

Virginia Beach's Segmentation Strategy

The secret to successful tourism marketing for Virginia Beach lies in its highly segmented marketing initiatives designed to drive prospective tourists to its easy-to-navigate website, and once there, enable each prospect to quickly locate the information of interest. This marketing strategy is uniquely customized and tailored to each demographic and behavioral consumer segment.

Here's how it works: first, Virginia Beach researches each consumer market segment's desires and develops a series of creative messages tailored to each segment's professed desires regarding *what each group lives for* in a beach vacation. Next, Virginia Beach places advertisements with unique website URLs created explicitly for each segment in specific media vehicles that strategically reach each traveler segment. Then, when each prospective traveler visits the Virginia Beach website, he or she immediately views select Web pages containing vacation information about Virginia Beach that is of specific interest. For example, prospective sports enthusiast travelers will view the Web pages featuring photos and descriptions regarding the wide variety of sports events and activities offered at Virginia Beach, as presented in Figure 3.20. Of course, each prospect is free to explore the entire website as it is easy to navigate and chock full of information and enticing photos and videos.

Figure 3.20 Virginia Beach Web pages. Used with permission of the City of Virginia Beach Convention & Visitors Bureau.

Let's take a look at precisely how Virginia Beach targets each leisure traveler segment.

Singles Without Children

So you are single, without children, and searching for a vacation destination for you and your friends. You might locate an advertisement and information about Virginia Beach on a travel website or via search engine optimization with Google, Yahoo/Bing or Facebook. As Figure 3.21 shows, the Virginia Beach advertisements that you find will contain messages tailored to your specific interests, such as taking a bike ride along the boardwalk. The ad encourages you to visit 'LIVEFORTHECRUISE.COM' to learn more about what a vacation in Virginia Beach has to offer you.

Figure 3.21 Virginia Beach LIVEFORTHECRUISE.com ad. Used with permission of the City of Virginia Beach Convention & Visitors Bureau.

Families

Pretend for a moment that you are a mom or a dad with a family of three young children and you're planning a beach vacation. As a parent, you might see an advertisement for Virginia Beach in a magazine such as *Good Housekeeping* or *Working Mother*. An example of the advertisement you will see is shown in Figure 3.22. The ad is targeting families with a specific call to action to come play on the beach and visit 'LIVEFORTHESPINCYCLE.COM.'

Figure 3.22   Virginia Beach LIVEFORTHESPINCYCLE. com ad. Used with permission of the City of Virginia Beach Convention & Visitors Bureau.

Sports Enthusiasts

If you are a sports enthusiast, you are likely interested in surfing, kayaking, running, or fishing when you visit Virginia Beach. Perhaps you want to learn more about its Annual Sand Soccer Tournament or its Rock 'n' Roll 1/2 Marathon. You may see ads such as those featured in Figure 3.23, those that provide unique URLs, here 'LIVEFORTHEBIGONE.COM' and 'LIVEFORCLOSEENCOUNTERS.COM,' encouraging you to visit the specific Virginia Beach microsite to obtain more information.

Figure 3.23 Virginia Beach LIVEFORTHEBIGONE.com ad; LIVEFORTHECLOSEENCOUNTER.com ads. Used with permission of the City of Virginia Beach Convention & Visitors Bureau.

Mature Consumers

Fast-forward your life by about 30 or 40 years and think about what you might want from a vacation at Virginia Beach when you are a bit older. You will still enjoy vacationing, but your desires will be different than they are now. You might see Virginia Beach advertisements in *Coastal Living* magazine or on WashingtonPost.com. Those ads will be tailored to your interests, which may include taking a walk along the boardwalk or enjoying a couple of afternoons spent on the fairways (see Figure 3.24).

Figure 3.24   Virginia Beach LIVEFORTHEFAIRWAY.com ad. Used with permission of the City of Virginia Beach Convention & Visitors Bureau.

Conclusion

When you are a vacation destination that offers something for everyone, you must carefully segment your market and identify the geographic, demographic, and behavioral subgroups that exist. As you have seen in this case, the Virginia Beach resort area offers an ideal example of how to employ effective market segmentation strategies by targeting specific segments or niches of consumers with customized and creative messages that appeal to each segment's precise needs, wants, and interests. So, what vacation interests do you have? Go to VisitVirginiaBeach.com and you will surely find whatever you desire in a weekend getaway or a vacation destination.

Case Discussion Questions

1. Identify the segmentation variables discussed in the case to classify potential tourists who vacation at Virginia Beach. Can you think of other variables that can group destination vacationers with common interests and attraction to Virginia Beach? Describe how such groups can be targeted. What role should social media play?
2. The case describes the target Virginia Beach vacationers as leisure travelers, meeting and convention planners, and group tour organizers/operators. Describe the marketing and media strategies Virginia Beach Convention and Visitors Bureau uses to target these groups.
3. Virginia Beach is described as a quality, year-round vacation destination. Yet the sports, entertainment, and leisure activities depicted on its website are all summer bound. Imagine a family is planning to vacation in Virginia Beach during the month of November. What recreational, sight-seeing, and cultural activities can you recommend to such a family?
4. Briefly describe how Virginia Beach could track its current customers/visitors and include database marketing in its strategic marketing activities. What data should it gather for its database? How can this data be obtained?

NOTES

1. www.usgs.gov/faqs/what-a-geographic-information-system-gis?qt-news_science_products=1#qt-news_science_products, retrieved September 22, 2019.
2. https://dema.az.gov/emergency-management/communications-and-technology/geographical-information-systems/geographic, retrieved September 22, 2019.
3. www.esri.com/en-us/about/about-esri/who-we-are, retrieved September 22, 2019.
4. Consumer Information Solutions – The Lifestyle Selector, www.equifax.com/pdfs/corp/EFS-779-ADV_TheLifestyleSelector_ProductSheet.pdf, retrieved September 15, 2019.
5. www.emarketer.com/Article/Whos-Boss-Teens-Influence-Household-Spending-Worldwide/1015039, retrieved May 9, 2019.
6. www.emarketer.com/Article/Whos-Boss-Teens-Influence-Household-Spending-Worldwide/1015039, retrieved May 9, 2019.
7. www.nielsen.com/us/en/insights/reports/2018/us-music-360-2018.html, retrieved May 9, 2019.
8. www.nonprofitpro.com/article/doctors-without-borders-uses-remarketing-retargeting-extend-reach/all, retrieved May 23, 2019.
9. www.equifax.com/business/customer-segmentation, retrieved April 28, 2019.
10. https://datadrivenmarketing.equifax.com/financial-cohorts/?web_010218_efx_cs_solution_finance, retrieved April 28, 2019.
11. https://datadrivenmarketing.equifax.com/economic-cohorts/?web_010218_efx_cs_solution_economic, retrieved April 28, 2019.
12. www.claritas.com/prizmr-premier, retrieved April 29, 2019.
13. www.census.gov/data/developers/data-sets/cbp-nonemp-zbp/zbp-api.html, retrieved September 16, 2019.

4

MARKETING ANALYTICS: TESTING AND MEASUREMENT

CHAPTER CONTENTS

CHAPTER SPOTLIGHT

THE NATIONAL GEOGRAPHIC SOCIETY OFFER TEST

The National Geographic Society (NGS) is one of the world's largest nonprofit scientific and educational organizations. Founded in 1888 to 'increase and diffuse geographic knowledge,' the Society works to inspire people to care about the planet. Like all direct and interactive marketing organizations, the NGS is always striving to maximize the rate of response it obtains on its membership offers. Its membership offer includes its 'product,' which is a subscription for 12 issues of *National Geographic* magazine (Figure 4.1).

In January, April, and October of each year, the NGS sends membership promotion mailings to approximately 18 million households in the United States and Canada. The NGS tests its offers, premiums, prices, mailing lists, payment options, and creative approaches to attract new members for its organization. The most common type of test is normally an **offer test**. When conducting a test, the NGS takes 10 percent of the total mailing quantity and uses that for tests. A test offer for the NGS will have no less than 25,000 recipients.

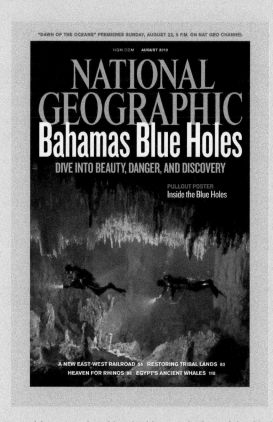

Figure 4.1 *National Geographic* magazine. Used with permission of the National Geographic Society.

The NGS conducted pricing and payment term offer tests to determine the impact that these offers had on response rates. As shown in Figure 4.2, the NGS tested two Bill-Me-Later price offers ($18 and $15) against its *control* Bill-Me-Later offer ($12 plus $3.95 for shipping, which totals $15.95) and a credit card payment offer. The control is the offer that has historically generated the highest rate of response for the organization.

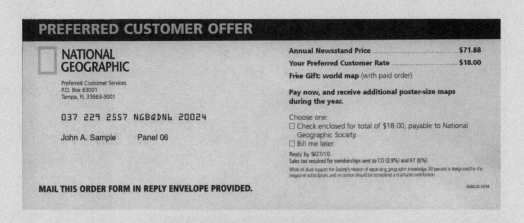

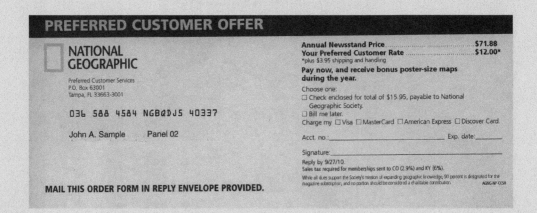

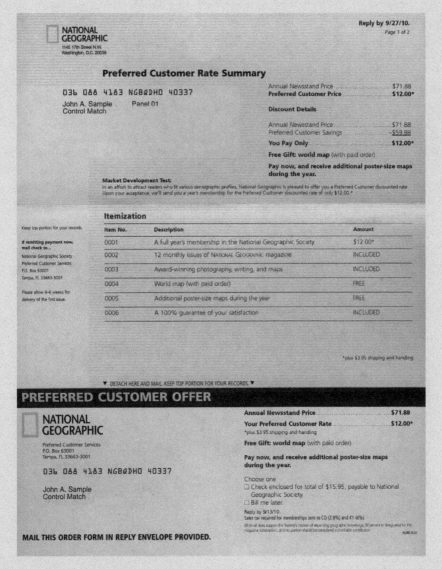

Figure 4.2 National Geographic Society offer reply cards. Used with permission of the National Geographic Society.

An analysis of the results of the offer test is used to determine the most effective offer to be sent to a larger sample of prospective members. How does the NGS decide 'what works best?' The NGS uses the following criteria:

1. The highest net per net subscription, which means how much money the organization obtained after it found the lowest cost per order, then adjusted for those who did not submit payment (as this was a Bill-Me-Later offer).
2. The offer that beat the control offer by at least 7 percent.

If two tests earned the same response rate, cost the same, and seemed like they would generate the same amount of renewal (repeat business), the NGS would consider the following additional factors:

1. Which one has a smaller environmental footprint–less paper, less trucking, less ink, etc.?
2. Which one more effectively extends its mission? For example, for several years, the NGS used a direct mail package that included a free world map in it. This package gave people a map with which to follow the news, trace their cultural heritage, locate earthquakes, etc. So the NGS educated 10 million people at a time. Even though 97 percent of the people who received the offer did not order the NGS magazine, they all got a useful tool to understand geography. And that is what the NGS is all about.
3. Which one takes the least amount of time to manufacture and get into the mail?

As can be concluded, response rates are the key metric used to make strategic campaign decisions, but there are other important factors to be analyzed as well. Analysis of the metrics generated from a test is critical to decision making. Direct marketers must conduct tests, measure response rate, and analyze results in order to make good business decisions to maximize profitability and meet organizational objectives. That's precisely what this chapter will discuss.

TESTING

Testing, also known as experimentation, manipulates one or more controllable factors, called independent variables, to determine their influence on various events or outcomes, called dependent variables. A common testing technique is A/B testing, also known as split testing, where you 'split' your audience to test a number of variations of a campaign element to determine which performs better. Thus, an A/B test is designed to compare the effectiveness of two alternatives (A vs. B) of marketing activities. In essence, you can show version A of a piece of marketing content to one-half of your audience, and version B to another, or you might compare two versions of a webpage against each other. Marketers may split the audience into more than two groups if there are more than two alternatives being tested.

For example, Quad, a worldwide marketing solutions company, helped an iconic retail chain[1] boost response rates for its catalog and direct mail. The retailer's direct mail and catalog marketing was rooted in the past and was no longer productive. It wanted to increase sales through tangible positive results from print channels. Quad conducted sophisticated research based on what real-world customers had responded to in the past. Quad designers built two test packages each for direct mail and catalog. Those packages included winning offers, taglines, images, and other elements for catalog covers and direct mail pieces. Quad printed and mailed the test packages along with a control, then measured results for three key performance indicators (KPIs)—response rate, sales value, and average order size. The results were outstanding. The text packages outperformed expectations for all KPIs, with response rates of 27.5 percent for catalog and 47.1 percent for direct mail. On top of that, the retailer experienced an increase in the average order size. (Check out the Readings and Resources at the end of this chapter for more detail on A/B tests.)

Testing is especially prevalent in direct marketing. In a test, the direct marketer creates an environment in which controls serve to pinpoint the causes of behavior differences among respondents. This method of gathering data requires close adherence to statistical techniques to ensure validity. Because direct marketers rely heavily on experimentation, we look closely at certain relevant tools and techniques of statistics in this chapter. Some examples of direct marketing questions that call for experimentation are the following:

- How does frequency of mailing to a particular record on a database affect total response?
- Which e-mail subject line generates the highest response rate?
- Is a direct mail piece more effective in color than in black and white?
- Which free gift with purchase garners the greatest consumer response online?
- What is the most profitable pricing strategy?

Independent variables could be the product or service offered, its price structure, or some attribute of the promotional strategy used in the offer. They can also describe the demography or geography of a market. Independent variables should reflect the situation in the real world, for example the age, gender, marital status, or ZIP code of residence of a respondent. Marketers should generally evaluate only one independent variable at a time.

Certain advanced statistical techniques, however, such as multivariate correlation and regression analysis, offer the opportunity to measure the interaction of many independent variables simultaneously. Although direct marketers may investigate many different independent variables, they commonly use the following four types of test: list, offer, creative, and contact strategy.

List Tests

Investigating whether certain lists will generate a higher response rate than other lists is an ongoing task for most direct marketers. Direct marketers constantly test the lists they use—for both prospective customers and current customers. Most will test a small sample of a prospect list prior to renting the entire list for new customer acquisition purposes. Most list brokers permit small samples of prospect lists to be rented for list testing.

Offer Tests

Offer tests assess whether incentives—such as free shipping or discounted shipping, percentage discount or dollar discount—have an impact on the rate of response to the offer. In other words, do the incremental sales generated by the promotional offer offset the forgone shipping revenue or discounts given?

Creative Tests

Creative tests address issues such as design, layout, copy, images, photographs, and much more. Most direct marketers have a printed catalog. One common creative test has to do with the design of the catalog cover. Thus, a test would be conducted to determine whether a test cover beat a control cover. This would require testing either a unique design or an alternative style of the control cover design. It could also include variations in images, such as a certain photographed model, or copy compared to the control design or norm. Let's take a closer look at an example.

The American Heart Association decided to test six copy approaches in the form of teasers displayed on the outside of the mailing envelope. These six envelope teasers would be tested against each other and also against the control—the envelope that the fundraiser had been using successfully in the past, but which had no teaser at all.

These seven envelope panels (six tests and one control) included a letter, a contribution form, and a reply envelope enclosed in each mailing envelope. These forms were essentially the same for all seven packages except for the beginning of the letter, which emphasized the teaser copy approach that was featured on the outside of the mailing envelope. The American Heart Association sent these mailings to their current donors as well as 'cold' prospects, those who had not given a contribution before. The response from each group and for each copy approach was tabulated separately through key coding appearing on the contribution form. These tested copy approaches are shown in Table 4.1.

The results of this test proved that teaser copy on the outer envelope was an effective creative approach to use in a fundraising campaign and enabled the American Heart Association to then utilize the most effective teaser copy in its subsequent mailings.

Table 4.1   Copy approaches tested by the American Heart Association

Effort		Copy approach
1		Use the enclosed FREE GIFT.
2		Emergency Heart Attack Card Enclosed.
3		4 years ago Billy Thompson's dad would have died …
4		If you have ever worried about having a heart attack …
5		You hold lives in your hands … TODAY … AND THAT'S IMPORTANT!
6		We'd like to show you how you can help save a life. YOURS.
7		(Control) No teaser copy.
The response results were these:		
The best package:	6	We'd like to show you how you can help save a life. YOURS.
Good packages:	4	If you have ever worried about having a heart attack …
	3	4 years ago Billy Thompson's dad would have died …
Poor packages	1	Use the enclosed FREE GIFT.
	5	You hold lives in your hands … TODAY … AND THAT'S IMPORTANT!
	7	No teaser copy.
	2	Emergency Heart Attack Card Enclosed.

Source: This case was originally developed by Freeman F. Gosden, Jr., president of Smith-Hemmings-Gosden, Direct Response Advertising, El Monte, California, who conducted the test from which it was derived.

Online marketing is another venue that uses a variety of creative tests. Online marketers test the effectiveness of e-mail headlines, social media posts, home page designs, and features of mobile apps. Two giants for online ads—Facebook and Google—provide features to create A/B tests in their marketing platforms.

For example, analytical research on a prominent healthcare delivery system's website[2] revealed that its site's existing Call-to-Action (CTA) button restricted users from easily accessing location-specific details, which hindered the appointment-making process. Quad, a worldwide marketing solutions company, designed an A/B test and split unique website traffic evenly (33.33%) among three 'Find Location' button variations to determine the optimal CTA button option. The three button variations were:

1. Original CTA: One 'request appointment' button at the top of the webpage under the navigation bar.
2. In-text CTAs: The original 'request appointment' button at the top of the webpage and three additional CTA buttons between each section of content on the page.
3. Top CTAs: Four horizontal CTA buttons statically located at the top of the webpage in addition to the original.

The A/B test was successful in identifying which CTA button option was the most effective in generating a response. Based on the outcome of this test, the healthcare system revamped its webpage to feature the most optimal CTA button option. The ultimate impact was an increase in the number of appointment requests.

Contact Strategy Tests

This common type of test is related to a direct marketer's customer database. Contact strategy tests investigate what type or combination of contacts will maximize the sales or profits associated with each particular customer or select market segment. Perhaps altering the number of catalogs sent to a group of customers over a specific period can have an impact on sales or profit.

For example, a leading craft retailer[3] wanted to investigate how its catalogs affect customer sales to determine whether catalogs are worth printing and mailing. Beyond its house mailing list, the company also wanted to know whether lapsed customers might still buy if prompted. Quad designed a contact strategy test by holding out a small number of names on the mailing list when distributing its catalog during the test period. If that customer group didn't purchase online during that period, catalogs might be important. At the same time, Quad mailed catalogs to customers who hadn't bought anything from the company in a year. The results of the test determined that catalogs lifted response rate by nearly 132 percent on average and increased revenue by 25 percent. In addition, catalogs brought 2,048 lapsed customers back into its active customer file. This contact strategy test provided evidence that catalog mailings generate sales.

Direct marketers often include additional variables, such as using e-mail or other types of direct mail contacts, in the contact strategy tests. In direct marketing, the number of responses or transactions is often the dependent variable. In other research situations, the dependent variable could be favorable or unfavorable reactions to a product or overall rating of a brand preference. At least three levels of observation are normally needed for measurement. Direct marketing tests usually take place in a field setting, but marketers do sometimes conduct them under laboratory conditions. In a laboratory, marketers must be sure that the setting is realistic and that the subjects are representative. It would not be appropriate, for example, to use college students in a laboratory setting to test a product geared to the senior citizen market.

Designing the Test

Valid experiments are characterized by (1) the presence of a **control group** on which the experiment is not conducted but that is otherwise identical to the test group, and (2) **random assignment** of subjects to both test and control groups so that differences between groups occur by chance alone. Particularly, in A/B tests, instead of using a control group, two groups receive different alternatives of marketing stimuli (A vs. B) and responses between the two groups are compared.

Let's examine an example of an e-mail offer test. In an effort to drive visitation to its Food & Wine Festival, Busch Gardens incentivized Pass Members with free festival food via e-mail. The park created an offer test to determine how much free food it would need to give away to see a significant difference in visitation. Its Pass Member e-mail database was split up randomly to form two groups. As shown in Figure 4.3, Group A's offer contained one free food and wine dish (the control group), while Group B's offer contained three free dishes. The results showed that the e-mail containing the three free dishes offer performed 34 percent higher than the first group. Busch Gardens concluded that the additional cost of the extra two dishes per member was worth it.

Figure 4.3 Busch Gardens offer test. Used with the consent of Busch Gardens/Water Country USA. All Rights Reserved.

It is naive to compare responses from two groups that are not randomly selected and may not be similar in their composition. Consider, for example, the often repeated statement that those who receive a college education earn more in their lifetimes than those who do not. The two groups are not comparable, and thus it would be foolish to draw a conclusion that college education in and of itself causes higher lifetime income. It is conceivable that the drive that caused the student to enter college in the first place also affects lifetime income.

Common forms of experimental design measure the effect of an experiment as the difference between what is observed about the dependent variable of the test group and what is observed about the dependent variable of the control group. But even with control and randomization, there is still no guarantee that the two groups are identical. Differences between them that arise by chance alone may be substantial.

Adequate scheduling of experiments, their timely release, and key coding are vital. Marketers should devise a comprehensive schedule to describe the purpose of the experiment and also its various components, costs, and expected results for the test segment as well as the control.

Tracking Responses and Measuring Test Results

Obviously, response differences to a product offering—between tests and control—cannot be measured unless there is a complete record of results for all segments of the experiment. There must be a means to identify the sources of these results. This is accomplished through **key codes** placed on each response device, such as an order form, to make it easy to record results. In direct mail, the key code can be a unique number or other identifier placed on the order form. When the phone is used for response, the key code can be a unique telephone number, a departmental number, or an individual's name. Many direct marketers using the phone or a website ask respondents for the key code printed in the advertisement or on the label of a catalog to which they are responding. This is an excellent tracking device where the code will vary based on the element being tested.

Let's examine a test that utilized a highly specific tracking device. Busch Gardens wanted to determine how much it needed to give away in the form of a price discount on its single pass tickets. Busch Gardens runs various types of promotions and offers throughout its operating season and wanted to test offer thresholds to determine whether they were giving away more than necessary. One way in which this offer variation was tested was for summer discounts, specifically for Pass Members to use for visiting friends and relatives. The primary objective was to determine how much a free ticket would influence visitation versus a 50 percent discounted ticket. Due to the significant level of the discount, offers were uniquely bar-coded and included in summer newsletters mailed to each Pass Member household. The shaded grey area that appears at the bottom-right corner of each coupon, shown in Figure 4.4, contained the unique barcode. The two offers were equally split and randomly sent to a total of 100,000 households, each offer representing 50,000. The test results showed that 75 percent of visits were made by the free ticket, and Busch Gardens was able to conclude that the free offer was a significantly higher motivator to generate a visit.

Figure 4.4 Busch Gardens discount ticket coupon test. Used with the consent of Busch Gardens/Water Country USA. All Rights Reserved.

Today, most direct marketers are multichannel merchants, and their customers' orders are often placed via the company's website or at a retail location without a key code. Tracking these responses and correctly linking the results of tests back to a customer database are crucial. The objective is to find ways to match the orders placed on the website or in the retail stores that were driven or caused by the specific catalog, offer, or direct mailing that is being tested. Typically, direct marketers use 'matchback' rules to track most accurately the results of these tests when key codes are not used. Matchback simply refers to the process by which an order response is tracked back to the original source (catalog or offer) from which it was generated. For example, suppose a customer places an online order for a pair of shoes. The direct marketer's task is to determine what specific offer or catalog was responsible for motivating that customer to place the order.

Measuring results involves comparing the response rate generated by the control format versus that of the test format. In direct marketing, the control is normally that direct mail format, package, offer, creative, and so on that has proven time and time again to generate the highest rate of response. When the results of a test show that a test format or package 'beats' or surpasses that of a control format or package, the direct marketer faces a strategic decision. At this point, many direct marketers decide to perform additional testing to validate that the new test format is repeatedly more successful in generating a higher response rate than that of the control format, prior to determining which format to use for its rollout. Therefore, the validity in measuring test results is crucial to direct marketers.

Let's look at how a direct marketer conducts a creative test. Calico Corners, a high-end retailer of custom draperies, furniture, and home accessories, recently conducted a **split test** on a direct mailer. A split test is where two or more samples are taken from the same list, each considered to be representative of the entire list, and used for package tests or to test the homogeneity of the list. An A/B split was performed on the prospect database, with the A group receiving the control piece presented in Figure 4.5 and the B group receiving the same postcard and offer but an alternative creative design. Both the control and the alternative piece contained a key code to track which piece was responsible for the response and order. The control creative design won, with a response rate that was 11 percent higher than the alternative creative design. This sizable difference in response rate qualified the control creative piece for rollout.

Figure 4.5 Control piece. Used with permission of Calico Corners and MindZoo, LLC.

Source: Photo by Jim Kirby, www.jimkirbyphoto.com.

In summary, direct marketers must track responses and measure results carefully to ensure the validity of a test. Assuming that the direct marketer has properly selected a sample of adequate size and designed and conducted the experiment itself in a valid manner, he or she must also know how to validate the difference between the results of the experiment group and its control group. Only by understanding this can direct marketers decide to change from one promotional strategy to another, from one market segment to another, or to adopt a new product in place of an old one.

Typically, in direct marketing experimentation, the mean response to a direct mail solicitation is expressed as the average number of responses for all 1,000 pieces of mail sent out and attributable to the test (in which a single variable has been injected) in relation to the control. That variable could be the mailing list used, a pricing variance, or a product difference.

When we compare the test and the control, we must determine whether in fact the difference is real, in a statistical sense, or whether it might have occurred through chance alone. The difference in results must be further related to difference in cost, if there is any. In effect, one tests the hypothesis that there is no difference between the test and the control.

Hypothesis Testing

In testing a hypothesis—an assertion about the value of the parameter of a variable—the researcher decides, on the basis of observed facts such as the relative response to a test of variation in advertising copy, for example, whether an assumption seems to be valid. The way that the assumption is stated for purposes of testing is called the null hypothesis, meaning that the researcher must state the hypothesis in such a way that it can be proved wrong. Assuming that the null hypothesis proves, in fact, to be *true* (meaning that the original hypothesis was not borne out by tests, but when stated negatively—as a null hypothesis—it proves to be borne out by tests), we can determine the probability that should be assigned to an alternative hypothesis. Hypotheses are typically stated in negative terms; that is, a null hypothesis (H_0) versus an alternative hypothesis (H_a) in a form such as the following:

- H_0: Direct mail response from the test promotion is at or below direct mail response from the control promotion.
- H_a: Direct mail response from the test promotion is above direct mail response from the control promotion.

The null hypothesis then states that direct mail response *will not* be better than the control. Measurement sets out to *disprove* this null hypothesis. The probability of this happening might be very small, considering that the experiment involves new and untried copy intended to outperform the control, which presumably is the best copy now available.

In the event the direct marketer decides to *reject the null hypothesis*, it is rejected in favor of the alternative hypothesis. In this instance, if the null hypothesis is rejected, it is done in favor of the alternative hypothesis because that test response is significantly better than the control response.

Some results, obviously, are more significant than others. A statistician puts a special interpretation on the word *significant*, associating it with a specific probability, often denoted by the Greek letter alpha (α), which is decided on prior to testing the hypothesis. The researcher might state that the null hypothesis will be rejected only if the result is significant at a level of, say, 0.05 (5 percent). That is, the test result must diverge enough from the control result so that such a result would occur with the probability of 0.05 or less if the hypothesis were true. The statement of a level of significance should be made prior to testing the hypothesis to avoid vacillation on the part of the researcher when the actual response is observed.

Two types of error can occur in tests of hypotheses. A **Type I error** results when the decision maker rejects the null hypothesis even though it is, in fact, true. In this instance, the 'wrong' decision allows an action when it should not. The probability of doing this is fixed and equal to (α). Note that this determines a critical result so rare that it is preferred to reject the null hypothesis rather than believe that an event so rare actually occurred.

A **Type II error** occurs when the decision maker accepts the null hypothesis when it is, in fact, not true. In this instance, the wrong decision is to not do something when something should be done. The probability associated with a Type II error is called beta (β) and it is more difficult to measure than (α), prior to conducting an experiment, because it requires a fixed value, other than the one assumed within the null hypothesis, around which confidence intervals associated with an alternative hypothesis can be based.

Statistical Evaluation of Differences

Frequently, when evaluating the results of an experiment and comparing the response from a test with the response from a control, we need to know whether a difference is (or is not) *statistically significant*. The **chi-square (χ^2) test** is one way to determine such a difference.[4] The null hypothesis offered in making the determination is that there is, in fact, no difference between the response from the test and the response from the control. A statistic χ^2 is computed from the observed samples and compared with a chi-square distribution table that lists probabilities for a theoretical sampling distribution.

The shape of a χ^2 distribution varies according to the number of **degrees of freedom**, defined as the number of observations that are allowed to vary. The number of degrees of freedom is determined by multiplying the number of observations in a row (minus 1) times the number of observations in a column (minus 1), thus $(r-1)(c-1)$, where r is the number of rows and c is the number of columns. For example, the contingency table in Figure 4.6, expressed as '2 × 2' (and read '2 by 2') would involve just one degree of freedom, $(2-1) \times (2-1) = 1$. A table of this form can be used for evaluating the significance of the difference between a test and its control in an experiment.

The typical chi-square table, found in most statistical textbooks, will show critical values for 30 (or more) degrees of freedom for reference when as many as 30 observations are measured *against one another*. Because direct marketers are urged to test just one variable at a time (i.e., a single test against a single control, only the top row of the table)—that for one degree of freedom— it needs to be referenced. Here, then, are the critical values of a chi-square distribution for one degree of freedom along with the associated probabilities:

Chi-square critical value of 0.00016 = 0.99 probability; 0.00063 = 0.98; 0.0039 = 0.95; 0.16 = 0.90; 0.064 = 0.80; 0.15 = 0.70; 0.46 = 0.50; 1.64 = 0.20; 2.71 = 0.10; 3.84 = 0.05; 5.41 = 0.02; 6.64 = 0.01; 10.83 = 0.001.

	Test	Control	Totals
Response	A	C	A + C
Non-response	B	D	B + D
Total mailed	A + B	C + D	A + B + C + D = N

The statistic χ^2 is computed as follows:

$$\chi^2 = \frac{N[|(A \times D) - (C \times B)| - N/2]^2}{(A+B) \times (C+D) \times (A+C) \times (B+D)}$$

Here is a sample calculation:

	Test	Control	Totals
Response	200	100	300
Non-response	800	900	1700
Total mailed	1000	1000	2000

$$\chi^2 = \frac{2{,}000 \times [|180{,}000 - 80{,}000| - 1{,}000]^2}{1{,}000 \times 1{,}000 \times 300 \times 1{,}700}$$

$\chi^2 = 38.4$ which is significant at the 99++% level since it exceeds the critical value in the χ^2 table for one degree of freedom for a significance level of 0.001, given as 10.83.

Figure 4.6 An example of chi square

Put simply, the actual level of response of even a meticulously controlled experiment may not always be projected into the future. Conditions might be different. Thus, whereas the relationship between a test and its control may be the same—that is, one is still better than the other—the entire level of response for both might be either higher or lower than that originally experienced.

Structuring and Evaluating a Test

We conduct a test to make an adequate decision. To do this, the direct marketer must:

- sample a population
- measure the relevant variables, ideally one at a time
- compute statistics using these measurements
- infer something about the probability distributions that exist in the population
- make a decision mindful of the chance of incurring a Type I error (when the decision maker rejects the null hypothesis even though it is true) or a Type II error (when the decision maker accepts the null hypothesis when it is not true).

Let's say that a direct marketer wants to test a new promotion strategy against his or her present strategy, to be offered to the control group in the experiment. Past experience indicates that they can expect a 2 percent response rate from the present promotion.

151

Here is a framework for implementation of the test:

1. State the hypothesis and convert it to a null hypothesis.
2. Develop, by a priori analysis, the assumptions required and compute the appropriate sample size.
3. Structure and perform the experiment.
4. Develop, by a posteriori analysis, statistics for judging hypothesis validity.
5. Make the decision.

This procedure sounds simple and appears to be reasonable. Let's follow it step by step:

Step 1: State the hypothesis. State the hypothesis and convert it to a null hypothesis. The null hypothesis is:

- H_0: Direct mail response from the test promotion is at or below direct mail response from the control promotion.

Although it is not necessary to state an alternative hypothesis at this stage, doing so could imply that the direct marketer is hoping to reject the null hypothesis in favor of the alternative, that is, the test promotion would be better than the control, so that:

- H_a: Direct mail response from the test promotion is above direct mail response from the control promotion.

Step 2: A priori analysis. The response level of 2 percent is the first of three assumptions. The second assumption is the significance level, which, when $\alpha = 0.05$, describes a confidence level of 95 percent. (The confidence level is equal to 1.0 minus α, thus 1.0–0.05 = 0.95, or 95 percent.) The final assumption relates to limit of error or variation around the mean or, more descriptively, the error limit we wish to maintain around the assumed level of response. In this example, we will assume 15 percent. Having established figures for our three assumptions—2 percent response, 95 percent confidence level, and 15 percent limit of error—we can use the formula given earlier in this chapter to establish the sample size. The three assumptions and resultant sample size are summarized in Figure 4.7, which shows the effect of the 15 percent error limit. At a 95 percent confidence level, any response below 2.3 percent would not be better than a control response (as assumed) of 2.0 percent.

Step 3: Structure of the test. Having determined (in the manner demonstrated earlier in this chapter) an objective sample size of 8,365 pieces to be mailed for the control and a comparable volume for the test promotion, and having obtained the sample in a valid manner, the direct marketer conducts the experiment through release of the test mailing versus the control mailing.

Step 4: A posteriori analysis. When all results are in, the direct marketer examines the response from both the test and the control promotions. One evaluation procedure for determining whether an observed difference is (or is not) statistically significant is the chi-square (χ^2) test, as demonstrated earlier in this chapter.

Step 5: Make the decision. The decision to accept or reject the promotion tested in the experiment should be clear-cut, based on the a posteriori analysis.

Expected (Assumed) Response Rate: 2%, 20/M pieces mailed

Significance Level (α): .05

Confidence Level ($1.0 - \alpha$): 95%

Limits of Error:

    Percent Response/M Pieces Mailed

    +15% 20/M + 3/M = 23/M (2.3%)

    −15% 20/M − 3/M = 17/M (1.7%)

Sample Size: 8,365 mailing pieces (determined separately)

Figure 4.7 A priori assumptions and sample size

Conducting tests and measuring and analyzing test results to make good business decisions are only a part of the analytics involved in direct marketing. Today's modern digital world has brought about a digital revolution to testing print media. Traditional testing takes time and tends to be expensive. Quad has developed an online testing platform, *Accelerated Insights*,[5] as an alternative to conducting testing. Accelerated Insights digs deeper than traditional testing. It combines demographics with the cultural and emotional factors to pinpoint how to motivate targeted customers. Its sophisticated persona matrix pinpoints how to motivate consumers. With Accelerated Insights, Quad's clients can predict which combination of format, offer, message, and images will be most effective in print and digital campaigns.[6] Figure 4.8 shows Quad's Accelerated Insights process.

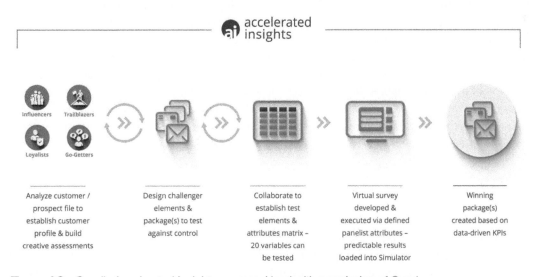

accelerated insights				
Influencers Trailblazers Loyalists Go-Getters				
Analyze customer / prospect file to establish customer profile & build creative assessments	Design challenger elements & package(s) to test against control	Collaborate to establish test elements & attributes matrix – 20 variables can be tested	Virtual survey developed & executed via defined panelist attributes – predictable results loaded into Simulator	Winning package(s) created based on data-driven KPIs

Figure 4.8 Quad's Accelerated Insights process. Used with permission of Quad.

The value of Accelerated Insights can be seen by one of Quad's clients, a leading footwear retailer. This retailer didn't have insight into how its direct mail campaigns performed with its target audience. Sales had lagged and marketers were unsure whether its direct mail offers, copy, images, and formats could make a difference. The Accelerated Insights predictions achieved a 200 percent greater response rate than did the retailer's control package, and improved all KPIs by a minimum of 19 percent.

In the following sections, we'll explore more analytic concepts, including response rates, conversion rates, and how to calculate them; customer lifetime value (CLTV); the concept of a lift; fixed and variable costs; margins; net order contribution; break-even and how to calculate it; and return on investment/return on advertising investment.

Direct marketing can be called successful, that is, it creates *benefits*, when it gains new customers (or new orders from existing customers) for a company. We need to remember that direct marketing also has *costs*, for example conducting research, acquiring lists, creating advertising campaigns, and fulfilling orders. The goal is to create a marketing campaign that not only breaks even—that is, gains enough sales to pay for all costs—but also results in a profit. To figure out how to be profitable and whether marketing activities are profitable, we need to understand a number of different concepts, terms, and formulas.

USING MATH AND METRICS TO DETERMINE THE 'RIGHT' TARGET MARKET

As we have already established in earlier chapters, all consumers are not alike. They can be grouped into market segments on the basis of similar needs and wants. Most companies build profiles of their customers on the basis of the customer data they gather and store in their databases. We discussed the different types of data used for segmenting customers in Chapter 3. The actions taken by consumers are certainly a viable base for market segmentation. The most valuable customer information a company can collect is that which comes after the first sale or transaction. The specific types of products and services consumers have purchased, the time the transactions took place, the method or location of their purchases, and the method of payment they choose can all reveal similarities among consumers. Each behavioral factor can indicate a consumer preference that may be shared by other consumers, consequently identifying a market segment. The creation of a database enables direct marketers to analyze customer transaction data to determine the value of each customer. How does a database help you quantify customer value? How do you measure and calculate customer value? How do you use transaction data to determine customer value? Those are the questions we address in the next section.

Determining Customer Value

It is well established that some customers generate the majority of a company's transactions. We refer to that as the 80/20 principle—approximately 20 percent of a company's customers generate 80 percent of its profits. If that is true, then shouldn't marketers identify those top 20 percent and concentrate on keeping them happy and loyal to the company? Of course! But how do you identify which customers are in the top 20 percent? There are a number of different methods for calculating customer value, such as recency/frequency/monetary assessment, which was discussed in Chapter 2. Another method is to calculate customer value quantitatively via a value equation. Let's take a look at this method. To calculate average customer value, you should follow this four-step process:

1. Take a random sample of customers (active and inactive) who first bought from you about three years ago.
2. Add up the total dollar amount they have purchased in the three years since the date of their first purchase.
3. Divide by the number of customer records in your sample.
4. Multiply by the percentage that represents your average profit margin.

For example, let's pretend you now own a catalog operation selling household gifts. You are in your fourth year in business and want to calculate the average value of your customers. What do you do?

- You randomly select 1,000 customers who have been purchasing with your company for a minimum of three years and obtain a computer printout of their buying history. You see that these customers have placed 1,775 orders during this period, with a total value of $89,300.
- You calculate your average profit margin on your household gift lines and determine it to be 20 percent.
- Now let's do the math! Dividing total sales by customers ($89,300 by 1,000) results in average sales of $89.30 per customer. Then, by multiplying that figure by the average profit margin percent (20 percent), you determine that average customer value is $17.86.

That figure represents what the average customer you acquired three years ago was worth to you in terms of future profits.

What if you were able to motivate your customers to spend twice as much? How much do the 1,000 customers now account for in terms of total sales? The answer is $178,600. Therefore, what is the average value of these customers now? Going through the rest of the calculations, the average customer is now worth $35.72. That figure tells you that you'll now be able to spend twice to acquire a new customer—$35.72 instead of $17.86!

The real benefit of calculating customer value is that it can be calculated on a segment or cluster basis, or on an individual basis. The process for calculating individual or segment customer values is basically the same; however, you would not select a 'random' sample of customers but concentrate on the segment or cluster of interest. On the basis of these customer value calculations, you can determine which customers or customer segments are generating the most profitability for your company and concentrate on retaining those customers.

Why calculate the value of customers? Because:

- It determines how much each customer is worth to your organization.
- It tells you how much money you can afford to spend to acquire a new customer like your current customers.

- You need to identify your best customers in order to seek out new prospective customers who match the customer profiles of your best customers.

Determining customer value is important, but, as described, it is based on past purchasing behavior. Customer lifetime value (CLTV) takes on more of an investment view where you regard your customers as investments in future profitability. Let's explore how to calculate customer lifetime value.

Calculating Customer Lifetime Value (CLTV)

As we discussed in Chapter 2 (as lifetime value), customer lifetime value (CLTV) is the present value of profits to be realized over the life of a customer's relationship with an organization. Customer relationships translate into customer retention, which usually means repeat customer purchases or transactions over time. When a customer is retained, it is not only the revenue generated in a one-month or one-year period that constitutes the value of that customer, it is the present value of the future stream of revenue that must be taken into consideration. This is the basic premise behind CLTV. Let's see how CLTV can be calculated. Refer to the equation shown in Figure 4.9.

$$LTV = \$[1-(1/1+i)^f/i]$$

Where:

$\$$ = Annual revenue from a loyal customer

i = Annual relevant interest rate

f = Frequency or number of periods in which a customer makes a purchase.

Figure 4.9 Customer lifetime value equation

Source: Adapted from Anton and Petouhoff, *Customer Relationship Management: The Bottom Line to Optimizing Your ROI*, Prentice Hall, 2002.

Now let's look at an example to apply the formula and calculate CLTV. Let's assume that you own a fitness business. Based on customer database analysis, you can determine the following about a given customer:

- The stream of revenue from a specific customer is level across time at $25 per month or $300 per year.
- The interest rate (opportunity cost) is the bank rate paid on the money for which no other specific use is made and will be assumed to be 9 percent.
- The amount of time a typical customer stays with a company is three years. Based on these assumptions, you can calculate CLTV using the formula where:

$\$$ = 300; i = 0.09; and f = 3. Therefore, the CLTV of this customer is $759.39.

You might increase a customer's LTV by enticing the customer to spend more on each transaction, thus increasing their annual stream of revenue. In addition, you might increase the length of time a customer stays loyal to a firm, which in turn would lengthen the investment period. In summary, calculating CLTV is critical for those direct marketers who view their customers as investments.

Predicting Buyer Behaviors

Recent developments in collecting, storing, and processing a large set of data (a.k.a. big data) help businesses to utilize their customer data not only to understand the past behaviors of customers, but also to predict customer behaviors in the future. An array of statistical techniques, broadly called predictive analytics, including traditional machine learnings and the latest neural networks, bring marketers the probabilistic information of behavioral responses of customers, including product purchase, future spending, brand loyalty, and so on. Thus, marketers can segment customers based on their likelihood of accepting a particular promotional offer. Then, beyond the benefits of having lower communication costs and expecting better response rates, marketers can zero in on those prospects that exceed a certain level of probability to likely respond to an offer.

Also, predictive analytics enables marketers to identify those profitable customers who are expected to shop more frequently, spend more money, and/or remain loyal to a given organization for a longer period of time. As previously discussed in Chapter 2, predictive analytics enables marketers to execute segmented marketing strategies. For example, a telecommunications company may offer a special incentive to select customers who are renewing their service plans if they are predicted to meet certain established profit generation levels. The company would not offer the same deal to all customers since predictive analytics can reveal that retaining some customers will negatively affect the company's profitability. Amazon.com was one of the direct marketing pioneers using predictive analytics. In addition, many information technology companies utilize predictive analytics to be able to provide product recommendations to their customers, such as Netflix for movie recommendations and Spotify for music recommendations. In sum, modern techniques in data analytics have presented new ways to segment and target customers via predicting their future behavioral responses with a higher degree of precision.

Determining the 'Right' Customer to Target

Quantifying customer value and CLTV can help marketers determine which current customers or prospective customers to target for future direct marketing campaigns.

An example of a company that understands the value of marketing analytics is that of an iconic fashion brand[7] and the coveted label for adorable, luxury women's apparel and accessories. When this global brand needed an effective way to acquire new customers, it turned to Baesman Group. To support the company's customer acquisition goals, Baesman put together a testing strategy that leveraged a variety of sources. This unique multi-sourced approach gave the brand the opportunity to zero in on its most valuable prospect types. After targeted prospect segments were determined, Baesman was leveraged to create and execute supporting strategies. With this new prospect strategy in place, the company exceeded its goals for revenue and brand growth. As this example demonstrates, even the strongest brands are using testing, customer acquisition matchback logic, and data analytics to acquire and retain the next generation of shoppers.

However, it is important to note that customer retention strategies normally generate greater profitability for companies than do new customer acquisition strategies. This is partially due to the value of the established relationship that current customers have with a given company. You must keep in mind that strong customer relationships are directly correlated to strong customer loyalty, and loyal customers are less price-sensitive, spend more per transaction, cost less to serve, and generate positive word-of-mouth referrals! The bottom line: loyal customers are more profitable!

Table 4.2 Acquisition versus customer retention

Customer acquisition focus	Customer retention focus
$150 to acquire customers = 6	$75 to acquire customers = 3
$25 to retain customers = 5	$100 to retain customers = 20

Many marketers claim that it costs at least five times more to replace a customer than it does to retain a current customer. Mathematically, this can be easily calculated. For example, let's say it costs $5 to keep a customer happy and loyal to your firm (a customer retention strategy) and it costs $25 (five times $5) to replace a customer (a new customer acquisition strategy). Let's perform the math given a budget of $175. Table 4.2 shows that if we allocate the majority of our budget to acquiring new customers, we net 11 customers. However, if we allocate the majority of our budget to retaining current customers, we net 23 customers. Given the same budget, the mathematical difference is significant.

The calculations show that it is more cost-effective to concentrate your direct and interactive marketing efforts on customer retention and customer relationship building than it is to concentrate on new customer acquisition. Of course, you will want to first focus on your most valuable customers and then search for customers who possess similar characteristics to these highly valued customers.

It sounds simple, right? But where do you look? How do you begin? How do you know which markets, market segments, or clusters of customers will be more likely to respond to your offer? One method is by conducting market penetration analysis. Let's examine that concept in greater detail.

Analyzing Market Penetration

Modeling techniques can correlate market penetration with demographics, lifestyle research, transaction data, and buyer behavior to reveal those markets that contain the largest proportion of a company's customers. **Market penetration** is the expressed percentage relationship of customers to some benchmark universe. Thus, it tells what percentage of the total universe of potential buyers are customers. Market penetration analysis may be performed on any universe, including ZIP code areas, product lines, customer market segments, or specific demographic categories, such as gender, age, or education. Market penetration is calculated by dividing the number of customers in a specific category (such as a ZIP code area) by the total number of people in that category (or ZIP code area). Let's take a look at the following example to better understand how market penetration is calculated and used.

Betty's Bakery is located in Erie, Pennsylvania, and is well known locally for offering delicious baked goods. Betty was able to create a customer list and collect information about her customers by offering weekly drawings for a free pie over the past year. She has determined that the 52 free pies were well worth the customer data she has now collected. Looking over the 5,000 customer cards, she noticed that her customers primarily reside in four ZIP code areas, as shown in Table 4.3.

Let's calculate the customer market penetration for each ZIP code area by dividing the number of Betty's customers in each area by the population for each respective ZIP code area. Table 4.4 shows the market penetration for each ZIP code area.

Based on an analysis of these market penetrations, we can conclude that ZIP code area 16502 contains the largest proportion of Betty's customers, while area 16501 contains the smallest proportion. Thus, market penetration analysis can assist Betty in determining which ZIP code area should be targeted for future direct mail promotions. Because it is well known that prospective customers are similar to current customers, Betty should target ZIP code area 16502 for new customer acquisition efforts. As shown in Figure 4.10, marketers often map their customers according to ZIP code area market penetration in order to visually reveal those geographic areas that should be targeted for future promotions.

Table 4.3   Betty's Bakery customer distribution

Zip code area	Population	Betty's customers
16501	17,050	1,384
16502	11,288	1,785
16503	10,035	876
16504	9,398	1,010

Table 4.4   Betty's Bakery ZIP code market penetration

Zip code area	Population	Betty's customers	Market penetration %
16501	17,050	1,384	8.1
16502	11,288	1,785	15.8
16503	10,035	876	8.7
16504	9,398	1,010	10.7

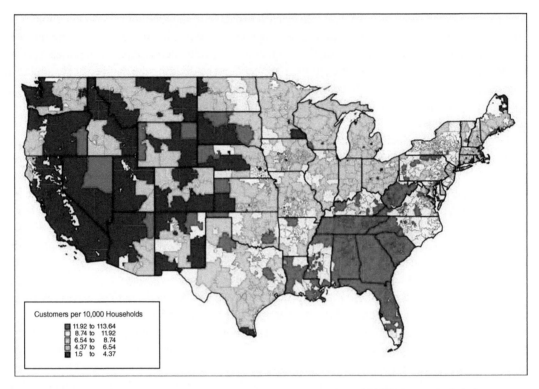

Figure 4.10 ZIP code area penetration map. Used with permission of RUF™ Strategic Solutions.

Often, companies make the mistake of targeting the market in which they have the least penetration in an attempt to increase the presence in that specific market segment (for example, ZIP code area 16501). This is not normally a wise strategy because there is usually a reason that the consumers in that market are not responding to company offers in the first place. Perhaps these customers do not have a need or desire for the company's products or services. Therefore, a more effective strategy is to concentrate future marketing efforts on those market segments that contain larger customer penetrations.

MEASUREMENT IS THE KEY

The single most notable feature of direct and interactive marketing is that it always seeks a measurable response. A variety of online advertising platforms such as Google and Facebook provide their own analytical features (Google Analytics and Facebook Insights), measuring the performance of keywords or online display ads. Also, there exist many commercial programs that help marketers to measure user responses toward online marketing using search keywords (e.g., SpyFu, SEMrush), social media (e.g., Hootsuite, Sprout Social), and mobile apps (e.g., AppsFlyer, Appsee). Regardless of whether that response comes via a website, or from an in-store visit, or is a phone call to place an order or request additional information, all responses can be measured and evaluated. Thus, determining *what* to measure becomes the challenge. First and foremost, let's discuss how to calculate response rates to conduct response rate analysis.

Calculating Response Rates and Conducting Break-Even Analysis

Possibly the most frequently asked question in direct and interactive marketing is 'What response rate should I expect to my offer?' In reality, there is no universal or normal response rate. The rate can vary relative to such important considerations as the product itself as well as the demand for it, price competition, market preference, and the nature of the promotional offer. A preprinted insert in a Sunday newspaper will generate more response if there are no directly competitive offers in the same issue. A product in the early stages of its life cycle will create more attention and more interest than one that is generally available and displays little if any differentiation.

A more realistic question to be asked in evaluating the response to an offer is probably 'What response do I *need*?' What would it take to just **break even** on a particular offering? And what response rate will give me a *profit*? We will discuss the concept of break-even in more detail in the next section, but let's look here at how knowing the number of sales it takes to break even allows us to calculate what we need to sell to earn a profit.

The formula for determining the break-even point for a single promotion to a new customer is shown in Figure 4.11. If the marketer recovers the promotion cost from the gross profit (beyond the cost of goods sold and the overheads) of the total number of units sold, they will break even *on those sales*. Figure 4.12 provides a worksheet for calculating the break-even point and profit at various levels of unit sales per thousand pieces of direct mail promotion. A variation of this worksheet can be used for any medium.

Lines 2 through 8 of the break-even calculation in Figure 4.12 represent production costs, totaling $17.69 (line 9) per copy of a book, *Practical Mathematics*. Order processing/collection costs (line 5) and costs of returns (line 6) are amortized and allocated to net sales, in the manner shown at the top of Figure 4.12.

Unit margin (also known as unit profit or unit contribution), calculated by subtracting $17.69 (line 9) from the selling price of $39.95 (line 1), is $22.26 (line 10). Unit margin divided into total promotion costs of $345.83 per thousand pieces mailed (line 11) provides break-even net sales (line 12). This is 15.54 units per thousand (M), or 1.55 percent. That is the answer to our earlier question: 'What advertising response is needed to just break even?' Having calculated a break-even response rate of 1.55 percent, lines 13 to 20 of Figure 4.12 present alternative profit amounts at assumed alternative levels of net sales.

The calculation assumes the offering of only a single item and anticipates a desirable net profit at various levels of response beyond the break-even point. However, a more likely and realistic calculation for direct marketers uses *continuity*, and is applicable to the long-term recovery of future time periods, such as that experienced by magazine publishers, insurance companies, fundraisers, and catalog merchandisers who expect repeat orders from new customers.

Response rates will also vary widely according to prequalification of the mailing list or the narrowness and appropriateness of market segments targeted. Typically, all other factors being equal, current customers will respond to an offer for a new product at a much higher level than will prospective customers. In addition, a company's more valuable customers, with whom a stronger customer relationship has been cultivated, will likely respond at much higher rates to company offers than will all other customers. This phenomenon is called a *lift*, and it can be mathematically measured and evaluated. Let's learn more about this valuable concept.

$$\text{Break even number of sales} = \frac{\text{Promotion cost}}{\text{Unit margin}\,(\text{or profit})\,\text{per sale}}$$

Figure 4.11 Break-even formula

Product/Offer: *Practical Mathematics* @ $39.95, net 30 days

Assumptions:		Order Processing/Collection Costs:		Cost of Returns:	
# Promotions Mail'd	9,508	Gross Orders	100@$1.80=$180.00	Return Servicing	$1.30
Shipments Return'd	8%	Less: Returns	8@8% of 100	Shipping/Delivery	$2.20
Sales Uncollectable	6%	Net Sales (A)	92@$0.50=$ 46.00	Total (C)	$3.50
		Total (B)	$226.00	Returns Project'd(D)	8%
		Cost Per Net Sale (B/A) =	$2.46	Cost Per Net Sale	$0.30
				(C x D/1.00-D)	

Break-Even Calculation:

Line	Description		
1	Selling Price		$39.95
2	Cost-of-Goods Sold	$5.99	
3	G&A Allocation	$3.80	
4	Shipping/Delivery Costs	$2.20	
5	Processing/Collection Costs	$2.46	
6	Cost of Returns	$0.30	
7	Sales Uncollectable	$2.40	
8	Premium Gift Cost	$0.54	
9	Total Production Costs		$17.69
10	UNIT PROFIT (Line 1–Line 9)		$22.26
11	Total Promotion Costs per M Pieces Mailed (includes database, print, mail, postage, overhead)		$345.83
12	BreakevenNtSales/M PiecesMailed(Line11/Line10)		15.54

Total Profit at Alternative Levels of Net Sales:

Line	Description							
13	Projected Net Sales per M Pieces Mailed	17	20	25	30	35	40	45
14	Less: Break-even Sales (Line 12)	15.54	15.54	15.54	15.54	15.54	15.54	15.54
15	Net Sales Earning Full Unit Pro (Line 13–Line 14)	1.46	4.46	9.46	14.46	19.46	24.46	29.46
16	Unit Profit (Line 10)	$22.26	$22.26	$22.26	$22.26	$22.26	$22.26	$22.26
17	Net Profit per M Pieces Mailed (Line 15 x Line 16)	32.61	99.39	210.69	322.00	433.30	544.61	655.91
18	M Pieces Mailed	9,508	9,508	9,508	9,508	9,508	9,508	9,508
19	Total Net Profit (Line17 x Line 18/1000)	$310.01	$944.98	$2,003.26	$3,061.55	$4,119.83	$5,178.11	$6,236.40
20	NtPr'fit %NtSales: Line19/Line1 x Line13 x Line18/1000	4.80%	12.44%	21.10%	26.87%	30.99%	34.08%	36.49%

Figure 4.12 Break-even worksheet

Calculating the Impact of a Lift

A lift is an increase in the average response rate due to making an offer to only those market segments or clusters that are predicted to be most responsive. A lift can be applied to any direct-response communication where selectivity is involved. For example, if you are creating a direct mail campaign, a lift can decrease the mailing quantity needed (via selectivity) and increase the overall response rate. Thus, a lift will produce a double cost advantage for a company in its direct and interactive marketing efforts.

How is a lift calculated? Figure 4.13 shows that a lift is basically the *new* response rate divided by the *old* response rate (achieved prior to selectivity).

For example, let's say we distributed a direct mail package to all of the 10,000 clients in our database and it garnered a 2.0 percent response rate. Not bad, right? But could it be improved?

Maybe, via database analysis! Let's say we analyzed our database to identify those clients who purchased from our organization within the past month. Based on our analysis, we determine that 3,255 clients actively purchased from our company during that time period. For our next direct mail campaign, we decide to selectively mail to those 3,255 individuals instead of our entire client population. We have now decreased our costs (printing, production, postage) and achieve a response rate of 3.52 percent. What happened? That is what we call a lift. As Figure 4.14 shows, the lift for this example was 176 percent.

$$\text{Lift} = 100 \times \frac{\text{New response rate}}{\text{Old response rate}}$$

Figure 4.13 Lift calculation equation

$$\text{Lift} = 100 \times \frac{3.52}{2.00}$$

Figure 4.14 Example of lift calculation

Most companies are striving to maximize response rates to their direct and interactive marketing campaigns. All else being equal, a lift can generally generate an increase in response rate due to greater selectivity, and produce lower costs associated with the more precise, targeted niche promotional effort. Beyond increasing response rates, most companies want to generate sales and maximize profitability.

For example, a U.S.-based company[8] providing outstanding professional residential and commercial cleaning services for carpet, tile, upholstery, and more, wanted to analyze its customer transaction data to better align its corporate and franchise e-mail and direct mail programs. The company asked Baesman Group, the company's marketing agency, to analyze its customer database metrics and produce actionable insights for targeting its final consumers. Baesman upgraded and streamlined the company's customer database and produced a profile analysis that illustrated a clear view of the customer and key opportunities in the purchasing life cycle. From these, key insights were leveraged to roll out a strategic e-mail and direct mail marketing plan. Was this database analysis successful in generating a lift? Yes! A remarkable 200 percent increase in response rates in just one direct mail campaign and a 23 percent lift in online booking.

Marketers evaluating the concept of a lift will normally seek to reduce any extraneous variables that may factor into the difference in response rates. Therefore, in an attempt to isolate and measure the impact of a lift, many marketers use a control group and an experimental group. These concepts were presented earlier in this chapter, but apply here as well. Once a direct marketing effort has been made to two different groups at the same time, the lift in response rates can be calculated. Marketers will also create and impose rules to more accurately measure lift on the marketing effort.

Beyond using a control and test group, some marketers have created a panel group that is reserved for calculating the potential lift in response rates. This method may be used to determine the impact that a catalog or mailing has had (if any) on customer response rates and transaction amounts. Thus, the concept of a lift can be applied to the measurement of almost any medium. For example, let's say we want to investigate the impact of catalog mailings on a company's website sales. We plan on mailing one million catalogs. So, we take a random sample of 100,000 customers and these customers will *not* receive the catalog in the mail. We then review the 21-day website sales at the household level and factor out sales for the group that did not receive the catalog mailer. The results show that those customers treated with the receipt of a physical catalog generated sales of $1.10 per online catalog, and those who did not actually receive the mailed catalog generated sales of $1 per online catalog. Therefore, the implied Web lift due to catalog receipt is 10 percent. At the source code level, which identifies the medium by which the customer has responded to a given promotion, the measurement of a lift is complete. However, many marketers want to know additional details about responses at the customer or household level, which is a bit more sophisticated and entails more detailed database analysis.

Often, consumer responses are in the form of an inquiry or a request for additional information. These responses, called leads, afford the marketer the opportunity to convert those inquiries or leads into sales. This is called lead conversion and it is the topic of our next section.

Determining Conversion Rates

Conversion refers to the transfer of a prospective customer to an actual buying customer. Many consumers do not actually place an order or make a donation during their first interaction with a company or an organization. In fact, the initial objective of a company's offer is often to entice the prospective customer to request additional information. This is the process of lead generation. These initial inquiries are then followed up with additional interaction between the company and the prospect, with the ultimate goal of new customer acquisition. The rate by which a company converts these leads into sales is called its conversion rate.

As Figure 4.15 reveals, a conversion rate is calculated by dividing the number of buyers by the number of inquiries, expressed as a percentage.

For example, let's say you have 1,000 inquiries and 300 of them have subsequently become buyers. You have a conversion rate of 30 percent. Achieving a high conversion rate is important because each direct marketing effort will likely cost the company additional dollars and will need to be allocated in a company's promotional budget. The concept of planning the direct marketing budget is the topic of our next section.

$$\text{Conversion Rate} = \frac{\text{Buyers}}{\text{Inquiries}}$$

Figure 4.15 Conversion rate formula

PLANNING THE DIRECT MARKETING BUDGET

To help us put together all the concepts we will be working with in this next section, let's create a mythical company: Permanent Wear (PW). This company produces all kinds of clothing from microfibers. Its director of marketing is Charlie Perry. This year, PW is introducing a new line of jeans for men and women. These jeans will be more expensive than some other brands, but they can be washed and worn for a much longer time than regular cotton fabric jeans, and they look good! As part of its new line introduction, PW has to conduct research, evaluate its probable market, create a marketing campaign, prepare a budget, and decide how it will measure the success of its direct marketing campaign. Let's see how Charlie and PW do, using marketing math.

PW has conducted its research, segmented its market, rented and created lists, prioritized the media it wants to use for advertising, and generated some preliminary ideas for creative materials, so it's time for Charlie to develop his direct marketing budget. Many companies will use one of the following traditional approaches to establish how much money to allocate to marketing:

- Establish a percentage of probable sales revenue.
- Use last year's marketing budget, plus a small percentage increase.
- Make a good guess on how much is needed.

In direct marketing, the budget is a function of:

- net order contribution of the item(s) sold
- media/sales costs
- response rates
- desired level of profitability.

Another difference between traditional marketing budgets and direct marketing budgets is that, in direct marketing, campaign results are constantly monitored and changes can be made in strategy even while the campaign is in progress—or before the next one is executed. Remember: direct marketing is *always* measurable and accountable.

How to Begin: Estimating Costs

Each advertising campaign needs to be treated as an individual cost/profit exercise. So, in the case of PW, if Charlie is planning to use the Internet for one major introductory campaign of the new jeans, he will need to work up a budget for that campaign.

Where does he start? One way is to list all the elements he would like to use in the campaign as if he had an unlimited amount of money. For example, maybe he would like to run banner ads for one month on three major websites. Here are some of the elements he would have to include in his preliminary budget.

For the ad itself:

- creative/production/cost of hiring a designer
- cost of the banner ad for 30 days on three websites
- cost of hiring someone to record and analyze the hits.

For the campaign:

- fixed costs
- cost of goods sold
- variable costs (including fulfillment costs, credits, and returns).

Table 4.5 Costs of creative elements by media

Medium	Creative cost elements	Related costs
Broadcast	Script writer(s)	Cost of air time
	Talent (announcers, actors)	Cost of distributing or disseminating finished product to broadcast outlets, e.g., by mail, satellite
	Studio time/rental to film/tape	
	Recording equipment	
	Crew (camera people, engineers, etc.)	Time buyer (if used)
	Duplication equipment	
	Discs, film, tape for duplication	
	Rights to use copyrighted material	
	Pre-produced sound effects, pictures	
Internet/Digital media	Artists/writers/videographers who create ads, Blogs, Tweets, etc.	Cost of placements
		Cost of site maintenance
	Computer design software	Cost of maintaining accounts
Catalogs	Writers, artists, photographers	List creation/rental
	Rights to use copyrighted pictures, photos	List maintenance
	Materials: computer software, drawing boards, artists' supplies	Production/duplication costs of catalog
Direct mail	Writers, artists, photographers	Duplication costs
	Production equipment, e.g., computers, design software, printers	List creation/rental
		List maintenance
	Paper stock/photo stock	Lettershop
		'Nixies' and returns
Out-of-Home*		
Billboards	Writers, artists, photographers	Billboard rental
	Production equipment	Billboard maintenance
	Paper stock (if not provided by billboard co. as part of rental)	
Buses	Writers, artists who create copy	Bus side rental
	Production equipment	Duplication costs
	Paper stock	
Point of sale	Same as for buses	Duplication costs
Print	Writers, artists, photographers	Space buy, e.g., in newspaper, yellow pages, magazine
	Production equipment and costs	
	Rights to copyrighted material	
Telephone marketing	Writers to create scripts	Telephone lines
		Salaries for staff making/taking calls
		Computers and programs for call makers/takers

Notes: For several of these media, e.g., broadcast, out-of-home, and print, there may be additional costs of working with personnel at an ad agency, if one is used.

* Other 'out-of-home' media may include: posters in subways, airports, other public places; aerial banners or other mobile media displays; table-top ads at large events. Generally, all of these will share the common creative costs of artists, writers and photographers, plus any special space/place rental costs.

If Charlie wanted to create campaigns using other media, for example direct mail, national television, and magazine advertising, his advertising costs would involve different elements.

As Table 4.5 shows, each medium has its own costs, but two constants are the costs of the *creative materials* (both the personnel to create them and their production and duplication) and the *media buy* (the cost of time or space to present the creative materials). The exceptions are in direct mail and telephone marketing, where, instead of media buy costs, Charlie would have mailing costs or personnel and telephone line-rental costs.

The First Calculations: Margins, Fixed and Variable Costs

Let's say Charlie has added all his costs for his ideal Internet campaign and they come to $3 million. Can PW afford this campaign? How many jeans can they sell and at what price to afford it and make money? Charlie has to look at some other factors. First, he needs to understand what the likely margins on sales of the new jeans are likely to be.

Let's start with total sales. If the new jeans retail for an average price of $88 a pair, and the company expects to sell 100,000 pairs in a year, then their gross sales or total sales would be: $88 × 100,000 = $8,800,000. But, of course, it costs the company something to make and distribute the jeans. Therefore, we use the term cost of goods sold to include the variable costs that come into play when making and selling the jeans. PW knows that its cost of goods sold for this line of jeans will be $22 per pair. This includes the cost of manufacturing the fabric, sewing the jeans, shipping them out, processing orders, allowances for bad debt, and handling returns. Variable costs are those costs that vary with production. Fixed costs are those costs that do not vary with production. (See Table 4.6 for examples.)

Another important concept here is the unit margin or trade margin (also called unit contribution or unit profit) that each sale provides. Remember, we talked about this in discussing response rates. This is like the concept of the gross margin except that the unit contribution is simply the amount that *each sale* provides to cover all other costs. In our example, the unit margin of each pair of jeans is $66:

$$\$88 \quad \left(\text{average selling price for one pair of jeans}\right)$$
$$\underline{-\$22} \quad \left(\text{cost of goods sold/variable costs}\right)$$
$$\$66 \quad \left(\text{unit margin}\right)$$

This $66 is what is left over after a sale to cover all fixed costs, which, as we have seen, include the overheads necessary to run the entire business. Why do advertising costs count as fixed costs? Because the advertising dollars will be spent regardless of how many units are produced and sold. It is going to cost Charlie the same amount to advertise on the Internet whether the company gets three orders or three million. The same is true of his advertising budgets for all other media: if he plans to spend $2 million this year on network television, that is a fixed cost, regardless of how many orders he gets as a result of this particular advertising campaign.

Table 4.6 Types of general fixed and variable costs

Fixed costs	Variable costs
Rent/mortgage on facilities	Cost of goods sold, tied to production
Salaries of permanent staff	Commission to sales people
Amortization of facilities	Order processing
Overheads of running company	Shipping, delivery, returns, restocking
Advertising	Cost of money (financing)
	Bad debt
	Fulfillment activities

Another important concept comes into play here: the **allowable margin**. Many companies will establish an allowable margin for each promotional campaign. Basically, this represents the amount of money you have left over to cover advertising/promotion and profit after *all* other expenses have been deducted. It can be the same as the unit contribution or less, depending on whether fixed costs have been allocated to the product sales before the unit contribution has been figured. In our example with PW, we will assume that the allowable margin is the same as the unit contribution, that is, $66 per pair of jeans.

Net Profit and Breaking Even

The next concept we encounter is **net profit** or net profit margin. This is the amount of money the company will have (before taxes) after the fixed costs have been subtracted from the gross revenues. Often, a company will set a goal for its net profit margin and measure its success for a product line in terms of whether this goal was obtained or not.

To know how many jeans have to be sold to make a profit, Charlie first needs to know how many jeans PW has to sell in order to break even before he adds in the cost of his advertising campaign. The simple formula for calculating break-even is as follows:

$$\text{Break-even in units sold} = \frac{\text{Fixed costs in \$}}{\text{Net unit margin in \$}}$$

We don't know what PW's fixed costs are on a per unit basis, but let's say the total fixed costs allocated to the jeans line are $6 million a year. Therefore, to break even on the new line of jeans:

$$\text{Break-even in units sold} = \frac{\$6,000,000}{\$66}$$

$$\text{Break-even} = 90,910 \text{ pairs of jeans}$$

However, PW wants to do better than just break even: it wants to make a profit. So, let's say that the company wants a 20 percent profit before taxes over and above recovery of the fixed costs. (It could establish its profit target in other ways, e.g., as a percentage of the sale of each pair of jeans, or as a fixed dollar number for the year based on increasing the profit percentage from a previous year.) Then we have to add 20 percent of the fixed costs to the fixed costs and recalculate the units to be sold:

$$\$6,000,000 = \text{fixed costs}$$

$$\underline{\times .20}$$

$$\$1,200,000 = \text{profit}$$

$$\underline{+6,000,000} = \text{fixed costs}$$

$$\$7,200,000 = \text{new target to be achieved}$$

$$\text{New target in units to be sold} = \frac{\$7,200,000}{\$66}$$

New target units: 109,091 pairs of jeans

Remember: always add the desired profit margin (in dollars) to your other fixed costs to give yourself the new number to divide by the unit margin (in dollars).

This is the number of jeans PW would have to sell over one year to not only recover all fixed costs, but to also arrive at a 20 percent net profit before taxes. In our example of Charlie's Internet campaign, all he has to be concerned about is how many jeans *this particular campaign* will sell—and whether he can do better than break even. He has initially calculated his costs for Internet advertising as $3 million. His boss has told him that he expects to see a 10 percent profit on this specific campaign. That means adding $300,000 to the fixed costs of $3 million, giving Charlie $3,300,000 to work into our formula. We need to know how many total pairs of jeans it will require PW to sell to meet this target. Again, we can use our break-even formula, realizing that we have already added a profit amount:

$$\text{Target units to be sold} = \frac{\$3,300,000}{\$66}$$

Target units to be sold: 50,000 pairs of jeans

At this point, Charlie needs to consult with others in the company. Is it reasonable to expect this one campaign to sell 50,000 pairs of jeans, which allows for covering fixed costs (before advertising), plus a profit, plus Charlie's Internet advertising campaign? If the company has no previous experience in the clothing field, it may be that it will want to test the market with a smaller campaign to start with. Or, Charlie's boss, the president, may feel that she has enough knowledge to predict that this is too ambitious a sales goal for the first campaign. We'll talk about how to compare a test with a roll-out later, but, at this point, let's assume that Charlie's boss tells him to cut back on the costs of his Internet advertising campaign so that he can have a less ambitious sales target. He does this by cutting back to one Internet provider, AOL, which has quoted him $100,000 to run a banner ad on its home page for one month. He also has to pay a designer $15,000 to design the ad, and he has a contractor who will charge $5,000 for recording the hits. His new fixed-costs budget for the Internet campaign is $120,000. Because this is going to be a two-step campaign—in other words, PW will advertise on the Internet, then send samples to people who respond before actually getting any orders—Charlie is told that he can budget up to $1.2 million for the second step of the campaign, the mail-out of samples.

Since Charlie now has the advertising budget that he needs for this campaign, he recalculates the number of jeans he needs to sell to achieve his target of break-even:

$$\text{Units to be sold:} \frac{\$1,320,000 \text{ (fixed costs plus profit)}}{\$66 \text{ (unit margin in this campaign)}}$$

$$\text{Units to be sold:} 20,000 \text{ pairs of jeans}$$

As we can see, if the variable costs in this campaign had risen even more, so would Charlie's target for sales have risen. Or, if he can reduce his fixed costs (or his profit margin), then the total number of pairs of jeans to be sold would be reduced.

Cost per Inquiry/Cost per Order

In direct marketing, it is important to know how much it costs us to obtain a new customer and a new order. We can have basically four kinds of possible prospective customer behavior:

- People are exposed to the campaign but do nothing (nonresponse).
- People are exposed and inquire (inquiry response).
- People are exposed, inquire, and buy (buyer response).
- People are exposed and buy immediately (no inquiry).

Since there is a cost to doing any kind of marketing, we need to know how to calculate it for those who inquire and those who buy (those who do nothing don't figure into our calculation). We also need to understand that calculating costs and responses varies from medium to medium. Table 4.7 shows the special calculations that need to be made in measuring the results in different media.

Let's look at an example in which PW uses Charlie's Web campaign to target 12 million customers. The campaign has two steps: the first step is intended to get people to request a sample of the jeans fabric. When PW mails back the fabric sample, they also send an order form. The next step is to sell jeans based on this inquiry/mail-out campaign. The company will have a **cost per inquiry (CPI)**, which is sometimes called a **cost per lead (COL)**, and then a **cost per order (CPO)** or **cost per response (CPR)**. Figures 4.16 and 4.17 detail the elements included and the process involved in the calculations of CPI and CPO.

Table 4.7 Special calculations for different media

Medium	Special calculations
Broadcast (radio/TV)	Cost of the schedule is the marketing cost
	Measurement of viewers reached based on rating points, e.g., number of responses divided by gross rating points*
Internet/digital media	Cost of website(s) and account(s) maintenance are the marketing costs

Medium	Special calculations
Catalogs (treat each item as its own campaign)	Divide the number of pages by cost to determine cost per page
	Divide the number of items per page by cost per page to determine the marketing cost of each product
Clubs/continuity programs	Higher advertising allowables used here because customers are expected to buy beyond their first purchase
Direct mail	Use total number mailed as basis to determine net profit
Print advertising	Use circulation figures to determine net profit, e.g., number of responses divided by circulation

Note: *Gross rating points are calculated by the 'reach' of a commercial–how many people watch or listen to the program in which it is inserted (as measured by commercial ratings services such as Arbitron and Nielsen) times the frequency (number of times) the commercial is presented in a given program vehicle.

AOL subscribers:	12,000,000
Response rate:	5%
Total number of people responding:	600,000
Banner ad cost:	$120,000
Banner ad cost per thousand:	$10*
Cost per inquiry:	$.20**

Figure 4.16   Cost per inquiry of a banner ad on AOL

Notes: *In marketing, costs are generally quoted in terms of how much it takes to reach 1000 people via a given medium. In this example, PW knew that via AOL it could reach 12,000,000 people. If we divide 12,000,000 by 1000, we get 12,000 'groups' of 1000 people each. Therefore, we take the total banner ad cost of $120,000 and divide it by the 12,000 'groups' and say the 'cost per thousand' is $10.

** To derive the 'cost per inquiry,' we take the total cost, $120,000, and divide it by the total number of people who inquired, 600,000, giving us a cost per inquiry of $.20. Note that this is a pure cost at this point–there is no profit associated with it.

Mailings of fabric to AOL inquirers:	600,000
Response rate (% who ordered):	4%
Number of orders:	24,000
Average order price:	$88
Gross sales:	$2,112,000
Gross profit before advertising: @75% margin:	1,584,000*
Cost of fabric mail-out campaign @$2.00 per mailing:	1,200,000
Advertising cost (inquiry campaign):	120,000
Promotional costs total:	1,320,000
Profit (or loss):	264,000
Cost per order:	55.00**
Contribution to fixed costs and profit	11.00***

Figure 4.17   Cost per order based on the AOL ad campaign

Notes: *The company has a cost of goods sold (COGS) total of 25%, so it has a profit margin of 75% before advertising costs.

**The cost per order is derived by taking the total marketing costs ($1,200,000 + $120,000) and dividing their sum of $1,320,000 by the total orders of 24,000.

***Since there was a profit of $264,000 from the campaign, we divide that by the number of orders, 24,000, to get the 'profit per order.'

We don't know whether Charlie was given targets for CPI or CPO in this campaign or a number of new customers to be obtained, but we do know that he achieved the following:

- His target for breaking even was 20,000 pairs of jeans sold, and PW sold 24,000.
- In addition to making a profit on his campaign, the sales covered all the variable costs (at 25 percent of revenue) of the 24,000 pairs of jeans *before* the advertising costs were subtracted.

There is one more measure of success that we need to know about.

Return on Investment/Return on Advertising Investment

It is important to note that the goal of an advertising campaign may not be to make a profit if, for example, the campaign focuses on a product introduction, achieving penetration in a new market, or even gaining market share. In these cases, the number of new customers acquired, new orders acquired, or total market share gained may be the measures of success. However, what is important is that these goals be clearly stated when the budget is being planned. At some point, of course, the company has to make money on the products it sells, so understanding the basics of how to calculate profit and loss are important.

One popular measurement tool in the business world is **return on investment**, or **ROI**. This is a simple calculation: net profit divided by the average amount invested in the company in a year. When we look specifically at calculating ROI for an advertising campaign, we need to know what the gross profit is for that campaign; remember: gross profit or margin is total sales less cost of goods sold (COGS). Then we subtract from the gross profit all the promotional (advertising) costs, which gives us a net profit (but without consideration of other fixed costs that the company incurs). We then divide this number by the total promotional costs. To express the answer in percentage terms, which is how we talk about ROI–for example 'his ROI in that campaign was 20 percent,'—we multiply the answer by 100. We can do this for Charlie's Web campaign for the jeans:

Gross Sales:	$2,112,000
Less COGS:	−528,000 (25% of gross sales)
Gross Margin:	$1,584,000
Less Promo:	−1,320,000
Net Profit:	$ 264,000
ROI calculation:	$\frac{\$264,000}{\$1,320,000} = .2$
ROI = .2 × 100 = **20%**	

Is this a good ROI for Charlie? Well, we don't know whether his boss gave him an ROI target. Since the jeans are a new product, it's possible that one of the company's goals was to gain a minimum number of orders while not losing money. Of course, a higher ROI is always better. If, for example, Charlie's campaign had sold two pairs of jeans for each order (without any additional promotional expenses), the gross margin would have doubled, and we would have the following numbers:

Gross Sales:	$4,224,000
Less COGS:	$-\underline{1,056,000}$ (25% of gross sales)
Gross Margin:	$3168,000
Less Promo:	$-\underline{1,320,000}$
Net Profit:	$1,848,000
ROI calculation:	$\underline{\$1,848,000}$ = 1.4
ROI = 1.4 × 100 = **140%**	$1,320,000

Also, if Charlie had been able to cut his advertising costs, the ROI would have improved. Overall, though, it looks like Charlie did a reasonable job with his first campaign for the new jeans!

One more note: in doing the math to arrive at the proper ROI for an advertising campaign, there is another way to calculate the ROI. We can take the total number of units sold and *subtract* the units we know it takes to break even on the cost of the campaign—in other words, the number of units it will take to pay for the entire advertising campaign. We then multiply the remaining number of units sold, which will be earning full profit by the net unit contribution. Then, we can divide that net profit number by the cost of the campaign and arrive at the same ROI answer as we did above. Let's see how Charlie would calculate this:

Charlie's break-even units: 20,000

Total units sold: 24,000

Units earning full profit: 24,000 – 20,000 = 4000 units (pairs of jeans)

Net profit: 4000 units × $66 net unit contribution = $264,000

$$\text{ROI for the advertising campaign} : \frac{\$\,264,000\ \text{profit}}{\$1,320,000\ \text{ad costs}} = .20$$

ROI = .2 × 100 = **20% ROI**

Budgeting for Tests

Sometimes, a company will want to test a planned campaign on a small scale to see whether the assumptions about costs and response levels are reasonable. In the case of PW and Charlie, he believes that direct mail might be a good way to market the new jeans, but he wants to run a test with a small sample. He has in mind a mailing that includes color pictures of people actively working and playing in the jeans, plus a small fabric sample—and, of course, an order form that can be returned, although he will also provide the website address, a fax number, and a toll-free number for ordering.

Charlie first has to determine his advertising allowable (sometimes called allowable margin), or the amount that can be spent to get an order while still allowing for media costs and the designated profit to be made. From previous experience and his budget projections, he believes that he can use an advertising allowable of $6 per unit (pair of jeans) ordered via direct mail. He has bought a mailing list from the magazine *Field and Stream*, and he plans to use just the portion of that list (people subscribing in four northeastern states) for his test campaign. This portion of the list has 2000 names. The cost per thousand is $900 for the test. We could also express this cost as $.90 per name:

CPM = $900 for the test

2000 names on the mailing list

2000 divided by 1000 = 2 'groups' of 1000 names

2 (groups of 1000) × $900 (per group of 1000) = $1800 for the test

$1800 divided by 2000 = $.90 per name

What Charlie is looking for is a response rate that comes in at a cost of $6 per response or less.

Charlie sends out the mailing in April, with an offer that expires by the end of May. He gets a 5 percent response, or 100 orders:

2000 mail pieces ×.05 response rate = 100 orders

It cost him $1800 to run the test. Did he achieve his $6 cost per order?

$1800 divided by 100 orders = $18 per order

No! It cost him $18 per order, so he decides to run a second test. This time, he eliminates the fabric sample from the mailing, which saves him the cost of the sample and also lowers his postage costs. He now has a CPM of $600. He picks 3,000 names from the *Field and Stream* list, this time people from four southwestern states. This time, his budget looks like this:

CPM = $600 for the test

3000 names on the mailing list

3000 divided by 1000 = 3 'groups' of 1000 names

(groups of 1000) × $600 (per group of 1000) = $1800 for the test

Charlie sends out the new test mailing in May and gets a 10 percent response, or 300 orders:

3000 mail pieces × .10 response rates = 300 orders

It cost him $1800 to run this test. Did he achieve his $6 cost per order?

$1800 divided by 300 orders = $6

Yes! It cost him exactly $6 per order. You will note that he did several things that improved his CPO. He lowered his actual costs by not sending the sample. He used a different mailing list, perhaps with people more interested in the product. He ran the test later in the spring, perhaps a better buying time. He used more names.

Sometimes, of course, companies are willing to take a chance on rolling out a large campaign, even if the test has not quite met their goals. Like Charlie, they may know of ways to cut costs, reach better prospects, or even pick a better time of year for the campaign. As we already know, varying the creative format, the message, and the price of products can make huge differences in how people react to advertising, but it's always a good idea to test first.

ANALYTIC APPLICATION: SUPER BOWL ADVERTISING

Suppose you are the marketing vice-president for a company that has just produced a truly revolutionary running shoe. You have a marketing budget of $10 million for the coming year, and since you are introducing the product next year, you decide to spend half of your budget, or $5 million, on one 30-second direct-response television ad during the Super Bowl in February. The ad provides a website address that will allow your company to know when a hit has resulted from people seeing this particular ad. You get one million hits on that website after the Super Bowl telecast. Is this good? How many shoes did you eventually sell as a result? Did the ad pay for itself or not? Could you have done better by spending your money on some other form of advertising?

Let's say that of the one million visitors to your site, .05 percent ordered a pair of the shoes by visiting your website. You, of course, created a special Web address *just* for this commercial, so you could accurately evaluate how many responses and orders this one ad produced. Let's also say that a pair of the shoes at the price offered in this ad sold for $110, including shipping and handling. The variable costs come to $50. You had an advertising allowable of $12 per order. So, you can now make some calculations:

Selling price: $100

Variable costs: $50

Unit margin: $50

One million prospects (hits) × .05 response rate = 500,000 orders

Cost of your ad: $5,000,000

Break-even in units ordered: $5,000,000/$50 = 100,000 units to break even

Pairs of shoes sold: 500,000

Break even needed: −100,000

Units at full profit: 400,000

Unit margin: × $50

Net profit: $20,000,000

ROI: Profit divided by ad costs = $20,000,000/$5,000,000 = 4.00 or 400% ROI

CPO: $5,000,000 divided by 500,000 = $10.00 versus an allowable of $12

We now know you beat your advertising allowable and came in with a healthy profit, although we do not know whether your boss gave you a higher ROI target. But 400 percent looks good! The point is not the numbers themselves, but that you now know how to make calculations that tell you how successful you have been—and, very likely, what you might want to consider doing (or not doing) in the future. In this case, it looks like the one-time Super Bowl ad worked well for your product introduction.

SUMMARY

Direct marketing is research-oriented and is especially susceptible to the tools and techniques of testing and experimentation. In this chapter, we have looked at how valid tests can be constructed to manipulate the variables that a direct marketer would be likely to test, including lists, offers, and creative materials. Experiments must be designed and sampling must be controlled so that results are measurable and accountable. Hypothesis testing enables such measurement. It is important to schedule experiments carefully and record results utilizing key codes to identify sources of response for accurate evaluation. Statistical differences in the results of tests may or may not be significant, and the direct marketer must know how to determine statistical significance.

Direct marketing mathematical calculations can also help you to determine which customers to target based on the calculation of customer value and CLTV. By calculating and analyzing response rates, lift, market penetration, and conversion rates, you may be able to create more effective future marketing strategies to grow the profitability of the organization. We saw, for example, how critical analyzing market penetration was to increased sales for Betty's Bakery. Indeed, quantitative analysis is important in direct and interactive marketing!

Finally, we looked at the steps Permanent Wear and Charlie, its director of marketing, would take to plan the marketing budget. We discussed key concepts such as break-even analysis, net profit, cost per inquiry/cost per order, return on investment (ROI), and budgeting for tests. The point of this extended example is that calculations can help you analyze how successful you have been with tests and campaigns, and therefore what you might want to consider doing (or not doing) in future campaigns. The numbers themselves are necessary to success, but alone are not sufficient. Marketers must measure and analyze them; that is to say, knowing how to do marketing math means everything to the direct marketer!

KEY TERMS

A/B test	conversion
allowable margin	conversion rate
alternative hypothesis	cost of goods sold
break even	cost per inquiry (CPI)
chi-square test	cost per response (CPR)
control group	customer lifetime value (CLTV)

degrees of freedom	net profit
dependent variable	null hypothesis
experimentation	random assignment
fixed costs	return on investment (ROI)
gross sales	source code
hypothesis	split test
hypothesis testing	test
independent variable	Type I error
key codes	Type II error
lift	unit margin
market penetration	variable costs
matchback	

REVIEW QUESTIONS

1. Why do we bother to examine the costs of marketing? What should result from spending money on marketing?
2. Why calculate the value of customers?
3. What steps would you take to calculate average customer value?
4. How much more does it cost to replace a customer than to retain a current one?
5. How is a lift calculated? Why is it important to know about lifts?
6. Why is the concept of break-even important? Is this always a goal in a direct marketing campaign? What might be another goal of the campaign?
7. What are some examples of fixed costs and variable costs in a clothing manufacturing business like PW?
8. Why do advertising costs count as fixed costs?
9. In a specific direct marketing campaign, if we want to improve the ROI, what are some ways to do this?
10. Why would a marketing manager run a test of a direct marketing campaign before rolling it out? What would he or she be hoping to learn from the test?

EXERCISE

Let's see where Charlie at PW is with his direct marketing campaign for the new jeans. After two years, he has learned that using the Internet and direct mail are effective ways to attract new customers and retain current customers who make repeat buys. But he would like to gain market penetration. How might he plan to do this? How could he achieve a lift in response during the third year of the campaign? By now, his boss is looking at the increased costs of producing the jeans and tells Charlie to work toward a better ROI. What steps could Charlie take to do this?

CRITICAL THINKING EXERCISE

Jack Stafford, director of a summer tennis camp, wanted to determine which offer he should use in promoting his tennis camp next summer. He wanted to determine which offer would work best to attract tennis players to register for the camp. He created the following two offers: (1) free court time for a week at the country club; and (2) free tennis balls and a gift card to the country club tennis pro shop. Construct a test to help Jack determine which offer to use. What are the steps that must be taken in determining which offer to implement? Beyond the actual test results, what additional issues should be analyzed in order to make a good business decision?

READINGS AND RESOURCES

- A/B Testing guide: https://conversionxl.com/blog/ab-testing-guide
- Similar Web for Web analytics: www.similarweb.com
- Online tools for statistics including A/B test: www.evanmiller.org/ab-testing
- Benchmarks for e-mail marketing: https://mailchimp.com/resources/email-market ing-benchmarks
- Marketing analytics: http://buildfire.com/marketing-analytics
- Customer value: https://blog.smile.io/easy-way-to-calculate-and-increase-customer-life-time-value

CASE: HI-HO SILVER

Hi-Ho Silver began as a traveling store, selling products wholesale to various vendors. Leslie and Chris Sink (shown in Figure 4.18) had the opportunity to open a small retail store operation in Newport News, Virginia, and seized the moment.

The Sinks quickly developed a 'growth' business model and began opening retail stores across the Hampton Roads, Virginia, area (see Figure 4.19). Each of their four different retail locations is led by a manager who reports back to the home office. All administrative duties, including marketing, purchasing, and accounting, are handled by the executive team led by Chris and Leslie Sink.

Hi-Ho Silver quickly became one of the area's largest sterling silver retailers. 'It's not fine jewelry; it's not fake jewelry–it's fun jewelry,' says Chris Sink. Hi-Ho Silver sells handmade sterling silver and gemstones at affordable prices, offering its customers a product that falls somewhere between the fine and not-so-fine jewelry stores. The company carries a line of silver rings, necklaces, and bracelets that can be engraved by any member of the Hi-Ho Silver staff. Its product lines include both sterling silver items and pewterware pieces.

Figure 4.18   Chris and Leslie Sink, owners of Hi-Ho Silver. Published with the consent of Hi-Ho Silver. All Rights Reserved.

Figure 4.19   Hi-Ho retail store. Published with the consent of Hi-Ho Silver. All Rights Reserved.

Hi-Ho Silver sells sterling silver pieces sourced from Taxco in Mexico, India, Indonesia, and other international locations. Many items are handcrafted. The sterling silver items range from basic necklaces and bracelets to original pendants. In addition, the company is host to three nationally branded lines: Chamilia, Kameleon, and Alex and Ani (see Figure 4.20). Hi-Ho Silver began carrying the Chamilia beads in 2006 in response to consumer interest. Since that time, the category has exploded in sales. Leslie Sink declares:

> Chamilia constitutes a strong percentage of our sales, simply because it gets customers to come back again. It's viral. Not only do customers return for self-purchases, but they also buy gifts for others, and get friends and family to come in and buy gifts for them. Lots of new customers have come to us by way of the Chamilia line.

Figure 4.20 Ads of nationally branded lines of merchandise featured at Hi-Ho Silver. Published with the consent of Hi-Ho Silver. All Rights Reserved.

Customers

Hi-Ho Silver customers are primarily middle-aged females who are financially secure. The following data will provide a glimpse of the profile of typical Hi-Ho Silver customers:

- 97 percent are female.
- 82 percent are 36 years old and above, with 57 percent being 46 years old and above.
- 73 percent have an average household income of $51,000 and above.
- 40 percent read women's or cooking magazines, such as *InStyle, Lucky, O, The Oprah Magazine, Cooking Light,* and *Food & Wine.*
- 41 percent listen to alternative and contemporary music stations (*101.3 2WD, 93.7 Bob FM, 92.9 The Wave*).
- 73 percent describe their jewelry style as 'classic' and 'traditional'.
- 58 percent are on Facebook.

Leslie regularly conducts customer surveys to gather pertinent data in order to better serve Hi-Ho Silver customers. The survey findings are also used to determine new or continued marketing strategies. For example, information about radio station preferences is compiled to better understand which radio stations Hi-Ho Silver customers are listening to, and thus which radio stations should be considered for radio advertising allocations. Research has also uncovered the fact that Hi-Ho Silver customers both budget for and actually spend considerably more money when purchasing for themselves and as gifts for family members ($50) as opposed to the amount spent ($30) on non-family gifts. Finally, research shows that Hi-Ho Silver customers rank 'Quality of Product' and 'Price/Affordability' as the two most important factors when purchasing jewelry. Leslie uses customer research data whenever possible to help create store promotions and determine the most effective advertising strategies.

Customer service functions as the underlying value that guides everything the Sinks do in their business. They strive to find new, fresh, exciting, and affordable products for their customer while maintaining their singular focus on making the customer happy. This level of customer service is what gives Hi-Ho Silver its competitive edge in the jewelry industry. An important part of Leslie's job is to constantly gather and analyze the figures associated with and produced by the various marketing activities and to use those figures to make solid business decisions. While quantitative analysis is critical to the success of any business, it is especially important for a small entrepreneurial company such as Hi-Ho Silver.

Hi-Ho Silver Marketing Challenges

As with most small entrepreneurial businesses, the biggest marketing challenge for Hi-Ho Silver is to spend its limited marketing budget in the most efficient and effective manner possible. This decision process begins with understanding the marketing and advertising budget limits within which they are to market. Hi-Ho Silver budgets for mass media advertising expenditures on an annual basis, as presented in the following:

Mass Media Expenses	
Newspaper	6,000
Radio	5,000
Television	12,000
Total	**$23,000**

In addition, the company budgets for the following marketing activity expenditures on an annual basis:

Marketing Expenses	
E-blasts	4,000
Trunk shows	3,000
In-store events	2,000
B-Day coupons	2,000
Thank You cards	1,000
Total	**$12,000**

Having a limited budget encourages precise measurement of each and every advertisement and promotional activity in order to determine whether the respective return on advertising investment (ROAI) deems that the advertisement or activity is profitable and worthy of repeating or not. As Leslie explains:

Let's say we spend all of the budgeted expenditures for mass media and marketing and we project to achieve $1 million in sales. That means that we will obtain a ROAI of 3.5 percent. How did we calculate that? Based on the data contained in these tables, $35,000 is the total budgeted promotional expenses ($23,000 + $12,000) divided by $1,000,000 (which is our projected sales for the period). Mathematically, as shown in the following calculation, that generates a 3.5 percent return on our promotional investment:

$$\frac{\$35,000}{\$1,000,000} = 3.5\%$$

In addition, the ability to make comparisons between the ROAI of one ad versus another is important to be able to make smarter future marketing investments. Leslie claims that *getting the biggest bang for your marketing buck* is of paramount importance for a small entrepreneurial business. Let's look at how each marketing program and activity are measured and analyzed.

Cooperative Advertising Allowances (Co-ops)

'Each one of the nationally branded product lines that Hi-Ho Silver carries offers a cooperative advertising agreement where each brand will share in the cost of our advertising whenever we feature one of the respective brands in our ads,' explains Leslie. Although that is one sure way to stretch an advertising budget, the challenge is that each advertising co-op is different and has unique stipulations associated with each. Leslie must know how to calculate the way to maximize the value of each co-op.

A challenge often faced by Hi-Ho Silver is determining which branded line should be featured in which advertisements so that the maximum amount of co-op dollars can be used to defray the cost of the advertisement. For example, if Hi-Ho Silver's yearly purchases of Chamilia jewelry are roughly $300,000, then the co-op cap for Chamilia is $15,000 for the year. If Hi-Ho Silver wants to run a television campaign and feature Chamilia, the cost of the television commercials is about $20,000. Therefore, since that cost exceeds the cap for Chamilia, Leslie might select another line to be featured, or else pay the additional $5,000 for the television spots. The number crunching conducted beforehand is tied to the fact that some caps are based on a percentage-of-sales figure, while others are a fixed amount. Leslie constantly manipulates the numbers within each co-op criteria to determine smarter marketing decisions.

Hi-Ho Silver's Marketing and Advertising Activities: the .925 Club

Many of the company's promotional strategies are database-driven by its customer loyalty program, the .925 Club. The name '.925' represents .925 silver, which is an indicator that the jewelry at Hi-Ho Silver is the highest quality sterling silver possible.

The customer database is only usable as a marketing medium if it contains valuable customer data that has been updated and maintained over time. Customer data must be collected, segmented, analyzed, and then used to target select customers or groups of customers with promotions that match customer interests and desires. Hi-Ho Silver collects customer data when customers sign up for its .925 Club. The company then creates a customer record by keying the data into its database. The data Hi-Ho Silver collects includes customer name, contact information (to include both telephone number and e-mail address), date of birth, spouse name (if applicable), and customer interest, including the specific brand or type of jewelry the customer desires.

Based on an analysis of the customer data, such as the date of the customer's last transaction (recency), how often they shop in one of Hi-Ho Silver's retail stores (frequency), and how much they spend (monetary), Leslie can determine her most valuable customers based on a Recency-Frequency-Monetary (RFM) assessment. The RFM analysis enables Leslie to assign each customer a 'Loyalty Number' that is recorded in

Figure 4.21 Hi-Ho Silver $10 birthday card. Published with the consent of Hi-Ho Silver. All Rights Reserved.

each customer record. Leslie remarks: 'Determining the value of our customers helps us to spend our marketing budget most effectively by communicating more often with our more valuable customers who generate greater profitability for our company.'

Hi-Ho Silver also segments its .925 Club customer database in order to enable its marketing communications to target different customers. The ways Hi-Ho Silver segments its customers include the following:

1. Top sales customers in the last 120 days
2. Top Chamilia customers
3. New customers in the last month
4. Customers who spend more than $100 within a year
5. Customers who spend more than $200 on necklaces within a year.

Hi-Ho Silver uses the database to send targeted, tailored, and timed communications to its customers. For example, on a monthly basis the company sends $10 birthday cards to customers who have spent $100 within the last year. As shown in Figure 4.21, these birthday cards can be redeemed at any of its four retail store locations.

Leslie and her team also analyze Hi-Ho Silver's customer data in order to discern which customers have not shopped in their stores in the past year. They then use that information to mail 'Miss You' postcards to these inactive customers to encourage them to shop with Hi-Ho Silver (see Figure 4.22). Leslie and her associates track the response that they get on their 'Miss You' mailings to determine whether the 'Miss You' campaign is productive or not. Here again, crunching and analyzing the numbers associated with this campaign provides great insight:

For example, we recently mailed 'Miss You' postcards containing a special 20% discount offer to 536 inactive customers. In response to that mailing, 29 coupons were redeemed and generated $2,208.18 in sales, for a net profit of $304.91. More important than the profit earned was the fact that 29 of those 536 inactive customers are now active again.

'We also track and compare the monthly response rates on our 'Miss You' mailers,' explains Leslie. 'It's interesting; the response rates vary considerably by month and we haven't precisely figured out why that is the case. This is an area that requires additional analysis that's for sure.' Leslie holds up a spreadsheet:

Here's a table that contains the data from our annual 'Miss You' Postcard Campaign. Do you see the monthly fluctuations? We need to better understand the impact that timing has on our promotional campaign. For example, if we analyze several years of our 'Miss You' campaign data and determine that year-after-year the response rates and sales generated on the postcards are higher during given months, perhaps we should reexamine our distribution strategy and distribute the cards during specific months, or, perhaps on a quarterly basis instead of monthly. Just think, we might send five months worth of postcards out in May and mail seven months worth in December, if we think it would provide a larger return on our campaign investment (see Table 4.8).

Figure 4.22 'Miss You' postcard. Published with the consent of Hi-Ho Silver. All Rights Reserved.

Month	Postcards mailed	Postcards redeemed	Sales generated	Mark down dollars	Cost to mail postcards	Gross profit
Jan	491	21	$1,050	$(210)	$294.60	$545
Feb	486	49	3,725	(758)	291.6	2,675
Mar	495	25	1,402	(256)	346.5	800
Apr	479	58	3,463	(692)	335.3	2,436
May	498	87	5,201	(1,063)	298.8	3,839
June	490	22	1,320	(248)	294	778
July	499	25	1,250	(250)	299.4	701
Aug	468	23	1,379	(275)	289.2	815
Sept	482	18	1,009	(201)	289.2	519
Oct	477	32	2,100	(420)	286.2	1,394
Nov	495	79	4,356	(897)	297	3,162
Dec	462	102	6,129	(1,226)	277.2	4,626

Leslie asserts:

> One more thing to consider is that we might want to test various timing options associated with our 'Miss You' campaign . . . . Testing advertising and promotional campaigns before rollout to all of our customers is another way we use math and metrics to determine strategy. Direct mail campaigns are perfect for testing since we can select random samples and establish control groups and test groups. Testing is not limited to direct mail tests, because we can test almost any promotional campaign and media format.

Print Advertising Campaigns

At Hi-Ho Silver, Leslie and her team track, measure, and analyze the impact and profitability of each and every advertising campaign. Let's examine a few previous ad campaigns.

Leslie often places ads in specific publications to target customers in select geographic areas for her different retail store locations. These are **geographically targeted ads**. The two ads shown in Figure 4.23 are similar in layout and design; however, they have a different offer, objective, and geographic target market. The first ad was specifically designed for *Beacon* readers who reside in Virginia Beach and read that particular publication; the second ad was placed in the Williamsburg edition of the local newspaper and promotes the New Town store in Williamsburg. Both of these ads were measured and analyzed to determine their effectiveness.

Think about the various reasons why Leslie might offer a larger discount in one geographic area versus another and the impact that the discount offer has on company profitability. This is another area where Leslie needs to grind some numbers in order to determine the response rate needed on each offer in order to break even on each geographically targeted advertisement.

Figure 4.23 Hi-Ho Silver's geographically targeted advertisements. Published with the consent of Hi-Ho Silver. All Rights Reserved.

Leslie is able to conduct ZIP code market penetration analysis for each geographically targeted advertisement by training her store sales associates to collect each customer's ZIP code area whenever a coupon ad is redeemed at one of the retail stores. By calculating the market penetration by ZIP code area, Leslie can determine which areas are more likely to respond to Hi-Ho Silver offers, enabling Leslie to more effectively and efficiently target these customers with future advertisements. Table 4.9 shows the results of her geographically targeted advertisement.

Table 4.9 Geographically targeted advertising results. Published with the consent of Hi-Ho Silver. All Rights Reserved.

ZIP code area	Pieces mailed	Responses	Market penetration% [response/mailed]
23451	5,793	60	1.04
23452	2,735	33	1.21
23454	6,731	136	2.02
23456	4,341	119	2.74
23461	7,212	240	3.32
23462	3,308	92	2.78

Unlike decades ago, today's marketing world is chock full of figures and statistics that must be analyzed on a regular basis. In planning the marketing activities at Hi-Ho Silver, Leslie finds herself constantly analyzing data–and that has only increased in recent years given the rise of digital and social media marketing activities.

Digital and Social Media Marketing

Leslie distributes many Hi-Ho Silver e-mail blasts to select customer segments. Examples of these e-mails are shown in Figure 4.24. These e-mails are promoting two of Hi-Ho Silver's nationally branded lines. The first promotes the Chamilia brand and was sent to all of Hi-Ho Silver's Chamilia customers. This e-mail offered select customers an opportunity to have an 'exclusive sneak preview' and be the first to own the new Swarovski collection created by Chamilia. The second e-mail blast example features a creative Kameleon compact that also promotes breast cancer awareness. This e-mail was sent to all of Hi-Ho Silver's Kameleon customers.

The campaign statistics for the Kameleon e-mail blast are: 9,479 e-mails distributed; 2,060 opened (18.4% open rate); 76 recipients clicked through the e-mail (.7% click-through rate), and 13 people unsubscribed. As with every e-mail blast, Leslie and her team analyze the statistics and determine whether the e-mail met its established objectives.

Leslie started the Hi-Ho Silver Facebook page in October 2009, and within three months the company had 500 fans. Today Hi-Ho Silver has more than 3,000 fans. Leslie offers Hi-Ho Silver fans monthly giveaways and new posts on a daily basis. Leslie and her team track and analyze each product they feature in daily posts to determine whether the post may have had an impact on company sales.

Figure 4.24 Hi-Ho Silver e-mail blasts. Published with the consent of Hi-Ho Silver. All Rights Reserved.

In conclusion, all of Hi-Ho Silver's marketing activities rely on precise measurement and analysis. That's the secret to success in today's modern marketing analytical world.

Case Discussion Questions

1. Determine some effective uses and allocations of cooperative advertising agreements. If you were a marketing intern at Hi-Ho Silver, what suggestions might you provide to help Leslie be even more proactive and efficient in the use of co-op advertising dollars?
2. Leslie is always striving to improve Hi-Ho Silver's .925 Club. While the database marketing strategies she has undertaken thus far with .925 Club members have been very successful, might there be more that she should be doing? She wonders whether there might be additional ways to segment the customer database in addition to the five strategies she is currently employing. If so, what other segmentation strategies should she employ? What additional customer data might Hi-Ho Silver collect in order to better serve its customers? What additional incentives or benefits might Hi-Ho Silver offer to its .925 Club members?
3. Calculate the response rates for each month of the 'Miss You' campaign. What months have the highest and lowest response rates? Based on your assessment of monthly response rates, what might you conclude about the timing of the mailers? What recommendations would you make for revising the 'Miss You' campaign? How might you implement a test strategy to determine the optimal timing for distribution of the 'Miss You' postcards?
4. Based on the market penetration data provided in the case, think about the various reasons why Hi-Ho Silver would offer a larger discount in one geographic area versus another. Think also about the impact that the discount offer has on the company's profitability. Based on the market penetration data, which ZIP code area would you recommend targeting to prospect for new Hi-Ho Silver customers? Why?

NOTES

1. The discussion of this feature is based on case studies by Quad. Used with permission.
2. The discussion of this feature is based on case studies by Quad. Used with permission.
3. The discussion of this feature is based on case studies by Quad. Used with permission.
4. Other statistical techniques used for measuring significant differences include ANOVA (analysis of variance, the F-test), the t-test (for sample sizes through 30), and the Z-test (for sample sizes larger than 30).
5. The discussion of this feature is based on case studies by Quad. Used with permission.
6. www.quad.com/solutions/marketing-strategy/customer-insights-analytics/accelerated-insights (retrieved on May 20, 2019).
7. This example is based on a case study by Baesman Group, the company's marketing agency. Used with permission.
8. This example is based on a case study by Baesman Group, the company's marketing agency. Used with permission.

PART 2

Create and Place Direct Marketing Campaigns

5

THE OFFER

CHAPTER CONTENTS

CHAPTER SPOTLIGHT

MOUNTAIN GEAR

Do you enjoy being outdoors? Do you like fresh air and beautiful scenery? How about hiking up a mountain on a crisp sunny afternoon? Or backpacking for days at a time? Are you interested in camping? How about partaking in a rock-climbing adventure? Or maybe you're fond of snow sports and enjoy the thrill of snowboarding or cross-country skiing? Perhaps you get pleasure out of cruising around a river or a lake in a kayak or canoe? How about fishing? Do any of these sound like fun? If so, go get your gear!

There are so many different ways to enjoy the outdoors, but to do so you'll need the right gear, clothing, accessories, and equipment. Meet Mountain Gear, an outdoor cataloger with one retail store located in Spokane, Washington. Mountain Gear is considered a national and international expert in climbing, mountaineering, and backpacking gear. It offers many different lines of products and myriad product items to serve just about any desire associated with outdoor adventures.

Mountain Gear offers the following five product categories: men's clothing, women's clothing, footwear, outdoor gear, and sale items. The company also offers the following seven product lines based on the outdoor activity type: climbing, camping and hiking, snow sports, trail running and fitness, canyoneering, paddle sports, and travel. Within each of these product lines, the company offers many different product groups. For example, in the camping and hiking activity line, Mountain Gear's customers may purchase tents, packs, sleeping bags and pads, headlamps, poles and tools, navigation and electronics, cookware and water filters, first aid and hygiene products, and chairs and furniture. Of course, the company offers a selection of different colors, models, and brands for each of these product groupings. Mountain Gear offers its customers a one-stop shopping haven when it comes to outdoor adventure products. However, Mountain Gear's customers are incredibly diverse in their needs and wants. For example, a customer who enjoys snowboarding may or may not be interested in camping, fishing, trail running or rock climbing. The challenge? How to target customers with relevant offers that match their outdoor adventure interests.

Mountain Gear wanted to expand its direct marketing efforts as a way to increase response and enhance its customer relationships. With the help of QuadDirect, an integrated communications provider, Mountain Gear implemented a highly segmented and personalized direct-response campaign. The company segmented its customer base and created customized offers tailored to each segment's interests.

QuadDirect created a double-fold card that featured one of three different images to target different customer segments based on purchase histories. See Figure 5.1 for Mountain Gear's customized direct mailers. Each card also contained a personalized URL built around a product assortment targeted to the customer's interests. The card was mailed to 57,000 customers. The personalized URLs also promoted either e-mail sign-up with a sweepstakes promotion or a 'refer-a-friend' offer if the customer had already signed up for e-mail notifications.

This campaign was a huge success for Mountain Gear. Customized offers tailored uniquely to customer's interests and behaviors proved to be highly effective. Response to the personalized mailer was 67 percent higher than response to postcards previously mailed to these same customer groups for similar marketing campaigns. Nearly 1,200 customers signed up for Mountain Gear's e-mail list during the 14-day period of the promotion. Creating compelling and need-satisfying offers is how Mountain Gear is able to help thousands of people start amazing adventures and enjoy lifelong hobbies.

(Continued)

Figure 5.1   (Continued)

Figure 5.1   Mountain Gear customized direct mailers. Used with permission of Mountain Gear.

In summary, planning and creating a value proposition or offer take creative and strategic thinking. This must satisfy a need or want and entice consumers to take action. That is the topic of this chapter. We define the offer and discuss what comprises an effective offer, the components of an offer, and how to create, target, and test the offer. In addition, this chapter examines a variety of different types of offers that have been successfully used by direct marketers through the years. Because creating the offer is both a science and an art, we can learn much from examining offers that have worked *as well as those* that have not worked.

WHAT IS THE OFFER?

The offer is the value proposition to the prospect or customer, stating what you will give the customer in return for taking the action your marketing communication asks him or her to take. In essence, it is the terms under which a direct marketer promotes a product or service. The offer encompasses both the manner of presentation by a direct marketer and the all-important request for a response.

Creating need-satisfying offers is a part of ongoing customer relationship management (CRM), which drives the direct marketing process. Without an attractive offer, consumers would not initially respond to an organization, and thus the customer relationship would never originate. Without continuous monitoring of customer needs and wants, direct marketers could not create appropriate offers to keep their customers satisfied and encourage them to return and purchase again and again. The offer is the all-important 'front-end' activity in the CRM process.

The offer is the element of the direct marketer's strategy that can be most quickly and easily revised for an improved result in the direct marketing effort. Even the slightest change in the price may produce a dramatic difference on consumer response. Just think about all of the products that are priced at odd numbers, such as $19.99 or $199.97. These figures are pennies away from the even dollar amounts; however, consumers often perceive them to be far less. Research has proven that odd prices are very effective in generating consumer response; therefore, many direct marketers use odd prices in their offers.

Other direct marketers believe in the '40-40-20 rule,' which states that the success of any direct marketing effort is 40 percent reliant on using the right lists, 40 percent reliant on having an effective offer, and 20 percent reliant on creating the right creative mix (copywriting, photographs, illustrations, and so on) in your direct marketing effort. However we may try to quantify its importance, the offer is clearly a major contributor to the success or failure of any direct marketing campaign.

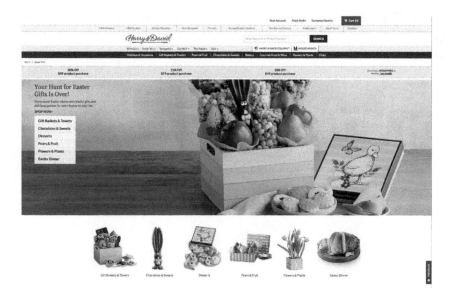

(Continued)

Figure 5.2 (Continued)

Figure 5.2 Harry and David seasonal offers. ©Harry and David, LLC.

Making an Offer Effective

To create an effective offer, the direct marketer must research and really know the target audience and the customers' likes, dislikes, 'hot buttons,' and, most of all, needs and wants. Without this information, it is difficult, at best, to create an effective offer. In addition, marketers must research how consumer needs and wants change. Direct marketers must constantly revise their offers, including the creative materials used to convey each offer. This normally requires printing a number of different catalogs or changing a company's website throughout the year to provide timely offers that appeal to consumers during a particular season or holiday. Figure 5.2 features a few of the various catalog covers used by well-known specialty food and gift direct marketer Harry and David when marketing to its customers. Note that the creative appeal used and the products offered are appropriate for each season or holiday.

According to Lois Geller, author of *Response: The Complete Guide to Profitable Direct Marketing*, effective offers have three characteristics: believability, involvement, and creativity.[1]

1. Believability: using common sense when creating the offer can go a long way toward making it believable. An offer has to make sense to the consumer. It cannot give so much in the form of gifts or 'freebies' that it makes the consumer wonder what's wrong with the product or service. For example, a sale offering 80 percent off at the end of a season makes sense to the consumer, because we all know that marketers need to make room for new inventory, but 80 percent off at any other time makes the consumer wonder 'What's wrong with this product that it didn't sell?' Therefore, the offer should be believable.

2. Involvement: Geller believes that most shoppers suffer from what she calls the 'glaze-over effect.' She claims that some offers are so common that consumers' eyes simply glaze over when they see one.[2] For example, an offer of a 10 or 15 percent discount is very common. It usually gets passed over. However, the offer that promises 'buy one, get one at half price' is more exciting and appealing and may motivate the consumer to calculate their potential savings. The offer must attempt to get the consumer involved.

3. Creativity: the most creative offers usually get the highest response. Creativity can set your offer apart from all the other offers bombarding consumers. Geller believes that 'exclusive offers' are very appealing and should be featured prominently if the product or service is really exclusive to the market. 'Exclusive' means that the product is in limited supply or not available in stores and is special to your company.[3] An example of an exclusive offer is:

The recipe for these peanut butter balls has been in the Stafford family for 50 years. For decades, friends and neighbors have been savoring these tasty sweet treats. Buy one box of these peanut butter balls and we'll throw in Grandma Stafford's special recipe for oatmeal cookies with a cinnamon swirl. You can't find this recipe in any cookbook or baker's magazine. We keep it so we can give it to our special customers. Enjoy!

Now you have an understanding of what the offer is and what makes it effective, let's explore the components of the offer.

COMPONENTS OF THE OFFER

The components of the direct marketing offer fall into two categories: required (must be present in all offers) and optional (may be included depending on strategy and costs). The four *required* elements are product or service, pricing and payment terms, risk-reduction mechanisms, and time limits or length of commitment. The *optional* element is incentives.

Product or Service

The actual tangible product or intangible service is critical to the success of any offer, of course. It must satisfy the needs or wants of the target consumer to whom it is being presented. Although brand names, packages, and labels, along with advertising and other promotional strategies, create product and supplier preferences, it is the quality of the product itself that must ultimately lead to repurchases. The quality (and this includes any warranty and service) must be consistent with customer expectations, and it is the offer that creates those expectations. Therefore, it is critical to meet (and even exceed) the product or service expectations that are presented by the offer.

Physical features such as weight, dimensions, color, model, accessories, and any extended properties such as gift wrapping, alterations, delivery, and service are very important, as is the basic benefit the product will provide. Services have unique properties such as type of service, length of time or duration of the service, location, and frequency or schedule of the service. Appropriate timing of the offer can also affect the consumer's response, particularly if the product or service is seasonal.

Marketers must understand these product or service features well in order to create an effective offer that garners a response from the target consumer. If the product/service itself does not satisfy the needs or wants of the consumer, then no matter how attractive you make the rest of the offer, it will be to no avail. Simply stated, consumers are not interested in purchasing products and services for which they have no need or desire.

Direct marketers must consider five specific product details, as follows, when determining the terms of the offer:

1. A choice of sizes: whether the direct marketer will make the product available in a wide array of sizes, including extra small, extra large, and half sizes, is a specific detail that must be determined. Another term of the offer pertaining to product size is whether the direct marketer will allow consumers to place a special order for an unusual size if desired. Direct marketers must spell out these specific product terms.

2. A choice of colors: whether the direct marketer will make the product available in a wide variety of popular colors is an important product detail. In addition, can the consumer select certain colors to be mixed and matched with other colors when ordering products with more than one component or piece? For example, when placing an order with Victoria's Secret, can a consumer select a bathing suit top in one color or design and a bathing suit bottom in a different but coordinating color or design? Will the direct marketer allow consumers to place special orders for a unique color if desired? Direct marketers make these and similar determinations when creating the terms of an offer.

3. Product specifications: direct marketers must disclose the dimensions of the product, including such elements as the weight, height, length, texture, and scent of the product in the offer. Direct marketers often use photographs or illustrations to depict the product; however, they must also be careful to spell out the exact specifications in words as well as photographs.
4. Product accessories: direct marketers must specifically state what product accessories are available. It is also important to specify which accessories are included with the purchase of the product and which can be purchased separately, if so desired. Once again, the more specific the product details identified in the offer are, the smaller the chance of unmet consumer expectations.
5. Personalization: personalization enhances the sale of a direct-marketed product, and thus should, if possible, be made available to the customer. The cornerstone of some very successful direct marketing companies has been offering personalized products.

Pricing and Payment Terms

Direct marketers must decide whether their price objective is to maximize profit or maximize sales. If the price is meant to generate the largest possible return on investment (ROI), that is, the objective is to maximize profit, then the direct marketer must use a **price skimming** strategy. This strategy establishes the price at the highest possible level to 'skim the cream' off the top of the market and target only a select number of consumers who can *afford* to buy the product/service. Of course, a high price will result in fewer sales transactions but greater profitability per sale.

A **price penetration** strategy will help the direct marketer maximize sales volume. This strategy sets the price at a very low level so that almost any consumer who wants to buy the product can afford to do so.

The price elasticity of a product is another factor to take into account when establishing the price of the product. **Price elasticity** is the relative change in demand for a product given a change in its price. It measures the consumer's responsiveness or sensitivity to price changes. For example, let's pretend Gap decreased the price of its jeans from $35 to $25. Would consumers buy two pairs of jeans instead of one? Let's also pretend Starbucks coffee increased the price of its coffee by $2. Would consumers continue purchasing Starbucks, or would they switch to either a different brand of coffee or a substitute product, such as hot cocoa or tea, instead of coffee? The direct marketer, in initially estimating the demand for products, first determines whether there is a price the market expects and then develops an estimate of the sales volume they expect at different price levels. If the consumer's demand for a product doesn't change substantially regardless of price increases, the product has an inelastic market demand. If, however, the consumer is very sensitive to price changes and market demand for the product decreases greatly as price increases, then the product has an elastic market demand. A product with an *elastic* market demand should usually be priced lower than an item with an *inelastic* market demand.

It is not just price level that is important. Equally important is the manner in which we state the price. Is it a buy-one-get-one-free offer? Is it a sale? Table 5.1 shows various ways to present price in an offer.

Table 5.1   Examples of price in an offer

Basic price statement	'One-year supply for only $12.99'
Price stated as a fraction	'One-half off when ordered by May 1st'
Price stated by unit	'Now only $2.49 an issue'
Price savings stated by percentage	'Save 30% when ordered by May 1st'
Price savings stated by unit	'First two issues are free'
Price savings stated by dollar amount	'Save $25'
Price savings based on introduction	'Save $15 on your initial subscription'
Price savings based on multiple purchases	'Save $2.98 on two'
Price based on promotional offer	'Buy one, get one free'

Finally, payment method is a vital part of the offer. The payment methods direct marketers have offered in the past, cash with the order and collect on delivery, lacked convenience and often were a deterrent to ordering. On the other hand, an offer to absorb shipping costs if cash payment is sent with the order can be a distinct incentive.

A bill-me-later (BML) payment offer that includes credit card options, either the direct marketer's own, a bank card, or a travel and entertainment card, not only provides convenience but also spurs the customer not to procrastinate when placing an order. In certain cases, such as a free trial offer with full return privileges, the BML offer isn't just nice to have, it's a necessity. Today, mobile payment tools make paying for products and services quick and easy. More will be discussed on those convenient payment options later, in Chapters 9 and 14.

Delayed payment is sometimes extended to provide installment terms. This option is usually confined to higher priced products and can be with or without an interest charge. Payment in installments is an attractive incentive to many consumers and such an offer can be a strong one. However, marketers must weigh the advantages of this incentive against the cost of financing the resulting accounts receivable, the potential for bad debts, and the ultimate return on the direct marketer's investment.

Sometimes marketers don't really offer an installment payment plan, but rather make reference to the overall price of a product or service broken down on a weekly or monthly basis. This is an effective strategy to present the price of a product or service while demonstrating the affordability of the offer. The Busch Gardens advertisement, shown in Figure 5.3, stating that its Pass Membership is 'Only $11 per month' is an excellent example of this price promotion strategy.

Risk-Reduction Mechanisms

The direct marketing consumer bears risk, usually greater than in traditional retail buying, whenever he or she purchases a product without the added benefit of actually seeing, touching, feeling,

Figure 5.3 Busch Gardens advertisement. Used with the consent of Busch Gardens/Water Country USA. All Rights Reserved.

and personally examining it. Therefore, the goal of the direct marketer is to reduce the perceived risk associated with purchasing the product unseen and unfelt.

Two basic mechanisms of the offer are designed to reduce the risk: they are a *free trial* or *examination period* and a *money-back guarantee*. Let's examine both.

Trial or Examination Period

The free trial or free examination offer helps overcome the distinct disadvantage of ordering a product via a remote location. For example, Dollar Shave Club, a company that delivers razors, razor blades, and other personal grooming products to customers by mail on a monthly basis, offers prospective customers free trial-size products so they can experience the quality of its shaving goods. Then, two weeks later, the company will ship the customer a restock box with full sizes of all those products, at a discount. The customer is in complete control and can add and remove products, plus adjust how often they receive restock boxes.[4]

Guarantees

Direct marketers have been using guarantees for many years. A guarantee of 'complete satisfaction or your money back' is an inherent necessity of direct marketing. This assurance, and the manner in which it is presented, is a vital part of the offer. L. L. Bean offered this '100 percent guarantee' in one of its catalogs:

> Our products are guaranteed to give 100% satisfaction in every way. Return anything purchased from us at any time if it proves otherwise. We will replace it, refund your purchase price or credit your credit card. We do not want you to have anything from L.L. Bean that is not completely satisfactory.

Some direct marketers even guarantee to buy back their products at a later time. Guarantees have been developed for extended time periods. Some even offer 'double your money back' if the buyer is less than completely satisfied. Of course, full return privileges are a fundamental part of any offer.

Time Limits or Length of Commitment

A limited time offer typically specifies a deadline, an enrollment period, a charter membership, a limited edition, or a prepublication offer. An example of an effective limited time offer can be seen in Figure 5.4. Busch Gardens sent an e-mail to its fans promoting a 'two parks for the price of one' offer with a live countdown clock inside to create a sense of urgency. The park saw a 27 percent increase versus the same offer the previous year. After the promotional period ended, the message of the e-mail changed to indicate the offer had expired and directed customers to other ticket options.

Incentives

Generally, the more attractive you can afford to make the offer, the better the response will be. How do you make an offer attractive? You dress it up with lots of freebies! This component of the offer is optional and entails close examination of both the objectives of the offer and the budget constraints within which the direct marketer must operate. Direct marketers must be careful that the cost of the incentives does not outweigh the added profit of the additional orders. Direct marketers commonly use two types of incentives—sweepstakes or contests and free gifts or premiums. Let's examine both.

Sweepstakes and Contests

Direct marketers have used sweepstakes and contests as an ordering stimulus. To avoid being considered a lottery, which requires a purchase as a condition for entry and is illegal in many

(Continued)

Figure 5.4 (Continued)

Figure 5.4 Busch Gardens limited time offer e-mails. Used with the consent of Busch Gardens/Water Country USA. All Rights Reserved.

states, a contest or sweepstake must guarantee a winner and making a purchase must not be a requirement, though it can be an option for entering. In addition, the law requires that the odds of winning the sweepstake or contest be published on promotional materials. You should readily see that attractive prize offerings, such as trips to lavish resorts or big-ticket electronic devices, yield a large response in terms of contest or sweepstake participation.

Random drawings to select winners are sometimes done in advance of distributing the sweepstakes offer, so that the contest will not be construed as a lottery. How can a direct marketer choose a winner before people enter the contest? That may seem odd; however, based on the consumer list that will be used to distribute the contest or sweepstakes offer, the direct marketer can actually select a name or multiple names and then if that person does not enter the contest, they will not be awarded the prize. Remember, lotteries require a prior purchase, whereas contests and sweepstakes only require an entry form to be submitted. A key to the success of sweepstakes and other forms of contest is getting the respondents involved in some way, such as by returning perforated tear-offs, die-cuts, tokens, and stamps, as well as by giving answers to questions, problems, or puzzles. Direct marketers should be creative when designing contest or sweepstake entry forms.

Gifts and Premiums

An effective device for stimulating response to a direct marketing promotion is the offer of a free gift or premium, either for purchasing or for simply examining or trying the product. Although such incentives increase response, as do sweepstakes and contests, they may also attract less qualified respondents in terms of creditworthiness or final product acceptance.

Some gifts are termed 'keepers,' meaning that the customer can keep the premium whether or not they keep the product. To be most effective, the premium should be related to the product or the specific audience. Sometimes, direct marketers offer customers a choice between multiple gifts. In other situations, direct marketers keep the gift 'a mystery' and consumers do not know what particular gift they will receive until it is delivered. It can have tangible and apparent value or the value can be intrinsic, such as a booklet containing advice. Sometimes the free gift offer can be as nominal as information or a price estimate. An example of a free gift offer by Barnes & Noble appears in Figure 5.5. Note that this online offer is for two free gifts, valued at $32.99.

Do all offers possess all the components we've discussed? Probably not. However, these are the essential parts of most basic offers. Now you know the pieces of the puzzle, what do you do with them? You begin creating an offer for your consumers.

CREATING AN OFFER

The offer is not independent of the entire direct marketing strategy. While creating it, marketers must keep the other strategic elements of direct marketing in mind, especially the needs and wants of the customer. Let's discuss the five steps direct marketers should follow when creating an offer.

Step 1: Perform Market Research

When direct marketers attempt to predict and determine consumer needs and wants, they often rely on certain indicators, such as the geographic, demographic, social, psychological, and behavioral characteristics of the consumer. (These were overviewed in Chapter 3.) Direct marketers strive to understand consumer needs and wants, not merely predict them. Thus, they often conduct consumer research to determine what motivates the consumer to purchase a given product/ service. After all, consumer motivations drive the purchase process. **Motivations** are needs that compel a person to take action or behave in a certain way, such as purchase a product/service. Consumers have both internal and external motivations for their behavior. Internal motivators can stem from basic physiological needs, such as hunger or thirst, or other needs, such as the need for acceptance. However, external motivators can take the form of advertisements, free samples, a sales pitch, or even a persuasive offer.

Figure 5.5 Barnes & Noble offer. Used with permission of Barnes & Noble Inc.

In any event, direct marketers must understand what needs the consumer is attempting to satisfy in order to effectively create offers that will meet these needs and wants. Direct marketers are concerned with creating, caring for, and keeping customers. They want to create a customer, not just make a sale! The difference between the two is that a sale means a one-time purchase, whereas a customer is someone who will come back and make repeat purchases from an organization throughout his or her lifetime. Thus, long-term CRM is a constant focus of direct marketers.

Therefore, the underlying theme in creating any offer is the consumer. The development of an offer cannot occur without an understanding of the consumer's needs and wants. Think of it in this way: creating an offer without careful analysis of consumer needs and wants is like driving off in a car without making sure there is gasoline in the tank! Not a good idea, right? It is only by carefully researching the consumer and the competitive situation that the direct marketer will have the needed information on which to create an offer. The market research data collected by the direct marketer also provides specific details pertaining to the consumer's desired elements of the offer.

Windstream Communications launched a direct marketing campaign called the Windstream Movers program that featured customized offers based on consumer analysis. Intuitively, Windstream knew that movers into single-family dwelling units (SFDUs) were more likely to be new homeowners, and therefore more likely to need landline, broadband, and television services. Movers into multi-family dwelling units (MFDUs) were more likely to be younger renters, and therefore they might eschew traditional landlines in favor of cell phones. As a result, Windstream employed duplex laser printing to customize the offer and text to the moving consumer segments. As Figure 5.6 reveals, this was achieved by preprinting a single self-mailer format that allowed for individualized and customized messaging to pre-movers, new homeowners, and movers/renters. In addition, these unique offers were mailed on a weekly basis to be in-home as close to the move date as possible so that the timing of the offers would correspond to consumer needs.

Step 2: Determine the Objectives of the Offer

What is the offer designed to do? Get orders? Generate sales leads? Sell subscriptions? Encourage repeat purchases or renewals? Introduce and sell new products? Increase the amount that the customer is presently purchasing? Raise funds? Without clearly established objectives, you won't be able to measure the success or failure of the offer—and remember that measurement is imperative in direct marketing.

The underlying objective of any offer is to maximize profitability for a company or organization. Two of the most common methods of achieving increased profitability are (1) encouraging repeat purchases from existing customers, and (2) encouraging a company's current customers to purchase additional related or unrelated products beyond what they normally buy. The three direct marketing strategies that achieve this profit-maximization objective are *continuity selling*, *cross-selling*, and *up-selling*. Let's take a look at each of these strategies in turn.

Continuity selling describes offers that are continued on a regular basis, whether weekly, monthly, quarterly, or annually. These offers are also called 'club offers' and are a hallmark of direct marketers who want to acquire customers who will remain active for an extended period of time. In continuity selling, customers buy related products or services as a series of small purchases, rather than all at a single time.

Figure 5.6 Windstream Communications offer. Used with permission of Windstream Communications and MindZoo, LLC.

Source: Photo by Jim Kirby, www.jimkirbyphoto.com.

Books, magazine subscriptions, insurance policies, and many other products are sold by means of club offers, as are periodic shipments of cosmetics or beauty products, and food products such as meats, cheese, fruit, and desserts. An example of continuity selling is provided in Figure 5.7. Harry and David's Fruit-of-the-Month Club offers consumers an opportunity to receive select fruit throughout the year. The customer can choose to give or receive the 3-Box Club, 5-Box Club, 8-Box Club, or 12-Box Club.

The continuity selling offer includes a **positive option**, where the customer must specifically request shipment for each offer in a series, or a **negative option**, where the shipment is sent automatically unless the customer specifically requests that it not be. The negative option is a controversial marketing technique because some consumers don't realize that they must request the shipments be stopped or else they are responsible for paying for the products delivered. Most consumers normally expect to pay for what they order, but, with a negative option, they pay unless they request the shipment to be stopped. For example, Guthy-Renker, a prominent direct marketing company, offers consumers an opportunity to receive a quality facial cleansing and acne treatment system, Proactiv. The customer decides whether to purchase a 30-day supply or a 90-day supply and product refills are shipped automatically. Proactiv is an example of a negative option club offer. The refill products are shipped either every 30 days or every 90 days based on the customer's order choice, and they must call if they want

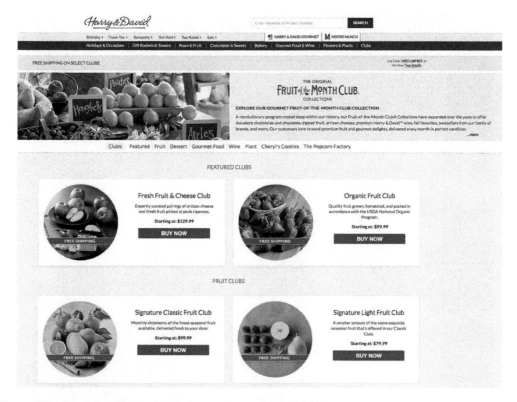

Figure 5.7   Harry and David club options. ©Harry and David, LLC.

to cancel. Of course, if the consumer receives an undesired shipment, it can be returned at any time for credit.

Another example of a negative option offer is a til-forbid. A **til-forbid (TF)** is an offer that prearranges continuing shipments on a specified basis and is renewed automatically until the customer instructs otherwise. TF offers are commonly used with insurance policies or magazine subscriptions. Other examples include some clubs, such as book clubs, wine clubs, and automobile clubs, which may also include specific services with an annual membership fee. An example of a til-forbid offer is that of the Wine Club of the Williamsburg Winery, featured in Figure 5.8. The Winery offers three tiers of membership: the Classics Club, the Discovery Club, and the Connoisseurs Club, designed to meet all budgets and levels of interest. Depending on the level of membership, club members receive varying quantities of unique bottles of wine hand-selected by the Williamsburg Winery winemaker, along with varying discounts on all vintages and merchandise in the Williamsburg Winery retail shop and online wine shop. Once a customer signs up, membership in the wine club is ongoing, with the customer's credit card billed automatically each quarter. After two shipments of wine, members may cancel their membership by calling the Direct Shipping department at the Williamsburg Winery or by writing the Wine Club Director an e-mail requesting cancellation. Cancellation must be done at least 30 days in advance of the next billing cycle.

Figure 5.8 Williamsburg Winery wine. Used with permission of The Williamsburg Winery. All Rights Reserved.

Cross-selling offers new products to existing customers. The products may be related or unrelated to those the customers are already buying. For example, a purchaser of books and software might be offered other books and software or possibly an insurance policy, a home power tool, or a vacation package to a tropical resort. The most important element of successful cross-selling is the manner in which the customer views the direct marketer's reputation, reliability, and overall image.

Up-selling is the promotion of more expensive products or services over the product or service originally discussed or purchased. You might think of up-selling as suggestive selling, since the marketer is suggesting the more expensive product or service as opposed to the consumer requesting it.

In summary, continuity selling, cross-selling, and up-selling are important direct marketing strategies used to achieve different objectives when creating the offer. Each strategy has been used by direct marketers and has met with great success. It is important that the direct marketer decides which strategy they will employ when creating an offer.

Step 3: Target the Offer

In creating an offer and developing the copy or jargon that will position it, Donna Baier Stein and Floyd Kemske in their book, *Write on Target*, insist that every direct marketer or copywriter must ask themselves four essential questions:[5]

1. What am I selling?
2. Whom am I selling to?
3. Why am I selling this now?
4. What do I want my prospect to do?

They believe the key to effective direct marketing is unlocking the selling power that comes from knowing to whom you are targeting your offer. Knowing the target consumer requires market research on that target profile of consumers. It is only by knowing and understanding the target consumer that the offer can be 'right on target' to generate the maximum response rate. Of course, not all consumers are the same. There are differences (and similarities) between them. That is the basis of market segmentation and is also the starting point of effectively targeting an offer. Examples of targeted offers are shown in Figure 5.9. Busch Gardens markets to different niche groups, such as corporations, emergency personnel, healthcare professionals and educators, and must create targeted offers and customized promotional materials personalized for each respective segment.

(Continued)

Figure 5.9 (Continued)

Figure 5.9 Busch Gardens targeted offers. Used with the consent of Busch Gardens/Water Country USA. All Rights Reserved.

The process of targeting the offer is directly related to the important concepts of market segmentation and positioning (reviewed in Chapter 3), as well as creative appeal. Market segmentation enables a marketer to view consumers as belonging to certain select groups based on shared characteristics and/or needs and wants. Thus, instead of trying to target a product or service to the total market, most marketers select certain groups of customers, called market segments, to which they will target their promotional efforts.

Positioning is a marketing strategy that enables marketers to understand how each consumer perceives a company's product or service. This perception is based in part on the strengths and weaknesses of the product or service compared with other competing products or services. By knowing what that perception is, we can more effectively create an offer and target it toward a particular consumer segment.

The appeal of an offer can be described as its message content that addresses consumer's needs, wants or interests and entices action. The most commonly used appeals are either rational or emotional. The rational appeal targets a consumer's logical buying motives. It presents facts in a logical, rational manner and targets basic needs such as those for food, shelter, clothing, and safety. An example of a rational appeal is the National Association of Letter Carriers' Food Drive. This organization distributes a direct mail postcard to residents asking them to help 'stamp out hunger' by placing a food donation at their mailbox on a certain day before their letter carrier arrives. The carrier will pick up the food donation and deliver it to a local food bank or pantry. The offer is clear, logical, and does not attempt to invoke great emotion on the part of the local resident who is being asked for a food donation. Rational appeals are normally used for business-to-business (B2B) direct marketing offers. With B2B offers, direct marketers are targeting organizations or groups where often the purchase decision is based on exact specifications and technical data, as well as being made by a buying committee or a team of decision makers. For example, check out Salesforce.com and you might see offers such as free information, special discount pricing for new small business users, and free demonstrations of Sales Cloud, its CRM online platform. These Salesforce.com offers appeal to the rational buying motives of small business owners. Much more will be discussed regarding B2B direct marketing later, in Chapter 11.

The emotional appeal focuses on a consumer's desires and feelings. It targets the consumer's wants—such as social status, prestige, power, recognition, and acceptance—as opposed to physical needs. An example of an emotional appeal is the Guinness 'Friendship' commercial. This TV spot depicted a group of friends playing wheelchair basketball and, at the end of the game, all but one stood up from their wheelchair. The tagline used was 'Made of More.' It related how our choice of friends, like our choice of beer, reveals the nature of our character. Check out this excellent emotional appeal ad at: www.ispot.tv/ad/7bSd/guinness-wheelchair-basketball.

Another great example of an emotional appeal is an ad by Zillow, an online real estate database and marketplace. Zillow's 'Returning Soldier' ad followed a husband and wife communicating about their house search via several different online platforms, such as video chat and instant messaging. They debated about the number of bedrooms needed for visiting relatives and school zone ratings for their daughter. When the mom and daughter walked into their new house for the first time, the father was waiting in his military camouflage uniform holding flowers. The daughter ran to him and the mother stood in shock as she looked at her soldier who had finally returned home. You can see this ad at: www.ispot.tv/ad/7nQa/zillow-returning-soldier. Both of these offers play on the viewer's emotional connection to their friends and family, making them feel more connected to the ad and the product.

The type of appeal selected must be appropriate to the media used to distribute the offer. For example, if a direct marketer is making an online offer to regular or prospective customers, the offer must be direct and to the point because most people only spend a few seconds on websites. In addition, the offer must enable the consumer to respond via a quick click of the mouse or keyboard. The offer must include direct messages that encourage the consumer to 'forward to a friend' or, as in the Busch Gardens offer in the banner ad shown in Figure 5.10, to 'buy now.'

Figure 5.10 Busch Gardens banner ad. Used with the consent of Busch Gardens/Water Country USA. All Rights Reserved.

Of course, offers may or may not generate a positive reaction or consumer response. This is why direct marketers normally test different offers to determine which one is most effective with a particular consumer market segment.

Step 4: Test the Offer

As presented in the previous chapter, testing is of great importance to the success of the offer. We might consider testing to be the ultimate consumer opinion poll. The research question we are asking each consumer is, of course, 'Does the offer make you want to buy the product or service?' If the offer is not attempting to sell something but trying to obtain a specific outcome, such as a vote for a politician or attendance at an upcoming meeting, does it make the target individual want to take the action for which the offer is requesting? The test determines the effectiveness of the offer and provides an answer to the critical question—does the offer *work*?

How do direct marketers conduct the tests? The answer is simple. They first determine what they want to test or investigate. For example, direct marketers may want to determine the free gift or premium they will offer consumers who make a purchase during some specified time period. Let's say a local restaurant wants to distribute direct mail offers to local residents in a particular ZIP code area to encourage consumers to patronize the restaurant. Prior to creating the offer, the restaurant wants to determine whether consumers will respond more readily to an offer for a free appetizer or a free dessert. Next, the direct marketer creates two direct mail cards, one containing the offer for the free appetizer and the other the offer for a free dessert, and mails these cards to a sample of consumers in the ZIP code area of interest. When consumers present these cards to the restaurant waiter or waitress, the cards are kept. At the end of the time period specified for the test, the direct marketer counts how many responses each free gift offer generated. The offer that generates the largest response wins the test. Direct marketers then use the test results to determine which free gift to include when creating the offer. Of course, direct marketers may perform multiple tests if they want to investigate other terms or components of the offer.

Lois Geller has offered a simple, four-step approach to testing the offer.[6]

1. Test only one feature at a time. When you are testing an offer, be sure to change only one variable at a time. If you change more than one variable, whether it is creative, product or service, or price, you will not know what variable change caused the change in consumer response.
2. Code your tests so you can measure results. Each version of a promotion must have its own specific/individual code so that you will know which offer has generated the best response. For example, if you are testing the same offer in two different magazines, the only difference between them should be the code printed on the response device so that when consumers respond to the offer you will know which magazine was responsible for generating that consumer's order.
3. Keep accurate records. Record all coded tests so that you can measure and analyze the test results. Recording test results can be as simple as writing them in a ledger book, or as sophisticated as computing an ongoing summation in a computerized database.
4. Analyze test results and take action. Whenever a test for an offer is complete, you will want to know which offer polled best—in other words, generated the largest consumer response rate—so that you repeat the most effective offer.

Marketers should test their offers on an ongoing basis. In fact, early testing of an offer on a small market segment, rather than waiting until the offer is complete and ready to be rolled out to the entire consumer market, saves time and money. Remember that, given time and preparation, all components of an offer can be tested—one at a time. Keep in mind that the ultimate goal of testing is to determine what will work the best in generating a response from the consumer.

Step 5: Execute the Offer

Once the direct marketer performs marketing research, decides on the terms of the offer, appropriately targets the offer to the right consumer market segment, and employs tests on various components of the offer, it is time to execute the offer. The first part of offer implementation is where the direct marketer uses the results of each test to revise the offer and make it more attractive to consumers. Once the direct marketer makes the necessary revisions, they are now prepared to put the offer into action.

What does executing the offer mean? It means that the direct marketer must be ready to implement the decisions made thus far. The direct marketer must be poised and prepared to fulfill the terms of the offer at the time of implementation. This means that if a free gift is offered with a purchase, the direct marketer must have an adequate supply of the free gifts to distribute to those consumers making a purchase. If the direct marketer is offering a new, innovative color of a given product, that new color of product must be ready to be packaged and shipped as soon as an order is received from a consumer.

In summary, creating the offer is a step-by-step process that culminates when a consumer accepts the offer and carries out the action that the direct marketer has asked him or her to take. Direct marketers who follow the steps described in this section should find greater success in both the execution of the offer and consumer acceptance of that offer. Creating the offer is a bit of science and art. The science is the logical sequence of steps that direct marketers should follow when creating the offer and the art is the many different kinds of offers that direct marketers can create. Let's take a look at some popular offers that are used in direct marketing.

POPULAR OFFERS

Although some offers may be unique and no offer is 'right' for all situations, most are extensions of common offers that have stood the test of time. With that said, the following is an overview of nine categories of proven direct-response offers:

1. Free gift offers: providing a gift for inquiring, trying the product, purchasing the product, or for spending a certain dollar amount can be very effective, given the right situation.
2. Other free offers: offering a free catalog, information booklet, estimate, demonstration, tour, delivery, and more is generally effective.
3. Discount offers: everybody loves a bargain! Discounts can come in many different forms: cash discounts, quantity discounts, seasonal discounts, early bird discounts, and trade discounts, to name a few. Discounts are most effective when the product or service has a well-established value. However, discounting the price can also generate a negative image. If a watch is priced at $15, consumers may perceive either that it is a bargain or it is simply 'cheap.' Therefore, direct marketers must use discount offers in conjunction with the promotional message that the offer is trying to convey.
4. Sale offers: these are similar to discount offers. There has to be a reason for the sale, such as preseason sales, postseason sales, and holiday sales. Direct marketers often repeat seasonal sale offers on an annual basis if they are successful. Examples of sale offers include the Mother's Day sale or Presidents' Day sale. Sale offers, such as inventory reduction or clearance sales, provide an explanation for the sale and thus make it more believable to the prospect. Unlike discount offers, sale offers tend to be held at certain times of the year and usually provide explanatory terms for their existence.
5. Sample offers: these are designed to get the product into the hands of a prospective buyer. Usually, they are offered in conjunction with continuity selling. An example is a free sample issue of a magazine offered along with a trial-year subscription.
6. Time-limit offers: these work because they force the consumer to make a decision by a certain time. It is normally more effective to use an exact date, as opposed to a time period (ten days), when implementing a time-limit offer. Examples of time-limit offers include magazine

publishers who offer consumers a special price on a subscription if the consumers place their order by a specified date, and amusement parks that offer consumers a free gift for purchasing a season pass by a specified date. In addition, book publishers commonly extend prepublication offers to consumers who place an order for a new book prior to the official publication date of the book. In this case, the publisher uses the prepublication orders to help in determining the printing quantity.

7. Guarantee offers: we've seen that guarantees are very common in direct marketing. Direct marketers commonly use money-back or extended guarantees. However, it is important to use common sense when offering time limits with the guarantee. For example, when selling fishing lures, be sure to allow enough time for the consumer to use the lures for a fishing season, prior to returning them, if not satisfied.

8. Build-up-the-sale offer: the objective of a build-up-the-sale offer is to increase the dollar amount of the average order. An example is offering a volume of books for $19.95, and then offering the same volume of books, leather bound, for $24.95.

9. Sweepstakes offers: contests or sweepstake offers add the element of excitement to an ordinary direct marketing appeal. There are, however, certain rules that must be followed in executing a sweepstakes offer. In addition, they may not be used in some geographical areas due to local restrictions.

Within each of these nine offer categories are many specific types of offers that direct marketers have effectively used throughout the years, such as subscription offers.

Subscription Models

Subscription offers, also referred to as **subscription models**, such as those offered by Dollar Shave Club, Amazon, Netflix, Spotify, and Ring, to name a few, are popular forms of a time-limit offer. With subscription models, consumers must pay an up-front subscription price in order to receive regular delivery or access to the products and/or services for a specified period of time. Subscription models are different from typical pay-per-service models. Subscription models offer consumers extra conveniences, such as free and/or timely delivery, easy access to services, and up-front knowledge of the cost of the products/services to which they subscribe. Basically, a subscription model simplifies the business process for both consumers and companies. Subscription models also enable marketers to focus on customer retention, as opposed to new customer acquisition, which, as was presented in Chapter 4, is a more effective and profitable business strategy. Subscription models are geared to customer needs and wants and typically offer various options or levels.

For example, Netflix, an international provider of on-demand Internet streaming media, offers three streaming plans to consumer needs. The plan selected determines the number of devices consumers can stream Netflix on at the same time. Regardless of which plan is selected, consumers can install the Netflix app on as many devices as they want, and enjoy as many television shows and movies as they want, anytime, anywhere.[7]

Direct marketing giant Amazon offers an extremely popular subscription model, Amazon Prime. More than 100 million Amazon Prime customers worldwide receive 31 distinct benefits, which include exclusive shopping deals and selection, streaming of movies, TV shows and music, and free fast shipping for eligible purchases, among many others.[8] In addition, Amazon, like many other companies employing subscription offers, extends multiple offers to consumers. For example, Amazon offers a free 30-day trial period of Amazon Prime, and, for students, a 50 percent discount.[9] Direct marketers often use multiple offers to entice consumers to respond, especially when promoting subscription models, since the initial commitment tends to be for an extended period of time.

Subscription models are not limited to final consumers, as B2B subscription offers are quite effective as well. For example, creative software manufacturer Adobe offers two subscription-based services: Creative Cloud for business (ideal for small to midsize businesses) and Creative Cloud for enterprise (ideal for large businesses and institutions), both with different service features that are designed for type of client.[10] Business customers pay a monthly subscription fee to access Adobe's customized products.[11]

Another value-creating offer that is emerging, especially for B2B direct marketers, is that of platform business models.

Platform Business Models

Platform business models create value by enabling direct interactions between two or more customer or participant groups.[12] In essence, platforms connect two or more multi-sided parties, where the parties are dependent on the platform. For example, the participants in platform business models may include connecting sellers with buyers, service providers with service seekers, hosts with guests, and content creators with consumers.[13]

Let's explore an example, such as Uber, to better understand the value created by a platform business model. Uber must provide offers to people to become Uber drivers, because, without drivers, Uber couldn't offer its valuable services. Uber must also promote its mobile app to prospective riders because, without riders, Uber drivers would not have any customers. Of course, without both offers, there would be no revenue for Uber. This example shows that platform business models offer value by serving as a type of middleman, but their value extends much farther. (Check out the Readings and Resources at the end of this chapter to learn more about platform business models.)

In summary, there are many different value propositions that may be used by direct marketers depending on their specific business objectives. Jim Kobs, a leading authority in direct marketing, developed an extensive listing of tested, successful propositions. See Figure 5.11 for Kobs's 99 proven direct-response offers.

99 PROVEN DIRECT RESPONSE OFFERS	
Basic Offers	**Free Gift Offers**
1. Right Price	9. Free Gift for an Inquiry
2. Free Trial	10. Free Gift for a Trial Order
3. Money-Back Guarantee	11. Free Gift for Buying
4. Cash with Order	12. Multiple Free Gifts with a Single Order
5. Bill Me Later	13. Your Choice of Free Gifts
6. Installment Terms	14. Free Gifts Based on Size of Order
7. Charge Card Privileges	15. Two-Step Gift Offer
8. C.O.D.	16. Continuing Incentive Gifts
	17. Mystery Gift Offer

99 PROVEN DIRECT RESPONSE OFFERS

Other Free Offers

18. Free Information
19. Free Catalog
20. Free Booklet
21. Free Fact Kit
22. Send Me a Salesman
23. Free Demonstration
24. Free "Survey of Your Needs"
25. Free Cost Estimate
26. Free Dinner
27. Free Film Offer
28. Free House Organ Subscription
29. Free Talent Test
30. Gift Shipment Service

Discount Offers

31. Cash Discount
32. Short-Term Introductory Offer
33. Refund Certificate
34. Introductory Order Discount
35. Trade Discount
36. Early Bird Discount
37. Quantity Discount
38. Sliding Scale Discount
39. Selected Discounts

Sale Offers

40. Seasonal Sales
41. Reason-Why Sales
42. Price Increase Notice
43. Auction-By-Mail

Sample Orders

44. Free Sample
45. Nominal Charge Samples
46. Sample Offer with Tentative Commitment
47. Quantity Sample Offer
48. Free Sample Lesson

Time Limit Offers

49. Limited Time Offers
50. Enrollment Periods
51. Pre-Publication Offer
52. Charter Membership (or Subscription) Offer
53. Limited Edition Offer

Guarantee Offers

54. Extended Guarantee
55. Double-Your-Money-Back Guarantee
56. Guaranteed Buy-Back Agreement
57. Guaranteed Acceptance Offer

Build-Up-The-Sale Offers

58. Multi-Product Offers
59. Piggyback Offers
60. The Deluxe Offer
61. Good-Better-Best Offer
62. Add-On Offer
63. Write-Your-Own-Ticket Offer
64. Bounce-Back Offer
65. Increase and Extension Offers

Sweepstakes Offers

66. Drawing Type Sweepstakes
67. Lucky Number Sweepstakes
68. "Everybody Wins" Sweepstakes
69. Involvement Sweepstakes
70. Talent Contests

Club & Continuity Offers

71. Positive Option
72. Negative Option
73. Automatic Shipments
74. Continuity Load-Up Offer
75. Front-End Load-Ups
76. Open-Ended Commitment
77. "No Strings Attached" Commitment
78. Lifetime Membership Fee
79. Annual Membership Fee

Specialized Offers

80. The Philanthropic Privilege
81. Blank Check Offer
82. Executive Preview Charge
83. Yes/No Offers
84. Self-Qualification Offer
85. Exclusive Rights for Your Trading Area
86. The Super Dramatic Offer
87. Trade-In Offer
88. Third party Referral Offer
89. Member-Get-A-Member Offer
90. Name-Getter Offers
91. Purchase-With-Purchase
92. Delayed Billing Offer
93. Reduced Down Payment
94. Stripped-Down Products
95. Secret Bonus Gift
96. Rush Shipping Service
97. The Competitive Offer
98. The Nominal Reimbursement Offer
99. Establish-the-Value Offer

Figure 5.11 Kobs's 99 proven offers. Used with permission of Jim Kobs, Kobs Strategic Consulting.

SUMMARY

In summary, planning the offer is a critical part of the success of any direct marketing campaign. It is reliant on a solid understanding of consumer needs and wants. All direct marketing offers are response-driven. Direct marketers must plan each offer. This planning includes establishing objectives, deciding on offer attractiveness, reducing offer risk, and selecting a creative appeal. Every offer consists of basic components and decisions that must be made by the direct marketer. These components include the product or service, pricing or payment terms, trial or examination period, guarantees, sweepstakes or contests, gifts or premiums, and time limits. Direct marketers must carefully create the offer to ensure success. The step-by-step process to follow when creating the offer involves performing marketing research, determining the terms of the offer, targeting the offer, testing the offer, and finally, revising and executing the offer. Direct marketers can create many different types of offers. Many direct marketers vary the offer based on the season. Some popular options include free gift offers, discount offers, sale offers, sample offers, time-limit offers, guarantee offers, build-up-the-sale offers, and sweepstakes offers. These different types of offers have been presented in this chapter. In the next chapter, you will learn how the creative strategy is used to position the offer to the target market.

KEY TERMS

appeal	positioning
continuity selling	positive option
cross-selling	price elasticity
emotional appeal	price penetration
market segmentation	price skimming
motivations	rational appeal
negative option	subscription model
offer	til-forbid (TF)
platform business model	up-selling

REVIEW QUESTIONS

1. Why is it important for direct marketers to understand consumer motivations when creating an offer? What can drive these motivations?
2. What is an *offer*? What constitutes an effective offer?
3. What are the main differences between *continuity selling*, *cross-selling*, and *up-selling*?

4. What are the basic components to include in planning an offer? Which component is optional and why?
5. What is a subscription model? What benefits do subscription offers provide for companies and customers?
6. There are several popular offers. Name a few of the popular offers described in this chapter. How can you determine which offer will work best in a particular situation?
7. In their book *Write on Target*, what are the four questions Donna Baier Stein and Floyd Kemske suggest every direct marketer or copywriter ask? What do they believe to be the key to effective direct marketing?
8. How do market segmentation, positioning, and creative appeal strategies play a role in planning an offer?
9. Review Lois Geller's four-step approach to testing the offer. Apply these steps in the creation of a test to determine the best price for a new set of golf clubs.
10. Name the five specific product details direct marketers must consider when planning the offer. Select any direct marketing catalog and determine whether it provides each of these important product details.

EXERCISE

If you could develop a subscription model business for some product or service specific to your college campus, what would it be? What would the subscription entail? Who would you target and with which specific offers? Review Jim Kob's 99 proven direct-response offers to give you some offer ideas, but don't let those deter you from creating new ones!

CRITICAL THINKING EXERCISE

Visit at least three websites of stores that are entirely virtual (i.e., have no bricks and mortar). Compare and contrast how each creates the offer, using the steps given in the chapter. Name the one you think is most effective and provide justification for your choice.

READINGS AND RESOURCES

* Effective offers: www.directcreative.com/the-top-8-direct-marketing-offers-of-all-time.html
* Value propositions: https://optinmonster.com/32-value-propositions-that-are-impossible-to-resist
* B2B offers: http://customerthink.com/creating-strong-b2b-offers-to-gain-attention-drive-response-6-key-criteria
* Subscription models: www.businessinsider.com/amazon-prime-benefits-what-is-included
* Adobe: www.adobe.com/creativecloud/business.html
* Platform business models: www.innovationtactics.com/platform-business-model-complete-guide

CASE: MIKE'S BIKE TOURS

Figure 5.12   Two Mike's Bike Tours logos. Used with permission of Mike's Bike Tour.

Do you enjoy sightseeing? Are you planning to participate in a study-abroad trip to Germany or Amsterdam in the near future? Maybe you're thinking about taking a trip after you graduate from college? Do you want a really fun and exciting experience? If you answered 'yes' to any of these questions, let me introduce you to Mike's Bike Tours, located in Munich, Germany and Amsterdam, the Netherlands.

Mike Lasher, a 27-year-old American entrepreneurial expat, launched the business back in 1995 and has led a virtual revolution in city sightseeing with his world-famous bike tours. A native of Long Island, New York, Mike moved to Munich in October 1993 and was working in management for McDonald's in the Tal, Marienplatz. One day, while riding his bike along the high shore of the Isar River through Maximilan's charming Anlagen, he had a 'eureka moment' as a brilliant idea struck him. He suddenly realized that no one in Munich was addressing the needs of the seemingly lost, lonely, bored, and often visibly frustrated English-speaking travelers. He thought about how many times he'd been asked the same question from tourists: 'Can you recommend something cool to do here?' It was in that moment that Mike decided to start 'Mike's Bike Tours of Munich' and offer English-speaking tourists something really cool and fun to do while visiting the area. The following May 1995, after conducting much research and buying 20 used bikes, Mike quit his job at McDonald's and began giving bike tours to tourists in Munich.

Mike's initial marketing activities included photocopied brochures and word-of-mouth communication from happy customers. And yet, business began to grow and grow and grow! Simply put, Mike identified an unfulfilled need and created an offering to satisfy that need. He expanded his business with a second location in Amsterdam in 1997.

Figure 5.13 Mike's Bikes in Munich. Used with permission of Mike's Bike Tour.

Figure 5.14 Mike's Bike Tours guide with tourists. Used with permission of Mike's Bike Tour.

Customers

Mike's Bike Tours aren't just for young and active people, as all activities are optional and there are many various touring alternatives. The company has several hundred bicycles, most of which are Cruisers with very comfortable seats. Mike's Bike Tours also has bikes for all ages and sizes, including bikes suitable for children aged 5–12 years old. To serve families with younger children, Mike and his staff offer a wide range of bike styles. Toddlers can be in a child seat, and children aged 4–6 years old may ride in tag-along bikes.

Most bike rides are relaxing and not strenuous at all. Select bike tours, such as the Amsterdam City Bike Tour, are more suitable for those 13 years and older because the tour route includes some city traffic and tourists should be able to ride a bike confidently. In addition, the Countryside Amsterdam Bike Tour requires tourists to possess a reasonable level of fitness, health, and biking skill as it is a longer bike ride.

Mike's Bike Tours caters to groups as well as individual tourists. Group size almost always ranges from 2 to about 25; however, Mike and his staff are happy to meet the customized needs of groups of any size. Any type of group is welcome, including school groups, social clubs, or just a bunch of friends or family members who want to enjoy a private bike tour together. Mike's Bike Tours has special rates available for school groups and travel agents.

Figure 5.15 Photos of two Mike's Bike Tours scenic tours in Munich and Amsterdam. Used with permission of Mike's Bike Tour.

Sightseeing Service Offers

The tour offerings vary between the two Mike's Bike Tours locations in Munich and Amsterdam.

In Munich, the original bike tour that made Mike's Bike Tours famous is its classic city bike tour that covers most of the landmark structures in the city center. Other standard Munich bike tour options include the Olympia Park and BMW Welt tour, Outdoor Adventure River Ride tour, Third Reich tour, and the Neuschwanstein Castle tour. In Amsterdam, Mike's Bike Tours offers different city and countryside bike tours throughout the year. City bike tours are a great way to discover the city of Amsterdam, while countryside tours take tourists out of town to explore the beautiful landscape surrounding Amsterdam. See Figure 5.15 for a sample of the sightseeing tours offered by Mike's Bike Tours.

Although Mike's Bike Tours began as an innovative service concept, Mike and his staff have mastered the business of offering fun and exciting sightseeing tours. They're now experts at offering their customers the most memorable experience possible. Mike's staff realizes that biking is thirsty work, so many of the bike tours often include stops at the end of the bike tour for a drink at the English Garden beer garden!

Figure 5.16 Photo of Mike's Bike Tours customers in the beer garden. Courtesy of Matthew Hettche.

Mike and his staff continue to raise the bar every chance they get. They now offer a variety of different sightseeing tours, along with tours that use alternative modes of transportation beyond bicycle riding. Today, tourists can enjoy the city sights by riding in a van or bus, or on foot via walking tours. Of course, bicycling is still a favorite among many tourists.

Mike and his staff truly cater to tourists' needs and desires and they pride themselves on their flexibility in meeting the needs of both individuals and groups. That's why in addition to standard tour options, they also offer a 'Private Make Your Own Tour' option where tourists can combine some of the standard tours or go to entirely different places. Mike's Bike Tours can also serve those tourists who want longer bike tours, such as for two or three days in a row. Mike's Bike Tours can arrange private sightseeing bike tours for small or large groups.

Each bike tour is rich in culture and history; however, this information will be mixed with the observations and opinions of the tour guide. Mike's Bike Tours understands the value of personal perspective, thus tour guides do not read from a script. Instead, each tour guide is entertaining, informative, and genuine. All tour guides are knowledgeable and are given the freedom to speak to their own passions; that means that each guide gives a different tour, sometimes varying day to day. However, all tour guides are intimately familiar with the respective sights and areas being visited, and their personal experiences inform their tour. The tour guides at Mike's Bike Tours are charismatic ambassadors who strive to show tourists a side of Munich or Amsterdam that tourists may not be able to find on their own.

Figure 5.17   Mike's Bike Tours guides. Used with permission of Mike's Bike Tour.

Mike's Bike Tours are usually in English; however, Mike has now also employed some fantastic multilingual guides and can now often offer private tours for tourists in Dutch, German, Spanish, and other languages as well. Tourists simply need to request their language preference when booking a bike tour.

Product Offers

In both the Munich and Amsterdam bike shops, Mike's Bike Tours offers a large selection of bike accessories and other cool bike-related goodies to serve customer needs. These product offerings include different and unique bells, valve caps, seats, handgrips, streamers, and mirrors. Customers can find local Dutch brands, such as BikeCap that produces the most amazing and colorful saddle covers, and Widek, Promobell, and Yepp that offer a wide selection of beautiful bells. The bike shops offer a great selection of Abus chain locks and back wheel locks, as well as a variety of local brands of bike bags.

Conclusion

Today, Mike's Bike Tours offers the most popular and best-known sightseeing tour for English-speaking visitors in Europe. The company has served more than half a million satisfied customers since the business was launched. Mike's Bike Tours has been able to earn top ratings from Trip Advisor.com thanks to all of the rave reviews from delighted customers. And, the business continues serving its customers by paying attention to detail and offering the coolest sightseeing experience possible. So, what are you waiting for? Start planning your trip to Munich or Amsterdam now to experience an exhilarating Mike's Bike Tour for yourself.

Case Discussion Questions

1. Beyond offering customized tours, what other offers can Mike's Bike Tours use to attract more individuals and groups to book bike tours?
2. How can Mike's Bike Tours more effectively promote its various bike tour options to entice groups to schedule sightseeing tours? What specific offers, beyond group discounts, might be used to target groups? What different groups might be approached?
3. What companies, organizations, and/or associations might Mike's Bike Tours partner with in an attempt to reach and attract visiting tourist groups? How might these partnerships work? What offers would be attractive in generating increased sightseeing tour bookings?
4. What specific promotional offers might Mike's Bike Tours use to encourage delighted customers to post user-generated content on social media platforms after they enjoy a sightseeing tour? What social media platforms would you suggest the company focus on and why?

NOTES

1. Adapted from Lois K. Geller (1996) *Response: The Complete Guide to Profitable Direct Marketing* (New York: Free Press).
2. Ibid., p. 26.
3. Ibid., p. 27.
4. www.toolsofmen.com/is-dollar-shave-club-worth-it, retrieved May 26, 2019.
5. Adapted from Donna Baier Stein and Floyd Kemske (1997) *Write on Target* (Chicago, IL: NTC Publishing Group).

6. Adapted from Lois K. Geller (1996) *Response: The Complete Guide to Profitable Direct Marketing* (New York: Free Press).
7. https://help.netflix.com/en/node/24926, retrieved May 26, 2019.
8. www.businessinsider.com/amazon-prime-benefits-what-is-included, retrieved May 26, 2019.
9. www.businessinsider.com/amazon-prime-benefits-what-is-included, retrieved May 26, 2019.
10. www.adobe.com/creativecloud/business.html, retrieved May 26, 2019.
11. https://mashable.com/2013/05/06/adobe-subscription-pricing-only, retrieved May 26, 2019.
12. www.innovationtactics.com/platform-business-model-complete-guide, retrieved May 26, 2019.
13. www.innovationtactics.com/platform-business-model-complete-guide, retrieved May 26, 2019.

6
CREATIVE MESSAGE STRATEGIES

CHAPTER CONTENTS

CHAPTER SPOTLIGHT

WILLIAMSBURG TOURISM

One of America's favorite family destinations, the Greater Williamsburg region of Virginia (see Figure 6.1), which includes Jamestown, Williamsburg and Yorktown, offers a unique juxtaposition of contemporary and historical experiences for all ages. Visitors can choose from hands-on, interactive attractions, scenic outdoor adventures, and sophisticated arts and culture experiences, making Greater Williamsburg a top choice among travelers. However, one of the destination's greatest strengths–its strong association with the history of America's founding–is also one of its major challenges, as young families show less interest in historical attractions. Since young millennial families encompass the new target market for Williamsburg tourism, that means it's 'outside-the-box' thinking time to create a compelling campaign with message strategies that connect with its target audience and motivate them to take action and plan a visit to the area. That's precisely what Williamsburg Tourism did.

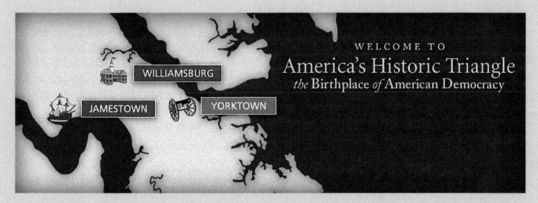

Figure 6.1 Map of the Historic Triangle area Published with the consent of Greater Williamsburg Chamber & Tourism Alliance. All Rights Reserved.

Destination research revealed that a majority of potential visitors who have decided against a trip to Williamsburg either cite a lack of interest in what the area offers (24 percent) or a belief that one visit is enough–a 'been there, done that' mentality (27 percent). Additionally, research on several attributes associated with vacations shows that Williamsburg has a strong association with characteristics such as *history* and *learning*, which are not deemed very important, while suffering from lower association with highly valued characteristics such as *fun*, *relaxation* and *affordable* (see Figure 6.2).

The creative challenge? To create a compelling appeal for millennial travelers to visit the Williamsburg area, overcoming perceptions that the destination is boring, not repeatable and focused solely on history.

235

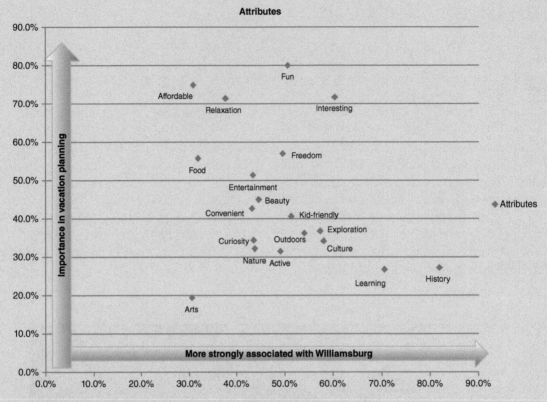

Figure 6.2 Importance of attributes when planning a vacation getaway. Published with the consent of Greater Williamsburg Chamber & Tourism Alliance. All Rights Reserved.

The task? Research was conducted that asked survey respondents to state how interested they would be in a vacation that focused on four different options of what Williamsburg has to offer. The findings revealed that more respondents are interested in a vacation that allows them to *chill (relax)* followed by to *be active*.

The result? A new Williamsburg destination marketing campaign targeting millennial family travelers was launched to reshape its image to be more appealing to millennial parents, whose young families are vital to the long-term growth of the destination. Based on research and analysis of visitor trends and consumer perceptions, a creative campaign was developed along with a new brand framework focused on *Williamsburg's Three Freedoms: Freedom to Have Fun; Freedom to Be Curious; Freedom to Relax*. See Figures 6.3–6.5 for some of the creative banner ads used in Williamsburg Tourism's new 'Freedom' campaign.

Creating promotions in direct and interactive marketing requires a special kind of creativity with which this chapter is concerned. With emphasis on the 'message' aspect of promotion, we discuss the need for conducting research and setting creative objectives. Then we explore copywriting and graphics techniques and strategies. Finally, we look at creating messages for specific media. The 'media' themselves–print media (direct mail, magazines, newspapers), broadcast media (television, radio), and digital and mobile media (blogging, e-mail, social networking, mobile and text)–will be dealt with in turn in later chapters, as will the adaptation of messages to all of them.

Figure 6.3 Williamsburg Tourism 'relax' banner ad. Published with the consent of Greater Williamsburg Chamber & Tourism Alliance. All Rights Reserved.

Figure 6.4 Williamsburg Tourism 'curiosity' banner ad. Published with the consent of Greater Williamsburg Chamber & Tourism Alliance. All Rights Reserved.

Figure 6.5 Williamsburg Tourism 'fun' banner ad. Published with the consent of Greater Williamsburg Chamber & Tourism Alliance. All Rights Reserved.

237

CREATIVE RESEARCH

The creative process to develop compelling messages for any direct-response promotion, in any format or in any medium, begins with research and leads to idea generation and finally copywriting. Direct marketers must really understand their target audiences. This includes customer preferences, buying patterns, offer and media preferences, contact preferences, and more. In the perspective of traditional economics, the demand from individual consumers is often viewed as a function of their monetary income or their accumulated wealth. In the real world, monetary income is not the *only* determinant of demand; in fact, it might not even be the major one. In addition to recognizing the real complexity of demand, the direct marketer also needs to study and understand buyer behavior.

What motivates buyers to take action? A buyer's ability to buy can be evaluated by well-understood demographic indicators such as income, wealth, age, gender, and marital status. However, buyer behavior is also influenced by environmental factors and psychographic indicators of lifestyle that are not readily identifiable or easily measurable. Marketers want to measure these environmental factors to determine the proneness to spend and the willingness to buy. To do this, they use such measurements as income in relation to what others are earning in some particular universe, such as a given ZIP code area. Or, marketers may study consumers' purchase behavior as well as their educational level and their social class standing. These can be important customer qualifications.

As social economist Thorstein Veblen observed,[1] the 'conspicuous consumption' of a neighborhood can also be a qualifier of behavior. The basic concept of human ecology that behavior is a response to environmental influences tells us that a household with a $20,000 annual income located in a ZIP code area in which the median household income is $30,000 is likely to emulate that median level. The reverse is also true, with a $50,000 household tending to behave like its $30,000 ZIP code area neighbors. This tendency contributes to homogeneity of behavior within such areas, even though there is a variance in characteristics among and between individual households.

Discretionary household purchases under such circumstances are dependent not just on the *ability to buy*, but also on the *proneness to spend*. Because this is such a potentially powerful economic force, direct marketers are well advised to understand it as they study the qualifications available within customer databases, the readership of magazines and newspapers, or the characteristics of television viewers and Internet browsers.

It is imperative for direct marketers to understand the economic and social differences among an infinite variety of consumers in the marketplace. They must also be aware of a vast number of factors motivating these individuals. The challenge to those responsible for creating compelling message strategies is to get inside the head of a buyer and to know what the benefits to the customer will be and what will motivate the customer to take action to gain them.

To plan effective messages, marketers must also understand how the consumer thinks and what he or she perceives. What are the key benefits each consumer is trying to obtain? In addition, direct marketers must research the competition to determine what other alternatives consumers have to fulfill their needs and desires. Armed with detailed knowledge about consumers, direct marketers can begin to plan and create effective messages that will not only get the attention and interest of consumers, but hopefully stimulate action—if action is the objective.

MESSAGE OBJECTIVES

Planning and creating compelling messages also relies on the objective of the message. Is it intended to generate a website visit, a telephone call, a text message reply, an in-store visit, to obtain a donation, secure a vote, generate a lead, or sell a product? Does the message have some other measurable intention? Is there more than one objective that must be taken into consideration? If so, there may be a need for more than one message strategy, based on differing consumer needs. In Chapter 3, we explored the need for segmenting consumers into homogeneous groups with similar needs, desires, and so on. Customer research can also determine which segments of consumers are more prone to respond based on the objectives of the message. Often, customized messaging is required in order to communicate effectively with different market segments of consumers. Therefore, long before you can create compelling messages, you must know all about your customers as well as the intention of your promotional message.

Mindful that a major goal of marketing is to convey product benefits to present and potential customers, advertising professionals have wavered in recent times between creative messages that create brand awareness, or are image building, and those more directed to immediate sales or response.

As our modern media channels, especially digital, social, mobile, and text, offer excellent opportunities for more customized and personalized communication, greater emphasis is being placed on ensuring that the direct-response copy relates to the target audience. However, relevant direct-response copy has always been the intended goal. According to direct marketing guru Jim Kobs, 'There are three mental exercises that are very important in the copy preparation stage: (1) Think about your objective; (2) Think about your offer; (3) Think about your market.'[2] Kobs goes on to state, 'The better you know your prospect and his or her needs, the better job you can do of appealing to that person. Naturally, your copy style should fit the audience.'[3] What's the bottom line? Writing engaging direct-response copy that resonates with its target audience, commonly referred to as *content marketing* for digital channels, is absolutely critical to successful direct marketing.

Many direct marketers do indeed feel that it's not creative unless it sells something! Though this is likely an exaggeration, we need to distinguish between advertising that promotes the brand and builds long-term image and advertising that seeks an immediate response or transaction. The response could be in the form of a website visit, text message reply, telephone call, in-store visit, product or service purchase, donation, vote, participation, and so on. Those creating direct marketing campaigns are more attuned to the latter objectives, but that is not to say they are oblivious to the former. Direct-response copywriters must not only possess skill as a wordsmith but also create copy to achieve message objectives.

This entails many different copywriting and graphics techniques. Let's delve into that topic.

COPYWRITING TECHNIQUES

Every successful promotion has at its heart a concept and an offer . . . and blends product, price, and place in a way that provides benefits to a target market. As we presented in the previous chapter, customers will respond to offers if they provide benefits that appeal to them. Such benefits can be the physical attributes of a product, translated into terms that meet customer needs. Customers don't buy quarter-inch drill bits; they buy the ability to make quarter-inch holes! They don't buy power steering; they buy ease in parking a car parallel to a curb. Direct marketers therefore use promotion that is benefit oriented. They sell benefits in a manner that matches a customer's motivation.

Features versus Advantages versus Benefits

When asked why he was so adept at writing copy for Scott's grass seed, Charles B. Mills, a direct-response copywriter at O. M. Scott's Lawn Products, replied, 'Because I like to talk about your lawn, not about my seed.' Airlines sell a vacation in some exotic place, not the trip to get there. Designers sell fashion and acceptance more than the practicality of clothing. Insurance companies sell security and peace of mind, not a paper contract. Elmer Wheeler, sales motivator, summed it up, saying, 'Sell the sizzle, not the steak.' Direct-response advertisers rely on copy that emphasizes such benefits to motivate responders.

Vic Schwab, a successful advertising copywriter with such ability, described the copywriting art as 'learning to think like a horse.' As an illustration, he told the story of a farmer who had lost his horse. 'How'd you find him so quickly?' asked a neighbor. To which the farmer replied: 'Well, I just asked myself, if I were a horse, where would I go? I went there and there he was!' Schwab used this story to drive home his copywriter's maxim that you have to 'show people an advantage.' This meant, to Schwab, that *you had to know them!*

Today, a database can provide the knowledge that enables the trained copywriter to 'think like a horse,' to relate the benefits of offers to customers. Direct-response copywriting is an art. Those who have the talent and have achieved a track record of success are much in demand. They have the ability to translate product features into advantages, these into benefits, and benefits into words, design, and graphics.

Phrases such as the following typify compelling promotional copy:

- 'An important message for persons under the age of 25.'
- 'Are you tired of the back-breaking work of caring for your lawn?'
- 'At last . . . a simple, effective way to rid your house of bugs.'
- 'Do you need more room in your house . . . or a new roof?'
- 'Here's good news for taxpayers!'

Offers incorporating customer benefits are structured to incite action and overcome human inertia. An analytical technique for identifying benefits, FAB (features-advantages-benefits), appears in Table 6.1.

As demonstrated in Table 6.1, the *features* of the iPad Pro included in its manufacture are a neural engine, face ID, A12X bionic chip, liquid retina display, edge-to-edge all-screen design, and being the thinnest iPad ever. But what value do these features offer to consumers? The direct-response advertising copywriter seeks to translate these product features into advantages and then from these into benefits. For example, face ID capabilities provide the advantage of the iPad being accessed with face recognition software, the benefit being that users won't have to remember passwords. The A12X bionic chip, as another example, provides the advantage of excellent performance and efficiency, with the resulting benefit being that users can quickly switch from page to page, which makes reading, photo editing, and gaming easy. Being the thinnest iPad ever offers the corresponding advantages of being extremely lightweight and exceptionally slender, which translate into the benefits of being easy to hold and tote. FAB provides the direct-response copywriter with a useful procedure for identifying benefits as a necessary prelude to actual copywriting.

Table 6.1 Features/benefits of the iPad Pro

Features ➡ (what the product has)	Advantages ➡ (what the features do)	Benefits (why customers buy)
Neural Engine	Smarter and capable	Provides faster and more powerful processing
Face ID	Won't need passwords	Don't have to remember passwords; can unlock and log in with just a glance
A12X bionic chip with Neural Engine	Excellent performance and efficiency–faster than most PC laptops	Can quickly switch from page to page; easy photo editing and gaming; great for multitasking
Liquid Retina display with ProMotion	Better clarity of images	Images look real with true-to-life color; pages feel responsive; easier to read; more enjoyable
Edge-to-edge all-screen design	Larger viewing surface area	Larger picture without larger iPad unit; can do anything you need any way your hold it; easier to read; more versatile
Thinnest iPad ever	Lightweight and exceptionally slender	Easy to hold and tote
Up to 1TB capacity	Has ability to store tons of content	No limits on what can be kept
Rounded corners (smooth, yet angular)	Better design	Easy to hold

Writing the Copy

Effective copywriting begins by determining the **big idea** and then creatively weaving that big idea into all aspects and elements of the creative campaign. Think of the big idea as a highlighted unique selling point or creative phrase that becomes the star or focal point of an entire promotional campaign. The big idea should become the company's tagline, logo, symbol, or slogan. Once the big idea is created, it must be used with unshakable consistency throughout the entire promotional campaign—across all media formats and featured in all creative executions.

An example of a global creative campaign that effectively communicates a big idea to consumers is that of 'Pepsi Generations' (Figure 6.6). The campaign celebrates the brand's rich history in pop culture for 120 years. The campaign uses old-fashioned graphics, retro cans, and music from several pop culture icons, such as Michael Jackson, Ray Charles, and Britney Spears. The Pepsi Generations campaign effectively attracts consumers of different ages and generations and engages them via the limited-edition retro packaging that was released in select markets around the world. Tied into the campaign was the return of the *Pepsi Stuff* loyalty program (in the U.S. only), where consumers could earn points through codes on participating limited-edition retro packages. Consumers could then enter the codes onto PepsiStuff.com to redeem limited-edition Pepsi apparel and premiums, such as vintage T-shirts, hats, LED signs, varsity jackets, coolers, bikes, and more.[4] The Pepsi Generations campaign was rolled out in more than 55 markets globally across the full Pepsi portfolio—Pepsi, Pepsi Zero Sugar, and Diet Pepsi.[5] The campaign was launched in the U.S. via a Super Bowl commercial, was featured in ads across the world, and came to life for consumers at the point of purchase in major retail stores featuring the retro packaging. Pepsi Generations was a highly successful campaign that consistently communicated the message that Pepsi is the choice of all generations of consumers and will continue to be for the future.

Figure 6.6 Pepsi Generations. PEPSI and the Pepsi Globe are registered trademarks of PepsiCo,Inc. Used with permission.

The big idea should be branded to create a synergy with real identity and meaning for the company or organization. In his book *Guerrilla Creativity*, Jay Conrad Levinson refers to the big idea as a 'meme.' He defines a meme as a self-explanatory symbol, using words, action, sounds, or pictures that communicate an entire idea.[6] Levinson also contends that the following three things should be understood about a meme:[7]

1. It is the lowest common denominator of an idea, a basic unit of communication.
2. It can alter human behavior, and in guerrilla marketing that means motivating people to buy whatever the guerilla offers.
3. It is simplicity itself, easily understandable in a matter of seconds.

How does a company create the big idea? In many different ways, including via the Internet, competitors, customers, distributors, books, movies, and more. The big idea is often the result of individual or group brainstorming sessions. However, some of the best big ideas are created by simply honing a wild, off-the-wall idea. Creative experts say that many off-the-wall or potential big ideas usually come to mind when they least expect them. Some of these different moments may include when a copywriter is out jogging, socializing, or taking a shower! Levinson claims that the key to creating a persuasive idea comes from the well-known 'shoes and eyes' theory. 'Walk a mile in your customer's shoes and see things through his eyes.'[8] Regardless of how the big idea is developed, it should be catchy, a real attention-getter, and brief—not too many words— easy to recognize and remember. Of course, the big idea usually ties in with the company's overall copy appeal.

Let's explore an example of a company that literally created a winning big idea and successfully used it to reinforce its branded products. When you think of winning, do you think of Gatorade (Figure 6.7)? Let's face it, earning a Gatorade shower after a grueling sports game is the ultimate symbol of winning. Gatorade, the beverage that sits in coolers on the sidelines of football fields and basketball courts all over the world, is firmly associated with both sports and winning. Gatorade is manufactured by PepsiCo and distributed in more than 80 countries. It commands 46 percent of the worldwide sports drink market, according to Euromonitor International.[9] Over the years, the company has been able to effectively capture and associate 'winning' in its many advertising campaigns, slogans and headlines, including 'Is it in you?' Gatorade's most recent campaign is 'Win From Within', which tells consumers that it's what's inside of them that counts, rather than the latest sports gear, apps, or technology. Gatorade hopes to highlight the message that sports nutrition really can help improve an athlete's game.[10]

Figure 6.7   Gatorade. Used with permission of Stokely-Van Camp, Inc.

Take a look at the ads in Figure 6.8 and you will see the use of effective persuasive copy. You might notice how the Virginia Beach *Live the Life* brand, or big idea, is consistently used. Also, each ad has brief and catchy copy that dares the tourist to 'be bold' or 'be daring.' Finally, in each ad both the 'Virginia is for Lovers' tagline and the Virginia Beach website are strategically placed in the same location.

Figure 6.8 Virginia Beach 'Be Bold' and 'Be Daring' ads. Used with permission of the City of Virginia Beach Convention & Visitors Bureau.

Copy Appeals

The **copy appeal** is the basic underlying theme of the promotion or campaign. Most copy appeals are timeless because they stem from basic human needs—what people want to gain, save, avoid, or become. Some examples are the following:

- **People want to gain** self-confidence, improved appearance, time, professional advancement, increased enjoyment, personal prestige, popularity, praise from others, financial wealth.
- **People want to save** time, money, memories.
- **People want to avoid** criticism, physical pain, trouble, discomfort, embarrassment, work, worry, effort, emotional suffering.
- **People want to become** good citizens, creative, efficient, knowledgeable, good parents, physically fit, influential over others, popular, successful, recognized authorities, respected.

Copywriters must determine and use the appropriate copy appeal based on the desired response. There are three basic types of appeals: rational, emotional, and moral. *Rational* appeals emphasize logic and reasoning. They usually present facts and figures. *Emotional* appeals are irrational and may focus on love, pride, joy, and humor. *Moral* appeals emphasize ethics and target consumers' feelings of what is 'right' or 'proper' from an ethical perspective. In some cases, copywriters may use a combination of the three basic appeals.

Figure 6.9 provides several creative examples of effective copy appeals used in direct-response advertisements. Each of these advertisements for Hauser's Jewelers, a family-owned, upscale jewelry store located in Newport News, Virginia, presents a simple message laced with subtle humor.

(Continued)

Figure 6.9 (Continued)

Cupid shoots!
He scores!

*For the gift that never misses its target,
come see us.*

HAUSER'S
JEWELERS
1898
City Center in Newport News ~ 757-595-6006
www.hausersjewelers.com

Birthday wishes
from a couple of studs

HAUSER'S
JEWELERS
1898
City Center in Oyster Point ~ 757-595-6006
www.hausersjewelers.com

Figure 6.9 Hauser's Jewelers ads. Used with permission of Hauser's Jewelers.

Each of these advertisements has an attractive and effective layout featuring a creative headline, a picture of the featured jewelry, the Hauser's Jewelers name, and its location, phone number and website to encourage action. Moreover, each headline offers a message appeal that stems from the basic human desire of most men—to give a truly special and memorable gift. The copy in each advertisement stems from basic human desires, and it is presented in a humorous tone. This combination is what makes copy appeals highly effective.

Copywriting Formulas

Successful copywriting often follows a formula to keep copy flowing in a logical sequence. Several of these formulas, which have been used extensively for many years, are presented here.

Bob Stone's Seven-Step Formula

1. Promise a benefit in your headline or first paragraph, your most important benefit.[11]
2. Immediately emphasize and build on your most important benefit.
3. Tell the reader exactly what he or she is going to get.
4. Back up your statements with proofs and endorsements.
5. Tell the reader what will be lost by not acting.
6. Rephrase your prominent benefits in the closing offer.
7. Incite action now.

A-I-D-A is of unknown origin and is a formula that has been used a great deal by direct-response copywriters for many years:

1. Attract Attention
2. Arouse Interest
3. Stimulate Desire
4. Call for Action

P-P-P-P, created by Henry Hoke, Sr. and popularized by Edward N. Mayer Jr., two pioneer direct marketers, is a tried-and-true formula for direct-response copywriting:

1. Picture—get attention early in copy to create desire.
2. Promise—tell what the product or service will do, describe its benefits to the reader.
3. Prove—show value, backed up with personal testimonials or endorsements.
4. Push—ask for the order.

L. E. 'Cy' Frailey, who authored many books on letter writing, described the STAR-CHAIN-HOOK, invented by another professional letter writer, Frank Dignan, as follows:[12]

1. Get the reader's favorable attention. Do it with an opening paragraph that is bright and brisk—*the star*.

2. Follow quickly with a flow of facts, reasons, and benefits, all selected and placed in the best order to transform attention into interest and finally into desire—*the chain*.
3. Suggest action and make it as easy as possible—*the hook*.

Figure 6.10 Calico Corners creative design. Used with permission of Calico Corners and MindZoo, LLC.

Source: Photo by Jim Kirby, www.jimkirbyphoto.com.

The **KISS PRINCIPLE**, of unknown origin, is a creative copywriting formula that stands for 'keep it simple, stupid!' The KISS copywriting formula has been effectively used by creative geniuses for centuries. The basic premise is to keep the message simple and easy to understand and remember.

Figure 6.10 presents an excellent example of the KISS copywriting formula in creative design. The creative design on this oversized self-mailer postcard for Calico Corners, a high-end retailer of custom draperies, furniture, and home accessories, is divided into three portions. Each portion features a photograph and a simple message shown in a shadow box for prospective consumers. The message is bold and punchy: 'Dream It.' 'Design It.' 'Done.' It conveys the ease and simplicity involved in the thinking, buying, and implementing processes when new homeowners shop at Calico Corners.

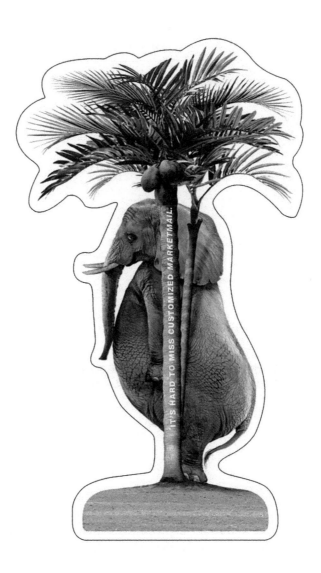

(Continued)

Figure 6.11 (Continued)

Figure 6.11 ShipShapes direct mail, elephant. Used with permission of ShipShapes™.

DESIGN AND GRAPHICS

Hand in hand with copy—the words, the expressions, the ideas, the meanings—go design and graphics—the art, the layout, the symbols, the effects. Here we include the impact of photographs, illustrations, type styles, paper, inks, size, and a variety of other attention-getting devices.

Through design and graphics, the designer, like the copywriter, creates mood and feeling while getting and holding attention. In direct marketing, the ultimate goal of the designer, like that of the copywriter, is to stimulate action, to generate measurable response. Thus, design (like copy) becomes a means and not an end—another element of the total promotion process.

The designer of direct marketing promotion has available a great many graphic techniques for use in a variety of media: direct mail, print, broadcast, digital video, and online, as well as posters and billboards. These include the following.

Layouts

A **layout** positions copy and illustrations, not only to gain attention but also to direct the reader through the message in the sequence intended by the copywriter. Compelling layouts make optimal use of type as well as white space, photographs along with illustrations, and other graphic techniques, including shapes, sizes, folds, die-cuts, and pop-ups. Figure 6.11 shows the effective use of a die-cut shape, as well as effective layout with multiple headlines, body copy, art, company logo, and response information.

Illustrations and Photographs

A compelling illustration can create attention. Photographs of products in use, especially showing people, can dramatize benefits. The designer, using graphic illustrations, can even extend to designed borders, highlighting copy elements for prominence, tint blocks, and emphasis of elements such as product features and response forms. An excellent example of the effective use of compelling photographs that draw your attention is that of Hi-Ho Silver's Southern Gates Facebook ad, shown in Figure 6.12. In addition, this ad effectively uses both white space and a horizontal grid layout to emphasize the photographs.

Figure 6.12　Hi-Ho Silver's Southern Gates Facebook ad. Used with permission of Hi-Ho Silver. All Rights Reserved.

Involvement Devices

Many direct-response advertising devices spur action by **involvement devices** that engage the reader in some way. These include tokens, stamps, punch-outs, puzzles, premiums, and gadgets that the reader returns to the seller. Links and click buttons are natural involvement devices of websites.

Type

Designers use typefaces to suggest boldness or dignity, Old English or Asian, antiquity or space age, movement or emphasis, masculinity or femininity. They know that typefaces need to be relevant to the message, and they also need to be easily and instantly readable. Sizes of typefaces are a factor to consider, as are the thickness and complexity of the type's structure. When the designer uses more than one typeface or type size, these should blend, and the variety should not become complicated. Sometimes, to create emphasis, typefaces can be overprinted on one another and sometimes they are reversed, that is, white on color. Certain special designs become recognizable logotypes for organizations, such as the typefaces used in advertising for Victoria's Secret, Nike, and IBM.

Paper

Here the designer is concerned with substance, texture, and finish as well as color, weight, size, and shape of paper. A linen or laid finish can denote elegance. A parchment stock can denote permanence. Paper can have a high-gloss finish for use in a catalog of upscale merchandise, or it can simulate the look of a newspaper to convey timeliness. Paper not only helps set the tone of a direct-response advertisement, but its texture, weight, and size can have substantial impact on cost. Paper can even be made to be earth-friendly by being printed and packed with plantable seeds. As Figure 6.13 shows, Bloomin seed paper comes in many different die-cut shapes, colors, and designs, and can be made with many different types of seeds. This plantable paper is sure to get noticed when customers sort through their mail.

Ink

Like paper, ink can convey impressions through color, gloss, intensity, and placement. Ink selection must consider the paper and the printing process as well as the design. Some inks are even available with fragrances, such as the smell of lavender or pine trees. Some can be embossed to simulate gold and silver coins. Some can be scraped off to reveal a printed message underneath. Some can be printed on unusual paper stock, such as cellophane, waxed paper, or foil.

Color

Much information has developed about the physical and psychological effects of color since Sir Isaac Newton first associated basic colors with sunlight. We know that light, heat, and color

Figure 6.13 Bloomin seed paper. Used with permission of Bloomin. All rights reserved.

have much in common. The darker the color, the more light and heat are absorbed. Certain colors, notably yellow, can be seen farther than others; black printed on yellow provides maximum readability. Some colors convey associations: purple implies royalty, red is associated with danger, green denotes safety, and blue evokes trust and leadership and is a 'health' color (e.g., health insurance provided by Blue Cross). Psychologically, the 'warm' colors (yellow, orange, red) stimulate and the 'cool' colors (blue, green, violet) sedate. Thus, the former might more likely encourage action if used in a direct-response advertisement. Colors have different meanings to various cultures, to various ages, in various geographic locations; the direct-response advertising designer needs to be aware of these.

CREATING MESSAGES FOR SPECIFIC MEDIA

The copywriting and graphics techniques discussed in the preceding sections apply to all the media used by direct-response advertisers; however, special considerations must be made when creating promotional messages that include sight, sound, or movement. We'll examine the video and audio creative elements associated with the design of print, direct-response television, radio, online video, and digital platforms in the next section. We will discuss each medium in greater length in subsequent chapters.

Print

All of the design strategies and techniques previously discussed apply to print media. Compelling print designs are those that successfully grab readers' attention, and hold it long enough to convince them to take whatever action is being asked of them. However, print media often has a short shelf life in that much of the printed promotional materials are thrown away soon after consumers read them. The challenge for direct marketers is to get consumers to hold on to the printed material to encourage multiple reads and impressions. Figure 6.14 presents an excellent example of creativity in print design that entices readers to retain the printed material. Hauser's Jewelers created its multi-page holiday direct mailer with a unique twist.

The beauty that is ruby: 18k, ruby & diamond clip/post earrings, $3,925. Art Deco inspired platinum, ruby & diamond ring, $7,195. Platinum, ruby & diamond bracelet, $11,750.

Red Velvet Cake

Ingredients: 1 cup margarine (2 sticks) ~ 1 1/2 cups sugar ~ 2 eggs ~ 1 oz. red food coloring ~ 1 tsp. baking soda ~ 1 tsp. vinegar ~ 2 tsp. cocoa ~ 1/4 tsp. cinnamon ~ 1/2 tsp. salt ~ 2 1/2 cups flour ~ 1 tsp. vanilla ~ 1 cup plus 2 Tbs. buttermilk

Recipe: Cream the margarine, sugar, and eggs on medium speed. Mix the food coloring, cinnamon, and cocoa in a separate bowl, then add to creamed mixture and mix well. Add salt and vanilla. Then alternate with the buttermilk and flour. Beat well. Add baking soda and vinegar. Mix well. Bake in 3 round cake pans at 350 degrees for 25 - 30 min. Cool well, then frost

Frosting: Mix 2 Tbs. cornstarch with 1 cup water. Cook until thick and cool. Mix 2 sticks of softened butter and 1 cup of granualted sugar. Add 1 tsp. vanilla and a few drops of lemon extract. Cream 10 min. well, then add cornstarch mixture. Blend until all lumps are gone. Frost.

when you cut into this cake, the smile on your face will reach all the way down to your tummy!
Joanne

(Continued)

255

Figure 6.14 (Continued)

Fabulous Faberge': The rich beauty of chocolate brown enhanced by 18k gold & diamonds.
Earrings, $7,730. Egg pendant, $6,150. Matching chain, $1,750. Cufflinks, $3,520.

Pecan Pie

3 eggs ~ 1/4 lb. of butter, melted (1 stick) ~
3/4 cup brown sugar ~ 3/4 cup dark Karo syrup ~
3/4 cup pecans, chopped ~ 1 tsp. vanilla ~
1 9-inch pie shell ~ pecan halves

Beat eggs thoroughly. Add melted butter, brown
sugar, and dark Karo syrup. Beat mixture. Add
chopped pecans and mix. Add vanilla and mix.
Pour into unbaked pie shell. Cover top with pecan
halves. Bake at 350 degrees for about 40 minutes
or until firm.

*a dollop of vanilla ice cream is
the perfect topping for this wonderful
combination of nutty pecan crunch
and delightful robust sweetness — Lee*

Figure 6.14 Hauser's holiday catalog recipe book. Used with permission of Hauser's Jewelers.

This 12-page booklet was designed to feature extraordinary jewelry collections as well as be a keepsake holiday recipe booklet for its customers. Each page contained a jewelry collection along with a corresponding page with a recipe and a picture of the baked good that coordinated with the colors of the jewelry. For example, the ruby collection was presented with a picture and recipe for red velvet cake, and the brown Fabergé collection was shown with a picture and recipe for pecan pie. The catalog itself was a holiday greeting from the Hauser's Jewelers family to each of its customers. Each recipe, shared by an associate of Hauser's Jewelers, featured a handwritten note about the recipe and how it brought back holiday memories. Let this example serve to inspire creativity and longevity in print media design.

Television

Television is especially suited to the visualization of action as well as demonstration. Products appropriate for direct-response TV include the following, which are often bought on impulse: innovative products, home goods, specialty items such as jewelry, and a variety of services. While younger generations are increasingly watching less TV (a 50% decrease in the past five years), older generations are much less affected by this decrease and prefer the medium.[13]

A major limitation in creating direct-response TV commercials is *time*. Commercial time is usually available in multiples of seconds: 10, 20, 30, 60, 90, and usually up to a maximum of 120 (two minutes). A maximum airtime of two minutes allows for approximately 200 spoken words. Because audio and visual images can be used simultaneously in TV, the old adage that 'one picture is worth a thousand words' applies *if* the product is one that can be demonstrated. For example, Ring video doorbell protection services effectively use TV commercials to demonstrate how Ring's home security video cameras can capture, on camera, everything that comes to the consumer's home – from package thieves to unexpected critters. Some of these television spots are hilarious.

Marketers generally feel they need 20 seconds for attention-getting, up to 75 seconds for demonstration, and the remaining 25 seconds of a typical 120-second spot announcement for specifying what action the customer can take by showing a mailing or website address, or telephone number. Because 120 seconds on prime-time television is usually too expensive for a direct-response advertiser, most of these commercials appear during low-cost fringe time (early morning, late night, and weekend hours). Often, markets can be segmented through specific programs, such as movies or wrestling, usually aired during non-prime times.

Many direct marketers have experienced profitable response rates using infomercials, which are program-style narrated commercials that may run as long as 30 minutes in other than prime time, usually on special-interest cable channels. Commonly featured products, such as exercise equipment or nutrition supplements, are those that can benefit from extensive demonstration and audience involvement.

Concept

The logical starting point in creating direct-response TV commercials is determining just what the advertising is about and what it is to do—its concept. The commercial might be used as support, to call attention to a newspaper insert or a forthcoming direct mail package. Or it may be used to generate website traffic or secure leads for sales follow-up. Or the commercial may be used to produce orders or create in-store traffic. Unlike the case for direct mail or print media, there is no written record of the product's features and benefits for the audience to refer to at a later time. The TV viewer can't be expected to remember too much, so logic and clarity are important.

Storyboards

The visual portion of a television commercial is shown through a series of illustrations, called **story-boards**, which outline the structure of the commercial, the graphics and photographs, and the video action. Most of these storyboards are now computerized, which makes commercial design much faster and easier. A storyboard essentially is a timeline that goes from top to bottom, with the top occurring first in the sequencing. The steps to creating a storyboard are as follows:

1. Objectives: Think of your story as a video and decide what you want it to accomplish.
2. Setting: Establish the backdrop for your story.
3. Major ideas: Outline the main ideas or frames that may be used to portray your story.
4. Characters: Identify the characters that will appear in your story along with each character's specific role.
5. Plot: Determine the story's problem and solution, along with its climax.
6. Message: Decide on the story's primary meaning or purpose—the action you want the viewer to take based on your story.

Figure 6.15 presents a storyboard created by White & Partners, a marketing and advertising agency located in Herndon, Virginia. The agency developed the storyboard for the production of a direct-response television commercial for one of its clients, Luray Caverns, a premier attraction in the Shenandoah Valley and Eastern America's largest and most popular caverns. This commercial was produced for the grand opening of its newest attraction, The Luray Valley Museum. The 'Treasure' commercial was 15 seconds long. The audio to accompany the video in the storyboard sequence, shown in Figure 6.15, included fun, simple and playful music, and the following:

> **Voice-over:** 'While the little ones are busy . . . sifting for gems . . . you get to discover . . . the real treasure. Family fun is easy to find at the Luray Valley Museum. Now open at Luray Caverns. What will you discover?'

This television commercial was extremely effective in generating a response. Within a month of the commercial airing on television, tourist traffic to Luray Caverns had increased more than 10 percent when compared with the same period during the prior year.

Script

Although a script for a TV commercial containing no more than 200 words cannot verbally 'explain' a product or service as thoroughly as a direct mail package or print advertisement can, the combination of words with pictures and graphics, audio with video, can exert considerable impact. That is why one of the most effective uses of direct-response TV is to support other

Figure 6.15 Luray Caverns 'Treasure' storyboards. Used with permission of White & Partners.

direct-response advertising media through copy, such as 'Watch your mailbox for . . .' or 'Watch for this offer in next Sunday's *Chicago Tribune*.' A visualization of the insert to which attention is being drawn often accompanies this copy. An effective TV script needs to be tightly woven and fully coordinated with the visual and graphic elements involved. Like good letter copy or well-written print ads, the script needs to first get attention, through audio coupled with video and graphics, and then do its job in presenting product features and benefits as it gets the viewer involved and geared into action.

Graphics

Direct-response TV graphics begin with the words or script coordinated with the other elements that bring the message to life in both audio and video: images, actions, effects, and direction. Actors who deliver the words must be credible, professional, and appropriate to the product. Filming and editing are important so that words are synchronized with pictures. Written words are often superimposed on video to present localized response addresses or phone numbers. Television graphics are concerned with the interaction of audio and video so that the ultimate effect of the message on the viewer will be maximized.

Production

The production team for a direct-response TV commercial consists of a variety of highly specialized technicians, coordinated by a producer. Typical concerns at this juncture are whether to use motion picture film or videotape and live actors, animation, or still illustrations. Directors, actors, and graphic designers become involved, as do camera people and film editors. Decisions as to which to employ must relate costs to response.

Radio

The process of developing radio commercials is less complex than that for television. Radio offers the additional advantage of flexibility in that live commercials, often read by a station announcer or known local personality, can be scheduled quickly. If need be, these can be revised right up to airtime. Radio commercials are far less expensive than TV, too, in airtime costs as well as production costs. Through use of particular radio station formats—easy listening, rock and roll, or news/talk programs—the direct-response advertiser can develop a substantial degree of market segmentation. Positioning adjacent to particular programs, such as early morning farm programs or a popular disc jockey, can further segment markets. Positioning during morning and evening drive times, when office or factory workers are driving to and from their jobs, is another means of market segmentation. Like other media, radio advertising must first get attention. Sometimes a radio personality reading a script, even in an ad-lib manner, can attract attention. If the product being sold involves music, a few bars or a few headline words can make an effective headline for a radio commercial.

The close and request for action are of special concern in using radio for direct response. Many times, radio listeners are performing another activity simultaneously, such as driving, reading a book, taking a shower, or doing household chores. Pencil and paper for writing down addresses and phone numbers are not readily available, nor is it feasible for a listener to stop everything and get them. As a result, the most effective response instruction is one that is easy to remember, such as '1-800-FLOWERS' or '1-800-PETMEDS.' Repeating the address or number helps, too.

As will be discussed later in Chapter 8, many consumers listen to audio ads through streaming services, such as Pandora, Spotify, or any podcast app. Music is commonly thought of as a key to a person's soul as it is very personal and is directly connected with a person's tastes, desires, moods, and preferences. Music is also an effective way to reach and engage with consumers via personalized creative content. Personalization is the core of Pandora (Figure 6.16) and its Music

Genome Project® is the most comprehensive analysis of music ever undertaken. For over a decade, Pandora has been gathering musical knowledge to bring listeners the best, most personalized listening experience out there. The algorithms, along with their data science team, ensure not only that the music is right for each individual listener, but also that the Pandora platform has been optimized on behalf of its advertisers—using music listening preferences and music listening data to get insights into who its users are. The goal is determining when and where to play ads, using intelligent ad search technology powered by AI and machine learning, as well as building custom targeting segments based on listening behavior and other behaviors, and improving measurement on whether or not an ad was heard and whether it was effective for the advertiser.

Figure 6.16   Pandora. Used with permission of Pandora.

Online Video

As we will explore in Chapter 8, millions of people are viewing videos online and the trend is poised to continue and grow in the coming years. Thanks to YouTube, Vimeo, Twitch, Dailymotion, and embedded videos in Facebook, Instagram, and Snapchat, marketers now have a new digital format with which to spread their promotional messages, and the best part—it's free. There are 400 hours of video uploaded to YouTube every minute and almost five billion videos are watched on YouTube every single day.[14] This equates to about 1 billion hours of video watched on YouTube each day.[15] Given that videos will continue to be a highly popular and productive format, marketers must make sure their videos are created in such a manner that they appeal to their target customers or prospects.

Creating a video requires an ordered process. From iMovie to Final Cut to Windows Movie Maker, there are many different computer programs that allow users to create customized videos. The following information is a generalized description of the steps used to create a video that can be distributed through e-mail, YouTube, or even burned onto a CD or DVD. A step-by-step process to creating a video is as follows:

1. The first thing to do is prepare a storyboard. As previously discussed, a storyboard is an illustration of your outline of the video. This includes the story line, examples of images or videos that will be included, timing of the video (i.e., how long each frame will last, etc.), and the dialogue or words that will be used. The information in the storyboard will guide the creation of the video and will make it easier to weave ideas together.
2. The next step is to **import** the images and videos that you will be featuring. Importing everything at once will make it easier to plan out the timing and sequence of your images and videos.

3. Next, put the videos and images in the **order** in which they should appear in the video. Some of your clips will need to be edited to decrease the time they will play or appear on the screen.

4. Now you may add in the transitions. **Transitions** are effects on the videos and images that allow the clip to move to the next scene or image. Most editing software will have different styles of transitions from which to choose.

5. Clipping the videos and images to perfect the timing is the next step in the process. **Clipping** is similar to cropping, but it relates to time instead of image size. By clipping the videos, the amount of time the video or image is shown can be extended or shortened. This process also includes selecting which parts of images or videos will be included. For example, if a video is four minutes long but you only want to include two minutes of the most exciting parts of it, you can use the clipping/cutting tool to select only those two minutes.

6. After clipping and transitions, a **sound overlay** can be added as part of the finishing touches. If the current videos or images have their own sounds and you would like to omit them, detach the audio files and then delete them. Depending upon the software used, each image or video segment with a sound file that may have to be detached will have to be deleted separately. After this is complete, import or add the audio file that will be played in the video. A voice recording may be used instead of music, depending upon the needs of the video.

There are many other features that may be included in a video to make it more appealing and effective, such as titles, captions, special themes, and other video effects; however, the above is a basic outline to get you through the process. The process of creating a video may be considered part art and part science. Despite what is involved in the process, creating an appealing video is important so that your videos don't get lost in the endless stream of available videos to be viewed.

Digital Platforms

Creating effective direct-response messages, or content, for the array of digital platforms is vital in today's marketing world. Let's explore content marketing in greater detail before examining how it is used on the various digital platforms.

Content Marketing

By definition, content marketing is a strategic marketing approach focused on creating and distributing valuable, relevant, and consistent communication to attract and retain a clearly defined audience—and, ultimately, to drive profitable customer action.[16] Content may be posts, photos, videos, infographics, podcasts, stories, events, and more. But, keep in mind that people process images 60,000 times faster than they do text.[17] As the old saying goes: a picture is worth a thousand words.

Good content should draw your target audience back time after time to engage with your digital platforms. Good content should motivate consumers to take some sort of action. As with writing copy for any type of media, good content begins with research and insight into your target audience. Without this critical insight, you cannot create content that appeals to their needs and wants and adds value to their lives with every interaction. Perhaps the most effective content is that which tells an authentic story with which the consumer can relate and be inspired.

Research shows that consumers seek out content from brands to be educated, inspired, informed, or entertained.[18] For some companies, it takes the average prospect to read 20 pieces of content before becoming a customer.[19] So, marketers must create a large amount of content in order to provide value and stimulate action. Here are some tips to follow to create engaging content:[20]

- Include images in your content as opposed to pure text.
- Share authentic stories as they will have a greater impact and be remembered.
- Share content that is beyond promotional.
- Focus on reaching your target audience as opposed to the largest audience possible.
- Personalize content to users' demographic profiles and browsing habits.
- Solicit feedback or reviews from users.
- Leverage user-generated content to engage users.
- Offer rewards to encourage user-generated content.

User-generated content is very powerful as it tends to be perceived as being more authentic. Content can be shared selectively or widely, and it may serve different marketing objectives, such as gathering input and ideas, generating site traffic, producing leads, and creating customers. To sum it up, consumers' digital devices are bombarded with marketing clutter today. The job of content, regardless of what form it is in or who produces it, is to break through, grab consumers' attention, engage and motivate them to take action.

Let's look at a few examples of engaging content created for different social media platforms.

YouTube: Blendtec Blenders runs a highly successful YouTube channel titled 'Will It Blend?', where it demonstrates the company's blenders by placing strange, and often expensive, items in the blender to see whether they will blend. Highlights include an iPhone X, an Amazon Echo, and an iPad. The content is entertaining while it conveys relevant information to the viewers, with the product itself taking a lower priority.[21]

Facebook: REI, the popular outdoor apparel and gear retailer, provides relevant content, such as product demonstrations, recovery drinks, ski pass recommendations, and camping food ideas, on its Facebook page. This enables Facebook analytics to track users' interaction with content or link to the blog section on the REI website.[22]

Instagram: Chaco, a popular outdoor sandal company, rolled out its new Z/Chromatic line of sandals by removing all other posts on its Instagram page and beginning the rollout with a lavender image highlighting the color of the Chaco sandal. The rest of the Instagram features presented pictures in the same chromatic colors, drawing awareness to the sandal.[23]

Direct marketers must be mindful of a variety of special considerations when creating content for digital platforms. Let's explore some of these.

The first item to address in creating digital promotions must be the dissemination of incentives for the prospect to visit a company's website in the first place. This is in contrast to the entrepreneur targeting the prospect, as is the case with direct mail or the telephone, as well as print and broadcast media. This is now typically being done through many formats, such as print, broadcast, mobile, SMS text messages, social media, and Internet search engines, all of which can let a prospect know the location of the website, as well as the benefits to accrue from browsing. We will discuss the Internet and digital and social media in greater detail in Chapter 10. There are many different tools and techniques that may be used to create digital ads, such as AdEspresso for social media ads. (Check out the Readings and Resources section at the end of the chapter for more detail.) However, for now, let's concentrate on the creation of compelling content for digital platforms.

AdEspresso is a Facebook Ads tool that makes ad creation and optimization easier and faster compared to the Power Editor. Since it was founded in 2011, it has grown to become a Facebook advertising partner and a preferred marketing tool for brands all over the world. With the platform, users can create Facebook and Instagram Ads right through the interface, which syncs with your pre-existing Facebook Ad accounts. It can even import active campaigns.

The copywriter and the graphic designer must design a website, starting with its home page, so that the visitor is motivated to becoming a customer. At this stage, everything we've said about creating promotions for all media—direct mail, print, and broadcast—apply as well to the Internet. Especially important, however, is the *sequencing* of each visit with clicks and links. *Information*, as needed, becomes a literal goldmine. The logic and convenience of ordering online is readily apparent. Of course, once a relationship has been established with a customer, then the Internet becomes an effective and efficient way of doing business.

Let's explore the message strategies used by Virginia Beach in its online promotion by reviewing its website.

Home Page

Virginia Beach's website, shown in Figure 6.17, uses the four basic design principles: *alignment*, *proximity*, *repetition*, and *contrast*. There is horizontal alignment across the main navigation bar on the top of the page as well as a vertical menu to enable visitors to quickly and easily locate desired information available on its website. The use of proximity and repetition in the vertical banner, such as the advertisements that run along the left side of the site, tie the various tourist features together, along with the bullet-point listing of recent news about what's happening in Virginia Beach. The eye is drawn to the page through the use of contrast with the different background colors, the various font styles, and the variety of colors in the primary image featured at the top of the page. This site also contains several key elements that consumers would expect to find on an interactive website. It enables prospective tourists to click on a file folder to request more information about accommodations, attractions, and packages directly from the site itself. The home page also offers visitors an opportunity to view a blog and select their preferred language.

Outbound E-Mail

One of the most important aspects of outbound e-mail messages is the subject line. If the subject line isn't creative, clever, catchy, and relevant to the consumer, they will likely delete the message before clicking through to open the e-mail. E-mail subject lines must be simple, brief or short, and convey a real benefit to the consumer. Marketers must limit the length of the subject line as more people are reading their e-mail on their mobile devices—61 percent in 2018, which is up from

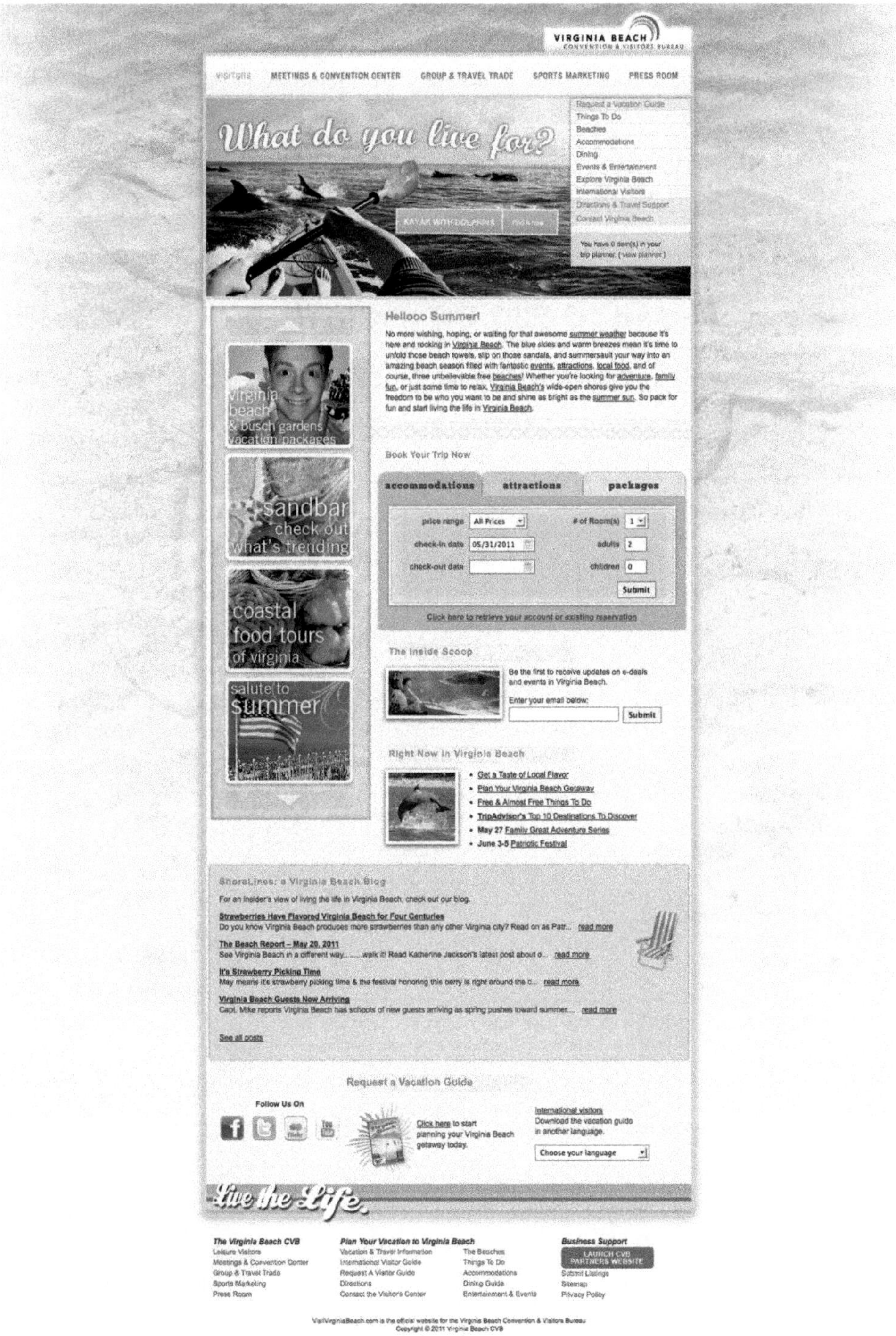

Figure 6.17 Virginia Beach Convention & Visitor's home page. Used with permission of the City of Virginia Beach Convention & Visitors Bureau.

55% in 2016.[24] This trend is expected to continue. Additionally, research shows that seven words, or 41 characters, produce the highest click-through rate (CTR) for e-mails, which is ten characters less than the average subject line.[25] Some marketers are including attention-grabbing emojis in their subject lines. A few good examples of catchy subject lines are shown in Figure 6.18.

"OMG, this bra!" – Victoria's Secret

 Meow! Woof! Take us with you! – Home Away

You Almost Missed It! $20 Off Online! – Dick's Sporting Goods Store

 Summer HOT Deals, Even HOTTER Gifts! – Harry & David

Figure 6.18 Attention-grabbing e-mail subject lines

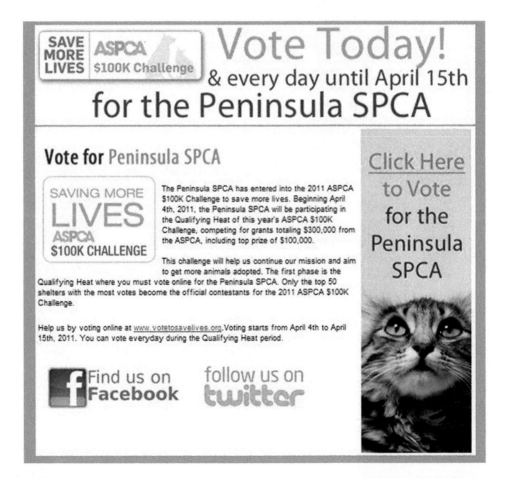

Figure 6.19 PSPCA 'Vote Today' e-mail. Used with permission of Peninsula Society for the Prevention of Cruelty to Animals.

Figure 6.19 provides an example of an outbound e-mail from the Peninsula SPCA. This e-mail utilizes the principles of design with contrast between the black, blue, and orange type and the use of an appealing image. The call to action, 'Vote Today!,' is presented with great passion and is repeated twice: 'Click Here to Vote' and in the 'www.votetosavelives.org' link. The e-mail also encourages viewers to connect with the PSPCA via the additional calls to action—'Find us on Facebook' and 'Follow us on Twitter'—set off at the bottom of the e-mail surrounded by generous white space.

Banner Advertisements

Banner ads, the digital equivalent of print ads, are created with the intent to engage the viewer and drive action. These ads have changed over time and now are truly interactive and integrated. These ads may use sound, video, and flash animation. The ads may also include special forms, such as floating ads, page takeovers, and tearbacks, designed to get the attention of the viewer. Let's examine an example of the creative design of banner ads. The banner ad for Busch Gardens featured in Figure 6.20 employs motion capture to gain the viewers' interest. The first frame was deliberately designed to feature a seemingly undisclosed photo by itself to spark curiosity, as the remaining frames uncovered the rest of the pertinent information one by one. The animated banner ad saw a 28 percent higher click-through rate than the static ad with the same message.

Figure 6.20 Busch Gardens animated banner ad. Used with the consent of Busch Gardens/Water Country USA. All Rights Reserved.

SUMMARY

Direct-response copywriting is both art and science, and those who have mastered it are very much in demand. FAB (features-advantages-benefits) analysis is often used by direct-response copywriters to position products so that these provide benefits to users. There is a variety of copywriting formulas available to guide creative development and many of these are set forth in this chapter. Design and graphics are important adjuncts to copywriting, used to create attention and guide the reader through copy. These include art, layout, symbols, and effects. Consideration should be given also to such factors as photographs, illustrations, type styles, paper, inks, size, and a variety of attention-getting techniques.

The development of direct-response advertising must be concerned with the special characteristics of the medium to be used: direct mail, catalogs, print (magazines and newspapers), broadcast (television and radio), digital videos, telephone, and the Internet.

KEY TERMS

big idea	layout
content marketing	meme
copy appeal	storyboards
involvement devices	

REVIEW QUESTIONS

1. How do measurability and accountability, characteristics key to direct marketing, apply to advertising?
2. What, specifically, is *direct-response advertising*? What makes it unique from all other types of advertising?
3. Why is an understanding of buyer motivations important in the creation of direct marketing promotions?
4. What do we mean by 'features, advantages, benefits'? Give an example of each for a product of your choosing.
5. Why are design and graphics important in the creation of direct-response advertising?
6. Name at least three elements of design that a direct marketer can use to create a message.
7. Name and explain one copywriting formula that has been successful throughout the years.

8. How do you create copy appeal? Give two examples.
9. Think about an advertising campaign you have seen recently. Who was the advertiser? What was the 'big idea' the advertiser was trying to convey? Was it successful?
10. What are some important considerations when creating message content for digital video? Provide an example of a compelling promotional video and explain why it was effective in your opinion.

EXERCISE

Busch Gardens, a well-known amusement park located in Virginia, is holding a contest for college students. The first-place prize is a season passport for two people to enjoy the park for a lifetime, for each member of the winning team! The challenge is to identify as many features of the park as possible and their associated advantages. Then, you must convert each advantage into a benefit that the amusement park may use in marketing the park to consumers. You may select your target market customer: either (1) families or (2) young adults. Have fun and good luck!

CRITICAL THINKING EXERCISE

Select one of your favorite advertisements and critically evaluate it according to the creative techniques and principles detailed in this chapter. Does it achieve its creative objectives? If so, how does it do this or in what way? If not, what is it about the ad that is hindering its effectiveness?

READINGS AND RESOURCES

- Copywriting: www.quicksprout.com/complete-guide-to-copywriting
- Design and graphics: https://blog.adobespark.com/2016/07/27/8-basic-design-principles-to-help-you-create-better-graphics
- Content Marketing Institute: https://contentmarketinginstitute.com
- Hub Spot: https://blog.hubspot.com/marketing/content-marketing-plan
- AdEspresso: https://instapage.com/blog/how-to-use-adespresso
- E-mail: https://rare.io/sales-email-examples

CASE: BARELY THERE

How does a creative idea for a direct and interactive marketing campaign originate? Is it a product of sheer genius? Or is it hatched when a bunch of brilliant minds get together and spit out off-the-wall ideas in a brainstorming session? Could it be the result of extensive research? Maybe it is based on a thorough understanding of the target customers' deepest desires? Or could it be just a stroke of good luck?

Whatever it takes, The Martin Agency in Richmond, Virginia, surely has it and demonstrated sheer ingenuity when it created the Barely There campaign for its client, Hanesbrands. This case is a success story of creativity that really worked. It demonstrates the exceptional things that can happen when you combine commonsense thinking with clever ideas.

In direct and interactive marketing terms, creativity encompasses the content of whatever media format is being used to convey the offer. Creative strategies include decisions about the words, terms, symbols, designs, pictures, images, and media format. The old cliché 'it's not creative unless it sells' implies that the creative strategies must attain the objectives set forth for the campaign. These objectives may be to generate a response, transaction, political vote, charitable donation, and so on. Regardless of the objectives, direct marketers must make many decisions about the creative elements included in a campaign. These decisions include brand and image building, copywriting and graphics, and message creation based on media selection. This case lets you explore how Hanesbrands and The Martin Agency made these decisions when they developed the direct and interactive marketing campaign for the Barely There Invisible Look collection of bras.

With a fraction of the advertising budget in comparison with category leaders, the company was intent on creating a more meaningful and intimate connection with women with the Barely There Invisible Look collection of bras. Hanesbrands challenged The Martin Agency to achieve this objective, and the company and agency worked together and did just that and more! After months of market research, positioning, and creative development, the end result was great success. Let's take a look at how this creative campaign was developed.

Research

The campaign was driven by innovative consumer research and then by the realization that the ultimate goal of bras for women was not to look sexy with their clothes off but to help them look and feel great with their clothes on. This realization was further developed when Hanesbrands began to gain consumer insights via research across the country.

The team flipped through a variety of fashion magazines, and all they saw were pretty women in pretty bras. In fact, the ads of the largest competitor in the lingerie industry, Victoria's Secret, featured beautiful models with perfect shapes and bras that fit perfectly. These models are often shown with slinky body parts, naked torsos, and stiletto heels. Where's the humanity? It seems that the intimate apparel category has been missing the mark for years, overlooking the underlying reason women wear bras in the first place–to help them look good in their clothes.

So, the team got busy, and they uncovered that women try to avoid the dreaded 'bad bra day' when bras don't fit right or don't look right. The team created a dictionary of 'bad bra moments' and began to completely understand the consumer's perspective (the mono-boob, the quadra-boob, the puffed-up chicken chest). These bad bra moments were extremely annoying for most women. Research also found that millions of women are wearing ill-fitting bras. What many consumers really need is a friend to help them avoid

270

bad bra moments. The solution? A new positioning strategy for Barely There intimates to be the bra brand to own, to solve the most common universal bra problems and allow women never to have a bad bra day. The Invisible Look bra collection addresses the practical concerns women have about shape and fit.

Positioning

Positioning Barely There intimates as the brand that can help women look and feel better in their clothes was a new direction for the lingerie industry. The new campaign is viewed as part sales pitch and part public service announcement. It doesn't focus on the supermodels, but illustrates the problems women often encounter with the wrong bra and provides practical solutions to correct the problem. The new positioning strategy fills a niche that is currently unfulfilled. Victoria's Secret may command the market segment of women desiring a sexier bra, but that still leaves a large portion of the consumer lingerie market to capture.

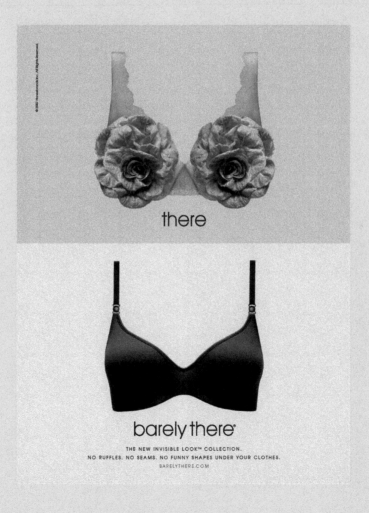

there

barely there®

THE NEW INVISIBLE LOOK™ COLLECTION.
NO RUFFLES. NO SEAMS. NO FUNNY SHAPES UNDER YOUR CLOTHES.
BARELYTHERE.COM

(Continued)

Figure 6.21 (Continued)

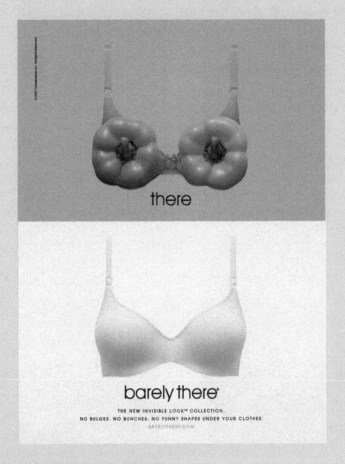

Figure 6.21 Barely There print advertisements. Published. with permission of Hanesbrands, Inc.

The Martin Agency team, armed with its new dictionary of bad bra moments, seized the opportunity, and history was made with a totally unique and entertaining creative campaign for the Barely There Invisible Look bra collection.

Creative Development

Due to the strategic direction and the desire to significantly drive brand awareness, the creative team found a simple way to convey the message using three words–two of which were the brand name. The result is a problem–solution campaign: your bra is either 'there' or 'barely there.' In each photo duo there is a bra that is bumpy or misshapen (labeled 'There') as well as a smoothly shaped bra (labeled 'Barely There'). The value proposition of the campaign was that other bras are painfully 'there.' Figure 6.21 shows a few of these creative executions.

The creative team at The Martin Agency had fun imagining all of the crazy shaped items that could be used to portray an ill-fitting bra. Of course, most women wouldn't intentionally stuff their shirts with cocktail umbrellas, red bell peppers, pine cones, or decorative bows, but many would be quick to admit that some bras do create the odd appearance of some of those items.

Color was also an important aspect to the creative development of the campaign. The creative team knew that the campaign needed to be both sophisticated and fashion-y as well as funny. They decided to photograph the items attached to the garments rather than composite the images of the items and bras in postproduction. The art director strongly felt that it would be more 'real,' and that this method would ensure that the color and reflections would work with each other. Therefore, the campaign entailed a photo shoot with each bra presenting its own set of different challenges for the creative team and the photographers.

The result? A company and agency partnership that produced a brilliant campaign that clearly passes everyone's giggle test. The campaign is nationally acclaimed, as it has won numerous creative awards. Finally, and most importantly, it effectively conveys a message along with a website (onehanesplace.com), where consumers can purchase a bra that will really make them feel and look good in their clothes.

Case Discussion Questions

1. What role did marketing research play in the development of the Barely There campaign? Could the campaign have been created without the background research? Why or why not?
2. Provide some examples of how this campaign converted the features of the Invisible Look bra collection into benefits.
3. Identify a few of the primary competitors for the Barely There Invisible Look collection of bras. What different copy appeals are being used by the various product line competitors? What makes the Barely There campaign different?
4. Would you categorize the copy appeal used in this campaign to be rational, emotional, or moral? Explain why. Do you think the use of a different appeal would have been more effective for marketing the Invisible Look bra collection?

NOTES

1. Thorstein Veblen (1917) *The Theory of the Leisure Class* (London: Macmillan), p. 110.
2. Jim Kobs (1993) *Profitable Direct Marketing*, 2nd ed. (Lincolnwood, IL: NTC Business Books), p. 189.
3. Ibid., p. 190.
4. https://csnews.com/pepsi-gives-nod-past-new-2018-global-campaign, retrieved May 17, 2019.
5. https://csnews.com/pepsi-gives-nod-past-new-2018-global-campaign, retrieved May 17, 2019.
6. Jay Conrad Levinson (2001) *Guerrilla Creativity* (New York: Houghton Mifflin), p. 10.
7. Ibid., p. 2.
8. Ibid., p. 13.
9. Euromonitor International, www.forbes.com/companies/gatorade/#70e3ff394b0b, retrieved May 14, 2019.
10. Euromonitor International, www.forbes.com/companies/gatorade/#70e3ff394b0b, retrieved May 14, 2019.
11. Bob Stone (2001) *Successful Direct Marketing Methods*, 7th ed. (New York: McGraw-Hill), pp. 294–395.
12. Ibid.
13. www.marketingcharts.com/charts/us-traditional-tv-viewing-trends-age-group-q2-2018/attachment/nielsen-traditional-tv-viewing-trends-by-age-group-in-q2-2018-dec2018, retrieved April 13, 2019.
14. www.tubefilter.com/2015/07/26/youtube-400-hours-content-every-minute, retrieved April 17, 2019.
15. https://youtube.googleblog.com/2017/02/you-know-whats-cool-billion-hours.html, retrieved April 17, 2019.
16. http://contentmarketinginstitute.com/what-is-content-marketing, retrieved July 29, 2016.
17. www.business2community.com/digital-marketing/visual-marketing-pictures-worth-60000-words-01126256, retrieved May 27, 2019.
18. https://insights.newscred.com/content-marketing-best-practices-from-top-brands, retrieved May 27, 2019.
19. Adapted from https://insights.newscred.com/content-marketing-best-practices-from-top-brands, retrieved May 27, 2019.
20. Adapted from https://insights.newscred.com/content-marketing-best-practices-from-top-brands, retrieved May 27, 2019.
21. www.youtube.com/watch?v=lAl28d6tbko&list=PLg6me2IluOEyI62HhvTeIm_URE2ON-n4wf, retrieved April 17, 2019.
22. www.facebook.com/REI, retrieved April 17, 2019.
23. www.instagram.com/chacofootwear/?hl=en, retrieved April 20, 2019.
24. www.campaignmonitor.com/blog/email-marketing/2019/02/best-email-subject-line-length, retrieved April 15, 2019.
25. www.campaignmonitor.com/blog/email-marketing/2019/02/best-email-subject-line-length, retrieved April 15, 2019.

7
PRINT MEDIA

CHAPTER CONTENTS

CHAPTER SPOTLIGHT

BAESMAN – SMART MARKETING; BEAUTIFUL RESULTS

Think print media is dead? Think again. Baesman Printing Company's success story is bound to change your mind.

The Baesman brothers, Rod and Tyler, pictured in Figure 7.1, are the current co-owners of the Columbus, Ohio-based printing company that their father, Dick Baesman, opened back in 1952. The brothers joined the family printing company in the late 1980s. At that time, the business had 30 employees and generated roughly $1.5 million a year in sales. Fast-forward 30 years to today when the company employs 140 people, has two separate divisions, and its annual sales exceed $30 million. That sure seems like solid proof that print is far from dead. To be fair, growth in the family business has not been a result of print media alone. About eight years ago, the company began offering its customers more than just printing services. However, Baesman's core business of printing and fulfillment still represents a huge chunk of its thriving business today.

Figure 7.1 Rod and Tyler Baesman. Published with the consent of Baesman Group, Inc. All Rights Reserved.

The Baesman brothers and their team of bright, talented associates focus on the complexities that come after the printing. Their focus is squarely on the precisely timed release of highly personalized direct marketing materials and the production and rollout of complex retail kits. The company offers its clients the convenience of on-demand printing and the assurance of getting the right offer into the right hands exactly when the client intended. Baesman's client list includes well-known brands such as Kate Spade, DSW, Lane Bryant, Victoria's Secret, Bath & Body Works, NY&C, Polo Ralph Lauren, and Stanley Steemer.

The company specializes in complex direct marketing programs. Baesman combines decades of experience with next-generation custom printing technology to enable its clients to send the perfect offer to their customers at just the right time. From digital color to ultra-violet (UV) offset, Baesman has the equipment and capacity to produce a variety of direct mail pieces. Its fleet of six-color presses and digital printers work around the clock to ensure that their clients' direct mail is completed on time and on budget. Baesman's expert printing craftspeople oversee traditional offset, UV offset, digital, and grand-format digital presses producing tens of thousands of sheets per hour, 24 hours a day. The company is G7 certified, maintaining strict quality control and color management across all printing methods to assure brand consistency for its clients. Some of the services and printing methods Baesman employs include the following:

- Variable data printing: picture a one-to-one campaign that goes beyond name, gender, and location to reflect a deeper connection with the customer: hobbies, past purchases, or other defining characteristics. Baesman's expert programmers transform their clients' databases into highly effective engines for one-to-one print marketing.
- Matched mailings and attachments: think personalized mailings are limited to a customer's name printed inside and out? Think again. Baesman has a wide array of mailing technologies to personalize letters, cards, envelopes, mailers, and more. Its high-speed attaching, ink jetting, and inserting equipment are complete with all the cameras, scanners, and bells and whistles to ensure the right card is attached to the right letter and in the right envelope, every time.
- Remote insertion and mail tracking: Baesman's clients never have to wonder whether their mail is in-home. Baesman saves their clients both money and worry as the company offers control over when their clients' direct mail reaches customer homes by shipping it to every destination post office. Baesman puts a special barcode on each piece to track client mail through the system and give clients real-time reporting by ZIP code.

The result: using early reads on redemption rates, marketers can project results and make decisions about their next promotion faster than ever.

Baesman is also a planner, producer, and distributor of in-store signage. The company offers floor sets, store bases, and personalized product display Plan-O-Grams. The company fulfills signs and other store essentials for a wide variety of well-known retailers, such as Victoria's Secret, Polo, NY&C, Bath & Body Works, and La Senza. Baesman's store attribution software lowers costs for their clients by printing the exact quantities needed–no more, no less. Baesman maintains detailed profiles of each store and sends only the point of sale (POS) materials, displays, fixtures, and even gift cards, as necessary. Baesman's state-of-the-art custom signage and Web-to-print portals give sales teams, franchise owners, and store managers an easy way to create custom signage and marketing materials. Clients just log in and order what they need–or customize them with graphics, text, contact info, maps, and more. Real-time proofing tools help clients get it right and fast with quick-turn printing and shipping.

Baesman associates love the complexity of packing every item each store needs, in the exact quantity, and getting them there safely and efficiently, as seen in Figure 7.2. The company's kitting accuracy is unmatched because Baesman associates know that a beautiful sign in the wrong store equals lost revenue and a big headache. Baesman's freight-analysis software compares weights and rates, ground and air, to find the best shipping option, whether their clients' kits are going to one store or one thousand.

Figure 7.2 Baesman in-store signs. Published with the consent of Baesman Group, Inc. All Rights Reserved.

Finally, Baesman offers store replenishment and fulfillment services. Baesman's clients will never run out of signs again. Regardless of whether clients need new store kits or need to replace damaged or lost signs, Baesman's online ordering system and massive warehouse make it easy for stores to replenish signs, fixtures, and other marketing must-haves. As a bonus, Baesman will run stock reports and send its clients notifications when inventory is running low. Print-on-demand options let clients make changes to their offer and get it in store fast.

Not convinced as to the value of print media yet? Maybe the following facts will help to convince you. While direct mail isn't as dazzling as digital marketing, as innovative as mobile marketing, or as recognized as e-mail marketing, it *does* achieve one important strategy better than any other medium: direct mail acquires customers. As a media channel, print outperforms digital channels in garnering customer response. The following response rates were presented in a 2015 Direct Marketing Association (DMA) report:

- direct mail: 1.0%
- mobile: 0.2%
- social: 0.1%
- paid search: 0.1%

Thus, print media may be undervalued in the digital age. With the cost of digital and social ads steadily rising, many brands are turning back to direct mail as an alternative to pricey digital options. Beyond that, direct mail is a great strategy for omni-channel and e-commerce retailers. Print media advertising is active, with customers actually holding a brand's collateral, where digital advertising is passive and intangible. With direct mail, consumers need to decide whether to toss it or keep it. By keeping it, consumers are much more likely to review, explore, and act on the direct mail advertised brand, such as the direct mailers of Stanley Steemer featured in Figure 7.3.

Figure 7.3   Stanley Steemer direct mailers. Used with permission of Stanley Steemer. All Rights Reserved.

In closing, print media isn't the front line of technology, nor is it as glamorous as some digital or social media channels, but it is successful. And while social may seem cooler, a Facebook 'like' simply can't compete with a tried-and-true purchase that is driven more directly via a print ad than a digital ad.

Note: Much of the content for this chapter spotlight has been provided by Baesman Group, Inc. Used with permission.

Direct mail, in its various formats, is a print medium. Publications, magazines, and newspapers represent another form of printed communication. In contrast with direct mail ads, which are delivered individually, magazines and newspapers convey direct-response advertising to groups of readers in a package along with other advertisements as well as editorial matter. In this chapter, we examine direct mail (including self-mailers, classic packages, and catalogs), newspapers, magazines, and collateral printed materials—and their characteristics and advantages and disadvantages. We discuss the potential for market segmentation through readership of specific parts of a particular print medium at a particular time—sports or obituaries in today's newspaper, as examples. Let's begin with direct mail as it has long been the basic promotion format for direct marketers. It relies on mailing lists and data about the individuals or organizations on such lists to most effectively reach market segments.

DIRECT MAIL

Direct marketers use virtually all forms of advertising media to generate measurable responses, including **direct mail.** According to the U.S. Postal Service, the average U.S. consumer receives about 15 pieces of mail per week, with 40 percent of households either reading or scanning the advertising mail they receive.[1] Postcards are the most read type of direct mail.[2]

Not all direct mail is carried by the U.S. Postal Service, however; some goes by private carriers, such as FedEx, UPS, or other door-to-door distributors, such as newspaper carriers on their circulation rounds. Some is enclosed within newspapers and magazines. Sometimes marketers also combine several offers into a single package, such as coupons or other inserts into newspapers, or enclose offers with other mail or parcels, such as statement stuffers or package inserts. Among the various shapes of direct mailers, postcards are most likely to be read.

Advantages and Disadvantages

Compared with other media, direct mail provides considerably more space and opportunity to tell a complete story. It can gain attention and develop an orderly and logical flow of information, leading to action by the reader. Direct mail, too, has a unique capability to involve the recipient and faces less competition for attention at the time it is received than other advertising media do. Direct mail inspires creativity and cleverness. Check out the Bloomin seed paper direct mail designs, shown in Figure 7.4, which encourage marketers to send their customers flowers through the mail. And customers will surely be involved when they plant the seed paper mailers and watch the flowers grow and bloom.

Direct mail is one of the most selective media and offers great potential for personalization. It is very flexible (mainly because of the many different formats available) and is also extremely suitable for testing. It is one of the most scientifically testable of all media because marketers can control experimentation with variables such as format, copy, and graphics.

The primary disadvantage of direct mail is that it is the most expensive medium per prospect reached. Direct mail costs normally include creative art and preparation, printing production, mailing lists, computer processing, letter shop production, allocated fees, and postage. This is true

Watch your response rates GROW!

Handmade PLANTABLE direct mail postcards, and mailings that get noticed in the MAIL, and in your GARDEN! Click on the flyer above to view more information.

Please contact quotes@bloomin.com for more pricing; or contact samples@bloomin.com to receive samples on a specific product

Figure 7.4 Bloomin seed paper direct mail designs. Used with permission of Bloomin. All rights reserved.

even though preferential postage rates apply to nonprofit organizations and to those large-volume mailers who presort their direct mail by ZIP code or by postal carrier route. However, direct mail costs vary by design. Let's investigate some options.

Designs

With adequate marketing research, direct mail affords the opportunity for positioning products and services to specific market segments and can, through computer and printing technology, personalize and individualize each piece to each recipient. This customized printing process is called variable data printing. **Variable data printing** (VDP), which is also referred to as variable printing or variable imaging, is a form of digital printing in which elements may be changed from one printed piece to the next, without re-setting the printing press or slowing down the printing process. What may be changed? Design elements such as text, graphics, images, offers, and more, are commonly changed during variable printing.

For example, Figure 7.5 shows two direct mailers that have been variably printed. Note the many subtle differences between the two mailers via variable printing technology. These differences include text (customer name, address, and source code that enable matchback to the actual direct mail campaign or mail piece to which the customer responds), images (products—male versus female sandal, unique barcodes that connect to Shoes, Inc. inventory, exclusive geo-tags that enable customers to use their smartphone to connect to a specific landing page based on their past purchases on the Shoes, Inc. website), and offers (different prices and unique promotional offer code based on customer value differences).

Figure 7.5 Shoes, Inc. direct mailers. Used with permission of Johnnie Gray.

Variable data printing enables print media to become a one-to-one campaign that goes beyond name, gender, and location, to reflect a deeper connection with the customer by addressing each customer's hobbies, past purchases, or other defining characteristics. As summed up by Tyler Baesman, president of the Baesman Group featured in the Chapter Spotlight, 'There is nothing we cannot print variably including images. Every sheet coming out of the press can be completely different.'[3] With variable printing, the customization of print media is endless!

There are many different direct mail designs that can be employed. Let's briefly discuss these. Let's begin with the three basic formats of direct mail: the self-mailer, the classic format, and the catalog.

Self-Mailers

A self-mailer is any direct mail piece mailed without an envelope. Self-mailers can range from simple postcards to tubes to a variety of different sizes and shapes of direct mail. Self-mailers can promote a single product/service or many products/services at one time. Mailing pieces promoting a single product or a limited group of related products are often called solo mailers. Figure 7.6 presents some examples from ShipShapes, a company specializing in the creation of unique self-mailers. ShipShapes provides customized self-mailers that really grab attention. Nearly any shape goes: a car, frog, elephant, cartoon character, floral bouquet—if you can imagine it, Ship-Shapes will create it! So think out-of-the-box and out-of-the-envelope and explore the many creative, colorful, and eye-catching designs associated with self-mailers.

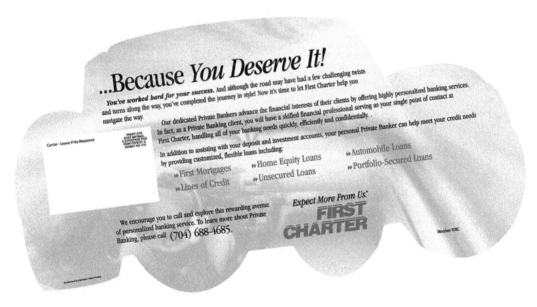

Figure 7.6 ShipShapes self-mailers, frog and car. Used with permission of ShipShapes™.

Classic Format

The **classic format** normally consists of six components: (1) an outer mailing envelope, (2) a letter, (3) a brochure, (4) a return device, (5) a reply envelope, and (6) a 'chit.' Let's address the purpose of each component. A **chit** is an additional enclosure card or separate slip of paper that highlights a free gift or some other information, which is often printed on a different color and size of paper to make it stand out from the rest of the mailing package. The **mailing envelope** is a vital component in the success of a direct mail package, for unless the envelope receives attention and is opened, the contents will never be revealed. For this reason, direct-response advertisers often use teaser copy on the outside of a mailing envelope in order to lead the recipient inside, to entice but not reveal. Figure 7.7 shows examples of how Valpak effectively uses teaser copy on its famous blue outer envelopes. In addition to teaser copy, the size, color, shape, and paper texture of the outer envelope can provide feelings of importance, urgency, prestige, or bargain to the recipient.

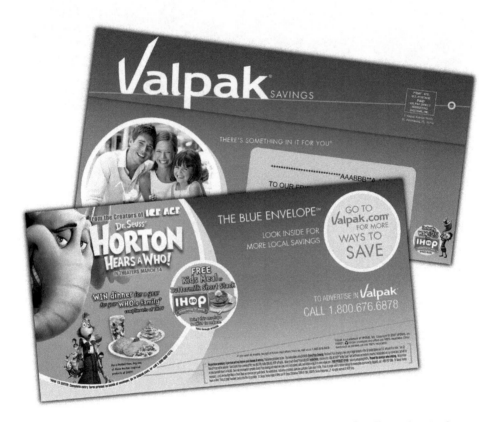

Figure 7.7   Valpak teaser copy. Used with the permission of Valpak. A Cox Target Media Company.

The principal element of the direct mail package, the **letter**, provides the primary means for communication and personalization. Databases enable the personalization of letters. Letters can be narrative and intriguing or they can be factual and staccato. The P.S. (**postscript**) at the end of a letter has high visual value. The recipient will frequently read this part of the letter first. For that reason, the copywriter often uses the P.S. to restate the offer, highlight benefits, and direct the reader to another part of the package. The **brochure** (also called a flyer, folder, or circular) is an optional piece that augments the letter (if needed) to provide product specifications, cover technical points such as pricing, provide scene-setting narrative and photographs, and dramatize and illustrate, while incorporating benefits to the reader. A brochure is sometimes a physical part of the letter itself—pages two and three of a four-page letter/brochure format, for example. It can be as simple as a single sheet printed on one side only or as complicated as multi-folded brochures, giant broadsides, or multipage booklets. Headlines and illustrations are vital parts of brochures, along with adequate subheads and body copy to provide full description and entice action. Sometimes testimonials or endorsements can lend credence to product claims, or report satisfied users.

Once the mailing envelope, letter, and brochure have performed their particular functions, the response device provides the means for action. This device can be as simple as a postage-paid return card with a mere 'check off' of instructions, or it can be an order form providing for remittance or credit instructions along with specific product selections, or it can be as complex as an application for insurance, a credit card, or an investment. In any event, it should be a selling piece. It should have a name to identify it, it should be well designed, and it should contain compelling and clear-cut copy. It should be easy to complete.

The real challenge to the direct-response advertiser in developing response devices is to provide, in a condensed format, all the necessary elements of the response/transaction, while at the same time keeping the form logical, orderly, and simple. Involvement devices should be constructed to lure the reader into action.

Finally, unless a card is used as a response device, a separate reply envelope is usually provided as an incentive and a convenience and to ensure privacy, especially if remittance is requested. Often, depending on the mathematics of the offer and whether curiosity seekers are to be discouraged, reply postage is prepaid. Sometimes wallet-flap envelopes incorporate an order form on the seal flap. Specialty envelopes provide an order blank combined with a reply envelope. Examples of such order forms can be found bound, as a convenience, into many mail-order catalogs. Like other elements of the classic direct mail package, the reply envelope should be designed to encourage action.

Catalogs

Certainly, one of the most challenging and popular formats for direct marketers is the catalog. A catalog is a multipage format or booklet that displays photographs and/or descriptive details of products/services along with prices and order details. A catalog can have just a few pages or hundreds of pages. Direct marketers may produce their catalogs in house or by contract with an outside agency or organization. We live in a world of catalogs. Catalogs offer almost every product imaginable, from art supplies to gourmet food and drink, children's clothing, games, toys, home furnishings, perfumes, gear for camping and sporting, automotive supplies, gardening tools, jewelry, and books. You can also find the latest, greatest fashions. We also have business-oriented catalogs for things like electronic components, office supplies, and industrial parts.

Targeting the right customer with the right catalog is easy today given that most marketers have amassed their own customer databases, and that industry databases, containing all sorts of information on households, are readily available. According to brand expert Denise Lee Yohn:

> As more products become more similar and as the Internet continues to provide increasing access to more products, print catalogs and their content will grow as a means to

differentiate brands and sustain existing customer relationships. Great brands integrate catalogs with e-mail marketing, social media, and other tactics into a distinctive, memorable, and valuable brand experience for their customers.[4]

A notable attribute of catalog copy is succinctness, brevity, and conciseness—few words and to the point. Catalog copy goes hand in hand with design, illustration, and graphics. Pictures show it, words describe it. Descriptive words often found in catalog copy include these: *quality, genuine, fine, full, comfortable, heavy, natural*, and *best*. Like all direct marketing promotional copy, the words are arranged to spell out benefits. The words inform at the same time as they sell.

Layout, including space allocation, is important. Like the store retailer who allocates shelf space and position according to the potential profitability of products displayed, a catalog retailer allocates space and position in print. Successful catalogers allocate space, including preferred positioning, such as covers, according to a product's potential profitability.

As you plan and design your print catalog, consider the best use of the prime selling spaces in your book. First is the *front cover*. Although this can be a prime selling space, many catalog marketers opt to use this first page as a 'theme setter.' They may show a group of merchandise items that are available for sale inside the catalog, a scene that characterizes the company and its goods, or a seasonal vignette. In any case, make sure that products shown on the front cover are readily identifiable for buying purposes. For example: a line that says 'see page 5 for details' on cover products. The *back cover* is the second hot spot. It should in most cases be used for selling products with high sales potential. Be careful that the products you choose for the back cover also characterize what's inside the catalog. If they are too different from the mainstream of merchandise in your book, prospective buyers may never make it past the front and back covers.

The *inside front cover spread* and the spread after that are next in the prime territory race, along with the *center spread* and the *inside back cover*. The *spread near the order form*—if you still provide a print order form (most catalogs no longer do so)—also carries high potential. And if you still provide a print order form, don't underestimate the power of the *order form* itself for selling merchandise. Talk with your printer about bind-in order form designs that give you some extra selling space at an affordable cost.

The copywriter must anticipate objections and overcome them in advance, at the same time holding the number of words used to a minimum. The catalog copy must be concise, yet it must be complete and clear. Notice the effective use of copy, design, and images in Cheryl's catalog, shown in Figure 7.8. The free shipping offer is clearly presented, as is the company's website and toll-free number for easy ordering. The pictures feature the products in an appetizing and appealing fashion. This catalog page inspires gift giving.

Catalogs and Multichannel Marketing

When *Catalog Age* changed its name to *Multichannel Merchant* (multichannelmerchant.com) some years back, the publication's editors explained the change with these comments: 'Once upon a time, catalogers sold through catalogs, and retailers sold through stores. But most

Figure 7.8 Cheryl's catalog page. Used with permission of Cheryl & Co®.

companies are now channel-agnostic. They realize that they must go well beyond their core channel to reach the largest pool of potential buyers.' The renamed publication was intended to 'serve catalog companies, online merchants, retailers, manufacturers and wholesale/distributors who sell via print catalogs and/or transactional Web sites.'

Some firms are able to translate their successful retail sales concepts to catalog and Web marketing. For example, the Crate and Barrel catalog and website (www.crateandbarrel.com) both echo the spare, contemporary good looks of the tabletop, cookware, furniture, and linen stores that preceded it. American Spoon Foods sells its jarred fruits, jams, salsas, and sauces in upscale grocery stores and its own retail outlets in Michigan resort towns, but broadens its reach with a colorful American Spoon catalog and a website at www.spoon.com.

Catalogs have become a vital and productive format of direct mail. Successful catalogs rely on databases to target specialized product lines to the market segments most likely to be interested. Today's catalogs are not confined to consumer products; they also play an important role in business-to-business distribution. Examples include the office product catalogs of Staples and Office Depot/Office Max and others, such as Bloomin Seed Paper, featured in Figure 7.9. Note the level of organization that is needed in business catalogs, including a table of contents, colorful page headers, detailed presentation of product items with respective item order codes, the variety of grades or types of products, an array of available colors, and pricing options that include ordering in bulk.

Table of Contents

1. Promote!   2. Plant!   3. Grow!

3

Coupons

Seed Paper Greeting Cards

Seed Paper Postcards

Seed Paper Postcard (PSP)

Send flowers through the mail at a postcard rate! The Seed Paper Postcard is a promotion that's as affordable as it is green. Your full-color, custom message is printed on the seed paper with Earth-friendly inks that won't damage the seeds. Our seed paper is made by hand from 100%-recycled material and embedded with a hardy mixture of wildflower seeds. Just plant the entire postcard, water and enjoy your flowers!

Size: 3.95x5.2" or 4x6"
Paper: Premium Seed Paper / Fully Plantable (Light Ink Coverage)

PSP	100	250	500	1000	2500	
1-sided	2.00	1.70	1.53	1.38	1.17	(A)
2-sided	2.60	2.21	1.99	1.79	1.52	(A)

$35 (G) set-up fee for each side of printing
Available on Signature for a 10% discount

3" x 4"	3.95" x 5.2"	4" x 6"	5" x 7"	4" x 8.5" (no bleed)

(Continued)

293

Figure 7.9 (Continued)

Seed Paper Grades

Premium Seed Paper

This top-of-the-line printable seed paper features a thick and rich texture, yet is still smooth and consistent for printing and handwriting. Inkjet printing is recommended for this paper, but it also works with silkscreen and letterpress printing.

Seed Mix: Dwarf Godetia, Lemon Mint, Maiden Pinks, Forget-Me-Not, Catchfly, English Daisy, Sweet Alyssum, Spurred Snapdragon, Corn Poppy and Black-Eyed Susan
Approximate Thickness: 12 pt., 250 gsm
Print Compatibility: Inkjet and Letterpress
Approximate Germination Rate: >75%
Color: White
Seed Mix Options: Annual and perennial wildflower seed mix, and herb mix. Custom mixes available (minimum charges apply)

Signature Seed Paper

Our Signature line of printable seed paper features a smooth finish. Packed with seeds and value, this is the grade that makes high-quality, 4-color printing on seed paper easy.
Inkjet printing is recommended for this paper.

Seed Mix: Catchfly, English Daisy, Sweet Alyssum, Spurred Snapdragon, Corn Poppy and Black-Eyed Susan
Approximate Thickness: 10 pt., 150 gsm
Print Compatibility: Inkjet, Digital and Offset (offset printing reduces germination)
Approximate Germination Rate: 50-75%
Color: White

ECOnomy Seed Paper

ECOnomy seed paper is loaded with visible wildflower seeds firmly embedded into tree-free fibers and convey your Earth-friendly messages. This paper is great for fast-turn, low-cost projects, with a low priority on achieving the high germination rates Bloomin's other papers are known for.

Seed Mix: Catchfly, English Daisy, Sweet Alyssum, Spurred Snapdragon, Corn Poppy and Black-Eyed Susan
Approximate Thickness: 12 pt., 150 gsm
Print Compatibility: Inkjet, Digital and Offset (offset printing reduces germination)
Approximate Germination Rate: <10%
Color: White

Seed Paper Shape Pricing

Quantity	250	500	1000	2500	
Small	0.30	0.26	0.22	0.18	(F)
Medium	0.37	0.32	0.28	0.23	(F)
Large	0.58	0.52	0.46	0.38	(F)

Set-Up $14 (F) • Add-On: cello bag and stock planting instruction card assembled $0.40 (F)

21 Original Seed Paper Colors

*PMS colors are approximate

White

BRIGHTS
Cranberry (PMS 206)*
Orange (PMS 172)*
Yellow (PMS 106)*
Lime (PMS 373)*
Sage (PMS 345)*
Forest (PMS 334)*
Teal (PMS 327)*
Royal (PMS 286)*
Violet (PMS Violet)*
Burgundy (PMS 228)*

NATURALS
Natural (PMS 4755)*
Desert Orange (PMS 1225)*
Chartreuse (PMS 617)*
Terra Cotta (PMS 693)*
Coffee (PMS 412)*

PASTELS
Light Yellow (PMS 607)*
Powder (PMS 5513)*
Light Blue (PMS 2915)*
Lavender (PMS 2567)*
Pink (PMS 1895)*

Herb Mix Sage
Herb Mix Forest
Herb Mix White
Hope Mix Pink
Evergreen Forest

Chili Pepper Lime
Tomato Cranberry
Carrot Orange
Lettuce Sage

Bulk Seed Paper Sheet Pricing

Original	100	250	500	1000	2500	
8.5x11"(untrimmed)	1.36	1.17	1.05	0.99	0.94	(F)
Premium						
14x19"(untrimmed)	3.12	2.88	2.69	2.50	2.25	(F)
13.25x17.95"	3.28	3.05	2.81	2.58	2.34	(F)
8.5x11"	1.64	1.41	1.26	1.17	1.13	(F)
Signature						
13.25x17.95"	2.25	2.06	1.69	1.43	1.31	(F)
8.5x11"	1.25	1.10	1.00	0.90	0.80	(F)
ECOnomy						
23x35"	3.19	2.63	2.44	2.18	1.95	(F)
8.5x11"	0.75	0.68	0.64	0.60	0.56	(F)

Figure 7.9 Bloomin seed paper catalog pages. Used with permission of Bloomin. All Rights Reserved.

Market Segmentation

Databases are most often the distribution vehicles for direct mail. Sophisticated techniques for compiling, warehousing, and mining such databases—coupled with computer technology for most effectively using transaction, demographic, psychographic, and other data inherent to them—can pinpoint prospects and identify market segments in a highly efficient manner. With such data, the direct marketer can efficiently segment house lists (active and inactive customers as well as inquirers) and compiled databases of other organizations. For example, Busch Gardens segments its database to target specific guests with customized offers and messages. Figure 7.10 shows a reacquisition self-mailer that was sent to lapsed Busch Gardens Pass Members, highlighting everything new the park had to offer.

Figure 7.10 Busch Gardens member reacquisition mailer. Used with the consent of Busch Gardens/ Water Country USA. All Rights Reserved.

Databases are at the heart of most print media, regardless of the type used. Let's now explore some other direct-response print media, including coupons, cooperative mailings, statement/invoice stuffers, package inserts, and take-one racks.

Coupons

As a promotional medium—primarily for grocery, health, and beauty care products—a **coupon** is an offer by a manufacturer or retailer that includes an incentive for purchase of a product or service in the form of a specified price reduction. A major objective of coupons is to motivate buyers to try a new product or to convert occasional users into regular customers. A further objective is to increase sales so the retailer will give the product greater display space.

Coupons may also be used to target select consumer market segments. For example, Busch Gardens wanted to attract discrete guests from the Virginia Beach area, so the park pushed a targeted coupon for a single-day ticket (seen in Figure 7.11) through its sales channels. After the coupon had reached the target market, the company saw its largest year-over-year increase for the region.

Coupons distributed by direct mail can be self-mailers for a single brand, enclosed in an envelope with descriptive literature, inserted in company newsletters, or combined with coupon offers—which will be discussed next. Coupon redemption rates are normally highest (slightly more than 18 percent) when coupons are instantly redeemable.[5]

(Continued)

Figure 7.11 (Continued)

Figure 7.11 Busch Gardens sales coupon mailer. Used with the consent of Busch Gardens/Water Country USA. All Rights Reserved.

Cooperative Mailings

Cooperative mailings provide participants, usually direct-response advertisers, with the opportunity to reduce mailing costs in reaching common prospects. Mass cooperative mailings frequently combine coupon offers with other direct-response offers, thus sharing the total mailing cost among several advertising participants. Some cooperative mailings provide opportunities to reach market segments such as new homeowners, new families, Spanish-speaking households, or consumers in particular ZIP code clusters. As many as a dozen or more offers might be contained in a cooperative mailed to a specific market segment. Such mass cooperatives are sometimes distributed through other print media, such as newspapers and magazines.

Valpak, the leader in cooperative mailings nationwide, allows its clients to select from a variety of format options—including coupons, flyers, and postcards—to fit each client's product or service, message, and budget. Valpak is a well-known and recognized cooperative direct mail program. Many consumers recognize its familiar blue Valpak envelope (shown in Figure 7.12) and look forward to sorting through the offers. Popular Valpak coupon advertisers most appealing to consumers include grocery stores, sit-down restaurants, fast food restaurants, mass retail stores, pizza parlours, and video rentals/movie theaters.

Statement/Invoice Stuffers

Periodic bills and reminder statements mailed to the customers of department stores, publications, utilities and credit card providers give an opportunity for distributing complementary (but not

Figure 7.12   Valpak envelope. Used with permission of Valpak, A Cox Target Media Company.

competing) offers of products and services with **stuffers** inserted in the envelope with the invoice or statement. Deliverability is ensured, because most bills travel via first-class mail, and virtually everyone opens their bills in a timely fashion. The billing company implies an endorsement of the offer and, in some cases, also offers credit to make the purchase. Marketers can segment these mailings by selecting the organization sending out the bills.

Package Inserts

Package inserts are related to stuffers but offer the additional advantage of arriving when the recipient has just made a purchase. Certain direct marketers offer the opportunity for one or more direct-response advertisers to include inserts with customer shipments. Gourmet meat purveyor Omaha Steaks, for example, might enclose an offer of gourmet coffee from Gevalia in its shipments. Some package shippers may even offer specific selection by product line or geographic location. Inserts might be loose or contained within a separate folder in the package.

Take-One Racks

Another method of print distribution is the use of **take-one racks** in supermarkets, restaurants, hotels, drug stores, transportation terminals, buses and trains, or other high-traffic locations. These might be placed in a cardboard display container adjacent to a cash register, or could be placed in a wire rack strategically hung on a wall in a supermarket and containing many offers. An advantage of such distribution is that those who voluntarily take a promotion piece from the rack are usually more than casually interested. Thus, the response rate from take-one rack inserts is relatively high when the lower cost is considered. Even though distribution within a single rack might be quite low—say, fewer than 100 pieces per month—the number of potential outlets for racks is quite large and distribution could total into the millions.

Other print media include magazines and newspapers, with which the following sections are concerned.

MAGAZINES

A key consideration for direct marketers, in the development of direct-response advertisements for use in print media, magazines, and newspapers, is space limitation when compared to direct mail. Because print advertisements must compete with other advertisements as well as the editorial content of the print media, the headline is the most important element. Like catalog copy, the headlines of print ads must gain attention quickly and the body copy must tell the story completely yet concisely. Copy must be benefit-oriented and the graphic design should lead the reader through the advertisement's elements in intended sequence. Illustrations augment copy.

Design

Direct-response print advertisements must contain an attention-getting headline, compelling body copy to stimulate interest and desire, and a strong call-to-action response device that can be traced, tracked, and measured. Let's explore each of these elements in greater detail.

Figure 7.13 Newport News/Williamsburg International Airport advertisement. Newport News/Williamsburg International Airport (PHF). Used with permission.

Headlines

Possibly the most important element of a direct-response print advertisement is the headline. Headlines must reach out and grab the consumer's attention and arouse interest. As presented in Chapter 6, you should promise a benefit in your eye-catching headline whenever possible. For example, the ad featured in Figure 7.13 has a catchy headline: Need a Vacation? Absolutely! Who doesn't need one!

Body Copy

Direct-response copy starts with benefits and ends with a request for action. Typical sentences are short and active, including phrases such as these:

* Today more than ever …
* Fortunately for you …
* There's a new way…
* Authorities have proved …
* Try it for ten days …
* Judge for yourself …

Refer again to the airport ad presented in Figure 7.13. Note that the body copy encourages readers to fly to warmer weather and respond by visiting its website, or connecting on Facebook or Twitter.

Response Devices

When all is said and done, the time comes to ask for the order. A good way to determine whether the advertisement can be categorized as direct response is to see whether it asks for action and how effectively it does so. Remember that a key characteristic of direct marketing is that it is measurable and accountable. Marketers measure transactions, that is, orders, inquiries, contributions, or votes. A direct response can be visiting a website, sending a text message, mailing a coupon or an order form, phoning in an inquiry or order, traveling by going to the seller's location, or placing a request for the seller to come to the buyer's location. Many otherwise good advertisements with effective headlines and compelling body copy fall down when they do not specifically ask the reader to order the product, fill out the coupon, click on the shopping cart, or call.

The terms of the offer, including price, need to be clearly stated. The response mechanism must provide a sense of action now. Although layout is not always easy to control, it is desirable to have right-hand coupons on advertisements that run on right-hand pages of print media (especially magazines) and vice versa for left-hand pages. The reason is obvious: it's easier to clip such a coupon if it adjoins an outside edge of the page.

Inserts

A popular form of print advertisement in a magazine is an insert. Printing technology has made possible a great many variations for such inserts, including folding, gumming, consecutive numbering, die-cutting, and personalization on a printing press. The insert might be a multipage piece, or it may be a simple reply card bound next to a full-page advertisement and serving as the response device.

Copy and format are important considerations for inserts in newspapers and magazines. Single-page or multipage formats are available along with special features, such as perforated coupons and gummed reply envelopes, incorporated right into the format. Inserts offer a chance for unbounded creativity for the writer and designer of direct-response print.

Market Segmentation

Special-interest magazines, through their selection of content and the resulting readership, serve to define market segments and even psychographic lifestyles for direct-response advertisers. Categories of special-interest magazines are virtually unlimited: class (*The New Yorker*, *Smithsonian*, and *Museum*), literary (*Atlantic*, *Harper's*, and *The New York Times Book Review*); sports (*Sports Illustrated*, *Ski*, and *Golf*), how-to (*Popular Mechanics*, *Popular Science*, and *Woodworking*), news (*Time*, *Newsweek*, and *U.S. News*), religious (*Christian Herald* and *Catholic Digest*), and many other diverse titles, such as *Entertainment Weekly*, *Self*, *Vanity Fair*, and *Playboy*. Figure 7.14 presents an example of a special-interest magazine, McDonald Garden Center's *Inspirations: Four-Season Solutions for Home and Garden*. This publication focuses on interior and exterior lifestyle trends and designs, and also contains advertisements related to home and garden improvement.

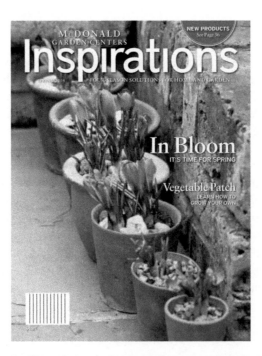

Figure 7.14 McDonald Garden Center's *Inspirations* magazine cover. Used with permission of McDonald Garden Center.

Certain national magazines—including, among many others, *The New Yorker*, *Businessweek*, and *Newsweek*—are available in demographic editions describing market segments, such as women, college students, and business executives. Some publications, including *TV Guide*, offer geographic editions that are described by ZIP code areas. Some, such as *Time*, combine both demographic and geographic market segmentation, offering selected advertisers access to these selected groupings. Occasionally, using laser printing technology, individual ads are personalized to individual subscribers.

Categories of Magazines

Magazines can be grouped by editorial content into five major categories:

1. General mass: Characterized by high circulation and relatively low cost per thousand readers, general mass circulation magazines include *Reader's Digest*, *TV Guide*, *People*, and *National Geographic*.
2. Women's service: Like the first category, women's service magazines are characterized by heavy circulation and reasonably low cost per thousand readers. Included are magazines such as *McCall's*, *Good Housekeeping*, *Family Circle*, *Seventeen*, and *Ladies' Home Journal*.
3. Shelter: With selected demographics and increased cost, shelter magazines (those that focus on homes, decorating, and gardening) include *Architectural Digest*, *Better Homes and Gardens*, *House & Garden*, and *House Beautiful*.
4. Business: This category includes *Fortune*, *Forbes*, *American Banker*, *Bloomberg Businessweek*, *Nation's Business*, *Fast Company*, and *Black Enterprise*.
5. Special interest: With highly selected demographics and even lifestyle definition, this category would include magazines such as *Travel & Leisure*, *Gourmet*, *Ski*, *Golf Digest*, *Jogging*, *Modern Bride*, *USA Hockey*, *Guitar Player*, *Hot Rods*, *Car and Driver*, *Game Informer*, and *National Geographic Kids* (see Figure 7.15).

Advantages and Disadvantages

Magazines can be selected to reach defined market segments: mass or class; rural, urban, or suburban; females or males; senior citizens or teenagers. Modern printing technology permits excellent reproduction at a relatively low cost per thousand circulation. Because magazines usually come out periodically—weekly, monthly, quarterly—they enjoy relatively long life and often many readers will read a single copy. Through split-run techniques, in which alternative advertisements are placed in every other copy, magazines can be tested relatively inexpensively for ways to maximize direct response.

On the negative side, however, magazines offer direct marketers less space in which to tell their story than direct mail does. Additionally, closing dates for magazines (the date by which the magazine must receive the ad) are often considerably in advance of the issue dates and, because of staggered distribution, over a long period of time, response is usually spread out over time and thus slower.

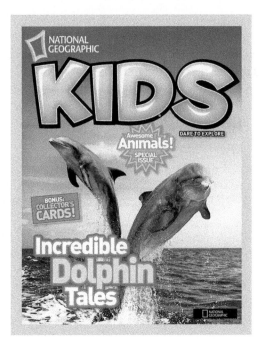

Figure 7.15 *National Geographic Kids* magazine. Used with permission of The National Geographic Society.

Factors influencing the cost of magazine advertising include: the amount of space purchased; whether the ad is in color or black and white; whether the ink bleeds off the edges of the page; and the use of regional, demographic, or test market selections. Certain magazines offer discounted rates for direct-response advertisers as well as special rates for categories such as publishers or schools. Sometimes, standby or 'remnant' space is available at publication deadline and at a substantial discount.

Position and Timing

Although the front and back covers usually get maximum readership in a magazine, many publications do not permit direct-response coupons in these preferred positions. The front portion of the magazine, assuming a full page, is preferable. A right-hand page is usually better for direct response than a left-hand page, but there are exceptions, such as the last left-hand page in the publication. Whether on a right-hand or left-hand page, the response coupon, if there is one, should always appear on the outside margin and never in the gutter (center fold) of the magazine. Inserts and bind-in response devices, reply cards or envelopes, serve to call attention to the advertisement. Many magazines offer advertisers an opportunity, along with a special cooperative advertising rate, to have their advertisement listed and highlighted on a bingo card. A **bingo card** (also called an information card) is an insert or page of a magazine that is created by the publisher to provide a numeric listing of advertisers. Bingo cards can be bound into the magazine or loosely inserted, and serve as a response mechanism for consumers to request additional information by simply circling or checking the number corresponding to each advertiser. Advertisers will often reference the bingo card in their ad with statements such as 'for further information circle item 27.' Consumers send completed cards directly to the publisher who, in turn, sends compiled lists of inquiries to the appropriate participating advertiser.

Aside from seasonal offers, the response from magazine advertisements usually follows the normal direct marketing cycle. The strongest response occurs in January–February and September–October, with the poorest response during June–July.

NEWSPAPERS

Along with magazines, newspapers represent a major medium for the distribution of printed direct-response advertising. A sizable number of weekly and free newspapers are also available for use by direct marketers. Figure 7.16 presents the cover of an issue of the *Oyster Pointer* newspaper. The *Oyster Pointer* is an example of a free monthly newspaper that provides direct marketers with excellent opportunities to promote to local consumers. The *Oyster Pointer* is a business publication that features stories about businesses and people who work within the Oyster Point Business Park. Direct-response advertisements are highly effective in this publication.

Market Segmentation

Like magazines, newspapers help segment the market for direct-response advertising, although not as finely as magazines. National newspapers, such as *The Wall Street Journal*, *USA Today*, *Capper's Weekly*, and *National Enquirer*, are directed to well-defined market segments. Some national newspapers are produced via franchises in local geographic regions.

Additional opportunities for market segmentation through newspapers include urban versus rural, dailies versus weeklies, commuter editions versus those home-delivered, morning versus evening editions, tabloids, comics sections, and Sunday supplements. Marketers can also select specific types of readers by choosing the placement of direct-response advertisements within the newspaper, such as in the sports, television, comics, or business sections, for example.

Categories of Newspaper Advertising

Aside from type and location of a newspaper's circulation, there are four distinct ways to reach newspaper readers: (1) run-of-paper, (2) preprinted inserts, (3) syndicated Sunday supplements, or (4) ad notes.

Run-of-Paper Advertisements

Run-of-paper or **run-of-press (ROP) advertisements** (also called 'space ads') are ads that are printed when the newspaper goes to press. This allows the editor or publisher to place the ads in the space where they fit the best in that edition of the paper, hence the term 'space ads.' Advertisers are given options for the size of their ad, and as they lay out the paper, editors use their discretion on which ads to place where. ROP ads are popular because they commonly have lower rates in newspaper advertising, compared with other options. Although ad position in a newspaper can many times be specified and paid for, positioning the ad at the will of the newspaper editor does not normally have the visual impact or dominance required for direct-response advertisers. Most ROP direct-response advertisements are small in size; however, full-page ads in newspapers will, of course, increase dominance wherever placed. An example of a direct-response space ad used to attract tourists to Williamsburg is shown in Figure 7.17.

Figure 7.16 Oyster Pointer newspaper cover. Published with the consent of Oyster Pointer. All rights reserved.

Figure 7.17 Williamsburg Tourism 'Freedom' space ad. Used with permission of Greater Williamsburg Chamber & Tourism Alliance. All Rights Reserved.

Preprinted Inserts

Preprinted inserts run typically in Sunday editions or on Wednesday or Thursday mornings. The direct-response advertiser usually prints them ahead of time and provides them to the newspaper according to the publication's specifications. Newspaper inserts abound and appear in a variety of formats, especially on Sundays and midweek, on Wednesdays and Thursdays, which are typically grocery shopping days for many newspaper readers. Coupons are a major response format used in such inserts. Direct-response advertisers using newspaper inserts include insurance companies, land developers, trade schools, retail stores, book clubs, magazine publishers, and film processors. A key advantage of newspaper inserts is controlled timing. In many markets, demographic selection, often by ZIP code definition, makes possible pinpointing messages to market segments.

The direct-response print advertisement from Hauser's Jewelers, shown in Figure 7.18, demonstrates many of the necessary elements of an effective print ad. This print ad was a newspaper insert, so it contained two sides of colorful copy. Direct-response advertisements often incorporate photographs to convey visually what the words describe. The call to action—'Drop everything! Head to Hauser's Jewelers'—is very strong, and it is creatively pictured on a clothesline to get the prospective customer to think about Mother's Day. The Hauser's Jewelers print

307

ad presents a compelling picture of 'Splendor in the Grass' followed by the announcement of Hauser's annual pearl event. The direct-response advertisement is measurable in that customers must present the ad to receive the 15 percent discount incentive on all pearl jewelry purchases. The advertised offer contains a time limit, May 7–12, which is clearly presented on both sides of the advertisement. Location and contact information is also provided on both sides.

Figure 7.18 Hauser's direct-response print advertisement. Used with permission of Hauser's Jewelers.

Sunday Supplements

Mass circulation **Sunday supplements**, such as *Parade* and *Family Weekly*, are edited nationally but appear locally in the Sunday editions of many newspapers. They offer large circulation and a great deal of flexibility at a relatively low cost. One variation of the Sunday supplement is the comics section, which reaches as many as 50 million households. Sunday supplements, both magazine and comics sections, have proven successful for many direct-response advertisers.

Ad Notes

An **ad note** is a small sticker that is placed on the front page of the newspaper that can be peeled off without damaging the newspaper. These notes offer a powerful front-page top position that truly catches the reader's attention. Ad notes are an excellent spot to place a direct-response ad, such as the Hi-Ho Silver ad note featured in Figure 7.19. Some companies offer ad notes in different shapes, two-sided printing, scratch-off ink, and barcoding for recording responses.

Figure 7.19   Hi-Ho Silver ad. Used with permission of Hi-Ho Silver. All Rights Reserved.

Advantages and Disadvantages

Key advantages of newspapers for direct-response advertisers include short closing dates and a relatively fast response. A wide variety of formats is available as well as broad coverage of geographic or demographic areas. Most newspapers now offer online editions that can be accessed from the Internet or from mobile devices via a free app, such as the *Daily Press*'s 'ON THE GO,' shown in Figure 7.20. The ON THE GO application allows you to view headline articles, see photos of the articles, add your favorite article, photo, or blog, view *Daily Press* tweets, and see breaking news stories. It has Facebook, Twitter, and e-mail sharing devices built in and offers mobile text alerts to any iPhone, Android, or mobile site.

Newspapers are well known for providing strong market penetration in a local geographical area. Most newspapers do not have the degree of selectivity or market segmentation that direct mail offers. Therefore, most direct-response ads in newspapers keep the message more generic. A disadvantage is that response from newspaper advertisements is usually short-lived because tomorrow brings another edition.

Position and Timing

There are many opportunities for positioning in newspapers. An obvious one is placement of a funeral service inquiry ad adjacent to the obituaries. Another is placement of automobile tire and hunting gear ads in the sports section. Most newspapers have food sections—usually on Wednesday or Thursday—and relevant ads are obvious candidates for placement there. Financial advisors and stockbrokers are appropriate advertisers in business sections.

Figure 7.20 The *Daily Press*'s On The Go copy. Used with permission of the Daily Press Media Group.

Timing can be important, too. Seasonal interests are obvious. Sunday editions typically are read at a more leisurely pace and in a family setting. Morning editions may be more appropriate for retailers than evening editions. As already noted, Wednesday and/or Thursday may be more favorable to grocery shopping ads, and weekend sport sections carry a lot of scores and other references for sports fans. Tuesdays may be relatively light days for advertising, so ads can be showcased. Friday editions may emphasize weekend activities. Of course, major news happenings (often unforeseen) can grab attention away from all the other content.

SUMMARY

Direct mail remains an important medium for direct marketers, relying on databases to effectively reach specific market segments. Direct mail is a selective, flexible medium, and it offers great potential for a high rate of response, although it is the most expensive medium per prospect mailed. Variations of direct mail include self-mailers, classic formats, catalogs, coupons, cooperative mailings, and miscellaneous distribution, such as statement/invoice stuffers, package inserts, and take-one racks.

Printed media, other than direct mail, include magazines and newspapers. Magazines, as they have moved away from mass circulation to special-interest circulation, offer increased opportunities for market segmentation through a definition of content and readership. We generally categorize magazines as general mass, women's service, shelter, business, and special interest. Thus, magazine readership can help describe markets. Although they offer high-quality printing reproduction, magazines provide direct marketers less space for their messages than in direct mail. The cost of circulation of magazines is substantially lower than that of direct mail, but response rates of individual advertisements are also much lower.

There are also a good many weekly and industry-specific newspapers (such as farm newspapers), which are also used extensively by direct marketers. Like magazines, newspapers can be segmented for direct-response advertisers by geographic location, special positioning within the paper, and other factors, such as morning or evening editions, and commuter or home delivery circulation. Response advertisers can use ROP (run-of-paper), preprinted inserts, or Sunday supplements.

KEY TERMS

ad note	package inserts
bingo card	positioning
catalog	preprinted inserts
chit	run-of-paper (ROP) advertisements
classic format	self-mailer
cooperative mailings	solo mailer
coupon	stuffers
direct mail	Sunday supplements
insert	take-one racks
letter	variable data printing

REVIEW QUESTIONS

1. What is the major advantage of direct mail over other media for direct response?
2. Discuss the attributes of a database that could be helpful for targeting direct mail to the most likely prospects. How can these be used in developing promotion copy?
3. In what ways do contemporary mailed catalogs differ from those pioneered by Ward, Sears, and Spiegel?
4. What are two attributes of mailed catalogs that give them an advantage in direct mail?
5. Why is a coupon considered to be direct-response advertising?
6. Evaluation of media for direct-response advertising must relate results to costs. How might this be done?

7. Describe and show examples of these alternatives to traditional direct mail: cooperative mailings, statement/invoice stuffers, package inserts, and take-one racks.
8. Discuss the relative advantages and disadvantages of direct-response advertising placed in magazines and/or newspapers.
9. Of what importance are position and timing of direct-response advertising placed in magazines or newspapers?
10. How are print media being used in conjunction with high-tech digital media? Provide an example.

EXERCISE

Congratulations! You have just been hired as a marketing director for a specialty magazine. Your primary responsibility is to increase the number of subscribers to your magazine. Your assignment is to: (1) describe the magazine and its target market; (2) create a media plan composed of only print media; and (3) develop the rough creative materials you plan to use in the execution of the media plan. Your new boss didn't give you a budget, so be creative!

CRITICAL THINKING EXERCISE

Find a print media advertisement that utilizes a multichannel call to action. Follow and comply with each of the calls-to-action and describe the synergy, or lack thereof, between the various channels.

READINGS AND RESOURCES

- Baesman: www.baesman.com
- Variable data: www.amazingmail.com/direct-mail-business-solutions/variable-data-relevancy
- Variable data: http://blog.ironmarkusa.com/variable-data-printing-examples
- Catalogs: https://windowsreport.com/software-create-catalogs
- Space ads: https://copywritercollective.com/howtobeacopywriter/7-tips-for-writing-more-effective-space-ads
- Print ads: https://blog.hubspot.com/marketing/interactive-print-ads

CASE: BUSCH GARDENS

SeaWorld Parks and Entertainment is one of the world's top theme park companies. Its ten parks, including the SeaWorld and Busch Gardens parks, play host to 25 million guests each year. One of the company's major bases of operation is Williamsburg, Virginia, where its Busch Gardens and Water Country USA parks are top attractions for family vacationers. Busch Gardens features some of the world's top-rated roller coasters, along with other rides, children's play areas, shows, animal encounters, and seasonal events. Water Country USA is the largest water park in the mid-Atlantic region, offering rides and slides from mild to wild, plus plenty of other water-soaked fun.

As leading regional theme parks, Busch Gardens and Water Country USA appeal to both tourists, who stay overnight in the destination, and residents, who visit the parks as a day trip. The majority of these guests are families, but the parks also cater to groups and niche audiences, such as seniors and members of the military. Although visitors come from across the United States and many other countries, the largest concentration of guests comes from the region stretching from New York through North Carolina, encompassing major cities including New York, Philadelphia, Baltimore, Washington, DC, Richmond, Norfolk, and Raleigh-Durham.

Media Mix

To reach potential visitors, the marketing team uses a comprehensive mix of paid media, direct marketing, public relations, promotions, and interactive communications. The media mix and level of activity are adjusted according to the potential of each geographic market and consumer segment. Television and radio advertising are used in most major visitor-source markets. Digital media, including online display advertising, pre-roll video, rich media and paid search, are key parts of the mix, which are targeted according to geography or behavior.

Although broadcast and digital media account for the largest portion of its marketing spending, Busch Gardens continues to use print media as a key component of its mix. Each year, the park produces hundreds of unique printed pieces, including advertisements, direct mail, and collateral materials. These elements provide a layer of communication that works in concert with other media by providing more information and specific purchase direction than are typically possible in a 30-second television spot or a Web banner advertisement.

Print Advertisements

Print advertisements are designed for newspapers and magazines and most have a specific call to action–a ticket offer, promotional discount, or limited-time event. As shown in Figure 7.21, some advertisements are targeted to specific audiences, such as parents of young children or military families. Others are designed to drive business through ticket-sales partners, which include travel agents, credit unions, and hotels.

One recent print piece ran as an insert in Thanksgiving Day editions of major regional newspapers and promoted the Christmas Town holiday event at Busch Gardens. The eight-page, four-color insert highlighted the special attractions, shows, dining, and shopping available during the event in high-impact format. The timing on Thanksgiving Day coincided with the start of Christmas Town and took advantage of the high readership of advertising inserts during this edition. Attendance for Christmas Town increased more than 30 percent year-over-year, with the print insert serving as the only paid advertising in some markets.

Figure 7.21 Busch Gardens 'Parent' and 'Military' ads. Used with the consent of Busch Gardens Water Country USA. All Rights Reserved.

Direct Mail

A significant part of Busch Gardens's direct-mail activity is aimed at its Pass Members, who purchase a pass good for unlimited admission for one or two years. To acquire new Pass Members, the park often uses self-mailers highlighting upcoming events and new attractions. To encourage existing members to renew their passes, the park communicates through a combination of e-mail, four-color postcards, and a statement-type letter offering a discount for continued loyalty. In addition, all members receive newsletters, postcards, and an annual 'Fun Tracker' calendar, featured in Figure 7.22, to encourage park visitation.

FUN TRACKER 2016 EVENTS CALENDAR

DON'T MISS ALL THE FUN
MEMBER-EXCLUSIVE OFFERS & EVENTS INSIDE

JULY

SUN	MON	TUES	WED	THURS	FRI	SAT
					1	2
3	4 INDEPENDENCE DAY	5	6	7	8	9
	CONCERT FIREWORKS					
10	11	12	13	14	15	16
17	18	19	20	21	22	23
24	25	26	27	28	29	30
31						

■ BG & WCUSA OPEN
■ 4th of July Concert

ALL FOR ONE™ PREMIERES

FIREWORKS

JULY 4 LEE GREENWOOD: Catch a FREE concert by this country star, known for his hit song "God Bless the USA"

SUMMER OF THRILLS
Presented by

ALL FOR ONE™!
NOW SHOWING
We're treating Members to FREE reserved seating in the Royal Palace Theatre premiere night, July 1. For your convenience, this Members-only benefit will be available for two show times. Stop by Guest Relations on July 1 for your reserved seating ticket.

(Continued)

Figure 7.22 (Continued)

Figure 7.22 Busch Gardens 2016 Fun Tracker. Used with the consent of Busch Gardens/Water Country USA. All Rights Reserved.

The Fun Tracker calendar was mailed to the active 'Pass Member' segment of Busch Gardens's customer database. The park decided to illustrate the value of a membership and entice its members to visit often by showcasing every month's events, concerts, and new offerings. The inside cover of the calendar showcased all of the benefits of a membership and stressed all the fun that could be had during the spring, summer, fall, and even winter seasons at Busch Gardens Williamsburg. Pass Members consistently cite these printed pieces as a primary source for their knowledge about events and new features at the park. It is a great piece because it stays on a Pass Member's wall or refrigerator all year long as a constant reminder of the park.

Direct mail also is effectively used by the marketing team to reach likely tourists. These mailers are targeted both geographically and demographically, and typically include a strong call to action for a vacation package or multi-day ticket for both Busch Gardens and Water Country USA. A direct mailing, shown in Figure 7.23, included a free, ready-to-use seven-day ticket to both parks as a powerful incentive to plan a getaway. While giving away a free ticket may seem like a money-losing proposition for the company, the mailing was successful because an average of two additional tickets were purchased for every free ticket redeemed, and each ticket resulted in almost three visits across Busch Gardens and Water Country USA.

INCREDIBLE RIDES, SENSATIONAL SHOWS, PLUS AN ALL-NEW, NIGHTLY FIREWORKS SPECTACULAR

This summer, treat your family to a world of fun at Busch Gardens. Feel the rush of Griffon, our heart-pounding, floorless dive coaster. Go on a thrilling and chilling adventure with Curse of DarKastle's dizzying drops, surprise twists and amazing 3-D effects. Get in on all the family-friendly festivities of Sesame Street Forest of Fun. From "just-right" rides for the kids to screaming coasters, unique dining to world-class entertainment and attractions, it's all available at Busch Gardens and it's all available at family-sized summertime savings.

(Continued)

Figure 7.23 (Continued)

Figure 7.23 Busch Gardens and Water Country USA 7-Day Tourist self-mailer. Used with the consent of Busch Gardens Water Country USA. All Rights Reserved.

Conclusion

Printed collateral ranges from small information cards to large posters. Almost all pieces include a direct call to action and many are customized for sales outlets, geographic markets, or customer segments. The pieces provide an important layer in extending the park's messages where potential visitors work, play, and seek vacation ideas. Busch Gardens's most widely distributed print piece is its annually updated park brochure, where more than one million copies are printed each year for use in visitor centers, hotels, and sales outlets.

Even with its strong presence in broadcast and digital media, Busch Gardens and Water Country USA continue to invest heavily in print media to reach diverse consumers with customized messages, captivating images, and compelling offers.

Case Discussion Questions

1. The case indicates that visitors to Busch Gardens are from all walks of life. Explain how the company segments its markets and what communication mix it uses to connect with potential visitors. What new promotional packages might Busch Gardens offer to attract different segments of its target market?
2. Describe the television and radio advertising media that Busch Gardens uses to attract potential visitors. How are they different from digital media, such as online display ads, pre-roll videos, and paid search, in reaching Busch Gardens's potential target markets?
3. What is the role of print media in the company's media mix? Explain how print media complement broadcast and digital media in Busch Gardens's current communication mix.
4. Provide three specific suggestions regarding how Busch Gardens could integrate its print media campaign with social media channels to increase visits to the park. How would you measure the impact of social media?
5. Busch Gardens focuses a significant part of its media on direct mail activities. Describe the different types of direct mail, such as self-mailers, newsletters, postcards, flyers, and annual 'Fun Tracker' calendars, which the company uses. Who are the target audiences for the company's direct mail? How do the marketing objectives of the various direct mailers differ?

NOTES

1. DMA (2016) *Statistical Fact Book 2016* (New York: Direct Marketing Association), p. 83.
2. DMA (2016) *Statistical Fact Book 2016* (New York: Direct Marketing Association), p. 70.
3. Personal communication with Tyler Baesman, president, Baesman Group, Inc., May 21, 2019.
4. Denise Lee Yohn (2015) 'Why the Print Catalog is Back in Style,' *Harvard Business Review*, February 25, 2015. https://hbr.org/2015/02/why-the-print-catalog-is-back-in-style, retrieved July 30, 2016.
5. DMA (2016) *Statistical Fact Book 2016* (New York: Direct Marketing Association), p. 100.

8

TELEVISION, RADIO, AND DIGITAL VIDEO

CHAPTER CONTENTS

CHAPTER SPOTLIGHT

PANDORA—MUSIC TO SUIT YOUR MOOD

pandora

Figure 8.1   Pandora logo. Used with permission of Pandora.

Need some music to wake you up for an early-morning class? How about some music to help you focus while studying? Perhaps you'd like some music to enjoy while strolling around on campus? Maybe you just need some music to allow you to chill while walking back to your dorm after a long day of classes? How about some music to help you get revved up before you play your favorite sport? Perhaps you need a little pre-gaming music before that blind date? Whatever mood you're in, Pandora has the tunes to suit your frame of mind and make life more enjoyable.

Pandora Radio (also known as Pandora Internet Radio or simply Pandora), a subsidiary of SiriusXM, is the world's most powerful music and podcast discovery platform, providing a uniquely personalized listening experience to approximately 70 million users each month. Pandora is the largest music streaming and automated music recommendation Internet radio service in the U.S., where its highly trained musicologists analyze hundreds of attributes for each recording, which powers its proprietary Music Genome Project® in delivering billions of hours of personalized music tailored to the tastes of each music listener.

Pandora is uniquely positioned to deliver experiences that cater to individual preferences and behaviors, effortlessly. Consumers can take their favorite music with them wherever they go, by listening to Pandora on their mobile devices, desktop, television, Apple Watch, using voice assistants, or in their car. Its new brand campaign reflects Pandora's heritage as the first streaming music service to create personalized radio, as well as its diverse and innovative newer product offerings, like Pandora Premium, which gives subscribers on-demand, ad-free listening, as well as the ability to create playlists and download music for offline listening.

In November 2018, Pandora rolled out its 'Sound On' brand campaign (Figure 8.2), initially centered on holiday travel and the ways music and sound can help people endure the associated challenges such as lost luggage, crowded airports or delayed flights or trains. The spring Sound On campaign that followed in 2019 was designed to inspire listeners to come out of winter hibernation and get into the spring exploration mode. 'Our brand mission is to connect listeners with the music and audio content they love to help them live their lives at full volume,' said Brad Minor, vice president of brand marketing and communications at Pandora. 'This campaign brings that notion to life by showcasing how universal life moments can be deeply enhanced with the right soundtrack.'

Figure 8.2 Pandora Sound On poster images. used with permission of Pandora.

The Sound On campaign was an exciting multi-channel campaign that initially ran in six main markets for 12 weeks, featuring some high-profile musical artists. The entire campaign was designed by its in-house creative team, with approximately 1,100 components developed, including billboards and live board screens in subway terminals and bus shelters. Pandora was the first advertiser to wrap the new AC Transit double-decker buses in Oakland, California. Pandora also executed site-takeovers with Thrillist, Vevo, and Vox online properties, as well as integrations with Facebook, Hulu, Instagram, Snapchat, and Twitter.

Pandora's new sonic logo also debuted throughout the campaign. Other key Sound On campaign components included the following:

- **Sound Wall**: Pandora has commissioned leading street artists to create wall murals that depict their unique interpretations of sound and spring discovery. The murals, which will appear in top markets across the country, will also include Quick Response (QR) codes that drive to custom playlists on Pandora, curated by the street artists and featuring music that inspired their work.
- **Sound Bites**: Pandora will give listeners exclusive opportunities to get up close and personal with private concerts, featuring artists from the campaign.
- **Sound Box**: Pandora has enlisted 20 leading social media influencers to share the spring sounds that inspire each of them, with weekly Pandora playlists for their followers.

Figure 8.3 Pandora Nashville billboard. Used with permission of Pandora.

- **Pandora Sound On Lounge:** Sound On will make an impact at this year's Stagecoach Country Music Festival and Hangout, Firefly, Electric Forest, and Bumbershoot Music Festivals through unique experiential activations.

In conclusion, Pandora's new Sound On campaign signifies the important role that the company plays in enabling consumers to access their favorite music anytime and anywhere to improve their quality of life. So, what are you in the mood to hear right now? Access Pandora, turn up the volume, and enjoy life!

Electronic media are the topic of this chapter. We explore how direct marketers use the media of television (TV), radio, and digital video to generate a response from customers and prospective customers. We also discuss the various formats available for each medium and the advantages and disadvantages associated with using each medium for direct and interactive marketing.

INTRODUCTION

Television and radio are commonly referred to as broadcast media. **Broadcast** is the most universal of communications media. Unlike telephone and print media, broadcasts reach virtually everyone and every location. Many people in the United States listen to the radio during some part of each day. According to Nielsen's National Television Household Universe Estimates, there were 119.9 million TV homes in the U.S. for the 2018–19 TV season.[1] The average household watches television for more than 7 hours and 50 minutes per day.[2] Almost 96 percent of U.S. homes are TV households.[3] Further, the Bureau of Labor Statistics reports that watching television is the leisure activity that occupies the most leisure time, on average, for those aged 15 and older.[4]

With its universality, broadcast reaches the full range of geographic, demographic, and psychographic market segments, which are not always easily separated. Relatively high costs associated with relatively low response rates result from reaching (and paying for) nonqualified prospects. Measurability and accountability, hallmarks of direct marketing, are difficult, if not impossible, with broadcast media. Still, the potential reach is there, if it can be harnessed.

In spite of their universality, however, broadcast media—television and radio—account for only a small percentage of total expenditures for direct-response advertising. Most TV advertising creatively emphasizes product brand and image rather than asking for an immediate response, the preferred advertising mode of direct marketers. However, this is changing as direct marketers experiment with and learn about the possible uses of television and radio.

Today, direct marketers are effectively using multi-media campaigns that combine the impact of television and radio advertising with print, digital, and social media content. The Virginia Living Museum re-branding campaign, *Protect What's Precious* (see Figure 8.4), was executed and supported via television, radio, print (newspaper, magazine, and arts programs), digital (online ads, website, viral video, and social media), direct (mail and e-mail), and public relations mediums. The campaign was a huge success. The campaign garnered a 25 percent increase in memberships as opposed to the 4.5 percent it had hoped to achieve, and a 29 percent increase in annual fund gifts compared to the previous year, which was far greater than the 3 percent the museum had stated as its objective.

Another multi-media campaign was the Dove 'Real Beauty' campaign, which utilized billboards, digital video, and social media.[5] Billboards were used to promote the natural female body, video was used to demonstrate a Photoshop retouching of a model, and discussions were held with Girl Scouts and other groups with influence over young women to discuss body standards.[6]

In this chapter, we look at the ramifications of television, such as network, cable, and satellite transmission, then we discuss radio. And finally, we look at digital video as a direct response and interactive medium.

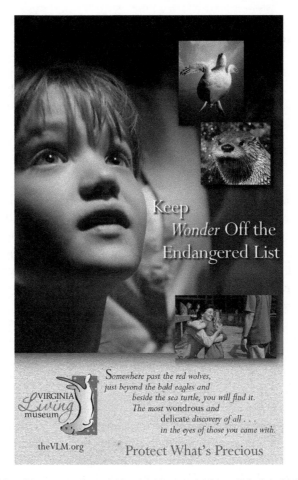

Figure 8.4 Virginia Living Museum print ad. Used with permission of Virginia Living Museum. All Rights Reserved.

TELEVISION

When it began, television, transmitted via established networks or local channels, was not an important medium for direct-response advertising. But its value has increased as direct marketers have learned how to use it. Cable and satellite transmissions now provide an almost endless variety of programming and special-interest channels, defining the potential for market segmentation. Interactive modes of television provide the immediate response—along with measurability and accountability—on which direct marketers thrive.

Direct-response advertisers use television in the following three ways, as we detail in this chapter:

1. To sell products or services or to promote a political candidate or non-profit cause.
2. To get inquiries: expressions of interest or sales leads for personal follow-up.

3. To support other media: driving website traffic, encouraging social media contacts, promoting newspaper inserts or announcing direct mail.

To accomplish these alternatives, direct-response advertisers need to be mindful that television viewers have one of two objectives: *entertainment* or *information*. It is also important that advertisers know how to direct their messages to defined market segments so as to minimize the high cost of reaching television audiences.

Market Segmentation

When a farmer 'broadcasts' seed, much of that seed lodges in moist, fertile ground and, under ideal growing conditions, it is nurtured into a living plant. Another portion of the seed is borne away by the wind or fails to achieve the proper conditions for germination for other reasons. Direct marketers using television are like the farmer sowing seed. Although television has the potential for reaching virtually everyone, it can achieve the objectives of the direct-response advertiser only if it is seen in the right place at the right time under the right conditions. Market segmentation, in television as in other media, is one way to maximize direct response.

Television programming plays an important role in defining specific audience segments. Sports, news, comedies, westerns, mysteries, variety, documentaries, wrestling, and opera or drama can categorize and appeal to market segments of viewers and thus provide a showcase for a particular direct-response offer. Other factors that can help segment markets include time of day or day of the week. Viewers of one of television's most-watched audience events each year, the Super Bowl, are large in number and broad in characteristics. On the other hand, viewers of a Clint Eastwood movie are a more narrowly defined group, and whether they watch late at night or mid-afternoon also can make a difference in the demographic and psychographic characteristics of the audience. The 'reach' of a local TV station can itself describe geographic markets differentiated by ZIP code characteristics.

Offering direct-response advertisers even greater opportunities for market segmentation is cable television, with hundreds of specialized channels. Highly specialized programming, 'live' news, sporting events, and a variety of movie fare can help define desirable segments of cable TV audiences, as can special-interest channels, such as CNN, ESPN, the History Channel, the Country Music Channel, or even the Golf Channel.

Let's check out a great example of how a company has innovatively used cable channels and social media to target a very specific market segment, build brand awareness, and drive product sales. STIHL, Inc., the best-selling brand of handheld outdoor power equipment in America, wanted to boost its brand awareness and promote both its products and its network of more than 8,000 servicing power equipment retailers to outdoor power equipment users. In 1985, STIHL established the STIHL® TIMBERSPORTS® Series, which brings together the world's top lumberjacks to compete in the Original Extreme Sports competition to determine the best all-around lumberjack. The STIHL® TIMBERSPORTS® Series is seen by more than 20 million viewers annually in more than 62 countries on targeted networks such as EUROSPORT and ESPN2 (see Figure 8.5).

Figure 8.5 Professional lumberjack athletes Mark Jones from Princeton, W. Va. And Jason Lentz from Diana, W. Va. Compete in the stock saw discipline in the STIHL® TIMBERSPORTS® Series Midwest Professional Qualifier hosted by Purdue University in West Lafayette, Ind. April 9, 2011. Slicing through 16 inches of white pine with only four inches of wood to work with using a MS 660 STIHL Magnum® chain saw, Jones finished the discipline in 12.45 seconds with Lentz right behind him with a time of 13.4 seconds.

Photo Credit: STIHLTIMBERSPORTS.US/ Adam Harbottle

Figure 8.6 Jason Lentz finishes the underhand chop discipline in 25.89 seconds at the STIHL® TIMBERSPORTS® Series Midwest Professional Qualifier hosted by Purdue University in West Lafayette, Ind. April 9, 2011.

Photo Credit: STHIL TIMBERSPORTS.US/ Adam Harbottle.

In an effort to connect with college-age consumers, STIHL created the STIHL® TIMBER-SPORTS® Collegiate Series, which airs on ESPNU (see Figure 8.6). Winners of the Collegiate Series events earn an opportunity to compete in the Professional Series. Consumers can learn more about the different competition disciplines and competitors and view pictures, video, live events, and check out ESPN air dates on its website (www.stihltimbersports.us). In addition, STIHL connects with followers and engages fans of both the professional and the collegiate series via Twitter and YouTube, and has almost half a million likes on Facebook.[7] Social media platforms are used to provide fans with event and athlete updates and promotional opportunities that feature local STIHL® TIMBERSPORTS® Series events. Social media is also used to coordinate with STIHL® TIMBERSPORTS®'s partners and sponsors to promote and highlight the Series.

The STIHL® TIMBERSPORTS® Series is one of the longest-running programs on ESPN, garnering more than 45 million media impressions, with an advertising value topping $1.77 million. Nationally, the STIHL® TIMBERSPORTS® Series has been featured in *The Boston Globe* and on The 700 Club, ESPN.com, National Public Radio (NPR), and The Colbert Report. So, if you want to become a fan and follow the action, check out STIHL® TIMBERSPORTS® on Facebook, Twitter, Instagram, or YouTube. It promises you a thrilling, action-packed, extreme sporting event.

Characteristics of Television Time

Like empty seats on a departing airplane, television time is perishable. Furthermore, once 24 hours per day have been used within a market, coverage cannot be extended, nor can more time be manufactured or imported. Only actual viewing can be increased. This penetration of the potential market, the number of viewers, is what determines the price of commercial television time.

This price usually peaks during prime time, the early evening hours, and drops to a minimum during the wee hours of the morning. The cost of TV time is highest when the viewing audience is the largest, although the cost is often set without regard to audience composition. Prime time may not be the best time for direct-response advertising unless an offer appeals to a large and diversified audience. Furthermore, large audiences attracted to a suspense-filled event like the Super Bowl are not inclined to break off watching to 'call this toll-free number *now*!'

The cost of a 120-second selling commercial, as typically used for direct-response advertising on television, is not an adequate indication of success unless it is related to anticipated (actual) response to the advertising. The key to maximizing such response lies in market segmentation: just who are the viewers at a particular time and how receptive are they to a direct offer?

Because television costs as well as audience segments vary, the most valid measurement for the direct marketer is cost per response (CPR), not cost per viewer (CPV). Nielsen audience ratings, gross rating points (GRPs), and areas of dominant influence (ADI)—the glossary of TV time buying for the general advertiser—have little or no relevance for the direct marketer who wants somewhat more from direct-response advertising than simply 'recall.'

For example, GRPs are a combination of reach and frequency measures. GRPs are determined by multiplying *reach* (the number of people exposed to vehicles carrying the ad) by *frequency* (the number of insertions purchased in a specific communication vehicle within a specified time period). GRPs may be able to measure the number of people exposed to an ad; however, they cannot determine whether that ad stimulated any subsequent action (response or order). As an example, the CPV of reaching one of television's largest audiences, those watching the Super Bowl, might be quite low, but because of the diversity of this audience, the CPR could be prohibitively high.

The acronym that counts is CPR, the total cost of a direct marketing campaign divided by the number of responses that campaign generated:

$$CPR = \frac{Total\ Promotion\ Budget}{Total\ Number\ of\ Orders/Inquires\ Received}$$

Direct marketers must always relate advertising results to costs.

Direct Marketing Uses of Television

We've said that there are three basic ways in which direct marketers use television. Let's now look at each in turn.

The first of these ways is to *sell something*: a product, a subscription, a service. Direct marketers usually require a 2-minute (120-second) commercial to achieve a direct sale. Customers respond by phone, online, or perhaps by mail.

The second purpose of television for direct marketers is to *generate* leads. These responses require a two-step process in which the commercial stimulates the original inquiry and the customer then follows up in some manner. This follow-up might be by e-mail, postal mail, telephone, SMS text, website visit, or personal visit. If television is used, 60-second television commercials are normally adequate to generate such leads, although in some cases the ad time may be shorter.

The third direct marketing use of television is as *support* of direct-response advertising in another medium. This includes online advertisements, or offline advertisements in newspapers or magazines such as *Cosmopolitan* and *People*. Usually 10- or 30-second commercials are adequate as reminders, with extensive repetition over a period of several days being the key to success. Support television, often purchased locally, creates interest in the offer and directs the viewer to the printed medium, which in turn provides detailed explanations as well as means for response.

Television Home Shopping

HSN (formerly known as the Home Shopping Network) and QVC (Quality/Value/Convenience) are notable examples of TV channels devoted to the continuous sale of merchandise. Though such programming does not yet provide random access for product selection—as would a printed catalog or a website—technology for such interactivity is emerging. For now, these networks primarily offer products such as jewelry, cosmetics, and electronics, which are frequently purchased on impulse. These products are extensively demonstrated, priced for quick sale, and sometimes rely on well-known personalities for credibility. Product demonstrations are often a prime motivating factor in influencing television home-shopper purchases.

Infomercials

Infomercials have become an important means of demonstrating and selling certain categories of products via television. These ads appear primarily on cable channels and often during early-morning and late-night time slots. They usually last for 30 minutes. Featured products typically include exercise machines, cookware, weight-loss programs, and sundry cleaning products. Table 8.1 provides the rankings of the top ten highest grossing infomercial products of all time.[8]

Table 8.1   Top ten highest grossing infomercial products of all time

Rank	Infomercial description	Revenue generated
1	proactiv	$1 billion (annual revenue)
2	P90X	$400 million (annual revenue)
3	Total Gym	$1 billion (total sales)
4	George Foreman Grill	$202 million (annual revenue)
5	Bowflex	$193.9 million (annual revenue)
6	Showtime Rotisserie	$1.2 billion (total sales)
7	Ped Egg	$450 million* (total sales)
8	Snuggie	$400 million* (total sales)
9	Sweatin' to the Oldies – with Richard Simmons	$200 million* (total sales)
10	ThighMaster	$100 million (total sales)

Note: *Estimated figure.

Source: https://worthly.com/business/10-successful-infomercial-products-time/ (retrieved April 20, 2019)

Infomercials allow customers to respond to marketers within moments of being exposed to the product and advertising. They are used by brands that are trying to sell high amounts of goods and increase brand awareness at the same time. Marketers should focus on the benefits of products and not the features when creating an infomercial. Individuals watching the infomercial can connect more easily with benefits and in turn be more likely to purchase, rather than just hearing a list of different features.

A benefit of DRTV infomercials is the fact that campaign results will be known in a quick and efficient manner. This makes tracking the ROI, cost per order, and other calculations easy to determine. Producing a half-hour infomercial can cost anywhere from $25,000 to $250,000, depending on the production values and the host or talent involved in the shoot. For the sake of comparison, the average cost of producing a 30-second national TV commercial is about $350,000. Of course, using well-known spokespeople drives the production cost up.[9]

One of the primary uses of infomercials is for testing. Companies can test products and offers in real time and make adjustments swiftly to produce the best results. If the test is successful, media expenditures will increase, which can translate into a larger ROI. For example, let's say you spend $10,000 per week on your infomercial campaign and it generates $20,000 in revenue. If you can maintain that same 2:1 media efficiency ratio (MER) and you spend $100,000 per week, then your infomercial campaign will generate $200,000 in revenue per week. It is also important to remember that there are additional costs associated with an infomercial campaign, such as card processing, telemarketing, fulfillment, and other, miscellaneous costs.

Advantages and Disadvantages

Television, when used for direct-response advertising, can provide a wide choice of cost alternatives and achieve quick (but short-lived) responses. It reaches an extremely large audience and uses the combination of video and audio, simultaneously providing a sales message along with a product demonstration to deliver a lot of impact in a short time.

Television's major disadvantage is the high cost to prepare and place the ads. Limited time is also one of the medium's disadvantages when product descriptions are complex or not subject to simple demonstration. Another major drawback is lack of a response device that the viewer can reference at a later time.

RADIO

When radio broadcasting was still in its infancy in the 1920s, it became a major medium for direct-response advertising. It was productive for books and records, as it is today, and also, in that early period, for proprietary medicines and health cures. A powerful radio station in Del Rio, Texas, with the call letters XERA, built its transmitter across the border in Mexico to circumvent curtailment of its power by the U.S. government, as well as regulation of its direct-response advertisements. These advertisements were often 'exaggerations of the truth' at best. XERA (and other stations) solicited orders for 'genuine synthetic diamonds' as well as inquiries for Dr. Brinkley's 'goat gland transplants' for those seeking perpetual youth. Mail-order nurseries, pioneers in direct marketing, offered their plants and trees, and religious groups raised funds for their evangelists through the medium of radio. Radio is still probably as effective a direct-response medium as it was then, although it is minimally used today.

Market Segmentation

Even more than TV channels, individual radio stations tend to develop strong images of programming, attracting particular types of listeners. Such program formats can segment markets into an array of specific subgroups that is virtually unlimited: all music, all news, and all talk. Program format doesn't stop with just 'music,' however. Music can be rock, classical, easy listening, country/western, show tunes, or nostalgic music-of-your-life programming. There are numerous different types of radio stations in the United States, each offering a different format or program available to satisfy the listening desires of all consumers.

Listeners are loyal to certain stations, so direct-response advertising, presented within an established program format by a well-known personality, derives an air of credibility or even an implied endorsement from the station announcer. (For many years, syndicated radio news commentator Paul Harvey provided a notable example, with his personally presented commercials for insurance and health products.) Unlike the case in television, in which viewers are constantly surfing among as many as a dozen or more favorite channels, according to the Radio Advertising Bureau, the average radio listener 'tunes in regularly to less than three stations—no matter how many he can receive.' Several thousand radio stations (AM as well as FM stations) provide a lot of choices, and there appears to be relatively little switching!

In addition to program format and station loyalty, another means of market segmentation through radio is by its use during particular times of the day or even days of the week. Unlike most TV viewers, radio listeners can be involved in another activity while listening to the radio, so direct marketers can reach them in an automobile, on arising, or in front of a mirror while shaving. Of course, the listener's attention is not always undivided at these times, and the real challenge to the direct marketer is to deliver a direct-response instruction that the listener will recall later.

Rate Structure

A major boost for radio in direct-response advertising is its relatively low cost. Whereas the economics of television dictate a maximum commercial length of two minutes, commercial messages on the radio can be melded with DJ chatter. Entire 15-minute information radio programs have been built around the content of a magazine, such as *National Geographic*, for which subscriptions are being simultaneously solicited. The same format has also been applied to advice for household repairs at the same time as orders are solicited for a *Home Handyman's Guide*.

Some radio stations accept per inquiry (PI) arrangements under which the station runs commercial messages, at its own discretion, in return for remuneration from a direct-response advertiser for each sale or inquiry produced in this manner.

Advantages and Disadvantages

Radio is the most flexible of all response media in that it requires relatively little in the way of preparation, and it can be scheduled or the copy can be changed right up to the time the message is aired. In contrast with the cost of direct mail or other print media and the high preparatory cost of television video, radio has minimal production costs. In fact, the direct-response advertiser accrues virtually no production cost if the message can be typed for reading by a local station announcer. Because the various program formats of radio are conducive to testing, the direct-response advertiser can readily test alternative copy and formats at relatively low cost.

A major disadvantage of radio, like that of television, is the absence of a response device that can be referenced at some later time. Radio also lacks the visual impact afforded by direct mail and the other print media as well as by television. Finally, increased competition, primarily due to the rapid growth and popularity of Internet radio competitors, has challenged the transmission of traditional broadcast radio programming. Let's briefly explore the impact these channels have had on radio as a direct and interactive marketing medium. Internet radio channels offer a personalized radio program that has significantly decreased advertising commercial radio air time and thus the opportunity to place ads. There are several satellite and digital music services that consumers may select for their listening pleasure as opposed to standard 'free' broadcast radio stations. Basically, these are commercial-free channels or are channels with limited advertising per hour compared with the minutes heard on 'free' channels. Consumers must subscribe to these Internet radio services, such as Sirius XM, Pandora, Spotify, Grooveshark, TuneIn, iHeartRadio, and others. Let's briefly examine a few of the current popular services.

Internet Radio Competitors

Spotify

Spotify is a digital music podcast and video streaming service that provides music of a wide variety of artists to its listeners. While Spotify's basic services are free, consumers pay for additional features via paid subscriptions. Spotify was launched in September 2008 by Daniel Ek. As of June 2016, it had more than 100 million active users and about 500 million registered users, with more than 30 million paid subscribers.[10] Spotify offers advertisers seven different types of ads, described in its ad specs as: Audio Ads, Display Ads, Billboard Ads, Homepage Takeovers, Branded Playlists, Lightboxes, and Advertiser Pages. These advertisements vary in size, type, and user engagement. Audio Ads run for a maximum of 30 seconds as a commercial in between streamed tracks. Display Ads, Billboard Ads, and Lightboxes appear during active and inactive use.[11]

Pandora

Founded in 2000, Pandora Media Inc. began as Savage Beast Technologies, and was founded by Will Glaser, Jon Kraft, and Tim Westergren. Pandora offers its subscribers musical selections of a certain genre based on the subscriber's artist selection. The subscriber then provides positive or negative feedback for songs chosen by the service, and the feedback is taken into account in the subsequent selection of other songs to play. Initially, Pandora offered a fee-based subscription-only service without commercials. However, the company revised its offering based on customer feedback and began selling radio commercials to advertisers. Today, basic Pandora services are offered free of charge to its subscribers and users will normally be exposed to some commercials unless the subscriber opts to pay a fee to enjoy commercial-free music. Pandora normally plays no more than three advertisements per hour for free users.[12]

Sirius XM

Given the merger between Sirius and XM Satellite Radio in 2008, Sirius XM has offered its Internet radio subscribers commercial-free music from every genre, live play-by-play sports, news and talk, and more. Consumers listen to Sirius XM via their car radio, their computer, or on their

335

smartphone or tablet. Sirius XM Radio is only one of the radio services provided by American broadcasting company Sirius XM Holdings. Sirius XM music channels are presented without commercials, while talk channels, such as Howard Stern's programs, have regular commercials. Sirius XM offers its advertisers an audience reach of more than 51.6 million radio listeners, with more than 25.8 million subscribers listening to its diverse talk programming, which includes sports, politics, and lifestyle topics, helping to differentiate it from its competitors.[13]

DIGITAL VIDEO

There are a number of different factors to consider with digital video marketing. The first factor is that in order to be successful in digital video marketing, the video content must fit with the culture of the brand. Without this necessary component, there will be no tie to the product or brand that is being marketed. This will help consumers understand where the brand is coming from and what it stands for. For example, Virginia Beach established its 'Livethelife' YouTube video channel to reinforce its Live the Life brand, as shown in Figure 8.7. Its YouTube site provides rich video content and entices viewers to want to learn more about Virginia Beach as a vacation destination. Its YouTube videos are an excellent way to communicate the many exciting features of Virginia Beach to prospective visitors.

Marketers must also have their target market in mind when creating digital videos, and video content should stem from consumer research. Sound consumer research will reveal the types of videos or products in which customers are most interested. Armed with that consumer information, marketers can identify other brands that already have a strong base of the customers that you wish to reach.

Ideas for video content may come from many different places. Regardless of the content, the video must have both a dialogue and a conversation to be effective. One of the most appealing features of digital video marketing is that it enables the company to connect its different marketing media.

Driving customer traffic from videos to websites, social networks, and other marketing platforms is easily accomplished with video marketing, particularly with 'live videos.' Let's examine how 'live videos' are used in various social media platforms. One of the first 'live video' apps was Periscope, launched in 2015. Since its initial release, and subsequent purchase by Twitter, multiple sites have incorporated some form of live video streaming. These streams are made by the user of the account and allow the user to share content as it happens, often with the option for viewers to comment in real time. Facebook, Instagram, and YouTube offer some similar services, with Facebook implementing the service soon after Periscope.[14] Live streaming is ideal for connecting content creators and brands to engaged consumers in an informal, immediate manner.

The final factor to mention is the importance of video metrics. There are many different ways to measure the outcome of a video. Typical metrics include the following:

- Views: the number of people who click on the video to watch it.
- Shares: the number of times the video content is posted to a server to be shared with others.
- Ratings: YouTube videos can be rated by users clicking red stars. The more and higher the ratings, the more people are viewing the video and like it.

Figure 8.7 Virginia Beach YouTube screenshot. Used with permission of the City of Virginia Beach Convention & Visitors Bureau.

- Comments: these are text responses to a video (on a watch page) or a user (on a channel page).
- Favorites: when people add the video to their own list of preferred videos on a YouTube watch page.

- Subscribers: those people who pledge to support the video channel by viewing video content on a regular basis.
- Links: on the watch page it displays the five websites within which your video has been embedded and is receiving the highest number of clicks or views.
- Active sharing: a YouTube feature that allows you to see who else is watching a video at the same time.

Let's now explore the marketing opportunities associated with the leading video marketing channel, YouTube (Figure 8.8).

Figure 8.8 YouTube logo

Note: The YouTube logo is owned by Google, Inc.

YouTube

YouTube was founded by three former PayPal employees: Chad Hurley, Steve Chen, and Jawed Karim. The idea of YouTube was proposed by Karim at a dinner party in San Francisco, and they all began working on the creation within a couple of days. YouTube was purchased by Google for $1.65 billion. When the largest digital advertising agency in the world acquires a video site, it conveys that video marketing is truly a dominant player in the digital marketing industry.[15] The first video on YouTube, 'Me at the Zoo,' was shot by Yakov Lapitsky at the San Diego Zoo. It was uploaded on April 23, 2005, and within a month it had more than 684,000 views, received more than 4,400 ratings, been 'favorited' more than 3,100 times, and generated nearly 5,200 text comments—all of which led to a public beta test version of YouTube that went live.[16] YouTube has grown rapidly since its inception in 2005 when only 8 million videos were watched each day. Today, more than five billion videos are viewed every single day.[17] In addition, YouTube is now localized in more than 102 countries.[18]

When YouTube was first created, the available features included the following:[19]

- searching by username
- linking videos from other Web pages
- showing related videos within comments
- introducing channels, categorizing, and grouping similar content
- embedding the YouTube video player into other Web pages
- rating videos between one and five stars.

As YouTube has grown, so have the number of features available to users. The following features have been added to the original list over the years and are very useful to marketers in this digital age of marketing:

- YouTube Studio: an analytical tool that tells you where users come from; their age and gender; how many times viewers rate your videos; how people discovered your video (what terms they searched on YouTube or Google); and where the hot and cold parts of your video are through the 'Hot Spot' feature.[20] The acquisition by Google has resulted in a user interface very similar to Google Analytics. One of the most recent upsides is the 'real-time viewers' tab, which allows content creators to monitor their uploads in real time, as soon as the video is released.
- Annotations: this feature allows you to insert text notes and bubbles, link to other YouTube videos or channels, and highlight areas, creating another way to drive traffic from YouTube to other marketing mediums such as websites. **Video annotation** is a way to add interactive commentary to videos by adding background information about the video and linking to related YouTube videos, channels, or search results from within a video.[21] In addition to providing links to related videos, annotations often go to the content creator's online store where merchandise is sold, which represents another income generator for many YouTube celebrities.
- Call to action: a call to action or requests can be created as overlays for all video plays across YouTube (whether the video play is triggered by a promotion or not). The overlay will appear as soon as the video begins to play and can be closed by the user. You can use the overlay to share more information about the content of your video or to raise interest in your channel, other videos, or additional websites. How it works is that when users click on the overlay, they are directed to a company's website as specified in the overlay's destination URL.[22] In addition, nonprofit organizations in the YouTube nonprofit program have the opportunity to insert ads within their own videos, which could be a link to their website, latest campaign, or a donation page.

You are encouraged to monitor YouTube to learn about the additional features it has to offer for video marketing, along with the tips available for setting up a video channel.

Setting up a Video Channel

Marketers can set up and utilize the YouTube channel to maximize their marketing efforts. A YouTube channel permits YouTube users to view your pinned videos, playlists, uploads, community, channels, and 'About' page. Your channel page also displays several links that let other people connect with you (or your brand) by sending you a message, sharing your channel with friends, or adding comments to your channel.[23] It allows all of their videos to be centralized in one location to create maximum exposure from both subscribers and channel visitors. A YouTube channel page serves as a profile page for a veteran marketer or new YouTubers.

Creating a YouTube account is as simple as creating a Google account. Registering for YouTube is free. You are then able to upload videos that will go directly to the users of the YouTube channel. New videos can be added at any time, which enables marketers to provide video content to reflect updated information, events, or interests. For example, the Virginia Beach video shown in Figure 8.9 might have been produced and posted in response to tourist feedback indicating that they wanted to learn more about how to pick crabs. Digital videos present an ideal format to serve both customers and prospects by providing timely information.

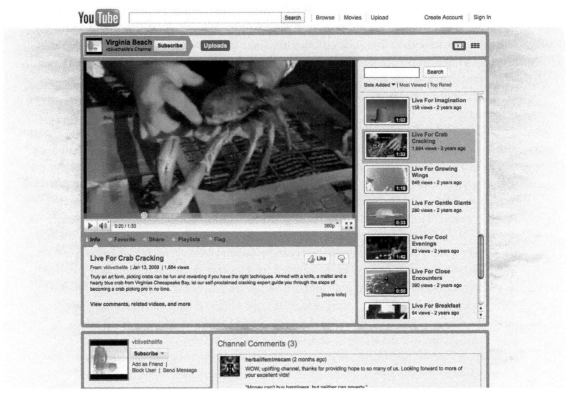

Figure 8.9 Virginia Beach YouTube crab-picking video screenshot. Used with permission of the City of Virginia Beach Convention & Visitors Bureau.

The YouTube channel allows individuals to have a unique URL code that they can share with others. Marketers can use this URL in all of their marketing activities, including printing it on promotional materials in order to drive traffic to their YouTube channel. The YouTube channel is virtually a hub for content marketers. Potential customers will be able to view valuable and engaging content and learn more about the company, as well as its products, brands, and services.

The YouTube channel also enables consumers to subscribe to a company's specific channel. Marketers can customize their YouTube channel so that it is more appealing to their audience.

The following are some of the different options YouTube offers for such customization:

- Users can click on the bell icon next to the subscribe button, which pushes notifications of any uploads directly to the user's device.
- A unique title for your YouTube channel can be created and your channel can be tagged with unique keywords. Individuals can type these keywords into the YouTube search and find your videos.
- Themes can be customized by selecting preset designs or by uploading unique images that will appear as the channel's background.

- Modules can be added and removed from the YouTube channel at any time. The available modules include comments, moderator, subscribers, event dates, other channels, subscriptions, friends, and recent activity.
- Uploaded videos, favorites, and playlists can all be chosen to be shown or to be hidden from subscribers. In addition, you can choose your featured video and how you wish your videos to be displayed on the YouTube channel.

In summary, customization is the key to success in digital video marketing. People often view videos to experience exclusive content or to get a 'sneak peek' of a new product or service. Here's a great example. Busch Gardens does not allow cameras on rides, so point-of-view ride footage videos, as seen in Figure 8.10, are exclusive to its own YouTube channel. These videos are often the company's most popular posts because people cannot obtain that kind of video experience anywhere else. Check out its YouTube channel and experience a few of the exciting rides you will find at Busch Gardens and Water Country USA.

YouTube channels can keep subscribers coming back for more and spreading the word. Individuals coming to the channel may have only come there to watch one video, but in turn may end up watching three or four. More importantly, videos are often viral or highly shared, which is very desirable for marketers today.

Going Viral

Going viral is something that is difficult to define. Typically, viral means creating an infectious video that individuals will want to share with their friends, thus further promoting the video and

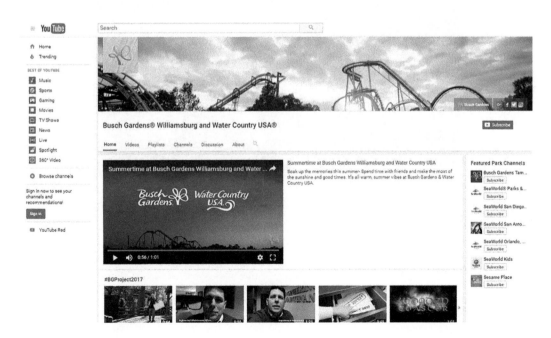

(Continued)

Figure 8.10 (Continued)

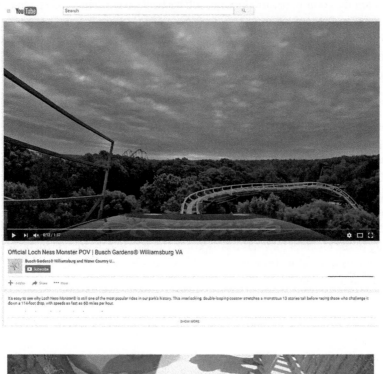

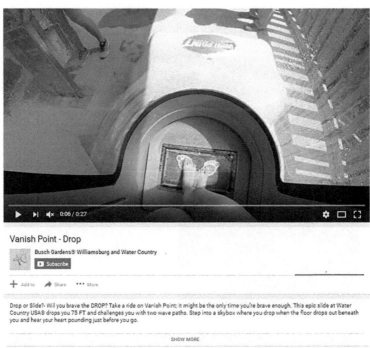

Figure 8.10 Busch Gardens and Water Country USA videos. Used with the consent of Busch Gardens/ Water Country USA. All Rights Reserved.

its featured product(s). **Viral videos** usually generate viewers on their own when individuals who have watched the video decide to pass along the link to others. This helps garner more awareness for marketers who are looking to expose their brands with viral videos.

Videos that go viral are most often those which evoke emotion.[24] Thus, those videos that contain an emotional appeal or a cute factor, such as animals or babies, spread more rapidly. Viral videos often have sex appeal or appeal to either the serious side of the consumer or to the humorous side. Humor has been effectively used in many videos that have gone viral. One of the most outstanding humorous videos shot was for Old Spice. The 'Return of The Man Your Man Could Smell Like' campaign generated the following results through the use of YouTube:[25]

- Day 1: The campaign received more than 6 million views.
- Day 3: The campaign received more than 20 million views.
- Old Spice released 8 of its 11 most popular videos online.
- Day 7: The campaign received more than 40 million views.
- The Twitter follower base increased by 2,700 percent, while Facebook fan interaction increased by 800 percent.
- The YouTube channel of Old Spice was framed as the most-viewed channel.
- The official website of Old Spice incurred more site traffic (300 percent).
- The campaign drove 27 percent more sales within six months of launching.
- Sales were increased by 107 percent by social campaigns.

These impressive results demonstrate the power of viral videos. They also show the importance of creating viral videos for marketing activities. Viral videos provide the opportunity to create tremendous results on a cost-effective basis.

Individuals view videos for different reasons. In the end, the propensity of a video going viral is based on consumer preferences. However, there is one item that can help to determine the viral nature of videos and that is social media. Think about it—videos go viral because people share them with their friends, family, and acquaintances. Social media sites are normally the battlefield where viral video fame is won. E-mail is another ingredient that should be factored into the equation of enabling a video to go viral.

Many people rightfully want to know the secret behind creating a video that will go viral and be widely viewed. Research conjures up many different tricks of the trade, but most seem to focus on keeping the video short, easy to share, and relevant and exciting to engage your target audience. According to creative director Mary Pedersen, marketers have just 10 seconds to capture and engage an audience before they continue to scroll down or click away; and engagement drops off significantly beyond that. If you have not fully engaged your audience after the first 30 seconds, you've likely lost 33 percent of viewers; and after one minute, 45 percent of viewers have stopped watching.[26]

In conclusion, video marketing, especially via YouTube, should be an important component in a direct marketer's media mix. Video watching and sharing is a rapidly growing habit among consumers, and marketers have the opportunity to tap into that force. In the words of Suzie Reider, YouTube Head of Advertising, 'The Internet gave marketers the opportunity to innovate. YouTube has given marketers a platform for celebrating and amplifying nearly every marketing activation.'[27]

SUMMARY

In summary, electronic media encompasses television, radio, and digital video. Television and radio are commonly referred to as broadcast media. Broadcast media are the most universal of communications media because broadcast reaches virtually everyone and every location. There are a number of different advantages and disadvantages associated with both television and radio, as well as a number of different formats from which direct-response advertisers may choose. Both media can be segmented according to different viewers and listeners. Direct-response advertising on television and radio can be highly productive for direct marketers. Digital video, exemplified by video marketing on YouTube, presents a new opportunity for the direct marketer. Digital videos can and should be designed to meet the interests and tastes of specific audience segments. Digital videos offer a number of response mechanisms, enabling marketers to judge their effectiveness. Creating a video that goes 'viral' can dramatically affect customer product awareness and lead to eventual purchase.

KEY TERMS

broadcast	infomercials
cost per response (CPR)	media efficiency ratio (MER)
cost per viewer (CPV)	reach
frequency	video annotation
gross rating points (GRPs)	viral videos

REVIEW QUESTIONS

1. Broadcast media (television and radio) are the most universal of all media, but what limits their effectiveness for direct-response advertising?
2. Suggest ways to segment markets through broadcast media.
3. In what ways do direct marketers use television as a medium?
4. What are some of the most common products or services featured in infomercials? Do you think infomercials are effective? Why or why not?
5. In what ways is radio more efficient than TV as a direct-response medium?
6. How has Internet radio changed the opportunities for direct-response advertising?
7. Compare and contrast the following Internet radio services: Sirius XM, Pandora, Spotify, Grooveshark, TuneIn, and iHeartRadio. Which one do you think offers direct marketers the best audience targeting opportunity? Why?

8. What are the advantages that digital videos offer to direct marketers?
9. Where are most digital videos seen today by prospective customers?
10. What characteristics are likely to help make a video 'go viral?'

EXERCISE

Have you ever wanted to be a 'couch potato'–even for a little while? Go ahead. Sit down this evening or weekend and watch television for a couple of hours. While you're watching, write down all of the TV commercials you view. How many of them are direct-response ads? What makes each advertisement a direct-response ad? For those ads that are not, identify how you could convert three into direct-response ads that are measurable and accountable.

CRITICAL THINKING EXERCISE

Go to www.youtube.com and locate a viral video of a specific company or organization. Identify the video's source. Evaluate whether the video created a positive or negative brand image for that company or organization. Provide justification to support your position.

READINGS AND RESOURCES

- Infomercials: www.therichest.com/business/economy/the-10-best-selling-infomercial-products-of-all-time
- Pandora: www.pandoraforbrands.com
- Pandora Sound-on: www.thedrum.com/news/2018/11/08/pandora-rolls-out-its-sound-brand-narrative-time-holiday-travel
- YouTube: www.hubspot.com/youtube-marketing
- Viral videos: www.wyzowl.com/branded-viral-videos
- DRTV: www.wordstream.com/blog/ws/2018/03/14/direct-response-marketing

CASE: GEICO

This case explores the benefits associated with innovative media buys for DRTV campaigns and how television can work with other media–especially telephone and online media. It will enable you to appreciate the risk and value associated with the unique positioning strategies implemented by a direct and interactive marketer.

What you are about to read is a success story about a company that effectively uses DRTV campaigns with humorous ad appeals and innovative media buys to sell a commodity–automobile insurance. The DRTV campaigns are the products of the creative minds at The Martin Agency, located in Richmond, Virginia. These campaigns and case study are a testament to the great things that can occur when a client and an agency have a collaborative relationship. It also affirms the fact that being different and trying new things with an established medium can really pay off. Are you ready to read, learn, and think out of the box? If so, we'd like to introduce you to the client, GEICO.

GEICO (which stands for Government Employees Insurance Company) was founded in 1936. Today, the GEICO companies insure more than 16 million vehicles and have assets of more than $30 billion. GEICO is ranked the third largest in the auto insurance market, behind State Farm and Allstate. It is the fastest-growing auto insurer and has more than 10 million policy-holders.

GEICO's success has been largely attributed to its widespread television and radio direct-response advertising campaigns. GEICO and its series of innovative and award-winning direct-response advertising campaigns use humorous ad appeals to entertain, inform, and connect with customers. Let's take a closer look at a few GEICO DRTV campaigns.

Campaign: '15 minutes could save you 15 percent or more on car insurance'

The initial GEICO '15 minutes could save you 15 percent' campaign took the idea of buying automobile insurance (which doesn't seem very exciting, and the insurance product itself is probably considered an unsought good by most consumers) and turned it into a personalized, quick process with a worry-free consequence. The Martin Agency's work with this campaign was among the more innovative campaigns of the 1990s. At the time, 60- and 120-second spots were the standard TV media buys in direct marketing. Instead, GEICO ran back-to-back 15-second spots in a 30-second media buy. This media strategy of pairing two 15-second DRTV spots did a number of smart things for GEICO, including the following:

1. It allowed smaller, customized messages to be tailored to individual market needs, creating a cafeteria menu of creative options. For example, a new market might get a spot with a message about how many new drivers sign up with GEICO every day, paired with a spot focusing on price. In Washington, DC, GEICO's hometown, a different pair of service and savings messages was teamed to address specific needs in that market. Thus, segmented messages were relatively easy to execute with this new media format.
2. It provided two opportunities for the toll-free phone number and website to appear in the 30-second media buy. This longer exposure allowed the number to make a better impression, while still leaving room for the creative work to stress the brand. Most important, it contributed to the ability of each DRTV spot to generate a consumer response–the ultimate goal of a DRTV campaign.
3. It enabled the message to break through. Different was good, especially when battling against giants who had worked for years to build their brands. Most insurance companies' ads were similar, many incorporating 'scare tactics' in their messages. However, there was no confusing a GEICO ad with another insurance company's. GEICO's unique positioning strategy effectively generated consumer awareness

and placed GEICO in the minds of millions of consumers as an exciting and easy-to-deal-with insurance company. The catchy tagline '15 minutes could save you 15 percent or more' became extremely well known by consumers and it branded GEICO as the most affordable choice for consumers making auto insurance purchase decisions.

Campaign: 'Gecko'

GEICO's Gecko trademark character–that cute little green lizard with a British accent–emerged to help people properly pronounce and remember the company's name, GEICO. Many people weren't sure how to pronounce it–was it pronounced 'geeko' or 'gecko' or what? So the company created the Gecko to teach the world that you pronounce the company's name as 'GUY-co' and history began for GEICO's Gecko. The continued use of the Gecko in GEICO advertisements was also due in part to an actors' strike at the time, which made it difficult to find humans to star in advertisements. So the little Gecko was fate for GEICO (see Figure 8.11).

Figure 8.11   GEICO's Gecko. Used with permission of GEICO.

The Gecko was used to deliver GEICO's message with humor. It uniquely positioned GEICO as an inexpensive and fun insurance company. This was the opposite of the perceptions of GEICO's competitors, which were thought of as more expensive and serious. This unique positioning strategy, combined with the cuteness and liveliness of the Gecko's personality, worked. In each ad, the Gecko makes a claim in a sassy manner. For example:

'I am a gecko, not to be confused with GEICO, which could save you hundreds on car insurance. So stop calling me!' Each commercial attracts the attention of the audience and generates a smile or a laugh. More important, consumers remember the little Gecko, his messages, and, along with it, GEICO.

The animated lizard quickly became both effective and popular for GEICO. In fact, the Gecko has been named one of America's top two favorite icons. The Gecko's charismatic personality and popularity made it a natural choice to become a symbol to promote wild-life conservation for the Association of Zoos & Aquariums (AZA). As a form of cause-related marketing, GEICO's Gecko has joined the AZA with a traveling live gecko exhibit and is featured in a series of TV commercials on behalf of the AZA.

Campaign: 'Caveman'

To continue the humorous appeal and drive home the fact that not only would GEICO save consumers money on car insurance, but consumers would find it easy to work with the company, GEICO introduced its 'Caveman' campaign. The campaign objective was to convince tech-savvy 25- to 49-year-olds that shopping for car insurance was easy with the company's website. The Martin Agency created a series of TV commercials, each playing on the theme of a fictitious slogan: 'GEICO.com. So easy, a caveman can do it,' to drive the message home. Each advertisement shows modern-day cavemen in various scenarios complaining about how offensive the slogan is. The cavemen are hairy, hostile, and dressed in designer clothes. They play tennis, they visit therapists, and order fancy meals like roast duck with mango salsa. They are much more sophisticated than one would have thought– and thus the simple message The Martin Agency was trying to get across (GEICO's website is really easy) was wildly effective in a humorous and fun-loving way (see Figure 8.12).

Figure 8.12 GEICO's caveman. Used with permission of GEICO.

GEICO's cavemen have quickly become a pop culture phenomenon. Their popularity in TV commercials is now being extended to the Web. Launched in January 2007, the flash site www.cavemanscrib.com allows visitors to get to know these cavemen–their personalities, preferences, and possessions. The primary purpose of the website is to entertain visitors. Selling auto insurance is considered secondary. GEICO receives fan mail for the cavemen and kids dress up like them for Halloween. The cavemen ads have been so effective that the cavemen have had to fend off groupies!

Campaign: 'Testimonials'

Another mini-DRTV campaign created for GEICO by The Martin Agency was the 'Testimonials' campaign, a series of TV ads featuring real customers providing testimonials to correct a misperception that lower price meant lower-quality service. To continue with GEICO's humorous appeals, each consumer was paired with a celebrity, such as Little Richard or Burt Bacharach, who helped 'interpret' the testimonials.

Each advertisement contained the tag line: 'Real Service. Real Savings.' Also, each advertisement ended with the GEICO website clearly displayed–causing people to process what they had just heard from a fellow consumer and encouraging them to visit the website to learn more about how their needs might be better served. Because these ads used real consumers, the messages were highly believable, yet fun. They were also quite effective.

Campaign: 'Sexy Grandpa'

Go to YouTube, type 'Geico commercial' into the search box, and see what you find. Millions upon millions of views for car insurance commercials? What's going on here?

What's going on is that the GEICO brand has become just as engaging in the online and social landscape as it is in traditional media by introducing GEICO's 'Sexy Grandpa' (see Figure 8.13).

Figure 8.13 GEICO's sexy grandpa. Used with permission of GEICO.

There are three keys to GEICO's success in the digital space. One reason is brand consistency. GEICO has the same fun, slightly irreverent personality on Facebook as it does on prime-time TV. Be entertaining, be engaging, and reinforce GEICO's core competency–saving people money on car insurance.

The second reason for GEICO's success is the element of surprise that has always been part of GEICO's multiple storyline approach to campaigns. This means that there is always a lot of fresh digital content for people to discover, share, and even parody. There's no better recipe for helping a brand go viral.

Thirdly, like other smart brands, as a marketer GEICO doesn't try to elbow its way into social conversations and digital interactions. GEICO believes that creating content that people seek out and that rewards them is a much better way to win friends and influence people.

Xtranormal is a favorite site where anyone with a computer and a keyboard can make their own movies. GEICO partnered with Xtranormal to make a series of inexpensive, lo-fi commercials in 15 minutes or less (the time it takes to save hundreds with GEICO).

By using a digital tool with which a younger, desirable demographic segment was already having fun, GEICO built an instant bridge between the brand and fans of the brand. Even with a limited media buy, 'Sexy Grandpa' quickly became a top-rated video on You-Tube, with more than one million views. Also, a full 90-second downloadable version of the 'Sexy Grandpa' song was made available on geico.com so people could make their own music videos, further seeding GEICO as a likeable, relevant brand in pop culture.

Conclusion

Because most of GEICO's customers work with the company through direct channels, the DRTV spots themselves needed to have personality. They were in fact the human voice for the company until the call was made and a real voice could answer. The fact that the GEICO marketing group understood this and was brave enough to be different from its competitors and embrace a humorous tone in each of its DRTV campaigns is an additional reason this brand has made its mark so effectively. Consumers were pleasantly surprised that an insurance company could make them smile. Humor can be a fine line to walk, and consumers' perceptions of humor can vary. The humor in GEICO ads pokes fun at or makes light of the human condition but does not belittle the serious nature of the product. The campaigns include everything from snappy one-liners to buttons at the end and over-the-top visual exaggeration.

These GEICO campaigns have proven you should never underestimate the value of a strong call to action and never change it if it's working. The modular media and messaging needed glue to hold it all together and keep the phones ringing and the Web visits coming. The glue for most of these campaigns was a strong call to action that remained constant in every spot–'15 minutes could save you 15 percent or more on car insurance.'

Have these innovative and humorous DRTV campaigns been effective in selling car insurance? You bet! While GEICO may be the number three company in the insurance business based on market share, it ranks number one in new customer acquisition and in recent polls; 91 percent of shoppers say they have seen or heard at least one GEICO message in the past 12 months. Finally, in 2010, GEICO achieved a 5.9 percent increase over the previous year in voluntary auto insurance business.

In conclusion, GEICO now owns its look, tone, and feel. No other name in the business can be substituted for GEICO. That has been the goal for the GEICO marketing group from the very first spot produced with The Martin Agency to the present. Indeed, the GEICO story is an impressive one–and one that most direct-response advertisers would like to emulate. So, the next time you are faced with the task of creating a DRTV campaign, think about doing something different. Think about GEICO.

Source: This case is based on information provided by The Martin Agency, Richmond, Virginia, and GEICO, Washington, DC.

Case Discussion Questions

1. A customer database is essential to direct and interactive marketing. How could GEICO's media, as described in this case, feed its database? Provide at least one idea regarding how you would use GEICO's database to increase sales.
2. With its heavy emphasis on humor, GEICO has managed to gain the attention of many prospective customers. Was this risky? Why or why not? Could GEICO have achieved the same success without the use of humor?
3. How did GEICO differ from the norm of TV advertising and was it effective?
4. What do the GEICO's 'Gecko,' 'Cavemen,' and 'Sexy Grandpa' campaigns have in common? Is the target market customer the same for all three of these GEICO DRTV campaigns? Why or why not?
5. In your opinion, what could GEICO do to integrate social media with its innovative campaigns to maintain its spectacular marketing performance in the future? Identify three specific ways you would use social media to increase GEICO sales.

NOTES

1. www.nielsen.com/us/en/insights/news/2018/nielsen-estimates-119-9-million-tv-homes-in-the-us-for-the-2018-19-season.html , retrieved April 20, 2019.
2. www.theatlantic.com/technology/archive/2018/05/when-did-tv-watching-peak/561464, retrieved April 20, 2019.
3. www.adweek.com/tv-video/nielsen-estimates-that-119-9-million-u-s-homes-have-tvs-for-the-upcoming-season, retrieved April 20, 2019.
4. www.bls.gov/news.release/atus.nr0.htm, retrieved April 20, 2019.
5. www.huffpost.com/entry/dove-real-beauty-campaign-turns-10_n_4575940, retrieved April 23, 2019.
6. www.dove.com/us/en/stories/about-dove/dove-real-beauty-pledge.html, retrieved April 23, 2019.
7. www.facebook.com/stihltimbersportsUSA/?brand_redir=1893301037562907, retrieved April 20, 2019.

8. www.therichest.com/business/economy/the-10-best-selling-infomercial-products-of-all-time, retrieved April 20, 2019.

9. http://theweek.com/articles/454561/lucrative-secret-behind-infomercials, retrieved July 30, 2016.

10. Marty Swant, 'Spotify Launches Display Ads that Guarantee Viewability.' www.adweek.com/news/technology/spotify-launches-display-ads-guarantee-viewability-170330, retrieved July 31, 2016.

11. Spotify Ad Specs, www.spotify.com/uk/brands/formats, retrieved July 31, 2016.

12. Rick Wilking, 'Yes, you're hearing more ads on Pandora these days,' *Quartz*. Reuters. http://qz.com/463470/yes-youre-hearing-more-ads-on-pandora-these-days, retrieved July 31, 2016.

13. www.siriusxm.com/advertise, retrieved July 31, 2016.

14. https://blog.twitter.com/en_us/a/2015/introducing-periscope.html, retrieved April 23, 2019.

15. www.nbcnews.com/id/15196982/ns/business-us_business/t/google-buys-youtube-billion, retrieved April 20, 2019.

16. Greg Jarboe (2009) *YouTube and Video Marketing: An Hour a Day* (Indianapolis, IN: Wiley Publishing), p. xxi.

17. www.youtube.com/yt/press/statistics.html, retrieved April 20, 2019.

18. www.youtube.com/yt/press/statistics.html, retrieved April 20, 2019.

19. Jarboe, *YouTube and Video Marketing: An Hour a Day*, p. 7.

20. www.youtube.com/t/advertising_insight, retrieved May 23, 2011.

21. www.youtube.com/t/annotations_about, retrieved May 23, 2011.

22. www.google.com/support/youtube/bin/answer.py?answer=150471, retrieved May 23, 2011.

23. Jarboe, *YouTube and Video Marketing: An Hour a Day*, p. 170.

24. www.convinceandconvert.com/content-marketing/4-rules-for-a-video-to-go-viral, retrieved July 31, 2016.

25. https://www.youtube.com/watch?v=owGykVbfgUE, retrieved May 23, 2011.

26. Mary Pedersen (2015) 'Best Practices: What is the Optimal Length for Video Content? Four Considerations When Determining the Length of Online Video Content,' *Advertising Age*, July 14. http://adage.com/article/digitalnext/optimal-length-video-content/299386, retrieved July 31, 2016.

27. Jarboe, *YouTube and Video Marketing: An Hour a Day*, p. 7.

9
MOBILE, TEXT, AND TELEPHONE FOR MARKETING

CHAPTER CONTENTS

CHAPTER SPOTLIGHT

CHIRP XM'S DIGICURB

Figure 9.1 Chirp XM's digicurb logo. Used with permission of Herbie Morewitz, Chirp XM. All Rights Reserved.

Have you ever been in a transportation jam and needed a ride somewhere? How about needing a designated driver after a fun night out on the town? Or, have you ever just wished you didn't have to drive yourself? And one final question: Do you like supporting your fellow college students? If you've replied with a resounding 'yes' to any of these questions, then read on and learn about digicurb.

What is digicurb? It's a new ride-sharing service smartphone application that is based on geographic location. Sure, you might be thinking that this new ride-sharing app isn't all too novel since Uber or Lyft might quickly come to your mind. However, what makes digicurb unique from other ride-sharing services is that it is exclusively designed for college students. It was built exclusively as a student-to-student network, for students, by students. Only students on your respective campus will be drivers and only students on your campus will be riders, essentially making it a closed network.

The two key selling points of digicurb are that (1) the service is about 30 percent less expensive than most competing ride-sharing services and (2) the transportation service may support college students on your very own campus. Digicurb provides a real 'sense of community' for each respective college campus on which it is available. In addition, digicurb fills a transportation need for those schools that do not permit freshman students to bring their cars to campus for the first semester or year.

The new mobile app (see Figure 9.2) was created by Herbie Morewitz and was launched in 2015 on a number of college campuses throughout Virginia. Digicurb is a spin-off of Chirp XM, where XM stands for 'extreme messaging.' Chirp XM focuses on a geo-social concept, which means that instead of selecting a group of people with whom to share information, Chirp XM selects a radius (in miles) based on ZIP code area, in which information may be shared.

The idea behind digicurb goes far beyond just giving someone a ride from point A to point B. The digicurb mobile app has the potential to connect and engage students across any given college campus in many ways, such as searching for a new roommate, selling your used textbooks, or sharing a ride home for the holidays. For starters, the mobile app is focused on providing safe, quality, and affordable rides for college students via their peers. Since digicurb has been designed to essentially act as a walled garden or gated community, you can have a reasonable expectation that every user you engage on the app is a fellow student.

If you think digicurb is an appealing concept for your campus, connect with Herbie on Facebook and download the app to get rolling. After all, digicurb is for students, by students, so why would you ever roll with anyone else?

Figure 9.2 Digicurb mobile app. Used with permission of Herbie Morewitz, Chirp XM. All Rights Reserved.

The chapter spotlight is just a brief glance at one of the newest mobile applications available for consumers today. New mobile apps are being developed daily to fit consumers' desires for a care-free, on-the-go lifestyle. Mobile marketing is a way of life in today's modern world, and marketers must strive to keep up with new mobile and text formats and applications in order to effectively use these channels to reach and engage with consumers. In this chapter, we will present a variety of concepts, strategies and applications associated with marketing via mobile, text, and phone.

INTRODUCTION

Never leave home without your keys, wallet, and now . . . your mobile device. In the future, you may not need your keys or wallet. Many consumers never leave home or go anywhere without their mobile devices. Direct marketers must recognize this and respond accordingly. The mobile industry is undergoing significant growth and change and, consequentially, so is mobile marketing.

In recent years, the number of people who own mobile phones, and smartphones specifically, has grown significantly. Research shows that the number of consumers solely accessing the Inter-net through their mobile devices is expected to grow to 72.6 percent by 2025. Most of the growth is expected to come in Asian markets, such as China, India, and Indonesia.[1] An increasing number of individuals have the Internet at their fingertips—constantly. The way that consumers access information is beginning to switch. Savvy marketers recognize the change and are responding in many cutting-edge ways.

EMERGING TOOLS AND TRENDS

Empowered by developments in Artificial Intelligence (AI), many mobile tools and trends are emerging that add value and convenience to consumers' lives. Let's explore two of these – Google Lens and mobile payment systems.

Google Lens

Consumers may now access information with a quick tap on their cell phone camera via Google Lens. In 2017, Google released a product called Google Lens, which uses AI to scan your envi-ronment through your mobile phone's camera, actively search the Web for matching images, and automatically provide you with information that matches whatever you initially scanned.[2] The valuable uses of Google Lens are unlimited. For example, if you are out shopping and you're looking at a specific plant in a store but cannot determine the plant's particular species, a quick Google Lens search will capture an image of the plant and use AI to match the plant to online articles, images, and references. You'll soon know the plant species and much more about the particular plant.

Google Lens can benefit marketers by enabling consumers to swiftly and easily identify prod-ucts which they may be interested in purchasing, and by providing similar – or exact – matches. Google Lens may also be utilized when attempting to discover where to buy the newest fashion item or a specific bag. Also, if a consumer cannot see a brand tag on a particular product, such as a sweater, a quick snapshot of the sweater via Google Lens and soon the consumer will know the identity of the sweater's brand and more information about the particular sweater.

Mobile Payment Systems

Mobile payment systems, such as Google Pay, Samsung Pay, and Apple Pay, represent one of the newest trends that utilize near field communication (NFC) chips. In mobile payment systems, also referred to as touchless payment systems, the phone connects to the card reader through NFC technology and transmits that appropriate payment information to the card reader. This effectively eliminates the need for the consumer to use their credit card.[3]

Another form of mobile payment system that does not utilize NFC technology is that of PayPal, Venmo, and WeChat. These systems establish a digital wallet that allows users to send or store values on their mobile accounts. Accounts are tied to the e-mail addresses or phone numbers of the users for quick access and ease of sending.

With these mobile payment systems, the payment method or methods are formed before the transaction by the digital wallet holder. Adoption rates of mobile payment systems are firmly established in foreign markets, such as China and Norway, which both boast usage rates of more than 40 percent. Unsurprisingly, the largest age segment that uses mobile wallets are the 18–34-year-olds, with nearly half stating that they possess a digital wallet. Digital wallets provide a form of security against physical financial institutions and allow the user not to worry about credit card theft or misplacement.[4]

New, emerging mobile tools and trends offer innovative marketing opportunities for mobile marketing.

MOBILE MARKETING

Mobile marketing is used for many different activities in today's modern world. Let's explore the more common ones.

Location-Based Search: Google, Yahoo, and Bing Places

Google, Yahoo, and Bing have introduced a feature that is primarily for people searching on their mobile devices, such as cell phones. Google may be the most dominant player in the Internet search market; however, key competitors, such as Yahoo and Bing, have been consistently holding approximately 15 percent each of the **search engine** market since 2008, with minor fluctuations of +/– 5 percent. While most millennials will immediately think 'Google' when something needs to be searched, alternatives are still prevalent. Therefore, it is important to address these search engine sites as well when discussing location-based search.[5] The three search engines started aggregating data from various directories such as InfoUSA to create their own search directories. What is the difference in these search directories versus traditional directories such as the Yellow Pages? There are many:

1. These directories are already mobile-ready, so when people search on their cell phone for a specific business, product, or service, these pages will show up on the mobile search. Plus, mobile ads can be used to drive people to specific local searches.

2. It is free for business owners to claim their listing and add contact information, information about the business, photos, and a link to their website, as well as to embed videos from You-Tube. Plus, business owners can make offers in the form of coupons, directly on the sites.

3. Google, Yahoo, and Bing aggregate other data about the business from across the Web, such as reviews from customers and the number of times the business is listed in other directories.

4. The search is location specific and geographically relevant to the place where the customer is searching. Plus, the person searching can push one button and call the business directly after searching.

5. There is a local map, included on the page, to show where the business is. And a person searching can get directions to the business based on their location via the GPS in the phone.

6. As the person searches, Google remembers the searches and the businesses they interact with, so in the future, Google will show search results that are relevant to the person's likes and interests.

7. Plus, statistics are aggregated, such as the number of impressions, number of clicks or number of calls, and the business owner has access to the data.

8. Mobile search engine optimization can be used to get a business ranked higher in mobile searches. All of these features give businesses a presence on the Web for FREE, whether they have a Web page or not, that shows up in mobile search.

Statistics reveal that more Google searches take place on mobile devices than on computers in ten countries including the U.S. and Japan.[6] In addition, 51 percent of all global Web pages were served to mobile devices in 2018.[7] A research study also found that 78 percent of local searches on mobile devices resulted in purchases, with 73 percent of those purchases occurring in a physical store, 16 percent on the phone, and 11 percent online. In addition, the study revealed that 76 percent of those purchases happened on the same day of the search and 63 percent of those transactions happened within a few hours of the search.[8]

Google has invested heavily in an open-source mobile operating system called Android. Built upon this platform is a system called Google Places. Part of the search engine system allows businesses to post a business profile on the search engine itself and be featured among local maps. Google Places has approximately one billion monthly users, all searching for local businesses.[9]

Google currently maintains a hardware line of mobile devices called 'Google Pixel.' Similar phones have previously been marketed under the title 'Nexus,' offering streamlined Google software while running on hardware developed by manufacturers such as HTC and Motorola. Presently, Google has made a shift to produce both software and hardware in-house under a unified brand, 'Pixel,' which started in 2016 with Pixel and Pixel XL.[10] Android currently runs on 75 percent of all devices globally.[11]

Mobile Websites

Many smartphone users are now accessing the Web on a regular basis through their mobile devices. This trend will likely continue in the future. Companies and organizations now have the technology to create a mobile version of their website. This enables consumers to easily connect with a given company at the convenience of their handheld devices. As Figure 9.3 presents, Virginia Beach has created a mobile version of its VisitVirginiaBeach.com website for consumers to use prior to and during their visit as a mobile research or planning tool.

Figure 9.3 Virginia Beach mobile website on a smartphone. Used with permission of the City of Virginia Beach Convention & Visitors Bureau.

Mobile Coupons

Mobile coupons are an effective way to track consumers and to microtarget. Research reveals that 25 percent of consumers redeem text coupons within three days of receipt and 60 percent redeem them within the week. Additionally, there is equal consumer preference (50/50) regarding the type of coupon (mobile versus paper) that consumers receive. However, research shows that 68 percent of consumers will join a brand/marketer's list if they receive an instant coupon.[12] The popularity of mobile coupons is likely to increase in the future.

According to David Wachs, President of Cellit, there are five steps to a strong mobile coupon program: offer creation, unique code generation, distribution, validation, and redemption. **Offer creation** for a mobile coupon campaign is the same as a traditional coupon campaign. Not only must the coupon be convenient, but the offer has also to be of worth to the consumer. If it is not a unique offer (i.e., a consumer can find it elsewhere), it will not be an effective mobile campaign. Secondly, Wachs stresses the creation of completely **unique coupon codes** for each coupon. If it is a standard barcode or the same coupon code for every consumer, tracking consumer redemption can only go as far as counting the number of people who use it. Step three, **distribution**, is also critical. The coupon must be delivered to the right consumers at the right time. This means understanding customers: when and where they make their purchase decisions. The fourth step, **validation**, refers to the way that the program minimizes fraud. This may include point-of-purchase technology. Finally, **redemption** may not mean only the scanning of a barcode. There are many ways to have consumers redeem mobile coupons, while still maintaining the coupon's uniqueness and creating an ease of use.

Click-to-Call

Mobile campaigns have the ability to combine the search and information functions of the Internet with the communication aspect of a mobile phone. Now, as consumers search for companies or services, they can also connect instantly through **click-to-call**. Many companies are using click-to-call in conjunction with sites such as Google Search, Google Maps, and so on. Click-to-call programs work as a liaison between the consumer and a business. A consumer can search for a specific type of business, in a specific area, and can take action by making a reservation, a booking, and so on, right from their mobile device. They can click an icon, and the third party (such as Google) will connect them to the business. The future of click-to-call in the case of booking and reservations is being pushed by Artificial Intelligence (AI) integration, using software such as Google Duplex, which will mimic a human being and automatically schedule and reserve tables at restaurants. Currently, the software is still in testing on select phones in key geographic locations.[13]

Prerecorded Messages

Prerecorded messages are another way to distribute information to consumers. This usually refers to a stored voice message that one may access through various triggers. There are many ways by which prerecorded messages can be used and delivered to individuals, including text messages with links to an audio piece or through the use of a QR code that can take the recipient to the message. 'QR' stands for 'quick response,' as these codes enable consumers to quickly connect with a company's website. QR codes will be covered in more depth in the following section. Prerecorded messages, if utilized carefully and sparingly, can prove to be a catchy medium to grab consumers' attention and prequalify the customer, prior to making contact with the business owner or sales team.

QR Code Campaigns

QR codes (quick response codes) are two-dimensional barcodes that can be read by barcode scanners on smartphones (see Figure 9.4 for an example). These unique codes offer marketers a wide range of opportunities to increase interaction and response to traditional direct-response ad campaigns and they can be created quite easily, while marketing to people instantly on their smartphones.

Figure 9.4 QR code example

QR codes can be used on traditional print media to drive response to a specific landing page on a website that makes a specific offer or asks for the individual to opt in to an e-mail list in exchange for something of value, such as a coupon, a report, a discount, an online presentation, and so on.

The possibilities for marketers to use QR codes are endless. For instance, retail stores can use them at the point of purchase display to drive traffic to a specific Web page to offer more information, product demonstrations, and customer reviews about a product. Businesses can use them to increase interaction within direct mail and postcard campaigns, by making specific, targeted offers on the landing page, once the QR code has been scanned with the smartphone. QR codes are spreading beyond most print advertisements, direct mail, and magazines, to billboards, magnetic car signs, tabletop displays, and on the products themselves. These codes will be placed nearly everywhere.

The direct marketer can measure the success of the QR code campaign with several metrics. Many QR code creators can measure the number of times the QR code was scanned by a smartphone or use Web-tracking software, such as Google Analytics, to determine how many people landed on a specific landing page. They can also compare how many people performed the requested action, such as opt in to an e-mail list or purchase of a product.

QR codes are used to drive response and increase interaction within direct marketing campaigns in a variety of ways. QR codes may affect how consumers shop, check out, and pay for products in supermarkets and other retail stores. A device that looks like a smartphone is being used in supermarkets and stores across the country. Perched on the handle of the shopping cart, the device scans grocery items as customers add them to their cart. Shoppers like it because it helps avoid an interminable wait in the checkout line. Retailers like it because the device encourages shoppers to buy more. The way to use QR codes in marketing is limitless because they are so easy to create and print, and because consumers like to use them.

Geo-Tagged Marketing

We briefly overviewed marketing with geo-tags and near field communication technology in Chapter 1. Before we expand on these, let's review the concepts. A **geo-tag** is a chip of data embedded in a digital media file to provide geographical information about the subject.[14] **Geo-tagging** basically implies that your physical location is registered from your mobile GPS tool or your computer's IP address. With geo-tags, marketers are able to target relevant communication to customers based on geographic location via interaction with their mobile phone or some other platform. Marketers are finding geo-tagging valuable to interact with customers based on prox-imity, time, interests, or behavior. Here's an example of how geo-tagging works. If you've got the Starbucks app on your mobile phone and you drive near your local Starbucks, you may receive a pop-up reminding you that you're near and prompting you to place a mobile order for your favor-ite coffee or espresso drink. Your phone may know you're craving Starbucks before you do, and it may prompt you to stop in for a fuel-up.

Another example of geo-tag marketing is seen in the implementation of Snapchat geo-filters and geo-fenced areas. Local business may set a specific geographic area around their business, referred to as a geo-fence, where this data is sent to Snapchat. When a user within this area takes a picture and scrolls through specific filter overlays, the local business ad will appear as a filter option.[15]

Near field communication (NFC) is location-based communication via short-range wireless technology that makes use of interacting electromagnetic radio fields.[16] NFC technologies are also used in various touchless payment systems, such as Apple Pay, Google Pay, and Samsung Pay. Marketers are creating NFC tags, placing them on printed materials such as signs, posters, direct mail, retail displays, business cards, etc., and using them to enable interactive communica-tion with customers and/or potential customers. In essence, NFC tags have the potential to con-vert a print material into a hot spot interactive medium with a call to action for mobile consumers. In addition, NFC tags effectively track analytics and generate valuable data and consumer insight for enhancing a company's database. Let's explore how mobile marketing with NFC technology works.

When consumers are near the NFC tag, they can tap, touch or wave an NFC-compatible device, such as their mobile phones, in front of the NFC hot spot to begin interactivity. The NFC tag triggers mobile engagement with its audience. NFC technology enables a variety of conve-nient applications. For consumers, some of the NFC mobile applications include opening a Web page, checking in on Foursquare or some other location-based mobile service (which will be discussed in the following section), mapping a location, sharing a contact, making a telephone call, sending a text message, connecting to social media, and more. For marketers, NFC tags provide location data on consumers, which can be vital information to assist them in delivering location-based advertising, differentiating between markets, spotting popular areas, determining where their brand presence is the strongest from a geographical perspective, and more. In sum-mary, the value and uses of both NFC technology and geo-tags for both consumers and marketers will likely continue to grow and evolve in the future.

Location-Based Mobile

Current mobile devices and software have allowed for the creation of location-based social networking websites such as Yelp, Foursquare, and WeReward. These can be referred to as **location-based mobile (LBM)**. Many of these programs enable smartphone users to 'check in' to a location, such as a business, and to see other friends' locations. For instance, one can use their smartphone to 'check in' to a restaurant on Facebook Places, Yelp, Foursquare, and many others to share their location with friends. Some, such as Foursquare, employ a point system, awarding points and statuses to those who check in to a location multiple times. There are also review and communication aspects to programs such as these. For instance, Yelp allows users to review businesses and share their experiences with others through rating the company and posting informative reviews.

Business owners can utilize this technology to their advantage and to drive traffic to their retail location. There are several benefits of doing this, including the following:

1. Business exposure—the technology will increase the exposure of the business via social media and within the application. Many of the apps have their own social networking aspect within them also, where people can friend each other and also see where their friends are geographically on their smartphones.
2. Loyalty/frequency programs—many of the apps allow the marketer to offer coupons. These coupons can be for first-time visitors, repeat visitors, and so on. This helps the business offer coupons to new customers or to repeat customers, similar to loyalty cards or the physical punch cards, but they are digital and available through a smartphone.
3. Customer data—the business can gather customer data, such as demographic and behavioral information. Many of these apps help the business profile of their customers by offering data in reports, such as the times people check in, ZIP codes with direction requests to the business, how many coupons each customer has claimed, average age of each customer, male versus female, and so on.

Foursquare is a leading geo-location network within the U.S. This app allows people to check in to the business, search for businesses within their geographic location, search for other friends within Foursquare who are close to them, redeem coupons, write reviews, and, most importantly, the app makes a game out of it for the users. This engages people's attention within Foursquare and makes it more interactive. One of the most compelling features is what is known as the 'mayor' of the businesses. The person who checks in to a business the most times each quarter is given the title 'Mayor.' The mayor can receive special discounts, coupons, and so on, that the business owner can offer the person for being the mayor.

Facebook Places is similar to Google My Business Maps, except it has a social aspect to it. Facebook gives the advertisers many tools and will be introducing many new tools for local businesses to target customers and drive people to their businesses and Facebook local pages. Facebook gives the business owner an advertising platform (see Chapter 10 on digital and social media) that is extremely targeted, enabling the business to grow a fan page or a Facebook Place page.

Companies can use these applications and websites as another way to track customers, gain feedback, and provide product offerings. The networking aspects of programs such as these include instant word of mouth regarding businesses. Many companies are taking advantage of these programs and providing special offers to customers who use them. These can be tailored to different customers, repeat customers, or first timers. This provides marketers with another form of segmentation. While location-based mobile continues to grow, direct marketers should adapt and increase their attention to this innovative segment of the mobile industry.

Mobile Application Development

An important topic with regard to mobile devices and the growth of smartphones is mobile applications. **Mobile applications**, or mobile apps, are Internet software programs that run on handheld devices such as smartphones. Applications can serve a number of purposes, such as connecting a consumer to a website, or providing the software that enables people to perform an action on their device that they otherwise may not have been able to do. 'Apps' can come in many different forms, with various programming and functions. Consumers can install apps onto their devices in order to tailor them to their preferences.

Many businesses are creating applications. As the mobile industry booms, applications will continue to become an important aspect in any business's marketing plan. Many companies are creating and offering their own free company mobile apps. Examples include Starbucks, Chick-Fil-A, and a number of grocery stores. These apps enable users to receive targeted communications, often in the form of valuable offers and services. For example, app customers receive pop-up notices ahead of Starbucks 'Double Star Days,' which means double customer loyalty program reward points will be earned for purchases made on the given day. The app also announces Starbuck's Happy Hour days, new product introductions, and much more.

Some companies are using micro-transaction strategies to encourage consumers to download a particular mobile app. The general strategy is that app developers will offer the base model of the app for free, but with some key features missing. This allows users to browse the app, understand its function, and eventually realize that they desire the locked functions. Developers will then offer either a subscription-based service plan in which all features are unlocked for a low cost per month, or a set price that allows the user to unlock and use all features. Presently, the subscription model is becoming the more dominant mode of capitalization.

Applications provide a consumer with better accessibility to the business and, ultimately, the product. As Oren Michels, CEO of Mashery, states in a Forbes.com article: 'Apps allow businesses to leverage nearly infinite resources of information and services by satisfying one highly targeted need at a time. This avoids brand confusion and builds brand strength.' One mobile app that has really caught on is that of Snapchat (Figure 9.5).

Figure 9.5 Snapchat ghost logo.

Note: The Snapchat ghost logo is owned by Snap Inc.

Snapchat

Snapchat is a platform that allows users to send photos or videos using its mobile app. Content lasts anywhere from 1 to 10 seconds, depending on what the user selects. After the recipient views the photo or video, it disappears and cannot be viewed again. Text can be added over top of the photos or videos and users have the option of communicating with each other through instant messaging or video chatting. Advertisements can be sent to users through the official Snapchat account. There are also live feeds, which every user can view, and marketers can use that to connect users to events.

Snapchat has more than 300 million active users sharing nearly 35,000 snaps every second.[17] Snapchat is currently valued at about $8 billion.[18] Snapchat originated in 2011 as a simple photo- and video-sharing app, but has quickly become a powerful social media marketing tool. Marketers must know their target audience and determine whether this mobile app might be an effective marketing channel for their products and services. Any marketer who wants to target millennials would likely find great success on Snapchat as currently 75 percent of Snapchat's users are between the ages of 18 and 34.[19] Marketers should also be aware of the casualness of the Snapchat messages that are typically shared via this mobile app. Snapchat makes advertising more of a 'soft sell,' which appears more integrated and natural, as opposed to a 'hard sell' where the advertisement is more forceful and appears to be pushed onto users' mobile phone screens.

For example, every Monday Busch Gardens takes its Snapchat followers on an adventure where a member of the Busch Gardens marketing team attempts to perform a challenge or a different department's job in the park (see Figure 9.6). The reoccurring feature has created a faithful fan base and helped the company grow its Snapchat following. It is consistently their most viewed and discussed Snapchat content.

Figure 9.6 Busch Gardens Snapchat. Used with the consent of Busch Gardens/Water Country USA. All Rights Reserved.

Snapchat offers marketers an opportunity to use filters with their images. **Snapchat filters** (also called **lenses**) are basically stickers, frames, images, and movement-sensitive animations that can be placed over Snapchat images or videos. Marketers may also use **geo-filters**, which are filters or lenses that change based on the consumer's geographical location. Snapchat filters enable greater customization of the Snapchat message, which can make the filter more personal and relevant to the consumer.

An example of a company that has used Snapchat filters with great success is that of Busch Gardens. Geo-filters on Snapchat let users share in real time where they are or what they are doing, in fun and visually interesting ways. Once a photo has been taken, a user can apply a location-based overlay to their photo that is specific to that area, attraction, or event. Figure 9.7 shows examples of geo-filters that can only be found and used at Busch Gardens Williamsburg and Water Country USA. For users, it makes sharing more exciting, and for companies, it means an increase in publicity and brand awareness.

Figure 9.7 Busch Gardens/Water Country USA Snapchat geo-filters. Used with consent of Busch Gardens/Water Country USA. All Rights Reserved.

Researchers have suggested several ways for marketers to effectively use Snapchat to engage consumers. These include presenting teasers, offers and promotions, stories, and competitions.[20] Let's briefly explore each:

1. Teasers—marketers can use the 10-second snaps to generate buzz around new products and ideas. Consumers like to be 'the first to know' the latest news.

2. Offers and promotions—consumers can screenshot company offers and use them either in store or online. Marketers can measure how many people took a screenshot of the snap or used the promotion code to measure campaign success.

3. Stories—by using 'My Story' on Snapchat, marketers can add snaps/videos that will be visible to users for 24 hours; or marketers can create a succession of videos (each 10 seconds long) that will generate a unique 'multi-storytelling' effect.

4. Competitions—getting your consumers to interact with you by sending in snaps of themselves doing various things to enter competitions is a clever promotional activity that will be both fun and potentially profitable.

Other Mobile Apps

Mobile applications are very empowering to consumers. For example, Red Laser, a mobile application designed by Occipital, allows consumers with an iPhone or an Android to scan a barcode and instantly receive information about the product. This application allows a consumer, with a click of a button, to learn the price of an item, where it can be found and purchased, or even what ingredients are in a specific food.[21] This allows consumers to have access to even more information regarding specific products.

Some mobile apps can help consumers live a healthier lifestyle. One such app is Calorie Mama AI. This app provides instant nutrition and calorie estimates from food photos. The app is updated, has 4,000 reviews, and averages 4.8 stars. The app utilizes AI, neural networks, computer vision, and image recognition and integrates with Apple Health.[22]

At the time of writing, legislation has been introduced to regulate the tracking (Do Not Track) of mobile devices, and major browser companies are implementing options for consumers to opt out of being tracked. However, this legislation has not passed into law. Only time will tell whether any laws that specifically address the sale or use of technologies that track the location of a cell phone or other geolocational data will be enacted. Be sure to keep an eye on the impact of global privacy legislation, such as the GDPR, which is discussed later, in Chapters 13 and 14.

In summary, there are many different types of mobile applications and they are a growing part of the mobile industry. Direct marketers should understand the significance of the applications' ability to provide consumers with greater accessibility to information and should learn to utilize and leverage those in existence, or consider creating one.

TEXT MESSAGING

SMS Text Messaging

One of the newer forms of direct marketing is **SMS text messaging** services. SMS (short message service) allows the marketer to track open rates, manage lists, allow customers to opt in and opt out, and perform many of the same functions as e-mail companies. There are some differences in e-mail and SMS text messaging services, but keep in mind, whether it is Twitter, SMS texting, or other forms of instant messaging services, they are all based on an e-mail type platform/system.

One of the biggest differences between e-mail marketing and text messaging is open rates. SMS text messages have an off-the-charts open rate of 98 percent, compared with only 20 percent for e-mail.[23] Although text message open rates may vary depending on the source, they are still much higher than those of e-mail. Most people automatically check their mobile device when it chirps or beeps.

So how does a marketer use SMS texting to drive sales? There are several ways, including the following:

1. Promote special events and remind customers about upcoming events: a winery hosting a monthly wine tasting event could send a text message about the wine tasting to its clients an hour before the event. This is a reminder that can get clients to visit the wine tasting.
2. Recoup lost sales: if a hairdresser has a client cancel an appointment, and the client was to get a perm in her hair, normally this dead time would now represent lost sales to the hairdresser. But with SMS texting, the hairdresser could send out a coupon to her clients letting them know she has a spot available. The coupon could be something to the effect of '25% discount on a perm to the first 5 people who show up at the salon and show this text message.' Depending on the size of her client list, this could actually get more people in store than just one person, which would result in additional revenue for the hairdresser, instead of having down time from a canceled appointment.
3. Coupons and special offers: this technique has to be used sparingly. SMS texting is still viewed by consumers as a means of personal communication, not a sales medium. So, the marketer has to be very careful not to burn out the list and have clients unsubscribe.

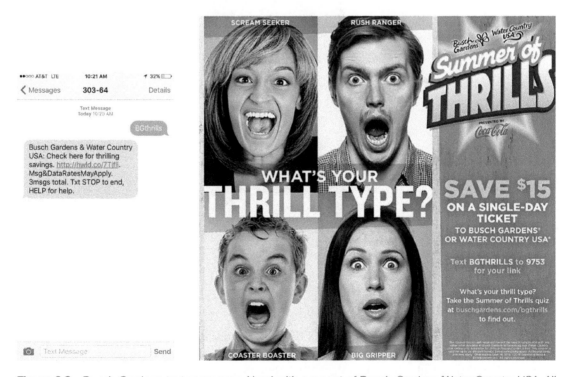

Figure 9.8 Busch Gardens text messages. Used with consent of Busch Gardens/Water Country USA. All Rights Reserved.

Any communication with clients has to be content driven and have value to the recipient, or the marketer risks upsetting the clients and having them opt out of receiving the text messages from the marketer. For example, Busch Gardens advertises special text offers, such as the one-time promotional interaction for savings shown in Figure 9.8. Consumers are encouraged to text 'BGthrills' to a number to receive a promo code that saves them $15 off a single day ticket. After they text 'BGthrills' to the specified number, they receive the text message shown in Figure 9.8.

4. Send people to a specific Web page on a website: most smartphones have Internet capabilities, so it is easy to send a text message to a customer with a link within the text message. This could be an opt-in to a squeeze page that requests a name and an e-mail address that would then give the customer access to a coupon, webinar, video, or some form of content. It could ask customers to comment on a specific page of a website, and so on. There are an infinite number of ways that marketers can use SMS text messages to engage customers and drive them to specific Web pages and content. As shown in Figure 9.9, the VIPER SmartStart phone app provides various messages that encourage prospective customers to visit its website to sign up for SmartStart services.

Figure 9.9 VIPER SmartStart 'go to' Web screen message. Used with permission of DEI Holdings, Inc.

There are many other ways that SMS can be used, such as polling and voting through text messages, using giveaways to entice consumers, sharing a little humor, requesting a donation, or providing tidbits of advice, such as the VIPER SmartStart tip provided in Figure 9.10. The methods of utilizing SMS have grown significantly and may continue to change.

Figure 9.10 VIPER SmartStart 'tip' Web screen message. Used with permission of DEI Holdings, Inc.

Non-profit organizations commonly use both text messaging and telephone calls to generate donor support. For instance, a text messaging campaign conducted by the American Red Cross generated 4.1 million text messages, valued at $10 per message, with 95 percent of responding donors being first-time donors.[24]

Finally, the other feature that makes SMS texting direct-response driven is the fact that most SMS texting services offer metrics to the marketer, such as open rate, who opened, click-through rate if there is a link in the message, opt-out rate, who opted out, and so on. Normally, the more expensive, premium text-messaging services offer these features to the marketer, which makes SMS texting a truly dynamic marketing platform.

In conclusion, SMS texting creates another way for marketers to interact with their clients and get them involved. It allows the business owner to drive sales, request e-mail addresses, and remind clients of events. As SMS texting evolves, business owners and marketers will find more and more ways to engage and retain customers, initiate sales, and increase response at a very low price.

Multimedia Messaging Service (MMS)

Multimedia Messaging Service (MMS) is very similar to SMS, but usually includes much more detail and elements. It may combine components such as text, images, audio, and even video to send to consumers. While SMS can be utilized by anyone who has a mobile phone capable of texting, MMS can be used in similar ways to SMS. Coupons and promotions can be sent through MMS, as well as special event reminders. Also, MMS provides the capability to market directly to the segmented consumer with more flashy effects.

How can businesses use MMS services to their advantage? With the ability to send multimedia-driven messages, the possibilities far surpass regular SMS texting services and are limitless.

For example, a travel agent visiting different locations around the globe could use his smartphone to record a personal video message, while on location. He could talk about what he has done, places he has visited, and then give a quick review about the destination. He could end the video with a link to his website, a call to action, and a link to the offer page with something to the effect of: 'If you book your travel package to Bermuda by August 12th while I'm still visiting, I'll give you and your family an additional adventure of *Free Parasailing*.' This allows the agent's clients to obtain a real-time review of the destination and follow him across the globe, and shows that the only reason the agent is offering this package is because the clients are virtually visiting the destination through the agent right now. Plus, the offer is automatically time sensitive, has a concrete deadline, and is only available while the agent is in Bermuda.

Response rates for both of these campaigns can be analyzed in several ways, such as:

1. The open rate of the MMS message.
2. The number of clicks on the link.
3. The number of people who purchased the offer.

The marketer can also provide incentives to clients or customers to share or forward the text message to friends and invite them to join. The marketer can then unleash the viral/word-of-mouth potential of the message. The opportunities to do so are endless and only limited by the imagination. The number of ways MMS can be used will only continue to grow as smartphones become more of a commodity and the norm of the cell phone industry.

TELEPHONE

The telephone occupies a dual position in direct marketing. Like print or broadcast media, it is a conduit for direct response marketing and, like mail or the Internet, it can carry the response itself. Thus, telephone marketing is both a marketing medium and a response mechanism. Telephone marketing is also referred to as teleservices or telemarketing. The objective of telephone marketing is to reach customers in a personalized interaction that meets customer needs and improves cost-effectiveness for the organization. Its scope is limited only by the imagination of the direct marketer, who can use it both for profit and nonprofit organizations as well as for individuals (such as political candidates), alone or with other marketing media, and targeted to both businesses (B2B) and final consumers (B2C). Compared to SMS and MMS, telephone communication is treated differently from regulatory points of view in terms of opt in/opt out, and the Do Not Call registry.

The telephone is an interactive medium, providing the flexibility and immediate response of a personal conversation. It can be especially effective when used in concert with other direct response media, such as direct mail or a website.

Experienced direct marketers report that the phone can generate many times the response achieved by mail alone if it is used correctly and in tandem with other media. Because of the live person-to-person power of a phone call, its cost is high. When calculating telephone marketing costs, the direct marketer needs to consider not only the line (minimal these days) and hardware, but also the program design, creative development, and labor costs. The latter should include supervisory as well as clerical support costs. If the telephone is used as an alternative to a personal visit by a salesperson, as is often the case, it can be tremendously efficient.

Telephone marketing has been woven into the planning of most direct marketers. To those who know how to use them, the interactive features of the telephone are, in many cases, replacing the face-to-face contact of a salesperson's visit to a prospect, or a buyer's visit to a retail location. The phone removes the need for travel and makes it possible to talk *with*, and not just to, customers and prospects. Now, click-to-chat is replacing some of the person-to-person contact of the phone. The application of the telephone to direct marketing efforts is a powerful combination. Telephone selling is a form of personal selling, because it occurs on a person-to-person basis but without the face-to-face aspect. Businesses use telephone marketing with the sole purpose of receiving results.[25] Let's take a closer look at the two basic ways direct marketers use the telephone.

Inbound versus Outbound Calls

Telephone marketing applications may be categorized as **inbound calls** when customers are calling to place an order, to request more information, or for customer service. Customer calls responding to DRTV or radio, service center calls, advertising responses, calls to catalog centers, after-hours sales calls, and dealer locator services requests are examples of typical inbound calls. The second category encompasses **outbound calls**. Here, organizations place calls to customers to make a sale or to offer information, hoping for a later sale. These calls often deal with lead generation, appointment setting, market research, fundraising, political calling, database verification, database appending, and, of course, sales. Outbound calls have become extremely regulated in the U.S. due to the National Do Not Call Registry and regulations. More will be discussed about this topic in Chapter 13. Let's discuss each application in greater detail.

Inbound Calls

Inbound calls are also referred to as **reactive telephone marketing** in that the initiator of the marketing communications is the customer. The customer places that call at his or her convenience to obtain information or to place an order, often using a toll-free number provided by the organization. In the US, the Federal Communications Commission (FCC) has designated not only 800 numbers as toll-free but also the area codes 888, 877, 866 and 855.

The recent surge of Web and Internet marketing strategies has also increased the number of inbound calls to marketers. Consumers have used the Internet to search for product or service information, and then have turned to the telephone to place orders for products and services that were presented in a company's website.

Toll-free telephone service has itself been a tremendous incentive to the use of inbound phone calls to respond to offers or transact an order. The marketer's direct response advertising in other media must provide incentives to encourage consumers to place inbound calls. Many of these ads point out the convenience of having a telephone order taker on hand 24 hours a day to answer questions and ensure faster deliveries or services.

The applications of inbound telephone marketing generally include: ordering or inquiring; clarifying or requesting assistance; responding immediately to an advertisement; expediting processing; locating a dealer or a product-servicing location; making reservations for travel accommodations, hotel rooms, or conferences; obtaining financial data, stock prices, yields; making pledges or contributions; and obtaining warranty information.

Outbound Calls

Outbound calls are also referred to as **proactive telephone marketing** because the company is the initiator of the marketing communications. Outbound calls are generally longer in duration and require more experienced and higher-paid personnel.

The large outbound telemarketers are using T1 service. **T1** designates bandwidth and denotes a giant pipeline or conduit through which a user may send multiple voice, data, and even video signals. It supports simultaneous voice/Internet connectivity, enabling telephone sales reps (or telereps) to speak to customers while also participating in their Internet session. Instead of simply carrying one voice conversation at a time, a T1 can carry almost 100 conversations or data connections simultaneously.

Although well-prepared scripts and well-structured offers can make telephone promotion highly effective, the medium is usually most efficient if calls are directed to persons who have been prequalified in some way. These are sometimes called handraisers or leads. The reason is that the cost of an individual phone call is expensive. Therefore, when telephone marketers properly segment the market (according to a wide variety of segmentation variables) and prequalify prospects, the length of the call may be reduced and the number of positive consumer responses may be increased. Prequalified outbound calls might include a response to an inquiry, a new product offer to an existing customer, or the generation of responses/transactions from a carefully selected list. **Cold calls** (which are calls made when there is no existing relationship with, or recognition of, the direct marketer) must be carefully structured in content because, by their very nature, they usually interrupt some other activity of the person being called and can create a negative response.

Direct marketers use the telephone for a great variety of outbound call applications, including the following: generating new sales, including reorders and new product introductions; generating leads and qualifying inquiries for personal sales follow-up; serving present accounts; reactivating old customers; validating the legitimacy of orders before shipping; responding to customer service needs, including responding to complaints; surveying customers, members, donors, voters, and so on; and substituting for a personal sales call. Most B2C outgoing calls are made by either non-profit or political organizations. These calls may be very effective as research reveals that one of the highest response rates for non-profit organization marketing is telemarketing at 53 percent.[26]

In summary, outbound calls have the ability to generate great profit when executed properly. Let's now explore the advantages and disadvantages associated with telephone marketing.

Advantages and Disadvantages

Some of the specific advantages of using the telephone as a marketing medium are as follows:

- It provides *two-way communication* and *immediate feedback*. This quick feedback, often in response to a test campaign, can be of great assistance to the direct marketer in making any needed changes before the entire marketing campaign is executed.
- It is a *very flexible medium*. Although a telerep may use a prepared script, this doesn't limit the number of changes you can make to that script as needed. You may also change the message for each caller.
- It is a *productive medium*. The telephone is actually more productive than traditional personal selling when you consider the sheer number of sales calls that a rep can make by phone on a daily or weekly basis.
- Telephone marketing is a *cost-effective medium*. Although the exact costs vary depending on the type of call being placed, the average cost per call is far lower for telephone selling than for traditional personal selling.

Some of the distinct disadvantages of telephone marketing are as follows:

- It is by far the most *intrusive marketing medium* used by direct marketers. Telephone marketing has a poor image among people who dislike the intrusion of marketers' outbound calling.
- Telephone marketing *lacks visual enhancement*. It is not a visual medium, and thus its power is often related to being integrated with other media.
- Telephone marketing does not provide a *permanent tangible response device*. Once again, it must be coupled with other media to provide a physical form for the customer to sign or a brochure to keep on hand to be reviewed at a later time.

Most direct marketers have concluded that although telephone marketing has its share of disadvantages, it can be a highly effective medium when properly planned and executed.

Planning a Telephone Marketing Program

In order to be successful in telephone marketing, telephone operators must convey a trustworthy, reliable image to the customer. Companies must train their operators to develop these skills and provide them with well-conceived scripts.

Preparing Telephone Scripts

A **telephone script** is a call guide to assist the operator in communicating effectively with the prospect or customer. Most do not have to be read word for word; in fact, the most effective scripts are more like a detailed outline that provides structure to the conversation. Each outbound telephone call aims to deliver a sales presentation to the potential customer or client. The purpose of each inbound call is to deliver information to the customer or receive the customer's order information. Thus, different types of scripts are needed for different types of telemarketing calls. In either case, developing scripts offers the dual challenge of determining the right words to gain a favorable customer response or impression and, at the same time, minimizing the length and the cost of the call. Writing a telephone script is both an art and a science. One valuable asset of a script is the flexibility it provides, allowing the telereps to change or experiment. While most marketing media call for copy to be finalized by a certain date, scripts can be revised after a few or a few dozen calls.

Training Telephone Operators

Many people might think that the best way to develop an effective telephone operator is to take someone with field sales experience and transfer that sales knowledge to the phone. However, in reality, this rarely works. One of the reasons field salespeople often do not make good operators is that they are accustomed to face-to-face interaction with their customers and dislike working behind a desk. These work qualities are the exact opposite of the requirements of a telephone marketing representative.

SUMMARY

In this chapter, we examined many concepts, strategies, and applications associated with marketing via mobile, text, and telephone. The mobile industry is undergoing significant growth and evolution and so is mobile marketing. Direct marketers must recognize and respond to this mobile movement if they are to take advantage of the new opportunities presented by the mobile, text, and telephone formats. These new media formats must be integrated into each marketer's marketing mix.

Text messaging is also used for a variety of marketing purposes and its use is rapidly growing. The chapter provided an overview of both MMS and SMS text messaging as well as an overview of their similarities and differences. Telephone rounds out the chapter as it remains an important medium to be used, especially for business-to-business. The uses of both inbound and outbound calls for telephone marketing are examined. As explained in the chapter, telephone marketing programs require planning and training to be executed in both a timely and cost-effective manner.

KEY TERMS

cold calls	outbound calls
geo-filters	prerecorded messages
geo-tag	proactive telephone marketing
geo-tagging	QR (quick response) codes
inbound calls	reactive telephone marketing
location-based mobile (LBM)	SMS text messaging
mobile applications (apps)	Snapchat filters
multimedia messaging services (MMS)	T1
near field communication (NFC)	telephone script

REVIEW QUESTIONS

1. What is an aspect of mobile marketing that has changed since this book was published? What does that say about the pace of mobile marketing?
2. What are the five steps to creating a strong mobile coupon program?
3. Define click-to-call and explain how consumers may use it in the marketplace.
4. Name and explain the many opportunities QR codes offer marketers. Explain what opportunities QR codes offer consumers.
5. How might business owners utilize location-based mobile (LBM) to drive traffic to their retail locations? What are the key benefits of doing this?
6. Identify three of your favorite mobile apps. How are these apps of value to you?
7. Name and explain the ways that marketers might effectively use Snapchat to engage consumers. Can you think of a few other ways?
8. Identify and explain some of the ways a marketer uses SMS texting to drive sales.
9. Compare and contrast SMS and MMS texting from a marketer's perspective. Why would a company use both types of text messaging?
10. Explain what near field communication (NFC) tags are and how they are being used by marketers. Name a few companies or brands that are successfully using geo-tagged marketing and explain why you think they are effective.

EXERCISE

The next time you are out shopping, jot down which businesses utilize geo-tags and geo-tagging. Which businesses are sending you ads based on your location? Which businesses are utilizing social media geo-tagging to drive business? Is geo-tagging effective in affecting your behavior as a consumer?

CRITICAL THINKING EXERCISE

When was the last time you truly listened to an outbound telephone sales call? The next time you receive a call, listen to the script and answer the salesperson's questions. See if you can distinguish between what is scripted and what is impromptu. After the call, evaluate its effectiveness.

READINGS AND RESOURCES

* Location-based mobile: https://www.blis.com/wp-content/uploads/2018/02/eMarketer_Location_Intelligence_2018-Consumer_Behavior_Data_Quality_and_Targeting_Tips.pdf Location_Intelligence_2018-Consumer_Behavior_Data_Quality_and_Targeting_Tips.pdf
* Mobile payments: https://thefinancialbrand.com/37408/monitise-cognizant-mobile-banking-segment-based-strategy

- Mobile payments: https://www.raconteur.net/finance/cashless-society-affects-consumer-spending
- Near field communications: https://blog.beaconstac.com/2019/03/5-companies-nailing-it-with-nfc-campaigns
- NFC examples: https://blog.beaconstac.com/2019/01/proximity-marketing-without-an-app-best-use-cases-of-nfc-to-implement-in-2019
- Mobile apps: www.linktexting.com/playbook

CASE: UBER — AN APP THAT MAKES LIFE BETTER[27]

Figure 9.11   Cell phone image

Think of a mobile app that has caused a total revolution in transportation and delivery. Did Uber come to mind? If so, you are likely among millions of other consumers who can honestly say that Uber has transformed the way they get around town and the way their dinner is delivered. Indeed, Uber has made our lives better. How did Uber first come to exist? What has it become? And where might it be headed next? If you are curious about any of these questions, you'll enjoy reading this case–which is all about Uber life in our modern world.

Background and Growth

Uber began as an idea between two entrepreneurs, Travis Kalanick and Garrett Camp, who couldn't find a ride in Paris back in 2008. They thought that a car-service app made good sense and would be much more convenient than the often frustrating and time-consuming activity of trying to hail a taxi. How easy it would be to summon a car by simply tapping the downloaded app on a smartphone, and entering a destination and pick-up location. The app could even allow users to store frequently used locations, such as a person's home or office. Plus, consumers wouldn't need to carry cash to pay for their rides, as payment happens through the app and riders will receive an online receipt documenting the route. Kalanick and Camp formally launched Uber in San Francisco in 2010 as 'UberCab' and, shortly after, changed its name to Uber.[28] In 2011, Uber returned to its birthplace and began operating services in Paris. Within a few short years, the company had expanded services to more than 100 metropolitan areas across the U.S., as well as to international locations such as Australia and Central and South America. Uber's service network had grown to 500 cities by December 2016, and by May 20, 2017, Uber had provided five billion trips.[29]

Uber experienced many firsts during its early years, including the following:[30]

- July 2012: Uber riders can request ice cream on demand in seven cities across the U.S.
- August 2014: Uber releases UberPool, its carpooling feature in San Francisco where riders can share the cost of an Uber ride
- September 2014: Uber unveils Uber Military where military personnel begin earning money as Uber drivers
- March 2015: the first baby is born in an Uber
- May 2015: deaf partners earn money as Uber drivers
- December 2015: Uber takes women in India to the voting polls for their first ever legal election
- September 2016: Uber riders can be matched with a self-driving vehicle in Pittsburgh, Pennsylvania.

Today, Uber offers far more than ride-hailing services. Uber has strived to make life better and more convenient for today's busy consumers with an array of Uber service apps.

Uber Services

Uber offers many services that provide great convenience and time savings for consumers. With a few taps on a smartphone, consumers can download additional Uber apps and enjoy food and package delivery services, or easily organize business travel for clients. These conveniences are made possible by the following mobile apps: Uber Eats, Uber Freight, and Uber Business.

Uber Eats

Uber Eats offers consumers food delivery services. How does it work? Three easy steps: browse, order, and track. Upon downloading the Uber Eats app, users can scroll through the list of partner restaurants or search for a particular restaurant or cuisine. Once the desired food is located, users simply tap to add it to their carts. Upon checkout, the individual user's address will appear, along with an estimated delivery time, and the price of the order including tax and delivery fee. If everything looks right, the user just taps 'Place

Order' and the user's credit card on file will be automatically charged. No cash needed. Users can follow their order in the app from preparation at the restaurant until their meal is at their doorstep.[31] Users can also see their Uber Eats delivery partner's name and photo and track logistics on the app's map. Delivery in some geographic locations may be via car, bike, or motorized scooter. Convenient? You bet!

Figure 9.12 Meal image

Part of the reason Uber Eats has found such great success is that more and more people are ordering delivered meals instead of cooking at home. Food delivery services save time in both meal preparation and clean-up tasks. Busy consumers today are willing to pay the nominal delivery fee for the added convenience that this app provides. Uber Eats meets the changing lifestyle needs of consumers and the phenomenon is predicted to continue and grow in the future.

Uber Freight

The Uber Freight app launched in May 2017. The app is designed to benefit both the carriers (truckers) and the shippers (freight customers) as they seek ways to streamline freight shipping and make it more transparent, efficient, and cost-effective for all. The app capabilities help carriers and shippers make informed business decisions. Carriers benefit from more flexible bookings, while shippers tender shipments easily.[32]

Figure 9.13 Truck image

Uber's website features a 'Freight Blog' where various carriers and/or shippers can post their experiences with Uber Freight. A quick visit there reveals comments from satisfied app users, such as that of Robert Fisher of Nestlé North America Procurement. According to Fisher:

> To maintain a healthy, efficient supply chain, it's key to prioritize carrier needs and feedback. The data that Uber Freight is providing with Facility Ratings in their platform is a great validator for making improvements to our operations, whether that means reorganizing personnel shifts or even moving to a bigger facility. I've never seen this granular breakdown and level of visibility into facility activity before–it's eye-opening, and exactly the kind of data we want to look into.[33]

Uber Business

Uber Business is an app that enables businesses and organizations to plan, organize, and provide transportation for their clients and employees. The uses of Uber Business are endless! The concept of making transportation services more efficient, with less paperwork and lower costs, is certainly attractive to the bottom line of all companies and organizations. Moreover, Uber Business provides an improved customer service experience in transportation over crowded shuttles and long taxi lines. In addition, Uber Business enables companies to have control over the transportation experience with the ease of a mobile app. It's a digital 'headquarters' for all your company's ground transportation. Get a clear view into all your trip activity and automate billing, expensing, and reporting.[34]

Figure 9.14 Business buildings image

Uber's website provides case studies of businesses that use its Uber Business app. One of those clients is Twenty Four Seven Hotels, which integrated Uber for Business under the title created for them of Uber Central into the operations of over half of the hotels in their portfolio, which includes brands by Marriott, Hilton, Hyatt, and IHG. Through an all-in-one dashboard, front desk associates can quickly and easily manage rides for hotel guests–no shuttle required. Alison Sansone, vice president of marketing and communications at Twenty Four Seven Hotels, claims: 'It's easy for our staff to use–at the touch of a button–reducing logistics and ensuring quick and responsive service to our guests.' Happy guests and happy clients–thanks to the Uber Business app.

Indeed, Uber strives to enhance the quality of life of its customers by offering many need-satisfying services with a few simple clicks of a cell phone. In addition, Uber strives to be a responsible organization and a good neighbor in the communities in which it operates.

A Good Neighbor: Supporting Many Non-Profit Causes

Uber has partnered with and supported many non-profit organizations to positively impact society. Some of its socially responsible activities are as follows:

* Teaming up with animal shelters across the U.S. to launch 'Uberkittens,' where riders received 15 minutes of snuggle time with kittens and free cupcakes. All of the proceeds of this campaign benefitted local animal shelters.
* Partnering with Goodwill for the #UberSpringCleaning campaign designed to provide donation pickups on demand. This program garnered more than 5,000 pounds of donated clothing.
* Aiding in the donation of #5MillionMeals to children in need.
* Teaming up with Mothers Against Drunk Drivers (MADD) in a campaign to reduce drunk driving.
* Partnering with Meals on Wheels to deliver healthy meals to those in need.

Recognizing the need to be part of a positive change for society, Uber uses the efficiencies created by its services in order to give back to the community in unique and creative ways.

Uber in the Future

Uber's future is dependent on the crowded competitive and uncontrollable environment in which it operates. Uber has had to make some tough business decisions in country markets around the globe. In some markets, Uber has responded by merging its business with local rivals in Russia, China, and Southeast Asia, while in other regions, particularly in the Middle East, Uber is acquiring competitive challenger businesses. In addition, Uber has had to battle a tough regulatory environment in Europe; however, the company has vowed to adjust to the uncontrollable variables in order to successfully operate in that region of the world. In Australia, ride-hailing services, including Uber, have had a slow start as consumers in that region have not yet actively used such transportation services.[35]

Uber has a number of competitors in the various service areas in which it competes. Lyft is its primary competitor in the ride-hitching business. Although the two services are similar, Uber is available in more cities and offers wheelchair-accessible cars in about 15 of its top cities.[36] Both Lyft and Uber offer a frequent rider program to reward loyal customers. Uber provides a tiered rewards system where riders earn two points for every dollar spent on most rides. The points cumulate and move riders up to higher statuses with different perks. For example, at 2,500 points, the rider reaches platinum status, where rewards include priority access to drivers at airports, among other things.[37]

The food delivery service arena is very competitive. Uber's largest competitors to date include Grubhub, Caviar, Postmates, and DoorDash.[38] As the food delivery service business continues to see explosive growth, more competitors are likely to enter the market and compete aggressively for their share. Uber Freight and Uber Business services are charting relatively new paths and thus the competition is not as fierce. These apps are trying to carve a new niche in the way the respective services add value to both the consumers and the companies involved. Marketing all of Uber's various apps and services will be critical to their future success.

Uber's use of hashtags has become a social phenomenon, especially on social media platforms, with the use of mobile devices bringing awareness to popular social trends and new campaigns. Uber's new 'Moving Forward' marketing campaign takes on an upbeat tone and focuses on the potentially emotional stories of its services.[39] Stories feature the exciting moments of life, such as an Uber driver taking a couple to the hospital to give birth to their first child, or a military spouse excitedly taking an Uber to meet her husband arrive back home from a deployment overseas. Indeed, storytelling is highly effective in engaging with consumers on an emotional level.

Additionally, Uber is constantly testing new app features and new services, which are likely to be the key to its future success. For example, one recently added safety feature in the app is the 'Check your Ride' notification. This serves to remind riders to check the license plate, car type, and driver description/photo to confirm the right car is their Uber ride before entering the car. In conclusion, Uber has diversified and created several different mobile apps to meet the needs of today's customers. Who knows what tomorrow will bring or where Uber will drive us?

Case Discussion Questions

1. What additional app features and ride-hailing services might Uber offer to its customers?
2. What could Uber drivers do to enhance the overall service experience for riders?
3. In addition to what Uber is already doing, how else might the company give back to the communities in which it operates? What other non-profit organizations or social causes should Uber support? Why?
4. In your opinion, what additional mobile apps should Uber develop? Why do you think these new apps would be attractive to consumers in today's world?

NOTES

1. www.cnbc.com/2019/01/24/smartphones-72percent-of-people-will-use-only-mobile-for-internet-by-2025.html, retrieved April 29, 2019.
2. https://lens.google.com, retrieved April 30, 2019.
3. www.paymentscardsandmobile.com/mobile-wallet-global-usage-statistic, retrieved April 30, 2019.
4. Ibid.
5. www.statista.com/statistics/267161/market-share-of-search-engines-in-the-united-states, retrieved April 29, 2019.
6. http://searchengineland.com/its-official-google-says-more-searches-now-on-mobile-than-on-desktop-220369, retrieved July 26, 2016.
7. www.statista.com/statistics/241462/global-mobile-phone-website-traffic-share, retrieved April 29, 2019.
8. http://searchengineland.com/study-78-percent-local-mobile-searches-result-offline-purchases-188660, retrieved July 26, 2016.
9. https://cloud.google.com/maps-platform/places, retrieved April 29, 2019.
10. www.pocket-lint.com/phones/buyers-guides/google/135451-google-nexus-vs-google-pixel-what-s-the-difference, retrieved April 29, 2019.
11. http://gs.statcounter.com/os-market-share/mobile/worldwide, retrieved April 29, 2019.
12. www.globenewswire.com/news-release/2018/06/12/1520471/0/en/New-CodeBroker-Research-Shows-Majority-of-Consumers-Redeem-Coupons-Received-via-Text-within-One-Week.html, retrieved May 19, 2019.
13. www.theverge.com/2018/12/5/18123785/google-duplex-how-to-use-reservations, retrieved April 29, 2019.
14. www.dictionary.com/browse/geotag, retrieved July 26, 2016.
15. https://marketingland.com/wp-content/ml-loads/2015/07/iPhone-Iso-Mastercard-e1436909546244.jpg, retrieved April 29, 2019.
16. http://tappinn.com/home/nfc-mobile-marketing, retrieved July 31, 2016.
17. www.omnicoreagency.com/snapchat-statistics, retrieved April 29, 2019.
18. www.cnbc.com/2019/01/16/snap-has-lost-more-than-20-billion-in-value-since-its-ipo.html, retrieved April 29, 2019.
19. www.omnicoreagency.com/snapchat-statistics, retrieved April 29, 2019.
20. http://curated-digital.com/snapchat-as-a-marketing-tool-is-it-worth-it, retrieved July 26, 2016.
21. Oren Michels, 'Why Businesses Need Mobile Apps' *Forbes.com*, Sept. 8, 2010 (Web: May 23, 2011). www.forbes.com/2010/09/08/mobile-apps-Internet-technology-mashery.html.
22. https://itunes.apple.com/us/app/calorie-mama-ai-diet-counter/id1121789860?mt=8, retrieved April 29, 2019.
23. www.campaignmonitor.com/blog/email-marketing/2019/01/roi-showdown-sms-marketing-vs-email-marketing, retrieved April 29, 2019.
24. www.nonprofitpro.com/post/dont-forget-telephone-fundraising-tool, retrieved April 30, 2019.
25. http://curated-digital.com/snapchat-as-a-marketing-tool-is-it-worth-it, retrieved July 26, 2016.

26. https://nonprofitssource.com/online-giving-statistics, retrieved April 30, 2019.
27. The views expressed here may not necessarily reflect those of Uber. Uber was not involved in the writing of this case.
28. www.uber.com/en-CA/newsroom/history, retrieved May 29, 2019.
29. www.uber.com/newsroom/media-assets, retrieved May 8, 2019.
30. Ibid.
31. https://about.ubereats.com, retrieved May 12, 2019.
32. www.uberfreight.com, retrieved May 29, 2019.
33. www.uberfreight.com/testimonials/nestle, retrieved May 12, 2019.
34. www.uber.com/business, retrieved May 29, 2019.
35. Biz Carson (2018) 'Where Uber is Winning the World, and Where it has Lost,' September 19. www.forbes.com/sites/bizcarson/2018/09/19/where-uber-is-winning-the-world-and-where-it-has-lost/#7d7ad55b4d6e, retrieved May 8, 2019.
36. Brian Chen (2019) 'Uber vs. Lyft: Which Ride-Hailing App is Better?', *New York Times*, April 17. www.nytimes.com/2019/04/17/technology/personaltech/uber-vs-lyft.html, retrieved May 8, 2019.
37. Ibid.
38. www.forbes.com/sites/bizcarson/2019/02/06/ubers-secret-gold-mine-how-uber-eats-is-turning-into-a-billion-dollar-business-to-rival-grubhub/#b5aa86d1fa9c, retrieved May 8, 2019.
39. https://adage.com/article/cmo-strategy/uber-breaks-biggest-campaign-history/314946, retrieved May 8, 2019.

10
DIGITAL AND SOCIAL MEDIA

CHAPTER CONTENTS

CHAPTER SPOTLIGHT

BUSCH GARDENS' 'DECIDE THE RIDE'

Figure 10.1 Busch Gardens logo. Used with the consent of Busch Gardens/Water Country USA. All Rights Reserved.

In early 2016, Busch Gardens Williamsburg started to tease its fans that something new was coming. A series of videos posted to its social media channels cleverly and mysteriously released small snippets of information regarding a new attraction set to debut the following year. Historically, Busch Gardens had never announced or discussed new attractions that far in advance, but the park made a conscious decision to be more transparent with its fans. The video series culminated in the announcement of a new wooden roller coaster as well as a new year-long campaign titled 'Decide the Ride' where the park turned to its fans to help plan the attraction. Touted as the world's first crowd-sourced ride, Busch Gardens gave an unprecedented look into what goes on behind the scenes of building a new ride and allowed its social media fans to make crucial decisions that would shape the attraction experience.

The campaign was kicked off with the announcement that the public would decide the name of the coaster. Naming an attraction is a permanent decision, a difficult challenge, and a legal nightmare, so the park had its trepidations but continued. Three name options were chosen and approved by the park's legal team and were left entirely for the public's decision. The park relied exclusively on its own social media channels and word of mouth to get the news out, instead of paid media. The news spread quickly and the park saw a record amount of engagement; new social media followers increased by 5 percent and online coverage grew as a result of its survey.

The coaster's theme and story followed a battle between Norse Vikings and Villagers. The public ultimately chose the coaster name 'InvadR,' the Norse spelling preference of the word invader. The verdict was announced on Facebook on April 4 (see Figure 10.2), almost an entire year before the coaster would open, but that didn't slow down the anticipation. The campaign continued throughout the year and kept the fans' excitement level high. Among other ride decisions, the park also paid homage to those who helped 'Decide the Ride' by making a large-scale collage of their names on the site of the coaster as it was being built. These types of campaign elements were announced and showcased on the park's Instagram and Snapchat profiles. A few lucky fans were even randomly chosen and given the opportunity to transform into Vikings to be the face of the ride and in future advertisements.

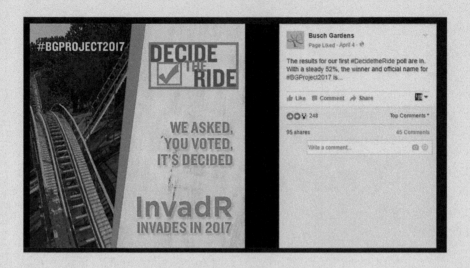

Figure 10.2 Busch Gardens Facebook page. Used with the consent of Busch Gardens/Water Country USA. All Rights Reserved.

The company leveraged its social media presence and empowered its fans from beginning to end by providing them with an unparalleled sense of ownership of the ride. The entire approach was very unconventional for the park, and even the industry, but it paid off in the end. Busch Gardens revealed that the public awareness and anticipation of the new attraction was 12 percent higher than that of its previous attractions, despite the lack of paid media.

INTRODUCTION

The digital and social media industry is evolving and growing at a rapid pace. Marketers must embrace this digital and social media revolution or they will forgo the most powerful, dynamic, personal, and cost-effective marketing force ever to emerge. This chapter will examine the concepts, strategies, tactics, platforms, and capabilities associated with marketing via digital and social media. However, a word of caution is in order: digital and social media techniques and capabilities are dynamic and continuously evolving at warp speed. You must keep abreast of the changes if you are to truly harness the power of digital and social marketing. Beware . . . the speed of change can be mind-boggling!

Growth and Transition

Direct marketers must not only keep up with the changes, but also be able to utilize digital and social media as they become vital in marketing plans. Sixty-nine percent of adults now use social networking sites—a nearly tenfold jump in the past decade.[1] Although the overall number of users of social networking sites has leveled off since 2013, there continues to be growth in social media usage among some demographic groups that were not among the earliest adopters, including older Americans. While 88 percent of young adults (ages 18 to 29) are users of social media,[2] 37 percent of those 65 years and older are now also using social media,[3] representing a huge increase from 11 percent in 2010 and just 2 percent in 2005.[4] Beyond age, no major differences in demographic composition with respect to gender, race, ethnic, and geographic groups of social media usage exists today. Comparable rates of social media usage include gender (males, 65 percent and females, 73 percent),[5] race and ethnic group (Caucasians, 68 percent; African-Americans, 69 percent; and Hispanics, 72 percent).[6] However, one demographic trend has continued: individuals possessing higher education levels and household incomes tend to be more likely users of social media.

The Internet also has enjoyed the fastest growth and acceptance rates of all media. Consider the time it has taken these technologies to reach 50 million users: telephone—40 years; radio—38 years; cable television—10 years; the Internet—5 years.[7] Yet Facebook hit 100 million users in four and a half years, while Instagram did it in under two and a half years.[8]

The Internet is an interactive marketing medium for direct marketers, offering information access and two-way communication with customers in real time via the computer. Interactivity is what makes marketing on the Internet different from other forms of direct marketing media. To be considered 'interactive,' a new medium must meet the following three criteria:[9]

1. Consumers must be able to control when they view the products and which types of products they are viewing.
2. Consumers must be able to control the pace at which they review products. They must be able to review the product content at their leisure, reading the product literature at a pace that is convenient to them, rather than being forced to progress to the next product.
3. Consumers must be able to place an order or request additional information directly via the medium rather than having to order through another method.

The Internet began as a high-tech tool for facilitating communication between scientists, and was developed under the sponsorship of the U.S. Defense Department's Advanced Research Projects Agency (DARPA). In 1969, the network, then called DARPAnet, became a reality when two nodes were linked together. By 1989, the National Science Foundation had replaced the Defense Department as the chief source of support for the network of networks, renamed NSFnet. Originally intended to facilitate research and communication within the scientific community, today the Internet has grown to include social networks and users across a wide variety of backgrounds and interests. The first widespread interest in the Internet as a vehicle for commerce occurred in 1993, when the first Web browser, Mosaic, was released and became freely accessible to the public.

Companies use the Internet to provide customer service, share information, sell goods and services, and build and strengthen customer relationships. However, most companies have established a website with the primary purpose of disseminating product/service information. Visit the website of the City of Virginia Beach Convention & Visitors Bureau, featured in Figure 10.3, to experience a well-organized and easy-to-navigate website.

In terms of functionality, websites are classified as informational and transactional. Providing customer support and service straddles the two, depending on the situation. Three primary marketing activities are well suited to the Web:

- making information available to prospective customers
- providing customer support, engagement, and accessibility
- enabling transactions to occur.

Direct marketers have been performing these activities for decades without the Internet, but now, due to technological advances, they are able to transfer their knowledge and experience to this powerful digital marketing medium. It is also very clear to many companies that merely having a Web presence is not enough. What it takes to succeed in digital marketing is a clear plan for the organization to follow and execute, a strong commitment of both human resources and capital for the technological infrastructure to support the various online applications and digital marketing activities, and *content* that engages consumers to respond. Liking, sharing, following, connecting, voting, requesting, donating, buying, and so on, are all critical actions that marketers want their digital audience to take. To obtain these actions, marketers rely on engaging digital communication or content marketing.

Content Marketing

Keep in mind that the most important element of creating relevant communication is to engage your digital audiences. Content marketing, as discussed earlier, in Chapter 6, is a strategic marketing approach focused on creating and distributing valuable, relevant, and consistent communication to attract and retain a clearly defined audience—and, ultimately, to drive profitable customer action.[10] Good content should draw your target audience back, time after time, to engage with your digital applications and platforms.

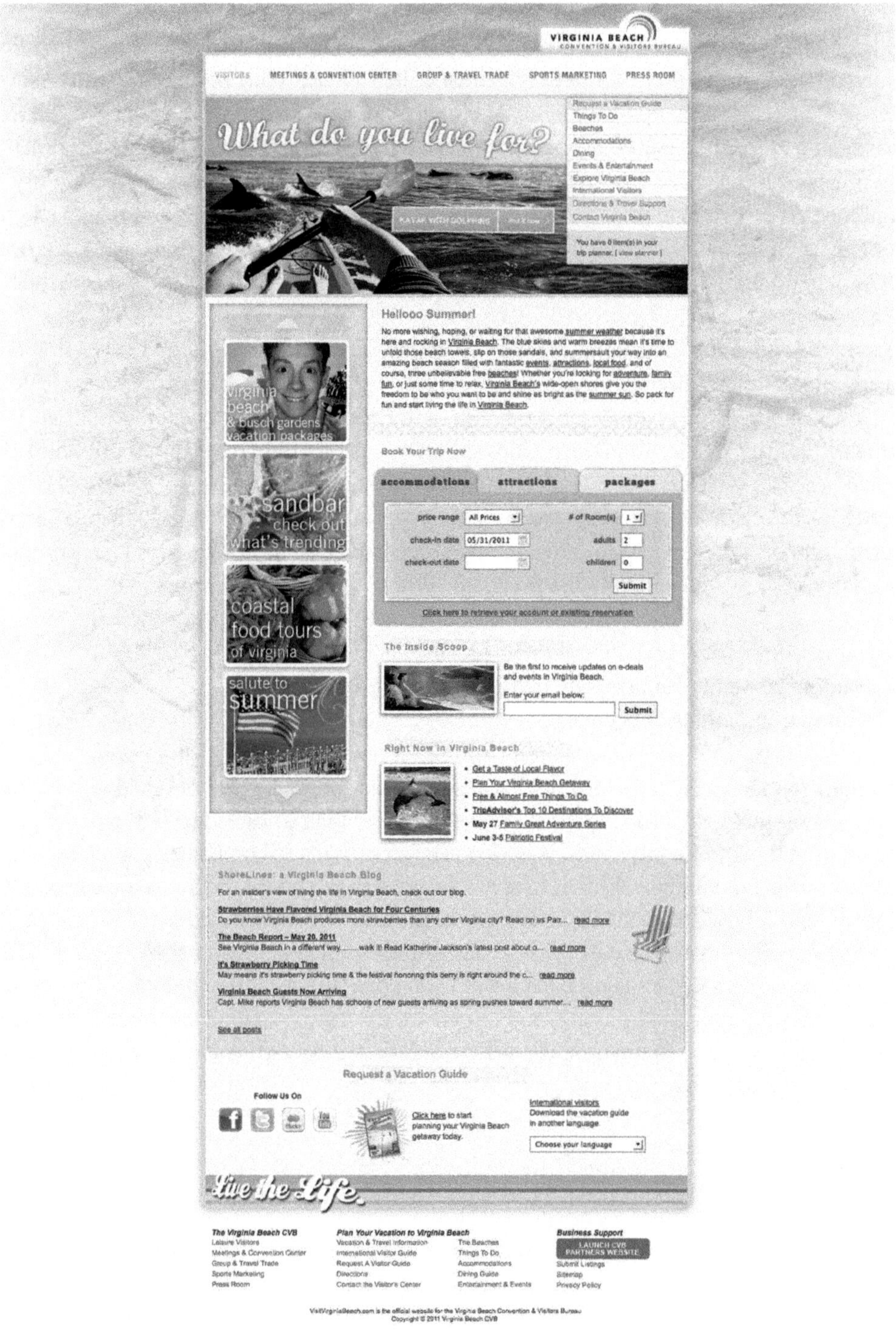

Figure 10.3 Virginia Beach website home page. Used with permission of the City of Virginia Beach Convention & Visitors Bureau.

Content may originate from many different sources – the company or organization, customers or users, distributors or channel members, and so on. Some individuals may be hired to create and share content to sway or help persuade a digital audience to take action. This is the topic of the next section.

Influencer Marketing

Influencer marketing is a form of content-driven marketing where the content shared is akin to an endorsement or testimonial by a third party or potential consumer. The 'influencers' can be anyone and anywhere. All influencers have one thing in common: they are influential because of their large followings on social media platforms and the Web.[11] In influencer marketing, an influencer or 'social media celebrity' is paid to promote a specific item or brand. This creates a cross between the traditional celebrity endorsement and the modern content-driven campaign. Some influencers got their start on other platforms, while others began their journey by becoming specialists in their field and leveraging social media to their benefit. Influencers can be utilized to promote a specific product in a manner that connects with audiences by identifying a trusting and familiar face with a brand or product.

Influencer marketing is not limited to any social media platform and may be executed in both B2C and B2B situations across all applications available in digital marketing. The bottom line: influencer marketing is very effective in swaying the behavior of large groups of consumers.

Let's explore another content marketing activity that digital marketers use to engage groups, while at the same time generating more content from the targeted groups.

Crowdsourcing

Crowdsourcing is defined as the practice of engaging a group for a common goal—often innovation, problem solving, or efficiency via technology. Crowdsourcing enables marketers to obtain new ideas and solutions and deeper consumer engagement.[12] Crowdsourcing is an efficient,

Figure 10.4   Lay's crowdsourcing example. Provided courtesy of Frito-Lay North America, Inc.

effective, and inexpensive method to mobilize a group. Crowdsourcing is an excellent strategy for companies to use in order to engage with consumers via their digital or mobile devices to identify new product ideas or product modifications, such as new designs, features, fragrances, and flavors. For instance, crowdsourcing is commonly used by craft breweries to engage customers in the development of new craft beer flavors.

An excellent example of successful crowdsourcing is that of the 'Do Us a Flavor' social media contests for Lay's potato chips. Through these contests, PepsiCo, the parent company of Lay's, encourages consumers to submit new flavor ideas via social media outlets or its website, www.DoUsAFlavor.com. Contestants pitch their ideas using a photo, name, ingredients, and a caption, explaining why their flavor of chip would be successful. Company executives judge the submissions, select the top three flavor ideas, and then send the top three ideas back to the public to vote on the best one. PepsiCo has held 'Do Us a Flavor' crowdsourcing campaigns in numerous countries, with consumers suggesting more than 12 million ideas for chip flavors around the world.[13] The company launched its first 'Do Us a Flavor' contest in 2012 in the U.S., which resulted in 3.8 million submissions and Lay's cheesy garlic bread chips. This 10-month campaign also resulted in the number of Lay's Facebook fans increasing to 1.2 million and the number of people talking about Lay's on Facebook rising by 4700%.[14]

Crowdfunding is a form of crowdsourcing where financial support is being requested of the group being contacted. Let's explore an example of crowdfunding. Imagine a group of entrepreneurs coming together to design a new home espresso machine that would produce the same high-quality espresso shot as one would obtain in a specialty café. The entrepreneurs could reach out to potential investors via a social media crowdfunding campaign that would offer these prospective backers various levels of investment opportunities in order to finance the new espresso machine business venture. Crowdfunding is a potentially powerful mechanism by which to digitally fundraise.

Indeed, the ingenuity of digital and social media is endless! Now, let's examine the various applications to be utilized in digital and social media marketing.

APPLICATIONS

E-mail Marketing

E-mail is a part of the Internet that operates independently from the Web, allowing global communication through the Internet without being indexed on any search engines. E-mail is an extremely successful and effective means of retaining current customers. For example, Hauser's Jewelers often sends e-mails, such as those featured in Figure 10.5, to its customers to promote special seasonal offers and events. Notice how the Touchdown e-mail cleverly ties into the fall football season.

Recent statistics show that e-mails average a 20.81 percent open rate, a 2.43 percent click-through rate, a 0.49 percent soft bounce-back rate, a 0.33 percent hard bounce rate, and an unsubscribe rate of 0.19 percent.[15] Now let's analyze these numbers. A 20.81 percent open rate indicates that more than one in five people open the e-mail they receive. Just think, these are average figures and when marketers target, customize, and use catchy subject lines with their outbound e-mails, even higher open rates may be realized. Research reports that e-mails where animation is utilized see a 15 percent lift in transaction rates.[16]

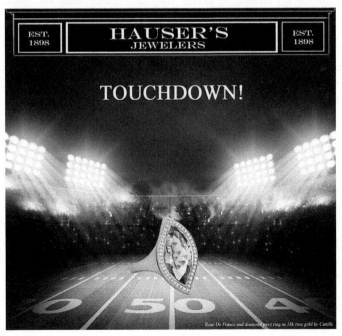

Figure 10.5 Hauser's Jewelers e-mails. Used with permission of Hauser's Jewelers.

In conclusion, all of these numbers are very good response rates and are comparable to some of the highest numbers in direct response. Now, these statistics are averages across many industries, so it is important for direct marketers to test and measure the response rates for their own industry and for their own house list. The highest performing industries for open rate and click-through rate include hobbies, e-mails sent by government entities, and arts and artists.[17]

Some of the methods for which marketers can use e-mail to grow their business, generate sales, and retain customers are as follows:

- staying in touch with current customers
- sending an e-mail newsletter
- announcing a new product or service
- sending an affiliate promotion
- promoting a sale or an event
- targeting specific promotions for loyalty programs
- announcing new content, such as a blog post, podcast, or video on a company website.

Today's marketers use **marketing automation** or software platforms and technologies designed to effectively carry out marketing activities on multiple online channels, including e-mail, social media, and websites. Marketing automation has omni-channel capabilities and has stemmed from the use of **auto responders**, e-mails that are automatically sent when triggered by some variable or some event. They enable the marketer to create and set it up and then forget about it. These can be triggered by all kinds of events, such as the purchase of a new product, opt in to a new list, registering for a webinar, or pretty much any other thing the marketer wants to use them for.

Here is typical scenario of how a marketer can use auto responders:

1. Consumers opt in to a new list.
2. They are immediately sent an auto responder welcoming them and offering them the promised item.
3. Two days later, each person receives a second e-mail with additional content linked to a teaser video.
4. On the third day, these consumers receive a third e-mail with a link to a third video. This video may be a sales presentation asking for the sale.

Marketers can use auto responders to increase sales, build rapport for a product, and provide information the person perceives as valuable. Most e-mail providers offer auto responders as part of their packages and services. As for measuring response rates, most e-mail providers can do this. Typical metrics that can be measured include deliverability rate, open rate, click-through rate, bounce rate, and the unsubscribe rate.

There are three basic types of e-mail of interest to marketers:

1. E-mail from companies targeting promotions to specific customers: this method is most effective when it is database-driven and customized to match the needs of specific market segments of customers. This includes both B2B and B2C e-mail.

2. E-mail from the consumer to the company: this is often used for placing an inquiry or a request for additional information.
3. E-mail from the consumer to another consumer: this is the electronic version of word of mouth. This form of e-mail has also been referred to as **viral marketing**, where e-mail messages are forwarded to other consumers by a consumer. In fact, the term **viralocity** has been coined to measure both the number of messages and the rate of speed by which e-mail messages are forwarded by a consumer to other consumers.

E-mail is similar to traditional direct mail in that it is conducted on a one-to-one, personal basis. However, e-mail costs a lot less than traditional mail and therefore enables companies to communicate on a more frequent basis, and creates a tendency to spam. In addition, consumers respond more quickly to e-mail than to direct mail, with replies normally coming from consumers within hours from the time they received the message. Likewise, this sets consumers' expectations to receive timely responses from companies when they send e-mail requests or inquiries.

E-mail direct marketing is most productive when companies use their own customer lists instead of lists generated by third parties. Many companies have developed an e-mail list of their customers and send e-newsletters and other communication on a regular basis. E-mail allows companies to send tailored and personalized messages to specific customers based on needs. This is both highly effective and efficient for direct and interactive marketers.

For example, the National Geographic Society (NGS) sent e-mails to its members who had opted in to receive notice about its entertainment offerings. Using data from its marketing database, NGS was able to match e-mail addresses to member ZIP code areas. With this information, NGS segmented its entertainment list to create geo-based clusters around theaters where its feature documentary, *Restrepo*, was going to show. When the members received the e-mail, shown in Figure 10.6, it told them where and when they could see *Restrepo*. The e-mail also had links to encourage people to watch the trailer, visit the *Restrepo* website and find show times. The very bottom of the e-mail featured the share options for Facebook, Twitter, and Forward to a Friend. NGS implemented many of these customized, geo-targeted e-mail campaigns. Using dynamic content techniques, NGS was able to basically design one e-mail, but code the e-mail to accept custom headlines naming the respective theater locations and dates, along with custom links. The main benefits of using dynamic content were that it allowed NGS to reduce the work involved in executing the e-mail campaign, and more importantly, it allowed the recipient to receive a customized, relevant message.

Because sending e-mail messages is easy, inexpensive, and fast, some marketers have misused this medium. Spam is the term for unsolicited e-mail messages. **Spam** is considered the junk mail of the Internet. Direct marketers can avoid sending spam by handling customer information carefully and adhering to ethical e-mail marketing practices. Providing a way for consumers to opt in to a mailing list is a starting point for practicing ethical e-mail marketing. Direct marketers must follow the established laws and should follow DMA guidelines for using e-mail. There are many rules that marketers should follow when creating and conducting e-mail marketing. However, when done right, an e-mail campaign can build profitable customer relationships at a fraction of the cost of other direct marketing methods. Customized e-mail marketing programs are most effective when combined with other digital media.

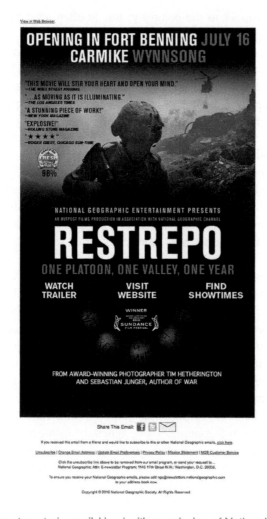

Figure 10.6 *Restrepo* geo-targeted e-mail. Used with permission of National Geographic Society.

Let's take a look at an excellent direct and interactive marketing campaign that combined e-mail with banner ads and a customized website to produce impressive results. The U.S. Department of the Navy used a 100 percent digital direct marketing campaign to change perceptions of the role of women in the U.S. Navy. An outbound e-mail campaign, targeting women aged 18–24 who were not attending a four-year college course, explained the benefits of joining the Navy, including training and money for college. Banner ads showed women in this age group in common jobs and then showed them in a Navy uniform doing exciting and important jobs like diving or fixing planes. As shown in Figure 10.7, on its website (Navy.com), a customized 'just for women' community showcased opportunities for women in the Navy. The combined digital campaign was extremely successful, with leads exceeding goals by 400 percent in 90 days, and the digital campaign increasing overall recruitment leads by 15.25 percent.

Figure 10.7 U.S. Navy Web page. Use of the Department of the Navy's Accelerate Your Life® and Life Accelerator® marks is granted with permission of the Department of the Navy and does not constitute an endorsement of any author, publisher, or product thereof, by the Department of the Navy or the Department of Defence.

In conclusion, e-mail offers the direct marketer an inexpensive way to grow a business, generate sales, and retain customers. It can be even more effective if the marketing company has a thorough understanding of its customers, based on market research. Let's discuss how this works.

Online Market Research

Primary data collection has also been enhanced by technological progress. Consumers seem to be more receptive to participating in surveys conducted via the Internet as opposed to mail and phone surveys. Thus, the Internet offers an alternative medium for executing marketing research studies on a one-to-one basis with customers. Some of the more common primary data collection techniques being implemented online are online surveys and online panels.

Online Surveys

Online survey research is carried out by either sending electronic questionnaires to customers via individual e-mails or by posting a survey on a company's website. Sending questions via e-mail allows for personalization and control over the timing and distribution of the survey. E-mail surveys are also the preferred method of data collection in countries where users must pay by the hour for Internet connection, because e-mail may be answered offline, whereas a respondent must be online to complete a survey on the Web.

However, Web surveys can be written in a more user-friendly fashion than e-mail, with reply buttons, drop-down menus, and blank spaces for each customer to record responses. Web surveys have become a relatively easy digital marketing tool that can be leveraged through e-mail, social media, website, QR code, or any other medium that allows a link to be inserted. Many sites, such as Google Surveys and Survey Monkey, allow for users to create comprehensive surveys with various forms of answer choices, including free response, sliding scale, numbering, and more. Best of all, most of these survey-creation sites are free! All data is then automatically situated in a spreadsheet for ease of visualization and analysis.

Online Panels

Online panels overcome the sampling and response problems associated with online surveys. Online panels, which are similar to focus group interviews, are discussions marketers conduct with people who have agreed to talk about a selected topic over a period of time. For example, a fitness magazine might conduct an online panel to discuss the latest available fitness equipment and obtain feedback as to the ease and effectiveness of the equipment. Normally, panelists receive a fee or gifts for their participation. Each person must complete a comprehensive survey after being accepted to participate as a panelist so that researchers have data about their characteristics and behavior. Online panels provide marketers with a supply of willing respondents about whom they already have extensive data. Thus, there is no need to ask demographic questions each time. Marketers contact panelists on a regular basis with high expectations of a positive response to their request for information. Many publishers have online panels to assist in the development of magazine content.

Conducting online research is important to better understand consumer behavior and to more effectively be able to connect with consumers to satisfy their needs and wants. This research is used to determine how companies can serve consumers via e-commerce.

E-commerce

The buying and selling of products online is known as electronic commerce, or e-commerce. However, e-commerce encompasses much more than the transactional portion of business. It can include every step of the supply chain, from advertising to order fulfillment, over the Internet. Many successful companies have been built through e-commerce.

Companies such as Amazon.com, Overstock.com, and Zappos are based entirely on the Internet. Amazon was started in 1995 as an online bookstore.[18] Amazon has evolved into the top Internet retailer in the country with more than 232 billion U.S. dollars in net sales.[19] Amazon prides itself on being customer centered by offering an extremely wide variety of products and increasing convenience. According to recent figures, Amazon has more than 304 million active customer accounts.[20] E-commerce has become a huge industry, creating a new type of convenience for consumers around the world. As we'll examine in the next section, the Internet offers consumers a way to unite with others—regardless of whether they are there to shop, make new friends, obtain information or just to connect.

Connecting Sites

Along with e-commerce, connecting sites are becoming increasingly popular. Connecting sites, which are similar to e-commerce sites, can be referred to as websites that serve to connect people for various reasons. They create market fronts to bring consumers to other consumers in order to trade products and information, or even to find relationships. Connecting sites serve two purposes: connecting people to products, and connecting people to people.

Product Connecting Sites

Auction sites and the like connect people to products. Major product connecting sites include eBay and Craigslist. eBay is an online auction website that serves as a liaison from consumer to consumer in order to trade products. Users can upload items to auction, view items to buy, or both. Similarly, Craigslist is a forum that allows users to post items for sale, view items, or both. Various social networking websites also have the ability to connect people with products, such as Facebook Marketplace and Etsy, which connect shoppers with local artisans and makers of craft products.

People Connecting Sites

There are also connecting sites that connect people to people, such as dating sites or job search sites. For instance, Match.com is an online dating company where one can create an account and profile and view the profiles of others in search of a relationship. Job sites, such as Indeed.com, allow job seekers to create accounts and upload a resumé and relevant information. They may search job listings and apply, or a company may search profiles and resumés and contact them. Connecting sites are a growing segment of the online industry and are designed to be easy, convenient, and need-satisfying for consumers.

Figure 10.8   Match logo

Note: The Match logo is owned by Match.com, LLC.

Driving Site Traffic

A company's website is designed to be a powerful destination for consumers to interact with the organization and its offerings. Great effort should be placed on website design to make the site easy to navigate so visitors can easily and quickly locate the desired information, products, services, or connections. However, even the most robust and well-organized website cannot be successful without visitors. All marketers realize that designing and launching a website is only one half of the equation. Attracting website traffic, recently referred to as 'customer development,' is the other crucial half of the equation for online marketing success. Think about it this way: creating and launching a company website without actively driving site traffic is similar to planning and hosting a party but forgetting to send out the party invitations. Unheard of, right? Thus, marketers must actively drive customer traffic to their websites. There are many ways a marketer can drive site traffic, including **search engine optimization**, banner ads, webinars, online sales letters, and various offline tactics. Of course, a variety of online activities, from blogs, social networks, and e-mail invitations to personalized websites, can be used to drive site traffic as well, and these options will be overviewed in this chapter.

Search Engine Optimization

In the past, people used to look for the products and services they needed in local phone books or directories such as the Yellow Pages. Today, the Internet has completely changed the way people search for just about any type of information. According to Google's mission statement,

'Google's mission is to organize the world's information and make it universally accessible and useful.'[21] With Google's technology, it is now easier and more convenient to search for these products and services via a search engine than to look things up in a local directory. **Optimization** is the *process* of improving website traffic by using search engines. In general, when the link to a website is listed in a higher position on the search engine results page, the user is more likely to view it. Thus, search engine optimization aims at moving the link to one of the top links on the results page.

Search engine marketing (SEM) is the entire set of techniques and strategies used to direct more visitors from search engines to marketing websites. The four most common purposes for SEM use include increasing or enhancing brand awareness of products or services; selling products, services, or content directly online; generating leads; and driving traffic to a website.[22]

Research shows that 64 percent of marketers are using paid search for lead generation.[23]

Let's explore the three different types of SEM that could be used by companies wanting to improve their website traffic:

1. Paid placement: sometimes referred to as 'pay-per-click' (PPC) or 'cost-per-click' (CPC), paid placement advertising uses text ads targeted to keyword search results on search engines through programs such as Google Ads and Yahoo!
2. Paid inclusion: paid inclusion entails the practice of paying a fee to search engines and similar types of sites, such as directories or shopping comparison sites, so that a given website or Web pages may be included in the service's directory, although not necessarily in exchange for a particular position in search engine listings. The fee structures will vary. One example of paid inclusion is evident in Google search results when searching for a flight. Instead of simply returning sites with flight options, Google shows a small widget that lists the available flights and the sites on which they are listed. These sites are part of a paid inclusion program.[24]
3. Organic search engine optimization: this form of optimization includes the use of a variety of techniques to improve how well a site or page gets listed in search engines for particular search topics.

Today, most consumers take the approach of typing in what they are searching for using keyword search engines such as Bing, Yahoo!, or Google. Before that, consumers often browsed through catalogs prior to visiting Internet retailers. Some consumers still do; however, that is certainly not the trend. Today, technological advances make it even easier to search for items online. Most of the major search engines now use visual search engine technology, also known as reverse image search, which allows a consumer to search for a product with only a photo. For example, when consumers see a photograph of a sweater they really like that is worn by a celebrity online, they can search for that same sweater online. Just imagine what other technologies lie ahead to help consumers save time and shop online.

Because of this shift in people's behaviors, it has become very important and valuable for a business to have its products and services or a company website show up on the *first page* of the search engines for a particular keyword that will benefit their business. How important is it to be on the first page of Google? Or, what is the number one position in Google worth to a company? The number one position on Google search achieves an average of a 58.4 percent of all clicks from users, according to a study from Optify. Websites ranked number one received an average click-through rate (CTR) of 36.4 percent, number two had a CTR of 12.5 percent, and number three had a CTR of 9.5 percent.[25] Thus, the closer the company is to the top, the more traffic they will receive from the organic search listing. Holding one of the top three positions on Goggle, a premium position to obtain, and maintaining this position has created a whole new opportunity for marketers known as **search engine optimization (SEO)**.

There are three components to getting a site ranked in most search engines, and specifically in Google. They are: content, links, and activity. The entire formula for reaching peak SEO is not something that can be summed up in a single chapter, as some marketing professionals devote their entire careers to SEO. For additional information regarding increasing a site's search engine results, please refer to Google's SEO guide on the company's website.

Content

Content consists of how relevant the content on the site is to the actual domain name and how relevant it is to the keyword search. For instance, a site with the domain www.dogtraining.com, if it has current, relevant information about dog training, would be very hard to beat for the keyword search 'dog training.' This website would be very hard to knock off the number one spot on Google by another site competing on the same dog training keyword. **Keyword density** is the number of times that the keyword in the search appears on that website. The keyword must be intertwined throughout the article or site naturally, but not so often that it can be viewed as spamming the searching engines. The more times the word appears, the higher the site will rank. Site structure primarily includes the content of the website.

Links

Links can be thought of as a popularity contest. This is based on the premise that the more valuable a site is, the more people will link to it. The other aspect of a link campaign is that not every link is the same. Each site has a PR (page rank) value. A **PR value** is simply how often Google or other search engines index or crawl through a site.[26] **Backlinks** involve the quality of links, the number of broken links, the anchor text, and the positioning of the link. How do you start establishing backlinks to a website? There are many ways of doing this and each can be used as an overall traffic building and linking strategy. And each medium can help the author establish himself as an expert in his field, drive traffic from each piece of content, with the overall objective of ranking on Google's first page. Links can be established from many sources, including the following:

- Videos: uploading videos to various video sites with links back to either a specific article or to the home page.
- Podcasts: uploading podcasts to various podcast hosting sites, such as Buzzsprout and RSS, feeds with backlinks on the download page and within the audio content to the site.
- Article directories: this is also known as article marketing. Writing articles with good, relevant content that is keyword driven will establish you as an expert within a field after you have uploaded several articles. Each article, of course, has a link back to your site at the bottom of the page or in the resource box. You can then take the same article and upload it to

multiple article directories, leveraging your time and content, while establishing you as the expert in multiple article directories.

- PDF directories: these work very similarly to article directories except they are saved as a PDF and then uploaded to a PDF directory. Keep in mind that one article can be sent to multiple directories, establishing multiple links and traffic sources, and people interact with each directory and download the PDF. It is worth considering that tracking PDF engagements through Google Analytics may be tricky, therefore a landing page or trackable URL is recommended. The advantage of saving in the PDF format is that people perceive PDFs to have higher value than articles. And often people will store PDFs that they find valuable on their hard drives. This adds to the shelf life of the PDF, often allowing the person who downloaded the PDF to go back later and reread the content, causing them to revisit the website. PDF files also provide the benefit of being available offline, if downloaded for later reading.
- Press releases: reformatting the article and PDF into a press release can establish two things: (1) the content can be syndicated across various media, such as online newspapers, radio stations, and television stations, which will allow multiple backlinks to the domain of the website; and (2) the owner of the site can receive free publicity about the company via content syndication, or radio and TV interviews.
- Commenting on other niche-related blogs and websites: adding value to other blogs by commenting and then posting a link in the website is a very good strategy for establishing backlinks to a website and encourages people within the niche to visit your site and interact with you.

The end result of all of the linking is twofold. First, if the content is good it will establish the author as an expert across multiple directories in various media. Second, it will create traffic from each of these directories back to the website. And this leads us to the third part of Google's triad for getting a site ranked, which is activity.

Activity

Activity includes the length of time people stay on a website and how they are interacting with the website. Activity also addresses how often a site is updated—every day, once a week, or once a month—the more often the better. **Aging** refers to the recency of the site and is based on the date by which it was established on the Web. The newer the site, the less weight it will be given compared to already established websites.

There are several ways of encouraging activity on a website, including:

- featuring video and MP3 content on a site that allows people to consume the content while they are on the site: this will increase the average time that people spend on the site
- allowing people to comment on a website by using a blogging platform as the website: having comments on a website from people visiting a site communicates social proof to other visitors (we will discuss blogging in greater detail later in the chapter)
- utilizing a social media feed that shows real-time follower engagement from Twitter, Instagram, Facebook, or any other social media of choice.

In conclusion, whether you decide to partake in search engine optimization for your own site or another company's site, keep in mind the importance of being listed on the first page of Google, because not only does it help a business on a local level, but it can quickly give a business a national presence as well. Another way to achieve awareness is by purchasing Google Ads, which is the topic of the next section.

Google Ads

Most of the ad platforms online that allow you to bid on keywords have one commonality: you bid on how much you will pay per click or per impression. So, for this section, we will focus on the most advanced and dynamic advertising platform and that is Google. For Google, there are two platforms that you can bid on: the search network and the content network.

Search Network

The search network is the part of Google AdWords with which most people are familiar. Traditionally, it is more expensive than the content network, but normally businesses that use the search network are bidding on terms that people are searching. This means they are placing ads based on keywords. The people that are searching using these keywords are looking for a solution to a need or want. This makes them red hot prospects, and if the ad can grab attention, generate interest, and get the person to click, then the marketer has a good chance of getting an opt-in lead and/or converting a sale.

When the person clicks on the ad, to incorporate a direct-response component, the visitor can be taken to a landing page or a sales page, or, if on a mobile device, there may be a direct link to a phone number. The ad can send the visitor to a standard Web page, but there needs to be some sort of funnel in place or call to action that will get the person to take the desired action of the marketer.

There are three metrics that Google considers when showing the ad and when establishing the cost of the ad. They are the cost per click, quality score, and click-through rate.

Cost per click is simply how much the person is willing to bid to show the ad. This can make a difference regarding whether the ad will be placed on page one of Google or some other page.

Quality score looks at a variety of factors to measure how relevant your keyword is to your ad text and to a user's search query. A keyword's quality score updates frequently and is closely related to its performance. In general, a high-quality score means that your keyword will trigger ads in a higher position and at a lower cost per click (CPC).

Click-through rate addresses the number of people who click on your ad. The higher your click-through rate, the more it improves your quality score. The higher the click-through rate, the more often your ad will show.

There are many strategies to maximize click-through rates, including the following:

- Ask for the click-through action: the easiest way to increase click-through is to simply ask for it.

- Animate a banner advertisement: animation increases the likelihood that the ad will draw the user's attention, and also generates more clicks than static banners, all else being equal.
- Involve the audience: the third generation of banner ads is interactive. Engage the viewers to allow them to personalize ads to their needs. Involving the viewer allows the advertiser to get to know them better, one of the primary goals of direct marketing!
- Change creative messages frequently: the nature of the Internet means that responses occur quickly, on the first few impressions. Therefore, online creative messages wear out more quickly than with traditional media.

Ad Structure

When utilizing Google Ads, many businesses mistakenly try to sell the product or do a branding ad to push the business. To make the ad more effective, remember to sell the click, not the product. There is not nearly enough space in Google Ads to do a sufficient job of selling a product or service. Keep in mind, as presented in Chapter 6, that consumers process images much faster than they do words. Google's new gallery ads combine words with images, with the goal of more effective marketing communications. Google gallery ads, interactive ads that feature swipeable image carousels, have been found to drive 25 percent more engagement (as measured by clicks and swipes) than standard text ads do.[27] Regardless of the type of ad being used, direct marketers seek a measurable response, thus effective ad structure follows the AIDA format (Attention, Interest, Desire, Action).

In conclusion, when using Google Ads, the search network can help businesses find prospects that are searching for their product and service, while growing their lists and driving sales.

Display Network[28]

Another service offered by Google related to AdWords is that of the content network. In the content network, either Google will place your ads on websites that it believes are a match for your ad or banner ad, or you can actually select the websites on which you want your advertisement to be shown. The content network is based more on interruption marketing, similar to Facebook ads or ads in magazines. The content network allows marketers to be more creative with their ads and also allows direct marketers to place ads in various positions that target their customers. An example of this is placing a banner ad for rap music on golf sites. Most people would not understand why a company would want to place a banner ad on a site that seems to not be suitably targeted. Once people understand that grandparents buy a lot of music for their grandchildren, then this ad makes much more sense. The content network allows the marketer to do just this type of advertising. People are not necessarily looking for the ad, but notice it as they are perusing content of interest.

Using Google suggestions of websites to place ads on within the content network can actually open up entire new markets for products, and it will allow the marketer to test whether the ad and product will actually pull. Once a converting offer is established, the marketer can actually start looking for other, similar sites to advertise on within the same market, either through the Google content network or by contacting the website owner directly.

Many people ignore and do not understand the content network and focus much of their campaign budget on the search network when using Google AdWords. By doing this they are missing out on a lot of traffic at a lower cost than the search network. The content network allows the direct marketer to place their ad on far more sites than the search network, which is extremely targeted, direct, and not nearly as creative as the content network. One additional benefit of the display network is the option for placing ads on YouTube channels. Ads can be specifically played on hand-picked channels, certain topics, or on the YouTube home page. Various cost structures exist for each placement option.

Banner Ads

Banners and buttons basically occupy designated space that is available for rent on Web pages. **Banner advertising** is the digital analog to print ads, targeting a broad audience with the goal of creating awareness about the product or service being promoted. Banner ads are similar to space ads used in print media; however, they have video and audio capabilities because they are designed for interactive media. There are a variety of sizes that have been standardized per the Interactive Advertising Bureau. Those primary sizes include rectangles, pop-ups, banners, buttons, and skyscrapers. Banner ads must have a strong call to action, as can be seen in the creative banner ads shown in Figure 10.9. The goal of banner ads is twofold: first, to increase brand awareness by exposing consumers to the banner ad, and second, to maximize the 'click-through' rate.

Figure 10.9 Busch Gardens banner ads. Used with the consent of Busch Gardens/Water Country. All Rights Reserved.

Embedded ads are gaining attention, too. Embedded ads allow the viewer to receive more information without having to link to other websites. These ads are designed to overcome the space limitations of banners.

Webinars

Imagine offering an hour-long presentation with up to 1,000 people watching, while you are delivering good content, controlling the entire sales process, then asking for the sale, and finally answering any questions at the end to overcome any objections. Now, imagine giving this same presentation to up to 1,000 people at the same time in the same hour, all over the world, who are targeted and already prequalified to purchase. This is the power of webinars. **Webinars** are essentially Web conferencing software used for sales presentations. These presentations can range from white-collar corporate presentations to the ever-growing popularity of social media influencer marketing through live-streams. Incorporating webinars into the digital media mix is wise and can be a productive method for building a prospect list, especially when combined with affiliate marketing and e-mail marketing. A more detailed examination of webinars and how they work will be presented in the next chapter on business-to-business marketing.

Online Direct-Response Conversion Pages

The Web allows the direct marketer to target specific traffic to a specific Web page. Many online direct marketers will send traffic to either a squeeze page, a long-form sales letter, or a video sales letter. Let's look at each of these three different types of pages that are known for converting traffic into either a prospect or customer.

Squeeze Pages/Landing Pages

Squeeze pages or landing pages are pages on a website that only allow the visitor to do one of two things: (1) opt in to obtain the lead magnet being offered, or (2) leave the page altogether. Squeeze pages can be presented in various formats, but the common elements of a squeeze page are:

- headline
- sub-headline
- bullet points about the features and benefits of the lead magnet
- opt-in form
- photo of the lead magnet (this can be optional, but photos often boost conversion).

Keep in mind that squeeze pages can come in various formats, including video squeeze pages, where instead of having the bullet points in print format, they are delivered in the video, either in presentation format or by a person speaking and delivering the bullet points.

The goal of the squeeze page or landing page is to get the person on the page to opt in. This is the only objective of the squeeze page. In conclusion, using squeeze pages to require people to opt in is a sure-fire way to grow your list, while keeping the lead magnet exclusive to only those who opt in.

Marketers often test different landing pages to determine which one is most effective. Figure 10.10 shows two different landing pages that were tested by Busch Gardens to promote its Christmas Town holiday event.

Figure 10.10 Busch Gardens Christmas Town landing pages. Used with the consent of Busch Gardens/ Water Country. All Rights Reserved.

Long-Form Sales Letters

One of the five components of a direct mail package is the sales letter. This is the part of the direct mail package that, if done correctly, builds intense demand for the product and has people yearning to grab their wallet and either visit a website, call a phone number, or mail in an order form to purchase whatever is being offered. However, since we are talking about digital marketing in this chapter, how can direct marketers take the same principles of the direct mail sales letter and apply them to the Web? Very easily actually, because long-form direct sales letters convert to the Web very well. Long-form direct sales letters are similar to squeeze pages, where there is just one page and the visitor to the page can only do one of two things: either purchase or leave.

The primary goal of the sales letter is to make a sale. But there are some differences to online sales letters, when compared to squeeze pages. The first is length, as these letters are much longer than squeeze pages and include more components, such as headline, sub-headline, testimonials, guarantees, videos, podcasts, sales graphics, bullet points, and, of course, the all important call to action. In addition, long-form direct sales letter layout may include '**Johnson Boxes**' (where copy is placed inside text boxes to highlight certain content and to enable the content to stand out in the letter) and an **offer box** (where the offer is stated and a buy button appears).

There are many other elements of an online long-form sales letter, but the most important thing to remember is that they traditionally follow the same format as a normal long-form direct mail letter. The main difference is the ability to incorporate a multimedia approach with graphical headlines, videos, podcasts, or any other digital aspect that will help increase the conversion rate.

Video Sales Letters

Video sales letters are very similar to long-form direct mail letters, except the sales letter is in the form of a video presentation. It is perceived as content and is more interactive than just reading a long-form sales letter. They are very similar to webinars, but not as long. Video sales letters can be created with PowerPoint slides that are turned into a video with screen-capture software. Or they can include actual video of the person doing the selling. Nearly any kind of presentation can be turned into a video sales letter. Furthermore, with a simple java script, the 'buy button' of the video sales letter can be hidden, until the appropriate time comes for the person to purchase. Other advantages of the video sales letters are that they:

- are much faster to create than long-form sales letters
- are less expensive—you do not necessarily have to hire a copywriter
- have a higher perceived value than a long-form sales letter
- can control the sales process by eliminating video controls
- can present the price correctly, because people cannot just scroll to the bottom of the presentation and see the price, like they can on a long-form sales letter
- have conversion rates that are normally higher than those for long-form sales letters.

In conclusion, video sales letters are the newest form of conversion page online today, but they are quickly becoming more popular as conversion rates outperform traditional online long-form sales letters.

Offline Tactics

Offline tactics are essential to drive website traffic. The words to remember are: consistency and omniscience. Marketers must be diligent in using their URL with unshakable consistency and place it anywhere and everywhere. Consumers should bump up against a company's brand and its URL at every turn. 'Outside-the-box' thinking should be used to be creative as to where to place your URL. To assist with your idea generation, glance over the creatively placed URLs presented in Figure 10.11.

Figure 10.11   Airport van. Photo by Adam Baker.

Placing an ad containing a 'call to visit a website' might be expected on transportation vehicles, such as vans and buses, but who would have thought it would be featured on a banana? (See Figure 10.12.)

Figure 10.12 Bananas with message sticker. Photograph by Adam Baker.

As Figure 10.13 proves, when it comes to innovatively promoting website traffic, the sky really is the limit! So, think outside the box and determine where your company's URL should be placed in order to effectively draw website traffic.

Figure 10.13 Southwest Airlines airplane. Photo by Adam Baker.

DIGITAL FORMATS AND TOOLS

Digital formats and tools are the context for information that is then generated, disseminated, and shared. There are several digital and online formats and tools that every direct marketer should be familiar with as the digital industry continues to mature. These include blogs, social networks, personalized URLs (PURLS), and click-to-chat capabilities.

Blogs

A **blog** is a Web log, or a website, that contains informal information and journal-like entries. There are many types of blogs, varying from those chronicling personal experiences to informational, article-like pieces from experts. Their scope also varies. Some blogs are about a very specific topic, such as baking cakes, while others can touch on a much wider subject, such as sports, or have no subject at all. In most cases, one can follow a blog and post comments to various entries. Important to marketing are product and company-based blogs, creating a type of discussion board. Direct marketers must be able to understand consumers' use of blogs, and how to utilize blogs.

Companies can utilize blogs as a means of providing information to customers and prospects. This is a form of online public relations. **Online PR** (also known as E-PR) refers to any type of public relations conducted digitally. Companies may also use social networking websites, such as Tumblr, as tools for sharing blogs. As touched on previously, increasing the number of links to and from your website will increase the SEO rankings of the site, hence another reason that blogs are invaluable.

Tumblr is a blogging platform and social networking website combined. The platform was launched in February 2007 by then-20-year-old founder David Karp and it has grown to host more than 200 million blogs today. Tumblr allows users to post content such as text, videos, GIFs, and MP3s. Users can follow other people's blogs and customize their page to fit their interests. Tumblr allows users to comment on and share other people's posts as well. This platform is all about expression and connecting with other users. It is designed for the user to create and connect with others. Tumblr also offers sponsored posts, which are just like regular Tumblr posts but are more visible and targetable by gender, location, and interest.

Blogs can be used to discuss new products, corporate-level decisions, product support, and much more. As Figure 10.14 illustrates, the City of Virginia Beach's *ShoreLines* blog (now www. visitvirginiabeach.com/blog) offered visitors an opportunity to share information with its guests about upcoming events and activities.

Companies can also use blogs as a way of obtaining feedback from consumers. Many consumers discuss products in blogs, and firms should constantly monitor this form of digital word of mouth.

Social Networks

Social networking sites are another way to engage with consumers, gain insights and feedback, conduct online PR, advertise, and drive site traffic. The current primary social networking sites discussed in this chapter are Facebook, Twitter, Instagram, LinkedIn, and Pinterest.

416

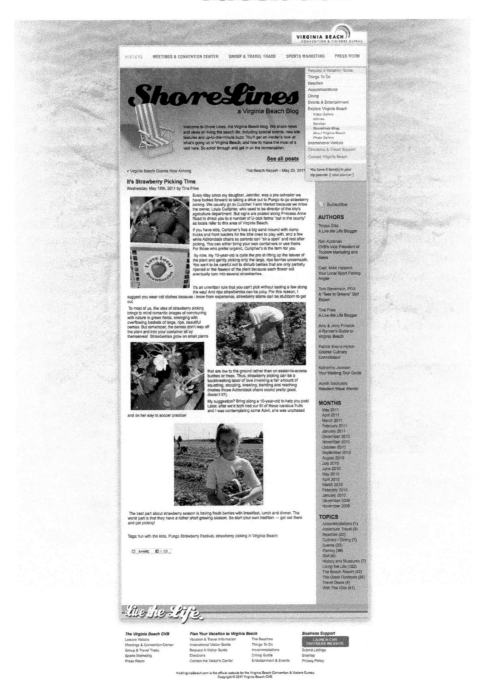

Figure 10.14 Virginia Beach *ShoreLines* blog site Web page. Used with permission of the City of Virginia Beach Convention & Visitors Bureau.

Facebook

Figure 10.15 Facebook logo

Note: The Facebook wordmark logo is owned by Facebook Inc.

Facebook is a social networking website created in 2004, which now has more than 2.38 billion monthly active users.[29] Approximately 85 percent of Facebook daily active users are outside the U.S. and Canada.[30]

Users create a profile and share personal information, which can be anything from interests and demographics to pictures. Facebook users also share information on preferred products through use of the 'like' button. Consumers can, with one click, show their preference for an advertisement, business, group, or topic.

Over the years, Facebook has added some new features for marketers and users. Marketers can pay to promote their posts to a selected audience. Who and how many people see their post depends on the budget they establish, and Facebook has tools to help marketers make these decisions. Promoted posts will be pushed onto users' news feeds. This is another useful form of advertising and promotion that can be carried out on Facebook.

Facebook can now be linked with Twitter and Instagram, so that all content posted on the other two platforms is automatically pushed to Facebook as well. This saves time for marketers, who do not have to post the same content on every platform but instead can post to one and have it appear on all of them. Facebook has begun to use hashtags, though not as extensively as Twitter. There is also a trending section on Facebook, similar to Twitter, that displays news and events that are being heavily talked about on Facebook. These both enable marketers to go viral more easily because once the marketer's content reaches the trending section, it appears on every user's page. (Both hashtags and trending will be addressed in greater detail in the following section on Twitter.) Facebook continues to innovate by offering its users more functions and interactive platforms.

Facebook's News Feed algorithm gives preference to native video content, meaning videos uploaded directly to Facebook, over linked videos, photos, or text posts. Short videos without sound or that feature subtitles so a user does not have to use sound, often perform the best. Figure 10.16 shows a 15-second, vertical video from Busch Gardens posted to its Facebook page. When watched on a mobile device, the video fills up the entire phone screen without any negative space to give a more immersive feel. The video featured edited footage of four different rides to make it look like one single drop—simple, fun, and, most importantly, effective. The video had more than 800,000 views in just 24 hours and drove the park's largest growth in Facebook fans from an individual post.

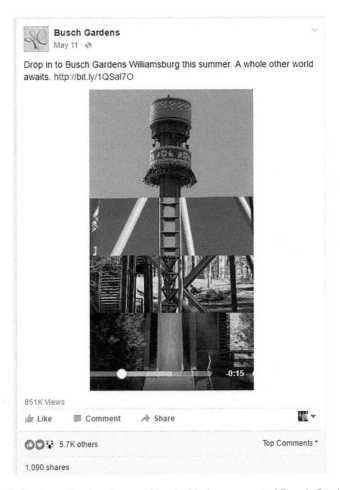

Figure 10.16 Busch Gardens Facebook page. Used with the consent of Busch Gardens/Water Country USA. All Rights Reserved.

Marketers can use the Facebook 'like' information to microtarget consumers on Facebook. An excellent example is that of the National Geographic Society (NGS) when it incorporated a Facebook 'like' button in the promotion of its feature documentary *Restrepo*. *Restrepo* is a film that chronicles the deployment of a platoon of U.S. soldiers in Afghanistan's Korengal Valley. Consumers were encouraged to discuss the film on the social networks. The Facebook 'like' button allowed consumers to virtually support the film and drove recipients to the fan page. The NGS microsite for *Restrepo* encouraged consumers to sign up for newsletters from the organization, contact their local theaters to book the film, or buy tickets to see the film. The page also urged consumers to follow the film on Twitter or become a friend of the film on Facebook. The campaign strived to draw attention to the Facebook page of the movie, which had by now attained a very engaged fan base (see Figure 10.17).

Facebook's ad platform allows you to segment your data by layering information. Facebook's segmentation features give marketers laser-like focus on targeting their best customers by geographic region, demographics, social factors, and psychographic and behavioral data.

Figure 10.17   Restrepo Facebook page. Used with permission of National Geographic Society.

Facebook introduced Facebook Fan Pages that allow businesses to set up a website within Facebook about their company, products or services. Each Facebook user can set up as many of these fan pages as they desire. This gives marketers a fantastic advantage, because not only can they establish a Fan Page for their company, but they could also create one for each product and service they offer. The ads can be targeted to individuals for each of these products and services.

Plus, Fan Pages can be customized using FHTML, which is Facebook's own hypertext markup language (HTML). You can also customize your Fan Page using apps. Apps make the page far more dynamic by being able to import blog posts from a website, import YouTube videos, Tweets from Twitter, stream live video, and offer exclusive content for fans only. Fan Pages can be used as another form of E-PR, providing information to, and staying in contact with, customers.

Organizations use Facebook Fan Pages to run different promotions and public relations activities. Some, such as Target and Kohl's, have used their Fan Pages to allow their fans to vote on which charity should receive the company's donations. The department store Kohl's gave away $10 million to various schools decided by the votes of their fans on Facebook. This was an excellent promotional campaign, as the 20 schools with the most votes were each given $500,000.

Kohl's Facebook page skyrocketed to more than a million fans, and the winning schools each tallied more than 100,000 votes.[31] Facebook is a dynamic and user-friendly networking site for both the marketer and the consumer.

Twitter

Figure 10.18   Twitter logo

Note: The Twitter bird logo is owned by Twitter, Inc.

Twitter is a microblogging social networking website on which users can receive real-time information through posts known as 'tweets.' Users can create a Twitter account and follow various accounts that interest them, as well as posting their own information. A 'tweet' is a 280-character statement that users share to stream publicly. A tweet can include a photo, video, or link.

Tweets often contain **hashtags**, which use the pound symbol (#) followed by a word or phrase. Hashtags are great for marketing campaigns because, when users clicks on a hashtag, they are brought to a page full of tweets from different users containing that specific hashtag. Hashtags are a way to organize content while also increasing the number of views the content gets. Hashtags are a major aspect of Twitter marketing. Tweets can contain multiple hashtags. These hashtags are then used to track what is trending. **Trending** occurs when a topic is talked about by many users in the form of re-tweets and hashtags. Trending measures what is being talked about the most on Twitter. Another way that Twitter is used by marketers is via promoted tweets. **Promoted tweets** are where marketers pay to have their tweets pushed onto people's feeds, regardless of whether those consumers follow the business or not. Promoted tweets are similar to promoted posts on Facebook, enabling marketers to advertise to select audiences, and helping marketers to achieve the message continuity they desire in social conversation.

Businesses can create Twitter accounts as a form of E-PR in order to provide information to their customers, and to gain feedback and insight through consumers' tweets. Many businesses are using this E-PR tool in order to create a connection with customers and positive word of mouth. For example, a consumer may tweet something either positive or negative about a product. The business may search for tweets that include its product, thank or reward those who have given positive feedback (with a coupon, shout out, etc.), or reconcile with those consumers who had something negative to say. For instance, if a consumer had an issue with a technical device, a company could tweet them a link with directions or a number to call.

With its real-time behavior, Twitter is great for responding to customer inquiries immediately and highlighting breaking news. As can be seen in Figure 10.19, Busch Gardens utilizes Twitter to ensure its fans are up to date on the latest weather conditions and park closings before they arrive at the park.

Due to persisting rain, #WaterCountryUSA will close @ 1:30 p.m. today 5/21. We apologize for the inconvenience.

Figure 10.19   Busch Gardens Twitter post. Used with the consent of Busch Gardens/Water Country USA. All Rights Reserved.

Here's another example that demonstrates both the power and the speed of Twitter. A few years ago, in anticipation of its annual *Christmas Town: A Busch Gardens Celebration*, the theme park's marketing team leaned on its Twitter account to generate some buzz. At the time of the promotion, Busch Gardens had been positioning its Twitter account (@BuschGardensVA) as the best place online for park guests to find exclusive offers, last-minute deals, giveaways, and promotional information. So, in October, the marketing department decided to sell Christmas Town tickets early through Twitter for $5—only a fraction of the normal $21.99 price of admission. With one tweet, the offer was live:

Hurry! Limited Time Offer. Buy a Christmas Town ticket for $5. Normally $21.99 Promo Code: BGVACT http://ow.ly/2Ws90

Without any public relations or other promotional support behind the offer, news of the deal spread quickly from the 4,400 Twitter followers and was accelerated by a posting on a local newspaper's blog dedicated to savvy shopping. Soon after, other news organizations picked up on the promotion, including another local newspaper and television station. In six hours, more than 18,000 tickets were sold! Additionally, the theme park had proof there was strong demand for the event, the promotion generated significant publicity, and the Twitter account's profile had been boosted. That's the power of Twitter. Companies shouldn't neglect to incorporate Twitter in their social media arsenal, as it's a growing force of social networking and word of mouth, not to mention an excellent opportunity for marketers to have real-time communication with their customers.

Some companies have found it strategically beneficial to have more than one Twitter account. Once such company is FedEx, a global shipping company with an interesting model for utilizing social media. The company has two Twitter accounts, each with a different focus. One Twitter account, @FedEx, serves as a platform for marketing and interacting with consumers. A second Twitter account, @FedExHelp, is a customer service page with specified hours during which representatives will be able to assist consumers. The splitting of these platforms allows FedEx to do many things. The first is to better assist customers by having a specified forum for complaints and questions, along with trained staff to answer them. Another benefit is that it frees up the general Twitter account for promotion and positive interaction. Complaints and concerns take place on one page, while promotion takes place on another. Splitting these tasks allows FedEx to accomplish both more effectively and to better interact with its consumers.

Instagram

Figure 10.20 Instagram app logo

Note: The Instagram app logo is a trademark of Facebook Inc.

Created in 2010, Instagram is a content-sharing platform combined with social media. On Instagram, users can post videos or photos and then their followers can see them, share them, 'like' them, and comment on them. Instagram can also be linked to Facebook and Twitter so that everything posted on Instagram is automatically pushed to the other plat-forms. Promoted images can also be used by paying to have certain photos placed in users' Instagram feeds.

Users can access Instagram online or on their phone via a mobile app; however, the site is optimized for mobile and app interaction. In 2012, Facebook bought Instagram, though it contin-ues to run as a separate site. Currently, Instagram is more popular among younger people, with 62.7% of users being under the age of 34.[32] On an average day, Instagram users post 95 million photos and videos per day and hit the 'like' button 4.2 billion times.[33]

Marketers can use Instagram by creating accounts designed to engage consumers and market their products or services. These accounts can promote products, run contests, create hashtags, and more. People tend to be creatures of habit and enjoy the idea of something reliable. Because of this, companies have found major success with weekly segments, webi-sodes, and content on social media woven through their normal, everyday posts. Users become more loyal and anticipation increases if a person knows when they can expect a certain piece of content. For example, Busch Gardens posts a small scavenger hunt on Instagram every Wednesday, which it has dubbed 'Where is it Wednesday?' (see Figure 10.21). The company posts a zoomed-in photo of a section of the park and challenges its followers to guess where the photo is located. The following day, Busch Gardens posts a full photo revealing the pho-to's location. No prizes are awarded and no extra money is spent, but week after week more followers engage with the segment. It provides Busch Gardens with two days of content on its Instagram account and gives the user a reason to stop scrolling through their news feed and engage with the brand for some fun.

Some tips for using Instagram for marketing include: (1) shooting high-quality, square pho-tos, which will load better and ensure that critical information isn't cropped out; (2) using a customized link exclusively for the URL in your Instagram bio so you can track and measure how well your Instagram account is driving traffic back to your website (Google Analytics can't accurately track this traffic when users visit your website from your mobile Instagram account); (3) using the link in your Instagram bio to connect to a landing page that holds the same posts you put on Instagram, which allows you to collect leads, promote your website, gain subscribers to your blog, collect entries for a giveaway, and so on; (4) tagging or cross-promoting others whenever possible, which results in higher recognition for everyone involved, increased followers (who in turn tag the businesses during visits) and increased traffic, and sales for the local businesses; (5) adding relevant hashtags to posts will ensure that posts are distributed across various users' accounts, even if they do not follow the business; and (6) adding a location to an image works in a similar fashion to a hashtag. Users can search by location and see photos that are tagged with the specific location. This is ideal for businesses, as business names are used interchangeably with the physical location.[34]

Figure 10.21 Busch Gardens Instagram photo. Used with the consent of Busch Gardens/Water Country USA. All Rights Reserved.

Figure 10.22 provides a glimpse of how Hi-Ho Silver uses Instagram to promote its variety of jewelry lines. Notice the descriptions, special offers, and hashtags that are provided for each of the featured pieces of jewelry to encourage customer engagement and entice customer purchases.

Figure 10.22 Hi-Ho Silver's Instagram page. Used with permission of Hi-Ho Silver. All Rights Reserved.

Pinterest

Figure 10.23 Pinterest logo

Note: The Pinterest logo is owned by Pinterest, Inc.

Pinterest is a social media site that allows users to create virtual corkboards where they 'pin' photos, text, and other graphics that interest them, such as cooking recipes, workout plans, or products that they like. This site can be accessed online or on smartphones via a mobile app.

425

There are different categories of pins, which users can search through, such as popular, humor, and products. Pinterest is the ultimate 'idea bank' where people browse for inspiration.

Users are able to pin to their own boards, send content to other pinners, and send content to nonusers via e-mail. They can also 'like' pins or comment on them. Users can also follow other users and see what they pin. Promoted pins are used by marketers to show up on more people's home feeds as well as the 'popular' tab. Almost all posts on Pinterest provide the option to click on the picture and be redirected to a website where consumers can read more or order the product if it is available for sale. Certain types of products and services, such as jewelry, cosmetics, and photography services, are well suited to be promoted via Pinterest. Figure 10.24 shows two of the Pinterest boards of Hauser's jewelry store. Hauser's uses Pinterest to promote the brands it carries, which are specifically chosen to complete the Hauser's experience and reflect the style and taste of Hauser's. Some of its Pinterest boards feature a select type of jewelry, such as engagement rings. Of course, consumers may click on any of the images to be taken directly to Hauser's website.

Figure 10.24 Hauser's Jewelers Pinterest boards. Used with permission of Hauser's Jewelers.

Some tips for effectively using Pinterest to market products and services are: (1) schedule your pins; (2) pin often and regularly; (3) create 'pin it later' links to enable consumers to have flexibility; (4) include both images and text; (5) write keyword-rich descriptions and boards; and (6) add a link to your pin descriptions.[35]

Linkedin

Figure 10.25 LinkedIn logo

Note: The LinkedIn logo is a registered trademark of LinkedIn Corporation.

LinkedIn is the world's largest professional network, with more than 575 million members worldwide and growing rapidly.[36] Some 22 percent of online adults are LinkedIn users. As a platform geared towards professional networking, its user demographics are unique from the other sites discussed above. LinkedIn remains especially popular among college graduates and those in high-income households. Some 50% of Americans with a college degree use LinkedIn, compared with just 9% of those with a high school diploma or less.[37] In 2008, LinkedIn launched its advertising platform, featuring enhanced targeting capabilities that included targeting users by geographic location, age, gender, industry, and other general information.

LinkedIn allows its registered users to maintain a detailed contact list of people with whom they have some level of relationship, called *Connections*. Users can invite anyone to become a connection. These connections can be used to find jobs, people, and business opportunities recommended by someone in one's contact network. Employers can join the network to list jobs and search for potential candidates.

Marketers can effectively use LinkedIn to market products and services, share various articles of interest with an audience, and distribute news blasts with noteworthy industry or company news. News blasts should have a link to another page.

Some tips for using LinkedIn for marketing include: (1) identifying potential consumers who may be interested in your product or service by creating a LinkedIn poll to survey prospects on topics that interest them; (2) investing in LinkedIn's Sales Navigator/Business Plus premium membership, which enables use of Profile Stats Pro to find out who has viewed your LinkedIn profile so you can follow up with them; (3) targeting key prospects with pay-per-click or pay-per-impression direct advertisements; and (4) choosing 'full view' on your public profile page to help boost your Google search engine page ranking.[38] In conclusion, when used effectively, LinkedIn can be a powerful marketing tool.

PURLs

Personalized URLs, commonly referred to as PURLs, can really boost response rates when employed in direct and interactive marketing campaigns. A **PURL** is a personalized Web page or microsite that incorporates the prospect's name and is tailored to their interests based on information known about them. Personalized URL marketing is the practice of engaging valuable prospects with their own VIP landing page. It begins with a specific Web address as one of the response channels in a mailer or direct-response ad, and follows it up with a series of extremely customized landing pages. When the individual visits the personalized landing page, they will find precisely the information they are looking for, which means they stay engaged at the site longer and are more likely to respond to the targeted offers presented to them. PURLs enable the unique creative messages of marketers to be linked with the interactive capabilities of the Internet. Let's examine the step-by-step process of PURLs:

Step 1: Attract—targeted prospects receive direct-response communication containing a call to action, encouraging them to visit a customized website or microsite.

Step 2: Connect—when prospects respond, they are taken to a VIP landing page established for them and containing relevant content based on their preferences.

Step 3: Engage—prospects provide additional information that guides them through customized landing pages based on their needs and wants. This enables more meaningful dialogue with the prospect.

Step 4: Retain—the personalized nature of the interactive communication enables the marketer to create a more direct relationship with each prospect and act according to each prospect's interests.

Figure 10.26 BlueSky Creative Level 10™ PURL–admissions and alumni postcards. Used with permission of BlueSky Creative, Inc.

Let's explore an example of a PURL marketing campaign that was developed by BlueSky Creative, Inc., in Cincinnati, Ohio, for one of its clients. BlueSky created a PURL marketing program, called Level 10™, for a university that was seeking to connect more effectively with prospective students as well as its alumni. Here's how it worked: Level 10™ started with a database and printed postcards. (The university could have provided the database or a prospect list might have been rented and used for the targeted mailing.) A customized postcard personalized to each recipient was designed for each target segment—admission candidates and alumni. The postcards encouraged each recipient to 'visit his or her personalized website today.' All of the copy and images on the postcards pertained to the university (see Figure 10.26).

Upon visiting their personalized URLs, individuals receive personalized thank you and welcome messages and a customized landing page designed just for them, as presented in Figure 10.27. It is important to note that the degree of personalization that can be offered on the initial customized landing page is determined by the amount of information the organization has about its target audience. Thus, in this case, the university would likely know more about its alumni than it would prospective freshmen students.

Welcome, Ryan!

Thank you for visiting your personal "Choosing a College" site.

Choosing a college is all about you; your wants, your needs, desires and future life plans and goals. Not your parent's, your friend's, your boyfriend's or girlfriend's, and not your sibling's either.

So, let's get started. Begin by assessing your wants and needs. **(please select all that apply):**

- ⦿ Campus Activities
- ○ Financial Aid and Cost
- ○ Size and Type of School
- ○ Majors
- ○ Campus Visits

First name: Ryan
Last name: Smith
Email: ryansmith@yahoo.com
Address 1: 123 Main Blvd.
Address 2:
City: Cincinnati
State: OH ▾ ZIP: 45237
☑ Please send me e-mail updates based on my selected interests.

(Submit)

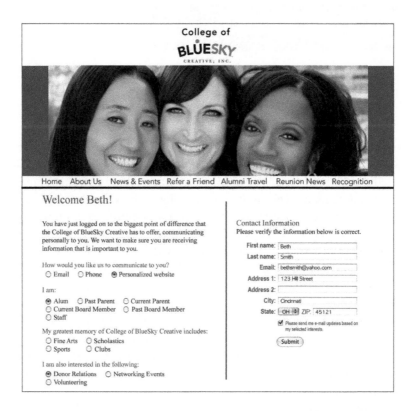

Figure 10.27 BlueSky Creative Level 10™ PURL–admissions and alumni customized landing pages. Used with permission of BlueSky Creative, Inc.

Visitors are asked to answer a few questions or provide information when they first visit their PURL Web page. The answers provided are used to determine the secondary pages to which each visitor is directed and the specific information that will be featured on these subsequent Web pages. Refer back to the interest questions to which Ryan and Beth responded in Figure 10.27 and you will notice that Ryan selected 'campus activities' and Beth selected 'donor relations' as their respective areas of interest on their PURLs. As shown in Figure 10.28, those responses determined the following personalized Web pages for Ryan and Beth. Now they will obtain the information in which they are most interested from the university (campus activities and donor relations, respectively) and the university can proactively communicate in order to build or strengthen its relationship with the two of them.

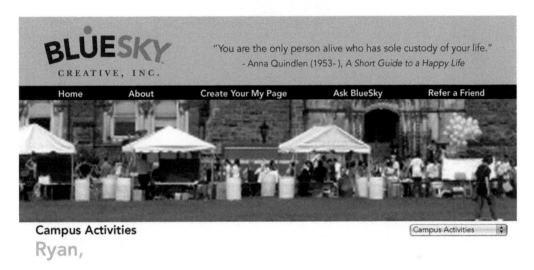

Campus Activities

Ryan,

You have many options to choose from when considering what activities to get involved in on campus.

We offer over 100 opportunities for involvement on campus, including student government, drama/theatre troupe, student newspaper and radio station, four national sororities, four national fraternities, one local fraternity and 14 intercollegiate athletic teams. We have two unique groups at College of BlueSky Creative:

• The President's Ambassadors program offers exemplary college juniors and seniors involvement in leadership training through college promotion.

• The Presidential Mentorship Program aims to provide leadership training for selected high school juniors. Both groups work under the personal mentorship of President William H. Crouch. In addition, the Marshall Center for Christian Ministry is helping students prepare for Christian leadership and service in the global mission of the 21st century.

>>>Learn more

(Continued)

Figure 10.28 (Continued)

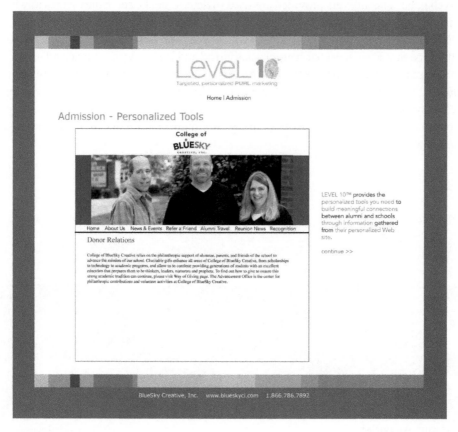

Figure 10.28 BlueSky Creative Level 10™ PURL–admissions and alumni personalized Web pages. Used with permission of BlueSky Creative, Inc.

BlueSky's Level 10™ program doesn't end there; in fact, it's just the beginning. Through the information provided on the personalized websites, the university can more effectively respond to prospective students and alumni, and engage in more meaningful dialogue with each on a personalized basis. The data reporting and analysis capabilities associated with BlueSky's Level 10™ program include dashboard reports captured in real time 24/7; individualized analysis by a unique PURL visitor, detailing the pages viewed and the number of visits; customized campaign reports based on the needs of the university; and hourly reports that can be used to determine future communications. In summary, one of the best ways to connect meaningfully with customers and prospects is via personalized communications. Beyond connecting with the customer or prospect, PURLs enable marketers to interact individually with prospects and respond to their expressed desires.

Deal-of-the-Day Online Offers/Coupons

Deal-of-the-day online offers/coupons, such as Groupon, Living Social, and others, are Web-based offers where typically one product is offered at a highly discounted price (50 percent or more) for a period of typically 24 hours or less. A customer may buy a $50 restaurant certificate for $25. The restaurant and the deal provider split the $25, with each typically taking 50 percent or, in this example, $12.50.

Amazon Local provides coupons and deals to consumers based on their geographic location. Coupons are sent through e-mails, its website, and a mobile app. These deals are for a wide variety of businesses, such as restaurants, entertainment, shopping, and health. Businesses can work with Amazon to promote their deals and content to consumers in the area. Amazon even provides metrics to measure the success of these marketing tactics. Businesses are able to gain a lot of exposure through a big name like Amazon, while specifically targeting consumers in their local area.

Click-to-Chat

Another customer contact channel that has emerged as an important method for engaging with visitors on a company's website and providing real-time customer service is click-to-chat. **Click-to-chat**, nicknamed '**chat**' for short, is a form of Web-based communication in which a person clicks an object (e.g., button, image or text) to request an immediate connection with another person in real time (see Figure 10.29). You may have experienced it while shopping online or conducting business with a bank.

Figure 10.29 Cisco chat messages. Used with permission of Paul Martson, Cisco Systems.

Click-to-chat has revolutionized the contact center, its agents' productivity, and the interactive marketing manager's options for meaningful dialog between the corporate website (or mobile sites, or SMS, Twitter, Facebook, etc.) and its visitors. It enables the kind of synchronous multitasking that customers want (personal enough to be helpful, but not as personal as a phone call). It has the added benefit of leaving behind a transcript for further review by either party, and it increases the productivity of the chat agents as they are able to handle multiple chats concurrently. Experienced agents should be able to conduct 2.5 chats, on average, concurrently with seamless consistency.

Chat was first seen in 1996 and, over the years, click-to-chat has become a common feature on B2B and B2C sites. Its uses range from cultivating leads in a pre-sales environment, to reducing abandonment within conversion, to technical support.

How does click-to-chat work? The two main types of chat are button chat and proactive chat. **Button chat** is where the call to action is resident on the page and the visitor initiates the chat. **Proactive chat** is where the visitor has triggered a business rule and the chat invitation 'pops in' to the page with a relevant call to action. Proactive chat is becoming increasingly common, as the method alerts the user that a representative would like to talk by showing a notification and stimulating the user's attention. Business rules can vary and include the time spent on a page or site, the aggregate pages viewed, the sequence in which the pages are viewed (known as **pathing**), or even specific page combinations, such as 'pogo-sticking' between product-oriented pages. One interesting business rule that many financial sites employ is the **abandonment rule**. This rule is when visitors start to complete a form and then stall or close the format, at which point a proactive Chat invitation can be issued to help complete the task.

There are a number of Chat providers. Current providers include Moxie Software, Right-Now, and Oracle. One of the category leaders is LivePerson. LivePerson is live chat support software designed for traffic monitoring.

MEASURING SITE TRAFFIC AND ANALYTICS

There are now other tools available online that will allow you to estimate how much traffic a keyword may generate for your site, website visitor search trends, and data about the types of people who are visiting your competitors' sites. These tools enable marketers to know who their target customers are and where to acquire new customers.

Google Analytics

Google provides many tools for its Ads program that marketers can use to their advantage and use to help target their customers. A few of these tools follow below.

Google Keyword Planner

The Google keyword estimator allows people to search for keyword terms, and it also offers additional keywords that are similar to the keyword. The tool also shows the level of competition for the keyword, the number of monthly global searches, and the number of searches within the USA (local search). This can give the marketer a good estimate of how many searches are being performed for a keyword and whether the market is large enough to even launch a product or business. Keep in mind that this tool was developed to help Google AdWords users target new keywords that they may not have thought about. But a marketer can use these same tools not only for this, but also to gauge organic traffic for SEO and the overall demand for a product or service. A business could put together a report or PDF for a product and create an offer based on just looking at the Google keyword planner.

Google Trends

Google Trends allows the marketer to type in keywords and see search results for that term based on the search volume, most popular countries and cities where the term is being searched for, and, finally, the months with the most searches. This allows the advertiser to target digital individual ads in those particular cities. This saves on advertising expenses by knowing the locations of the people who are searching for this key term. It is also helpful by knowing which months to spend on advertising or when to increase the amount spent on advertising during months of high numbers of searches.

Quantcast.com

This is an invaluable tool for targeting people and advertising. Quantcast will allow you to analyze specific websites and then reveal demographic and search data about the website. For instance, after conducting a quick search for 'books' on Google, the website www.barnesandnoble.com was in second position. Upon entering the URL into Quantcast, it revealed that almost six million people visited the site in January 2015. It also revealed the demographics of the visiting traffic, such as gender, age, race, marital status, family status, income level, and education. The site also provides information on traffic frequency and business type.

www.SpyFu.com

SpyFu reveals information about a site, such as how much the company is spending on AdWords, the clicks per day, and the cost per day. This is important because it is a gauge of the dollar amount that your competitors are spending and making each day with Google Ads. This site also reveals other keywords that your competitors are bidding on and the other competitors bidding on the same keyword. If we continue our example and put 'books' into SpyFu, it reveals that the cost per click is 22 cents; average clicks per day are more than 100,000; the cost per day ranges from $17.31 to $36.37, depending on the ad placement. It also gives you search data and organic search results.

Combining these tools will give marketers an ideal picture of who their customers are. This allows the marketer to target them more effectively, save on wasted marketing to people who are not likely to respond, and increase response rates. In the past, it would have taken companies a great deal of time, money, and testing to narrow down who their customers were and learn this much about them. Today, the data is at a marketer's fingertips and a customer profile can be generated for free in less than an afternoon for just about any product.

Clicktale

Clicktale.com is a website that provides marketers with a tremendous amount of information about their website and how their visitors are using the website. These analytics allow marketers to fine-tune their website to increase conversions and improve overall performance.

Clicktale will allow marketers to do four things:

1. Watch visitors: Clicktale will record visitors as they interact on the website. Clicktale will actually record a video screenshot of the visitor for the entire time they are on the site. This allows the marketer to know exactly how people are interacting with their site, by being able to watch the mouse move throughout the site.

2. View heatmaps: heatmaps allow marketers to see the areas of the site that are most popular and the location where the mouse is most often positioned or pointed.
3. Conversion analytics: this analyzes several aspects of a website. It looks at sales funnels, forms, and where people are leaving the sales funnel. This allows marketers to improve the site and test different pages.
4. Demographics: this feature provides a demographic analysis of the website.

In conclusion, Clicktale will allow direct marketers to fine-tune their website, increase conversions, and improve the overall website usability.

SUMMARY

This chapter examined the concepts, strategies, tactics, platforms and capabilities associated with marketing via digital and social media. As detailed in the chapter, digital and social media techniques and capabilities are dynamic and continuously evolving. These formats are both popular and powerful for direct marketers and must be utilized effectively to connect with customers. Marketers are challenged to keep abreast of the constant changes associated with these digital formats.

The chapter provided an overview of the marketing opportunities available with the digital media applications of e-mail, online market research, e-commerce, and connecting sites. The chapter also presented the importance of driving website traffic and detailed the various methods used by marketers to generate site visitors. These methods included search engine optimization, AdWords, banner ads, webinars, online direct-response conversion pages, and offline tactics. The chapter also examined the various digital formats available for marketers, such as blogs, social networks, PURLs, online offers and coupons, and click-to-chat. Finally, the chapter concluded with an important discussion of measuring site traffic and analytics.

KEY TERMS

abandonment rule
aging
auto responders
backlinks
banner advertising
blog
button chat
click-through rates
click-to-chat
connecting sites
content marketing
cost per click

crowdfunding
crowdsourcing
electronic commerce (e-commerce)
e-mail
hashtags
hypertext markup language (HTML)
influencer marketing
Johnson Boxes
keyword density
marketing automation
offer box
online panels

online PR	search engine marketing
optimization	search engine optimization
pathing	social networks
personalized URL (PURL)	spam
PR value	trending
proactive chat	viral marketing
promoted tweets	viralocity
quality score	webinars

REVIEW QUESTIONS

1. What is one of the first key things that a marketer must understand when utilizing digital and social media?
2. What are the different types of online market research? How are they alike? How are they different?
3. What are the two purposes of e-commerce connecting sites? Describe some of these.
4. Discuss the various digital and social ways that a direct marketer can drive site traffic.
5. Compare and contrast the three types of search engine marketing.
6. What are blogs? How are they different from other online formats?
7. How can online social networks be used by a direct and interactive marketer to segment consumers? Provide an example that addresses the market segmentation features of two different social networks.
8. Compare and contrast Facebook, Twitter, Instagram, Pinterest, and LinkedIn with regard to how they may be used by direct and interactive marketers. What are the unique strengths of each social networking format?
9. What are PURLs and how are they used by direct marketers?
10. Discuss the significance of programs such as the *Google Keyword Planner*, *Google Trends*, *Quantcast.com*, *SpyFu.com*, and *Clicktale.com*.

EXERCISE

Select two different products, such as cameras, camping gear, running shoes, or skateboards, and visit the websites of at least three different companies that sell these products. Compare and contrast the websites. How easily can you locate the style or model of the product in which you are interested? What types of offers or incentives are provided to encourage you to purchase? Do the sites offer a blog? Can you connect to Facebook or Twitter directly from the sites?

CRITICAL THINKING EXERCISE

Are you on Facebook? Twitter? Instagram? Pinterest? LinkedIn? Have you posted a blog anywhere in the past week or month or year? Why do you connect? What primary needs or wants are you satisfying by doing so? How much time are you spending on such digital and social media? Now, compare your digital and social media usage profile with that of your parents. How should marketers use both profiles to determine how digital and social media should be used as a component of its media mix?

READINGS AND RESOURCES

- News Cred: www.newscred.com
- Gallery ads: www.business2community.com/online-marketing/googles-new-gallery-ads-everything-you-need-to-know-02202364?MessageRunDetailID=317450421&PostID=5835621&utm_medium=email&utm_source=rasa_io
- Content marketing: https://insights.newscred.com/content-marketing-best-practices-from-top-brands
- Influencer marketing: https://sproutsocial.com/insights/influencer-marketing
- E-mail: www.emailmonday.com/future-of-email-marketing-automation
- Crowdsourcing: https://innovationmanagement.se/2015/01/07/10-commandments-of-effective-crowdsourcing

CASE: MUD PIE

Consistent growth of online retail sales drives heavy competition in the e-commerce realm. Consumers are demanding an exceptional user experience online, whether they are shopping from their smartphone, tablet, or computer.

How does a company beat the competition and increase online sales? By delivering the right offer to the right customer at the right time. It might be easy to segment a customer/prospect list into different audiences, but to deliver unique and relevant messages to each prospective customer in a company's online audience is a challenge. Brands naturally have unique personas, which help define who the customer is, what they value and how to speak to them. By identifying these personas, a company can better understand their many audience segments and determine the best content for each customer.

See how Mud Pie delivers this persona-based, omni-channel experience with help from the innovative digital agency Whereoware, located in Chantilly, Virginia.

Mud Pie is a B2B and B2C online retailer of trendy and seasonal baby clothes, women's apparel, gifts, and home décor. This case study focuses on the marketing tactics used to sell direct-to-consumer at Mud-Pie.com (see Figure 10.30).

Figure 10.30 Mud Pie website home page. Used with permission of Mud Pie. All Rights Reserved.

The Online Marketing Challenge

Mud Pie has three main lines of business, which translate to its three customer personas: baby, living, and fashion. Though most of Mud Pie's customers prefer to buy products in a single product category, they were traditionally receiving generic e-mails and seeing product images on the website that may or may not be relevant to them.

The solution? Create a customized, omni-channel experience that dynamically displays products and promotions relevant to each customer persona.

Mud Pie focused its efforts on three main areas:

1. Developing a personalized shopping experience on the website
2. Marketing automation (e-mail marketing)
3. Pay-per-click advertising.

439

Note: This feature is based on a case study by Whereoware, the digital agency of Mud Pie. Used with permission.

Personalized Shopping Experience

Mud Pie chose a website content management system (CMS) with advanced personalization functionality. The CMS connects to Mud Pie's marketing automation platform, so data is shared between the tools to deliver consistent information to the customer. This integration closes the data gap. All actions captured on the website are fed back into Mud Pie's database to personalize e-mail campaigns, and all e-mail behavior and data can be used back on the website to serve up content, imagery, and promotions tailored to individual site visitors.

This means that if customers in the fashion persona visit the website, they are immediately targeted with fashion-focused imagery across the site, pertinent to their interest and buying behavior. The shopping cart page effectively recommends additional products in the same product category as items in the shopper's cart, encouraging upsells throughout the checkout process.

Through every page visit on the website, customer data is captured, such as geographic location, device utilized, time spent on site, etc., and stored in website cookies. This tracked data, combined with order history information, is used to identify the relevant content to deliver to each website visitor.

E-mail Marketing

The second focus area, e-mail marketing, is a cost-effective way to deliver personalized content at the right time. E-mail blasts are sent consistently each week to deliver current sales and promotions to customers. By filling out e-mail preference forms, customers select the types of messages they want to receive, so they aren't overwhelmed and annoyed with irrelevant content. These preference forms, built into Mud Pie's website, continually capture data, such as product interests, birthdate, and e-mail frequency preferences. This data feeds directly into the marketing automation platform and is also passed through to the website, so both tools are working together to deliver an optimal customer experience.

As Figure 10.31 illustrates, Mud Pie also customizes automated e-mails to trigger a message to each customer based on their behavior, such as signing up for e-mail through a Web form, abandoning a shopping cart, browsing the website, and searching for a popular keyword. These e-mails result in a much higher return on investment, because they are programmed one time in the automation tool and then are triggered at the right time to deliver a compelling offer to each customer.

Pay-Per-Click Advertising

The third focus area, pay-per-click advertising, ensures Mud Pie delivers the same consistent message, regardless of where customers interact with the brand.

Once customers visit the website, Mud Pie easily retargets those customers with ads showing products and promotions pertaining to their respective persona through pay-per-click advertising platforms, such as Google AdWords and Facebook Ads. Mud Pie has

Figure 10.31   Mud Pie targeted e-mails. Used with permission of Mud Pie. All Rights Reserved.

found great success with Facebook advertising due to advanced audience segmenting. Using Facebook's segmenting tools, Mud Pie creates a look-alike audience that mimics buyers from the past, making it easy to generate new customers.

Marketing Results

Delivering the right product at the right price and time generates excellent results! Mud Pie saw a 56 percent increase in the e-commerce conversion rate on its website and a 120 percent increase in online sales with this new and improved omni-channel customer experience.

Case Discussion Questions

1. How does changing the content of the website, e-mail, or other ads affect the brand experience?
2. Browse the Mud-Pie.com site. What content would be effective to personalize your customer experience and why?
3. What is another good example of an omni-channel experience? Give an example where at least three different channels are involved.
4. Have you ever had a personalized experience through website, e-mail, or pay-per-click ads? Explain the scenario and describe how the company targeted you.

NOTES

1. https://blog.hootsuite.com/social-media-statistics-for-social-media-managers, retrieved May 14, 2019.
2. Ibid.
3. www.pewinternet.org/fact-sheet/social-media, retrieved May 14, 2019.
4. Andrew Perrin, 'Social Media Usage: 2005-2015,' www.pewinternet.org/2015/10/08/social-net-working-usage-2005-2015, retrieved July 22, 2016.
5. www.pewinternet.org/chart/social-media-use-by-gender, retrieved May 14, 2019.
6. www.pewinternet.org/chart/social-media-use-by-race, retrieved May 14, 2019.
7. Eloise Coupey (2001) *Marketing and the Internet* (Upper Saddle River, NJ: Prentice Hall), p. 5.
8. https://twitter.com/ValaAfshar/status/593805398219436034/photo/1, retrieved May 14, 2019.
9. *Interactive Direct Marketing: A DMA Guide to New Media Opportunities*, Introduction Section (New York: Direct Marketing Association, 2000), p. 5.
10. http://contentmarketinginstitute.com/what-is-content-marketing, retrieved July 29, 2016.
11. https://influencermarketinghub.com/what-is-influencer-marketing, retrieved May 15, 2019.
12. https://crowdsourcingweek.com/what-is-crowdsourcing, retrieved May 15, 2019.
13. Pepsico (2019) www.potatopro.com/news/2014/lays-relaunches-do-us-flavor-contest-united-states, retrieved May 14, 2019.
14. Penn State (2018) 'Do Us a Flavor,' Lay's Case Study, July 18. https://sites.psu.edu/lrstarker/2018/07/18/do-us-a-flavor-lays-case-study, retrieved May 14, 2019.
15. https://mailchimp.com/resources/email-marketing-benchmarks, retrieved May 14, 2019.
16. DMA (2016) *Statistical Fact Book 2016* (New York: Direct Marketing Association), p. 195.
17. https://mailchimp.com/resources/email-marketing-benchmarks, retrieved May 15, 2019.
18. www.brandinteractivism.com/2006/01/some_statistics.html, retrieved May 23, 2011.
19. www.statista.com/statistics/266282/annual-net-revenue-of-amazoncom, retrieved May 14, 2019.
20. www.statista.com/topics/846/amazon, retrieved July 29, 2016.

21. 'The Top 500 List—Internet Retailer.' Industry Strategies for Online Merchants—Internet Retailer. www.Internetretailer.com/top500/list, retrieved May 23, 2011.
22. 'Media Kit: Overview.' Amazon. February 2011. http://phx.corporate-ir.net/phoenix.zhtml?c=176060&p=irol-mediaKit, retrieved May 23, 2011.
23. DMA (2016) *Statistical Fact Book 2016* (New York: Direct Marketing Association), p. 175.
24. https://marketingland.com/wp-content/ml-loads/2012/05/flight-search.jpg, retrieved May 15, 2019.
25. www.smartinsights.com/search-engine-optimisation-seo/seo-analytics/comparison-of-google-clickthrough-rates-by-position, retrieved May 15, 2019.
26. https://support.google.com/webmasters/answer/7451184?hl=en, retrieved May 15, 2019.
27. www.business2community.com/online-marketing/googles-new-gallery-ads-everything-you-need-to-know-02202364?MessageRunDetailID=317450421&PostID=5835621&utm_medium=email&utm_source=rasa_io, retrieved May 15, 2019.
28. www.wordstream.com/blog/ws/2014/05/20/google-adwords-search-versus-display, retrieved May 15, 2019.
29. http://newsroom.fb.com/company-info, retrieved July 28, 2016.
30. Ibid.
31. www.jeffbullas.com/2011/03/01/the-10-best-facebook-campaigns, retrieved July 23, 2016.
32. www.statista.com/statistics/398162/us-instagram-user-age-groups/, retrieved May 15, 2019.
33. Ibid.
34. www.socialmediaexaminer.com/13-instagram-marketing-tips-from-the-experts, retrieved July 15, 2016.
35. https://blog.bufferapp.com/pinterest-marketing-tips, retrieved July 15, 2016.
36. https://kinsta.com/blog/linkedin-statistics, retrieved May 15, 2019.
37. www.pewinternet.org/2018/03/01/social-media-use-in-2018, retrieved May 15, 2019.
38. www.marketingtechblog.com/how-to-use-linkedin-for-marketing, retrieved July 18, 2016.

PART 3

Serve and Adapt to Customers and Markets

11

BUSINESS-TO-BUSINESS (B2B)

Lisa Spiller, David Marold, and Matt Sauber

CHAPTER CONTENTS

CHAPTER SPOTLIGHT

DUPONT PERSONAL PROTECTION

The DuPont Personal Protection group helps protect workers with its safety consulting services and a variety of protective apparel made from Nomex, Kevlar, Tyvek, and Tychem materials. DuPont uses direct and data-driven marketing to promote its protective apparel to two primary customer segments: emergency responders and industrial workers. Thus, DuPont is a business-to-business (B2B) direct marketer. What you are about to read is an example of an effective B2B direct and data-driven marketing campaign used by the DuPont Personal Protection group to increase end-user awareness and stimulate demand for its new line of protective apparel.

The Tyvek line of personal protection garments (see Figure 11.1) posed some unique marketing challenges. This product line has a lower price point and a broader range of applications than do DuPont's other personal protection products. In addition, end users were beginning to perceive all-white garments as Tyvek, so it was difficult to differentiate Tyvek from other white-colored general protective apparel. Finally, industrial workers were complaining that general protective garments did not fit well–a tremendous drawback for people who need mobility while they are performing work-related tasks. To solve these product issues, DuPont Personal Protection introduced its new line of Tyvek comfort-fit design apparel. The marketing challenge was to get these improved garments to potential consumers to experience first hand the garment's comfort and durability.

Figure 11.1   Tyvek personal protection garments. Used with permission of DuPont.

Although the line is sold through distributors, DuPont realized it needed to increase end-user awareness and interest to increase demand. The marketing team decided to launch a comprehensive direct and data-driven marketing campaign integrating offline and online marketing tactics to drive traffic to the DuPont Personal Protection website, where potential customers could request a free garment sample. DuPont's marketing team could then serve customer requests and convert these leads into sales. The budget for this multimedia campaign included the following allocations: approximately 30 percent was spent on Google AdWords, 30 percent on direct mail, and the remaining 40 percent on traditional print and online banner ads (see Figure 11.2).

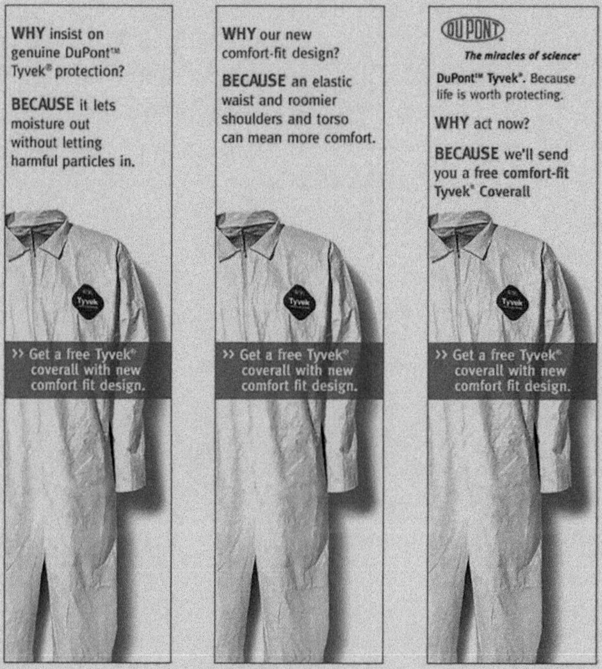

Figure 11.2 Tyvek online banner ad. Used with permission of DuPont.

The entire campaign was effective in generating leads for the DuPont Personal Protection group. Google AdWords proved to be the most successful tactic in driving traffic to the website. In fact, immediately after launching the Google portion of the campaign, the marketing team noted a 702 percent increase in page views. In addition, once visitors landed on the DuPont Personal Protection page, they spent 73 percent more time there than they did before the campaign began. DuPont Personal Protection's campaign is an example of the effective application of direct and data-driven marketing strategies in the B2B sector.

Direct and data-driven marketing can be successfully applied in B2B sectors, which is the topic of this chapter.

BUSINESS-TO-BUSINESS

Business-to-business, commonly referred to as '**B2B**,' marketing is the process of providing goods and services to organizational consumers and industrial market intermediaries, as opposed to ultimate, final individual consumers, or people like us. Collectively, business consumers consist of companies, government, and not-for-profit organizations. These include manufacturers, wholesalers, retailers, government agencies, as well as non-business organizations such as charities, churches, and foundations. In essence, any formal entity that purchases a product or service for further production, for use in its operations, or for resale, is considered a business consumer. Contrast that with final consumers, who purchase products and services for personal, family, and household consumption, which we refer to as business-to-consumer (B2C) transactions.

Although the distinction is not always easy to make, one way is to differentiate industrial or organizational products or goods from consumer products or goods—which is normally based on their ultimate use. Here's one way to think about it. Let's say you belong to a fraternity or sorority and have been tasked with going to a grocery store or Costco Wholesale Club to purchase supplies for your upcoming party or event. When you are at the store purchasing the 15 cases of soft drinks needed, you are there purchasing that quantity on behalf of your fraternity or sorority. Thus, you are acting as a business consumer, and you are purchasing products (tons of soft drinks, in this situation) for use in the operations (hosting a party or event) of your fraternity or sorority. Although you are making an individual purchase, it is one for which you will likely be reimbursed by your fraternity or sorority. After all, it is highly unlikely that you would purchase 15 cases of soft drinks in a single transaction for your own personal consumption. Remember, the key distinguishing factor between business consumers (formal entities or organizations) and final consumers (individuals or people) is the ultimate or end use of the product or service that is being purchased.

Here's a good example: Busch Gardens promotes its park to both final consumers and business consumers. When Busch Gardens promotes its early-bird picnic offer, as featured in Figure 11.3, the park is targeting companies, organizations, and groups, as opposed to final consumers.

(Continued)

Figure 11.3 (Continued)

Figure 11.3 Busch Gardens B2B direct mailer. Used with the consent of Busch Gardens/Water Country USA. All Rights Reserved.

Industrial goods are generally used as raw materials or in the fabrication of other goods. Whereas iron ore is almost always an industrial good, a personal computer can be either an industrial or a consumer good, depending on its ultimate use. As much as 50 percent of manufactured output is sold to the industrial market and as much as 80 percent of farm produce is considered industrial. Wheat, for example, is an industrial good when it is sold for the production of flour; flour is an industrial good when it is sold for the baking of bread; and bread is an industrial good when sold to a restaurant. But bread is a consumer good when sold to a household.

As a historical point of reference, John H. Patterson, who founded the National Cash Register Company (today's NCR), was the first to use direct marketing to get qualified leads for follow-up by salespeople. The firm's lead generation in the early 1900s was oriented to specific industries. The salesperson assigned to call on each prospect expressing interest was provided with sales literature directed to firms using cash registers: groceries, druggists, movie houses, and so on—each identified by a Standard Industrial Classification (SIC) code. This literature was often stored in the trunk of the salesperson's car for reference and delivery to a qualified prospect. Today, this method of sales prospect qualification, utilizing a variety of direct-response media (especially database technology and digital media), plays an important role in the total scheme of B2B direct and data-driven marketing.

Direct and data-driven marketing is employed throughout B2B distribution channels. This is not so much in the 'direct' sense of bypassing middlemen (via a website or a catalog order) as it is in the 'directed' sense of targeting prospects and communicating with end users, thus increasing the effectiveness and the efficiency of the salesperson. The salesperson, in fact, performs a critical role in the B2B direct and data-driven marketing process. In the case of selling consumer goods, the buyer usually visits the seller. The opposite is true of industrial goods—usually, the seller comes to the buyer. Thus, training sales representatives to effectively identify, acquire, manage, and retain clients or customers is a critical part of the B2B marketing process.

Here's an example of a company that raised the bar on sales representative training with real-time productivity data. Interlude Home, a premier design house and importer of four distinct product lines—accent furniture, accessories, wall art, and lighting (see Figure 11.4)—needed a better way to monitor the products and product categories its sales representatives showed during their sales calls. In addition, the company wanted to personalize and improve sales representative training and balance sales across all four of its product categories. At the time, its sales representatives often gravitated to one or two product categories and showed those lines more frequently on their sales calls, causing the remaining product lines to suffer. The solution? Interlude outfitted its sales teams with Whereoware's Spotlight Enterprise iPad sales application. Spotlight provides real-time insight into each sales rep's productivity. Real-time insight into representative sales calls enables Interlude to pinpoint areas where reps have weaknesses and develop measurable solutions to improve their performance.

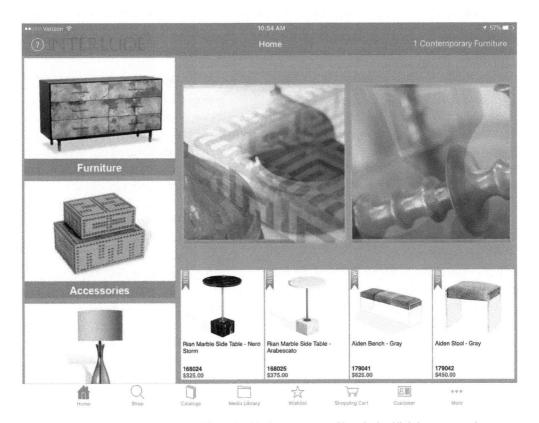

Figure 11.4 Interlude home page. Published with the consent of Interlude. All rights reserved.

BUSINESS-TO-GOVERNMENT

Although technically government consumers are a type of business consumer, they possess a number of unique qualities that differ from most other business consumers, which direct marketers must understand in order to successfully conduct business-to-government (B2G) marketing. We'll explore some of these differences; however, check out the Readings and Resources at the end of this chapter for more details on B2G marketing.

First, the government is *not* one big unified market, but rather, it is comprised of countless different market niches. The many unique government markets are based on the level of government agency, for instance federal, state, and local, as well as the form of government department, such as military, agriculture, education, health and welfare, transportation, and so on. In addition, each governmental agency may have its own set of public procurement procedures or processes by which they buy products and services. These procurement processes affect a wide range of governmental purchases, from buying routine supplies or services to securing competitive contracts for large infrastructure projects or military equipment. For example, the United States Government (USG) is bound by Federal Acquisition Regulations (FAR), whereas business consumers are not. This means that direct marketing to the USG may entail creating and submitting a proposal that cost-effectively solves a specified government problem. Another difference is government language or 'Gov-Speak' phrasing versus standard business terminology. For example, *webinars* are referred to as *distance learning* by government consumers.[1] One final difference worth mentioning is the value placed on certifications, accreditations, and proof of quality standards, which tend to be more important to government consumers than they are to most industry consumers.[2]

Thus, direct marketers must conduct detailed and thorough research to understand both the needs and the buying processes of the specific governmental agency or organization that is being targeted, in order to employ the relevant direct marketing strategies. Research reveals that there is great value in B2G search engine optimization (SEO), especially in conducting SEO website audits to ensure that a company's website contains the keywords about which prospective government decision makers are searching.[3] In addition, content marketing that is focused on educating government consumers and helping them to resolve their key challenges is very valuable.[4] Research shows that e-mail marketing is consistently rated as the most essential marketing tactic for both B2G and B2B marketers.[5] Of course, personalization is critical to e-mail effectiveness and that may only occur if relationships with prospective government decision makers are established.

B2G marketing is about building relationships with government decision makers, thus direct marketers need to focus their social media activities on those platforms where their target B2G consumers are active.[6] Research shows that GovLoop, LinkedIn, and Facebook seem to be the commonly preferred social media platforms to use.[7] Government consumers and influencers may also be targeted with direct-response advertisements in places such as highway billboards, train/subway/mass transit stations, airport terminals, and print media.[8] Targeting the geographic location of key decision makers and influencers is the objective. For example, placing ads at the metro station near the entrance to the Washington Convention Center, where the Association of the United States Army Symposium is taking place, makes good sense if you are targeting an Army customer with solutions to specific systems for which there is an established need.[9] Finally, keep in mind that thorough research on the target government consumer should produce good insight on where to best direct B2G marketing to engage prospective buyers and influencers.

DIFFERENCES BETWEEN BUSINESS AND CONSUMER MARKETS

In contrasting business buyers with consumer buyers, apparent differences between these groups are sometimes exaggerated. Individual buyers within business organizations are obviously also consumers in their own right. The primary differences between business (B2B) markets and consumer markets are the following:

1. **Market structure**: B2B markets follow the Pareto principle, widely known as the 80/20 rule. This rule states that 80 percent of the market value resides in 20 percent of the customer base. Although one may correctly argue that some consumer markets follow the 80/20 rule as well, business markets are aligned with it more often. Additionally, businesses are clustered around other, similar businesses geographically, taking advantage of industry/market infrastructure and support facilities. In contrast, consumer markets are dispersed among many buyers who are geographically scattered and attracted to differentiated market offerings. Markets are in monopolistic competition.
2. **Channel structure**: B2B marketing channels are more direct, with fewer intermediaries that act in a highly coordinated manner. In contrast, consumer channels are more indirect, with many levels providing a wide variety of consumer utilities of time, place, form, and possession. Channel relationships are also indirect and consumers are seldom involved in the channel design.
3. **Marketing communications**: B2B marketing communications are direct and heavily rely on personal selling aimed at establishing and maintaining long-term buyer–seller relationships. As such, communications in B2B markets are targeted and audience specific. In contrast, consumer markets are dominated by mass communications, such as advertising, and less personal dialogues. Messages are broad based and address mass audiences.

Some B2B organizations, recognizing this comparison, have gone so far as to look at the demographics of buyers within organizations at the same time as they look at the relevant features of organizations themselves. A comparison of database descriptive characteristics, contrasting consumer and business (B2B) markets, is shown in Table 11.1. These characteristics are not all-inclusive, of course, but they do indicate some interesting differences and, at the same time, similarities. Most list vendors, such as ListFinder.com, NetPostmaster.com, NextMark.com, SalesGenie, LeadCrunch, and LeadGenious.com, offer massive databases with multiple selection criteria to create custom leads to target businesses and professionals. Hoover's database, for example, offers a pool of more than 85 million companies with a list of more than 100 million professionals spanning 900 industries.[10]

Table 11.1 Comparison of descriptive characteristics in consumer and business direct marketing

Consumer	Industrial
Name/Address	Name/Address
Source code	Source code
Age	Year started
Gender	Gender of decision maker
Income	Revenue
Wealth	Net worth
Family size	Number of employees
Children	Parent firm or subsidiary
Occupation	Line of business
Credit evaluation	Credit evaluation
Education	Education of decision makers
Urban/rural resident	Headquarters/branch
Own or rent home	Private or public ownership
Ethnic group	Minority ownership
Interests	Interests of decision makers
Lifestyle of ZIP code area	Socio-economics of location
Mail respondent	Mail respondent
Transactions & R/F/M	Transactions & R/F/M

All buyers—consumers as well as business or industrial organizations—have a name and address. Beyond that identification, a consumer's age can be important in product differentiation, as can the years a company has been in business. A consumer's income can be looked at in the same light as an organization's revenue, just as a consumer's wealth can be looked at in the same light as an organization's net worth. Though many marketers see lists of business buyers being different from lists of consumers, some argue that there is as much sameness as there is difference.

Direct and data-driven marketing techniques are often used in lead generation among potential buyers of organizational products and industrial goods. For example, a company needing a new computer system does not usually shop for it in a retail store, but rather visits a well-designed Dell website or responds to an e-mail or a brochure from Dell. The Dell website or promotional materials can often entice an organizational prospect to invite a Dell representative to make a presentation. A further characteristic of industrial goods is that their purchase usually involves group decision making, also referred to as 'team-based buying' or committee decision making, because a particular component represents only a part of the whole.

Direct and data-driven marketing techniques are also used (and should be used) for **lead nurturing**, that is, connecting and interacting with the customer (de facto and potential) more effectively, and, over time, across all phases of the customer life cycle. At its core, lead nurturing is an integral part of relationship marketing where customer engagement is pursued with the communication of relevant information to all leads all the time. Today's B2B customers are well informed and judicious. They expect their interactions with the brand to be customized, personable, and timely. A 2015 IDC study reported that 65 percent of B2B customers engage with a sales rep only *after* they have made a purchase decision. Of these customers, 83 percent are willing to hear from the sales rep only if the information is relevant and contextual.[11] In this environment, marketers would very much like to develop a community of engaging and happy leads who can become their advocates. Likewise, sales reps would much rather call on warm, receptive, and engaging leads with whom they have meaningful relationships than cold call prospects.

Integrating B2B marketing into an existing consumer marketing organization is not an easy task. However, it can be carried out effectively given a keen understanding of the differences between industrial demand and consumer demand.

CHARACTERISTICS OF INDUSTRIAL DEMAND

Industrial demand differs from consumer demand by these four characteristics, which are worth noting and understanding:

1. **Derived demand**: demand for industrial goods is derived ultimately from consumer demand. The industrial demand for automobile tires, steel, or glass, for example, depends in part on the consumer demand for automobiles.
2. **Inelastic demand**: because a variety of industrial goods go into the manufacture of a single product, and thus each represents only a fraction of the product's total cost, there is not as much price sensitivity in industrial goods. The cost of tires for an automobile, for example, might double, but this increase would represent a relatively small part of the total cost of a car.
3. **Widely fluctuating demand**: the demand for industrial goods is subject to wide fluctuation, ultimately dependent on consumer demand, but also dependent on rises and falls in inventories as well as in the optimism of entrepreneurs.
4. **Knowledgeable demand**: industrial buyers are usually much better informed about their purchases than consumers are about theirs, have more specialized interests, and benefit from the process of joint decision making.

To better understand how B2B marketers experience the characteristics of industrial demand, let's look at this DuPont example. DuPont manufactures the well-known brand Corian® Solid Surface, a popular material used for countertops, sinks, and showers in both commercial buildings and residential homes. DuPont, working with a major designer, Mario Romano, produced an exclusive line of multi-dimensional walls—M.R. Walls designed with Corian® Solid Surface. As shown in Figure 11.5, the walls are exquisitely carved and textured in non-repetitive patterns and are sold to interior designers and architects for installation in upscale residential homes and commercial applications. These designers and architects are highly knowledgeable about the products that they recommend to their customers. They know that M.R. Walls designed with Corian® Solid Surface are very durable, highly functional, and extremely beautiful, with no painting, sanding, grout or seams needed. Demand for these customized multi-dimensional walls is derived from final consumers seeking uniquely patterned walls inspired by nature, such as the ripples of water, waves in the ocean, or a butterfly's wings.

Figure 11.5 Multidimensional M.R. Walls designed with Corian® Solid Surface image. Courtesy of DuPont. M.R. Walls designed by Mario Romano.

Although the number of industrial organizations is but a fraction of the number of consumers, the volume of purchasing is as great in the business market as it is in the consumer market. The buying power of industrial organizations is highly concentrated, however, within certain industries (e.g., manufacturing), and there are also heavy concentrations regionally and geographically. This buying power is often measured by various forms of activity, such as manufacturing, wholesaling, retailing, mining, agriculture, and construction.

In comparing B2B transactions with B2C transactions, we should note that consumer purchases are often consummated at the seller's location (e.g., clothing bought at a retail store). In industrial buying, the seller normally comes to the buyer's location (e.g., a computer installation sold to a chain of retail stores). A major factor contributing to the increasing use of direct marketing by businesses is the rising cost of these personal sales calls made to a buyer's location, coupled with the availability of online transactions via the Internet.

B2B APPLICATIONS

Researchers forecast that B2B e-commerce transactions will hit $12 trillion in sales worldwide by 2020, up from $5.5 trillion in 2012.[12] The main drivers leading the shift to B2B selling are:

- an expectation among a growing number of companies to conduct buying and selling online
- a shift from some companies to conduct procurement transactions through the Internet instead of through **electronic data interchange (EDI)**
- the growing interest of companies in placing orders through mobile commerce devices
- the increasing popularity of e-marketplaces such as Alibaba.com and AmazonSupply.com.[13]

Besides the Internet, lead generation for follow-up by salespeople, using the tools and techniques of direct marketing, has been a major contributor to the rapid growth of B2B direct and data-driven marketing. Spotting, qualifying, nurturing, and following leads now take place with the help of marketing automation where prospects are assigned to different tracks based on product interests, pain points, objections during the sales cycle, and more. They then are monitored (observed) based on their daily actions/interactions with the brand. They may go to the company website and download new content, request a live sales demo, engage in a chat, text, or e-mail with the sales rep, connect with the organization via social media, or call in for an appointment and/or conference meeting. At each step, they move in and out of various tracks based on the signals they send, and their status changes as they go through the funnel.

Even though the number of consumer households in the United States is at least 10-fold and the number of individual consumers is at least 25-fold that of the number of businesses, total B2B sales volume is more than double that of B2C sales. Because the average revenue per industrial response is typically larger, it follows that response rates from B2B direct-response advertising can be lower than that which is consumer directed and still be profitable for the direct marketer.

The tools and techniques of direct marketing and data-driven marketing used by businesses are basically the same as those for consumer direct marketing, as presented throughout this textbook. These tools and techniques are used in business markets to:

- generate qualified 'leads' for salesperson follow-up
- achieve direct sales remotely (i.e., via catalogs and websites)
- reinforce all sales efforts
- introduce new products
- develop new markets and applications
- build industrial customer goodwill
- conduct industrial market research
- build and maintain a robust database to better meet specific customer needs
- employ **customer relationship management (CRM)** activities.

Notable users of the tools and techniques of direct marketing have been makers of office products, industrial plant supplies, computers and their peripherals, building equipment, and even aircraft and the complex array of aircraft parts. Much has changed since John H. Patterson founded the National Cash Register Company and first used direct mail to get qualified leads for follow-up by salespeople. Today, the various online and offline methods of sales prospect qualification, as well as direct selling, when augmented by direct-response advertising in a variety of media, play an important role in the total scheme of B2B marketing. The opportunities for B2B direct and data-driven marketing are nearly endless.

As noted earlier in this chapter, an important feature of B2B distribution that makes it especially susceptible to the tools and techniques of direct marketing is this: producers and their middlemen are more likely to make sales calls on buyers of industrial goods, whereas buyers of consumer goods are more likely to make purchases at the locations of producers and middlemen. Direct marketing has been used effectively throughout industrial distribution channels—producer to agent to distributor to industrial user—to augment personal selling.

B2B marketers, like B2C marketers, combine relational databases to obtain information about their customers *as well as their customers' customers*. They perform statistical analyses to identify their own best customers and then seek prospects that look like these. Let's take a look at how FedEx used database information to conduct a successful B2B direct marketing campaign.

FedEx offers and prices its delivery services in a variety of categories, including, several years ago, a category called Priority 1. To expand its market, increase its penetration, and hold its present customers for this premium service, FedEx conceived a B2B direct mail campaign to announce a new discount schedule. Based strictly on its potential value in the immediate future, the program was divided into three segments:

1. Frequent users of Priority 1: 29,126 individual customers
2. Infrequent users of Priority 1: 121,705 individual customers
3. Other FedEx customers who had never used Priority 1: 63,431 individual customers.

The symbol to be used for dramatizing the Priority 1 service was the same for all three market segments: a five-pound reproduction of a 1913 exercise weight. Frequent users of Priority 1 received the exercise weight immediately as a goodwill gift; infrequent users had to request it; and nonusers received it as a premium with the purchase of the Priority 1 service for the first time. Frequent users were also asked to identify other prospects and decision makers within their own organizations. A total of 7,044 (24.1 percent) of the 29,126 frequent user recipients of the promotion did just that.

Of the 121,705 infrequent users contacted, a total of 25,985 (24.0 percent) responded by requesting the gift, and, in the process, they also supplied 14,723 names of new prospects within their own organizations. Of the 63,431 nonusers of Priority 1 among FedEx customers, a total of 9,300 (15 percent) actually purchased the service and submitted a copy of the FedEx air bill as proof of purchase to receive the exercise weight.

In summary, the following total results were tabulated:

- 21,767 new prospects
- 40,000 responses from *old* customers
- 25,985 'market research' forms returned
- 9,300 proven direct sales to new customers
- $500,000 in immediate traceable sales to these new customers alone.

Because each user of the Priority 1 service was known to average $4,000 in sales per year for an undetermined number of future years, the potential value of these new customers is impressive.

B2B MARKETING CHALLENGES

Changes in today's global economy are forcing B2B marketers to adapt to many challenges. In order to be successful, these marketers must be able to account for each nuance of change in their customers' organizations as well as in their own organizations and in the overall economy. In addition, they must find new ways to cultivate their current customer database, locate qualified prospects, and reduce marketing costs.

The primary challenges facing B2B marketers include:

- Face-to-face selling, down in efficiency, is up in cost. Travel expenses are up, and the cost of a salesperson's call on a prospect/customer is a larger part of revenue than before.
- Communication clutter brings individuals up to 10,000 messages per day and many have tuned out non-relevant marketing messages.
- Customer relationship managers often do not integrate an analytical approach to combining operations with marketing programs and campaigns. There is generally not nearly enough analysis of customer data.
- Industry classification of customers/prospects, most commonly used in the past, is not adequately predictive in the current business environment. Such market segmentation assumes that businesses within the same industry type are similar; however, a business in a rural area can be dramatically different from an inner-city business with the same industry classification.
- The security of customer information: trust is the number one prerequisite for any relationship, particularly a **customer relationship** in a B2B setting. Unlike final consumers who are primarily concerned about the safety and security of personal information and identity, businesses are concerned about data security at different levels. Businesses deal with transactional data whose security directly affects their customers and suppliers. They also deal with business data concerning intellectual property, business plans and implementation, and employment.

SEGMENTING BUSINESS MARKETS

B2B markets are much smaller in number than consumer markets, but they are certainly not smaller in sales volume. The descriptive characteristics of B2B firms, including sales revenue, number of employees, private or public ownership, and more, are called **firmographics**. These are comparable to the demographic characteristics of final consumers (B2C), such as age, income, and marital status. Similar to consumer markets, industrial markets break down into smaller, more homogeneous segments of the heterogeneous total industrial market. Market segmentation may be even more important in industrial applications than in consumer ones, because of the diversity of activities within each segment.

B2B market segments can be identified by industry, financial strength or size, number of employees, or sales volume. Geographic selectivity includes urban/rural orientation, city size, and location. There may also be selection by form of ownership or by branch/headquarters.

Within organizations, industrial markets are also segmented by job functions. Demand within firms is not generated by purchasing agents alone, but also by engineers, chemists, architects, and a good many other specialists. Direct marketers must appeal not only to firms as such, but also to many relevant individuals within them.

Maintaining accurate customer/prospect databases is a real challenge for B2B direct marketers. While approximately 15 percent of households move in a year, in a B2B list the change in individual, title, office location, and address is oftentimes 60 percent or higher in a year. The most important database, of course, is that of their customers. Such a compilation should include, in addition to names and addresses, prior purchase behavior, as well as the organization's—and possibly even the individual buyer's—demographic profile. Keep in mind, as previously discussed in

Chapter 3, that most list vendors offer massive databases with multiple selection criteria to create custom leads to target businesses and professionals. Let's discuss some of the more commonly used methods for segmenting B2B markets.

Standard Industrial Classification (SIC)

The **Standard Industrial Classification (SIC)** coding system is a means of industrial market segmentation developed by the federal government many years ago. The four-digit SIC codes, which identify businesses by industry and segment of industry and serve as a basis for statistical data about industries, are in broad use by government, trade associations, and business enterprises. Within SIC codes, which designate the primary and secondary lines of business, establishments can also be segmented on other bases: sales volume, credit rating, age of business, number of employees, net financial worth, subsidiary, and location.

Many businesspeople felt that the SIC system failed to recognize the growth of information technology, the service industry, high technology, and international trade. Thus, an updated system to provide uniform coding across North America was developed.

North American Industry Classification System (NAICS)

The **North American Industry Classification System (NAICS**, pronounced 'nakes') was basically designed to replace the SIC coding system, although both systems are still in use today. NAICS offers several improvements over the SIC system. Table 11.2 overviews the main differences between them.

The first improvement is relevance. NAICS identifies more than 350 new industries, including high-tech areas, and nine new service industry sectors that now contribute to the economy. The second improvement is comparability. NAICS was developed by the United States, Canada, and Mexico to produce comparable data for all three nations. Industries are identified by a six-digit code to accommodate a larger number of sectors and allow greater flexibility in designating sub-sectors. The first five digits denote the NAICS levels common to all three **NAFTA (North American Free Trade Agreement)** countries, while the sixth digit accommodates user needs in individual countries. NAICS is a two- through six-digit hierarchical classification code system. A complete and valid NAICS code contains six digits. Table 11.2 shows the hierarchical structure of NAICS.

Table 11.2 Comparison of SIC codes and NAICS codes

SIC codes	NAICS codes
SIC codes classify establishments by the type of activity in which the business is primarily engaged	NAICS is based on a production-oriented, or a supply-based, conceptual framework
SIC is a 4-digit code	NAICS is a 6-digit code
SIC system lacks current information	NAICS will be reviewed every five years so classifications will change with the economy

(Continued)

Table 11.2   (Continued)

SIC codes	NAICS codes
SIC has 10 classifying sectors:	NAICS has 20 classifying divisions:
agriculture, forestry, and fishing	agriculture, forestry, and fishing
mining	mining
construction	construction
manufacturing	manufacturing
transportation, communications, and public utilities	utilities
wholesale trade	transportation and warehousing
retail trade	wholesale trade
finance, insurance, and real estate	retail trade
services	accommodation and food services
public administration	finance and insurance
	real estate and rental and leasing
	information
	professional, scientific, and technical services
	administrative support: waste management and remediation services
	educational services
	health care and social assistance
	arts, entertainment, and recreation
	other services (except public administration)
	public administration
	management of companies and enterprises

XX	Industry sector
XXX	Industry subsector
XXXX	Industry group
XXXXX	Industry
XXXXXX	U.S., Canadian, or Mexican national specific

Figure 11.6   NAICS hierarchical structure

The third improvement is consistency. NAICS uses a consistent principle: businesses that use similar production processes are grouped together. This is entirely different from the SIC system, which focuses on the industries served. The fourth improvement is adaptability. NAICS will be reviewed every five years, so classifications and information keep up with the changing economy.

Other Industrial Market Segmentation Criteria

We can also categorize industrial organizations by financial strength or size as well as in terms of number of employees or sales volume. Geographic data are also often used, including city size and location. Other criteria differentiate the form of ownership and whether the enterprise is a headquarters or branch office, a parent or a subsidiary.

Direct marketers must appeal not only to organizations, but also to individuals within organizations. Purchasing agents alone do not generate demand. More likely, engineers, chemists, architects, production managers, and a host of other specialists make joint decisions. Personalities and the demographics of these decision makers and influencers are now also becoming a basis for market segmentation. With data on contacts within the business, further market segmentation based on titles and utility of the function can enhance response rates and build relationships with customers. To grow sales and profit, B2B marketers need to spend time and resources to acquire qualified customers at the right cost, which is the subject of the next section.

MARKETING FUNNEL

A **marketing funnel** (see Figure 11.7) is the progression or stages of the customer or client journey. The sales funnel begins with the awareness stage and continues through to the purchase stage. However, for direct marketers, the focus is on lifetime customer relationships, so the marketing funnel does not end when a sale is made; rather, it continues on through the stages of the customer's relationship with the company. So, the marketing funnel stages include awareness, consideration, purchase, retention, and advocacy. If you recall from Chapter 2, the customer hierarchy depicts the progression of a customer's journey using the following five levels: suspects

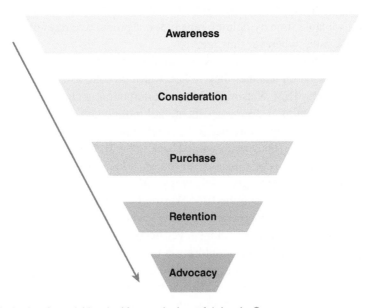

Figure 11.7 Marketing funnel. Used with permission of Johnnie Gray.

(prospective customers who are thought to have a need or want for your product or service), prospects (qualified leads, those with expressed interest in your company), customers (single-time buyers with your company), clients (repeat customers), and advocates (your most valuable customers who generate the most revenue for your business).

As you might have expected, marketing strategies and tactics vary according to each of the stages in the marketing funnel. For B2B marketers, the customer or client journey often takes much longer, perhaps years in some cases. However, B2B marketers are equally interested in both acquiring customers and retaining customers. The various strategies to accomplish both of these tasks will be discussed in the following sections.

B2B CUSTOMER ACQUISITION

Generating high-quality leads is the number one challenge of B2B marketing, according to Marketo.com.[14] Marketers should use lead generation to build brand interest, qualify leads, and generate profitable results. An example of a company that has successfully empowered its sales teams to be more efficient and effective in generating leads is that of Evergreen Enterprises.[15] Evergreen Enterprises is a B2B distributor of exceptional home and garden decor products known for their quality, beauty, and functionality. Evergreen employs more than 175 territory managers selling to retailers in territories across the United States and Canada. To support its expansive customer base, Evergreen needed a customized sales tool to meet the unique challenges of its complex sales team and national distribution channels. Evergreen Enterprises outfitted its team with Whereoware's 'Spotlight for Sales Teams' iPad application to increase sales and improve oversight of sales rep activity. With Spotlight, Evergreen Enterprises can showcase products, take orders, and monitor sales activity.

Three features in particular are making a huge impact on Evergreen's bottom line—proximity search, lead scoring, and address verification. Proximity search helps Evergreen save money in gas, mileage, and valuable time by helping reps plot out productive days of meetings to nurture customers and close sales, wherever they are.

In Spotlight, Evergreen reps can access a visual representation of leads and existing customers, color-coded based on whether they're hot, warm or cold, as shown in Figure 11.8. This information is passed into IBM Watson Campaign Automation, a cloud-based digital marketing platform for e-mail marketing, lead management, and mobile and social engagement solutions. With the IBM Watson Campaign Automation/Spotlight integration, sales reps can adjust a contact's lead score in Spotlight. This score is passed back to the IBM Watson Campaign Automation to reflect the rep's adjustment. The capability to 'bump' a lead's score higher or lower, based on interactions in their sales meetings, gives sales reps a 360-degree view of each lead's online and offline behavior. Since implementing the IBM Watson Campaign Automation/Spotlight scoring integration, Evergreen reps have increased their new lead close rate by 45 percent.

In addition, Spotlight's integrated address verification feature saves Evergreen Enterprises time and money by pre-checking postal addresses on the spot, to ensure products are shipped to the right person, at the right location, and on time. When a sales rep is placing and closing an order, the retailer's address is submitted to Spotlight and, behind the scenes, sent to UPS for verification. Spotlight instantaneously returns an exact match for correct addresses or suggests

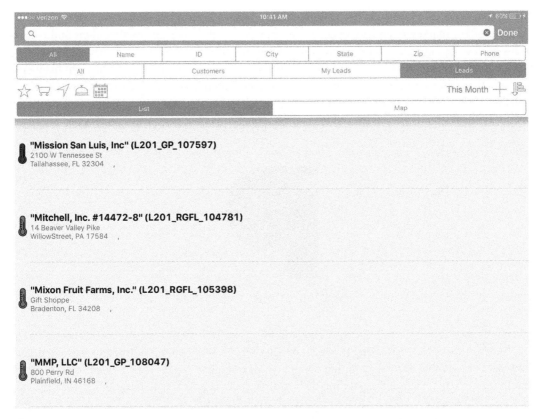

Figure 11.8 Evergreen's lead scoring screen. Used with permission of Evergreen Enterprises. All Rights Reserved.

alternative addresses in real time. When an address is invalid, reps cannot complete the order until the address has been corrected. Since using this feature, address verification has enabled Evergreen Enterprises to reduce returned package fees by more than 90 percent.

As practiced, *content marketing*, *in-person contacts*, *telephone calls*, *referrals*, *webinars*, and *social media* are primary strategies in B2B lead generation. Let's discuss each one.

Content Marketing

Content marketing refers to conveying and communicating valuable information to attract, engage, and retain a target audience to stimulate profitable action or behavior. As a term, content marketing has emerged as the way marketers primarily refer to online direct-response copywriting. Content marketing has become an effective lead-generating strategy for many B2B marketers. It keeps readers' attention, improves brand loyalty, and increases leads and direct sales. It is an ideal tool for building relationships with customers of products and services with long sales cycles.

Pandora encourages advertisers to include its streaming audio platform in the ad campaigns they develop for their clients. What advertiser wouldn't want to successfully connect with an engaged network of more than 70 million monthly unique listeners through their love of music? Pandora offers marketers and advertisers the opportunity to hyper-personalize their audio messages by leveraging rich listener data in real time. Intelligent ad technology optimizes various triggers such as location, weather, and time of day to serve the right message to the right listener at the right time. This custom audio execution allows the advertisers' creative executions to scale to hundreds, thousands, and even millions of variations. Business marketers and advertisers should visit www.PandoraForBrands.com to learn more about the latest from Pandora (Figure 11.9).

Figure 11.9   Pandora. Used with permission of Pandora.

Success in content marketing is reliant on sharing relevant content tailored to various digital formats. For example, Danish shipping company, Maersk, first began using content marketing by sharing stories that emerge from within its business, such as how it is helping to increase the sale of Kenyan avocados. Maersk utilized several digital platforms, with its content on each tailored to the respective platform. So on LinkedIn, Maersk promotes job vacancies, while on Instagram it encourages followers to post photos of its ships using the hashtag #Maersk. The use of content marketing was an effective strategy for Maersk as it now has more than 1.5 million Facebook fans (of which about 15 percent are customers) and 12,000 Twitter followers.[16]

Seventy-one percent of B2B marketers use content to generate sales, according to *Forbes*. Compared to traditional marketing strategies, 93 percent of B2B marketers believe that content marketing generates more leads. Seventy percent of business decision makers feel content makes them closer to B2B marketers, and 60 percent maintain B2B content helps them make smarter buying decisions. Finally, compared to traditional marketing, B2B content marketing costs 62 percent less and generates three times the leads per dollar spent.[17]

To generate qualified business leads, B2B marketers communicate their content via the company's landing page, blogs, and social media channels. Sixty-eight percent of B2B companies use landing pages to disseminate sharable content, such as white papers, infographics, videos, and other well-targeted and easily digestible content, to generate new sales leads.

An excellent example of a successful B2B marketer using its website effectively is that of Sullivans.[18] Sullivans is a B2B wholesaler of floral, seasonal décor, and home décor products. Sullivans had a deep understanding of its customer base and the product lines that were important to different retailers, but its website couldn't personalize content to specific retailers. Everyone saw the same content. The company enlisted the services of Whereoware to design and build Sullivans a new, responsive website. Sullivans's goal was to leverage retailer data, so each website visit and outbound e-mail would be relevant to users' current interests. By personalizing customers' shopping experience, Sullivans could nurture loyal customers while introducing Sullivans's exceptional products to new customers. As shown in Figure 11.10, Sullivans's new B2B e-commerce website now places the right product in front of the right customer at the right time to make shopping easy and intuitive for its retail customers. Sullivans's new website personalizes customers' online experience using behavior-based personas. The company currently has three core personas, based on product categories (Everyday, Seasonal, or Brands), along with select areas on its website for personalized content.

Figure 11.10 Sullivans's seasonal Web page. Published with the consent of Sullivan's. All rights reserved.

B2B companies also use blogs to provide information, trigger inquiries, and create dialogue. They generate 67 percent more leads compared to companies that do not. Finally, social media are gaining momentum among B2B marketers. Seventy-eight percent of small businesses seek and acquire a quarter of their new customers through social media, LinkedIn and Twitter in particular. According to market.com, 44 percent of B2B marketers have generated leads using LinkedIn.[19]

Content marketing does not have to originate from the company or organization itself. Rather, there is great power of persuasion for clients and prospective clients to hear from others, perhaps satisfied customers, distributors or employees, who share authentic content about the company or organization. As discussed in Chapter 10, **influencer marketing** is where content is derived from individuals who have influence over potential customers or clients. This type of marketing is very valuable as content is seen as even more factual and genuine when it is shared by an influencer, as opposed to company-shared content. B2B influencers often serve as unpaid endorsers for a company or an organization, thus B2B marketers should encourage influencer content whenever possible. The impact of the shared content is highly influential in moving a prospect or customer along in the marketing and sales funnel.

In-Person Contact

Although content marketing is an inconspicuous, far-reaching, and effective method of lead generation, it is still impersonal and may not be as effective as in-person contacts. Business practitioners still prefer to meet others in person and B2B marketers continue to report that some of their best new customer leads are developed from personal interaction with others. To wit, the most effective lead generation tools include inside sales contacts, executive events, telemarketing, trade shows, and conferences.[20] Trade shows generate the highest quantity and quality of leads, according to the annual B2B Demand Generation Benchmark report. In a survey of B2B marketing professionals, 77 percent of respondents said they generated a 'somewhat' or 'very high' quantity of leads, and 82 percent said they generated leads of 'good' or 'excellent' quality.[21]

Telephone Calls

Believe it or not, the telephone is still an effective method for B2B communication. As presented in Chapter 9, B2B marketers use the telephone for both inbound and outbound calls. Most businesses offer a toll-free number to customers/clients and encourage customer service inquiries. These inbound calls can provide the marketer with additional relationship-building opportunities. In addition, B2B outbound calls may be highly effective and are used throughout the marketing and sales funnel. Outbound calls are commonly used for generating leads, qualifying prospects, serving new customers, following up on personal sales calls, and surveying customers, among other uses. For example, Marketo, a leading provider of marketing analytics software, regularly holds free Web conferences to share information and generate leads. The company realized that while many people registered for their webinars, often some didn't attend. Marketo used outbound telephone calls with a simple recorded message, in addition to e-mail, as a reminder prior to the webinar date for which the client or prospect registered. Although the telephone reminder added $2 per registrant, it increased the conversion rate of people who attended from 26 percent to 46 percent.[22] While outbound calls add an incremental per-prospect cost to the client, it may be well worth the added investment.

Referrals

Referrals are the best type of lead to new customers. They carry credibility from someone who the prospect knows and trusts. According to *Chief Marketer*, 50 percent of B2B marketers thought referrals gave their business the largest number of qualified leads.[23] If asked, satisfied customers would be happy to refer prospects that might benefit from the B2B product or service.

Webinars

Traditionally, face-to-face sales have the highest close rate, but are also the most expensive strategy for a direct marketer to implement. Moreover, they consume the greatest amount of time. The time involved limits the number of people who can be shown the sales presentation and ultimately can be very limiting on sales, even if there is a very high close rate. However, what if you could leverage the same one-to-one relationship when selling, but multiply it times a thousand? webinars essentially allow you to do this. As briefly mentioned in the previous chapter, webinars are Web conferencing software used for delivering sales presentations. webinars are commonly used in B2B marketing as they are excellent for generating leads.

Here is how they work:

1. The presenting company establishes an account with a host company, such as https://www.gotomeeting.com.
2. Next, the presenting company establishes a time that the webinar is going to be delivered.
3. An opt-in landing page is created where people have to enter their information; in return, they will get the details of how to log in to the webinar.
4. After a person opts in to the landing page to view the webinar, an e-mail is sent from an auto responder giving the person the actual link and time and any other information needed to access the webinar.
5. At the start time of the webinar, the prospect logs in to watch.
6. The Web conferencing software connects all of the computers of all of the people logging in to watch the webinar to the presenter's computer. This way each person can watch the webinar at home, in the office, or wherever they are as long as they have an Internet connection.
7. The presenter normally uses a PowerPoint presentation to go through the sales process, while talking into a USB-connected microphone, plugged into their computer.
8. The presentation shows up on all of the people's computer screens that are logged in to watch the presentation as it is being delivered.
9. As the webinar is being delivered, the people watching can type in any questions, which are then sent to the presenter's computer. The presenter can answer the questions, either during the webinar or at the end of the webinar.
10. At the end of the webinar, there is a specific Web page that is shown where people can go and purchase the product or service being offered.

webinars can be effectively used to build a prospect list. Let's examine a four-step process for doing so:

1. The presenting company, A, sets up an affiliate link for the promoting company, B.
2. Company B sends an e-mail to its list with the affiliate link, asking its customers to join it on the webinar to learn about some topic of interest to the list.
3. The link in the e-mail that Company B sent to its list is a link to the opt-in page for the webinar.
4. When people opt in to the webinar, those names and e-mail addresses become an asset of Company A, because they can be downloaded from the webinar software and inserted into an e-mail program such as Icontact. This allows Company A to market to them whenever they desire in the future.

Traditionally, marketers will use a separate opt-in e-mail form for people to actually log in to the webinar when it is being delivered. This serves two purposes. First, it allows Company A to measure who registered for the webinar and how many people actually showed up. The company can then look at this number to determine its close rate and how many people actually purchased. Second, the company can segment the people who did not show up or purchase into a separate list and e-mail them details of the webinar when it is replayed.

Social Media

Social media is a highly effective format to use to reach and engage with B2B clients and prospects. Social media can be used to generate awareness and leads as well as to cultivate and strengthen client relationships. B2B companies primarily use social media with the objective of *leads* rather than *brand awareness*. In social media campaigns, the first objective is audience engagement and presence. If B2B direct marketers can develop engaging content, they should be able to use social media effectively. Of course, the ultimate objective of most B2B social media efforts is generating *leads*. According to the Content Marketing Institute, 9 out of 10 B2B companies use LinkedIn as their social media platform, followed by Twitter, Facebook, and YouTube. Obviously, the top B2B social media platforms attract the right audience and, as such, generate more leads.[24]

For example, AT&T put together a new sales team to re-build business relationships with a Fortune 100 company in Atlanta. AT&T used social media to implement content marketing strategies aimed at 'persons of interest' from the former customer. Inside of 18 months, $47 million in new business was awarded to AT&T, directly attributable to social media outreach.[25]

Let's look at another example. Dell EMC is an American multinational corporation headquartered in Hopkinton, Massachusetts. As a member of the Dell Technologies family, Dell EMC manufactures and sells data storage systems, information security, virtualization, analytics, cloud computing, and other products and services that enable businesses to store, manage, protect, and analyze data. As a computer technology company, Dell had a great deal of social media experience, especially with Twitter, with selling via microblogging, before acquiring EMC in 2016. After the acquisition of EMC, a new B2B division was established and social media communications became a priority to address and support customers. The B2B division now has an impressive presence on various social platforms: 1,072,000 fans on Facebook, 137,000 on Twitter, 36,300 subscribers on YouTube, and 850,000 followers on LinkedIn.[26]

Lastly, one of the best examples of a B2B company innovatively using social media content is Novartis, a pharmaceutical company in Switzerland. Novartis has built a strong presence on Instagram by creating engaging content that goes beyond the traditional B2B digital content of case studies and white papers. Novartis now includes compelling images, hashtags, podcasts, and videos, which are likely to go viral on social media.[27] Novartis avoids using Instagram to promote any of its medications; however, the company shares content such as photos of employees involved in volunteer activities, videos of authentic patients talking about the real-life impact of disease, and engaging stories of how the company is offering non-profit medical help to ordinary people.[28]

In summary, social media is effective in both securing and retaining business customers. Retaining customers is the topic of the next section.

B2B CUSTOMER RETENTION

It goes without saying that customers are value maximizers and, as such, they buy and keep buying from vendors that offer the highest value. So, a happy customer is a returning one and B2B marketers must make sure to keep profitable customers coming back, since losing them can dramatically affect their company's profit. In fact, the cost of attracting a new customer is often five to ten times higher than the cost of keeping a current customer happy. The key to retaining customers therefore is to engage them in meaningful relationships and to continue providing value, with the goal of ultimately turning them into the company's brand advocates.

B2B marketers must be cognizant of the lifetime value of their customer base to understand their profit implications. They must also be skilled in customer relationship management (CRM) to not only develop programs to attract and retain the right customers, but also to determine ways to increase the value of their customer base through up-selling and cross-selling.

Building a customer database and conducting data mining to detect trends, segments, and individual needs are essential in developing CRM insights. To build strong long-term relationships, B2B marketers should use the right information to differentiate, customize, personalize, and dispatch precision marketing to maximize **customer loyalty**.

Marketing to current or existing customers is a highly profitable B2B **customer retention** strategy. Beyond acquiring customers, B2B marketers should focus on their customer base and enhance customer lifetime value with their existing customers through up-selling, cross-selling, customer loyalty, and customer advocacy. Let's discuss each one of these in turn.

Up-selling

Increasing the sales and profitability of existing customers is the B2B tried-and-true best practice that can be done through offering additional quantities of products and services, and tailoring the process to the specific needs of each customer. Identifying and analyzing the needs of current customers are the first steps in the **up-selling** process. Vetting the most profitable and promising customer base, uncovering and profiling their specific needs, and fulfilling those needs through the addition of existing product and service offers, add value for the B2B customer. The up-selling activity can strengthen the customer relationship over time as the targeted customers enjoy the additional communications and attention they receive.

Cross-selling

Cross-selling is a bona fide customer base expansion technique that maximizes the selling efficiency and profitability of B2B marketing. It focuses on existing customers while encouraging them to ask for additional offers via cross-selling. The technique works when the B2B marketer suggests related additional products that can genuinely benefit the current customer's needs and requirements. It entails a careful assessment of the customer's business to understand their needs before developing solutions and suggesting additional products and services that the customer has not even considered or been made aware of. Cross-selling is a great opportunity for B2B marketers to raise awareness and promote their company's offerings while further serving loyal customers and enhancing relationships.

Customer Loyalty

B2B loyal customers maintain and solidify their relationship. They purchase additional products and services. Creating a strong, tight connection to customers should be the goal of B2B marketers and is the key to their long-term marketing success. Retention-building activities to help the customer benefit financially, managerially, technically, and entrepreneurially all enhance customer satisfaction, relationship, and loyalty. The key contributor, however, is listening to and interacting with customers to pave the way toward institutional ties, collaboration, and partnership. For example, Bloomin's attention to detail and reputation for producing seed paper with the highest germination rates make the company the obvious choice of marketing executives, wedding professionals, promotional product distributors, and many other types of B2B seed paper aficionados. Bloomin works with a network of distributors around the world (in the U.S., Europe, China, Canada, and more). These dedicated distributors are Bloomin's partners in serving B2B customers. Bloomin serves as a supplier of seed paper products to its distributors, thus the company values the strong relationships it has cultivated over time. As Figure 11.11 shows, Bloomin periodically seeks feedback from its distributors in order to continue to serve the needs of each distributor and to strengthen these relationships.

Customer Advocacy

Satisfied customers are expected to voice and share their passion for the company and its brands to the world. **Customer advocacy** is not only desirable and profitable to B2B marketers, it is also a reliable and believable decision factor in B2B customers' product and vender choice. Customer advocacy, including referrals, references, product reviews, and blog posts, is increasingly in demand, as reported in Demand Gen Report's *2014 B2B Buyer Behavior Survey* that 36 percent of those surveyed rely more on peer recommendations than they did previously.[29]

Frequently, marketers expect their happy customers to become evangelists for their products and brands. They provide these customers with resources and opportunities to communicate their insights. With the advent of the Internet, online customer ratings and reviews are predominantly playing an important role in B2B decision making. Satisfied customers provide the most powerful B2B influencer marketing.

SUMMARY

Business-to-business (B2B) marketing is the process of providing goods and services to organizational consumers and industrial market intermediaries. Collectively, business consumers consist of companies, government, and not-for-profit organizations. These include manufacturers, wholesalers, retailers and government agencies, as well as non-business organizations, such as charities, churches, and foundations.

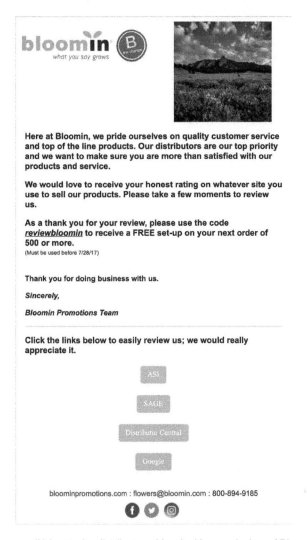

Figure 11.11 Bloomin e-mail blast to its distributors. Used with permission of Bloomin. All rights reserved.

Compared to consumer markets, industrial markets consist of fewer buyers who purchase large quantities. Buyers and sellers are geographically concentrated and have close relationships. Demand for industrial products is derived, less price-sensitive, and fluctuates across business cycles. Industrial buyers are trained professionals with specialized interests and technical knowledge. They benefit from the process of organizational decision support and joint decision making.

B2B transactions are dominated by electronic commerce and e-procurement. There is a growing interest among business buyers to place orders through mobile commerce devices. Lead generation and nurturing are benefiting from the Internet and the applications of digital communication in B2B customer acquisition and retention.

Major segmentation variables for B2B markets include firmographics, such as industry type (SIC and NAICS), company size, and geographic locations. Specific identifiers, such as

475

organizational functions (centralized versus decentralized) and influences, organizational relationship, purchasing policies, and criteria, are also used to further refine B2B segments. Ultimately, the personal characteristics of the buyer and/or the buying office, such as buyer–seller characteristic similarities, attitude toward risk, and supplier loyalty are taken into consideration for successful segmentation and targeting.

KEY TERMS

business-to-business (B2B) marketing

business-to-government (B2G) marketing

channel structure

content marketing

cross-selling

customer acquisition

customer advocacy

customer loyalty

customer relationship management (CRM)

customer retention

derived demand

electronic data interchange (EDI)

firmographics

industrial demand

industrial goods

inelastic demand

influencer marketing

lead nurturing

market structure

marketing funnel

North American Free Trade Agreement (NAFTA)

North American Industry Classification System (NAICS)

procurement

referrals

Standard Industrial Classification (SIC)

up-selling

webinars

REVIEW QUESTIONS

1. Distinguish between B2C and B2B markets and provide two examples of each market type.
2. What are the characteristics of industrial demand? How are these different from the characteristics of final consumer demand?
3. Name some of the challenges facing B2B marketers today. What new challenges do you think will arise in the future? Why do you think these challenges will occur?

4. What are the major factors contributing to the increasing use of direct and data-driven marketing for B2B?
5. What are the major uses of B2B direct marketing? Which of these do you think is the most important? Explain why.
6. How are B2B direct marketers using digital and social media platforms in their marketing arsenal? Provide a few real-world examples.
7. Describe how segmenting business consumer markets is different from segmenting final consumer markets. Provide at least three segmentation variables that you might use to segment each type of market.
8. Explain the important strategies of content marketing, in-person contacts, and referrals in B2B lead generation. How do these relate to one another?
9. What are the primary differences between B2B customer acquisition and B2B customer retention programs?
10. Select an industry (e.g., food, chemical, automotive) and its B2B vertical market maker (e.g., www.foodmarketmaker.com, https://e-chemex.com, www.covisint.com/industries/automotive). Investigate the site and report the size of the industry it serves, the services it provides, and the value it creates for buyers and suppliers.

EXERCISE

Korea International Trade Association (KITA) is an international e-marketplace where global business buyers and suppliers manage their contacts and conduct transactions electronically. Visitors can access KITA's extensive and detailed databases and acquire information on buyers, sellers, products, and services, and trade with more than 73,000 KITA member and non-member domestic and international companies. Visit KITA at www.kita.org and:

- identify KITA's core functional areas and services
- identify and explain the services that KITA offers to match global B2B buyers and suppliers.

CRITICAL THINKING EXERCISE

Describe the purchasing decision process for a road construction company in need of earth-removing equipment, such as bulldozers, articulated dump trucks, and haulers. Include typical personnel participating in the decision process, key specifications for the equipment, and requirements for equipment after-sale servicing and warranty.

READINGS AND RESOURCES

- Market growth opportunities: www.bain.com/insights/how-to-capture-the-b2b-growth-opportunity-in-telecom

- B2G: https://socialwebtactics.com/b2g-marketing-guide-government-contractors
- Content marketing: https://nealschaffer.com/marriage-social-media-content-marketing-imply-b2b-brands
- Content marketing: https://contentmarketinginstitute.com/2018/10/research-b2b-audience
- Digital media case studies: https://businessesgrow.com/2015/05/21/b2b-digital-marketing-case-studies
- Influencer marketing: https://insights.newscred.com/b2b-influencer-marketing

CASE: Cisco

Cisco, the networking technology giant in the top 60 of the *Fortune 500* ratings, is an excellent example of a B2B colossus. In this case, we will show how Cisco uses Click-to-Chat to increase lead generation and sales, and improve customer relationships. Web Marketing and Strategy is a discipline within Corporate Marketing at Cisco, and it is important to both lead generation and customer acquisition. Its charter is to run the product/solution/services sections of cisco.com as well as the home page, shown in Figure 11.12. It is also accountable for Search (on site and organic), Video, and Chat.

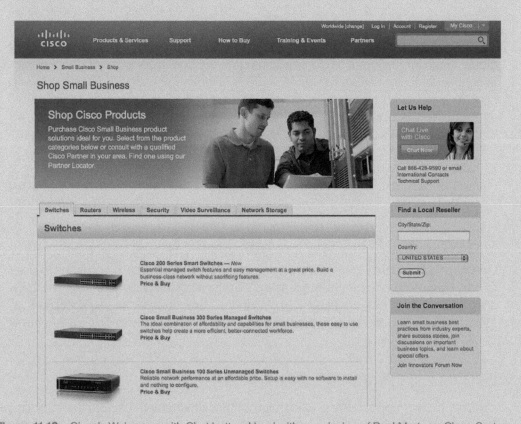

Figure 11.12 Cisco's Web page with Chat button. Used with permission of Paul Martson, Cisco Systems.

Cisco began a pilot Chat program in 2006. It started with just a handful of pages in a specific section of the site, focused on pre-sales product information for the small and medium business (SMB) market. Almost immediately, the executives at Cisco were surprised by the performance of Chat. Initial findings included the following:

- More people wanted to chat than Cisco expected.
- Importantly, more leads were generated than forecasted, with a higher conversion rate than other tactics, including telephone or e-mail communication (see Figure 11.13).
- Cisco agents were more productive because they were able to handle concurrent chats. Agents on the phone can only service one customer at a time, but agents online are able to 'multi-chat.'

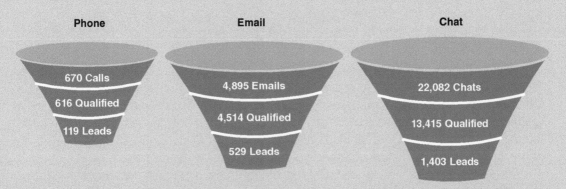

Figure 11.13 Cisco's lead comparison chart. Used with permission of Paul Martson, Cisco Systems.

Over the course of the next few quarters, the number of Chat placements expanded rapidly. At every checkpoint along the way, the ROI was extremely healthy. Customer satisfaction was in the 90th percentile as measured in the post-chat surveys, where Cisco routinely asks for level of satisfaction with the agents and the Chat experience overall.

At this time, Cisco's focus turned to chatting in other countries. Scaling the program to include 43 countries and 14 languages was, surprisingly, not that difficult. It took about one year of effort among a few Web marketing staff and the Cisco professional services team at LivePerson. There were some tricky points with the technology, like right-to-left languages such as Hebrew and Arabic. And, of course, the 'management' of internal stakeholders is always a challenge at a company of this size.

Optimization

With the expansion phase behind Cisco, it was time to work on optimization and innovation. Optimization included changes to business rules for better outcomes, including the number of visitors who move from Chat candidates to Chat leads, as shown in the Chat funnel in Figure 11.14.

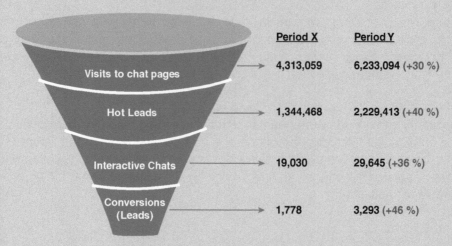

	Period X	Period Y
Visits to chat pages	4,313,059	6,233,094 (+30 %)
Hot Leads	1,344,468	2,229,413 (+40 %)
Interactive Chats	19,030	29,645 (+36 %)
Conversions (Leads)	1,778	3,293 (+46 %)

Figure 11.14   Cisco Chat funnel. Used with permission of Paul Martson, Cisco Systems.

At the Cisco contact centers–approximately eight globally–optimization included frequent reviews of transcripts to share best practices for agents. Innovation efforts came often as there was a whole universe of opportunity: What if Cisco could transfer chats to its partners to close the deal in real time? What if Cisco proactively invited visitors from other countries on its U.S. site in their local language? What if Cisco Chat could be placed on other websites that its customers frequent (referred to as 'watering holes')?

Today, the next big thing with Chat is establishing a handshake between Cisco's engagement scoring system and the Chat rules engine to move more leads to customers. The idea behind this is that Cisco can better target high-prospect chatters if it peeks into their structured data, such as purchase history, partner status, and so on, combined with their on-the-site behavior, such as including search terms or recency and frequency of visits.

Emerging Trends

Cisco has identified three emerging trends with Chat: *third-party apps* that harmonize with your chat deployment to enhance functionality; *unstructured data* to better manage the content of chat transcripts; and *skill matching* to provide more intelligent routing and matching of Chat users and subject matter experts. Let's briefly discuss each of these.

Third-Party Apps

Much like how a phone-based contact center might take advantage of new call features like recording or forwarding, Chat is experiencing a period of rapid innovation around capabilities for providing richer and more relevant experiences. Targeting by company domain is one example. If you were Cisco, wouldn't you want to know that the person chatting with you happens to work for Xerox? Add to this CRM data and it gets really exciting and offers an even more powerful way to turn leads into customers. If you knew what equipment your customers had bought from you in the past, you would be better positioned to make the best recommendations.

Unstructured Data

Chat leaves behind a vast amount of text. Mining Chat transcripts for business intelligence can be very rewarding from a sentiment-monitoring perspective or a training perspective or even a product development perspective. Cisco has begun to aggregate actionable data around opportunities to improve its Web content offerings.

Skill Matching

Chat should be moving from a many-to-many, homogeneous experience to one of great differentiation. We've already talked about knowing more about our visitors, and therefore being better able to target them. As shown in Figure 11.15, the opportunity is to match that high-value target with an equally capable agent who may not be located in a contact center. Think of it as connecting niche questions with niche expertise, or working the supply side of Chat along with the demand side. Cisco's customers consistently ask for greater access to its subject matter experts, whose time is extremely valuable.

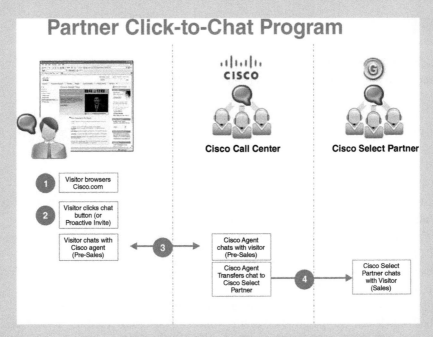

Figure 11.15 Cisco flowchart. Used with permission of Paul Martson, Cisco Systems.

Through these Chat trends, Cisco is attempting to create productive and friction-less conversations to convert more leads to profitable customers and support its brand promise.

Conclusion

Acquiring quality leads, converting them to customers, and retaining them are of key importance to business marketers. This example from the B2B colossus Cisco provides an excellent example not only of the important role that chat can play in customer acquisition, but also of the role of data to focus on the most important leads and bring the SMEs to the table to answer the customers' questions and help acquire the business.

Case Discussion Questions

1. In Cisco's B2B lead conversion and customer acquisition, what other methods are used to communicate with leads besides Click-to-Chat?
2. How did Click-to-Chat enhance the process from a B2B customer's point of view? From Cisco's point of view?
3. How can the addition of customer data help move leads to customers?
4. Discuss *unstructured data*, *skill matching*, and *third-party apps* and how they might help Cisco convert more leads to customers.

NOTES

1. www.dmnews.com/marketing-channels/direct-mail/news/13061379/five-ways-to-make-government-agencies-clients, retrieved May 25, 2019.
2. Ibid.
3. https://socialwebtactics.com/b2g-marketing-guide-government-contractors, retrieved May 25, 2019.
4. Ibid.
5. Ibid.
6. Ibid.
7. www.dmnews.com/marketing-channels/direct-mail/news/13061379/five-ways-to-make-government-agencies-clients, retrieved May 25, 2019.
8. https://socialwebtactics.com/b2g-marketing-guide-government-contractors, retrieved May 25, 2019.
9. Personal communication with Rick Pallen, Director of Sales, Government Technology Group, Johnson Controls Security Solutions, May 28, 2019.
10. http://products.hoovers.com/get-200-free-leads/?mm_campaign=8ba3a0d4c6f13535f20bd 2845b691438&utm_campaign=4129&utm_source=MSN&utm_mediu m=CPC&medium= TSA&serv=SEMMSN412996911-12370134432-1&keyword=business%20 leads%20list& gclid=CKnFtKnRkc4CFfRTMgod80EEYA&gclsrc=ds, retrieved July 26, 2016.
11. www.pardot.com/blog/new-research-reveals-how-to-turn-more-prospects-into-customers, retrieved July 26, 2016.
12. http://ecommerceandb2b.com/b2b-e-commerce-trends-statistics, retrieved July 26, 2016.
13. Ibid.

14. http://blog.marketo.com/2015/08/data-talks-2-proven-lead-generation-tactics-to-jump-on-now.html, retrieved July 18, 2016.

15. The discussion of Evergreen Enterprises is based on a case study by Whereoware, the company's digital agency. Used with permission.

16. https://businessesgrow.com/2015/05/21/b2b-digital-marketing-case-studies, retrieved May 6, 2019.

17. https://www.demandmetric.com/content/content-marketing-infographic, retrieved July 18, 2016.

18. The discussion of Sullivans is based on a case study by Whereoware, the company's digital agency. Used with permission.

19. http://blog.marketo.com/2015/08/data-talks-2-proven-lead-generation-tactics-to-jump-on-now.html, retrieved July 18, 2016.

20. Ibid.

21. www.softwareadvice.com/resources/demand-generation-benchmark-report-2014, retrieved July 18, 2016.

22. https://businessesgrow.com/2015/05/21/b2b-digital-marketing-case-studies, retrieved May 6, 2019.

23. www.statista.com/statistics/368739/b2b-lead-generation-most-effective-online-tactics, retrieved July 23, 2016.

24. www.articulatemarketing.com/blog/b2b-social-media-statistics, retrieved May 25, 2019.

25. https://businessesgrow.com/2015/05/21/b2b-digital-marketing-case-studies, retrieved May 6, 2019.

26. https://dmexco.com/stories/five-examples-of-social-media-marketing-in-b2b, retrieved May 25, 2019.

27. https://nealschaffer.com/marriage-social-media-content-marketing-imply-b2b-brands, retrieved May 25, 2019.

28. www.wegohealth.com/2018/07/23/instagram-for-patient-engagement, retrieved May 25, 2019.

29. http://marketingland.com/symbiotic-relationship-customer-loyalty-advocacy-120632, retrieved July 23, 2016.

12
FULFILLMENT AND CUSTOMER SERVICE

CHAPTER CONTENTS

CHAPTER SPOTLIGHT

LIDS—'ANY TEAM, ANY TIME, ANY WHERE'

When Glenn Campbell and Scott Molander began selling hats from a single storefront in the early 1990s, the consumer world was a different place. The Internet was in its infancy. Online shopping didn't exist. And most distribution channels were singularly focused.

Since then, Campbell and Molander's hat business, Hat World, has transformed into a leading nationwide provider of headwear and accessories. Now owned by Genesco, Hat World, Inc., operates the retail brand Lids, with more than 1,300 retail locations and 8,000 employees. Lids' headwear products are distributed through four brand outlets:

- Lids–offers officially licensed, branded, and specialty fashion headwear in the latest styles and colors, sold primarily through retail stores.
- Locker Room by Lids–retail locations that sell a full assortment of headwear and sportswear, including apparel, accessories, and novelty items.
- Lids Clubhouse–focuses on partnering with teams, both professional and collegiate, to operate team stores, online Internet retailing, and souvenir concessions at various athletic events.
- Lids Direct–an e-commerce network that provides state-of-the-art online merchandise for all Lids branded retail and many Clubhouse partners.

Driving Lids' success is its well-known customer promise: to deliver merchandise of 'any team, any time, any where.' Its Locker Room business increased 49 percent in one year. Its e-commerce business grew 10 percent in three years. Its online sales average rose to 20,000 orders per day.

Today, Lids sells more than 230,000 products with separate universal product codes (UPCs). Figure 12.1 shows a variety of some of the products Lids offers its customers. Its inventory includes more than 4.5 million units. It ships 35 million units annually. While growth propelled the company, it put greater pressure on Lids' warehouse operations.

All Lids' products were stored and distributed from the single, manually operated facility near Indianapolis, Indiana. Initially, the manual warehouse was set up for stores dealing with high numbers of picks per unit and a manageable number of stock keeping unit codes (SKUs). Personnel used RF (radio frequency) scan guns for batch picking and carousels for sorting. But Lids' current omni-channel retail environment required fundamental changes. Space limitations challenged its need to respond to multiple order types quickly. Fulfilling orders required labor-intensive, multi-line picking. Fulfillment tasks were difficult to batch across customer types. Inefficiencies threatened to have a negative impact on profitability and contradicted Lids' brand promise of immediate delivery.

In order to meet its new distribution challenges, Lids contracted Swisslog, a leading provider of automated inventory and order fulfillment solutions for warehouses and distribution facilities. Swisslog's Click&Pick™ solution was offered to meet the challenges of Lids' omni-channel operations and increase the efficiency and productivity of its

Figure 12.1 Lids' products. Used with permission of Lids. All Rights Reserved.

warehouse operations. Click&Pick™ combines components such as conveyor and lifting technology, warehouse management software, and preconfigured systems such as AutoStore, SmartCarrier, and CarryPick. The solution provides storage for 100,000 SKUs serviced by robots with highly efficient goods-to-person pick functionality.

The end results for Lids? Both cost efficiency and cost savings goals were met, including:

- ensuring 100 percent order fulfillment accuracy
- guaranteeing delivery times under 24 hours
- replenishing products quickly and efficiently
- streamlining employee training
- reducing manpower by 58 full-time equivalents annually.

Impressive? You bet! Not only did the new warehouse operations of Lids achieve each of these goals, but, at the same time, it supported the multiple distribution channels of Lids and enabled the company to quickly fulfill orders from consumers responding to its many attractive offers, such as the 'free shipping' offer shown in Figure 12.2.

Note: This feature is based on a case study by Swisslog. Used with permission.

Figure 12.2 Lids' free shipping ad. Used with permission of Lids. All Rights Reserved.

As we discuss fulfillment and customer service throughout this chapter, keep Lids' success story in mind as the company that provides fast and efficient delivery of a wide variety of products that meet the needs of each and every fan. Efficient fulfillment operations enable Lids to live up to its customer promise of 'Any Team, Any Time, Any Where.'

FULFILLMENT

What is Fulfillment?

Fulfillment is the act of carrying out a customer's expectations. Strictly defined, fulfillment means sending the product to the customer or delivering the service agreed on. Loosely defined, it includes the entire dialogue (all interactions with the customer) and delivery functions. Marketers also see fulfillment as a part of the 'extended product,' or the intangible part of the product. For example, think in terms of the dialogue that a customer has with an organization. A customer or potential customer may communicate with the direct marketer by making an inquiry or placing an order, and then expect to receive a response in a timely fashion. Likewise, customers expect their orders to be filled and delivered in a timely fashion. These dialogue and delivery activities are fulfillment.

Fulfillment is often referred to as the 'back end' of the direct marketing process—the fulfillment, call center, and customer service operations. Fulfillment entails anything and everything that happens *after* the customer or prospective customer responds to some form of direct response communication from a company or an organization. If a customer places an order, he expects delivery of the ordered item. If a prospective customer places an inquiry, she expects to receive the requested information. In some cases, consumers need additional information to make appropriate product or service selections. In those cases, the task of fulfillment is to provide information and assistance to empower consumers to make informed decisions. Of course, fulfillment of these requests should be handled in a timely manner. Direct marketers strive to fulfill customer and prospect desires and ensure customer satisfaction.

Many experts contend that back-end functions alone cannot make a sale but certainly can break one. More important, the lack of efficient fulfillment operations and good customer service can injure the relationship the direct marketer has with the customer and ultimately lead to the loss of that customer. Customer relationships begin when the firm receives an order. We also discuss the components of fulfillment, call centers, and customer service, along with strategies to help direct marketers maximize their customer satisfaction level.

Adequate fulfillment, by minimizing the time between ordering and receiving, can alleviate two distinct handicaps inherent in direct marketing: (1) a time lag between placing an order and receiving it, and (2) a lack of familiarity with the actual product, which has been purchased remotely by mail, telephone, or online. Ultimate success in direct marketing depends on adequate fulfillment. It has been said that 'The best copy, the best graphics, and the wisest choice of lists are all a sheer waste of money, time, and talent if they are not followed through with really outstanding fulfillment.'[1] Let's investigate the standards direct marketers must meet in order to provide really outstanding fulfillment.

Traditional Fulfillment Standards

Fulfillment standards have changed over the past couple of decades. The consumer is increasingly desiring, demanding, and expecting faster turnaround times on orders and all forms of communication with companies. This is especially true of those orders and inquiries that come to the organization via the high-tech media. Consumers are busier today, they are more astute, and they procrastinate. With overnight delivery, toll-free numbers, fax machines, and the Internet, direct marketers have inadvertently encouraged customers to wait longer before placing an order because the consumer expects an immediate delivery service from the direct marketer.[2]

Though not every direct marketer can provide immediate delivery services, all direct marketers must uphold certain delivery standards. The following are some typical fulfillment benchmarks that direct marketers strive to attain to ensure excellent customer service:[3]

- **Cost per order (fully loaded)**: the range is between $8 and $13, which includes both call center and warehouse costs, such as direct labor, indirect labor, benefits, occupancy, packing supplies, telecoms, and credit card processing. This does not include shipping and handling revenue or shipping costs.
- **Order processing turnaround time**: for in-stock products, 100 percent in 24 hours. Zappos. com has this down to a science and allows customers to book within a two-hour window of goods having to be passed off to UPS from its Kentucky distribution center.
- **Initial customer order fill rate**: this pertains to the percentage of customer orders shipped complete in 24 hours (or whatever its shipping standard is). Typically, good performance is based on product lines, such as advanced fashion: 70–80 percent; re-orderable apparel: 80–90 percent; gifts/home: 85–95 percent; and business supplies: 98–100 percent.
- **Order accuracy**: these targets are 99.5 percent without barcode and 99.9 percent with full inventory process barcode.
- **Inbound receipts, dock to stock**: products moving through all fulfillment processes should have 8–24 hour turnaround time.
- **Per-hour benchmarks**: these vary, but as noted by an industry expert, most systems should handle at least 3,100 units per hour.
- **Inventory accuracy**: the target is 99.8–99.9 percent for bar-coded products.

THE FULFILLMENT PROCESS

The fulfillment process consists of the following six basic elements: (1) offer, (2) response, (3) processing, (4) shipping, (5) billing, and (6) customer service. Figure 12.3 shows a model of the elements involved in the fulfillment process. Let us now take a closer look at each element.

Figure 12.3 Fulfillment process

The Offer

We saw in Chapter 5 that the offer encompasses the terms under which a direct marketer promotes a specific product or service to the customer. To create an offer, the direct marketer first undertakes a number of activities, such as a close examination of the target customer, market segmentation, product or service research, database analysis, price determination, packaging requirements, and others. Direct marketers should properly address and direct the product/service offer and ensure that it is relevant to the needs of the addressee. This description should be adequate and fair and communicate the offer's relevance to the prospect's needs. Direct marketers should clearly state all disclosures and all options, such as sizes and colors. Direct marketers must specify credit terms. They should leave nothing to the imagination of the consumer during this initial stage.

For example, employees of the well-known online retailer Zappos (see Figure 12.4) are striving to WOW their customers and will go the extra mile to contribute to the successful customer experience by presenting their offered products in an innovative fashion. Zappos revolutionized the online shopping experience by using amusing and useful videos to showcase its products. Zappos's employees participate in these videos by showing and talking about shoes, sandals, handbags, and clothing. Zappos's employees produce thousands of these short videos because the company determined that when a product includes a video explanation, especially one coming from a 'regular' person as opposed to a supermodel, it is highly effective in helping with the online buying process. Zappos's research has found that when a product includes an employee video explanation, sales increase and product returns decrease. Today, Zappos has a sizable crew of people creating hundreds of videos each week to present to its customers.

Figure 12.4 Zappos logo. Used with permission of 2012 Zappos.com©, Inc and its affiliates.

A relevant product offering is timely and clear. Because an order form is an essential contractual document, it should be legally correct as well as distinct, simply stated, and easy to follow. When creating the order form, the direct marketer may use check-off boxes, or something equally easy to identify, for allowing customers to select size, color, or style variations and any other specialized information, such as personalization.

The Response

Direct marketers generally receive consumer responses (inquiries) or transactions (orders) via mail, phone, fax, or the Internet. If an order or inquiry is placed by mail, fax, or Internet, it is critical that the consumer completes the order form in a full and accurate manner. The consumer must provide all information necessary for the direct marketer to fill the order. If the order or inquiry is placed via telephone, then operators need to be especially diligent in collecting order information. The way an organization handles the receipt of an order or inquiry is critical in the fulfillment process.

Processing

After receiving an order, the marketer undertakes editing and coding as well as credit checking and capturing of vital data for updating the database. The seller also prepares a series of documents such as shipping labels, billing notifications, and inventory instructions. At this stage, if there might be a delay in shipping an order, the marketer lets the customer know and anticipates any possible complaints.

Inventory control is another critical part of fulfillment operations. Direct marketers must examine inventory for quality checks prior to packaging and, if possible, after packaging as well. Computer technology can be of great assistance in processing orders. For example, at Lillian Vernon computers are programmed to catch errors, such as an invalid address or an invalid credit card. Furthermore, if an item can be personalized and the order information provided by the customer does not include personalization information, the computer flags the order and alerts the employee of the situation.[4]

Shipping

A computerized inventory control system is often the key to proper and timely shipment. Out-of-stock and back orders, requiring separate shipments later, are costly to the direct marketer and frustrating to the customer. For example, Zappos uses its one million square feet of storage space in its Kentucky fulfillment operations (seen in Figure 12.5) to physically warehouse every product item that it offers to its customers. That's quite a statement.

Back orders may even result in corrective action by governmental agencies. The Federal Trade Commission (FTC) trade regulations require all direct marketers to comply with its strict '30-day rule' guidelines regarding out-of-stock situations by notifying the customer if an item cannot be shipped within 30 days of the time it was placed. In addition, the customer must have the opportunity to cancel the order because of the out-of-stock condition. Direct marketers should not substitute a similar item to try to fulfill the sale, nor send a different color or size, without explicit authorization from the customer. If these FTC guidelines are not followed, the FTC may take punitive action, including fining the company.

Billing

Once an order is on its way, the organization should receive payment as expeditiously as possible. If the customer did not use a credit or debit card and payment did not accompany the order, then clear billing instructions, with appropriate follow-up, are vital to ensure not only payment but also customer goodwill.

Figure 12.5 Zappos Fulfillment Center building. Used with permission of 2012 Zappos.com©, Inc and its affiliates.

This need for clarity and accuracy also extends to proper receipt and posting of the payment, especially with extended-pay options. We often hear of computer errors, such as incorrect billings and incorrect postings, but more than likely these are human instruction errors.

Customer Service

The customer service function of the fulfillment process specifically refers to the handling of complaints, inquiries, replacements, and special problems. The high costs associated with this kind of customer service should be one of the incentives to getting it right the first time. Another, more important incentive is, of course, that only a satisfied customer comes back. Therefore, because direct marketers place great importance on repeat business, they should pay great attention to detail in all aspects of the fulfillment process so as to eliminate the need to handle complaints and special problems. This care will also eliminate the risk of losing a valued customer.

The following are some tips for providing excellent customer service:

1. *Conduct customer satisfaction research*: a simple survey asking customers to indicate how well the company and its competitors are performing should be conducted on a regular basis.
2. *Simplify your guarantee*: omit the confusing legal jargon and explain the refund and replacement policy in simple everyday language.

3. *Acknowledge orders*: if merchandise cannot be shipped immediately, send a postcard acknowledgment. Many customers probably won't mind waiting a short time period for their order if they know that their order has been received and is getting careful attention by the direct marketer.

4. *Ship merchandise more promptly*: most professionals believe that order turnaround time should be one week. Thus, the product should be in the customer's hands the week following the one in which the order was placed.

5. *Don't bill before you ship*: customers should be told that payment is not necessary until after the order has been received – just in case they receive an invoice prior to the merchandise they order.

6. *Acknowledge returns and cancellations*: when customers return merchandise, they want to be assured that the direct marketer has received it. Send a simple acknowledgment card telling the customer you received the returned goods or cancellation request, explain that it may take a couple of weeks to process it, and to disregard any invoice for the product(s) that they may receive in the interim.

7. *Answer correspondence promptly*: nothing is more bothersome to the customer than having to write multiple letters or make multiple calls to get a problem straightened out with the direct marketer. Direct marketers can use a form with check-off boxes, if necessary, to make it easier for the customer to reply. Most importantly, follow through to get the problem straightened out to minimize the inconvenience of the customer.

8. *Make complaint resolution a priority*: recent research points to the fact that customers who have a complaint or problem satisfactorily resolved become *better* long-term customers than those who never had a problem. In addition, it is well documented that an unhappy customer tells many more people about their dissatisfaction than does a happy customer about their satisfaction.

9. *Appoint your own consumer affairs manager*: this person might be called the 'customer service manager.' Their job is to keep customers happy, seeing that orders go out promptly and that complaints are handled properly. This person should be empowered by the organization to make changes in policy and procedures.

10. *Make customers your top priority*: everyone within an organization should understand the value of keeping customers satisfied and happy. Train and reward employees for good customer service.

However, because 100 percent quality control is often unattainable, shipping and billing errors inevitably occur, and only prompt handling and adjustment can overcome these. A customer might receive an incorrect shipment, be erroneously double-billed for a product, or be billed incessantly for a product that was returned. Though such occurrences can become extremely complicated, all should be meticulously adjusted as soon as possible.

Not all communications from customers relevant to fulfillment are complaints—many are inquiries. Many seek further information and some request additional orders. These, too, are a proper concern of the fulfillment operation and fall under the heading of customer service. Good customer service is simply good business.

FULFILLMENT OPTIONS

Options for fulfilling a customer's order include handling all of the processing within the company (in-house), outsourcing the fulfillment activities to an outside fulfillment service, and handling the fulfillment activities online, either in-house or with an outside agency. Let's see what each of these entails and how marketers choose among them.

In-House Fulfillment

Many traditional direct marketing organizations (L. L. Bean, Lands' End, Spiegel, Williams-Sonoma, Orvis, Avon, etc.) operate their own fulfillment centers. Most of these direct marketers have invested heavily in automation and barcode systems to make their fulfillment centers more efficient and improve customer service. However, as many professionals agree, automation in a fulfillment operation warehouse must benefit the customer as well as the company. Some direct marketers believe that the ability of an organization to deliver good customer service is not dependent on automation alone. They believe that new technology, coupled with a well-trained staff, can create good customer service.

The In-House Warehouse Process

Although some in-house fulfillment centers may differ, most traditional fulfillment warehouses operate in a similar manner. The fulfillment warehouse process normally follows the steps presented in Figure 12.6. Let's walk through the warehouse process step by step:

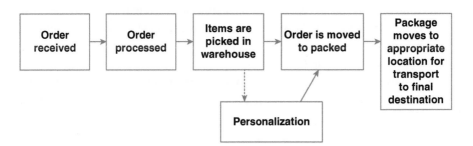

Figure 12.6 Flowchart of warehouse process

1. The direct marketer receives the customer's order via mail, phone, fax, or the Internet.
2. The marketer processes the order and checks inventory levels (if they have not already been checked while receiving the order).
3. The direct marketer sends several documents per order to the warehouse, including the packing slip and the picking list. The **packing slip** identifies the products to be included with the order and the **picking list** normally provides routing information regarding the most efficient way to physically move through the warehouse and assemble the items ordered by the customer.

4. Fulfillment center personnel, often called *pickers*, physically move through the warehouse and, as items are picked, the items are merged with the packing slip. The pickers check the items against the packing slip and indicate a correct match with their initials. The picker is responsible for order accuracy. Many fulfillment centers now use robots to pick the merchandise instead of having pickers physically walk up and down the aisles of the warehouse. For example, Swisslog, a leading warehouse operations systems provider, offers a robotics system (featured in Figure 12.7) to retrieve cartons and distribute them to appropriate picking stations. This system uses a 3D matrix of bins to store the goods, which are then retrieved by a series of robots. The bin is brought directly to the person doing the item picking, so there is no walking around searching for any item. These high-speed, goods-to-person workstations can be pick-only or one-step pick and pack.

5. The order then moves to a packing area, where the *packer* rechecks the products picked against the order and initials the packing slip before boxing the order. This is a second quality-control checkpoint.

6. The packer packs the items into an appropriately sized carton, enclosing a variety of materials, including a catalog, gift boxes, dunnage material (like foam or bubble wrap to protect products during shipment), and promotional inserts. These materials are within an arm's reach of the packer to ensure high productivity levels. As shown in Figure 12.8, warehouse employees must inspect, weigh, and scan each package before it is shipped to the customer.

7. Finally, the package moves via conveyor belt to the appropriate truck for transportation to its destination. Often, prior to the package leaving the warehouse, a warehouse supervisor randomly opens packages to check for order accuracy. This is the third quality-control checkpoint.

Figure 12.7 Swisslog Click&Pick® system. Used with permission of Swisslog, Newport News, Virginia. All Rights Reserved.

Figure 12.8 Swisslog robotic retrieval to picking stations. Used with permission of Swisslog, Newport News, Virginia. All Rights Reserved.

Other warehouse activities occur simultaneously. For example, the direct marketer is collecting customer database information and updating customer records. Additionally, the warehouse is receiving shipments of products and warehouse employees are responsible for restocking the inventory as well as replenishing the packaging stations with packing materials, such as tissue paper, inserts, and bulk packing material called peanuts. Sometimes a portion of a customer's order is sent to a specific location in the warehouse to be personalized. This may involve a wide array of sophisticated machinery and trained operators to fulfill the customer's request for personalization. Let's briefly explore what is involved in the personalization process.

Personalization

Free personalization is popular with many customers. Personalization operators must carefully read the packing slip to ensure accuracy in the personalization process. Personalization processes include engraving, stamping, sandblasting, heat press transferring, embroidery, and more. Though computers run many of the personalization machines, operators are responsible for ensuring accuracy and preventing malfunction. Once the operators personalize the product, the fulfillment process continues to order processors in the picking department, where the personalized product is placed with the rest of the customer's order.

Inventory availability drives the efficiency and success of the entire fulfillment process. Occasionally, a customer will not be shipped their complete order due to the inventory not being in stock. In this situation, the customer is informed that the product is on back order and will be shipped by a specified date. Most in-house warehouses store huge quantities of inventory, often stocked so high that special equipment is needed to obtain the merchandise cartons as needed. Figure 12.9 reveals the large quantity of inventory typically stored at a distribution center and the Swisslog High Bay automated storage vehicle used to retrieve merchandise from the warehouse shelves.

Figure 12.9 Swisslog High Bay automated storage. Used with permission of Swisslog, Newport News, Virginia. All Rights Reserved.

The warehouse processes of most in-house fulfillment operations are highly sophisticated and computerized. The Zone Pick-to-Light system from Swisslog, shown in Figure 12.10, is a good example of the automation involved in the warehouse process. This system reduces employee picking time dramatically by having a flashing light identify the bins from which the picker must secure an item for the order currently being packed. As goods are exhausted in the picking area, a system of storage-and-retrieval cranes behind each picking location automatically replenish inventory to allow non-stop order fulfillment.

Most distribution center operations use computer-originated barcodes to enable orders to be tracked and packages to be physically moved throughout the center and routed to appropriate distribution areas for timely delivery. Conveyor belts are used to swiftly transport the shipping cartons through the warehouse.

Figure 12.10 Swisslog Zone Pick-to-Light system. Used with permission of Swisslog, Newport News, Virginia. All Rights Reserved.

As with most fulfillment operations and warehouse processes, there is a demand for automation to ensure accuracy and speed while minimizing operating costs. Highly flexible and scalable systems are needed to respond quickly to changing demands. Warehouse automation must produce energy-efficient systems in order to reduce the impact of ever-increasing energy costs. Most fulfillment operations require high-density storage to better utilize warehouse space and lower building costs. Swisslog's innovative 'AutoStore' (shown in Figure 12.11) offers an inventory solution for warehouses today. With Swisslog's Click&Pick® system, products are picked via bins that are brought to the pick station by AutoStore robots in predetermined sequences with specialty software.

Figure 12.11 Swisslog's AutoStore. Used with permission of Swisslog, Newport News, Virginia. All Rights Reserved.

An excellent example of an in-house fulfillment center is that of Lids. Its warehouse stores more than 100,000 items in a robotic goods-to-person order-fulfillment system. This system utilizes autonomous robots on an aluminum grid to access products stored in plastic containers, which are stacked directly on top of one another. One bin can store up to eight different units depending upon the stored product. It eliminates long travel times for picking personnel, and most importantly, given the huge number of product lines, ensures that the correct Lids product is matched to each and every order. In a typical day, more than 10,000 orders are completed for all of the Lids stores and distribution channels, including direct-to-consumer business, ensuring that Lids customers can get the items they need for 'Any Team, Any Time, Any Where'—which is the Lids customer promise. This highly automated process aids in reducing fulfillment center operating costs, while maximizing the speed with which the orders are delivered to customers. As shown in Figure 12.12, its automated fulfillment system is very 'worker friendly,' which means that it is easy to learn how to operate, along with providing a very ergonomic work environment for Lids employees, ensuring they can work longer and still stay productive and safe. Finally, the Lids automated fulfillment system leads to a very efficient fulfillment operation.

Figure 12.12   Lids fulfillment system. Used with permission of Lids. All Rights Reserved.

However, some direct marketers do not believe in this traditional in-house fulfillment process. They do not support the storage of products and having inventories sitting in a warehouse waiting for an order to be placed by the customer. They support the concept referred to as 'integrated order fulfillment.'

Integrated Order Fulfillment

Integrated order fulfillment is an emerging business concept based on the idea that the process of building and delivering products should not begin until after the firm receives an order for them. This is in sharp contrast to the traditional fulfillment model, in which

502

assorted products are collected and stored in the distribution center warehouse until an order arrives.

The following eight steps describe the process of integrated order fulfillment:[5]

Step 1: The direct marketer receives a customer's order via mail, phone, fax, or the Internet.

Step 2: The direct marketer processes the order. This includes logging the order into the computer system and determining whether any special promotions or discounts should be noted on the customer's invoice.

Step 3: Next, sourcing occurs. This is where the direct marketer determines where the individual products or components needed to fill the order will come from. The primary choices are the company's own production lines or an outside contract manufacturer.

Step 4: Now it is time for the direct marketer to store the product. This is the brief holding of products or components in a warehouse until their scheduled delivery or manufacture times.

Step 5: The direct marketer assembles the product. Product assembly includes the gathering of parts in a central place where they are put together to form the finished product.

Step 6: Next, the direct marketer ships the product to the customer.

Step 7: The direct marketer tracks the distribution of the product and fulfills any after-sale service needs.

Step 8: Finally, the customer grades the company on how well it performs the entire process on each individual order.

Integrated order fulfillment will not work for every organization. It is primarily designed for those direct marketers who manufacture custom-made products on a customer-by-customer basis. According to Stig Durlow, chairman and CEO of the Swedish software company Industrial Matematik International, which manufactures a popular fulfillment software system called System ESS:

> Integrated order fulfillment helps companies make the jump from the industrial age to the information age by forcing everyone within the enterprise—including outside contractors—to think first about exactly what the customer has asked for before taking any action toward fulfilling a particular order.[6]

Integrated order fulfillment is carried out at the fulfillment center of well-known direct marketer and personal computer manufacturer, Dell. When a consumer places an order, Dell builds the computer precisely to the customer's specification. Dell's customers are able to select different performance options and add-ons. When a customer visits Dell's website or calls the company, he custom-designs his computer online or over the phone with a representative. The computer is built and shipped to the customer. Probably the most valuable thing Dell offers its customers is a customer-oriented approach to product customization that carries over to a comprehensive approach to customer service. Dell believes that each customer is unique and that integrated order fulfillment is one way to serve these distinct needs.

Outside Fulfillment Centers

Once upon a time, most traditional direct marketers had their own fulfillment or distribution centers to warehouse products until picked and packed for shipment to customers. However, this traditional fulfillment model is changing. Today, many direct marketers are extending their businesses to the Web and are realizing their need to quickly convert their operating models from shipping in bulk to processing thousands of daily online orders consisting of just a few items.[7] So they are outsourcing their fulfillment operations to third-party fulfillment centers or online fulfillment providers to obtain the customer service expertise they need. Many direct marketers are moving toward the business model that management experts have dubbed the **virtual enterprise**. According to this model, the company whose name appears on any given product is primarily a marketing and customer service entity, with actual product development and distribution being handled by a broad—and sometimes far-flung—network of subcontractors.[8]

Advantages of an Outside Fulfillment Service

There are certain distinct advantages of hiring an outside contractor to provide back-end support versus handling fulfillment in-house. Some of those advantages include the ability of the company to focus more specifically on marketing and sales activities as opposed to warehousing and distributing tasks. Another advantage is that outside fulfillment companies are likely to have state-of-the-art fulfillment software that most direct marketers would otherwise find it too expensive to acquire. A third advantage concerns financial risk. By contracting outside fulfillment services, direct marketers can treat fulfillment costs as variable costs. Thus, there will be less financial risk because fulfillment costs will be more predictable. A final advantage is that the direct marketer may receive equivalent fulfillment services at a lower cost per order than would have been the case with in-house fulfillment.

Some traditional retailers just getting started in direct marketing activities, especially those planning to use electronic media, have also decided to outsource their fulfillment operations to a third party. They quickly realize that fulfillment capabilities are outside their general core competencies. Many other direct marketers are outsourcing fulfillment operations so that they may concentrate on multichannel marketing activities, especially those tasks associated with the Web.

An Example of an Outside Fulfillment Company

DICK's Sporting Goods utilizes GSI Commerce for the outside fulfillment operations for its e-commerce division. GSI Commerce provides DICK's Sporting Goods with a full range of services associated with DICK's e-commerce, customer service, fulfillment, shipping, and marketing processes. DICK's Sporting Goods began its relationship with GSI in 2001, and sales through its website, dickssportinggoods.com, have grown substantially. GSI is also directing DICK's Sporting Goods toward greater innovation, such as in-store pickup and in-store ordering, to provide even more customer convenience and satisfaction.[9]

Online Fulfillment

Of all the changes that computers and information technology have brought to our modern society, few are more visible than the change in the way products and services are bought and sold. Digital media raise new managerial and customer service challenges for direct marketing organizations. Many organizations have learned the hard way that there is more to e-commerce than just opening a website and inviting consumers to come and shop. It is well established that the primary problem with e-commerce customer satisfaction is *fulfillment*.

Fulfillment guru Bill Kuipers sees little change in fulfillment as a result of electronic media: 'You still have to warehouse, pack, and ship.'[10] Kuipers believes that companies need to plan for the fulfillment process when they use the Internet. Customers shopping online have higher expectations and service standards than do their offline counterparts. Customers are looking for a quicker response to their order or inquiry. They often expect to receive a response to their online communication the same day—and no later than the next day—and they like to be able to investigate the shipping status of their orders online. These high consumer expectations can be a real fulfillment nightmare for the online direct marketer who isn't able to meet them.

Many of the benefits of the automated warehouse are provided by radio frequency identification (RFID). RFID is a technology that enables the wireless identification and subsequent tracking of products. RFID technology has been used by thousands of companies for more than a decade to support a variety of manufacturing, retailing, and warehousing processes along the supply chain. Through the transmission of radio frequencies between an RFID tag with a programmed microchip and a specialized receiving device, companies such as Target and Walmart can immediately locate items and determine inventory levels. This enables them to improve supply chain efficiency and ensure that a given product is in stock when customers want to buy it.[11] RFID can essentially provide a 70 percent improvement in counting efficiency over barcodes, and in the warehouse that means reduced labor and human error.[12]

Amazon has taken a strategic move toward its own fulfillment services. Amazon's fulfillment services can be tailored to meet the individual needs of businesses. The process to utilize Amazon's fulfillment services is quite simple. First, companies create a business account with Amazon. Next, the company adds its product listings to the Amazon catalog. Then, the company needs to identify any special shipping supplies, such as poly bags, shrink wrap, bubble wrap, special labels, and tape, to ensure that its products are 'e-commerce' ready. Then, the company creates shipping plans to Amazon fulfillment centers. Shipping plans include the product, quantity, and shipping method. Once Amazon has received the products in its fulfillment center, it is able to mail the products to the customers who have placed online orders. Amazon uses an advanced, Web-to-warehouse, high-speed sorting system in its fulfillment centers. Business owners and customers both benefit from Amazon's tracking system throughout the fulfillment process. Amazon's customer service team supports business owners with managing customer inquiries, refunds, and returns too.[13]

E-Fulfillment

E-fulfillment refers to the integration of people, processes, and technology to ensure customer satisfaction before, during, and after the online buying experience.[14] Online retailers have what may be the unique ability to extend the interaction with their customers by creating a memorable and distinct fulfillment experience.

Unlike passive traditional media, interactive media put the consumer in control, with both positive and negative consequences. The positive include a great opportunity for building brand awareness and enhancing the relationship between customer and company. An example of e-fulfillment is Amazon.com with its entrance into the e-fulfillment market in 2008. Through its Fulfillment Web Service, merchants can store their own products with Amazon's fulfillment centers and then, using a simple Web service interface, fulfill orders for the products when needed.[15] This frees merchants from the fulfillment process, but provides them with control over the inventory of their products, creating practically a virtual business.[16]

The major problem with many e-commerce organizations is that they lack the needed focus and emphasis on e-fulfillment. According to Kuipers, e-commerce organizations treat fulfillment and customer service as incidental rather than fundamental. They're interested in technical capabilities—instant messages, e-mail, click-to-talk, and so on—and they don't realize that what they need most to satisfy the customer and keep the customer coming back is a polished customer fulfillment infrastructure.[17] However, that may be in part due to the fact that most organizations wanting to attract and obtain customer orders electronically don't have the fulfillment systems or infrastructures and don't want to be in the warehousing business. Therefore, these organizations normally outsource or hire third-party service bureaus to sort, pick, pack, and ship the product.

Supplier Direct Fulfillment

Producers are taking part in direct fulfillment services to accommodate the high demands of supply chain management for sellers. With e-commerce continuously growing, product pricing, availability, and speedy delivery are drivers for earning customers. Supplier direct fulfillment helps sellers quickly ship products, while cutting costs associated with inventory levels and postal expenses.[18] For example, Quad, which first began as an American printing company called Quad/Graphics, offers more than just printing services. The company now offers fulfillment services, while it continues to produce relevant content to strengthen brands. Thus, Quad serves direct marketers at both the 'front end' and the 'back end' of the direct marketing process, as discussed back in Chapter 1. Quad specializes in warehousing, distribution, kitting, and fulfillment solutions for prompt, streamline deliveries. Also, Quad offers sourcing and procurement services to discover affordable, quality goods.[19] In Europe, Quad's warehouse of 4,000 m² is currently holding more than 5000 items, with packages leaving a minimum of twice a day every working day.[20]

DELIVERY OPTIONS

Because the delivery of products is such a vital part of the fulfillment operations of direct marketers, we should look at the alternative delivery options that are available, especially those that provide individual delivery to households and businesses rather than those that handle bulk shipments.

Curbside pickup delivery is growing in popularity among individuals who do not have time to spare by roaming through the grocery store aisles and dodging around customers. Walmart,

Target, and Kroger are among the many retailers heavily investing in grocery pickup services. Studies show that more consumers prefer curbside pickup versus shopping in-store.[21] Millennials and Generation X are the most active cohorts participating in curbside pickup.[22] The service seamlessly integrates online and offline commerce.

One popular grocery delivery service is Instacart, a company that operates as a same-day grocery delivery and pick-up service in the U.S. and Canada. How does Instacart work? Instacart is a platform that presents you with a set of one or more retailer virtual storefronts from which you may select goods for picking, packing, and delivery by individual personal shoppers to your location or, if available, for you to pick up in-store.[23] After creating an Instacart account, you can order groceries via your personalized landing page on its website, www.instacart.com, or through the downloaded app. You can order from a variety of grocery stores in your area. You shop, select your delivery time window, such as between 7:00 and 8:00 p.m., and the groceries are delivered to your doorstep. Your personal shopper may contact you if a product is out of stock to inquire what you may want to order as a replacement. You may also set up replacements on the website or app in advance. Additionally, if you don't reply to your personal shopper's inquiry, she may automatically replace the out-of-stock item with a similar one. Instacart also stores frequently purchased items in your account, so reordering groceries is quick and easy. Talk about convenient! Instacart is well worth the nominal subscription fee it charges.

Figure 12.13 Instacart logo. Used with permission of Instacart and Maplebear, Inc.

Another grocery delivery service is Amazon's PrimeNow, through which Prime Members may order groceries from WholeFoods (which is an Amazon-owned store), or Amazon, and have them delivered for a small service fee. The number of companies offering grocery delivery services will continue to grow as more consumers will desire this highly convenient and time-saving delivery option in the future.

Food delivery services via mobile applications are growing in popularity as well. Uber Eats, an online food ordering and delivery platform, is available to countries all throughout the world.[24] Go back and refer to the Uber case at the end of Chapter 9 to learn more about Uber Eats. Other food delivery services similar to Uber Eats are Seamless, Grubhub, and DoorDash.

Direct marketers are concerned with product delivery, but also with the delivery of advertising and other promotion materials. Let's explore some delivery options that currently exist for the delivery of promotional materials.

U.S. Postal Service

The volume and scope of operations of the U.S. Postal Service (USPS) is mind-boggling. The USPS processed and delivered more than 154.2 billion pieces of mail in 2015.[25] Approximately 47 percent of the world's mail volume is handled by the U.S. Postal Service.[26]

First-Class Mail

This category includes business reply envelopes and cards. The postage rate is higher than for the other classes, but so is the cost of priority handling and individual sorting. This category of mail is the largest source of mail revenue for the USPS, although that percentage has been steadily shrinking over the past few decades. It generated 70 percent of USPS revenue in 1977, 35.3 percent in 1987, 54.1 percent in 2005, 50.7 percent in 2010, and 41.1 percent in 2015.[27]

Periodicals

The periodical category consists of publications. It includes magazines, newspapers, and miscellaneous periodicals, such as classroom publications. It accounted for 4.3 percent of total mail volume in 2005. This category of mail generated 3.6 percent of USPS revenue in 1977, 4.4 percent in 1987, 3.2 percent in 2005, 2.8 percent in 2010, and 2.3 percent in 2015.[28]

Standard Mail

Standard mail is the category mainly used for the distribution of direct-response advertising. Although postage rates are lower per piece, mailers of this class must ZIP code their mail, sort and bundle, tie, bag, and personally deliver the sacks of mail to the post office. Thus, the direct mailer performs up to half the basic tasks normally performed by the postal service for first-class mail. Delivery is also deferred. This class accounted for 25.5 percent in 2015 and 25.8 percent of total mail revenue in 2010, compared with 28.4 percent in 2005.[29] This class represents the second largest source of revenue for the USPS. Standard mail accounted for slightly more than 51.8 percent of mail volume in 2015, compared with 47.8 percent in 2005.[30]

Special Mail Services

There are certain alternatives for expedited mail service of special interest to direct marketers. These include services such as Express Mail, which is a guaranteed overnight service to designated destinations for items mailed prior to 5:00 p.m. In addition, the USPS continues to offer more online services (www.usps.com) such as Mailing Online, Card Store, Certified Mail, and Postecs. Using NetPost, for instance, you can send professionally printed letters, postcards, and booklets that have been created on a personal computer. NetPost also offers CardStore, an ideal way to customize your business or personal message.

Alternative Delivery Systems

Although the Private Express Statutes grant the USPS a form of monopoly over first-class mail delivery, they have been in transition and now make private delivery services possible under certain conditions. Alternatives to first-class mail, permitted under the Private Express Statutes provided they meet certain criteria, include FedEx® and major airlines. FedEx® provides more than 12 million worldwide shipments daily using a fleet of 643 aircrafts and more than 100,000 motorized vehicles across more than 220 countries and territories.[31]

Other alternatives for the delivery of information include telephone and the Internet, as well as additional emerging forms of electronic message transmission. Certain publications, including *Better Homes & Gardens* and *The Wall Street Journal*, have been experimenting with delivery alternatives for the periodical category of mail. These alternatives have been increasing, as have the number of private firms distributing direct mail advertising, including samples, in selected markets.

Alternative delivery systems are rapidly evolving. The future of delivery systems lies in the sky—drones (Figure 12.14). Many companies are using **delivery drones**, unmanned aerial vehicles (UAVs), to transport lightweight packages to customers in record time. The top drone delivery systems around the world consist of Google Wing and 7-Eleven in the U.S., Airbus in Singapore, Rakuten in Japan, Amazon in the U.K., Domino's in New Zealand, and DHL in Germany.[32] These companies around the world are taking the lead by setting new trends in the market. Delivery drones are revolutionizing delivery systems by eliminating delivery complications such as late delivery arrivals. Importantly, delivery drones fully accommodate to high customer demands.[33] For example, companies across the world are currently using drones to quickly dispense vaccines and other vital medications.[34]

Figure 12.14 Delivery drone image. Image courtesy of Mollyrose89. Accessed via wikicommons.

There are many other added benefits of delivery drones, too. When compared with traditional delivery vehicles, drones are a safer option since they don't encounter hazardous road conditions and they have greater route flexibility as they can avoid congested areas. While more and more companies are jumping aboard with this cutting-edge delivery system, there are a few limitations to delivery drones to keep in mind. Currently, drones are able to transport lightweight packages, but not heavier or larger items. The limited battery capacity of drones reduces the duration of flight times. Also, unpredictable events in the environment may have the ability to negatively impact the reliability of delivery drones.[35] As delivery drones are becoming commonplace, direct marketers will likely find ways to combat these limitations in the future.

FULFILLMENT PROBLEMS

Everybody makes mistakes—and fulfillment centers are no exception. The crucial point for the direct marketer is becoming aware of the mistake and fixing it promptly—making it right for the customer so that the final impression is a positive one. Keep in mind that the fulfillment experience often determines whether the customer will respond to the next sales offer.

What are some common sources of fulfillment problems and how can direct marketers attempt to avoid these mistakes? Let's examine these two important issues.

Sources of Fulfillment Problems

Many of the most common fulfillment problems originate in the warehouse. These problems can occur in many ways. Let's look at some of the potential sources of fulfillment problems:

- Order accuracy: delivering the wrong product to the customer is a costly mistake. It may result in losing the customer's future business as the customer has lost a certain degree of confidence in the direct marketer.
- Package presentation: packaging is an extension of the company's image, and sloppy packaging communicates a poor image. Small details like the correct position of the label on the mailing carton and the neatness of the outer carton seal are important. Even more important is the product placement within the package—making sure that the product is upright or positioned the best way to ensure it reaches the customer in good condition.
- Speed of delivery: in today's electronic age, customers demand faster delivery than ever before. However, accuracy cannot be sacrificed for speed. Therefore, the fulfillment challenge is to process and fill orders as efficiently as possible.
- Stock availability: delivering what you offer is the ultimate role of fulfillment. Maintaining an accurate inventory system and an adequate amount of inventory is crucial to fulfillment success. Back orders commonly result not only in the loss of a sale, but also in the loss of a customer.
- Return processing: it would be wonderful if every product a customer ordered was received and kept. The fact is that many products get returned for many different reasons and direct marketers must process these returns in a timely and professional manner.

Other common fulfillment problems come from areas outside the warehouse and are commonly related to customer database files. Included in this category of fulfillment mistakes are not thanking the customer for the order, sending the customer an invoice after payment has already been sent, misspelling the customer's name, and using the incorrect prefix (for example, using Mr. or Ms. instead of Dr.). Mistakes like these can make the customer skeptical and could result in the loss of future business.

Ways to Avoid Fulfillment Problems

Fortunately, direct marketers can take simple steps to avoid fulfillment problems and actually assist the organization in exceeding consumer expectations. Although many of these may seem like commonsense marketing, not all direct marketers exercise these steps. The ways to avoid fulfillment problems include the following:

- Pay careful attention to the packing slips and picking lists to ensure that orders get filled accurately and expediently.
- Include a toll-free number for customer service in a prominent place on the catalog, direct-mail piece, Internet site, or packing slip with the order. If your toll-free phone line is too expensive because too many calls are coming in, then maybe you've got too many service problems. So fix them.[36] However, you should encourage your customers to call you even if the problem is small.
- Hire a professional, well-trained customer service staff. If your customers are important to you, make sure their interaction with your organization is a positive experience. Nothing is more frustrating for a consumer than dealing with an inept customer service representative. The more positive you can make the customer experience, the greater the probability the customer will return and purchase from your organization again. Smart direct marketers ensure repeat business by establishing customer service standards and monitoring customer service representatives (often via tape-recorded phone calls) to measure and control the service level.
- Establish quality control measures for each phase of the fulfillment process. From order receiving to warehousing, from order processing to shipping and delivery, from picking and packing to handling customer complaints, each part of the fulfillment process is important and you should establish and monitor quality control standards that focus on the customer. Service levels are shaped by the needs of the target audience, the desired image of the company, and management's ability to define and implement the necessary programs and systems in the operation.[37] Setting up these quality control standards, communicating them to all employees, and monitoring their performance and ultimate effect on customer satisfaction combine for a proactive approach to delivering quality service and to avoiding fulfillment problems before they begin.

CALL CENTERS

A **call center** is a dedicated team supported by various telephone technological resources to provide responses to customer inquiries.[38] Some marketers think of call centers as the 'telephonic front door' to the company or the main access point for obtaining information or placing an order. In essence, the call center is the formal entity of an organization, or representing an organization, that handles communication with any type of stakeholder. Regardless of whether a customer is placing an order, calling to check on the status of an order, inquiring about new products or services, seeking technical support, or placing a complaint, the call center should provide a seamless communication process and quality service.

In addition to receiving phone orders, the call center provides answers for customers who call with questions or problems they may have concerning a product or an order. For example, Pittsburgh-based PNC Bank has devised a customer rating program that automatically activates when customers contact its National Financial Services Center. It uses software that requires customers to enter their PIN or Social Security number. The bank determines the customer's identity, analyzes that person's past transactions with the bank, and places the customer into one of several preset segments. Callers with basic transactions are transferred to an entry-level representative. Callers with complex financial histories are given to handlers with a specific expertise. A 'most valuable customer' is routed to a relationship consultant—one of 30 or 40 service representatives deemed the bank's very best.[39]

Call centers can operate: (1) within the company or in-house; (2) outside the company, when calls are made or taken by a teleservice outsourcing firm; or (3) a combination of both. Each type of call center organization has similar functions, yet all have unique features and challenges. The decision about how to carry out telemarketing activities is, ultimately, a function of the company's financial situation and the nature of its telemarketing program. A major factor in determining whether to establish the call center in-house or outsource it is the expected pattern of calls. When customer orders are expected to come into the company all at once (or within a relatively short time interval), it becomes difficult to staff the call center to receive and process each order on a timely basis. This is when outsourcing begins to look attractive because nothing is worse than putting your customers 'on hold.' Only outsourcers with thousands of positions can handle such call volume effectively. According to Peppers and Rogers, 'Customers today are accustomed to having their needs met immediately, completely, conveniently, and inexpensively.'[40]

Organizations measure the level of customer dissatisfaction by calculating the rate of **call abandonment**, the number of callers who hang up before being served by a sales representative. Companies strive to keep this rate as low as possible. However, during peak calling times, consumers may abandon a higher percentage of the calls. To reduce customer frustration, many companies route incoming calls through interactive voice-response equipment to capture preliminary information and balance the workload among teleservice agents. Nonetheless, even one missed call can lead to the loss of a sale and, more importantly, the loss of a customer. At these times, outside service centers should handle customer orders. Let's examine both in-house and outsourced call centers.

In-House Call Center

In-house call centers require substantial investment in facilities and equipment. Direct marketers can place outbound calls or receive inbound calls from the same call center due to advances in telephone and computer technology. The process of setting up an in-house call center and managing an ongoing program entails many activities. These include (but are not limited to) obtaining support from top management, setting goals and objectives, developing scripts and guides, recruiting and training personnel, designing a productive work environment, developing measurement systems, testing systems and procedures, and reporting and controlling the operation. Personnel issues constitute a sizable portion of this process—from obtaining the support of top management to reporting and controlling the operation.

The biggest advantage of establishing an in-house call center is the degree of control the company has over its telemarketing operations. The biggest disadvantages of an in-house call center are the time it takes to properly train representatives and the large financial burden. Many in-house call centers, especially those B2C organizations that offer seasonal products, rely on a large number of seasonal, part-time, or flex-time employees.

Outside/Outsourced Call Centers

Outsourcing formally refers to the process of having all call center activities handled by an outside organization or a teleservice outsourcer. The primary advantage of outsourcing for the marketer is a reduction in expenses and capital outlays. Most call center outsourcers are larger than in-house call centers and can more easily accommodate a large volume of seasonal orders. And because of their size, they offer lower costs and provide better formal training for telephone operators than in-house call centers. In addition, most call center outsourcers tend to use the most advanced technology available to stay efficient.

There are five main advantages to using an outside service bureau to conduct a company's telemarketing program:

1. Low initial investment: marketers pay for the telemarketing program on a short-term basis only.
2. Elimination of hiring needs: marketers eliminate the day-to-day managerial tasks associated with hiring employees.
3. Fixed operating costs: with a defined rate schedule provided by the call center outsourcer.
4. Quick start-up: shorter lead times for implementing the telemarketing program.
5. Time flexibility: 24-hour, 7-days-a-week service for inbound calling and, as required by the FTC, restricted hours for outbound calling.

There are also disadvantages associated with call center outsourcers:[41]

1. Lack of direct control: the company does not have the same degree of control over an external organization.
2. Lack of direct security: because of the remote location of the call center outsourcer, the company cannot keep its customer information in its exclusive possession. However, most call center outsourcers take great security measures.
3. Lack of employee loyalty: employees possess greater loyalty to the call center outsourcer than to the company that they are representing on the telephone.
4. Mass-market approach: service bureaus are high-volume businesses, thus the quality of the sales pitch for any single company could suffer.
5. Caliber of personnel: often call center outsourcers pay less than in-house call centers, thus the quality of personnel is affected.

Regardless of the aforementioned disadvantages, many telemarketing companies successfully outsource their call center activities to service bureaus. In fact, many outsource their call center operations to call centers in international locations, as the geographic location has an impact on its operating costs.

THE IMPORTANCE OF CUSTOMER SERVICE

Each customer wants to be satisfied. **Customer satisfaction** has been defined as the extent to which a firm fulfills a consumer's needs, desires, and expectations.[42] Contrary to what many believe, the customer doesn't care about what has to happen behind the scenes to get the product or service delivered on time. The customer is primarily interested in what the marketer can do to satisfy their needs.

Direct marketers know that simply providing a quality product or service is not enough. So they have begun to create strategies designed to move goods from factories and warehouses directly to the customer in the shortest possible time and at the lowest possible cost, using the level of service to differentiate their organization from others. For example, Zappos moved its state-of-the-art fulfillment operations from California to the central location of Kentucky, in order to provide more timely shipping of orders to its customers across the United States. As a result, the shipping time required to send products from California to the East Coast was reduced from a week to only two days.

Customer service also enables the organization to exceed rather than simply meet the customer's expectations. Delivering high-quality customer service can enable the direct marketer to develop a long-term relationship with each customer, which is, after all, the ultimate goal of direct marketing. In essence, the task of customer relationship management (CRM), as discussed earlier in Chapter 2, is a big-picture approach that integrates sales, order fulfillment, call center operations, and customer service, and coordinates and unifies all points of interaction with the customer, throughout the customer life cycle and across multiple channels.

In addition, direct marketers use social media to provide customer service. Approximately 67% of consumers use social media platforms as a direct approach for support from businesses.[43] For example, Starbucks, Nike, and Spotify are three companies that use social media to engage on a personal level with consumers. Social media interaction works to establish brand loyalty and commitment. When a brand engages publicly and promptly, it establishes brand credibility. A study shows that approximately 25% of social media users expect responses within one hour and 6% expect a response within 10 minutes.[44] Timeliness is key to delivering premium customer service.

Business doesn't end when an order is received. In fact, most direct marketers believe that is when it begins. Let's take a look at the customer service strategies that direct marketers implement before and after a customer places an order.

ZAPPOS: AN ONLINE CUSTOMER SERVICE EXPERIENCE

When it comes to serving customers, Zappos.com is in a class all by itself. There may not be another company on our planet that is more consumer- and employee-oriented than Zappos. Given the opportunity, Zappos won't just meet your expectations, it will far exceed them. Zappos will delight you!

Zappos has a 'people-centered' culture bursting with employees who are motivated to serve each customer with complete attention to detail. New employees are given a Zappos culture book that describes the ethos of the company with short essays written by current employees. The company employs a life coach, maintains an on-site library to encourage employees to read books, and regularly offers its employees $2,000 to quit, just to make sure that Zappos employees are working for more than just a paycheck.

Zappos's associates are available and compassionate. They strive to make magic happen for their customers and want their customers to know that Zappos is 'only a wave of a wand away and is very willing to assist in every possible way.' To live up to that goal, Zappos regularly connects with its customers via numerous social media formats such as Facebook, Twitter, blogs, and its own YouTube channel. Customer testimonials linked to the Zappos home page prove that its associates have gone the extra mile to serve its customers. For example, one Zappos's customer service representative helped a caller locate a nearby pizza place that would deliver after midnight, while another rep helped a customer locate a pair of boots seen in a movie. That's 'WOW' customer service!

So, what does a customer experience when shopping online with Zappos?

Imagine you are sitting at your computer in the comfort of your own home. You have just connected to the Zappos home page (www.zappos.com), seen in Figure 12.15. Stop there for a moment. How did you get to this point? This is also a part of customer service—because serving the customer begins with researching and analyzing the customer's needs and wants. A great deal of business planning, consumer research, and historical sales analysis have gone into determining which products are offered to customers and how the items are displayed on the Web pages. In addition, great care has been put forth to organize and design the website so that you, the customer, can easily navigate and shop from it. Zappos strives to make the site easier for you to use by not having to enter information more than once. Zappos uses the customer information that you enter to help the company help you quickly find information, products, and services; create content that is most relevant to you; and alert you to new information, products, and services that might be of interest to you. The company also offers a 'How Do You Like Our Website?' feedback link to gather information that can be used to better serve you in the future.

Once you make a product selection, the website may offer additional, related products or services. This is an example of up-selling, cross-selling, and suggestive selling. Any of these suggested items may be added to your shopping cart with a simple click. Then the website visually displays your updated shopping cart. This point provides another cross-selling opportunity, with an offer to purchase some inexpensive unrelated items. Think of this as offering impulse items—similar to those that are located near the checkout counters in traditional retail stores.

Once you make your final selections, you proceed to a checkout stage where the website totals the order, adds shipping and handling fees, and verifies personalization (if applicable). The shipping and billing addresses are determined, as is the method of payment. Most direct marketers offer several payment methods to enable each customer to select their preferred method. Next, Zappos sends you an order confirmation. This is an opportunity for the company to thank the customer and to provide the order number in case the customer has an inquiry about that particular order. It also enables Zappos's customers to sign up for its weekly newsletter.

What happens next? Within a day or two, Zappos may send you an e-mail providing details about the status of your online order. This is an additional opportunity for the direct marketer to thank you for your order and to provide an update. In addition, it allows the company to remind you about its customer service priority and how its products carry a 100 percent money-back guarantee. In sum, it enables the direct marketer to strengthen the relationship it has with the customer.

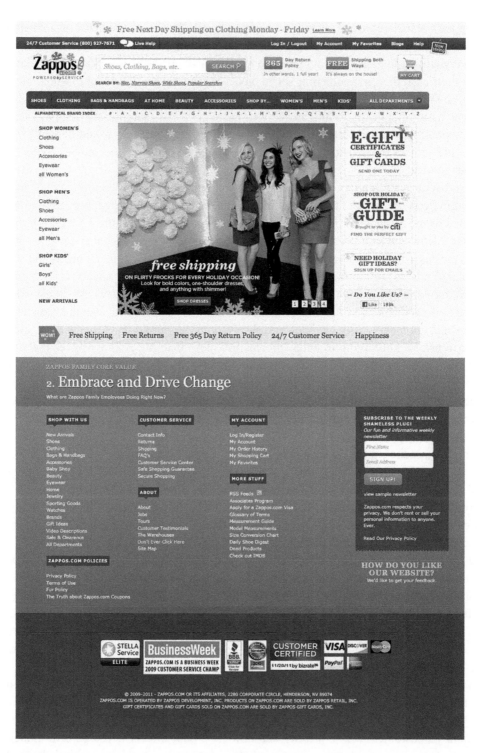

Figure 12.15 Zappos.com home page. Used with permission of 2012 Zappos.com©, Inc and its affiliates.

Zappos enters the information collected about you and your transaction data into its customer database. The company will use this information to target future direct response communications to you and better serve you in the future. From this point on, the direct marketer will communicate with you on a regular basis. Each time Zappos contacts you via some direct-response media (e.g., an outbound e-mail, phone call, or catalog), the contact and response (if applicable) will help further the customer relationship.

Although we've used an online example here, all customer service activities are similar, whether online, through a catalog, or via a telephone contact. The main purpose of all back-end functions is to serve the customer more effectively. When carried out well, such back-end functions can strengthen customer relationships and encourage customers to continue to purchase from the organization.

Beyond waiting for the customer to repeat purchase, how do direct marketers determine the strength of their relationship with the customer? How does a direct marketer assess the level of service the customer is receiving from their organization? How will direct marketers determine whether their relationship with each customer can be improved? How can they know what is best for the customer? The next section details how direct marketers can evaluate customer satisfaction levels.

Evaluating Customer Satisfaction Level

Direct marketers can evaluate the level of customer satisfaction in a number of ways. First, they might begin by pretending they are the customer. Every organization likes to think they are doing a good job of serving their customers. But savvy direct marketers investigate this from both sides of the relationship. Are inquiries processed in a timely manner? Are customer complaints addressed as quickly and as professionally as they should be? Is delivery time as expedient as you promised the customer it would be? Direct marketers determine the answers to these questions in two ways:

1. Place an inquiry, order, or a complaint with the organization under a fictitious name and experience first hand the level of customer service your organization really delivers.
2. Send periodic follow-up surveys consisting of only a few questions designed to address a customer's fulfillment experience. Questions might address the speed, accuracy, and degree of staff friendliness the customer experienced when interacting with the organization. An example of a brief customer survey designed for assessing the fulfillment experience is shown in Figure 12.16.

Regardless of how you obtain this information, it is critical to perceive the fulfillment experience from the customer's point of view. This experience and any subsequent action you take should lead to an improved relationship with the customer.

A strong focus on CRM is crucial to the success and profitability of every direct marketing organization. Many professionals believe that it may be necessary to make CRM part of the broader concept of customer management, because the whole organization must support and participate in customer relationship maintenance. These words from Robert McKim, CEO of MS

Please tell us how we rated:	Excellent	Good	Fair	Poor
Knowledgeable phone operators	❏	❏	❏	❏
Promptness of delivery	❏	❏	❏	❏
Overall impression of service	❏	❏	❏	❏
Other comments:	_____			

Figure 12.16 Sample customer survey

Database Marketing, sum up the value of customer relationship marketing:

> Gone are the days of empty 'customer is king' lip service. The key to the new rules of success is the ability to address each customer's idiosyncrasies and needs, balanced with their current and future value to the company. Firms that do this can differentiate themselves from the competition, forge long-term customer relationships, engender customer loyalty, stop attrition and enjoy success in the 21st century.[45]

The next section provides suggestions and examples of how to keep customers happy.

Keeping Customers Happy

At the foundation of customer service is the simple notion of *keeping the customer happy*. Only a satisfied customer is a happy customer. Only a satisfied customer will come back and purchase from your organization again and again. However, keeping customers happy does not happen by accident. Direct marketers need to constantly keep abreast of the customer's changing needs and wants and must always strive to satisfy these. Some classic suggestions for keeping customers happy are shown here:

- Remember that the customer is always right.
- Don't promise something you cannot deliver.
- Inform your customers about how to return products.
- Inform your customers about how to complain.
- Test your own service.
- Date and record all customer correspondence.
- Investigate your competitors' offerings on a regular basis.
- Exercise care in billing and collection.[46]

Many companies go out of their way to exceed customer expectations and delight the customer. Let's look at an example of great customer service. One holiday season, a customer ordered two 'Towers of Treats' from the Harry and David Specialty Foods and Gifts catalog to have delivered to two neighbors. The customer had placed the order in time to have the packages arrive a day or two prior to seeing the neighbors at a dinner party. The packages didn't arrive before the date of the dinner, nor did they arrive before the holiday. When the customer found this out, she phoned the company. The customer service department was very professional and apologetic and offered to resend the ordered items that had not arrived. Within a week, the packages were received by each of the neighbors and the customer received a note of thanks both for her order and her patience, another apology for the inconvenience, and a free gift. Mistakes happen, but how they are handled can either contribute to a positive customer experience or reinforce a negative one.

Good customer service is an important part of fulfilling the customer's expectations.

SUMMARY

Fulfillment encompasses all the activities a company has with a customer after the initial order has been placed. It can also be defined as the final impression left with the customer. In the fulfillment process, there is a chance for additional communication with a customer, including making available promotional materials and/or new catalogs included in the shipment of an order. Being attentive to detail in the fulfillment process should generate satisfied customers and future business for the organization. Customer service and fulfillment activities are vital to the success of any direct marketing organization. They may not be glamorous, but they are the guts of direct marketing. There are six steps in the fulfillment process—(1) offer, (2) response, (3) processing, (4) shipping, (5) billing, and (6) customer service. Direct marketers may select from various fulfillment options, including in-house fulfillment, outside fulfillment centers, and online fulfillment, to serve its customers. In addition, direct marketers must select from the various delivery options available for shipping products to consumers. These delivery options include multichannel distribution, USPS, and alternative delivery systems.

Direct marketers should recognize the most common fulfillment problems along with ways to avoid these problems.

Another key aspect of fulfillment involves call center operations. Call centers can operate within the company, outside the company, or a combination of both. Regardless of where the call center is located, qualified personnel are the key to effectively serving the customer.

The importance of customer service begins with an understanding of customer satisfaction and CRM. Direct marketers follow a step-by-step process to ensure customer relationships are managed properly. Direct marketers use personal experience and surveys to determine whether the organization is providing good customer service and keeping customers happy. Good customer service, correct order entry, and prompt order delivery generate satisfied customers and repeat buyers.

KEY TERMS

call abandonment	fulfillment
call center	integrated order fulfillment
customer relationship management (CRM)	offer
	outsourcing
customer satisfaction	packing slip
delivery drones	picking list
e-fulfillment	virtual enterprise

REVIEW QUESTIONS

1. List and describe the six steps of the fulfillment process.
2. Discuss some common fulfillment problems along with actions direct marketers may take to avoid future fulfillment problems. Why don't all direct marketers exercise these preventive measures?
3. What are some of the ways a firm can keep their customers happy? Describe from your own personal experience the actions direct marketers have taken to keep you happy.
4. Describe the relationship between fulfillment and customer service.
5. Describe how the traditional fulfillment model is changing.
6. Compare the advantages and disadvantages between in-house fulfillment and outside fulfillment services. Name some companies that are using the different types of fulfillment services.
7. List and explain the eight steps of the integrated order fulfillment concept.
8. What is the function of a call center? How does it fit within the fulfillment process?
9. Explain some of the primary challenges associated with operating a call center.
10. Describe the ways a company can interact with its customers to strengthen those relationships and maximize customer satisfaction.

EXERCISE

You are an employee of a small clothing boutique that also distributes a catalog. You work in the fulfillment department. Currently, the company uses in-house fulfillment, but you learn that your boss is considering using an outside fulfillment service to meet demand, in part because it may be less expensive. Business has grown rapidly since the company has gone online and is now receiving online orders. Voice your opinion on the matter of outside fulfillment. Should the company keep fulfilling orders in-house or should they use an outside fulfillment source? What about the call center functions–should those also be outsourced? What variables would impact your decision? Be sure to give specific reasons to support your position on the matter.

CRITICAL THINKING EXERCISE

Visit www.zappos.com and any other online retailer and examine how each company addresses customer issues and concerns. Compare and contrast. What strategies and tactics are being effectively employed? Explain. What might each company do to enhance its customer service?

READINGS AND RESOURCES

- Quad: www.quadgraphics.eu/capabilities/direct-marketing/fulfilment#
- Customer service: https://sproutsocial.com/insights/how-to-improve-customer-service
- Alternate delivery service: www.nielsen.com/us/en/insights/news/2017/the-digital-growth-opportunity-in-curbside-pick-up-click-collect-subscription-services.html
- Fulfillment process: https://visual.ly/community/infographic/economy/amazon-fulfillment-process
- Drones: http://dronesonvideo.com/drone-delivery-around-world
- Drones: www.fehrandpeers.com/drone-delivery

CASE: 1-800-FLOWERS.COM

This case provides real stories of how 1-800-FLOWERS.COM has made its customers the top priority and how it has been able to motivate its employees to embrace this customer orientation. The roles of changing technology and changing consumer needs have led the company to become a successful multichannel direct marketer. This case illustrates the important role that high-quality customer service and employee motivation play in building a successful enterprise. Jim McCann, CEO of 1-800-FLOWERS.COM, demonstrates how his company combines recognition of people with technology to build a highly profitable direct marketing business.

The original 1-800-FLOWERS was started by a group of successful businessmen from Dallas, Texas. The founders spent $30 million during their first year of business and built the world's largest telemarketing center. This call center consisted of million-dollar telephone switches, state-of-the-art computer systems, 700 workstations, and a detailed bridge command center to oversee the entire operation. The operation was housed in 55,000 square feet of office space. A network of 6,800 'fulfilling florists' were paid on a commission basis to create, package, and deliver the orders received by the 1-800-FLOWERS telecommunications call center.

Sounds great? You bet! Was it profitable? No way! With that kind of killer overhead and nobody with a burning desire to manage the business on a daily basis, the company lost money right from the start. What was missing in the business start-up was a focus on the customer. The original owners failed to establish relationships with their customers.

One day, in walks Jim McCann, then owner of Flora Plenty, a successful 14-store retail chain of florists in New York. Flora Plenty was doing extensive telemarketing for its retail chain, plus it was one of the fulfilling florists for 1-800-FLOWERS. McCann had a passion for serving the customer, and he sincerely believed in the 1-800-FLOWERS concept. He thought the company could be highly successful if managed properly. Thus, on November 6, 1984, after a few years of negotiation, McCann bought 1-800-FLOWERS for $7 million, and managed it first as a partnership, then later as a sole proprietorship. The acquisition gave McCann the right to use the 1-800-FLOWERS phone number but left him buried in debt and scrambling to create a makeshift operation for the new company with very little overhead. In the beginning, McCann himself went back to answering the phone: 'Thank you for calling 1-800-FLOWERS. How can we help you today?'

McCann knew the three big challenges that were ahead for this troubled business:

1. At that time, toll-free numbers were still new to most consumers, and it was going to take time to build consumer confidence in purchasing via toll-free technology.
2. Most consumers were not aware of 1-800-FLOWERS, yet often had a need to purchase flowers. Thus, brand awareness would need to be developed such that consumers thought about 1-800-FLOWERS whenever they had the urge to buy flowers.
3. Most importantly, there was the challenge of building relationships with customers– one at a time–to gain their loyalty for a lifetime. McCann realized that if he was going to make a business out of something impersonal like buying flowers over the telephone, he would have to create a personal relationship with every caller. The sale would be almost secondary.

When McCann first bought the business, it was a lousy deal: several million dollars of debt and a telephone number with a not very good track record. One of the keys in turning 1-800-FLOWERS into a success story in the world of telemarketing has been getting people to want to buy flowers over the phone for someone they really care about. In 1992, as 1-800-FLOWERS entered online commerce (www.1800flowers.com), the company had to give people a reason to want to be in its virtual store (see Figure 12.17).

The company added personal contact and entertainment to the value equation to make people want to visit its site. McCann credits the fact that 1-800-FLOWERS was named the single most successful business operation on the Web in 1996 to the lessons he learned ten years earlier in telemarketing. He believes the Internet fulfills the same functions as any other retail system, so the jump from telemarketing to modern marketing was a natural one for 1-800-FLOWERS. On the Internet, as with telemarketing, a company must have strong infrastructure to keep track of inventory, process orders, secure billing, and deliver the product. Above all, the business must focus on people.

Today, the company is called 1-800-FLOWERS.COM and people are still its top priority. Training and motivating customer service representatives to provide top-notch customer service are critical to ensuring long-term customer relationships. How does 1-800-FLOWERS. COM motivate its customer service representatives? Here are a few examples:

- It is not uncommon for managers to place smiley face stickers on a customer service representative's computer whenever the customer service representative has been seen smiling while on the phone with a customer. Customers can tell a smiling, happy person over the phone, and it makes the customer experience more enjoyable. Thus, the customer service representative is rewarded simply for smiling.
- Like many companies, 1-800-FLOWERS.COM monitors customer service representatives' phone calls. However, the primary reason for the monitoring is to reveal strengths to be shared with others. This ensures the quality control of customer service representatives and provides clues on how to sharpen the script and improve customer service.
- Public praise of the customer service representative is also common at 1-800-FLOWERS.COM. In fact, the company purchased a refrigerator door and mounted it on the wall at the entrance to the customer service area. Whenever a customer service representative was found doing something noteworthy, the manager wrote it up and stuck it to the door with a magnet.

Figure 12.17 1-800-FLOWERS.COM website. Used with permission of 1-800-FLOWERS.COM®.

- There is a *Legends* book at 1-800-FLOWERS.COM. This book is filled with stories of associates going the extra mile to please a customer. This book is given to new customer service representatives as a part of their training–it provides the rules for working in customer service. The new employees are told that if what they are doing to serve a customer is not worthy of being included in the *Legends* book, then they are probably not doing enough.

In summary, old-fashioned rules have been the guiding light to McCann in building 1-800-FLOWERS.COM into a successful business. McCann believes in putting a premium

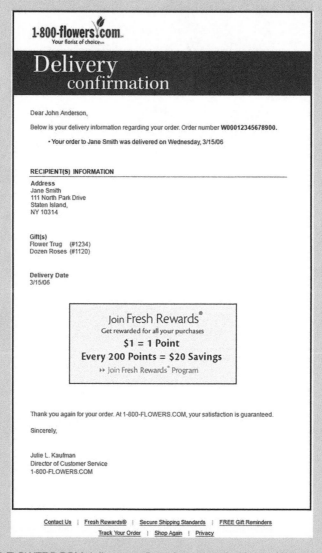

Figure 12.18 1-800-FLOWERS.COM delivery confirmation example. Used with permission of 1-800-FLOWERS.COM®.

on people and making an emotional contact–by planting emotional seeds that will yield sales and build customer relationships far in excess of a simple sale. The company tries to please each and every customer. If a customer isn't happy, company policy is to 'find out what it will take to make the unsatisfied customer happy, then do it.' The 1-800-FLOWERS. COM '100% SMILE Guarantee™' policy is unique to the floral industry:

If at any time, you are not satisfied with the product you ordered, we will replace it. Or refund your money. Or do whatever it takes to ensure that you, the customer, are happy and will continue to be a customer of ours in the future, as we are here to help you deliver a smile.

Technology also plays a key role in the success of 1-800-FLOWERS.COM. The company uses technology to:

- process orders more quickly
- confirm product delivery more accurately
- remind customers of birthdays and anniversaries more faithfully
- free employees to devote themselves to creating customer relationships.

Figure 12.18 shows an example of how 1-800-FLOWERS.COM communicates with its customers. Once a customer places an order, she instantly receives an order confirmation and thank-you e-mail. Follow-up e-mails are sent to update that customer on the status of her order and ultimately confirm delivery.

(Continued)

Figure 12.19 (Continued)

Figure 12.19 1-800-FLOWERS.COM outbound e-mail offers. Used with permission of 1-800-FLOWERS. COM®.

In addition, 1-800-FLOWERS.COM sends out regular e-mail offers to its customers, featuring weekly specials or holiday reminders. Figure 12.19 presents examples of these special offers. Notice how the company effectively promotes its free reminder service.

As McCann puts it, 'Computers aren't friendly, people are.' Technology is very effective at improving a business, but too much technology can depersonalize a business–which is a bad thing. Over the years, 1-800-FLOWERS.COM has investigated new telephone technology and has experienced both positive and negative outcomes. Technology allowed the company to adjust the length of the phone ring. During the busiest times (Mother's Day, Valentine's Day, and Christmas), customer service representatives had the alternatives of putting people on hold with canned music or letting the phone ring. Since it was already established that people like to have their telephone call answered by the third ring, 1-800-FLOWERS.COM simply extended each ring from 6 seconds to 9 seconds. The

(Continued)

Figure 12.20 (Continued)

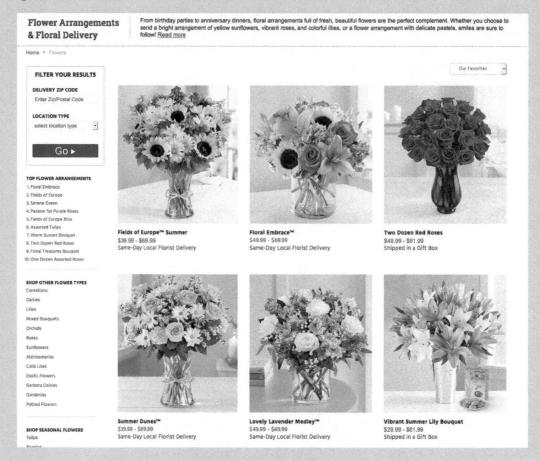

Figure 12.20 1-800-FLOWERS.COM catalogs. Used with permission of 1-800-FLOWERS.COM®.

company found that there was no perception of a longer wait, so with the same number of rings, it was able to serve customers during peak seasons without turning them off with too many rings or too much 'elevator music.' This same technology enabled the company to pick up the phone before the caller even heard a ring–but callers thought it was downright creepy, as if the company knew what the customer was doing before they did it. Therefore, although technology would allow the company to eliminate phone rings, 1-800-FLOWERS. COM chose to stay with the old-fashioned ring cycle because people felt comfortable with it.

What began as a simple, toll-free number is now a well-established brand. 1-800-FLOWERS.COM has blossomed into a successful direct marketer with a database of loyal customers and a nationwide network of BloomNet florists who have been handpicked to fulfill their orders. The company has become a multichannel direct marketer. It now sells its products via phone, Internet, on-site retail stores, and even catalogs. Figure 12.20 shows both a print and an online catalog of 1-800-FLOWERS.COM.

The 1-800-FLOWERS.COM call center, once a bunch of crates and boards and telephones down in the basement of a Queens, New York, floral shop, now has the capability to handle millions of calls and Internet orders per week. With unparalleled attention to customers, motivated employees, and modern technology, 1-800-FLOWERS.COM, the world's largest florist, is poised to continue its direct marketing success story well into the future.

In conclusion, according to McCann, 'Today 740,000 people are celebrating their birthdays, tomorrow another 740,000 will be celebrating theirs. If you'd like to make one or two of them feel terrific on their special day ... I know a 1-800 number you can call!' Of course, if you prefer, you may place your order by visiting its website instead at 1-800-FLOWERS.COM.[47]

Case Discussion Questions

1. Discuss how 1-800-FLOWERS.COM became a direct marketing success story. What were the main ingredients in its success?
2. Why did 1-800-FLOWERS.COM become a multichannel direct marketer, instead of specializing solely in telemarketing? How should the company use these channels to support one another?
3. What role did technology play in assisting the company in achieving its goals? Has improved technology always led to success for 1-800-FLOWERS.com? Support your answer with specific details and examples.

NOTES

1. Robert D. Downey, 'Proper Fulfillment—Image with the Proper Stuff,' *Direct Marketing* (July 1985), p. 28.
2. Jack Schmid, 'How the Back End Drives the Bottom Line,' *Target Marketing* 13, no. 5 (May 1990).
3. F. Curtis Barry & Company, Benchmarking Fulfillment ShareGroups, 2007, www.fcbco.com/articles-whitepapers/trends-in-fulfillment.asp, retrieved May 5, 2011.
4. Lillian Vernon (1996) *An Eye for Winners* (New York: HarperCollins).
5. Sidney Hill, 'Integrated Order Fulfillment for the Virtual Enterprise,' dmnews.com, February 1998, www.manufacturingsystems.com, retrieved May 10, 2000.
6. Ibid., p. 3A.
7. Susan Reda, 'Customer Service, Brand Management Seen as Key Aspects of On-Line Fulfillment,' *Stores* (October 2000), p. 44.
8. Hill, 'Integrated Order Fulfillment for the Virtual Enterprise.'
9. www.bizjournals.com/pittsburgh/stories/2008/08/25/daily9.html, retrieved April 7, 2017.
10. Jonathan Boorstein, 'Customer Service: Fulfillment 101,' *Direct*, May 2, 2000, www.directmag.com/Content/monthly/200/2000050119.htm, retrieved May 2000.
11. www.aimglobal.org/technologies/RFID/what_is_rfid.asp, retrieved May 12, 2011.

12. http://ezine.motorola.com/ezine/enterprise?title=Indiana+Jones+and+the+Automated+%0AWare-house&a=554, retrieved May 12, 2011.

13. https://services.amazon.com/fulfillment-by-amazon/how-it-works.htm/ref=asus_fba_snav_how, retrieved May 12, 2019.

14. Reda, 'Customer Service, Brand Management,' pp. 40–44.

15. www.informationweek.com/news/206905010, retrieved May 12, 2011.

16. http://aws.amazon.com/fws, retrieved May 12, 2011.

17. Boorstein, 'Customer Service: Fulfillment 101.'

18. www.retailitinsights.com/doc/supplier-direct-fulfillment-accelerating-e-co-0001, retrieved May 12, 2019.

19. www.quad.com, retrieved May 12, 2019.

20. www.quadgraphics.eu/capabilities/direct-marketing/fulfilment#, retrieved May 12, 2019.

21. www.produceretailer.com/article/news-article/walmart-snagging-these-shoppers-grocery-pickup, retrieved May 12, 2019.

22. www.forbes.com/sites/pamdanziger/2019/04/07/walmart-is-in-the-lead-in-the-soon-to-be-35-billion-curbside-pickup-market/#237792dd199e, retrieved May 13, 2019.

23. Instacart, www.instacart.com/terms, retrieved May 18, 2019.

24. https://about.ubereats.com, retrieved May 13, 2019.

25. https://about.usps.com/who-we-are/postal-facts/size-scope.htm, retrieved July 28, 2016.

26. Ibid.

27. Ibid.

28. Ibid.

29. Ibid.

30. Ibid.

31. http://about.van.fedex.com/our-story/company-structure/corporate-fact-sheet, retrieved July 29, 2016.

32. http://dronesonvideo.com/drone-delivery-around-world, retrieved May 30, 2019.

33. www.fehrandpeers.com/drone-delivery, retrieved May 30, 2019.

34. www.nytimes.com/2019/03/19/technology/drone-deliveries-faa-pilot-programs.html, retrieved May 13, 2019.

35. www.fehrandpeers.com/drone-delivery, retrieved May 30, 2019.

36. John M. Chilson, 'The Top 10 Fulfillment Mistakes,' *Folio: Magazine for Magazine Management*, 27, no. 7 (May 1998), pp. 61–62.

37. Jeffrey A. Coopersmith, 'Customer Service: The Final Link,' *Catalog Age*, 5, no. 7 (July 1988), p. 76.

38. Bobette M. Gustafson, 'A Well-Staffed PFS Call Center Can Improve Patient Satisfaction,' *Healthcare Financial Management*, 53, no. 7 (July 1999), p. 64.

39. *Sales & Marketing Management*, 151, no. 9 (September 1999), p. 26.

40. Ibid.

41. Ibid., pp. 39–40.

42. William D. Perreault Jr. and E. Jerome McCarthy (2009) *Basic Marketing: A Global Managerial Approach*, 17th ed. (New York: McGraw-Hill/Irwin), p. 5.

43. www.jdpower.com/business/press-releases/2013-social-media-benchmark-study, retrieved May 13, 2019.

44. http://downloads.sproutsocial.com/Sprout-Guide-Customer-Service.pdf?utm_medium= Email&utm_source=Sprout+Social&utm_content=Send+Guide&utm_campaign=L-N&utm_term=text, retrieved May 13, 2019.

45. Robert McKim, 'Is CRM Part of Customer Management?' dmnews.com, March 13, 2000, www.dmnews.com/archive/2000-03/7058.html, retrieved May 10, 2000.

46. Adapted from Stanley J. Fenvessy (1979) 'Introduction to Fulfillment,' *Direct Marketing Manual* (New York: Direct Marketing Association), p. 500.

47. Case adapted from Jim McCann and Peter Kaminsky (1998) *Stop and Sell the Roses: Lessons from Business & Life* (New York: Ballantine Books). Updated based on information provided by 1-800-FLOWERS.COM, 2008.

13
ENVIRONMENTAL, ETHICAL, AND LEGAL ISSUES

CHAPTER CONTENTS

CHAPTER SPOTLIGHT

ENVIRONMENTALLY FRIENDLY SEED PAPER BY BLOOMIN

Figure 13.1   Bloomin logo. Used with permission of Bloomin. All rights reserved.

D o you think all direct mail ultimately ends up in giant landfills somewhere? If so, think again and read on! That myth will clearly be dispelled after reading about Bloomin, one of the most environmentally friendly companies in the world. Bloomin is the worldwide authority on and original pioneer of plantable seed paper since 1995. The company produces more seed paper than anyone on the planet. Consumers who receive seed paper just need to soak the paper in water, plant it under a thin layer of soil, water daily, and watch the seed paper take root and sprout in a couple of weeks.

Bloomin seed paper is the most eco-friendly promotional option available. The company is certified and authorized by the United States Department of Agriculture (USDA) and other agriculture departments around the globe. Bloomin works closely with the USDA, who tests and inspects its non-genetically modified organism (non-GMO) seeds and paper, to ensure only the highest quality seeds are used in the firm's plantable seed paper promotions. The company produces millions of seed paper products each year, with more than 200 die-cut seed paper shapes. Figure 13.2 shows the many shapes and designs available via Bloomin's online catalog at bloominpromotions.com. Plus, if customers want a customized shape or design, all they have to do is request it.

Bloomin's seed paper is made by hand in Boulder, Colorado. From a backyard chicken coup production facility that started back in 1995, the small family business has grown from a specialty greeting card niche business, into the worldwide authority on all things seed paper. Employing a diverse mix of eco-minded, creative individuals, along with some Boulder hippies, the company now employs anywhere from 20 to 60 people who perform a multitude of tasks and duties depending on the season and specific opportunities at hand.

Bloomin's seed paper is crafted from 100% post-consumer, post-industrial, recycled paper. It is either natural white (the base pulp color), or colored with all-natural, vegetable-based pigments. When printed, most sheets are printed with water-soluble, four-color process inks or soy-based inks, when letterpress printed. The company uses old-school paper-making techniques and handmade molds and deckles to handcraft each sheet. Bloomin paper is packed with flower, vegetable, herb, grass, tree, and many other varieties of seeds, so it's easy to grow and cultivate. If packaging is required, the company uses corn-based packaging.

Bloomin doesn't just make plantable papers that blossom into flowers, herbs, vegetables, grasses, and trees. The company has cleverly figured out how to make an even

535

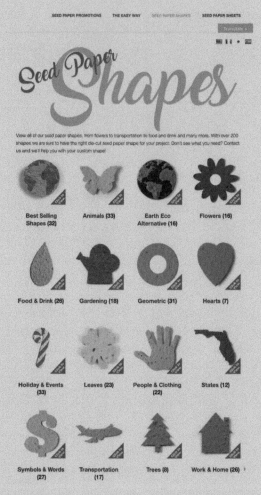

Figure 13.2 Bloomin's assortment of seed paper designs.

greater positive impact on our environment by creating custom seed mixes that save our pollinators. These special seed mixes aim to help sustain our bee and butterfly population. Check out Bloomin's e-mail blast (shown in Figure 13.3), encouraging consumers to join the company in its mission to save our pollinators.

On top of its ecologically friendly production process, Bloomin's production facility is powered by a 30KW solar power system. In fact, in 2017, Bloomin was certified as a Benefit Corporation (also called B Corps) community. B Corps are for-profit companies that have adopted a new type of company structure, to ultimately solve social and environmental problems. In a nutshell, B Corps are required to consider the impact of their decisions on shareholders and stakeholders equally. In this way, B Corps actively seek to improve standards for company stakeholders, including workers, suppliers, the community, customers, and the environment. Additionally, each company hoping to become a B Corp must score at least 82 points on a rigorous impact assessment proctored by B Labs in

Figure 13.3 Bloomin's 'Save the pollinators' e-mail blast. Used with permission of Bloomin. All rights reserved.

order to become certified. Certified B Corporations meet the highest standards of social and environmental performance, transparency, and accountability.

Today, there are more than 1,300 Certified B Corps around the globe, including Patagonia, Namaste Solar, and Klean Kanteen. Bloomin has joined these companies in the movement to redefine corporate success, so that eventually all business will become of benefit to society and to the environment. Bloomin is to be commended for its extraordinary environmentally friendly business behavior.

In this chapter, we will discuss the environmental, ethical, and legal issues and regulations that affect the business practices of marketers. Raising environmental consciousness and exercising environmentally friendly behavior are two of the more recent focuses of most marketers today. We will also explore 'The Green 15,' which is a set of business practices that the DMA established to assist its members in becoming more environmentally friendly.

The regulatory environment of direct marketing includes the two very important areas of ethical and legal issues. **Ethics** are the moral principles of conduct governing the behavior of an individual or a group. **Morals** are often described in terms of good or bad. To be *ethical* in marketing means to conform to the accepted professional standards of conduct. However, you might ask, what exactly are the 'accepted professional standards of conduct'?

This chapter discusses ethics and the ethical behavior expected of direct marketers as set forth long ago by the Direct Marketing Association (DMA), now the Data & Marketing Association, a division of the Association of National Advertisers,[1] along with the law as it pertains to direct marketing activities. The legal regulations affecting direct marketing activities at the federal, state, and local levels primarily deal with three broad legal issues: intellectual property, security, and privacy. We detail the legal issues in each of these three areas in this chapter, after an overview of the ethical aspects of direct marketing.

ENVIRONMENTAL ISSUES

Protecting the environment is an important issue for direct marketers. DMAs around the world are taking a leading role in shaping the industry by partnering with other organizations to create environmental standards. The U.K. DMA, for instance, has developed an alliance of like-minded member companies to partner with BSI British Standards to create the first standard for environmental performance in the field of direct marketing.[2] The U.S. DMA has taken a lead on this issue, starting in 2005 with the formation of a Committee on Environment & Social Responsibility (CESR) composed of DMA member organizations. In January 2007, the DMA launched an Environmental Planning Tool & Policy Generator. In May 2007, the DMA board of directors passed an Environmental Resolution. That same month, the DMA also announced a nationwide 'Recycle Please' campaign. For more information on these major milestones, please visit the DMA's Environmental Resource Center at: www.recycleplease.org. The following section provides an overview of the key environmental issues.

The DMA's Environmental Resolution and 'Green 15' Program

The U.S. DMA has taken a stance on protecting the environment by promulgating greener marketing practices with its Environmental Resolution and new green goal to reduce waste, including digital waste, such as mobile devices and carbon. The main areas of this initiative are the following:[3]

1. Resource procurement
2. List hygiene and data
3. Design and production

4. Packaging
5. Recycling, and pollution reduction.

The DMA has also created a nationwide public education campaign called 'Recycle Please,' which asks all DMA members to display prominently one of the 'Recycle Please' logo options, shown in Figure 13.4, in their catalogs and direct mail pieces to encourage consumers to recycle them after reading. In addition, DMA members should create benchmarks to measure organizational performance with respect to the above five environmental initiatives. The DMA coordinated with the Envelope Manufacturers Association and the Magazine Publishers of America and launched this campaign back in 2007.[4] The DMA hopes this campaign will overcome the lack of public awareness that catalogs, magazines, and mixed paper can be recycled.

VERSION 3: BLACK BIN (grayscale)
• Should be used on a light or white background
• Should NOT be used less than 30% of its original size.

VERSION 3: BLACK TEXT (grayscale)
• Should be used on a light or white background
• Should NOT be used less than 15% of its original size.

Figure 13.4 DMA 'Recycle Please' logos. Used with permission of the Direct Marketing.

The other objective of this campaign is to improve the overall recovery/recycling rate of used catalogs, magazines, and direct mail in the United States. In addition, the DMA's 'Recycle Please' campaign seeks to increase awareness that electronic communications have a waste impact and recycling need as well, given the breadth of computers, mobile telephones, and equipment used to support e-mail, search, social media, and Internet marketing. Overall, increasing recycling and recovery activity benefits our environment by:

• making efficient use of raw material
• reducing the amount of new fiber that must be obtained from wood to make new paper products
• conserving valuable global resources
• decreasing landfill waste
• reducing greenhouse gas emissions from incinerators and landfills.[5]

The DMA enacted a resolution calling on members to implement and benchmark a set of 15 business practices called 'The Green 15.'[6] The Green 15 is a checklist of best practices attuned to current data-driven direct marketing science and environmental issues. The DMA commits to public green goals to reduce environmental and social impacts associated with marketing through awareness and a widespread adoption of the 'Green 15.'[7] Figure 13.5 provides an overview of the Green 15. Thus far, the program has met with success.

DMA Green 15

Resource Procurement:

1. Develop a policy that ensures legal and ethical paper sourcing.
2. Require suppliers to increase environmental protection by expanding certification programs.
3. Identify additional environmentally preferable attributes for paper you buy: reduced weights, recycled, etc.
4. Conduct energy audits of facilities and offices to reduce costs.
5. Make renewable energy choices for offices, production, and data centers.

List Hygiene & Data:

6. Comply with all DMA requirements for list management.
7. Maintain 'clean' mailing lists.
8. Apply predictive models and RFM analytics to improve targeting.

Design & Production:

9. Test into new designs that reduce size and wasted materials.
10. Use links instead of attachments when sending files or content.
11. Ensure that all labeling is clear, honest, and complete.

Packaging:

12. Work with suppliers to develop environmentally preferable packaging solutions.

Recycling & Pollution Reduction:

13. Purchase supplies and materials made with post-consumer recycled content where possible.
14. Participate in the DMA Recycle Please campaign to help increase direct mail recycling rates.
15. Implement processes to responsibly recycle electronic devices throughout your organization.

Figure 13.5   DMA Green 15. Used with permission of the Direct Marketing.

In summary, the DMA is making a concerted effort to move its members along the continuum of ongoing environmental improvement. These standards are a part of its commitment to corporate responsibility and its efforts to promote sustainable and ethical business practices, which is the topic of the next section.

ETHICS OF DIRECT MARKETING

A different kind of e-business is receiving an increasing amount of attention from the direct marketing community. In this case, the 'e' doesn't stand for electronic, it stands for ethics, and direct marketers are paying close attention. Ethics are concerned with morality: the rightness and wrongness of individual actions or deeds. As former Supreme Court Justice Potter Stewart once said, 'Ethics is knowing the difference between what you have a right to do and what is the right thing to do.' A code of ethics is a set of guidelines for making ethical decisions.

The DMA's Guidelines for Ethical Business Practice

For more than 100 years, the DMA has been proactively promoting ethical business practices and standards of conduct for its members.

The DMA has established a detailed code of ethics for direct marketers. These guidelines are intended to provide individuals and organizations in direct marketing in all media with generally accepted principles of conduct. These are self-regulatory measures as opposed to governmental mandates. Visit www.dmaresponsibility.org to obtain updated versions of these guidelines. In addition, you may contact the DMA Corporate & Social Responsibility (CSR) Compliance Network at ethics@thedma.org to tap into the many resources the DMA has available to promote and support responsible marketing. Figure 13.6 provides an overview of the DMA's guidelines for ethical business practice.

DMA Ethical Guidelines

The Terms of the Offer

Honesty and Clarity of Offer: Article #I

Accuracy and Consistency: Article #2

Clarity of Representations: Article #3

Actual Conditions: Article #4

Disparagement: Article #5

Decency: Article #6

Photographs and Artwork: Article #7

Disclosure of Sponsor and Intent: Article #8

Accessibility: Article #9

Solicitation in the Guise of an Invoice or Governmental Notification: Article #10

Postage, Shipping, or Handling: Article #11

Advance Consent/Negative Option Marketing: Article #12

Marketing to Children

Marketing to Children: Article #13

Parental Responsibility and Choice: Article #14

Collection and Use of Information from or about Children: Article #15

Marketing Online to Children Under 13 Years of Age: Article #16

Special Offers and Claims

Use of the Word 'Free' and Other Similar Representations: Article #17

Price Comparisons: Article #18

Guarantees: Article #19

Use of Test or Survey Data: Article #20

Testimonials and Endorsements: Article #21

(Continued)

Figure 13.6 (Continued)

DMA Ethical Guidelines

Sweepstakes

Use of the Term 'Sweepstakes': Article #22

No Purchase Option: Article #23

Chances of Winning: Article #24

Prizes: Article #25

Premiums: Article #26

Disclosure of Rules: Article #27

Fulfillment

Unordered Merchandise or Service: Article #28

Product Availability and Shipment: Article #29

Dry Testing: Article #30

Collection, Use, and Maintenance of Marketing Data

Consumer Choice & the Collection, Use, and Transfer of Personally Identifiable Data: Article #31

Personal Data: Article #32

Health Information Privacy and Protection: Article #33

Promotion of Marketing Lists: Article #34

Marketing List Usage: Article #35

Responsibilities of Database Compilers: Article #36

Data Security: Article #37

Digital Marketing

Online Information & OBA: Article #38

Mobile Service Commercial Message Solicitations Delivered to a Wireless Device: Article #39

Commercial Solicitations Online: Article #40

E-Mail Authentication: Article #41

Use of Software or Other Similar Technology Installed on a Computer or Similar Device: Article #42

Social Media & Online Referral Marketing: Article #43

E-Mail Appending to Consumer Records: Article #44

Telephone Marketing to Landline & Wireless Devices

Reasonable Hours: Article #45

Taping of Conversations: Article #46

Restricted Contacts: Article #47

Caller-ID/Automatic Number Identification Requirements: Article #48

Use of Automated Dialing Equipment/Robocalls: Article #49

Use of Prerecorded Voice & Text Messaging: Article #50

Use of Telephone Facsimile Machines: Article #51

Promotions for Response by Toll-Free and Pay-Per-Call Numbers: Article #52

Disclosure and Tactics: Article #53

542

DMA Ethical Guidelines

Mobile Marketing

Obtaining Consent to Contact a Mobile Device: Article #54

Providing Notice about Mobile Marketing Practices: Article #55

Mobile Opt-Out Requests: Article #56

Sponsorship or Affiliate Marketing: Article #57

Location-Based Mobile Marketing: Article #58

Mobile Subscription & Premium Rate Services: Article #59

Fundraising: Article #60

Laws, Codes, and Regulations: Article #61

Figure 13.6 DMA ethics guidelines. Used with permission of the Direct Marketing.

The DMA Corporate Responsibility Department

In addition to providing guidelines for ethical business practices, the DMA sponsors several activities in its Corporate Responsibility Department. The Mail Preference Service (MPS) offers consumers assistance in decreasing the volume of national advertising mail they receive at home. The Telephone Preference Service (TPS) offers consumers assistance in decreasing the number of national phone calls received at home. The E-Mail Preference Service (EMPS) is designed to assist consumers in decreasing the number of unsolicited e-mail offers received. In essence, the DMA supports a consumer's right to choose the channel by which they would prefer to shop. The DMA's consumer page for registering with the Preference Services is https://dmachoice.thedma.org/. The DMA also publishes a variety of publications designed to assist direct marketers in complying with federal and state regulations. Visit the DMA website at www.the-dma.org to obtain a list of such publications and information sources. The DMA has established both the Guidelines for Ethical Business Practice and an office of corporate responsibility to assist direct marketers in developing and maintaining consumer relationships that are based on fair and ethical principles. With these ethical guidelines, the DMA is encouraging all direct marketers to act in a morally correct business manner and to safeguard basic consumer rights.

BASIC CONSUMER RIGHTS

Consumers possess the following basic human rights: (1) the right to safety, (2) the right to be informed, (3) the right to selection, (4) the right to confidentiality, and (5) the right to privacy.[8] Direct marketers should respect and safeguard these rights. Let's look at each of these in turn.

The Right to Safety

The **right to safety** entitles consumers to be safe from both physical and psychological harm. They cannot be harassed or made to feel bad if, for example, they decline a phone request to purchase a product or service. These circumstances may cause the consumer to experience undue stress.

The Right to Information

The **right to information** includes the consumer's right to receive any and all pertinent or requested information. This includes the right to be informed about all stages of the direct marketing process. It is an obligation of direct marketers to fully disclose what they intend to do with the consumer's name and address once they are put on a mailing list. In addition, direct marketers should provide the consumer with an explanation of why they collect information about consumers and their lifestyles.

The Right to Selection

The **right to selection** includes a consumer's right to choose or make decisions about their buying behavior. In other words, the consumer can accept or reject any offer from a direct marketer or a telemarketer, be it a request to purchase a product or service, subscribe to a magazine, attend a meeting, donate to a charitable organization, or vote for a political candidate. Consumers cannot be made to feel forced into taking an action against their wishes.

The Right to Confidentiality

The **right to confidentiality** is a consumer's right to specify to a given company that information they freely provide should not be shared. Like information disclosed in a physician–patient or attorney–client relationship, information a consumer provides to a direct marketing organization with expressed confidentiality must not be shared. Savvy direct marketers know that in order to be successful they must build long-term relationships with their customers based on trust. This trust must not be betrayed. Direct marketers can uphold the consumer's right to confidentiality by developing proper security measures (electronic watermarks, firewalls, digital signatures, authentication, data integrity, encryption, etc.), to protect the security of the proprietary data the direct marketer has promised to safeguard.

Suppose a nonprofit organization specifically stated in its printed materials that it will not share the names of donors with other charitable organizations, and then it turns around and rents its donor lists! This is unethical and constitutes a breach of confidentiality.

The Right to Privacy

The final basic consumer right, the right to privacy, is probably the most noteworthy consumer right affecting direct marketers. The **right to privacy** has been defined as the ability of an individual to control the access others have to personal information. Because of the heightened awareness and controversy over the matter, along with the legal ramifications of the consumer's right to privacy, later in the chapter we discuss privacy issues in more detail than the other four basic consumer rights.

LEGISLATIVE ISSUES

The three primary areas where legislation has been designed to safeguard consumer rights are intellectual property, security, and privacy.

Intellectual Property

Intellectual property is defined as products of the mind or ideas.[9] Examples include books, music, computer software, designs, and technological know-how. The protection of intellectual property afforded by copyrights, patents, trademarks, and databases is the province of several governmental agencies. Under copyright laws, a copyright owner has the exclusive right to distribute copies of the protected work. Thus, third parties are not permitted to sell, rent, transfer, or otherwise distribute copies of the work without the express permission of the copyright owner. Several channels currently exist for businesses to prevent unauthorized usage of protected material. The American Intellectual Property Law Association (AIPLA) is a national bar association constituted primarily of intellectual property lawyers in private and corporate practice, government service, and the academic community.[10] The AIPLA is one of the organizations available to assist direct marketers in protecting intellectual property.

Given the freedom of the Internet, the protection of trademarks has recently become even more difficult. The Internet's focus on visual advertisements will increase the likelihood of a conflict over trademark rights as more company logos, slogans, brand names, and trademarks are appearing in websites. Therefore, this area of intellectual property protection must also be one of the top concerns for direct marketers.

With the introduction of faster computer applications and hard drives with larger capacity for data storage, a new kind of intellectual property has emerged—the database. Data collection, both online and offline, has soared in the past decade. However, intellectual property protection of an organization's database is a volatile area. Businesses are being caught between the threats of unauthorized access by hackers (which we discuss with regard to security in the next section), requirements to disclose certain data collected to law enforcement agencies, and consumer privacy concerns about data collection (which we discuss later, in the privacy section).

Security

In addition to creating and storing databases, companies must also secure their databases from unauthorized access and outside damage. Failure to do so may cause the direct marketer much embarrassment, pain, and potential liability for breaches in security. Although the technology exists to provide security via password controls and firewalls, these are not completely dependable, and security breaches may still occur.

For example, publishing giant Ziff-Davis Media suffered a security lapse that exposed the personal data of thousands of magazine subscribers. In restitution, the company agreed to pay $100,000 to three states as well as to the New York State Department of Law and $500 each to the 50 customers whose credit card information had been disclosed.[11]

In response to these types of incidents, a California law known as SB 1386 became the first state law to address security breaches. This law requires government agencies, businesses, and anyone else who stores personal information to notify the California resident when the data have been accessed. The purpose of SB 1386 is to give California residents adequate time to check their credit ratings and protect themselves against identity theft.[12]

Privacy

Consumers are more concerned about privacy today than ever before. There are two terms that should be distinguished concerning privacy today. Privacy and the data/security breach are both discussed in this section, however they are two separate and distinct issues that may require separate legislation. **Privacy** refers to the level of control consumers have over the information provided. A **data/security breach** pertains to the safeguarding and securing of data from unauthorized access or damage, as mentioned in the security section above. Privacy legislation has existed for a long time. Let's review the history of this important legislation.

PRIVACY LEGISLATION

Privacy protection actually began being discussed over a century ago, in 1890, when Samuel Warren and Justice Brandeis wrote a law review article advocating that a person should be protected from having personal matters reported by the press for commercial reasons. That marked the beginning of what many know today as a consumer's right to privacy. In the 1950s, laws protected citizens from allowing public organizations to intrude on their private matters. However, these laws did not protect consumers against a private organization's use of personal information. Still, it wasn't until recent years that privacy issues became increasingly visible.

From the explosion of credit cards and personal computers to the advent of smartphones to the new marketing realities in social media today, the process of direct marketing has attained new heights of marketing success. With this phenomenal success, businesses have also faced scrutiny on numerous aspects of the privacy issue. Whatever the root, the concern over information privacy has been going on for decades. Back in the late 1970s, prior to most technological advances, the following appeared in a newspaper:[13]

They know about you. They know how old you are.

They know if you have children. They know about your job.

They know how much money you make, what kind of car you drive, what sort of house you live in and whether you are likely to prefer paté de foie gras and champagne or hot dogs and a cold beer.

They know all this and much, much more. And you know how?

They know your name.

What they have done with it is very simple: they have added it to a mailing list.

Though it was an exaggeration (at the time), this excerpt is evidence of a widely held concern that a list is a conduit through which personal information is transferred from one direct marketer to another. Although this may be true, as you should realize from the material contained in Chapters 2 and 3, to a direct marketer a list is an instrument for describing a market segment. Market segments enable direct marketers to target appropriate promotional offers to consumers, thus reducing the amount of irrelevant marketing communication each consumer receives. This is good for both direct marketers and consumers. Information technology has made it possible for marketers to design promotional campaigns directed at different segments of prospective and current customers. From a marketing and customer service perspective, the purpose of gathering consumer information is to achieve greater selectivity and to make direct-response advertising more relevant to the recipient. The use of personal information enables marketers to develop closer relationships with customers that foster brand loyalty and provide better customer service. However, regardless of the noble purpose information serves for direct marketers, privacy issues have now become legal matters.

Marketers have always had an interest in knowing consumer information, dating back to the days of corner 'mom and pop' stores when everyone knew everyone else and their families and their business. Today is no different. Marketers still want to know about their customers in order to serve them better. Technology makes it easier to do that. With the swipe of a customer loyalty card, consumers receive discounts on purchases or earn bonus points toward free gifts, while retailers download information about customer purchasing preferences and habits. From there, with a few clicks of the mouse or strokes on the keyboard, the purchase information can be shared with any number of interested parties—for a fee.

Modern digital and social media platforms have brought about an increase in privacy concerns. The threat of having social media users' personal data shared beyond their desires has become a reality. For example, in 2018 it was publicly revealed in the Cambridge Analytica case, that data collected from Facebook users for one purpose was being redeployed for all sorts of purposes by actors nefarious and otherwise.[14] Cambridge Analytica gained access to information from more than 87 million Facebook users, thanks to a personality test called thisisyourdigitallife.[15] The inability of Facebook (and to a certain extent the researchers at Cambridge Analytica) to exert any kind of meaningful control over that data is indicative of grave missteps in digital privacy.[16]

Technology has made direct marketing database activities easier and more efficient. However, before direct marketers start thinking beyond this, they have to realize that along with advances in technology come additional legislative regulations. Perhaps the best-known legislation regarding privacy has come from the Privacy Protection Study Commission.

Privacy Protection Study Commission

The concern of the U.S. consumer and Congress over the broad issue of privacy, including the subject of mailing lists and databases, culminated in the **Privacy Act of 1974**. This act established the Privacy Protection Study Commission to determine whether the various restrictions on what the federal government could do with personal information, as provided in the Privacy

Act, should also be applied to the private sector. Significantly for direct marketers, Section V (c), B (i) of the Act directed the Commission to report to the president and Congress on whether an organization engaged in interstate commerce should be required to remove from its mailing list the name of an individual who does not want to be on it.

In July 1977, after months of hearing testimony and studying the issues, the Commission issued its 618-page *Report from the Privacy Protection Study Commission*. Chapter 4 of this report was devoted entirely to the subject of mailing lists. The Commission basically concluded that the appearance of an individual's name on a mailing list, so long as that individual has the prerogative to remove it from that list, was not in and of itself an invasion of privacy. In reaching this conclusion, the Commission observed 'that the balance that must be struck between the interests of individuals and the interests of direct marketers is an especially delicate one.' The Commission also noted the economic importance of direct mail 'to nonprofit organizations, to the champions of unpopular causes, and to many of the organizations that create diversity in American society.'

Agreeing that the receipt of direct mail is not really the issue but instead how the mailing list record of an individual is used, the Commission further recommended that a private sector organization that rents, sells, exchanges, or otherwise makes the addresses or names and addresses of its customers, members, or donors available to any other person for use in direct mail marketing or solicitation should adopt a procedure whereby each customer, member, or donor is informed of the organization's list practice. In addition, each consumer should be given an opportunity to indicate to the organization that he or she does not wish to have their address, or name and address, made available for such purposes.

These were the privacy issues of the past. Now direct marketers must prepare for handling the privacy issues of the future. Let's take a look at privacy today.

Privacy Today: Antispam Laws

California has recently enacted two landmark pieces of consumer rights legislation regarding data security and privacy. These new regulations will directly affect the companies doing business with California residents. The first, Senate Bill No. 1386, requires any company that stores customer data electronically to notify its California customers of a security breach to the company's computer system if the company knows or reasonably believes that encrypted information about the customer has been stolen. The second, Senate Bill No. 1, also known as the California Financial Information Privacy Act, creates new limits on the ability of financial institutions to share nonpublic personal information about their clients with affiliates and third parties.[17]

Spam is defined as unwanted, unsolicited bulk commercial e-mail messages. It has also been referred to as junk e-mail. Most people today complain about spam. Recipients find it annoying; Internet service providers say it clogs up and slows down the online systems; and many direct marketers claim it is ruining e-mail as a legitimate media channel. The minutes e-mail recipients spend clicking through unwanted e-mail messages add up quickly in a nation with millions of Internet users. However, spam is a worldwide issue. Recent statistics show that spam messages account for 57 percent of e-mail traffic worldwide.[18] This worldwide phenomenon of spam had to start somewhere. There is some speculation about who actually sent out the first spam e-mail and when it happened. The first 'tasteless' spam e-mail was most likely sent out in 1996 by Dave Rhodes. Rhodes was a college student who advertised a pyramid scheme in his e-mail messages. The message was relayed to all newsgroups on Usenet. Thousands of users were hit with a message that read 'MAKE MONEY FAST!' It's said that Rhodes made a substantial amount of money from several people chasing an elusive dream. The most interesting twist of the story is the great possibility that Rhodes never existed. The university that he supposedly attended had no record of him. Because chain letters began as early as the 1970s, it's very probable that someone else copied the format onto a computer and distributed it via Usenet under an alias.[19]

Internet providers have tools for blocking spam; however, these filtering programs are often time-consuming and ineffective. Senders of spam are finding ways to defeat the filtering software simply by misspelling keywords that trigger the filters. To get consumers to open these e-mail messages, the senders of spam also use a variety of attention-getting subject lines and sender names in the 'from' field of the e-mail message. Examples include 'Claim Your Prize,' 'Payment Past Due,' and 'You Have Won.' This is where the law comes into play. When the subject line of an e-mail message misrepresents its point of origin or the nature of the message itself, it is considered deceptive.

The CAN-SPAM Act of 2003 sets requirements for everyone involved in sending commercial e-mails. This act also states various penalties for spammers and companies whose products are advertised as spam. The CAN-SPAM Act gives power to the consumer to ask the e-mail sender to stop sending e-mails to the consumer's address. The U.S. Federal Trade Commission (FTC) has the power to enforce the act, which came into effect on January 1, 2004. CAN-SPAM gave the Department of Justice (DOJ) the power to enforce criminal sanction for noncompliance. The CAN-SPAM Act also contains compliance obligations and prohibitions for transactional or relationship messages; however, these are less rigorous than the rest of the requirements specific to commercial messages. For commercial messages, the main provisions of the CAN-SPAM Act are that it:

- bans false or misleading header information
- prohibits deceptive subject lines
- requires that the advertising e-mail give recipients an opt-out method
- requires that commercial e-mail be identified as an advertisement and include the sender's valid physical postal address.[20]

Additionally, the Digital Advertising Alliance (DAA) icon (shown in Figure 13.7) is placed on billions of online ads that are behaviorally targeted. Consumers may click on the icon to discover why they received an ad, and continue to opt out of a majority of behavioral advertising. The goal of this program is to enable consumers who desire to 'opt out' of receiving online ads the opportunity to do so. Visit www.aboutads.info to learn more about DAA principles and this program. The DAA's most recent ad campaign directs consumers to a revamped home page presenting the ADChoices program.

Figure 13.7 The DAA ADChoices program icon. Published with the consent of Digital Advertising Alliance. All Rights Reserved.

In addition, the Internet-based advertising (IBA) opt-out process will aid consumers in being removed from online ads that they receive based on their viewing or browsing history. However, this 'Ad Choices' program does not affect the content or placement of the ads themselves, as that is beyond the scope of the program. Data Standards 2.0 is expected to address high-profile and emerging data issues, such as 'on-boarding' of offline data online; use of television viewing data; information service provider transparency; and more.[21]

Federal and state legislation covering the broad range of privacy issues today is rapidly changing. The legal environment concerning spam is also constantly changing. For updated legislative information, contact the Internet Alliance at https://digitaladvertisingalliance.org/ or visit the spam laws website at https://www.spamlaws.com/. Direct marketers must constantly monitor key information sources.

On May 25, 2018, the most strict and broad-reaching data privacy law went into effect across the European Union (EU)—the General Data Protection Regulation (GDPR). Under the GDPR, if a company has a customer living in an EU country and collects data from that customer through any type of contact, that company must inform the customer about how the data will be stored and used. The regulation applies to any company, regardless of its location, to abide by the law or face stiff penalties. The GDPR affects all companies located within the EU as well as any with an 'establishment' in the EU. Establishment is a broad term but can be considered as simple as promoting a product that is targeted at an EU consumer.[22]

The GDPR focuses on regulating personally identifiable information, such as name, photo, address, social media posts, computer data, and more. Repercussions for violating GDPR regulations are significantly more expensive than previous legislations permitted. Maximum fines for smaller breaches are €10 million or two percent of a company's annual revenue, whichever is greater. Maximum fines for larger breaches are €20 million or four percent of a company's annual revenue, whichever is greater.[23]

To avoid hefty fines and ensure compliance with GDPR regulations, here are some primary requirements to comply with:[24]

1. Create a plan for if a data breach were to occur.
2. The individual from whom you captured data has the right to revoke consent at any time and be removed from all records.
3. The data collected must be accurate, minimized, and portable.
4. One must obtain informed consent from an individual before storing any personal data.

Annoyance and Violation

To get at the heart of privacy concerns, you have to understand two basic consumer perceptions: annoyance and violation.[25] People feel annoyed because they receive too many unsolicited marketing communications, and they feel violated because they believe too much information about their personal lives is being exchanged between marketers without their knowledge and/or consent. Many consumers want to place restrictions on the amount of information that may be collected, warehoused, and shared about them. However, not all consumers feel the same way. Some are willing to disclose personal information to marketers, providing they receive something in return. This may include a targeted offer that meets the consumer's needs and desires, or informative updates on a certain topic of interest to them. In fact, it has been determined that a consumer's willingness to disclose personal data may actually depend on the type of information being disclosed.

Type of Information

The degree of control or the amount of restriction an individual wants to have over their personal information may depend on the *type* of information requested. We can divide personal information into four different categories: general descriptive information, ownership information, product purchase information, and sensitive/confidential information.[26] Let's discuss each of these types of information and look at some examples of each category.

General Descriptive Information

General descriptive information is the easiest to obtain. Often considered demographic or classification information, it includes race, height, age, gender, level of education, and occupation. Consumers are the least restrictive with this category of information and usually provide marketers with easy access to this data.

Ownership Information

Ownership information contains data about the various products the consumer owns. Consumers consider some belongings to be status symbols, like a home, an expensive automobile, or an American Express Platinum travel and entertainment credit card. Consumers generally place moderate restrictions on the release of these data, and it is believed that some may want to share this data to achieve greater self-esteem or status.

Product Purchase Information

The information contained in the product purchase information category includes a variety of purchase activity data, including magazine subscription information, credit record information, and lifestyle information obtained from such purchases as vitamins, cat food, hunting and fishing equipment, or certain medications. This category is similar to the ownership information category; however, these purchases are not necessarily considered to be status symbols. Consumers generally place moderate restrictions on this information category.

551

Sensitive/Confidential Information

The final category of information contains facts about an individual that are considered to be most private: sensitive/confidential information such as annual income, medical history, Social Security number, driving record (including any motor violations), and home value. Consumers are most restrictive with this category of information and usually exercise the strongest control over the release of these facts.

Consumer Privacy Segments

Not all consumers have the same feelings and opinions about privacy issues, regardless of the type of information. Just as information can be grouped into categories, consumer opinions and behaviors toward information privacy can be categorized as well. In fact, research conducted by Alan Westin of Columbia University and Lou Harris Organization/Equifax has concluded that consumers may be grouped into three possible segments (the privacy unconcerned, privacy fundamentalists, and privacy pragmatists) when it comes to their feelings about privacy.[27] Let's take a closer look at these segments.

Privacy Unconcerned

The **privacy unconcerned** group represents about 20 percent of the U.S. population and consists of those who literally do not care about the issue of privacy at all. They are aware of the benefits of giving information for marketing purposes and enjoy the information and opportunities they receive in exchange for it. These consumers say their lives are an open book. They feel they have nothing to hide. They welcome most contacts by businesses, non-profits, and others and have little concern about information about them being transferred from one organization to another. This group is most likely to be receptive to the activities of direct marketers.

Privacy Fundamentalists

The **privacy fundamentalists** also make up approximately 20 percent of the U.S. population. These individuals are likely to take the point of view that they own their name as well as all the information about themselves, and that no one else may use it without their permission. This group includes activists who will write letters to their congressional representatives or the editor of a local newspaper about privacy. They may call companies and file complaints on this issue. Direct marketers should be certain to purge these consumers from their lists because they are the least receptive to direct marketing activities.

Privacy Pragmatists

The **privacy pragmatists** represent approximately 60 percent of U.S. consumers. They look at the contact, the offer, and the methods of data collection and mentally apply a cost–benefit analysis to make a determination about a marketer's use of information. They ask themselves:

- What benefits can I get from this?
- Are there choices that I would not otherwise have?
- Is there an opportunity for me?
- Can I get a product or an offer that is valuable to me?
- What harm can come from this? For example:

  ○ Will I be inconvenienced in some way?
  ○ Will I be embarrassed or feel discomfort?
  ○ Will I be disadvantaged in some way?

Pragmatists will allow their buying patterns to be tracked by supermarkets, if they get valuable coupons or other deals in return. They have no problem with a catalog company providing its list to another organization or company so long as they appreciate the subsequent offers they receive. They will receive telemarketing calls from an organization they patronize and respond to an offer they consider valuable. The privacy pragmatists represent the majority of consumers in the United States. Developing relationships with these customers is an important strategy for the direct marketer to take.

So what have companies done to respond to consumers' privacy concerns?

Corporate Response to Privacy

The **chief privacy officer (CPO)** is the newest arrival in corporate hierarchies, the new white knight of the twenty-first century. Like the CEO and the CIO, the CPO is overseeing something very important in the corporation: *privacy!* The CPO is responsible for protecting the sensitive information the corporation collects, from credit card accounts to health records.

Privacy executives have an open-ended job. They must guard against hackers and articulate uses for sensitive personal, financial, or medical information. They must not only set guidelines, they must figure out how to communicate those guidelines to customers and employees. Figure 13.8 shows a portion of the detailed privacy policy of SeaWorld Parks and Entertainment. Hiring CPOs to oversee privacy matters may be the price of doing business in today's corporate world as consumers and government officials more aggressively sue companies over breaches of privacy.

Many companies already have information privacy policies and actively communicate these to their customers. Take, for example, the following privacy notice provided to customers at Universal Bank:[28]

Keeping customer information secure is a top priority for all of us at Universal Bank. We are sending you this privacy notice to help you understand how we handle the personal information about you that we collect and may disclose. This notice tells you how you can limit our disclosing personal information about you. The provisions of this notice will apply to former customers as well as current customers unless we state otherwise.

Universal Bank goes on to provide its customers with a 'Privacy Choices Form,' which allows them to select one of the following four choices, then return the form to the bank:[29]

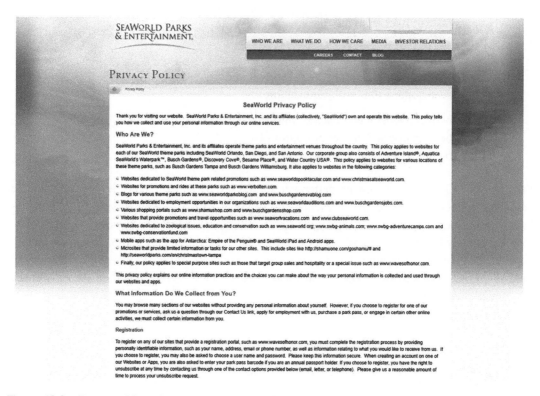

Figure 13.8   Excerpt of the privacy policy of SeaWorld Parks and Entertainment. Used with the consent of Busch Gardens/Water Country USA. All Rights Reserved.

1.   Limit the personal information about me that you disclose to nonaffiliated third parties.
2.   Limit the personal information about me that you share with Citigroup affiliates.
3.   Remove my name from your mailing lists used for promotional offers.
4.   Remove my name from your telemarketing lists used for promotional offers.

Like Universal Bank, many direct marketers have become proactive in handling information privacy issues. Perhaps no organization is more proactive than the DMA. The DMA initiated a Privacy Promise in 1999 that provided public assurance that all members of the DMA follow certain specific practices to protect consumer privacy. The practices were designed to have a major impact on those consumers who wish to receive fewer advertising solicitations. The DMA updated and expanded its Privacy Promise and now requires its members to adhere to the Commitment to Consumer Choice (see www.DMACCC.org).

The DMA Commitment to Consumer Choice

In 2008, the DMA initiated its redefined preference website, DMAchoice. This site addresses consumers' need for choice across a multitude of channels, not just mail. The primary mission of DMAchoice is to give consumers the opportunity to make what they receive more relevant to their needs and interests. This website's purpose is to educate consumers and enable them to make more informed decisions about their preference choices. The Commitment to Consumer Choice (CCC) includes the following six components:[30]

1. Provide existing and prospective customers and donors with notice of an opportunity to modify future mail solicitations from their organization. The notice should contain access to an option to eliminate future commercial mailings, and may also offer additional modification options. (See Figure 13.9 for examples of notice language.)
2. Accept and maintain consumer requests to be on an in-house suppress file to stop receiving solicitations from organizations you do not currently do business with. This means that if you ask a DMA member to stop sending you marketing promotions, the member is required to honor this request.
3. Provide customers with annual notice of their ability to opt out of information exchanges. This provides you with an opportunity to let companies know if you don't want your name, address or other information shared with other companies. This requirement is even stricter for online marketers, which are required to provide notice of their own online privacy practices on their website. (An example of an opt-out notice is shown in Figure 13.10.)
4. Honor customer opt-out requests not to have this contact information transferred to others for marketing purposes.
5. Upon request by a consumer, disclose the source from which it obtained personally identifiable data about that consumer, thus explaining why a marketing communication from that company was received (see Figure 13.11 for examples of in-house suppress language).
6. Use the DMAchoice suppression files on a monthly basis.

A. 'We make our customer information available to other companies so they may contact you about products and services that may interest you. If you do not want your name passed on to other companies for the purpose of receiving marketing offers, just tell us by contacting us at _____, and we will be pleased to respect your wishes.'

B. 'We make portions of our customer list available to carefully screened companies that offer products and services we believe you may enjoy. If you do not want to receive those offers and/or information, please let us know by contacting us at _____.'

Figure 13.9 Examples of notice language. Used with permission of the Direct Marketing.

UNSUBSCRIBE: Please use this link to unsubscribe. Or please write UNSUBSCRIBE in the e-mail subject heading and reply to this e-mail.

Figure 13.10 Example of opt-out notice

A. 'If you decide you no longer wish to receive our catalog, send your mailing label with your request to _____.'

B. 'We would like to continue sending you information only on those subjects of interest to you. If you don't wish to continue to receive information on any of the following product lines, just let us know by _____.'

C. 'If you would like to receive our catalog less frequently, let us know by _____.'

Figure 13.11 Examples of in-house suppress language. Used with permission of the Direct Marketing.

See Readings and Resources at the end of this chapter to obtain full details of the DMA CCC guidelines. In addition, the DMA has developed privacy principles and guidelines for those direct marketers operating online sites. The next section explores these principles.

The DMA Interest-Based Advertising (IBA) Guidelines

While millions of consumers have been quick to embrace technology, they have also called for regulation. Some consumers view online data collection as an invasion of privacy that, at best, inundates them with spam and, at worst, risks putting their financial or personal information in the hands of potential employers, lenders, or insurance companies. Most consumers freely provide their e-mail address or shopping preferences in exchange for better customer service. However, they don't expect marketers to share the information without their consent and to use it to target them for other offers (especially from other companies).

In today's modern digital world, consumers generate data with every action they make. This information is gathered, stored, shared, and used at lightning speed. As discussed in Chapters 2 and 3, companies use data to drive precisely targeted marketing communications to prospects and customers. Digital data-driven activities have led the DMA to create interest-based advertising (IBA) guidelines. **Interest-based advertising** refers to the collection of information about consumers' online activities and Web-viewing behaviors, over time and across non-affiliate websites, to deliver tailored ads.[31] The DMA IBA guidelines have been created to help digital marketers ensure the appropriate collection and use of IBA information, thereby building consumer trust in the online space[32] (see Readings and Resources at the end of this chapter to obtain full details of the DMA IBA guidelines). These guidelines include the following:[33]

1. Publish a privacy policy and abide by it.
2. Provide an enhanced notice link to consumers and honor their choices.
3. Ensure reasonable security and limited data retention.
4. Offer notice and choice for material changes to your policies.
5. Obtain express consent for sensitive information collection.

With these privacy principles for digital marketing activities in place, it is up to direct marketers to ensure that their programs include responsive personal information protection practices.

Third-Party Privacy Intervention: Infomediaries

Infomediaries are companies that act as intermediaries, or third parties, by gathering personal information from a user and providing it to other sites with the user's approval. These companies vary in their methods; each attempts to provide consumers with a type of privacy assistance by enabling consumers to control and limit access to their personal information when shopping online. Critics of infomediaries claim that these companies fail to provide enough protection and that they have the potential to exploit what they claim to protect. The World Wide Web Consortium, the Washington-based organization that sets standards for the Internet, has developed a 'Platform for Privacy Preferences Project,' also known as P3P. This program enables Web browsers and consumers to easily read a company's privacy practices and even to 'automate decision making based off of these when appropriate.'[34]

Now that we have reviewed the main privacy issues affecting direct marketers and the various DMA and corporate responses to these issues, we explore the regulatory authorities that are charged with enforcing these rules.

REGULATORY AUTHORITIES OF DIRECT MARKETING

By their very nature, direct marketing promotional activities, as they inform and persuade, often in very large numbers, are highly visible. The volume of direct mail has grown rapidly over the past few decades. As it grew, some of it was branded as 'junk mail' by those people who received it and did not find it relevant, by those individuals who resented its intrusion, and even by those businesses that represented competing advertising media. This, coupled with the development of and advances in telephone equipment, fiber optic cables, satellite transmissions, and the Internet, enabled direct marketers to transfer consumer data from internal or external databases to user databases quickly, easily, and at low cost. During this period of proliferation of direct marketing, some abuses by individual organizations ultimately resulted in the intervention of regulatory authorities.

The Federal Communications Commission (FCC), the Federal Trade Commission (FTC), the Consumer Financial Protection Bureau, and the Food and Drug Administration (FDA) have issued several very important trade regulation rules and guides that affect direct marketing, as well as advisory opinions about unfair competition in the form of misleading or deceptive acts or advertising. State and local governments also intervene in advertising and selling practices, as do the U.S. Postal Service, Better Business Bureaus, trade associations, the advertising media, and, ultimately, consumers themselves. Some industries are more highly regulated than others. The pharmaceutical, banking, and higher education industries, and especially for-profit advertising, are all highly regulated at the federal level. Let's look more closely at each of the regulatory bodies that affect direct and interactive marketing and advertising.

Federal Communications Commission

The FCC is an independent U.S. government agency directly responsible to Congress. It was established by the Communications Act of 1934 and is charged with regulating interstate and international communications by radio, television, wire, satellite, and cable.[35] The FCC enforces the Telephone Consumer Protection Act (TCPA), originally passed in 1992, and its rules governing telephone marketing.[36] From a telephone marketer's point of view, the most significant part of the TCPA regulations concerns commercial solicitation calls made to residences. Direct marketers making those calls are required to do the following:

- Limit calls to the period between 8:00 a.m. and 9:00 p.m.
- Maintain a do-not-call list and honor any consumer request to not be called again. The FCC permits one error in a 12-month period. The FCC worked closely with the FTC in

enforcing the National Do Not Call (DNC) Registry, which we will discuss a little later in this section.

- Have a clearly written policy, available to anyone on request.
- If you are a service bureau, forward all requests to be removed from a list to the company on whose behalf you are calling.

A call is exempt from the TCPA if the call:

- is made on behalf of a tax-exempt nonprofit organization
- is not made for a commercial purpose
- does not include an unsolicited advertisement, even if it is made for a commercial purpose
- is made to a consumer with whom the calling company has an 'established business relationship.'

The TCPA prohibits both for-profit and nonprofit marketers from using an automatic phone dialing system (including predictive dialers) to call any device when the called party is charged unless that called party has given prior express consent. Therefore, marketers using automatic dialing systems should not call consumers' or businesses' cellular phones, pagers, or toll-free numbers unless they have been given permission to do so. The FCC also has created strict rules concerning the use of fax machines for marketing purposes.

In addition, the FCC, in concert with the FTC, enforces the National Do Not Call Registry. This registry permits consumers to sign up via the telephone by calling (888) 382-1222, or online at www.donotcall.gov, to declare that they do not wish to receive telephone marketing calls. Section 310.2 of this new federal DNC legislation provides for an established business relationship exemption. Thus, direct marketers may still call customers who appear on the registry providing they are calling on them:

- within 18 months of their last purchase, transaction, shipment, end of subscription/membership, or
- within three months of their last inquiry or application.

Exemptions to the DNC legislation have also been made for most business-to-business calls, including nonprofit organizations, airlines, some financial institutions, and insurance companies (to the extent regulated under state law), as well as third-party marketers calling on their behalf, are required to honor in-house suppress requests.[37] (Visit the FCC website at www.fcc.gov/cgb/donotcall to obtain updates on the National DNC Registry.)

Federal Trade Commission

The major federal legislation regulating the promotional activities of direct marketing is the FTC Act, together with its Wheeler-Lea Amendment. The FTC is charged with regulating the content of promotional messages used in interstate commerce. In Section 5(A), intended to prevent unfair competition, the Wheeler-Lea Amendment to the FTC Act strengthened this provision by making it a violation of the law whenever such competition injured the public, regardless of its effect on a competitor. The amendment also prohibited false, misleading, or deceptive advertising by enumerating four types of products in which advertising abuses existed and in which the public health could be directly affected: foods, drugs, cosmetics, and therapeutic devices.[38]

In October 1995, the FTC and the DMA produced a checklist for direct marketers. It was written for mail, telephone, fax, and computer order merchandisers to give them an overview of rules or statutes that the FTC enforces. Figure 13.12 provides a brief overview of these rules.

Advertisements: Product offers and claims All products and/or services advertised must be advertised truthfully. The FTC Act prohibits unfair or deceptive advertising.

Mail and telephone orders In order to comply with the Mail or Telephone Order Merchandise Rule ('MTOR'), you must have a reasonable basis for stating or implying that you can ship within a certain time when you advertise mail or telephone order merchandise.

Telemarketing If your business uses either inbound or outbound interstate telephone calls to sell goods or services, you must comply with the new Telemarketing Sales Rule (TSR) and Do-Not-Call laws.

900 Numbers All providers of 900 numbers must comply with the FTC 900-Number Rule, requiring that they disclose the cost of the call.

Delayed Delivery Rule This rule provides that, if the marketer believes that goods will not be shipped within 30 days of receiving a properly completed order, an advertisement must include a clear and conspicuous notice of the time in which delivery is expected to be made.

Negative Option Rule This trade regulation rule, effective June 7, 1974, governs pre-notification negative option sales plans. Under negative option plans, sellers notify buyers of the periodic selection of merchandise to be shipped.

Guides against Deceptive Guarantees The FTC promulgated seven guides on April 26, 1960, for the purpose of self-regulatory adoption by marketers in their advertising of guarantees. These guides are intended to ensure that the buyer is fully apprised of the conditions governing any guarantee.

Guides to Use of Endorsements and Testimonials These FTC guides, which became effective May 21, 1975, relate to the use of expert and organizational endorsements and testimonials in advertising.

Advisory Opinion on Dry Testing An advisory opinion issued by the FTC on March 27, 1975, allows such dry testing under very strict guidelines to ensure that the potential customer is in no way misled about the terms of the offer.

Mailing of Unordered Merchandise Coming under a category of fraud and deception is the mailing of unordered merchandise, sent without the prior expressed request or consent of the recipient, an unfair method of competition, and an unfair trade practice in violation of the FTC Act.

Guides against Deceptive Pricing Made effective January 8, 1964, these guides cover offers stating reductions from a 'former,' 'regular,' 'comparable,' 'list price,' or 'manufacturer's suggested retail price.'

Guides against Bait and Switch Advertising The four guides against bait and switch advertising that were issued by the FTC on December 4, 1959, define this type of advertising as that which is 'alluring but insincere in offering to sell a product or service which the advertiser in truth does not intend or want to sell.'

Guide Concerning Use of the Word 'Free' This guide issued by the FTC on December 16, 1971, is intended to prevent deceptive or misleading offers of 'free' merchandise or services if, in fact, such is available only with the purchase of some other merchandise or service.

(Continued)

Figure 13.12   (Continued)

Advisory Opinion on the Use of the Word 'New' This advisory opinion, issued January 4, 1969, is concerned with merchandise that has been used by purchasers on a trial basis, returned to the seller, refurbished, and resold as new.

Advisory Opinion on Disclosure of Foreign Origin Merchandise Direct marketers, when advertising or promoting goods of foreign origin, must clearly inform prospective purchasers that such goods are not made in the United States if, in fact, the goods originate elsewhere.

Warranties The FTC is empowered by the Magnuson-Moss Warranty Act, effective July 4, 1975, with enforcement. Although no organization is required to give a written warranty and state a minimum duration for a warranty, the National Retail Merchants Association, in summarizing the act and the FTC rules relative to it, describes the following responsibility of direct marketers under the act: catalog or mail order solicitations must disclose for each warranty product either the full text of the warranty or notice that it may be obtained free upon written request.

Online Direct Marketing Due to the information explosion, online direct marketing activities have become one of the focal points of the FTC. In fact, the FTC has produced a four element 'Privacy Policy' in an effort to assist companies in telling their customers what information they are collecting, how they will use it, what security is in place, and how consumers can opt out of providing information.

Figure 13.12   Overview of the FTC rules and regulations for direct marketers

Those direct marketers using online media must be aware of and comply with the FTC regulations. The four elements in the FTC's privacy policy for online direct marketing are:[39]

1. Notice: websites should provide consumers with clear and conspicuous notice of their information practices, including what information they collect, how they collect it, how they use it, whether they disclose the information to other entities, and whether other entities are collecting information through the site.
2. Choice: consumers should be offered choices as to how their personal information will be used beyond completing a transaction.
3. Access: consumers should be offered reasonable access to the information that a website gathers about them, including the opportunity to review such data and correct or delete data.
4. Security: organizations that have websites should take reasonable steps to protect the security of information they gather from their consumers.

The FTC is constantly updating its consumer privacy protection. On March 26, 2012, the FTC issued its final report setting forth best practices for businesses to protect the privacy of American consumers and give them greater control over the collection and use of their personal data. The report expands on a preliminary staff report released in December 2010, which proposed a framework for consumer privacy in light of new technologies that allow for the rapid data collection and sharing that are often invisible to consumers. The goal of the FTC Privacy Policy is to balance the privacy interests of consumers with innovation that relies on information to develop beneficial new products and services.[40] The FTC also offers tips and advice for businesses to ensure the privacy and security of consumers across a number of different areas, including the following:[41]

- **Children's privacy**: the Children's Online Privacy Protection Act (COPPA) gives parents control over what information websites can collect from their kids. On July 1, 2013, the FTC added new provisions for marketers to follow. Those companies operating a website designed for kids, or having a website geared to a general audience but collecting information from those under the age of 13, must comply with COPPA's requirements.
- **Consumer privacy**: the FTC privacy policy ensures businesses are honoring the promises they have made to their consumers regarding what personal information they are collecting and regarding how the company will use consumer data.
- **Credit reporting**: the FTC provides information about company responsibilities under the Fair Credit Reporting Act and other laws when using, reporting, and disposing of information in consumer reports or credit reports.
- **Data security**: the FTC has free resources for businesses to help them establish a security plan to safeguard sensitive personal information about their customers or employees in their files or on their network.
- **Gramm-Leach-Bliley Act**: this Act addresses financial institutions and requires them to explain their information-sharing practices to their customers and to safeguard sensitive data.
- **Red Flags rule**: the Red Flags rule requires many businesses and organizations to implement a written Identity Theft Prevention program designed to detect the warning signs, or red flags, of identity theft in their day-to-day operations.
- **Privacy shield**: the EU–U.S. Privacy Shield Framework provides a method for companies to transfer personal data to the United States from the European Union (EU) in a way that is consistent with EU law. The Framework replaces the U.S.–EU Safe Harbor program, which is no longer valid. Companies working with Europe must understand the provisions of this Framework. A company's compliance with the principles is enforceable under Section 5 of the FTC Act, prohibiting unfair and deceptive acts.
- **Tech**: the FTC has resources to assist any company that designs, develops, or sells mobile apps, smartphones, or other tech tools, in considering the privacy and security implications of their products and services.

In conclusion, all direct marketers should take note of the FTC rules and regulations prior to carrying out their marketing activities and utilizing various media. Visit the FTC website (www.ftc.gov) to obtain complete details and updates on FTC rules and regulations. Keep in mind that these regulations are constantly being updated.

Consumer Financial Protection Bureau

The Consumer Financial Protection Bureau (CFPB) is a governmental agency that was created in response to the 2008 financial crisis to protect consumers. The CFPB, established in 2011, addresses the serious problems the United States has with debt collection, including creditors:

- debiting accounts without authorization
- making excessive and harassing telephone calls
- calling consumers at all hours of the day or night

- threatening consumers with arrest or criminal prosecution
- threatening consumers with physical harm.

The CFPB has estimated that, in the U.S., one in three consumers—meaning more than 70 million people—are contacted by a creditor or collector seeking to collect a debt each year.[42]

The role of the CFPB is to create tools and resources, answer common questions, and provide tips that help consumers conduct informed comparative shopping so they can navigate and evaluate the financial choices available and determine the financial services that are best for them. Thus, the CFPB is the agency that oversees and ensures that banks, lenders, and other financial companies treat consumers fairly.

Food and Drug Administration

The marketing activities of companies in some areas, such as in the pharmaceutical industry, are highly regulated. Pharmaceutical marketing is closely regulated by the U.S. Food and Drug Administration (FDA) to help ensure that promotional materials are accurate, fairly balanced, and limited to information that has been approved by the FDA.

The FDA Center for Drug Evaluation and Research has a division dedicated to establishing and policing guidelines for all pharmaceutical marketing communications. The Office of Prescription Drug Promotion (OPDP) is the FDA office responsible for monitoring external communications. The OPDP has a team of reviewers who are responsible for ensuring that all pharmaceutical communications and promotional materials are:

- consistent with FDA-approved labeling (on-label)
- truthful and accurately communicated
- fairly balanced between risks and benefits
- supported by substantial evidence.

OPDP contains two divisions: the Division of Professional Promotion and the Division of Direct-to-Consumer Promotion, which recognizes some of the differences between the two types of promotions and audiences. The OPDP goes beyond the monitoring of pharmaceutical print and broadcast advertisements as its staff members also travel to major medical meetings and pharmaceutical conventions to monitor promotional exhibits and activities.

Let's discuss some of the above legal restrictions in greater detail:

- **Substantiation of claims**—claims stated in the approved Product Information (PI) have been proven in several phases of clinical trials prior to approval. The FDA reviews the data and convenes panels of experts to review the findings prior to approving the drug to be manufactured and marketed. FDA rules mandate that when pharmaceutical company ads talk about treatment, they stay within the approved product label. In other words, the advertisement cannot suggest that a given pharmaceutical drug is 'safe' or 'more effective' or 'more convenient' than the package insert demonstrates. FDA rules also do not allow for any comparative statements that imply superiority or inferiority, as such statements would need to be supported by substantial evidence, such as two adequate head-to-head clinical trials.

- **Fair balance**—FDA rules mandate that when speaking about treatment, a pharmaceutical marketer must provide 'fair balance' in the advertisement or promotional material. That means that both a medication's benefits and important side-effects (formally called adverse events) must be presented. The side-effects cannot be minimized in any way. Pharmaceutical marketers must avoid minimizing words such as 'little, only and just.' Part of the 'balance' has to do with placement. Safety should follow efficacy immediately as opposed to waiting until the end of the advertisement to be discussed. Finally, fair balance also implies that the risk and benefit information shared should be given relatively equal weight. In other words, a pharmaceutical marketer cannot spend two minutes talking about benefits and ten seconds mentioning side-effects.
- **Overstatement of efficacy**—this regulation pertains to an overstatement of efficacy or quality of life (QOL) claims. FDA rules mandate that when speaking about treatment, pharmaceutical marketers must avoid 'quality of life claims' in advertisements and promotional materials. 'Quality of life' includes being able to do activities, hobbies, or anything else that makes life worthwhile and enjoyable, which are not typically measured in clinical trials of a given pharmaceutical drug. No statements beyond those in the Product Information are allowed, nor are superlative interpretations of those claims. The FDA regularly sends warning letters or issues fines for promotional materials that exaggerate the efficacy of a product or make an unsubstantiated claim of superiority over another product.

Check out the pharmaceutical advertisement shown in Figure 13.13. Notice how this advertisement has been evaluated to ensure that it complies with all of the previously discussed OPDP regulations. This intense scrutiny of ads is required in the pharmaceutical industry.

Not so long ago (in the 1990s), pharmaceutical sales representatives of various pharmaceutical companies would call on physicians with an arsenal of free gifts and offer plush benefits, such as free lunches, dinners, weekend trips, tickets to theater productions, and even circus tickets or amusement park passes for the physician and their entire family. In 2002, Pharmaceutical Research and Manufacturers of America (PhRMA) established specific guidelines that affect the direct marketing practices of pharmaceutical companies to physicians.

The *Code on Interactions with Health Care Professionals* is PhRMA's guidelines specific to live interactions between pharmaceutical companies and medical providers. These guidelines have imposed spending limits on meals, speaker training and speaker program guidelines, and the distribution of promotional merchandise. To comply with PhRMA guidelines, pharmaceutical sales representatives cannot leave a single pen, notepad, or mug bearing the name or logo of a pharmaceutical brand behind after they make an office sales call or they will be in violation of PhRMA regulations. Items given to healthcare professionals must not be of substantial value ($100 or less) and they must be educational in nature (such as medical reference books) and benefit patients in the long term.

State and federal government regulations govern the marketing of pharmaceutical products and serious consequences exist for noncompliance. Only a product's scientifically proven properties, verified by the FDA, can be discussed in its marketing. Furthermore, pharmaceutical representatives strive to provide the most accurate information in order to build credibility and earn the trust of physicians over time.

Figure 13.13   Pharmaceutical advertisement Creative design by Nicole Hoadley. All Rights Reserved.

Many doctors find that, overall, direct-to-consumer (DTC) advertising benefits patients and helps strengthen the patient–physician relationship. Getting patients into needed therapy is one of the most important roles of DTC advertising. By helping to reduce underdiagnosis and under-treatment, DTC ads benefit patients and the healthcare system.

U.S. Postal Service

Through its Inspection Service, and in compliance with the Private Express Statutes, the U.S. Postal Service has established rules and regulations that impact the promotional activities of direct marketers. The Inspection Service is constantly on the lookout for fraud and deception through the mail; the Private Express Statutes, by granting the U.S. Postal Service a form of delivery monopoly, determine the classification and cost of promotional matter that can be circulated outside the postal monopoly.

State and Local Regulation

Certain organizations using direct marketing strategies, including insurance companies, small lending associations, banks, and pharmaceutical companies, are closely regulated by state legislation, especially relative to promotion and pricing tactics. State legislators have become increasingly active in consumer issues and in privacy matters, such as those that affect mailing lists and promotional use of the telephone. The matters of state sales and use taxes, as they relate to taxation of advertising and promotional services, are also of vital concern to direct marketers.

An example of state and local regulations that affect direct marketing activities is the Truth in Advertising legislation. Truth in Advertising was fashioned after a model statute first proposed in 1911. Most states have so-called truth in advertising legislation that governs the conduct of promotional activities in intrastate commerce.

Private Organizations

Better Business Bureaus, the history and influence of which go back more than half a century, are located in most major cities and are sponsored by private businesses and organizations to prevent promotional abuses though commonsense regulation. Likewise, trade groups, along with the DMA, have promulgated ethical guidelines for use by their members and others desiring to adhere to them.

THE FUTURE: SELF-REGULATION OR LEGISLATION

Many believe that these issues are merely generational, and, as technology continues to advance, the concerns will fade away. Many privacy debates may seem irrelevant down the road. However, while these issues remain hot topics today, there are two methods for dealing with them—self regulation or legislation.

Self-Regulation

The preferred method for dealing with the issues of the regulatory environment is self-regulation by direct marketers. Years ago, Donn Rappaport, chairman of the American List Counsel, presented an eight-step self-regulation plan for direct marketers to follow. The basic guidelines of that plan are still relevant today. Figure 13.14 provides an overview of Rappaport's plan.

Legislation and Permission Marketing

Permission marketing obtains the consent of a customer before a company sends out a marketing communication to that customer via the Internet. In other words, permission marketing gives the consumer control over what online communications come to them. It is a parallel to opt-out procedures, whereby the consumer must opt in to receive marketing messages from select organizations seeking to communicate with the consumer. Permission marketing must start with consumers' explicit and active consent to receive online commercial messages, and must always give consumers the option to stop receiving messages at any time.

1. Allow the consumer some measure of control over what lists or types of lists their name is on. Include a notice in every marketing communication, stating your list rental practices and offering to remove the name of anyone who prefers that their name not be released to other mailers.

2. Ensure that we know who's renting our lists and what they are planning to do with them. Direct marketers must pay close attention to list renters that plan to combine your file with other files, abstracts, or overlays.

3. Review all third-party cooperative arrangements with regard to list rights. From time to time, a credit card processor will lay claim to the names of people who charge mail-order purchases to their credit cards. Remember, they are your customers regardless of how they paid. Be wary of any arrangement that dilutes your rights of ownership.

4. Make sure that information is used for the purpose for which it was gathered. In other words, if you sell women's clothes and happen to sell a significant volume in large sizes, use that information to develop more large-size business. Don't rent your large-size customer names to a weight-loss program.

5. Stop scaring consumers unnecessarily over how much personal data on them is actually available. For example, Pacific Bell Telephone Company once began promoting its customer file with the announcement: 'Now a business list from the company that has everyone's number.' Is this kind of claim really worth the scare it may instill in the consumer?

6. Eliminate deceptive or misleading direct mail. Does direct mail that looks like an official document from the IRS really work in the long run? Even if it did, it's deceptive and it raises suspicion about the direct marketing industry.

7. Use personalization wisely. There is a fine line between familiarity with the consumer and an invasion of their personal privacy. Keep in mind that certain types of personal data should not be included in personalization.

8. Make sure that the consumer is not ripped off or compromised by the dissemination of personal data. Since consumers are serious about the issue of personal privacy, direct marketers must safeguard against privacy abuses.

Figure 13.14   Donn Rappaport's Eight-Step Plan for direct marketers. Used with permission of Donn Rappaport.

Source: Adapted from Donn Rappaport, 'What We Should Say (and Do) About Privacy,' *Direct Marketing News*, October 11, 1993.

Online Legal Issues

Today, companies have easy access to more data than ever before; especially given all of the metrics that are generated by digital and social media analytics. While they collect some of this data directly from their own websites and mobile apps, they must rely on third parties for much of this data. This is especially true when it comes to social media, where companies typically have little to no ability to access the raw data associated with the interactions their accounts and content generate on these companies' platforms.[43] Third-party data providers use data to generate metrics that companies rely on to gauge the productivity of their efforts on popular platforms.[44] Companies must trust the accuracy and integrity of the measurements that are being provided to them. This is where additional online legal issues may arise, such as ad fraud.

Ad fraud is the process of creating fake traffic, clicks, impressions, and other engagements to generate revenue through ads. The methods of fraudsters are always changing. As one form of ad fraud is discovered and remedied, another pops up in its place. The five most common forms of ad fraud are as follows:[45]

1. Bots: **bots** are computer programs that are designed to mimic human interaction on a website or ad. Bots can be programmed to play videos, click certain places, and interact with ads to generate engagement.
2. Click farms: **click farms** are the human side of bots. Instead of bots being programmed to engage with certain ads or content, humans are paid to click on the content and engage with the ad in ways that remove the predictability inherent in bot interactions. Most click farms are based in developing or underdeveloped nations and are notoriously hard to pinpoint and solve.
3. Ad injections: **ad injections** operate by replacing ads on a specific website with malicious ads or ads not intended by the publisher. These are often done with browser extensions or user-installed software.
4. Domain spoofing: **domain spoofing** occurs when advertisements are created that effectively mimic a trusted domain and generate traffic and engagement to the falsified website. This can lower trust in the publisher's site and open users to forms of privacy breaches.
5. Cookie stuffing: cookies, as previously explained in Chapter 3, track how a user behaves on a certain website and can be used for remarketing purposes. For these specific reasons, they can be beneficial to the user. If a user visits a shoe website and views a specific style repeatedly, the site will now show ads for that model. **Cookie stuffing** maliciously utilizes the website tracking system by placing cookies from other websites on the original publisher's website without the user being informed. This means that the users' interactions on this site are no longer limited to being utilized by the original publisher, but various undisclosed third-party sites may now see the products with which the visitor interacted, information that was entered, and so on. This creates issues with user consent and data infringement.

Emerging Privacy Concerns

As new technologies emerge, so do accompanying concerns about consumer privacy rights. One clear example lies in the use of facial recognition. Governmental agencies have been using facial recognition technology to identify threats and prevent crime for years. In fact, China is the leader in facial recognition software which is used for securely entering buildings, monitoring large spenders in retail stores, and also identifying criminals.[46]

Facial recognition technology has now been extended to the marketing field, which brings about associated consumer privacy concerns. Retailers are integrating facial recognition technology into cameras to estimate a customer's age, gender, or mood so stores can target them with ads on in-store video screens.[47] Much of the privacy concerns regarding facial recognition are grounded in ethics. These ethical concerns raise questions such as: Is it ethical for retailers to monitor large spenders and deliver targeted ads based on the consumer's profile? And what kind of consent should transpire for facial recognition tracking and marketing? These questions and more regarding the use of facial recognition in marketing will need to be addressed in the future as facial recognition software becomes more widely available.[48] As with most new technological innovations, new legislation will likely be created to ensure ethical and legal compliance.

SUMMARY

Upholding ethical guidelines in carrying out direct marketing activities is crucial to the present and future success of the direct marketing industry. The three primary areas of legislative oversight are intellectual property rights, security, and privacy. Privacy is the area of greatest concern for direct marketers. Privacy issues encompass personal privacy, information privacy, and offline and online privacy—including spam. The opt-in and opt-out mechanisms, along with permission-based marketing, are some of the ways consumer privacy issues are being addressed. In addition, security concerns have arisen greatly over the past few years because of security breaches; companies are addressing these concerns as well. Direct marketers must be mindful of the consumer's right to safety, information, selection, confidentiality, and privacy.

The regulatory environment is both dynamic and uncontrollable. Direct marketing regulatory authorities include the FCC, FTC, U.S. Postal Service, state and local entities, and private organizations. The FCC oversees the Telephone Consumer Protection Act. The FTC rules govern advertisements, mail and telephone orders, telemarketing, delivery, the negative option rule, guarantees, endorsements and testimonials, testing, merchandise mailing, pricing, bait and switch advertising, use of the words 'free' and 'new,' disclosures of foreign origin merchandise, warranties, and online direct marketing. The marketing activities in some industries, such as pharmaceuticals, are governed by the FDA or other federal regulatory bodies. Direct marketers must maintain compliance with the many laws affecting direct marketing activities, while not losing sight of the bottom-line objective: maximizing customer relationships and customer satisfaction while sustaining a profitable business. The preferred method to deal with issues in the regulatory environment is through self-regulation by direct marketers.

KEY TERMS

ad fraud	fair balance
ad injections	infomediaries
annoyance	intellectual property
bots	interest-based advertising
chief privacy officer (CPO)	morals
click farms	overstatement of efficacy
code of ethics	permission marketing
cookie stuffing	privacy
data security	Privacy Act of 1974
domain spoofing	privacy fundamentalists
ethics	privacy pragmatists

privacy unconcerned	right to selection
right to confidentiality	spam
right to information	substantiation of claims
right to privacy	violation
right to safety	

REVIEW QUESTIONS

1. What is the purpose of the DMA's guidelines for ethical business practice?
2. List and briefly explain the five consumer rights.
3. What is a chief privacy officer (CPO)? What is their primary role in an organization?
4. What are the four components of the DMA's Commitment to Consumer Choice?
5. Explain the role of infomediaries and why some consumers might object to them.
6. What are the names and recommendations of some of the private organizations that provide ethical guidelines for direct marketing?
7. Explain the impact of federal regulations on direct-to-consumer marketers in the pharmaceutical industry. Provide another example of a specific industry where marketing activities are highly regulated.
8. What is spam? Why are there so many negative feelings toward spam? What is currently being done to eliminate spam?
9. What is the current status of the FCC/FTC Do Not Call Registry?
10. Using the online legal sources provided in the chapter, provide a legal update on permission marketing and spam as they affect direct marketing activities.

EXERCISE

Imagine you are the first CPO for a major credit card company. Your organization, like all credit card companies, unfortunately, has the typical reputation of selling your customers' information to various firms. You want to change the reputation your company has regarding this matter so that you may gain a competitive edge over your competition. What do you think are some of the regulations and ethical codes you are subject to follow set forth by legislation, private organizations, and organizations such as the FTC? Also explain any steps that your company may take to regulate itself that aren't currently being taken by other companies.

CRITICAL THINKING EXERCISE

How might the continuing technological developments in marketing affect the ethical or legal issues pertaining to consumer privacy? What can direct marketers do to alleviate these concerns? Identify a company or an organization that is responding to consumer privacy concerns today. Provide an overview of what that company or organization is doing and predict what it might do in the future to continue to address consumer privacy concerns.

READINGS AND RESOURCES

- Data & Marketing Association: https://thedma.org/accountability/ethics-and-compliance/dma-ethical-guidelines
- Data & Marketing Association: https://thedma.org/resources/compliance-resources/online-behavioral-advertising-compliance/iba-data-compliance-checklist/
- ANA Nonprofit Federation: www.nonprofitfederation.org
- Facial recognition: www.cnbc.com/2019/05/16/this-chinese-facial-recognition-start-up-can-id-a-person-in-seconds.html
- GDPR: https://martechtoday.com/privacy-design-deeper-dive-gdpr-requirement-212463?utm_source=zest.is&utm_medium=referral&utm_term=zst.5abb83fe69c4a
- Digital legal issues: https://econsultancy.com/when-data-metrics-cause-company-bad-decisions

CASE: SNOW COMPANIES

Very few marketers have more ethical and legal regulations imposed on their marketing activities than those who operate in the pharmaceutical and biotech industry. This industry is highly regulated, both externally and internally. Compliance is the name of the game.

Just think of the sophisticated web of key players in this industry and how each player affects the actions of another. Those key players include patients, doctors, pharmaceutical companies, medical trade associations, insurance companies, and the government.

The need for ethical use of patients' medical information is quite obvious in this industry, as each patient's medical records are private. These are highly sensitive documents that must be kept strictly confidential. However, the barrage of legal restrictions imposed on the marketing of branded pharmaceutical drugs is simply mind-boggling. This case will present the challenges and marketing strategies associated with pharmaceutical marketing.

The ethical and legal regulations associated with pharmaceutical marketing make 'business as usual' vastly different from that of nearly any other industry.

With a decrease in the variety of marketing activities legally and ethically permitted by pharmaceutical sales reps visiting doctors, many pharmaceutical marketers are now placing more emphasis on direct-to-consumer (DTC) marketing. Investments in direct marketing activities in this industry have been rising for decades and are expected to continue to grow in the future.

Direct-To-Consumer (DTC) Marketing

Have you ever wondered about the drug your doctor prescribed to you or a loved one? Do you ever wish you could talk to someone who has a similar condition? Have you ever researched a disease or condition you or a loved one has in advance of a doctor's visit to be better prepared to ask the right questions? If you've answered 'yes' to any of these questions, you are among the hundreds of millions of people across the nation who have helped to make direct-to-consumer (DTC) or direct-to-patient (DTP) pharmaceutical and biotechnology marketing a burgeoning endeavor. DTC/DTP pharmaceutical advertising is considered to be any marketing communication for prescription drugs that directly targets the final consumer, or individual patient, as opposed to promotions that target the physicians who write prescriptions. DTC/DTP marketing is currently allowed only in the United States and New Zealand. Other countries allow a variety of unbranded educational programs, such as grants for support groups or disease-awareness events.

While most consumers desire more information on the products they take or have been prescribed, the U.S. Food and Drug Administration (FDA) closely regulates this type of communication. In addition, the industry body PhRMA has created specific guidelines which pharmaceutical companies must follow. PhRMA's *Direct-to-Consumer Advertising about Prescription Medicines* are guidelines specific to direct promotion to consumers of prescription medications. These guidelines address the use of actors in television and print advertisements, the content of advertisements, and the lead times before DTC advertising for a new product may begin.

Products in other industries that pose significant health and occupational risks to individuals do not have the same level of scrutiny as do pharmaceuticals. Before a promotional piece can be created for a pharmaceutical product, it needs to undergo an internal review by the pharmaceutical company. Typically, there is a review team for each brand or therapeutic area within the company. These review committees may be called different things:

- Joint Review Committee (JRC)–typically used when two companies co-promote a product
- Promotional Review Committee (PRC)
- Review Committee (RC)
- Communication Committee Review (CCR).

Most review committees are made up of the same key players–legal, medical, regulatory–each tasked with different prime directives and each viewing the promotional material through the lens of their personal experience.

Each and every pharmaceutical advertisement or item that will be seen by either a physician or a consumer must go through an extensive and rigorous review process. Although the exact process varies by pharmaceutical company, the main point to be made is that getting a pharmaceutical advertisement through the review process entails a long and tedious process. An example of this detailed process is revealed in Figure 13.15. This process may take months and require several revisions before the ad or item obtains the necessary approval to be used in marketing.

Given the stringent federal regulations and scrutiny imposed on the direct marketing of pharmaceutical products, innovation is a prerequisite for success in this space. One company that has found a way to innovate and create value for clients is Snow Companies, a DTC/DTP and word-of-mouth healthcare marketing agency.

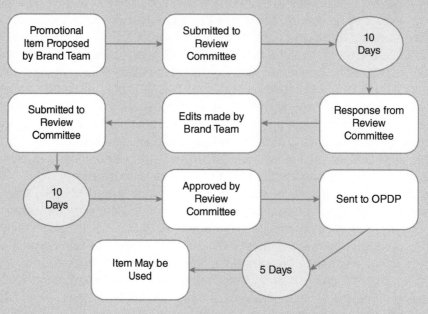

Figure 13.15　Review process flowchart. Used with permission of Snow & Associates.

Snow Companies Patient Ambassador® Program

Brenda Snow, pictured in Figure 13.16, founded Snow Companies in 2001 and developed its proprietary Patient Ambassador® program. After Snow was diagnosed with multiple sclerosis, she became frustrated at how little was being done to help educate, empower, and engage people like herself.

Figure 13.16　Brenda Snow, founder of Snow Companies. Used with permission of Snow & Associates.

Snow Companies provides its clients with a wide variety of services, including graphic design and layout, account services, event management, video production and editing, marketing research, copy and creative writing, call center services, database management, and analytics. As can be seen in Figure 13.17, the company's services include live, digital, and print offerings.

Figure 13.17 The services of Snow Companies. Used with permission of Snow & Associates.

Snow Companies also offers a unique Patient Ambassador® program. The company sources, develops, trains, and manages Patient Ambassadors, who are people with a medical condition who have undergone legal, regulatory, and storytelling training. They help provide a human face to the disease conditions and the brands they represent. Patient Ambassadors help raise awareness of treatment options and educate others about therapy choices by sharing their personal stories. In this role, they become a resource for other patients with the same condition under the guidelines established by the FDA. This powerful and persuasive personal communication has proven to be a success and has helped Snow Companies become a leading marketing force in the pharmaceutical and biotech industry.

Snow Companies employs a variety of direct marketing strategies in the execution of tactics to support clients, including direct mail, outbound and inbound telephone marketing, e-mail marketing, Internet marketing, and social networking to reach target audiences. Patient Ambassadors are used in a mixture of online features, including webisodes, YouTube videos, and features on sponsored websites. Web initiatives, as a percentage of a brand's tactical mix, continue to rise due to decreasing brand budgets. This means that there is increasing scrutiny for effectively measuring marketing spending and the desire to target specific patient segments.

To date, Snow Companies has conducted Patient Ambassador programs in 25 countries, trained tens of thousands of Patient Ambassadors, and connected more than eight million people with their stories. Moreover, it is currently active in more than 150 disease categories and has 75 industry partners. Most importantly, the program gives patients and care partners the knowledge and motivation they need to successfully manage and live with their respective health conditions. Telling and listening to stories is so powerful and has the potential to alter behavior and improve health. That's quite an impact! Further, although face-to-face interactions have the greatest impact on behavior, patients are increasingly leveraging the Internet, and specifically social media, for health topics such as a specific disease or treatment.

Despite successfully using Patient Ambassadors in content online, such as posting approved material on a program Facebook site or listing Local Patient Outreach Programs (LPOPs) for their social network to attend, there are still restrictions. Although DTC marketing has moved online and will remain there for the foreseeable future, social media continues to be an area where communications are limited or tentative. Pharmaceutical companies producing online video content have disabled YouTube commenting, for example, due to HIPAA concerns over the 'friends' and 'subscribers' functions, which might reveal the identity (and diagnosis) of those parties. Depending on the content of a channel's posted videos, that is, branded versus unbranded information, additional restrictions may be made related to disclaimers, share functions, and friend/subscriber options.

Besides patient privacy issues, another major concern for the pharma and biotech industry is the reporting of adverse events (AEs), or side-effects, via the Internet. Members of the industry are required to report AEs within 24 hours of receiving information that fits four criteria: an identifiable reporter, patient, drug name, and adverse event. These requirements increase the burden on any marketing initiatives from a financial and resource perspective, as constant surveillance would be mandatory.

The subsequent surveillance and anticipated results must be weighed to determine if this is an avenue that is positive for the brand. Additionally, Facebook has made screening responses more challenging by lifting the ability to prescreen comments in 2011. This decision makes it even more challenging for pharmaceutical companies to engage with their consumers directly, due to the increased risks related to other regulatory guidelines. The FDA has been studying social media for several years, and in 2014 it made available draft guidelines for the industry entitled 'Internet/Social Media Platforms with Character Space Limitations: Presenting Risk and Benefit Information for Prescription Drugs and Medical Devices.' The agency continues to work in this ever-evolving digital landscape, with more regulations likely to come in the future.

In any case, whether a brand chooses to engage in digital and social mediums or not, in order to remain authentic, real patients should be a major part of the brand's tactics. The more involved these brand ambassadors are, the stronger the messages, brand resonance, and subsequent marketing results. Snow continues to look for new, yet safe, approaches to social media and pharma marketing, and will continue to propose and develop new ways to leverage the conversations patients are having online.

Because of the highly regulated nature of the industry, all of the company's activities come under tough scrutiny from regulatory, legal, and medical reviewers who closely monitor all of these activities to ensure compliance. One of the most effective methods used by Snow Companies is live events, which are high-touch and very resonant with the people who attend. LPOPs are targeted educational symposia for patients, caregivers, family members, and friends to learn about a specific condition and possible treatments for that condition. Snow uses direct marketing tactics to promote LPOPs and find people who are interested in learning more about their condition and interacting with others living with it.

At these events, a Patient Ambassador shares their personal story–not just their trials and tribulations of living with a chronic medical condition, but also the inspiring, the funny, and the elevating parts of their journey. They also share their philosophy of taking charge of their health to inspire others, as well as sharing tips and advice for their specific condition. Disease and treatment information is presented by a healthcare professional. The program attendees can also meet others living with the same condition or opt in for relationship marketing programs for more information. Through these programs, Snow is able to amplify brand messages, such as treatment compliance, not settling, and being proactive with healthcare providers, while still remaining compliant with the industry guidelines.

Conclusion

Snow Companies is an excellent example of an organization that has found a way to be highly successful by effectively employing myriad direct and interactive marketing strategies and tactics within the constraints of a strict regulatory environment.

Case Discussion Questions

1. Discuss the factors contributing to the popularity of direct-to-customer (DTC) marketing in the pharmaceutical industry. Explain the advantages and disadvantages of direct-to-customer marketing of prescription drugs to patients, physicians, and pharmaceutical companies.
2. Describe the number of reviews a pharmaceutical product has to go through before it is marketed to the public. Explain how each review committee is made up and the rationale behind it.
3. Discuss Snow Companies and the Patient Ambassador® program developed by Brenda Snow. Who are the Patient Ambassadors and what role(s) do they play in the marketing of pharmaceutical and biotech products? Explain the communication techniques that they use.
4. Check out the most recent FDA policies on social media usage by pharmaceutical marketers to reveal the latest legal regulations that are in place to police the marketing activities of this highly regulated industry. What future directions do you think the FDA will take?
5. Why are pharmaceutical and biotech marketers wary about using large-scale social networking to promote their products? Explain the advantages and disadvantages of social networking in marketing pharmaceutical and biotech products.

NOTES

1. In October 2016, the DMA rebranded itself and became the Data & Marketing Association. In July 2018, the DMA joined with the Association of National Advertisers (ANA) to form the largest and most influential advertising and marketing association in the world. However, the industry standards and ethical guidelines that the DMA has established remain relevant today (https://thedma.org/ana-driving-growth, retrieved May 25, 2019). The DMA is now a division of ANA, serving both membership bases with its network of educational and professional development resources channeled through the DMA's strategic center for data-driven excellence (www.ana.net/content/show/id/49074, retrieved May 25, 2019).

2. New Environmental Standard on Direct Marketing, September 21, 2007, www.bsi-global. com/en/About-BSI/News-Room/BSI-News-Content/Disciplines/Environmental-Manage ment/DMA-PAS, retrieved May 7, 2008.

3. Direct Marketing Association, https://thedma.org/wp-content/uploads/Green15-Digital-Final-9.14.pdf, retrieved July 25, 2016.

4. Melissa Campanelli, 'EMA Unveils "Please Recycle" Campaign,' July 2007, www.dmnews. com/EMA-unveils-Please-Recycle-campaign/article/html, retrieved April 16, 2008.

5. Direct Marketing Association, 'Recycle Please,' www.the-dma.org/recycle, retrieved April 16, 2008.

6. Direct Marketing Association, 'The Green 15: Benchmarking Environmental Progress,' www.the-dma.org/green15/overviewDMAgreen15.pdf, retrieved April 16, 2008.

7. https://thedma.org/wp-content/uploads/Green15-Digital-Final-9.14.pdf, retrieved July 25, 2016.

8. Adapted from Carl McDaniel, Jr. and Roger Gates (1993) *Contemporary Marketing Research*, 2nd ed. (New York: West Publishing Co.).

9. Charles W. L. Hill (2002) *Global Business Today* (New York: McGraw-Hill/Irwin), p. 50.

10. American Intellectual Property Law Association, www.aipla.org.

11. www.nytimes.com/2002/08/29/business/technology-briefing-internet-ziff-davis-settles-security-breach-case.html, retrieved May 19, 2019; 'Help Wanted: Steal This Database,' Wired News, January 6, 2003; Elaine M. LaFlamme, 'Know the Liabilities of Data Collection,' *New Jersey Law Journal*, March 14, 2003, www.law.com.

12. ZDNet.co.uk, California's S.B. 1386 Requires Notification of Customers When Unencrypted Data Are Stolen: Law Exempts Encrypted Data, November, 2005. http://whitepapers.zdnet. co.uk, retrieved April 11, 2008.

13. James Kindall, 'Lists Help Build Dosier on You,' *Kansas City Star*, September 5, 1978, p. 1.

14. https://techcrunch.com/2018/05/14/anyone-could-download-cambridge-researchers-4-mil lion-user-facebook-dataset-for-years, retrieved May 19, 2019.

15. www.theverge.com/2018/5/14/17352900/facebook-data-exposed-personality-quiz, retrieved May 19, 2019.

16. https://techcrunch.com/2018/05/14/anyone-could-download-cambridge-researchers-4-million-user-facebook-dataset-for-years, retrieved May 19, 2019.

17. http://corporate.findlaw.com/law-library/california-raises-the-bar-on-data-security-and-privacy.html, retrieved July 27, 2016.

18. www.statista.com/statistics/420391/spam-email-traffic-share, retrieved May 19, 2019; www. statista.com/statistics/420391/spam-email-traffic-share, retrieved July 25, 2016.

19. Spam Laws, Spam Origin; www.spamlaws.com/spam-origin.html, retrieved April 16, 2008.

20. www.kelleydrye.com/publications/articles/1418/_res/id=Files/index=0/Ervin_Loeffler_ CAN-SPAM%20Act%20Compliance%20(0-503-5278)%20(2).pdf, retrieved July 26, 2016.

21. DMA Annual Ethics Compliance Report 2016, https://nonprofitfederation.org/wp-content/ uploads/2014/05/DMA-Ethics-Compliance-Report_Final.pdf, retrieved July 26, 2016.

22. www.wired.co.uk/article/what-is-gdpr-uk-eu-legislation-compliance-summary-fines-2018, retrieved May 19, 2019.

23. https://adprofs.co/beginners-guide-to-gdpr, retrieved May 19, 2019.

24. Saul Hansell, 'Virginia Law Makes Spam, with Fraud, a Felony,' *The New York Times*, April 30, 2003, sec. C, p. 1, col. 5.

25. Karl Dentino, 'Taking Privacy into Our Own Hands,' *Direct Marketing* (September 1994).

26. Richard A. Hamilton and Lisa D. Spiller, 'Opinions about Privacy: Does the Type of Information Used for Marketing Purposes Make a Difference?' *International Journal of Voluntary Sector Marketing* 4, no. 3 (September 1999), pp. 251–264.

27. Page Boinest Melton, 'Business Trends to Watch,' *Virginia Business* (February 2001), pp. 78–81.

28. Universal Bank, Important Information Regarding Your Privacy (2001), p. 1.

29. Ibid., p. 5.

30. https://dmachoice.thedma.org/static/pdf/CCC_other_DMA_requirements.pdf, retrieved May 19, 2019; 'Online Marketing Privacy Principles and Guidelines,' July 1997 (New York: The DMA), pp. 3–9.

31. https://thedma.org/resources/compliance-resources/online-behavioral-advertising-compliance/dma-oba-guidelines, retrieved May 30, 2019.

32. Ibid.

33. Ibid.

34. W3C Platform for Privacy Preferences Initiative. Technology and Society Domain. 'Enabling Smarter Privacy Tools for the Web,' May 21, 2011. www.w3.org/P3P.

35. www.fcc.gov.uk.

36. Adapted from the Direct Marketing Association, Telephone Consumer Protection Act (TCPA), www.the-dma.org/guidelines/tcpa.shtml, retrieved September 17, 2003.

37. Direct Marketing Association, 10 Steps to Making a Sale under the FTC's New Telemarketing Sales Rule, DMA Telemarketing Resource Center, www.the-dma.org/government/teleresource center.shtml, retrieved September 12, 2003.

38. The Federal Trade Commission, *Privacy Online: Fair Information in the Electronic Marketplace* (Washington, DC: GPO, May 2000).

39. Direct Marketing Association, 'The FTC's New Telemarketing Sales Rule: Q & A's,' www. the-dma.org, retrieved September 12, 2003.

40. www.ftc.gov/news-events/media-resources/protecting-consumer-privacy/ftc-privacy-report, retrieved July 26, 2016.

41. The following list comes from www.ftc.gov/tips-advice/business-center/privacy-and-security, retrieved July 26, 2016.

42. www.consumerfinance.gov/about-us/blog/were-working-improving, retrieved July 26, 2016.

43. https://econsultancy.com/when-data-metrics-cause-company-bad-decisions, retrieved May 25, 2019.
44. Ibid.
45. The following list comes from www.adpushup.com/blog/types-of-ad-fraud, retrieved May 19, 2019.
46. www.cnbc.com/2019/05/16/this-chinese-facial-recognition-start-up-can-id-a-person-in-seconds.html, retrieved May 19, 2019.
47. Ibid.
48. Ibid.

14
INTERNATIONAL DIRECT MARKETING

Lisa Spiller and Carol Scovotti

CHAPTER CONTENTS

CHAPTER SPOTLIGHT

BODY PARTS DIRECT

I f you are like most college students, you are often strapped for cash. What that small detail translated into was an opportunity for Bank of New Zealand to target college students with a wildly creative direct marketing campaign called 'Body Parts.' The name of the campaign alone arouses curiosity, right? Well, allow us to satisfy your curiosity and reveal the details about this brilliant direct marketing campaign.

Most banks believe that students are a highly important market to target. Are you wondering why? It seems odd since most students do not have much money to be saved or invested. However, it is as a student that most customers begin a relationship with the bank that they are likely to stay with for many years. Establishing relationships with them is seen as investing in future profitability for banks. It makes good sense. Most banks offer lucrative incentives, such as MP3 players or cash sign-on bonuses, to get students to open an account. In New Zealand, many students are a bit cynical toward overt marketing, therefore banks have to be extra creative and strategic when developing and executing their marketing campaigns.

Bank of New Zealand sought out AIM Proximity to help it meet the challenges associated with marketing to students. The campaign objective was to open 6,500 new accounts, with a stretch target of 10,000 accounts–which was the same campaign objective as the previous year, but with the added challenge of a 10 percent reduction in the promotional budget over last year. With the student consumer culture in mind, AIM Proximity and Bank of New Zealand constructed a campaign to appeal to students' desire to *get something*. They wanted something different and unique–something that would really appeal to students. The answer was to develop a program where students could obtain discounts and get free stuff all year (as opposed to just once) to make their frugal life more enjoyable.

The offer featured Bank of New Zealand's Campus Pack, which is a student bank account with a free student discount card. The bank offered additional incentives to students to encourage them to open a Campus Pack account. The campaign was executed through a variety of traditional direct-response media, such as print and direct mail, as well as some nontraditional media, such as mobile bank stands on campus, street posters plastered around campus, banner ads on student websites, inserts in new student orientation bags, and street theater-style stunts on campus. The campaign was creative, bold, and fun. As Figure 14.1 presents, all of the creative materials used in the campaign featured the same basic message–'You don't have to sell your body parts for cash–don't get desperate, get a Campus Pack instead.'

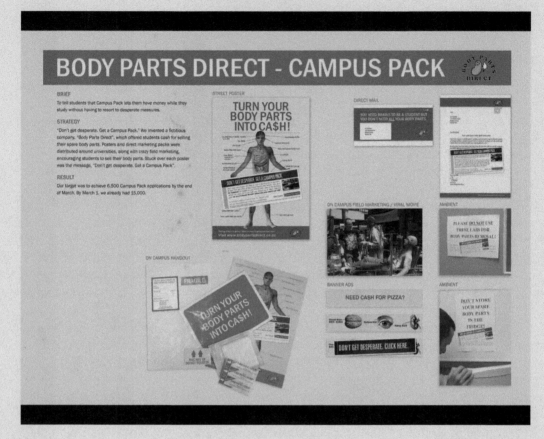

Figure 14.1 Body Parts Direct campus pack. Used with permission of Bank of New Zealand.

The agency invented a fictitious company, Body Parts Direct, which offered students cash for selling their spare body parts. This was crazy marketing–but fun! Need extra cash for pizza? Consider selling an eyebrow! The call to action was to visit Bank of New Zealand's website, visit a branch office, or text-message the company. The campaign was so effective that Bank of New Zealand opened 18,138 new accounts, far surpassing the stretch target of 10,000.[1]

The Bank of New Zealand campaign is proof that highly creative and effective direct and interactive marketing campaigns are being used all over the world. That is the topic of this chapter. We explore international versus domestic direct marketing strategies, factors entering into the decision to market internationally, modes of market entry, and the international direct marketing infrastructure needed in order to be successful in international direct and interactive marketing. In addition, this chapter enables you to explore how direct and interactive marketing strategies are being employed in geographical regions around the world. We hope you enjoy the international voyage!

DIRECT MARKETING AROUND THE WORLD

The world is getting smaller. Facing saturated U.S. markets, many companies are looking overseas to achieve increased sales volume and greater profits. Over the past two decades, global trade has climbed from $200 billion a year to more than $20 trillion.[2] Although those are the two reasons frequently named by organizations seeking international business, other reasons are the hope of expanding into new markets, diversification, achieving economies of scale, and business survival. World exports of merchandise products increased (from $15.8 trillion in 2016 to $19.3 trillion in 2017) after two years of decline; world exports of commercial services increased 7 percent (from $5.4 trillion in 2017 to $5.8 trillion).[3] The United States's trade with the world was $4.2 trillion in 2018.[4] The top trade partners for the United States in 2017 were China at $635.4 billion, Canada at $581.6 billion, Mexico at $557.6 billion, Japan at $204.1 billion, and Germany at $171.5 billion.[5]

Today, nearly half of the global brands are headquartered outside of U.S. borders. According to a study by Goldman Sachs, it is estimated that by 2050 the 'BRIC' economies of Brazil, Russia, India, and China will, in all likelihood, surpass that of today's six largest economies, thus creating a new world order.[6] Revenue generated by international direct marketing activities has continued to increase over the years.

The Internet has helped many companies enter international markets because of its worldwide access. It has also prompted the rise of Internet-dependent businesses such as Uber and Amazon. Marketing on the Internet through a website is the same thing today as opening a global business with a worldwide audience. Unlike traditional exporting, which began with brokers and other intermediaries that assisted companies in generating international sales from preselected foreign countries, a website is immediate and inexpensive. However, it does not permit much selectivity in choosing markets. Research has shown that 77.1 percent of the population in North America has Internet access, and that 88.9 percent of Internet users are located outside of North America.[7] This may often lead to fulfillment problems for direct marketers, who don't have the distribution network or capability of fulfilling international orders in some countries.

There are four compelling reasons for direct marketers to decide to go international in their marketing efforts. These are limited growth opportunities in the domestic market, shared global values, the high cost of new product development, and competitive forces.[8] The potential of many international markets is extremely attractive for direct marketers and has been for a number of years. International direct marketing is not new. Let's take a short look at the use of direct marketing around the world.

According to the Direct Marketing Association (DMA) *Statistical Fact Book*, the oldest known catalog was produced by Aldus Manutius of Venice in 1498 and listed the titles of 15 texts Manutius had published.[9] Next came seed and nursery catalogs, the earliest known mercantile gardening catalog being a printed price list issued by William Lucas, an English gardener. But it was in Germany that direct marketing truly has its roots. Germany had a parcel post system by 1874, and a collect on delivery (COD) system by 1878. The first known European consumer catalog was distributed in 1883, about the same time that Richard Sears was creating his first catalog in the United States.[10] In 1912, a German businessman, August Stuchenbrok, produced a 238-page catalog—which was five years before Leon Bean (of L. L. Bean) sold his first pair of boots.[11] The largest mail order company in the world is a German company, Otto Versand, which owns Crate & Barrel, and operates in more than 20 countries.

DIFFERENCES BETWEEN DOMESTIC AND INTERNATIONAL DIRECT MARKETING

What makes international direct marketing different from domestic direct marketing? Market uncertainty is one of the biggest differences. The uncertainty of different foreign business environments is due to differences in infrastructure, technology, competitive dynamics, legal and governmental restrictions, customer preferences, culture, accepted payment methods (such as the use of credit cards), and many additional uncontrollable variables. These risk factors make many direct marketers hesitate to leap into international markets, regardless of their potential.

To ensure success in foreign markets, direct marketers must first research the cultural differences of the prospective market. Primarily, the culture being examined needs to be recognized as being either a collectivist or individualistic society. In a collectivist culture, emphasis is placed on the group as a whole. History, family ties, loyalty, and tradition are revered above individual accomplishments. Societies sharing strong attributes of collectivism include cultures like those of Latin America, Asia, and the Middle East. In individualistic cultures, the value lies in the achievements and successes of the individual person. Independence and a strong sense of self take priority over any group focus. Cultures such as the United States, Europe, Canada, and Australia display this individualistic quality. For example, Tang, the orange-flavored powdered drink, was marketed successfully in the United States as a substitute for the common orange juice breakfast drink. However, in France, Tang had to be marketed as a refreshment beverage because the French do not normally drink orange juice at breakfast. Thus, customer preferences driven by cultural differences dictated the marketing strategy.[12]

Different country laws can also dictate marketing strategies. For example, in Europe there are many restrictions on advertisements for cigarette and tobacco products, alcoholic beverages, and pharmaceutical products. Ads for other products may also be regulated. Advertisements in the U.K. cannot show a person applying an underarm deodorant. Therefore, ads are modified to show an animated person applying the product.[13] German law bans comparative advertising. In addition, many Western European countries allow partial nudity in late-night television advertisements. There may be tremendous opportunities in foreign markets, but direct marketers must conduct careful, calculated research before they venture abroad.

The high prevalence of different languages is a growing obstacle for marketers with domestic and international direct marketing. Recent technology in natural languaging processing (NLP) enables and enhances the auto-translation of foreign languages. It uses artificial intelligence with computer science and computational linguistics to manipulate human language. In addition, NLP encompasses various methods and approaches for analyzing human language such as statistical and machine learning, rules-based, and text- and voice-based data.[14] NLP may affect aspects of consumer behaviour in global markets. One way that businesses use NLP techniques is to understand customer complaints. Royal Bank of Scotland, for example, uses text analytics to summarize common trends from customer review pages on electronic forms.[15] E-mails, surveys, and call center conversations are sources of data for analysis of customer complaints.

Other new advancements in information technology related to direct and digital marketing include mobile payments, unmanned stores, and facial recognition. The evolution of mobile payments has shaped the future of consumer purchasing behavior. By 2030, mobile payments are expected to make cash and credit cards unnecessary for final consumers, according to The Institute of Electrical and Electronics Engineers (IEEE).[16] Storefronts such as Amazon Go are revolutionizing offline shopping experiences. Customers no longer have to wait in long checkout lines—simply, grab and go! Apple, Facebook, and Snapchat are among numerous companies using facial recognition technology to enhance user experiences.

MAKING THE DECISION TO GO INTERNATIONAL

Various researchers have offered tips or processes to follow when deciding to begin international direct marketing activities. Today, it has become increasingly important to pursue global market segmentation (GMS) as a starting point for going global. GMS can be defined as the process of identifying specific segments, country groups, or individual consumer groups across countries of potential customers who exhibit similar buying behaviors.[17] The following five-step approach is a synthesis of the many processes suggested for screening, selecting, and marketing to another country.[18]

Step 1: Assess Your International Potential

Direct marketers must analyze their domestic position in their industry to provide an indication of the strength of their foundation and resource base from which they can expand. A part of this assessment is determining whether there are adequate internal and external resources to assist them in penetrating international markets. For example, when eBay started expanding abroad in the early 2000s, it limited expansion because it didn't have the 'internal bandwidth,' meaning enough internal expertise, to support fast expansion. Despite its internal limitations, it managed to expand into more than a dozen countries by acquiring existing companies, forming partnerships with local companies already established in the marketplace, or starting from scratch. Some of these external resources may include *expert advice* and *counseling*. Many organizations exist in the private and public sectors to assist firms in beginning an international marketing program. Such resources include the following:

- Bureau of the Census (www.census.gov)
- CIA—Country Fact Sheets (www.cia.gov)
- Forefront Corporation (www.forefrontinternational.com)
- GroupM (www.groupm.com)
- Market Development Cooperator Program (MDCP) (www.ita.doc.gov/td/mdcp)
- Partners International (www.partnersinternational.com)
- U.S. Chambers of Commerce (AMCHAMS) (www.uschamber.org/intl/amcham.la.htm)
- U.S. Department of Commerce—Foreign Trade Highlights (www.doc.gov)
- U.S. Department of State (www.state.gov)
- U.S. Market Development Group (www.usmarketgroup.com)
- U.S. Small Business Administration (www.sba.gov)
- U.S. Trade Information Center (1-800-USA TRADE).

In addition, many industry trade associations and graduate business programs at universities provide assistance to companies beginning their international marketing activities.

Step 2: Conduct Market Research

Conducting market research is critical to understanding the cultural differences and market nuances that may exist between and among countries. Identifying potential overseas markets involves a great deal of time, effort, and research. However, given the vast amount of data available about each foreign market, researching a single market is likely to provide information overload. Savvy direct marketers sort through all the data and determine the pertinent information they need to analyze the potential of a foreign market.

Direct marketers must determine whether consumers have a basic need for their products/ services and whether the resources necessary for them to carry out local business activities are available. International direct marketers must understand the local color of the destination country, including such information as what consumers buy, why they buy, how they pay for it, and what motivates them to make a purchase. At a minimum, direct marketers must understand local buying behavior, typical payment methods, advertising practices, and privacy laws. The customers in other countries are not Americans who simply live abroad. They have different cultures, different tastes, and different needs and wants, and must be segmented accordingly. For example, Europe is highly diverse in terms of geography, language, economic development, spending habits, disposable income, and so on. Even packaging varies by country. In Belgium, it is common to see a playful baby in a diaper, while just across the border in Germany, showing a baby in a diaper is considered repulsive. Instead, packages typically show a mother cuddling the baby. Therefore, direct marketers structuring their approach as if there were one unified European Union will likely fail.

Direct marketers must also research the national business environment of the target country, including its cultural, political, legal, and economic situation. They must determine as well whether the language, attitudes, religious beliefs, traditions, work ethic, government regulation, government bureaucracy, political stability, fiscal and monetary policies, currency issues, cost of transporting goods, and the country image are understandable and conducive to doing business there.

The state of a country's infrastructure must be factored into the potential for success in that country's market. Infrastructure is normally a leading indicator of economic development and must be in place to support the direct marketer. A country's **infrastructure** represents those capital goods and services that serve the activities of many industries. At a minimum, the infrastructure analysis should include the following essential services: transportation, communications, utilities, and banking. There are really four infrastructure pillars that support the international direct marketing industry—the publishing industry, the transportation industry, the banking industry, and advances in high technology.[19] Because of its importance, we discuss infrastructure in greater detail later in this chapter. Market research should also investigate the potential market or site to determine the suitability of the market for the particular product or service. Would the product succeed in this market? Certain locations may not be acceptable due to the lack of resources available for marketing a specific product or service. Therefore, direct marketers must conduct a detailed country-by-country analysis to properly select which markets to penetrate. Market research for each country under consideration can be boiled down to the following primary international market indicators: population, political stability, GDP/inflation, distribution of wealth, age distribution, currency, tariffs and taxes, and computer ownership. Let's look briefly at each. While each of these factors is important in their own right, even more important is how they interact with each other.

Population

Direct marketers should consider the size of the population segments that fit their targeted prospect profile. They should consider a country's population along with its overall wealth. For example, direct marketers should be cautious in entering a country with a large population but little monetary wealth. They may prefer entering a market with a small population that has a high per capita gross domestic product (GDP), such as Singapore or Sweden.

Political Stability

The political stability of a country becomes extremely important for those direct marketers planning to establish a physical presence there. In addition, political shifts in power and leadership may affect foreign exchange rates and tariffs. A reliable source for details on political corruption is Transparency International (www.transparency.org).

GDP/Inflation

The rate of inflation of a country affects the purchasing power of consumers within a country and is closely related to the country's GDP. GDP stands for **gross domestic product**, which is the total market value of all final goods and services produced within a nation's borders in a given year. When assessing a country's GDP and inflation rates, most direct marketers look for annual trends going back as far as five years.

Distribution of Wealth

Direct marketers must assess the distribution of wealth in a country to determine whether there are a substantial number of consumers who are able to afford the product or service. As in the United States, some international countries, such as Mexico, have a situation where the top 10 percent of the population possesses more than 50 percent of the wealth. On the other hand, just over 25 percent of the population is considered 'middle class' when considering purchasing power parity. Yet with almost 1.4 billion people, that equates to more than 400 million in that economic strata. Thus, the size and viability of a market in any country depend on the target market customer's disposable income.

Age Distribution

An analysis of age distribution assesses both the average longevity of the citizens and the age breakdown of the population. The age structure of a population affects the nation's key socioeconomic issues. Countries with young populations (with a high percentage under age) need to invest more in schools, whereas countries with older populations (with a high percentage aged 65 and over) need to invest more in the health sector.[20] For example, a population comprised primarily of young adults is great if you are marketing soft drinks; however, if you are marketing automobiles, the likelihood of these young people having the income to purchase the product is considerably lessened. Age distribution is typically illustrated with population pyramids. The CIA *World Factbook* contains population pyramids for every country and nation-state.

Currency

An assessment of the currency of a foreign country includes an evaluation of the stability, convertibility, and ease of exchange of currency, inflation rates, and credit card penetration. While currency and payment method may be separate issues, they may be related in some countries. For example, the Venezuelan bolívar hyper-inflated in the mid-2010s because oil prices dropped and its president, Hugo Chavez, died. When a currency has no value, consumers cannot pay. Without the ability to pay, there can be no commerce, direct or otherwise![21]

Tariffs and Taxes

How difficult and expensive is it to bring goods across a country's international border? Do local regulations such as tariffs and taxes favor locally produced goods and services over imported ones? These are typical questions that direct marketers must consider when deciding to go international.

Computer Ownership

How widely are computers used, and how many computer users have Internet access? In many countries, the majority of consumers do not have easy Internet access. This poses a problem for direct marketers who seek to create a virtual business.

Postal/Delivery Services

This category includes the postal system as well as private delivery alternatives. Areas to consider include the following:

- adequacy of the change-of-address system available
- the existence of a parcel COD system
- the existence of a track-and-trace system for parcels
- the level of sophistication and format of the postcode system.

If any of these researched items do not satisfy a business's requirements or justify the modifications necessary to carry out the necessary marketing activities in that country, then perhaps that country should be eliminated from further business consideration.

Step 3: Select Your Trading Partners

Based on the research collected and analyzed in Step 2, careful analysis should indicate which markets would be receptive to the particular product and/or service. Direct marketers should select the country or region that holds the greatest potential for successful international marketing. Although many companies are anxious to get an international direct marketing campaign started, it can be extremely taxing on a company. Most experts suggest targeting only one country at a time. Multi-country rollouts are difficult to execute successfully, especially to those new to international marketing.

This step of the process typically requires traveling to those countries or markets that have been selected. When companies 'go in blind,' they miss important nuances that impact success. During these field trips, direct marketers should investigate the nuances of the market and perform a competitor analysis. Many countries select neighboring countries for trading partners or they select those countries that share a common language and culture.

Step 4: Develop an International Direct Marketing Plan

Direct marketers should create a detailed marketing plan itemizing their long-term goals along with the competitive niche the firm is attempting to fill. They should structure the marketing plan to cover a two- to five-year period, along with a competitor analysis. This plan should detail product, communication, and distribution strategies. For example, product and package design can change dramatically from country to country. Homes in European cities are substantially smaller than their counterparts in the United States. Therefore, people buy less per shopping trip, but make more shopping trips per week. It is not uncommon for a German to shop daily for food. Direct marketers must also determine the media mix for communicating the promotional message.

Regarding distribution strategies, direct marketers must determine whether they will have a physical presence in the country. Customers worldwide want the feel of a local presence. This translates into the need to have a local in-country return address along with customer addresses without country codes, response call centers handled in the native language, country- and

589

language-specific websites, prices quoted in local currencies, and so on. However, given today's technological advances, it is possible for U.S. direct marketers to create a 'virtual' local presence if the firm cannot attain a physical presence. This is attained by making the intangible tangible.

The Peruvian Connection is an example of the many direct marketers using multi-channel fulfillment. It obtains inquiries for its catalog from its website, direct mail, and magazine ads. It has retail stores in selected locations, where it sells surplus stock. A good many new sales now originate at its website, the home page of which appears in Figure 14.2.

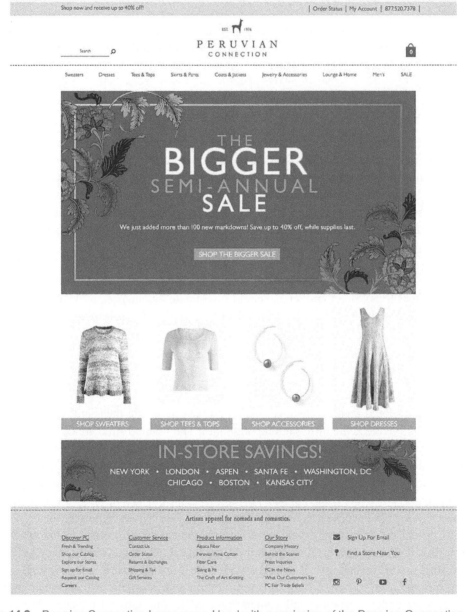

Figure 14.2   Peruvian Connection home page. Used with permission of the Peruvian Connection.

Step 5: Begin International Direct Marketing Activities

Implementing a direct marketing plan is expensive and time-consuming. However, for many direct marketers, it is very well worth it. As direct marketers begin to implement their strategies, revisions may be necessary. The international business environment is extremely unpredictable. It is a dynamic environment that must be constantly monitored. Therefore, as direct marketers begin international direct marketing activities, they will need to continue researching and analyzing the changing business environment.

With all the necessary research and preparation, of course, direct marketers entering foreign markets still do so with greater risk than they face when entering the domestic marketplace. Thus, they should slowly, not hastily, penetrate one country's market at a time. International direct marketing is all about differences. It should be no surprise then that different foreign market entry strategies exist. We now turn to market entry modes.

MODES OF MARKET ENTRY

There are six basic modes of market entry for penetrating an international market: exporting, licensing, joint venture, contract manufacturing, direct investment, and management contracting.

Exporting

An **exporting** company sells its products from its home base without maintaining any of its own personnel overseas. Many successful, well-known direct marketers, such as L. L. Bean, conduct their international marketing via direct exporting from their respective home bases. L. L. Bean is located in Freeport, Maine, mails its catalogs to customers in more than 170 countries, yet it fulfills orders all over the world. However, in some circumstances the company must have a local mailing address because some customers are reluctant to place orders and send money overseas. For example, in Japan, L. L. Bean works with McCann Direct, the specialized direct marketing division of McCann-Erickson Hakuhodo, Japan's largest foreign advertising agency. When L. L. Bean places ads for its catalogs in Japanese media, those catalog orders are sent locally to McCann Direct. McCann Direct then forwards the orders to L. L. Bean's headquarters in Maine, where all the orders for catalogs or products are fulfilled.[22] L. L. Bean also has a distribution arrangement with UPS for parcel fulfillment.[23]

Licensing

Licensing occurs when a **licensor**, a company located in the host country, allows a foreign firm to manufacture a product or perform a service for sale in the **licensee's** country. Licensing is similar to franchising in that a local business in an international country becomes authorized to manufacture or sell specific brand products for another company. Franchising is a form of licensing that has grown rapidly in recent years. The right to use a patent or trademark must be granted to a foreign company under the license agreement contract. The most common licensing agreements occur when a direct marketer allows a firm in a local country market to reproduce a direct marketing catalog in the local language. An example of a direct marketer using licensing agreements to market internationally is that of Orvis. It markets its outdoor clothing, accessories, and fishing equipment by mailing 50 million catalogs a year through four different titles, and operates about 80 retail stores in the United States.[24] In addition, it has more than 20 stores in the U.K.[25] Orvis sells through catalogs, a network of 500 independent dealers worldwide, and its website. It also partners with select licensees.[26] In fact, if you go to its website (www.orvis.com), you can obtain a listing of its worldwide dealer network along with a listing of international market opportunities that Orvis wants to pursue in the future.

Joint Venture

A **joint venture** is created when two or more investors join forces to conduct a business by sharing ownership and control. It is similar to a partnership. Companies understand that marketing alliances with a foreign company can provide a number of benefits. These benefits include easy access to a foreign market, the elimination of tariffs and quotas, faster growth and market coverage, and the ability to penetrate markets that normally would have been closed to wholly owned enterprises. Joint ventures are normally a win-win situation for each of the partners. For example, Recreational Equipment Inc. (REI) and Austad's, a golf supply cataloger, worked out a cooperative venture with one another and mailed their catalogs together to names on both of their Japanese lists.[27] Another example of a joint venture is that of E*TRADE. E*TRADE, a U.S. Internet-based stockbroker, entered into a joint venture with Softbank Corporation of Japan to offer online investing services in Asia. E*TRADE also entered into a second joint venture with Electronic Share Information in Great Britain.[28]

Contract Manufacturing

Many times, a company will outsource or contract with a local manufacturer to produce goods for the company. This strategy, known as **contract manufacturing**, enables companies to take advantage of lower labor costs and faster market entry, to avoid local ownership problems and to satisfy legal requirements that the product must be manufactured locally for it to be sold in that country. For example, visit the website of Texas Instruments at www.ti.com and click on TI Worldwide, and you will learn that TI has manufacturing sites and sales and support offices located in Europe, Asia, Japan, and the Americas.[29] While you're there, take note of the selection of TI websites featuring different languages designed to serve its international customers.

Direct Investment

Direct investment occurs when a company acquires an existing foreign company or forms a completely new company in the foreign country. For example, Walmart currently has more than 11,300 retail stores, with 58 banner names, in 27 countries. Sales in 2019 were $510.3 billion and the company employed 2.1 million associates worldwide.[30] For the fiscal year that ended in

January 2019, Walmart International drove $121 billion in sales, which is almost 24 percent of the company's three business units (Walmart U.S., Walmart International, and Sam's Club).[31] The German company Otto Versand, for example, became the largest mail order company in the world by buying existing companies and building new ones. Otto Versand owns or co-owns over 120 mail-order companies and direct marketing firms in more than 30 countries worldwide.

While direct investment typically yields the highest returns on investment, it also presents the highest risk of failure. For example, when Uber started expanding into foreign markets, it appeared that it was destined to dominate the global ride-sharing industry. However, it also hit major road blocks around the world. Taxi drivers in Spain went on strike, which prompted the government to allow only one Uber permit for every 30 taxi permits. In 2016 Uber chose to sell its Chinese operation to rival Didi, rather than continue to incur losses. Its expansion efforts were thwarted in Germany, France, Russia, Japan, India, South Korea, and even sub-Saharan Africa.[32]

Management Contracting

In **management contracting**, local businesspeople or their government sign a contract to manage the foreign business in their country's market. An example of management contracting is Day-Timers, a U.S. firm located in East Texas, Pennsylvania. Day-Timers uses direct mail to market to millions of businesspeople in the United States. However, it opened offices in Australia, Canada, and the U.K. and hired local employees to manage its foreign business locations because it needed to have people who were familiar with the culture and who could handle incoming phone calls.[33]

Direct marketers must carefully weigh the advantages and disadvantages of each entry method and determine which is best for their company. The choice of mode of market entry depends in the end on many factors, one of which we address next.

INTERNATIONAL DIRECT MARKETING INFRASTRUCTURE

Direct marketers must assess the degree of sophistication of each country's direct marketing infrastructure, with the goal of determining how well they can use it to implement direct marketing activities. Some questions and issues direct marketers might investigate are the following:

- Does the country or region have an active DMA?
- What is the degree to which support services (printing and publishing services, transportation or package delivery services, postal services, and technological services) are present?
- How sophisticated is the credit card and banking system in the country?
- Is there an established pattern of purchasing via familiar direct channels?
- What legislative issues will affect direct marketing activities?

Figure 14.3 provides an itemized list of the direct marketing infrastructure needed to support international direct marketing activities. Let's briefly look at some of the infrastructure supporting international direct marketing activities.

List availability

Quality of postal service

Average postage costs

Percentage of mail-friendly households

Internal or external database

Average direct mail cost per price

Availability of in-line personalization

Standardized addresses

Postal codes

Inbound telemarketing availability

Outbound telemarketing availability

Availability of credit cards

Response channel opportunities

Figure 14.3 Direct marketing infrastructure

Lists and Databases

Lists of both consumer and business customers are normally available for most countries, although different kinds of lists are available in different countries. Direct mail and e-mail lists are important tools for a global direct marketer. However, the list industry (with the exception of Australia, the U.K., Canada, and New Zealand) remains far less developed than that offered within the United States, and list sharing among mail-order companies is nearly unheard of.[34] For example, in Europe, there are multinational lists and local lists. In China, lists of factories, ministries, professional societies, research institutes, and universities are available, though quite expensive.[35] A number of vendors in the US offer international lists, but the quality will vary. It is good practice to test a small representative sample of any list before renting it. Because mailing lists in Russia are so unreliable, Hearst Corporation bypassed direct mail and opted for newsstand sales to distribute the first issues of *Cosmopolitan* to the consumer market.[36] However, Magnavox CATV, which markets cable television equipment, has increased its international mailings to support its many trade shows in developing regions.[37]

Also be aware that a number of laws pertain to information privacy—which normally affects direct marketing list and database activities. Canada's 'Personal Information Privacy and Electronic Documents Act' has had significant impact on direct marketers on both sides of the border.[38] As previously discussed in Chapter 13, the European Union enacted its General Data Protection Regulation (GDPR), requiring companies who gather customer data to inform customers how the data will be stored and used. The regulation applies to any company, regardless of its location, to abide by the law or face stiff penalties. For example, Google was fined €50 million for collecting personal data without letting consumers know how the data was to be used. Lists and databases are clearly key areas of importance to international direct marketers, but it is critical that businesses worldwide protect their data and be transparent about how they use the data they collect.

Fulfillment

Distributing products to the customer is one of the prime difficulties associated with international direct marketing. Direct marketers have two main distribution options available to them—ship products from the home location or establish a bulk distribution operation overseas. Those direct marketers using their home location have three basic options for distributing products: (1) the U.S. Postal Service (USPS) international mail; (2) non-USPS postal delivery via a foreign postal administration, such as the Royal Mail or DHL; or (3) consolidators within the United States (such as Worldpak, Global Mail, and FedEx) that act as service agents for the international direct mailer.

Besides distribution issues, fulfillment concerns also include the determination of payment options. In the United States, most direct marketers offer consumers the option to pay by credit card, check, or money order. These are not necessarily the standards in foreign markets. Credit card penetration is considerably lower in other countries than it is throughout the U.S. In addition, and unlike the U.S., many consumers in foreign countries primarily use their credit cards for vacation purposes only. Debit cards, direct debit, bank transfers (wire services), and invoicing are other payment options to be considered.

Another growing option for transferring money between buyers and sellers is through online transactions facilitated by companies such as PayPal—the former company of the online auction website eBay. The company, through online processes, enables its members to 'send money without sharing financial information, with the flexibility to pay using their account balances, bank accounts, credit cards or promotional financing.' Nearly 98 million active user accounts are maintained in some 190 worldwide markets. The company customizes its website for 21 individual markets and handles 25 different international currencies.[39]

Venmo is a mobile payment service owned by PayPal, which has shown substantial growth since its initial release in 2009. During the fourth quarter of 2018, Venmo had $19 billion in payment volume through Venmo, which equates to an 80 percent increase year-over-year.[40] With Venmo, users can make and share payments, connect with people, make purchases, and even transfer money to their bank! The social commerce platform allows users to share their shopping purchases with their friends. The connection with a network of friends is a new take on online shopping. Users can view, like, and comment on shared purchases, which is an added bonus for businesses by exposing their brand to a network of friends.[41]

An additionally important fulfillment issue is customer service. Direct marketers must make their return policies simple and easy to understand, as well as have toll-free numbers available for consumers to place inquiries or file complaints. Local fulfillment centers should be established to handle orders for foreign countries with language barriers. For example, U.S. inventory for Lands' End's U.K., German, and Japanese catalogs is shipped in bulk to local operations in the U.K. and Japan. The U.K. fulfillment center handles orders originating from its U.K. catalog and German-language catalog, and the Japanese fulfillment center handles orders for its Japanese-language catalog.[42]

Determining the locations for fulfillment centers and deciding whether to centralize fulfillment operations are among the other decisions international direct marketers must make. Garnet Hill and Paper Direct have centralized fulfillment. Garnet Hill is a consumer apparel cataloger that fulfills orders to customers in about 20 different countries from its centralized facility in Franconia, New Hampshire. Paper Direct is a leading direct marketer of preprinted papers and supplies for the laser and desktop publishing industry and offers more than 3,000 items through four separate catalogs to customers in 35 countries, fulfilling all orders from three distribution centers located in Lyndhurst, New Jersey; Hinckley, England; and Northmead, Australia.[43] Visit the website of Paper Direct (www. paperdirect.com) and you will learn that Vista Papers, based in Leicestershire in the U.K., is the exclusive European supplier of Paper Direct products https://www.paperdirect.com/.[44]

Media

Direct marketers must determine the most effective media mix based on consumer preferences in each foreign market. Media decisions are based on a number of market-specific factors, such as media availability, legal restrictions, literacy rates, and cultural factors. A country's level of economic development may also enter into the media mix decision. For example, literacy rates, TV and computer ownership, and sophisticated technology usage tend to be lower in less developed countries. Mature countries with high broadband usage appear to be converging on a norm. However, Internet advertising revenue does not include all investments, like advertiser investment, in building websites.[45]

Canadian tourists represent a sizeable portion of summer travelers to Virginia Beach. Thus, a media plan specifically to attract Canadians from Ontario and Quebec is executed via radio, print, television, and targeted online formats such as e-mail. As presented in Figure 14.4, Virginia Beach offers its Canadian tourists a dedicated microsite in French.

Mike's Bike Tours of Amsterdam uses Facebook and Instagram extensively to generate interest in its tours. As Figure 14.5 reveals, the company also follows up with every customer after the tour and solicits online reviews. These authentic reviews or digital word-of-mouth advertising are very valuable as a form of influencer marketing, as previously discussed in Chapter 10.

Shipping products overnight and using telephone marketing may also be difficult in less developed countries. In these countries, the establishment and maintenance of databases may prove difficult. In some countries, the price of postage is very low; in others, it is quite expensive. In many developing countries, the mail system is slow and not secure. For example, in Mexico, there is a dearth of mailboxes and the system is very slow, although improving. In Argentina, mailboxes are considered a luxury and most residents do not have them. Therefore, mail is often delivered directly underneath the door. In an effort to increase delivery to residents, the Argentinean postal service charges lower rates for items that should fit underneath residents' doors. Telecom Argentina saved on postage and chose to capitalize on this cost-saving opportunity by creating innovative mail pieces targeting different market segments. A variety of designs were created, including flat items such as pencil cases that were mailed to students, along with innovative flat sea waves washed under doors promoting 'a flood' of Internet savings through the company's website. This campaign won a Silver ECHO award for its creativity and achieved a response of 3.2 percent, which was more than double the goal set by Telecom Argentina.[46]

Figure 14.4 Virginia Beach French site. Used with permission of the City of Virginia Beach Convention & Visitors Bureau.

Figure 14.5 Mike's Bike Tours online review. Used with permission of Mike's Bike Tours.

E-mail marketing can offer direct marketers lower development costs and excellent targeting. E-mail is an efficient and cost-effective alternative to direct mail. E-mail marketing across Europe is the fourth most effective channel for customer acquisition, behind word of mouth, SEO, and online local directories.[47] Because of the international growth of e-mail usage, companies such as IBM Watson Campaign Automation, formerly known as Silverpop, a major e-mail marketing provider, have begun preparations to extend their services outside North America.[48]

In addition, e-mail marketing can provide a faster response—just compare a direct mail campaign that typically takes months to roll out to an e-mail campaign that may take only weeks to execute. E-mail newsletters are a recommended first step into international e-mail marketing, because their circulation tends to be greater than that for solo campaigns. However, to successfully implement e-mail marketing, direct marketers must be aware of GDPR as well as each country's local privacy laws. International acceptance for direct response television (DRTV) has grown. Latin America has become one of the first regions outside the United States to be explored. To successfully use DRTV, direct marketers must be keenly aware of the media landscape, including the key TV stations, cable, and satellite opportunities; the role of third-party negotiators (representatives); federal regulations concerning advertising and infomercials; audience trends; media penetration; and viewing share.[49] Direct marketers normally have two options when launching a DRTV campaign: (1) set up local operations on their own, or (2) use an established DRTV international company.

General Motors used a DRTV campaign in Argentina, supported by a series of follow-ups via direct mail, phone, and fax. The campaign, designed to increase test drives and sales of the Astra, offered consumers a free video by calling a toll-free number. The results were phenomenal. Astra's market share in Argentina increased from 5 to 11 percent.[50]

Telemarketing is another medium for direct marketing overseas; however, it is more limited than in the U.S. and varies greatly from country to country. Toll-free telephone number formats vary significantly by country. In many countries, such as Japan, telemarketing is perceived to be too aggressive. As is the case with other types of media, the successful use of telemarketing depends on the level of sophistication of the telecommunications infrastructure.

SMS text messaging is being met with great success in some international markets. In the Chinese capital of Beijing, Coca-Cola executed a summertime campaign where participants could text their predictions of the following day's high temperature. The participant who had the most accurate predictions won the first prize of a year's supply of Coke. The 34-day campaign generated four million SMS messages and 50,000 mobile downloads of a new Coke ringtone.[51] Another effective SMS campaign was that of Smirnoff's mobile sweepstakes in the U.K., where Smirnoff offered a free dance CD in every six-pack of Smirnoff ICE. Inside the CD was also a unique code and instructions to SMS the code to a special number to learn whether they might have won a vacation package. This successful campaign generated more than 200,000 responses.[52]

Creative

In the process of developing the creative materials for any international direct marketing campaign, the four words of wisdom seem to be *research*, *test*, *translate*, and *adapt*. Visit the website of Nestlé in Peru (www.nestle.com.pe) and you will see how the company effectively translated its website for Peruvians. It is critical to present your promotional message in words and images to which your audience can relate. That is why direct marketers must properly research their audience, testing the offer and the copy, carefully translating the message into the proper language, and adapting to the local nuances of different cultures. Words that are entirely appropriate in one country's language may be inappropriate and insulting in another. Certain colors, symbols, and designs may also be inappropriate to use in a marketing campaign.

One well-known example of a company adapting to local cultural differences is that of the Coca-Cola Company. In Japan, the word *diet* has a negative impression, because Japanese women do not like to admit they are drinking a product for weight loss. Therefore, the Coca-Cola Company revised the brand name of Diet Coke to 'Coca-Cola Light' and successfully introduced and positioned the product in Japan as a soft drink for figure maintenance as opposed to weight loss.[53] Another example of the need to adapt to different cultures and consumer lifestyles is that of N. W. Ayer's Bahamas tourism campaign designed for the European market. While the overall campaign focused on clean water, beaches, and air, it incorporated different appeals for select European markets. It emphasized sports activities to the German market and it used humorous ads in the U.K.[54]

To get maximum results, direct marketing campaigns must use promotional appeals that motivate prospects. However, consumer motives vary country by country, and what works in one market may not work in another. There are myriad cultural nuances, including different foods, languages, social interactions and shopping habits, which must be understood and taken into consideration in order to effectively market to a given country's consumer market. Studies on the effectiveness of different advertising styles found that individualistic cultures enjoy humor, how-to, and lifestyle approaches, while collective cultures prefer dramatic metaphors, symbolism, and a play on words.[55] For example, the promotional products that are created by Bloomin, the worldwide manufacturer of seed paper, are translated into different languages and promotional appeals that are both appropriate for and effective in each country market. As shown in Figure 14.6, these Bloomin seed paper advertisements have been designed for use in China, Europe, Asia, and France.

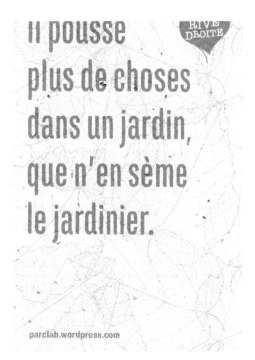

Figure 14.6 Four international examples of Bloomin seed paper. Used with permission of Bloomin. All rights reserved.

Direct marketers using the Web as a marketing medium must also be aware of the legal regulations that vary by country. For example, Germany sued Benetton for 'exploiting feelings of pity' in one of its online campaigns.[56] Again, careful market research and cultural adaptation are the keys to developing successful creative materials. For example, U.S. consumers are more receptive to advertisements that affect the emotional, or even sensual, aspects of their decision-making process, whereas the Japanese are more comfortable with logical and rational appeals. Then again, U.S. consumers are said to be far more conservative than are Canadians and Europeans. Regardless of whether the message appeal is emotional, rational, conservative, or liberal, it must be produced to maximize the response from the targeted customer. Cultural adaptation is crucial to the success of the direct marketing campaign when developing the creative appeal.

An excellent example of creativity that was effective was a direct mail campaign executed in India. Seagrams wanted to reinvigorate the image of its Chivas Scotch whisky brand in India. Therefore, the company invited the country's most famous figures to an elite art show and sale in which Chivas would be promoted. To convince famous guests to attend, a lavish invitation was created. The invitation was designed to look like an artist's portfolio and contained high-quality miniature prints as a preview of the works on sale at the show. The campaign was a great success. The invitation itself became a collectible item, and 90 percent of those invited attended the event. Furthermore, 60 percent of the art displayed was sold.[57]

One of the first measures a direct marketer can take to ensure cultural adaptation is to determine the country's receptiveness to direct marketing activities. Let's look briefly at the indicators used in this assessment.

GEOGRAPHICAL AREA ANALYSIS

Canada

Most Canadians are very familiar with products and services from the United States because the majority of Canadians reside within 100 miles of the U.S. border. In fact, Canada and the United States have many things in common—they even share a professional ice hockey league. However, there are some distinct differences that direct marketers should bear in mind when marketing to Canadians. For example, Canada is officially bilingual in English and French. However, in Quebec, local language laws require all advertising materials to be printed in French. As Figure 14.7 shows, Virginia Beach banner ads were translated into French to be used to promote its vacation destination to prospective tourists in Quebec, Canada. Both ads creatively encourage Canadians to take a vacation to Virginia Beach and leave the cooler Canadian climate behind.

Figure 14.7 Virginia Beach banner ads. Used with permission of the City of Virginia Beach Convention & Visitors Bureau.

Taxes and duties assessed in Canada are another area of difference. Three taxes may come into effect when a U.S. company ships products to Canada. These are as follows:[58]

1. The Goods and Services Tax (GST): a 5 percent tax on the total value of the parcel. This tax is applied to all goods imported into Canada, with the exception of prescribed property such as magazines, books, or similar printed publications.

2. The Provincial Sales Tax (PST): a province-dependent tax (around 8 percent) on the parcel's total value. The provincial retail sales tax rates vary from province to province, as do the goods and services to which the tax is applied and the way the tax is applied.[59]
3. The Harmonized Sales Tax (HST): this is dependent on the province and includes a single tax which combines both GST and PST.

Duties, or charges imposed on shipments based on a country of origin and commodity, are also imposed by Canada. In 2018, the North American Free Trade Agreement (NAFTA) concluded and was replaced with a new U.S.–Mexico–Canada Agreement (USMCA). The new agreement inhibits the increase of existing customs duties as well as the establishment of new duties on any products traded among the three countries.

Canadians are experiencing the same societal pressures as their neighbors in the United States (single-parent families, two parents working outside the home, constant time pressures) that make the ability to shop from home appealing. Privacy issues are also on the rise. However, unlike the U.S. DMA, which has been a proponent of industry self-regulation with regard to privacy, the Canadian Marketing Association has been active in calling for federal privacy legislation. There are also cultural differences between the United States and Canada. For example, Canadian direct marketing appeals don't normally include appeals to patriotism and vanity, as U.S. appeals often do.

When marketing to Canadian consumers, often companies may use two versions of the same advertisement, with one translated into French for those Canadians who speak French. An example of two ads promoting Busch Gardens as a family vacation destination for Canadian residents appears in Figure 14.8. Note that the ads are identical with the exception of language.

(Continued)

Figure 14.8 (Continued)

Figure 14.8 Busch Gardens Canadian ads in English and French languages. Used with the consent of Busch Gardens/Water Country USA. All Rights Reserved.

Europe

The European Union currently represents almost 513 million consumers.[60] According to European Union External Action, together the European Union and the U.S. represent 12 percent of the world's population, but account for almost half of global GDP.[61] The European Union is currently made up of 28 different countries with 24 official languages, cultures, and legal systems.[62] (However, at the time of writing, the United Kingdom is due to leave the EU, reducing its membership to 27 countries.) Direct marketers are advised to conduct an in-depth study of each country prior to conducting business in that country.

Differences between U.S. and European markets also exist. For example, European stores are not open seven days a week, as many are in the United States. In fact, many European stores maintain hours and service levels that most U.S. consumers would find unacceptable. Another example is that when actual vacation time is calculated, workers average 7.9 weeks in Italy, 7.8 in Germany, and 7 weeks in France, whereas in the United States, the average is 3.9 weeks.[63] Is Europe still an attractive avenue for direct marketing? The answer is, you bet! There are many successful U.S. direct marketers in Europe, including Lands' End, Viking, and Allstate Insurance, as well as successful European direct marketers.

An example of a successful direct mail and print campaign in Europe is that of Diageo Ireland's Guinness relationship marketing program. Diageo Ireland needed to regain lost market share from competing lagers and ciders that were strongly associated with sporting and music events through sponsorship. To accomplish this task, the company created its own event, 'poker night,' and chose to communicate with customers on a personal level by sharing stories about the history and heritage of the Guinness product and its bond with consumers. As shown in Figure 14.9, this campaign, 'A Passion Shared,' helped convert in-pub drinkers of Guinness to also become at-home Guinness drinkers, a vital change in the market, and generated an increase of 17 percent in Guinness consumption.[64]

Figure 14.9 Guinness's 'A Passion Shared' direct marketing campaign. Used with permission of Diageo Ireland.

French direct marketing for consumer products and services is one of the world's largest, growing at a rate of 10 percent annually to reach €71.4 billion in 2016. The total number of Internet users in France and the total number of commercial websites has increased drastically. Currently, there are approximately 47 million Internet users in France, 36 million of whom made an average purchase of €1,780 in 2016.[65] Despite the high level of spending on mail-order products, most Europeans are not bombarded with direct mail as are U.S. consumers. The U.K.'s national postal service, Royal Mail, has tried to counter this trend of using fewer direct mailings, however. Through use of 'DM Sales,' Royal Mail has launched discounts of 20 percent for direct mail items in an effort to encourage marketers to utilize new, expanded campaign tactics, such as the distribution of samples.[66]

Some factors affecting direct marketing activities in Europe are the following:

- **Postal requirements**—formats, location of the window, teaser copy on the outer envelop— must comply with local postal regulations, which differ by European country. Euro Inter- mail, the leading full-service direct mail company in Italy, is finding great success by designing innovative direct mail pieces for its clients while still complying with the local postal regulations. Many of the direct mail packages it has created have used clear, see- through outer envelopes, personalized messages, compelling copy, and small premiums, such as a free pencil or coin. Figure 14.10 provides an example of one of Euro Intermail's creative direct mail pieces.
- **Data protection** is far more stringent in Europe than it is in the United States. Throughout Europe, an opt-out provision is mandatory at the point where you collect data. Until recently, individual countries had their own privacy legislation—which varied from country to coun- try. However, now a Europe-wide privacy directive is in place and must be adopted by every European Union country.[67]
- **Mailing restrictions** and policies may differ by European country. For example, in the U.K., each direct mail package must be approved by the Advertising Standards Authority.
- **The list industry** is strong in Europe. Multinational lists include names and data about individuals who are usually responsive to direct mail offers, speak English, and are inter- nationally minded. The list selections available, output formats, and guarantees equal U.S. standards. Multinational lists allow the direct marketer to test many countries at the same time without incurring additional fees. Local lists tend to be more numerous and offer greater selections.
- **The Benelux**, which is composed of the countries of Belgium, Netherlands, and Luxem- bourg, is ideal for direct marketing because of its well-developed direct marketing infrastruc- ture. Lists, payment options, and call centers are all quite advanced in this region of Europe.[68]

Figure 14.10   Euro intermail direct mail. Used with permission of Marco Mori, Eurointermail.

Latin America

The population of Latin America is more than 652 million across 26 countries.[69] Total trade with the U.S. approached $1.9 trillion in 2018, with $945 billion in exports and $929 billion in imports. Different dialects of Spanish are spoken across Latin America, and Portuguese is spoken in Brazil.[70] The number of Internet users has grown from 16.6 percent in 2005 to 62.3 percent in 2016.[71] Latin America is a continent of countries made up of very different direct marketing infrastructures. It cannot be treated as a single market except on paper.

For direct marketers, Brazil is the most sophisticated market in Latin America. Brazil accounts for nearly half of the total South American GDP, and has grown continuously through 2017. It has the ninth highest GDP worldwide. With growing per-capita income and almost 209 million consumers, Brazil offers great opportunity for direct marketers.[72] The lists and databases available there are of fairly high quality. However, fewer public sources of data are available in Latin America than in the United States. With the exception of Brazil, direct marketing is largely underdeveloped in terms of the number of agencies and telemarketing companies in Latin America. However, Latin America is not expected to follow the path the U.S. did in slowly developing sophisticated direct marketing machinery. The Internet will likely enable Latin America to make revolutionary strides quickly in direct marketing development.[73]

Although the direct marketing industry in Latin America trails that of the U.S., the outlook is promising. One reason for this is that the amount of communication one Latin American consumer receives is much less than that received by a typical U.S. or European consumer. For example, the average household in Mexico receives only about three pieces of mail per month.[74]

Therefore, the amount of communication clutter is significantly reduced. It is also true, however, that mail services in Mexico are considerably slower than in the United States.

Latin American consumers are very receptive to products made in the U.S. and have recently shown acceptance of DRTV media as well. Two successful DRTV marketing campaigns in Latin America are the following:[75]

- AB Flex, one of the fitness industry's top-performing products, generated more than $10 million of sales in a nine-month period.
- Murad International Skin Care generated more than $7 million in sales in Mexico alone. The brand awareness generated created an extremely successful continuity program and catalog.

More than 46.2 percent of Mexico's 126 million people subsist below the poverty line. It's the top 10 percent that commands 40 percent of the nation's wealth. This may be of concern to direct marketers. Though the percentage of the population under the age of 15 has fallen in recent years to 30 percent, this relatively high figure still provides strong opportunity for direct markers to make inroads with younger consumers and build lasting relationships.[76]

Building relationships is important in direct marketing, and this is especially so in Latin America, where consumers crave personal contact and *confianza* (trust). Many Americans find the Latin American perspective on personal space and physical interaction somewhat alarming. Latins are not nearly as conscious of personal space as Americans are, thus physical contact is quite common. For example, in most Latin American countries, it is expected for men conducting business from the second meeting onward to greet one other with an *abrazo*, or hug, or sometimes even with a kiss on the cheek. Most business deals will not develop until a friendship has been established. Unlike in the U.S., time is not money in Latin America.

Asia/Pacific

Asia has a population of more than 4 billion consumers and millions of businesses.[77] Companies such as consumer products leader Procter & Gamble Co. have capitalized on growing product demand in this massive market, accelerating growth and extending its customer base. The Asia/Pacific region generated 17 percent of P&G's $65 billion in net sales in 2016, but the company hopes to rely even more extensively on the region in the coming years.[78] Considering Asia's diverse population and unique culture, P&G is intent on offering products for all levels of buying behavior—from billionaires to those living on less than one dollar per day. P&G's Asia Group president, Deb Henretta, states:

I don't believe you can win in Asia by simply taking Western mindset and Western business models and plopping them into Asia. We've taken on a bit of a rallying cry—'being as common as possible, but as different as needed'—to satisfy varying cultures and customer demands.

By offering both 'pennies-priced' shaving tools and advanced, high-end cosmetics and shampoos, P&G is accomplishing this balance necessitated by the Asian market.[79]

Catalog marketers have struggled with the Asian market for more than a decade. The major challenges include the lack of reliable mailing lists, a scarcity of local talent, inadequate phone systems, and the inability to fulfill orders through traditional retailers. Among the lessons many direct marketers have learned in Asia is the fact that you must treat each country separately and understand the local laws and policies. All Asian markets are not equally attractive. Recent research shows that the more accessible Asian countries for direct marketers are South Korea, Taiwan, Hong Kong (China), and Japan.[80]

However, one of the major challenges faced by Americans and other Western international companies is a propensity to lump together these markets and assume that all Asian consumers have similar tastes and preferences. This is not true and is an unwise assumption made by companies seeking to enter these markets. Each market demonstrates different preferences toward marketing and often differs in its consumer buying behavior. Let's take a closer look at each of these markets.

South Korea

Direct buying in South Korea is growing considerably, with South Koreans importing almost $80.9 billion in U.S. goods annually, and importing over $457 billion in 2017.[81] Sales from direct selling have grown by 2 to 3 percent annually in recent years, leading some companies to adopt more appropriate marketing strategies.[82] For instance, Hong Joon-Kee, Chairman of the Korea Direct Selling Association and CEO of Woongjin Coway Co. Ltd, a global leader in health- and environment-related lifestyle products such as water purifiers, notes strong increases in both door-to-door sales and multi-level marketing strategies. 'The Korean direct selling market is one of the largest markets around the world,' he says. Indeed, ecommerce via the Internet and mobile devices became the largest sales channel in the country in 2016, with over 12.6 billion in sales.[83]

Furthermore, U.S. products are desirable to South Koreans because most of the population is concentrated in cities, especially near Seoul, which accounts for about 20 percent of the entire population.[84] These urban consumers tend to possess a stronger desire to keep up with the latest innovations in technology and trends in fashion. For example, Life's Good (LG), the world's top producer of air conditioners and one of the top three players in washing machines, refrigerators, and microwaves, introduced the Kimchi refrigerator into this market. Kimchi, a spicy cabbage concoction, is very popular in South Korea. However, the problem was that the dish's odor is so strong it penetrates all surrounding food items when it is stored in the refrigerator. Therefore, LG used in-depth localization to target the South Korean community. This approach emphasizes understanding the idiosyncrasies of key local markets by opening in-country research, manufacturing, and marketing facilities. LG's efforts paid off when the new Kimchi refrigerator became all the rage in South Korea.[85]

Taiwan

The direct marketing infrastructure in Taiwan has developed substantially over the past decade. Over 82 percent of the population has Internet access and virtually everyone has at least one smartphone. Almost half of the population has a Facebook account, but virtually no one uses Twitter. List availability has improved and telemarketing is available. While many use direct marketing methods for legitimate purposes, telemarketing fraud is a major concern. In 2015, there were 590,000 registered complaints from Chinese authorities, with total losses of over $3.4 billion (22.2 billion yuan).[86]

China

Direct marketing in China is relatively new, but growing. With 1.4 billion people, China has great potential for direct marketers, with heavy concentrations of wealth in mostly coastal cities.[87] However, like Taiwan, its direct marketing infrastructure is lacking. Although the middle class is growing, the vast majority of the Chinese population have little money, no credit cards, no telephones, and no direct way to receive merchandise. Surprisingly, information privacy is very strict in China, and there are privacy code laws in place. Anyone caught breaking the privacy code laws may be subject to a prison term.

Japan

Japan is one of the most advanced countries in the Pacific Rim. Its direct marketing infrastructure is superior to that of its Asian counterparts. Direct mail, telemarketing, home-shopping programs, and even infomercials continue to grow in popularity. While television remains the top medium for advertising, companies spent almost 27 percent of their advertising budgets online. Direct mail represents almost 6 percent of total advertising expenditure.[88] Online retail in Japan grew to almost US$148 billion in 2019, but the country's consumers have lagged behind other developed markets in their willingness to embrace the electronic method of shopping. Instead, consumers in Japan enjoy more of a physical shopping experience. That said, e-commerce has experienced a sharp increase from the $1.3 billion in online sales in 1999.[89]

Regarding direct marketing, an example of a highly successful marketing campaign in Japan is that of DHL Japan. Faced with customers who increasingly regarded air express services as commodities, DHL Japan wanted to build loyalty among its customers via a campaign in 2019 with an emotional appeal. The campaign included year-round greeting cards mailed to customers depicting a seasonal scene with a DHL vehicle or airplane in one of the major international cities of the world, such as Melbourne in the summer or New York at Christmas. Customers were captured by the beautifully illustrated cards and the campaign exceeded all targeted projections, garnering an ROI of 700 percent.[90]

Middle East

Direct marketing in the Middle East is in the early stages of development. While many countries are war-torn, limited opportunities for direct marketers exist in Saudi Arabia, Egypt, Israel, and the United Arab Emirates (UAE). Lists of business organizations are available in a directory referred to as KOMPASS. This list contains information such as the nature of business, address, phone number, and key personnel. Also, some key highlights about each company are offered, such as number of employees, annual revenue, date of establishment, and legal form of operations. Most direct marketing activities are based on outbound telemarketing calls to customers. These databases are based on purchases of databases. Laws about information privacy vary by country. Many companies share information with other companies, maybe for a fee.

Africa

The African continent is home to about 1.29 billion people.[91] The largest country in terms of population is Nigeria, with a population of more than 203 million.[92] More than 40 percent of the population on the continent of Africa is under the age of 15. With the highest infant mortality rates in the world and a large percentage of the population uneducated, the literacy rate varies from one country to another.[93] There is very limited computer access and also low Internet penetration. That said, the middle class in Africa has increased notably. Today's middle class consists of 40 percent of the population—about 480 million people—compared to 27.2 percent of the population— about 196 million people—in 2000. The emergence of a stronger middle class has increased consumption expenditures in Africa to a third of those in developing European countries.[94] In fact, Africa's middle class has grown larger than that of India, and the 'invasion' of stores such as Walmart and KFC has begun. High commodity prices have helped drive Africa's economy, while 'better infrastructure, improved governance and the creation of jobs through private investment have helped drive the growth of the middle class.'[95]

Africa has the fastest growing mobile market in the world. Seven out of ten telephones in Africa are mobile. Direct marketing is considered to be a new phenomenon for many African countries and does not exist in most African markets.

South Africa is considered the most developed nation in the African continent. The Direct Marketing Association of South Africa helps to regulate direct marketing practices in the country. It also promotes networking and business opportunity development for its members.[96]

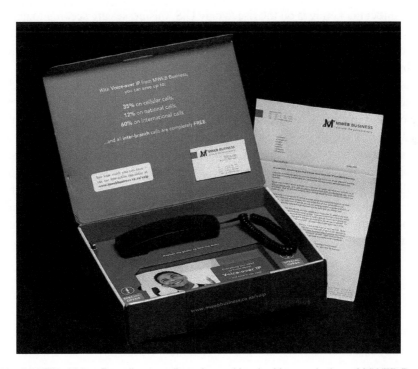

Figure 14.11   MWEB's Voice Box direct mail package. Used with permission of MWEB Business and primaplus.

Direct marketing activities in South Africa are growing rapidly. Examples of effective campaigns are those of MWEB, one of the country's largest Internet service providers. Recently, MWEB executed the following two unique direct marketing campaigns with totally different objectives and target markets. 'The Voice Box' campaign, created by the Primaplus Agency, targeted a business community in South Africa that was paying extremely high telephone rates but was shy about adopting new technologies. MWEB introduced its ADSL VOIP product to select CFOs and medical doctors, sending them a substantial 3D pack that gave them a unique way to try the new phone service. As shown in Figure 14.11, the pack came with a telephone, which rang as soon as the box was opened and directed them to a designated account manager. The campaign was highly effective with this hard-to-convert audience and achieved an outstanding 60 percent response rate.[97]

The other successful direct mail campaign, called 'Babushkalopes,' was created for MWEB by OlgivyOne Cape Town. In the South African market, where broadband services are new, the objective of this campaign was to ensure that MWEB's dial-up customers converted to its new broadband service before the competition reached them. To achieve this, a direct mail campaign was built around the theme of the bigger world available through broadband. The mailing conveyed that message with a series of envelopes within envelopes, each of which unfolded to reveal a larger envelope, which resulted in a large poster promoting the product. The campaign was a success, with 9 percent of all consumers receiving the mailing opting to upgrade their service to broadband.[98]

SUMMARY

International direct marketing is on the rise. Many U.S. businesses are seeking to expand by penetrating international markets. In doing so, direct marketers must keep in mind the many unique differences between domestic and foreign markets. Many researchers offer suggestions for how to enter a foreign market. These steps include assessing your international potential, conducting market research, selecting your country markets, developing an international marketing plan, and implementing your international marketing strategies. Careful market research, including an assessment of consumer needs, direct marketing infrastructure, and political, economic, and business environments, is necessary prior to commencing international direct marketing activities.

Direct marketers must make decisions involving the mode of market entry—direct exporting, licensing, joint venture, contract manufacturing, direct investment, or management contracting—that they will employ. Direct marketers must make a careful examination of the unique infrastructure needed to support direct marketing operations, including an analysis of lists and databases, fulfillment operations, media, and creative executions. The direct marketing infrastructure varies by country market and each market must be thoroughly researched and analyzed.

KEY TERMS

collectivist culture	direct investment
contract manufacturing	duties

exporting
global market segmentation (GMS)
gross domestic product (GDP)
individualistic cultures
infrastructure

joint venture
licensee
licensing
licensor
management contracting

REVIEW QUESTIONS

1. What makes international direct marketing different from domestic direct marketing?
2. Why are companies looking outside the United States to do business?
3. Describe the different modes of market entry that can be used to enter a foreign market.
4. Discuss the primary infrastructure necessary for international direct marketing activities to be carried out with success.
5. Name some of the ways direct marketers have adapted to cultural differences when marketing internationally.
6. Identify and explain the five-step approach direct marketers should follow when marketing to an international country.
7. How do the media preferences vary by country markets? Which country is attractive for DRTV?
8. Compare and contrast direct mail and e-mail as international direct marketing media. Which one would be most appropriate to use when marketing in Canada? Europe? Latin America? Asia?
9. Discuss fulfillment operations. What advantages do both centralized and decentralized fulfillment operations offer international direct marketers?
10. Provide an overview of the history of direct marketing around the world. Be sure to explain when and where it began and how it grew.

EXERCISE

The U.S.-based motorcycle company that you are now employed with wants to expand its business overseas. Using the market research issues discussed in this chapter, describe how the company should go about doing this. Based on your analysis, which countries might be considered likely candidates for international expansion? Provide an explanation to support your selections.

CRITICAL THINKING EXERCISE

Many marketing campaigns translate effectively across international markets, while some do not. Select two different direct marketing campaigns that were successful in the United States and apply them to three different country markets. Discuss whether or not each would be effective in the respective country and how each one might be modified to be successful in each market.

READINGS AND RESOURCES

- Global Road Warrior: www.globalroadwarrior.com
- CIA *World Factbook*: www.cia.gov/library/publications/the-world-factbook
- GlobalEDGE: https://globaledge.msu.edu
- China's online consumers: www.bain.com/insights/chinas-e-commerce-the-new-branding-game
- Uber global: www.forbes.com/sites/bizcarson/2018/09/19/where-uber-is-winning-the-world-and-where-it-has-lost/#7d7ad55b4d6e
- Natural language processing: https://www.sas.com/en_us/insights/analytics/what-is-natural-language-processing-nlp.html

CASE: COCA-COLA IN PERU

Freddy Rosales, Universidad de CEMA

Peru is a Latin American country in northwestern South America on the shores of the Pacific Ocean. Ecuador lies to the north and Chile to the south. The country's identity emanates from a combination of Inca and other related ancient local cultures, the influence of Spanish colonization, and its 200-year history as an independent democracy. Its economy is booming, with foreign investment and steady growth. Beyond 2000 miles of sandy coast are mountainous areas inhabited by indigenous Quechua-speaking people, as well as tribes that live in the rainforests. The entire population's deep sense of belonging and tradition has made the local soft drink, Inca Kola, the preferred beverage. This yellow, sweet, carbonated concoction has deep national roots.

Coca-Cola is the global leader in carbonated and non-carbonated soft drinks, juices, and juice-based beverages. Consumers in more than 200 countries enjoy its beverages at a rate of nearly 1.6 million units per day. While Coca-Cola has always focused on protecting the environment, saving natural resources, and contributing to the economic development of the countries in which it operates, its recent global marketing theme has focused on happiness (see Figure 14.12). This happiness theme has been tailored to fit the needs and interests of local markets across the globe.

In spite of the high level of brand awareness achieved by this branding strategy, Inca Kola still leads in connecting Peruvians with their roots and local identity. Prior efforts to

Figure 14.12 'Uncover Happiness' campaign ad in Peru. Used with permission of Coca-Cola Peru.

connect with happiness didn't register with the population. The values Peruvians identify with are friendship or creativity, which have become the foundation for solid images of many brands. Key brand engagement indicators were especially low among teenagers, Coke's customers of tomorrow.

Its challenge was formidable: to mobilize teens in a way that uses Coca-Cola's international positioning to connect with Peruvians and their way of life. Peruvians consider themselves to be happy. The country meets every condition used to determine degree of happiness. Yet Peru has the lowest score of any country in its region, ranking 16th in the happiness index.

Coca-Cola decided to change this, one Peruvian at a time. The marketing department set a goal to improve brand association with happiness by at least 5 percent, and the attitude key performance indicator (KPI) 'For Someone Like Me' by 5 percent when compared to levels researched prior to the start of the campaign. The company considered these important steps to effectively challenge its primary Peruvian rival, Inca Kola.

Happiness is commonly associated with smiling. A relaxed smile is the most visible sign of happy people, or at least a happy moment. Yet the personal identity cards of Peruvians typically show stern faces. Given the dramatic appearance changes that occur as a child grows into a teenager, Peruvian teens must update the ID cards issued to them as infants.

Coca-Cola saw the ID cards as a branding opportunity. With the help of McCann Lima and MRM/McCann, it launched a unique campaign to put happy, smiling faces on the new ID cards issued to teenagers . . . on behalf of Coke, of course.

The first step was to negotiate an agreement with the National ID and Marital State Registry (RENIEC) to install free photo booths in key strategic points throughout the country (see Figure 14.13). Those who needed to update their national ID cards would be invited to take their updated photographs in those booths for free. These booths had smile recognition technology. The only way to receive an ID photo was to smile at the camera lens. The card, called the 'DNI' (Documento Nacional de Identidad–'National Identity Document') was renamed 'DFI' (Documento Feliz de Identidad–'Happy Identity Document') for the campaign.

Figure 14.13 Coca-Cola Happy ID photo booth. Used with permission of Coca-Cola Peru.

More than 30 percent of the people of Peru live in Lima, the capital city on the Pacific shore. Thus, Lima was a focal point in the media and operations strategy. The campaign used the following promotional tactics:

- Several videos promoting the concept of the DFI, showing celebrities flashing their own DFI cards and explaining the procedure, were produced and digitally deployed on YouTube, Facebook, and the Coca-Cola Web page, generating considerable buzz.

- Open-air devices were also deployed in urban areas, inviting Peruvians to become part of the 'movement.'
- There was extensive coverage on TV and radio programs. Many popular shows joined the campaign and promoted participation using live and recorded messages.
- Photo booths were strategically deployed in shopping malls and dense commercial areas around the country, and hosts with iPad tablet computers prepared to register users (see Figure 14.14).

Figure 14.14 Coca-Cola advertisement promoting photo booth locations. Used with permission of Coca-Cola Peru.

- Press ads were placed in the *Somos* magazine distributed with the *El Comercio* national newspaper.
- Display ads were placed on the publimetro.pe news portal.
- Bus stop billboard advertisements were displayed.
- Key accounts that sell Coca-Cola products were provided with point-of-purchase materials and displays to promote participation.
- Several celebrities were hired as DFI ambassadors. These celebrities posted invitations and details within their social networks.
- Agreements were made with traditional photo-taking shops. If they took smiling ID photographs, the customers received a free Coke on the spot.

See Figures 14.15–14.17 for some of the advertisements used for the Coca-Cola 'Uncover Happiness' campaign.

Coca-Cola also made alliances with several local and global brands to offer additional benefits to Happy ID-card holders. Some of the benefits included the following:

- Key retailers offered high-demand products exclusively for smiling DFI clients.
- Membership into the benefit club. DFI cardholders accessed a microsite to register. Members could receive discounts in key accounts like McDonald's and Pizza Hut. They also received discounts for packs of Coca-Cola products, and tickets to events and activities sponsored by Coca-Cola, such as Mistura food festival and the World Cup Trophy Tour (see Figure 14.15).

Figure 14.15 This billboard invites Peruvians to smile for their ID card, uncovering a happier Peru. It uses the informal 'tu' command which is more direct and personal. Used with permission of Coca-Cola Peru.

Figure 14.16 This print ad introduces viewers to the 'Happy ID,' an initiative to change the face of Peru through the power of smiles. It also gives information on how to join in. Used with permission of Coca-Cola Peru.

Figure 14.17 This billboard asks Peruvians to smile for their ID card, uncovering a happier Peru. Used with permission of Coca-Cola Peru.

Conclusion

The value of public relations efforts alone resulted in about $300,000 of free publicity for Coke. The campaign results included (as informed in https://vimeo.com/) the following:

- Of the 50,000 ID cards issued, 45,000 (90 percent) were of smiling people.
- Association of the brand with happiness grew 8 percent, which was 60 percent over the target set prior to the start of the campaign.
- The indicator 'For Someone Like Me' (FSLM) grew by 10 percent, which was 100 percent higher than the expected growth.
- The level of awareness of the campaign had reached 58 percent by the end of the campaign (campaign recall), and the association of the campaign with the brand was at 75 percent (brand recall).
- In follow-up research, 62 percent of those who didn't obtain the DFI said they intended to do so at a later date.
- Other brand indicators improved. Association of the brand with unhealthy beverages dropped 2 percent. Differentiation with other brands increased 12 percent.
- Many of the traditional photo shops that did not carry Coke products before the campaign sold them by its conclusion.

Interviewed after the campaign, Gabriel Chavez, Senior Marketing Manager, expressed his satisfaction in having generated 'a social movement putting happiness in the agenda and helping to extend it to all Peruvians, inspiring them to a collective change towards a better Peru.' He added: 'In Peru there is no law prohibiting to smile on a photo ID. Even so, all Peruvians appeared in their IDs with a stern face. Then, playing with the initials of our DNI (in Spanish: Documento Nacional de Identidad), we decided to turn it into a DFI (Documento Feliz de Identidad), inviting all to contribute to a more happy Peru by smiling in their ID photos.'

Case Discussion Questions

1. Would you consider this to be a direct/interactive marketing campaign? Why or why not? How can the goal of increasing awareness of the brand be connected to increasing response and sales?
2. Do you think the cultural change Coke inspired is a fad or a trend? Is this a true national movement?
3. What, if any, response would you expect from Inca Kola?
4. What do you recommend Coca-Cola do in the future? What should happen to the campaign if the company selects a theme other than happiness?
5. What would you recommend if Coke's global campaign changes?

NOTES

1. Adapted from the *Direct Marketing Association International ECHO Awards 2006*.

2. Central Intelligence Agency (2019) *The World Factbook*. www.cia.gov/library/publications/the-world-factbook/geos/xx.html.

3. World Trade Organization (2019) International Trade Statistics 2018. www.wto.org. Online interactive database. May 23, 2019.

4. United States Census Bureau (2019) Trade in goods with world, not seasonally adjusted. *Foreign Trade*. www.census.gov/foreign-trade/balance/c0015.html

5. United States Census Bureau, 2017 Top Trading Partners. *Foreign Trade*. www.trade.gov/mas/ian/build/groups/public/@tg_ian/documents/webcontent/tg_ian_003364.pdf.

6. Bob Stone and Ron Jacobs (2008) *Successful Direct Marketing Methods*, 8th ed. (New York: McGraw-Hill), p. 148.

7. Internet World Stats (2019) *Internet Users and 2019 Population in North America*, https://internetworldstats.com/stats14.htm.

8. Richard N. Miller (1995) *Multinational Direct Marketing: The Methods and the Markets* (New York: McGraw-Hill), pp. 7–8.

9. Ibid., p. 2.

10. Ibid.

11. Ibid.

12. Michael R. Czinkota and Ilkka A. Ronkainen (2004) *International Marketing*, 7th ed. (Mason, OH: South-Western), p. 539.

13. Ibid., p. 545.

14. www.sas.com/en_us/insights/analytics/what-is-natural-language-processing-nlp.html, retrieved May 5, 2019.

15. Ibid.

16. www.primeindexes.com/indexes/prime-mobile-payments-index/whitepaper.html, retrieved May 5, 2019.

17. V. Kumar and Anish Nagpal (2007) *Marketing*, 29th ed. (New York: McGraw-Hill/ Irwin), p. 174.

18. Adapted from John J. Wild, Kenneth L. Wild, and Jerry C. Y. Han (2003) *International Business*, 2nd ed. (Upper Saddle River, NJ: Prentice Hall); adapted from William J. MacDonald, 'Five Steps to International Success,' *Direct Marketing* 61, no. 7 (November 1998), pp. 32–35; Rainer Hengst, 'Plotting Your Global Strategy,' *Direct Marketing* 63, no. 4 (August 2000), pp. 52–54; and Richard N. Miller, 'Where in the World . . . How to Determine the Best Market for Your Product or Service,' *Target Marketing* 24, no. 3 (March 2001), p. 57.

19. Miller, *Multinational Direct Marketing*, pp. 6–7.

20. Central Intelligence Agency (2007) *2008 World Factbook* (New York: Skyhorse Publishing), p. 346.

21. Patrick Gillespie (2016) '5 Reasons why Venezuela's Economy is in a "Meltdown".' *CNN Money*, http://money.cnn.com/2016/01/18/news/economy/venezuela-economy-meltdown.

22. Czinkota and Ronkainen, *International Marketing*, p. 318.

23. Ted Reed (2009) 'UPS: We Took L.L. Bean Account From FedEx.' Stock Market Today—Financial News, Quotes and Analysis—*TheStreet*, 9 February. www.thestreet.com/

story/10462893/1/ups-we-took-ll-bean-account-from-fedex.html?puc=_tscrss, retrieved May 23, 2011.

24. Hoovers Website, www.hoovers.com/orvis-company/—ID__89473—/free-co-profile.xhtml, retrieved February 2008.

25. 'Orvis Stores: Retail Locations in the UK.' Orvis U.K. Official Store: Quality Men's Clothing, Women's Clothing, Fly Fishing Gear, Dog Beds, Luggage, Travel, Shooting, and Gifts; Since 1856. www.orvis.co.uk/intro.aspx?subject=328, retrieved May 23, 2011.

26. 'The Orvis Company, Inc. Company Profile from Hoover's.' Hoovers Business Solutions. www.hoovers.com/company/The_Orvis_Company_Inc/ xsckyi-1.html, retrieved May 23, 2011.

27. H. Katzenstein and W. S. Sachs (1986) *Direct Marketing*, 2nd ed. (New York: Macmillan), p. 417.

28. Gitman and McDaniel, *The Future of Business*, p. 83.

29. Texas Instruments website, www.ti.com, retrieved September 2003.

30. 'Walmartstores.com: About Us.' http://walmartstores.com/aboutus, retrieved May 23, 2019.

31. 'Walmart's net sales worldwide from 2008 to 2019, by division.' *Statista: The Statistics Portal*, www.statista.com/statistics/269403/net-sales-of-walmart-worldwide-by-division, retrieved May 23, 2019.

32. Biz Carson (2018) Where Uber is Winning the World, and Where it has Lost. *Forbes* (September 19). www.forbes.com/sites/bizcarson/2018/09/19/where-uber-is-winning-the-world-and-where-it-has-lost/#7d7ad55b4d6e, retrieved May 19, 2019.

33. Terry Brennan, 'Day-Timers Makes Foray into U.D. with First 100,000-Piece Mail Test,' *DM News*, November 15, 1989, p. 14.

34. Stone and Jacobs, *Successful Direct Marketing Methods*, p. 164.

35. Czinkota and Ronkainen, *International Marketing*, p. 318.

36. MacDonald, 'Five Steps to International Success,' p. 35.

37. Czinkota and Ronkainen, *International Marketing*, p. 318.

38. Beth Negus Viveiros, 'As the World Turns,' *Inside the DMA* (2002), D19.

39. 'About PayPal—PayPal.' PayPal Press Center. www.paypal-media.com/about, retrieved May 23, 2011.

40. www.cnbc.com/2019/01/31/venmo-had-a-break-out-quarter-but-wont-make-money-for-paypal-until-at-mid-2019--.html, retrieved May 5, 2019.

41. https://venmo.com/business, retrieved May 5, 2019.

42. Lawrence Chaido and Lisa A. Yorgey, 'The Back-End of Global Delivery: How to Transport Your Products around the World,' *Target Marketing* 21, no. 9 (September 1998), pp. 64–66.

43. Paper Direct Websites, www.paperdirect.com, retrieved February 2008.

44. Ibid. and www.paperdirect.com.uk.

45. 'All Change: Marketing in Addressable Media,' *Interaction* (April 2007), p. 24.

46. *The DMA ECHO Winners Program 2007* (New York: Direct Marketing Association), p. 39.

47. Statista (2017) Most Effective Marketing Channels. www.statista.com/statistics/380720/most-effective-marketing-channels-according-to-smbs, retrieved November 2019.

48. 'Secrets and Lies about International E-mail Marketing.' *BtoB Magazine: Marketing News and Strategies for BtoB, Direct & Internet Marketing*, May 8, 2008. www.btobonline.com/apps/pbcs.dll/article?AID=/20080508/FREE/922962543/1116, retrieved May 23, 2011.

49. Priya Ghai, 'Southward Bound,' *Target Marketing* 24, no. 5 (May 2001), p. 64.

50. Stan Rapp, 'Something New Under the Advertising Sun,' *DMA Insider* (Fall 2002), pp. 10–14.

51. NewPhase Mobile Marketing (2008) http://newphasemobile.com/campaign_examples. php.

52. Ibid.

53. Czinkota and Ronkainen, *International Marketing*, p. 257.

54. Ibid., p. 552.

55. Tom Altstiel and Jean Grow (2013) *Advertising Creative: Strategy, Copy, Design*, 3rd ed. (Thousand Oaks, CA: Sage Publications), p. 93.

56. Rose Lewis, 'Before You Advertise on the Net—Check the International Marketing Laws,' *Bank Marketing* (May 1996), pp. 40–42.

57. *The DMA ECHO Winners Program 2007*, p. 87.

58. Lisa A. Yorgey, 'Navigating Taxes and Duties,' *Target Marketing* 22, no. 10 (October 1999), p. 76.

59. Susan Munroe, About.com: Canada Online, Provincial sales tax-PST, http://canadaonline. about. com/od/personalfinance/g/pst.htm, retrieved February 2008.

60. United Nations Population Division (2019) Population Total – European Union, Online Interactive Database, https://data.worldbank.org, retrieved May 23, 2019.

61. European External Action Service (2019) The United States and the EU, https://eeas.europa. eu/delegations/united-states-america_en/27291/The%20United%20States%20and%20 the%20EU, retrieved May 23, 2019.

62. Ibid.

63. Charles W. Lamb, Joe F. Hair, and Carl McDaniel (2012) *Marketing*, 12th ed. (Boston, MA: Cengage Learning), p. 112.

64. *The DMA ECHO Winners Program 2007*, p. 81.

65. Ecommerce Europe (2018) 'French e-commerce turnover.' www.ecommerce-europe.eu/ wp-content/uploads/2016/08/France-PDF.pdf, retrieved May 23, 2019.

66. 'Keeping you up to date.' *Royal Mail—Personal Customers*. www2.royalmail.com/cus tomer-service/customer-news#Royal%20Mail%20announces%20DM%20sale%20to%20 help%20advertisers, retrieved May 23, 2011.

67. Erika Rasmusson, 'The Perils of International Direct Mail,' *Sales & Marketing Management* 152, no. 4 (April 2000), p. 107.

68. Lisa A. Yorgey, 'Direct Marketing in the Benelux,' *Target Marketing* 22, no. 7 (July 1999), p. 40.

69. www.worldometers.info/world-population/latin-america-and-the-caribbean-population, retrieved May 5, 2019.

70. Office of the United States Trade Representatives (2019) Western Hemisphere. https://ustr. gov/ countries-regions/americas, retrieved ?.

71. Digital Element (2019) Marketing in Latin America's Growing Digital Economy. www. digitalelement.com/marketing-in-latin-americas-growing-digital-economy, retrieved May 23, 2019.

72. Central Intelligence Agency (2019) Country Comparison: GDP. *The World Factbook*. www. cia.gov/library/publications/the-world-factbook/rankorder/2001rank.html, retrieved ?.

73. 'Fact Sheet on U.S. Relationship with Central and South America' (March 15, 2011). United States of America Embassy—IIP Digital. http://iipdigital.usembassy.gov/st/english/article/2011/03/20110315105216su0.2035443. html#axzz1MiWvpPKT, retrieved May 23, 2011.

74. Universal Postal Union, and the Organisation for Economic Co-Operative Development, www.upu.int/en/resources/postal-statistics/query-the-database.html, retrieved April 13, 2017.

75. North American Publishing Company, 'Southward Bound,' *Target Marketing* 24, no. 5 (May 2001), p. 64.

76. Central Intelligence Agency, *The World Factbook: Mexico*, www.cia.gov/library/publications/the-world-factbook/geos/mx.html, retrieved May 23, 2019.

77. Ibid., p. 845.

78. Procter & Gamble (2016) Annual Report. www.pginvestor.com/interactive/newlookandfeel/4004124/2016_Annual_Report.pdf, retrieved ?.

79. Procter & Gamble (2015) Annual Report. www.pginvestor.com.

80. Hengst, 'Plotting Your Global Strategy,' pp. 52–57.

81. Central Intelligence Agency, *The World Factbook: South Korea*, www.cia.gov/library/publications/the-world-factbook/geos/ks.html, retrieved May 23, 2019.

82. 'Direct Selling—South Korea—Market Report—new market research report.' (30 March 2011). Wooeb News. http://news.wooeb.com/NewsStory.aspx?id=713452, retrieved May 23, 2011.

83. Export.gov. (2018) Korea—Direct Marketing, www.export.gov/article?id=Korea-Direct-Marketing, retrieved May 23, 2019.

84. Hengst, 'Plotting Your Global Strategy,' p. 55.

85. Elizabeth Esfahani (2006) 'Thinking Locally Succeeding Globally,' *Annual Editions International Business*, 14th ed. (New York: McGraw-Hill), p. 86.

86. Michael Martina and J. R. Wu (2016) 'China blames Taiwan criminals for surge in telephone scams.' www.reuters.com/article/us-china-telecoms-fraud-idUSKCN0XJ022, retrieved?.

87. S. Janssen (ed.) (2017) *World Almanac and Book of Facts*. (New York: Infobase Learning), p. 730.

88. MVF (2016) 'Lead Generation and Internet Marketing in Japan.' Web publication. www.mvfglobal.com/japan.

89. Statista—The Statistics Portal (2019) Internet Usage in Japan: Statista Dossier. www.statista.com/statistics/379122/e-commerceshare-of-retail-sales-in-japan, retrieved ?.

90. *The DMA ECHO Winners Program 2007*, p. 27.

91. World Population Review (2016) 'Africa Population 2016.' http://worldpopulationreview.com/ continents/africa-population, retrieved ?.

92. Central Intelligence Agency (2016) Nigeria. *The World Factbook*. www.cia.gov/library/publications/the-world-factbook/geos/ni.html, retrieved ?.

93. Ibid.

94. Mthuli Ncube, Charles Leyeka Lufumpa, and Désiré Vencatachellum (2011) 'The Middle of the Pyramid: Dynamics of the Middle Class in Africa.' *AfDB Chief Economist Complex*, April 20. www.afdb.org/fileadmin/uploads/afdb/Documents/Publications/The%20Middle%

20of%20the%20Pyramid_The%20Middle%20 of%20the%20Pyramid.pdf, retrieved May 23, 2011.

95. Direct Marketing Association of South Africa (2016) www.dmasa.org.
96. Peter Wonacott (2011) 'Continental Shift—Global Businesses Battle to Tap Africa's New Middle Class Wealth.' *The Wall Street Journal—Classroom Edition*, May. www. wsjclass room.com/cre/articles/11may_intl_africa.htm, retrieved May 23, 2011.
97. *The DMA ECHO Winners Program 2007*, p. 42.
98. Ibid., p. 55.

PART 4

Applications, Examples, and Careers in Direct, Digital, and Data-Driven Marketing

Comprehensive Case A

DOMINO'S: MEETING CUSTOMERS WHEREVER AND WHENEVER TO GROW SALES

Matthew H. Sauber and David W. Marold

Figure CA-1 Domino's Pizza logo with tagline. Domino's® is a registered trademark of Domino's IP Holder and used with permission.[1]

With 31 consecutive quarters of same-store sales growth in the United States and 100 consecutive same-store sales growth internationally, Domino's continued strengthening its position as the world's largest pizza brand, with 15% market share, in 2018, by adding franchisees, advancing high-quality menus, focusing on operations and technology leadership, and creating shareholder value. Innovations included a voice-ordering function on Domino's app called 'Dom,' along with the ability to order through smart TVs, smartwatches, and even a tweeted emoji. Domino's expansion continued in the U.S. with the addition of 291 new stores, the highest in the past 15 years. Globally, Domino's continued its growth by adding 769 stores. At the end of 2018, Domino's had a total of 15,914 restaurant units in 85 markets around the world (see Table CA-1).

Table CA-1 Domino's store counts for the fiscal year ended December 30, 2018

Fiscal year	Year end store counts		
	2018	2017	2016
U.S. franchise	5,486	5,195	4,979
U.S. company owned	390	392	392
International	10,038	9,269	8,440
Total	**15,914**	**14,856**	**13,811**

Domino's international retail operation listed 10,038 franchise stores, an increase of annual 8.3% in 85 markets in 2018. The international segment accounted for 36.5% of Domino's consolidated franchise royalties and fees. Franchise stores in Domino's top ten international markets accounted for 64% of the total number of international stores led by India. Stores in eight of the top ten international markets are publicly traded master franchise companies (Domino's 2018 Annual Report).

Table CA-2 Domino's top 10 international markets, as of December 30, 2018

International market	Number of stores
India	1,195
United Kingdom	1,100
Mexico	760
Australia	693
Japan	550
Turkey	535
Canada	487
South Korea	447
France	387
Germany	283

One could say the digital revolution at Domino's began in 2007, with customers being able to visit its website and browse the menu to build their own pizza and add sides such as buffalo chicken wings or chocolate lava crunch cake. This was when customers first began to watch the simulated image of the pizza they were ordering. The image changed as they selected a different pie size, chose a sauce, and added pepperoni, black olives, or other toppings. They could also watch the price when the order changed and ingredients were added or removed and when they applied a coupon. In 2018, over 65 percent of all Domino's global retail sales were realized via online ordering through the company's website and mobile applications (Domino's 2018 Annual Report).

Technological innovation at Domino's has been relentless ever since. In 2008, the company made the strategic decision to develop its own online ordering platform. Over the next five years, the company launched mobile applications that cover 95% of the smartphones and tablets in the U.S. market. In 2013, it launched an enhanced online ordering profiles platform, allowing customers to reorder their favorites in 30 seconds or five clicks. In 2014, Domino's introduced a voice-ordering application, 'Dom,' the first in the restaurant industry, and made the Domino's Tracker® available on its ordering platforms. In 2015, Domino's added more innovative ordering platforms, including Samsung Smart TV®, Twitter, and text message using a pizza emoji. In 2016 it introduced zero-click ordering and added Google Home, Facebook Messenger, Apple Watch, and Amazon Echo to its ordering platforms. In collaboration with Ford Motor Company, in 2017 Domino's began testing pizza delivery using self-driving vehicles, an industry first. In 2018, Domino's launched its Delivery Hotspots, featuring over 200,000 non-traditional delivery spots, including parks, beaches, local landmarks, and other unique gathering locations.

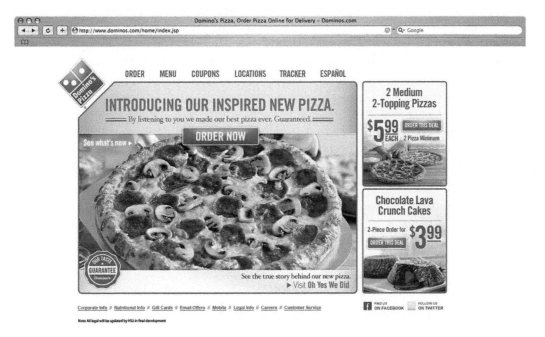

Figure CA-2 Domino's home page. Domino's® is a registered trademark of Domino's IP Holder and used with permission.

COMPANY BACKGROUND

In 2018, Domino's reached 15,914 stores globally; just five years before that, the company had celebrated the opening of its 10,000th store. Domino's is the largest pizza company in the world based on global retail sales. In addition to being the largest pizza chain in the world, it is number one in pizza delivery and approaching number one in carryout (Domino's 2018 Annual Report). The company has come a long way since its humble beginnings. In 1960, brothers Tom and Jim Monaghan borrowed $900 to purchase DomiNicks, a local pizzeria in Ypsilanti, Michigan (Boyer, 2007). Eight months later, Jim Monaghan traded his share of the restaurant for a Volkswagen Beetle. In 1965, Tom renamed the business 'Domino's Pizza, Inc.' (Our Heritage, 2008a).

The restaurant had minimum seating, making delivery essential for success. Initially, Tom Monaghan hired laid-off factory workers as drivers, compensating them based on commission. With an efficiency focus, the menu was reduced from subs and small pizzas to only 'regular pizza.' The business concept took off, leading to expansion through franchising and the first franchise store opened in 1967 (Domino's Pizza, Inc., 2008a).

Expansion

The company continued with its expansion, overcoming challenges, including a fire destroying company headquarters in 1968, and a legal battle headed by Domino's Sugar over trademark infringement (Amstar Corporation, 1980). Originally, Monaghan added dots to the logo for each new franchise opened. With an aggressive expansion rate, the idea became impractical. There were 200 franchises in operation by 1978. Domino's opened its 1,000th store five years later. In 1983, Domino's opened its first international store in Winnipeg, Canada. This paved the way for a global expansion of 1,000 pizzerias overseas—in Europe, Australia, South America, Africa, and Asia—by 1995. In 2018, Domino's celebrated the opening of its 10,000th international store (Domino's 2018 Annual Report).

In 1998, after 38 years of ownership, Tom Monaghan announced his retirement and sold Domino's Pizza to Bain Capital, Inc. (LA Times, 1998). A year later, the company named David A. Brandon chairman and chief executive officer (Domino's Pizza, Inc., 2008b). The company went public in 2004. (See Table CA-3 for a timeline from 1960 to 2010.)

Table CA-3 Domino's milestones. Domino's® is a registered trademark of Domino's IP Holder and used with permission.

1960	Tom Monaghan and his brother, Jim, purchased 'DomiNick's,' a pizza store in Ypsilanti, Michigan. The Monaghans borrowed $900 to buy the store.
1965	Tom Monaghan renamed the business 'Domino's Pizza, Inc.'
1967	The first Domino's Pizza franchise store opened in Ypsilanti, Michigan.
1968	The first Domino's store outside of Michigan opened in Burlington, Vermont.
1978	The 200th Domino's store opened.
1983	Domino's first international store opened in Winnipeg, Canada. The 1,000th Domino's store opened. The first Domino's store opened on the Australian continent, in Queensland.

1985	The first Domino's store opened in the United Kingdom, in Luton, England.
	The first Domino's store opened on the continent of Asia, in Minato, Japan.
1988	The first Domino's store opened on the South American continent, in Bogota, Columbia.
1989	Domino's opened its 5,000th store.
1990	Domino's Pizza signed its 1,000th franchise agreement.
1995	Domino's Pizza International opened its 1,000th store.
	The first Domino's store opened on the African continent, in Cairo, Egypt.
1996	Domino's launched its first website (www.dominos.com).
1997	Domino's Pizza opened its 1,500th store outside the U.S.
1998	Domino's launched HeatWave®, a hot bag using patented technology that keeps pizza oven-hot to the customer's door.
	Domino's Pizza opened its 6,000th store in San Francisco, California.
	Tom Monaghan announced his retirement and sold 93% of the company to Bain Capital, Inc.
1999	David A. Brandon was named chairman and chief executive officer of Domino's Pizza.
2000	Domino's Pizza International opened its 2,000th store outside the U.S.
2003	Domino's became the 'Official Pizza of NASCAR.'
	Domino's was named Chain of the Year by *Pizza Today*.
	Domino's introduced its Pulse Point of Sale, a touch-screen ordering system.
2005	Domino's Pizza Australia opened its 400th store in Aspley, Brisbane.
	Domino's Pizza UK opened its 400th store in Wadsley Bridge, Sheffield.
2006	Domino's opened its 8,000th store by simultaneously opening the 5,000th U.S. store in Huntley, Illinois and the 3,000th international store in Panama City, Panama.
2007	Domino's rolled out online and mobile ordering in the U.S.
2009	Domino's was ranked no. 1 in customer satisfaction per the annual American Customer Satisfaction Index (ACSI).
	Domino's introduced Pizza Tracker.
2010	Domino's changed its pizza recipe 'from the crust up'.
	J. Patrick Doyle became Domino's chief executive officer.
	Domino's opened its 9,000th store in New Delhi, India.
	Domino's was ranked no. 1 in Keys Brand taste test.

At the end of the fiscal year 2018, Domino's had 15,914 stores in operation worldwide, of which 10,038 were international and 5,876 were domestic stores. As Table CA-4 reveals, Domino's global retail sales, from 2015 to 2018, grew from $10.87 billion in 2016 to $13.54 billion in 2018 (Domino's 2018 Annual Report).

Table CA-4 Domino's financial highlights (2016–18). Domino's® is a registered trademark of Domino's IP Holder and used with permission

Fiscal year	Domino's global retail sales (in millions)		
	2018	2017	2016
U.S.	6,591.6	5,925.1	5,335.2
International	6,953.6	6,327.0	5,538.4
Total	**$13,545.2**	**$12,252,1**	**$10,873.6**

INDUSTRY OVERVIEW

Categorically, Domino's Pizza belongs to the quick-service restaurant (QSR) industries. The QSR industries consist of restaurants with fast-food service and limited menus of moderately priced and cooked-to-order items. The QSR pizza category in the U.S. is large and fragmented—the second-largest category within the $299.6 billion QSR sector—and comprised of delivery, dine-in, and carryout. The category grew unevenly from $33.9 billion to $36.5 billion between 2008 and 2018, as shown in Figure CA-3.

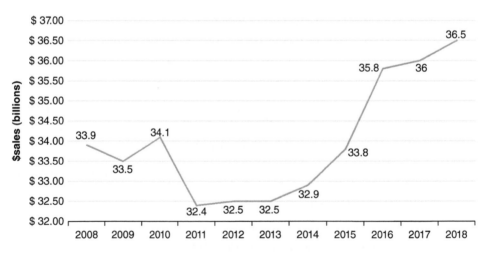

Figure CA-3 U.S. QSR pizza sales (2008–18). Domino's® is a registered trademark of Domino's IP Holder and used with permission

In fact, QSR pizza registered more sales in 2008 and 2010 compared to 2015. Sales dropped by 5 percent in 2011 and did not rebound until 2015. Sales grew by 8 percent between 2015 and 2018. About 54 percent of U.S. pizza outlets are independently owned, and these controlled 41 percent ($18.78 billion) of industry sales in 2018 (Figure CA-4).

A recent survey found that consumers rate independent pizzerias superior to chains in operational and emotional attributes such as personalized service, customer value, and community

U.S. Pizza Stores 76,993
Year Ending September 2018

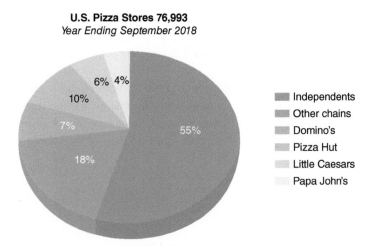

Figure CA-4 U.S. pizza stores pie chart. Domino's® is a registered trademark of Domino's IP Holder and used with permission.

orientation (PMQ Pizza Magazine, December 2017). As Figure CA-5 shows, the chains, the Big Four—Domino's (22%), Pizza Hut (20.45%), Little Caesars (13.80%), and Papa John's (11.17%)—kept steady growing sales and market share (58.93%) as a collective unit after the recession (PMQ Pizza Magazine, December 2018).

Pizza Sales: U.S. Chains $26.95 Billion
Year Ending September 2018

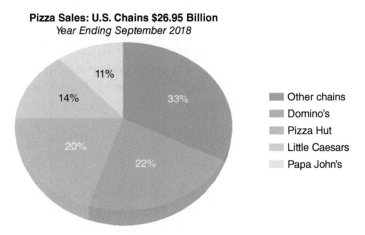

Figure CA-5 Pizza sales (U.S. chains). Domino's® is a registered trademark of Domino's IP Holder and used with permission.

A closer look at the performance of independently owned pizzerias indicates that their sales growth was marginal (1.5%) in 2018, while chain restaurants increased sales by 7.99 percent. Similarly, the chains added 1,452 stores to the 33,515 they already had (an increase of

4.3%), whereas independent operators added 298 stores (.71%) to their numbers (41,728). As a result, the market share for independent operators shrank to 41 percent (from 42.5%) against 60 percent for the chains in the QSR pizza category in 2018 (PMQ Pizza Magazine, December 2018).

Plausibly, one can argue the slow adoption of digital, mobile, and social ordering technologies among independent pizza stores, compared to big chains, as one reason for the market share loss. According to a white paper by the National Restaurant Association, consumers who place orders online, visit restaurants 67 percent more frequently than those who do not (Payment HQ, 2015).

Pizza Hut

Pizza Hut is a division of Yum! Brands, Inc., the world's largest restaurant company in the world in terms of system restaurants—48,000 globally. McDonald's had nearly 38,000 restaurants (McDonald's Corporation 2018 Annual Report). Yum! is ranked no. 472 on the Fortune 500 List, with over $49 billion in revenue in 2018. The Yum! Brands management team lately spun off the company into an independent, publicly traded company (Chinese division, Yum! China) and a high-margin franchise company (New Yum!) focusing on global growth (Yum! Brands 2018 Annual Report).

Pizza Hut, based in Dallas, Texas, is America's first national pizza chain, established in 1958. It is the world's second largest pizza chain, with 16,000 units in more than 100 countries and territories around the world. Pizza Hut became the first national chain to offer pizza delivery on the Internet in 1994. It offered online ordering in all its U.S. locations in 2007, and mobile ordering, through text messaging and Web-enabled cell phones, in 2008. In April 2015, it introduced a new technology, 'Visible Promise Time,' that allows customers to view an estimated timeline of when their food will be ready prior to actually placing an order (QSR, 2016). More recently, Pizza Hut launched a social ordering platform that allows its customers to place orders using a 'Chabot' on Twitter and Facebook Messenger (Huddleston, 2016). In 2018, Pizza Hut became the Official Pizza Sponsor of the NFL (blog.pizzahut.com).

Papa John's

Since opening its first pizzerias in 1985, Papa John's has grown to be the fourth largest U.S. pizza chain, after Little Caesars, in terms of market share and the number of stores. Headquartered in Louisville, Kentucky, the company had 5,303 restaurants in operation as of December 2018, operating in all 50 states and in 46 countries (Papa John's 2018 Annual Report). In 2018, Papa John's North American sales decreased by 10.5% compared to the previous period, reflecting negative publicity and consumer sentiment challenges as a result of statements by Papa John's founder and former chairman, John H. Schnatter. The company is addressing the negative sales impact through brand initiatives and a new advertising and marketing campaign (Papa John's 2018 Annual Report).

Papa John's long-term business goal is to build the strongest brand loyalty of all pizza restaurants. The company's key strategies are based on a menu of high-quality pizza along with side items, efficient operating and distribution systems, team member training and development, national and local marketing, technology initiatives, developing and maintaining a strong franchise system, and international operations (Papa John's 2018 Annual Report).

Papa John's 'traditional' domestic restaurants are a delivery and carryout operation that serves defined trade areas. As such, Papa John's is the closest competitor to Domino's. Potential and active competition exists for management personnel, drivers, and hourly team members as well as attractive commercial real estate sites suitable for a pizzeria.

Papa John's advertising slogan and brand promise is 'Better Ingredients. Better Pizza.' Domestic Papa John's restaurants offer a menu of high-quality pizza along with side items, including breadsticks, cheese sticks, chicken strips and wings, dessert items, and canned or bottled beverages. Papa John's traditional crust pizza is prepared using fresh dough (never frozen). Papa John's pizzas are made from a proprietary blend of wheat flour, cheese made from 100 percent real mozzarella, fresh-packed pizza sauce made from vine-ripened tomatoes (not from concentrate) and a proprietary mix of savoury spices, with a choice of high-quality meat (100 percent beef, pork and chicken with no fillers) and vegetable toppings. The 2015 American Customer Satisfaction Index gave Papa John's the highest rating among its competitors (Papa John's 2018 Annual Report).

In 2001, Papa John's became the first national pizza company to offer online ordering and was the first pizza company to surpass $1 billion in online sales. In 2018, 60% of Papa John's sales were from digital channels. In addition to placing orders online at papajohns.com, customers can place orders via text messaging and the mobile Web capabilities of cell phones. Papa John's completely redesigned its website and mobile app to significantly improve its rating and mobile ordering. It is the only national pizza chain with an e-commerce help desk. Its PAPA REWARDS® program is a customer loyalty program designed to increase loyalty and frequency. It is offered domestically, in the U.K., and in several international markets.

In 2018, Papa John's relaunched its digital rewards program. Papa John's introduced electronic PayShare in 2015, a digital solution that allows customers to split their pizza bill while ordering online (Papa John's 2018 Annual Report).

Domino's

Based in Ann Arbor, Michigan, Domino's is the number one pizza company in the world, number one in delivery and number two in carryout. The company pioneered the pizza delivery business and has built the brand into one of the most widely recognized consumer brands in the world.

Domino's is the largest pizza brand in the world, with a global market share of nearly 15% in the quick-service pizza category, operating a network of almost 16,000 franchised and company-owned stores in all 50 states and 85 international markets. As Table CA-5 reveals, the company had global retail sales of about $13.55 billion in 2018—$6.59 billion in domestic and over $6.95 billion in international sales.

Table CA-5   Domino's global sales in millions for the fiscal year ended December 30, 2018. Domino's®
is a registered trademark of Domino's IP Holder and used with permission.

Global retail sales	2018	2017	2016
U.S.	6,591.60	5,925.10	5,335.20
International	6,953.60	6,327.00	5,538.40
Total	**$13,545.20**	**$12,252.10**	**$10,873.60**

Domino's business model emphasizes on-time delivery of quality pizza. The model entails: (1) delivery-oriented store design with low capital requirements, (2) a concentrated menu of pizza and complementary side items, (3) a network of committed owner-operator franchisees, and (4) a vertically integrated supply-chain system. Revenues are largely driven by sales through company-owned stores and at franchise level, made up of royalty payments and supply-chain revenues.

Domestically, Domino's competes against regional and local pizzerias as well as national chains on the basis of product, service, image, value, effective advertising, and leading technology. The company is no. 1 in total pizza and delivery market share in the U.S. and is closing in for the same top spot in the carryout pizza market. The industry is often affected by changes in consumer tastes, economic conditions, demographic trends, and consumer disposable income (Domino's 2018 Annual Report).

In the U.S., Domino's primarily competes in the delivery and carryout segments of the QSR pizza industry. Domino's is the leader in the U.S. pizza delivery market where it collectively commands, together with Pizza Hut and Papa John's, a 58 percent share of that market. In 2015, Domino's $9.8 billion sales accounted for approximately 27 percent of the total U.S. QSR pizza delivery segment.

Domino's also competes in the carryout market, which together with pizza delivery make up the largest components of the U.S. QSR pizza industry. From 2008 to 2018, the U.S. carryout pizza segment grew from $14.1 billion to $17.1 billion. Although Domino's primary focus is on pizza delivery, it is also favorably positioned to compete in the carryout segment, given its strong brand identity, convenient store locations, and affordable menu items (Domino's 2018 Annual Report).

Together with Pizza Hut, Domino's has had a significant presence in pizza markets globally over the past 35 years. Although international pizza delivery is relatively underdeveloped, the demand for pizza in general and pizza delivery in particular—fueled by international consumers' emphasis on convenience—is large and growing throughout the world.

For the first time, Domino's total sales surpassed those of Pizza Hut in 2018. Global retail sales expanded 8.3%, domestic same-store sales grew 6.3%, and international same-store sales advanced 3.3%. The chain experienced a global net store growth of 232 units in the third quarter of 2018, according to Domino's 2018 Annual Report.

Domino's has been commanding a consistent growth pattern in the past decade. The company stock has risen 2,000 percent, from $3 in 2008 to $305 per share in 2018. Kelly Garcia, Domino's SVP of e-commerce development and emerging technologies, attributes Domino's success to two critical factors: fundamentals and 'surprise and delight.' Fundamentals focus on the basics, namely product, service, image, value, and mobile technology that are contributing to half of their digital sales that make up the majority (over 65%) of overall sales. And 'surprise and delight,' a strategy that enables customers to order using any device, including in-home assistants such as Amazon Echo, smart TVs, smart watches, and social media platforms. Meanwhile, the emphasis on new platforms attracted top talent to work on product development. Garcia also notes that Domino's loyalty program rewards customers and keeps them away from the competition (PMQ Pizza Magazine, December 2018).

Customer Profile

According to the Smart Flour Foods (2015) study, 'Pizza Lovers in America 2015: Unexpected Findings from a Generational Look at Pizza Trends,' 35 percent of Americans, called 'pizza lovers,' order pizza and buy grocery-store pizza at least once per month; 63 percent of pizza lovers are women and 41 percent of those women are millennials (born between 1980 and 1995), while 68 percent of all pizza lovers exercise two or more times per week. More than half (53 percent) are aged 25 to 44, and 8 percent are 65 or older.

The typical pizza lover may not be white. As a recent study from research firm Mintel shows, Hispanic, black and Asian populations are growing faster than whites. The Hispanic population is predicted to grow by nearly 27 percent between 2009 and 2019, and Hispanic households will have more kids and are more likely to choose pizza when they go out for fast food as compared to the general market (PMQ Pizza Magazine, December 2015).

Buying Behavior

Other buying trends indicate that consumers are shifting dining-out occasions toward breakfast and lunch and away from dinner in recent years: 72 percent of pizza lovers—and 77 percent of millennials overall—think it is completely acceptable to eat pizza for breakfast and dinner on the same day.

Consumers are also being attracted to alternative dinner meals from non-pizza QSR chains, including the ones focusing on fresh sandwiches. Many casual diners began using 'fast-casual' restaurants[2] that emphasize carryout and curbside meals. *Nation's Restaurant News* (NRN) hails 'fast casual' as the growth engine of the restaurant industry. The segment has expanded 550 percent since 1999 and registered $30 billion in sales in 2014. The fast-casual segment is expected to continue its growth 'in the double digits' through 2022 (PMQ Pizza Magazine, December 2015).

In its report 'A Look into the Future of Eating,' the NPD group forecasted that healthy foods, especially the ones labeled 'organic,' will be among the fastest growing consumption trends in the foreseeable future. Consumers increasingly expect fresher, healthier ingredients and a higher degree of customization from quick serve restaurants. In the pizza category, 'fast-casual pizza is the fastest-growing segment in the restaurant business,' says Sean Brauser, founder of the traditional Romeo's Pizza (romeospizza.com) chain as well as Pizzafire (pizzafire.com), a new fast-casual concept with locations in Akron and Cleveland, Ohio. 'We have grown [Pizzafire] to $5 million in just over a year, and we plan on opening 12 to 18 more stores next year' (PMQ Pizza Magazine, December 2015).

Promoters of the new fast-casual pizza segment are not in direct competition with traditional pizzerias. Their position is to compete with the mainstream fresh-casual restaurants, such as Chipotle, Jimmy John's, and Panera Bread, where the sales volume and ROI are significantly higher. Pieology Pizza, the fastest growing fast-casual pizza chain in America, according to Technomic's annual ranking of the 500 largest restaurant chains, currently has 140 pizzerias in 23 states, with more than half located in California (pieology.com). The chain appeals to those consumers who prefer to customize their pizzas (making it similar to Chipotle)—from wheat crust to gluten-free crust to vegetarian pizzas to dairy-free cheese (Schlossberg, 2015). Other fast-casual pizza chains MOD and Pie Five Pizza doubled their sales in 2104, and Pizza Rev tripled its sales and the number of stores in 2014 (PMQ Pizza Magazine, December 2015).

Although growth of fast-casual restaurants has slowed significantly since 2016, this category continues to be an important and growing segment of the pizza industry. A Technomic study found that 28 percent of consumers frequent fast-casual establishments (visiting at least once per month), according to a Technomic study. Fast-casual pizzerias are also expanding their menus, offering dishes such as chicken wings, sandwiches, and salads.

A survey of 1,000 consumers by AlixPartners, a global consulting firm, in May 2018, reported that 20% of millennials intended to visit fast-casual establishments twice a week or more, compared with 24% in the 2017 survey. Similarly, the same survey found that 32% of diners preferred fast-casual for lunch, a 5% drop from the 2017 survey. By comparison, fast food was the preferred lunch destination for 35% of respondents, an increase of 5% on the previous year (PMQ Pizza Magazine, December 2018).

Granted its phenomenal success, the fast-casual pizza boom has yet to hurt top pizza chain sales and their market share. Domino's, Little Caesars, and Papa John's all reported gains of 11.1%, 2.1%, and 2.8% respectively in their 2017 sales. A notable exception, Pizza Hut lost 4.2% in sales in 2017 (PMQ Pizza Magazine, December 2018).

There are several plausible reasons as to why fast-casual pizzerias are not hurting the sales of the traditional chains. First, fast-casual pizza chains are competing against other fast-casual restaurants where the segment is new, expansion is faster, and competing brands are not entrenched as compared to the traditional top pizza chains. Second, the traditional chains are not focused on the lunch crowd the way fast-casual brands are. With their brand recognition, digital-ordering, and advertising clout, the national chains are pursuing the dinner crowd and delivery occasion, while fast-casual pizza chains are after the workday lunch crowd. Third, fast-casual pizza chains are very new and their brands are unknown among the pizza-loving consumers who are exposed and accustomed to national brands. This market share picture, however, might change significantly if more fast-casual pizza brands crash Technomic's top 500 annual ranking of the largest restaurant chains.

DOMINO'S SWOT ANALYSIS

Strengths

The *cost-efficient store model* is characterized by a delivery- and carryout-oriented store design, low capital requirements, and a focused menu of quality, affordable pizza, and other, complementary items. At store level, the simplicity and efficiency of operations provide advantages over competitors who, in many cases, also focus on dine-in.

Strong brand equity: Domino's is the largest pizza brand in the world in terms of retail sales and is one of the most widely recognized consumer brands in the world. It is the world leader in pizza delivery and has a significant business in carryout. Consumers associate the brand with timely delivery and quality food that is affordable.

Technological leadership: pioneering in digital technology has been vital to Domino's long-term success. This recognition includes the following:

- Domino's 65% of U.S. sales were completed using digital platforms in 2018.
- Domino's is one of the top U.S. e-commerce retailers in terms of number of annual transactions.
- Digital ordering was launched in 2008 (Figure CA-6). This included Domino's PULSE™ point-of-sale system—installed in all company-owned stores, in more than 99% of domestic franchised stores, and in nearly 75% of international stores. The PULSE™ point-of-sale system features:

  ○ the franchisee's ability to implement centralized promotional activities throughout the marketing mix, including couponing and flyers as well as communicating back to consumers in the manner they communicated
  ○ touch-screen ordering, which improves accuracy and facilitates more efficient order taking
  ○ a delivery driver routing system, which improves delivery efficiency
  ○ improved administrative and reporting capabilities, which enable store managers to better focus on store operations and customer satisfaction.

- In 2007, an enhanced online ordering capability, including Domino's Pizza Tracker, was introduced, while Pizza Builder emerged in 2008.
- In 2010, an online ordering platform was launched, whose mobile applications covered 95% of mobile devices, such as smartphones and tablets, in the U.S.
- In 2013, an enhanced online ordering profiles platform was launched, allowing customers to reorder their favorites in five clicks or 30 seconds.
- In 2014, 'Dom,' a voice-ordering application and the first in the restaurant industry, was introduced. Also, Domino's Tracker® became available on the Pebble smartwatch platform (Figure CA-7).
- In 2015, innovative ordering platforms such as Samsung Smart TV®, Twitter, and text messaging using a pizza emoji were introduced.
- Also in 2015, 'Piece of the Pie Rewards,' an online loyalty program, was launched. Upon signing up for the program, customers become rewards members and can earn points for online ordering.
- In 2017, Domino's began testing pizza delivery using self-driving vehicles, in collaboration with Ford Motor Company.
- In 2018, Domino's launched its Delivery HotSpots, featuring over 200,000 non-traditional delivery spots, and an artificial intelligence (AI) voice-ordering system.

641

Figure CA-6 Online order pizza builder. Domino's® is a registered trademark of Domino's IP Holder and used with permission.

Figure CA-7 Domino's pizza tracker. Domino's® is a registered trademark of Domino's IP Holder and used with permission.

Product innovation: in 2009, Domino's changed its core pizza formula from scratch and came up with a new recipe, beginning with the crust up. In the new crust, it added butter, garlic, and parsley. The new cheese was shredded, instead of diced, mozzarella, with a hint of provolone. And the new sauce was made sweeter, with a red pepper kick. It was well received and achieved growth in customer reorder rate, customer traffic, and increased sales.

In a national taste test, sponsored by Domino's and appearing on its website, three out of five people preferred the taste of Domino's pepperoni pizza, sausage pizza, and extra cheese pizza over Papa John's and Pizza Hut's. Domino's used social media to announce the new arrival with a 'Pizza Turnaround' documentary on YouTube, showing how the company listened to customers who complained about the 'old' recipe, and how it developed the 'new' recipe.

Domino's successful recent product innovations include handmade pan pizza, specialty chicken, parmesan bread bites, stuffed cheesy bread, and marbled cookie brownie. Domino's new product innovation stretches over its international markets as well, where master franchisees have the ability to recommend new products, such as Mayo Jaga in Japan and Saumoneta in France, suitable for local market tastes.

Weaknesses

Quality perception: up until 8–9 years ago (Domino's launched a new pizza recipe in January 2010), many consumers ranked Domino's pizza near the bottom on taste, healthy nutritional value, and quality. However, it is important to realize that perception generally lags behind reality when change is made.

Promotion failure: in 2014, Domino's partnered with the MLB to run a promotional event for the first and second no-hitters of the season. The first 20,000 fans who logged on to their MLB. com accounts could win a free pizza. Unfortunately, because there was so much digital traffic all at once, the site could not handle the volume of loggers and consequently many upset fans did not receive their free pizza.

Operational uniformity: since about 97 percent of stores are owned and operated by independent franchise owners, it is sometimes hard to get all franchisees on the same page. With every new operational and promotional improvement initiative, there can be process and implementation headaches.

Healthy alternatives: the consumers of the twenty-first century are changing and moving towards a health-conscious craze. Consumers demand healthy, nutritional food. Domino's does not offer any healthy alternatives such as salads or grilled chicken.

High turnover: Domino's does not offer many promotion opportunities to its store workers. There is a high turnover rate among team members and franchisee employees.

Opportunities

According to a Technomic study, 83 percent of consumers eat pizza at least once per month. The industry census reported a 60.47% increase in sales over the previous year in 2018.

Internationally, pizzerias are expected to grow by 10.7% based on five-year forecasts (PMQ Pizza Magazine, December 2018).

The world pizza market was estimated to be worth $144 billion in 2018, and continued growth over the next five years is forecast across the world:

- North America + 10.2%
- Latin America + 19.2%
- Western Europe + 5.5%
- Eastern Europe + 18.3%
- Middle East/Africa +8.7%
- China +21.6%
- Russia +9.4%
- Asia Pacific +22.7%
- Australia/New Zealand + 9.1%

Source: PMQ Pizza Magazine, December 2018

Food quality, technology, and the youth culture are the driving forces in the food industry and the QSR pizza group in particular. Consumers are increasingly insisting on the freshest, healthiest ingredients, a trend largely driven by millennials and Generation Z, who also demand advanced technology to facilitate an ease of ordering and delivery. Because of its sheer size, the younger generation's demand is likely to outpace and outspend the boomers in the foreseeable future. This generation has the least established brand loyalty, and millennials are the most 'up for grabs' new retail customers. Millennials and Gen. Z are digitally savvy and heavily use electronic communications when they network, shop, purchase, and pay bills. They are most likely to tell their friends about a great pizza experience; the majority have taken a photo of their pizza and posted it online.

Fast-casual is the fastest growing segment in the pizza group. The QSR fast-casual segment has expanded 550 percent since 1999 and raked in $30 billion in sales in 2014, according to Nation's Restaurant News (NRN). The growth is expected to continue in double digits through 2022.

Social responsibility: patrons expect restaurants to be socially conscious, especially in regard to the environment and sustainability. In a 2014 Techonomic study, 63 percent of all consumers said they would more likely eat at a restaurant they view as socially responsible.

Growth opportunities overseas: emerging economies such as Brazil, Russia, India, and China (BRIC) are being watched closely as the hot growth centers for the pizza industry.

Threats

- As the most diverse and soon to be the largest generation, millennials pose major challenges for marketers in general and the pizza industry in particular:
  - Millennials communicate and shop heavily, relying on social media and mobile technology.
  - Millennials are more likely to search for digital coupons when they order and use ePay when they purchase in stores.

- Millennials display resistance to 'corporate' brands, those that don't authentically commit to a purpose beyond earning money. Well-established restaurant brands such as McDonald's and Chili's that are not adequately socially and environmentally conscious may be at a disadvantage, given millennials' perception of established 'corporate' brands.

- Slow economic growth and lack of income growth in the middle class hamper profitability and growth.
- Stronger competition from fast-casual pizza chains, independents, and take-and-bake options as well as QSR categories other than pizza.
- Healthy-eating trend and organic food consumption.
- With rising minimum wages and depleted labor force, pizzerias struggle to keep their operation staffed as their profit is squeezed by stagnant pizza prices.

Menu-based Growth Strategy

Domino's has revamped and expanded its menu since 2008. It introduced its core hand-tossed pizza in the U.S. with a new recipe in 2009. The new recipe has contributed to continued growth in customer traffic, reordering, and increased sales. More recent innovations of handmade pan pizza, specialty chicken, parmesan bread bites, stuffed cheesy bread, marbled cookie brownie, and bread twists have significantly contributed to U.S. sales over the years. Product innovation also has contributed to the expansion of global sales, where master franchisees recommended products to suit local market tastes by country and culture. Products including the Mayo Jaga in Japan (bacon, potatoes, and sweet mayonnaise) and the Saumoneta in France (light cream, potatoes, onions, smoked salmon, and dill) have been well received in their respective markets (Domino's 2018 Annual Report).

Figure CA-8   Honolulu Hawaiian pizza. Domino's® is a registered trademark of Domino's IP Holder and used with permission.

Figure CA-9 Pacific veggie pizza. Domino's® is a registered trademark of Domino's IP Holder and used with permission.

Technology-Based Growth Strategy

Domino's has developed a reputation for innovation in business processes. It pioneered the corrugated cardboard boxes and 3-D car-top signs that are synonymous with the pizza industry. The company strengthened its efficiency with the time-saving invention of the Spoodle, a combination of a spoon and a ladle. To ensure that customers received the best pizza, the Domino's HeatWave Hot Bag was introduced. This technology utilizes electro-magnetic energy and 3M Thinsulate Insulation to deliver pizza hot and without excess moisture (Corporate Profile, 2010). To improve its daily operations, the Domino's Pulse Point-of-Sale system was introduced in 2003 (Pizza Marketplace, 2003). The touch-screen ordering system significantly improved the accuracy and efficiency of order taking. More than half of Domino's sales in the U.S. are placed digitally.

In 2018, more than 65% of Domino's all global retail sales were derived from digital channels, through online ordering websites and mobile applications. In 2013, it launched an enhanced online ordering profiles platform, giving customers the ability to reorder their favorites with five clicks, or in 30 seconds. Domino's 'Dom,' a voice-ordering application, was the first in the restaurant industry in 2014. Domino's expanded its ordering platforms to include Samsung Smart TV®, Twitter, and text message using a pizza emoji. It introduced zero-click ordering in 2016 and added Google Home, Facebook Messenger, Apple Watch, and Amazon Echo to its platforms. Domino's continued its technological pioneering in 2017 by using self-driving vehicles to deliver pizzas. It launched Domino's Delivery HotSpots and included more than 200,000 non-traditional delivery locations in 2018 (Domino's 2018 Annual Report).

New Media Strategy

Although television accounts for more than 90 percent of Domino's media spending, the company is increasingly utilizing new media, such as online advertising, e-mail, mobile, search, and social networking, to connect with its younger customers. Domino's recently tripled its online advertising spending to promote its new menu and delivery service across a broad range of sites, such as Amazon, Ask, Facebook, Instagram, Yahoo, College Humor, Yellow Pages, as well as sites from local newspapers.

E-mail marketing at Domino's ranges from a variety of special deals, promotional offers, and coupons to new menu item introduction and menu suggestion for special occasions (e.g., lunch, family gathering, gift) to just a simple reminder to order from Domino's. Established customers typically receive a weekly e-mail with promotional deals and suggestions.

Domino's search marketing was catching up with its archrival, Pizza Hut. It demonstrated a strong showing in organic search—a testimony to the company's effective advertising and strong website experience—as opposed to paid search where Pizza Hut made a bigger commitment.

Mobile is one of the fastest growing elements of new media that all the three pizza chains are paying attention to. Mobile marketing at Domino's has been growing and includes 50% of its online marketing via the Internet. The growth rate dovetails mobile commerce, the fastest growing area of retail purchases in the United States (Figure CA-10).

Figure CA-10 Domino's mobile site. Domino's® is a registered trademark of Domino's IP Holder and used with permission.

Domino's 'Surprise and delight' strategy, which allows customers to order from any of their favorite devices, has led to the development of its new ordering platform, Domino's AnyWare, which enables customers to order through any number of devices, including in-home assistants such as Amazon Echo, smart TVs, smart watches, and social media platforms.

Domino's social media strategy is broad ranging. It uses major social media platforms such as Facebook (Figure CA-11) and Twitter to promote its brand and sell pizza. Domino's integrated its social media campaign on Facebook by encouraging consumers to try its new-recipe pizza. An interactive contest, 'Taste Bud Bounty Hunters,' rewarded Facebook users with free food for getting their friends to try the new pizza recipe. On the website (pizzaholdouts.com), photos were displayed of the top bounty hunter contestants and those pizza holdouts with 'wanted taste buds.' Domino's recent 'tweet-to-eat' campaign encouraged customers to order their pizza via Twitter. The campaign was part of Domino's marketing strategy that said customers can stay within whatever media form they are using—social media, mobile, desktop, Apple Watch, etc.—and order a pizza without having to switch media. Although ordering a pizza via Twitter isn't faster or more convenient than submitting the same order through Domino's mobile app, it has added promotional value for Domino's since using Twitter is a public announcement, visible to followers of the person who orders Domino's pizza.

Figure CA-11 Domino's Facebook page. Domino's® is a registered trademark of Domino's IP Holder and used with permission.

CHALLENGES AHEAD

As a $13.5 billion company with 400,000 employees and more than 16,000 stores in more than 85 countries, Domino's has done well in its almost 60 years in business. Basking in the company's success, the management is realistically thoughtful about the list of challenges ahead. Concerns about competition, the economy, and the maturity of the U.S. pizza market remain at the top. The question before the management is whether the same-store growth performance is domestically sustainable and achievable in the near future. Per company reports, U.S. sales rose over 11 percent, from $5.9 billion in 2017 to $6.6 billion in 2018. With a 31.1% share in pizza delivery, Domino's is the number one pizza delivery company in the U.S., where it covers a majority of U.S. households (Domino's 2018 Annual Report).

International growth is one area that management remains hopeful about. Currently, over 51 percent of the company revenues are from the international operation. Domino's International has experienced 101 consecutive quarters of positive same-store sales growth (Q1 2019).

The success of Domino's new recipe has created momentum for the brand, and maintaining that momentum is subject to proper marketing strategy and execution. Since 2008, Domino has significantly expanded its menu and more than 70% of the items on Domino's menu are new. Items include multi-variety oven-baked sandwiches, bread bowl pasta, and the American Legends line of specialty pizza.

Domino's had a very successful 2018 when it became the dominant number one pizza company in the world. It has every intention to maintain its number one position as it looks ahead. Domino's goal is to have 25,000 stores operating around the world, driving more than $25 billion in global retail sales, by the end of 2025, via focusing on fundamentals—namely, product innovation, brand image and value, customer care, pioneering technology, and effective marketing—and front-footed investments that benefit both its customers and franchisees (Domino's 2018 Annual Report).

The question is whether Domino's can continue its phenomenal market and sales growth in the face of the fast-casual movement, local sourcing and healthier ingredients, and the rising costs of running a pizza business.

CASE DISCUSSION QUESTIONS

1. As the largest pizza brand in the world, in terms of retail sales, Domino's is using 'fortressing' strategy to protect its market position. Explain how Domino's fortresses its markets. What activities does fortressing entail? How would fortressing affect Domino's carryout and delivery operations?
2. Assume you are the account director of an IMC agency specializing in data-driven and digital marketing. Domino's has asked you to develop a test plan to increase:

    o   Domino's carryout business without decreasing its delivery business: at the time of writing, Domino's is close to overtaking Little Caesars to become number one in the carryout business.

    o   The number of orders placed through its mobile app: Domino's is near capacity for drivers/delivery but has room to grow in carryout. Over 65% of Domino's sales are now digital (computer, tablet or mobile) and these orders are larger, more profitable, and have higher customer satisfaction. The budget is $500,000 and the tests must be completed in three months and results presented in four months.

3. In 2018, Domino's introduced Hotspots and Paving for Pizza. What innovations have their three major competitors had lately, if any, and how do they compare to these? Investigate the details of each of these innovations for Domino's and formulate an opinion with supporting rationale as to their success.

4. Domino's has expanded into salads and has a gluten-free pizza. Develop a position on expanding into healthier products, farm to table, and be sure to address salads as well as gluten-free and organic foods.
5. Develop three measurable direct/interactive tests designed to increase Domino's mobile sales to a defined target market and test market(s) of your choice (both carryout and delivery are acceptable).

BIBLIOGRAPHY

Allen, A. (2018) 'How Domino's turnaround gained nearly $12b in enterprise value.' Blog. https://aaronallen.com/blog/dominos-turnaround, retrieved May 20, 2018.

Amstar Corporation (1980) Plaintiff-appellee v. Domino's Pizza, Inc. and Atlanta Pizza, Inc., Pizzaenterprises, Inc. and Pizza Services, Inc., Hannacreative Enterprises, Inc., Defendants-appellants, 615 F.2d 252 (5th Cir. 1980).

Boyer, P. J. (2007) 'The deliverer,' *The New Yorker*, February 19. www.newyorker.com/maga zine/2007/02/19/the-deliverer, retrieved September 13, 2019.

Bryant, C. (2018) 'Quick service restaurants—US—May 2018,' Mintel. http://academic.mintel. com.ezproxy.emich.edu/display/860445, retrieved September 14, 2019.

Butcher, D. (2009) 'Domino's Pizza exec: mobile commerce growing at astounding rate,' *The Mobile Marketer*, September 4. www.mobilemarketer.com/cms/news/commerce/4102, retrieved September 14, 2019.

Connor, D. (2000) 'QuickOrder brings Domino's Pizza to you in 30 minutes or less,' *Network World*, March 6.

David A. Brandon (n.d.) Biography. https://en.wikipedia.org/wiki/Dave_Brandon, retrieved September 14, 2019.

Domino's 2010 Annual Report, 2011.

Domino's 2015 Annual Report, 2016.

Domino's 2018 Annual Report, 2019.

Domino's Investor Relations (2010) 'Corporate profile.' www.annualreports.com › AnnualRe portArchive › ASX_DMP_2010, retrieved September 14, 2019.

Domino's Pizza, Inc. (2008a) 'Our heritage.' https://dominos.gcs-web.com/financial-informa tion/annual-reports, retrieved September 14, 2019.

Domino's Pizza, Inc. (2008b) Datamonitor company profiles. *Datamonitor*, November 12. www. datamonitor.com/store/Product/dominos_pizza_inc?productid=1744376E-79E5-49F9-9298-F128768A73E5, retrieved November 12, 2008.

Domino's Pizza, Inc. (2010) 'Domino's Pizza rewards the "taste bud bounty hunters",' *Restaurant News.Com*, May 11. www.restaurantnews.com/dominos-pizza-rewards-the-taste-bud-bounty-hunters, retrieved September 14, 2019.

Domino's Pizza, Inc. (n.d.) 'Making pizza since 1960....'. www.dominosbiz.com/Biz-Public-EN/ Site+Content/Secondary/About+Dominos/History, retrieved September 14, 2019.

Domino's Pizza Investor Presentation, January 2010. https://dominos.gcs-web.com/financial-information/annual-reports, retrieved September 14, 2019.Domino's Pizza UK (2007)

'Domino's Pizza launches UK's first ever text message pizza order service'. Press Release. www.dominos.uk.com/media_centre/pdf/Text%20Ordering.pdf, retrieved September 14, 2019.

Dow Jones (2004) 'Agency of the year: digital agency of the year – best of the rest'. *Dow Jones*, December 15.

Gartner (2015) 'Gartner says by 2017, U.S. customers' mobile engagement behavior will drive mobile commerce revenue to 50 percent of U.S. digital commerce revenue.' Press Release, January 28. www.gartner.com/en/newsroom/press-releases/2015-01-28-gartner-says-by-2017-us-customers-mobile-engagement-behavior-will-drive-mobile-commerce-revenue-to-50-per-cent-of-us-digital-commerce-revenue, retrieved September 14, 2019.

Horovitz, B. (2010) 'New pizza recipe did wonders for Domino's sales,' *USA Today*, May 5. www.us atoday.com/money/industries/food/2010-05-05-dominos05_ST_N.htm, retrieved June 28, 2010.

Huddleston, T., Jr. (2016) 'Now you can order Pizza Hut on Twitter and Facebook, too.' *Fortune*, July 13. http://fortune.com/2016/07/13/pizza-hut-chatbot-twitter-facebook/?iid=recirc_f500profile-zone1, retrieved September 14, 2019.

Jargon, J. (2009) 'Business technology: Domino's IT staff delivers slick site, ordering system—pizza chain rolls out point-of-sale system in U.S. stores to woo customers, streamline online orders,' *The Wall Street Journal*, November 24.

LA Times (1998) 'Domino's founder to retire, sell stake,' *Los Angeles Times*, September 26. https://www.latimes.com/archives/la-xpm-1998-sep-26-fi-26500-story.html.

Liddle, A. (2008) 'Domino's pioneers "couch commerce," expands its ordering options with new TiVo partnership,' *Nation's Restaurant News*, December 1.

Litterick, D. (2008) 'Colin Halpern sells £4m slice of Domino's Pizza,' *The Daily Telegraph*, February 23. www.telegraph.co.uk/finance/newsbysector/retailandconsumer/2784914/Colin-Halpern-sells-4m-slice-of-Dominos-Pizza.html, retrieved September 14, 2019.

Mattioli, D. (2010) 'Retailers answer call of smartphones,' *The Wall Street Journal*, June 11. www.wsj.com/articles/SB10001424052748704749904575292910414412650, retrieved September 14, 2019.

McDonald's Corporation (2018) Annual Report.

National Restaurant Association (2016) 'Restaurant industry forecast.' www.restaurant.org/research/reports/state-of-restaurant-industry, retrieved September 13, 2019.

NMA (2007) 'Domino's Pizza enables ordering by SMS,' *New Media Age*, July 26.

NRN (2010) 'Domino's opens 9000th store,' *Nation's Restaurant News*, March 11. www.nrn.com/archive/dominos-opens-9000th-store, retrieved September 13, 2019.

Nyse (2010) 'Change at Domino's,' *nyse magazine*. www.nysemagazine.com/dominos, retrieved.

Packaged Facts, New York, 2010.

Papa John's 2009 Annual Report.

Papa John's 2015 Annual Report.

Papa John's 2018 Annual Report.

Payment HQ, "White Paper: Mobile invasion", National Restaurant Association, May 11, 2015.

Phone interview with Dennis Maloney, Domino'sMulti-Media Marketing Vice President, 2011.

Phone interview with Dennis Maloney, Vice President, Domino's Chief Digital Officer, 2016.

Pizza Marketplace (2003) 'Domino's Pizza & breakaway roll out of new pulse POS system,' *Pizza Marketplace*, February 5. www.pizzamarketplace.com/news/dominos-pizza-and-break away-rollout-new-pulse-pos-system, retrieved September 13, 2019.

Pizza Today (2010) 'Chain of the year,' June, www.pizzatoday.com.

PMQ (2009) 'Pizza Power Report, 2009,' *PMQ Pizza Magazine*, September, www.pmq.com.

PMQ (2015) 'Pizza Power Report, 2015,' *PMQ Pizza Magazine*, December, www.pmq.com.

PMQ (2018) 'Pizza Power Report, 2018,' *PMQ Pizza Magazine*, December, www.pmq.com.

PR Newswire (2008) 'Domino's launches revolutionary customer tool: pizza tracker™; industry-leading technology allows customers to follow progress of their order online—even if they order by phone,' *PR Newswire (U.S.)*, January 30.

QSR (2015) 'The QSR 50,' *QSR Magazine*, August. www.qsrmagazine.com/reports/qsr50-2015?page=2, retrieved September 14, 2019.

QSR (2016) 'Pizza Hut now shows "visible promise time" on orders,' *QSR Industry News*, April 27.

QSR (2017) 'How Domino's loyalty program is paying off,' *QSR Magazine*, October 12. www.qsrmagazine.com/news/how-domino-s-loyalty-program-paying, retrieved September 14, 2019.

Revolution (2006) 'Revolution Awards 2006: Is your work in the running?' *Revolution*, February 28.

Ross, J. (2007) 'Domino's, Papa John's look to build clientele via text message ordering,' *Nation's Restaurant News*, December 10.

Schlossberg, M. (2015) 'The fastest-growing restaurant in America should terrify traditional pizza chains,' *Business Insider*, June 25. www.businessinsider.com/pieology-pizza-business-story-and-expansion-2015-6, retrieved September 14, 2019.

Smart Flour Foods and The Center for Generational Kinetics (2015) 'Pizza Lovers in America 2015,' LLC, June, www.smartpizzamarketing.com/wp-content/uploads/2015/07/Pizza-Lovers-in-America-2015.pdf, retrieved September 14, 2019.

Standard & Poor's stock report (2010) 'Strategic play–Domino's Pizza: Speedy delivery,' *New Media Age*, May 15.

Vesco, M. (2018) How Domino's pizza is mastering data, one pizza at a time – Talend. Talend Real-Time Open Source Data Integration Software. Available at: www.talend.com/blog/2018/06/13/how-dominos-pizza-is-mastering-data-one-pizza-at-a-time, retrieved September 14, 2019.

Wohl, J. (2018) Domino's unseats Pizza Hut as biggest pizza chain. Available at: https://adage.com/article/cmo-strategy/domino-s-unseats-pizza-hut-biggest-pizza-chain/312463, retrieved December 8, 2018.

Yum! Brands (2009) Annual Customer Mania Report.

Yum! Brands (2018) Annual Report. www.yum.com/annualreport, retrieved September 14, 2019.

NOTES

1. All copyright material for figures was supplied to the case authors.
2. 'Fast-casual' is the fastest growing QSR group that offers a higher quality food with fresh ingredients compared to its fast-food alternative. It is an intermediate concept between fast food and casual dining, and priced accordingly. The category is exemplified by chains such as Boston Market, Bruegger's, Captain D's, Chipotle Mexican Grill, Culvers, El Pollo Loco, Five Guys, Freddy's Frozen Custard & Steakburgers, Newk's Eatery, Noodles & Co., Panera Bread, Pizza Ranch, and Vapiano.

Comprehensive Case B

OOZLEFINCH CRAFT BREWERY: A SMALL BREWERY WITH GLOBAL PLANS

Used with permission of Oozlefinch Craft Brewery and Russel Tinsley.

Figure CB-1 Oozlefinch logo.

Craft breweries have been launched all over the world in recent years, with many entrepreneurs following their dreams of starting their own craft breweries. Oozlefinch Craft Brewery is one example of this growing phenomenon. What you are about to explore is the story of an entrepreneur and his bold new craft brewery venture. This case will enlighten you to the many marketing opportunities and challenges that are associated with the pursuit of craft brewery business success.

   Meet Russel Tinsley, founder of Oozlefinch Craft Brewery, LLC, located in Southeastern Virginia. Russ is a Virginia transplant, having been born in Chicago; he grew up in the Johnson City area of East Tennessee. After two years of school at East Tennessee State University, he joined the U.S. Navy where he served as a military police officer for a total of ten years of both active and reserve duties. Russ's military career took him to Iceland before bringing him to Virginia, where he met his wife Rebekah, and where he began a new career as a police officer where he worked for eight years. In just under two years of service for the police department, Russ was moved from a regular street officer position to an undercover narcotics detective role. Russ's time as a detective was truly successful and rewarding, where he worked with federal and state agencies on high-level drug cases throughout the Hampton Roads area.

Throughout Russ's time in the police department, his love for craft beer grew from simply enjoying a well-crafted beer to insisting on learning the art for himself. He obtained a Sabco BrewMagic brewing system and began brewing beer at home. As his knowledge and passion for the craft increased, he dreamed of starting his own craft brewery. That opportunity presented itself after a near-death experience one night in 2012, while he was working as an undercover detective. Russ and Rebekah (shown in Figure CB-2) both decided to immediately stop putting off their dream and pursue opening their own brewery. Within a couple of days following the incident, they were being shown buildings in their dream location of Fort Monroe in Virginia.

Figure CB-2 Photo of Russ and Rebekah

Fort Monroe is a historical location with 400 years of history. The land known as Old Point Comfort, which now includes Fort Monroe, was the key defense site that sits on the mouth of the Chesapeake Bay. Fort Monroe was a strategic defensive site for four centuries. The area has history from pre-colonial times, the War of 1812, the Civil War, tourism and social history, and the numerous visits to Fort Monroe from various U.S. presidents.

COMPANY HISTORY

Oozlefinch Craft Brewery first opened its doors in 2016 and it has been a successful microbrewery in the Hampton Roads area of Virginia ever since. The Brewery is situated in a 100-year-old 10,000+ square foot building on Fort Monroe. Oozlefinch Craft Brewery has exclusive use of the large field in front of the building and the use of large parking lots that are located within a short walking distance from the brewery (see Figure CB-3).

Figure CB-3   Brewery building in surrounding environment

From its waterfront view to the history that comes with being the sole brewery operating on America's 'Freedom's Fortress,' Oozlefinch Craft Brewery has quickly become a significant piece and adds to the already rich history that exists on the Fort, joining the likes of Harriet Tubman, Abraham Lincoln, General Robert E. Lee, Edgar Alan Poe, and, of course, the imprisonment of Jefferson Davis following the end of the Civil War. Between the waterfront view, the vast amount of space, the seclusion from city life, and almost 400 years of history that come with being located on Fort Monroe, Oozlefinch truly is one of the most unique brewing destinations on the East Coast of the U.S.

The Brewery is named 'Oozlefinch' to honor and retain the rich history of the brewery's location. The legend of the 'Oozlefinch' began in Fort Monroe, Virginia in 1905 (Porter, 2018). Captain H. M. Merriam reported seeing a bird with large, all-seeing, bloodshot eyes and a long neck. Around the year 1906, Mrs. Tilton, wife of Colonel E.R. Tilton, went shopping in Hampton, Virginia and came across a model of a bird that matched the Captain's description. She purchased the bird and brought it back to Fort Monroe; the officers placed it behind the bar of the Fort Monroe Officers Club. In 1908, the Oozlefinch model moved to a special gambling room, famously known as the 'Oozlefinch Room,' and later, the Gridiron Room where the Artillery Board and eventually the Gridiron Club would meet. Since the Oozlefinch was present at all meetings, he became a member of the club.

During World War II, the Oozlefinch was a guardian for artillerymen fighting overseas and had many adventures in locations such as California, Texas, and even Hawaii (Porter, 2018). Reportedly, the original Oozlefinch currently resides at Fort Bliss in Texas. However, a figure made in his image now sits behind the bar at the Oozlefinch Craft Brewery in Fort Monroe, Virginia, the location of the first Oozlefinch sighting.

Russ and Rebekah have created a trademark character to brand the Oozlefinch Craft Brewery. Meet 'Tilton' (Figure CB-4), the cute, long-necked, bug-eyed Oozlefinch bird that represents Oozlefinch Craft Brewery. 'Tilton' consistently appears in all branded promotions, and on most brewery merchandise and craft beer products. Tilton is used to create brand awareness and recognition, and to drive brand engagement for the brewery.

Figure CB-4   The oozlefinch figurine

Oozlefinch Craft Brewery Operations

Since Oozlefinch's opening in September of 2016, Russ has been the sole managing member of the brewery. He oversees everything from the day-to-day financials to the management of all employees. Russ can also be credited with overseeing the implementation of the vision and goals he has set for the brewery.

Rebekah's work at the brewery is focused on sales and marketing. Shortly after the brewery opened, she started doing chalkboard art in the taproom for upcoming beer releases and events. Then, Rebekah started managing the Instagram and website components of the brewery's media advertising. Later, she took on an official role within the brewery as the marketing and sales manager, and absorbed the additional Facebook and Twitter accounts to round out her work on the social media pages. Rebekah is responsible for all photography, graphics, band flyers, advertisements, website updates, e-mail blasts, and online customer communication. She is also establishing new ways to expand advertising methods that are outside of social media, which initially were the only platforms used for brewery promotions.

Rebekah's predominant role in sales is overseeing all festivals and events outside of the brewery. She seeks out festivals for the brewery to attend with its tap truck (shown in Figure CB-5), and establishes communication between the festival coordinators, distributors, and sales/festival representatives. She also prepares all of the equipment for the festivals, and ensures that staff are knowledgeable about the beers they will be serving at the event. The other aspect of managing outside sales is to guide the brewery sales representative as needed, and maintain account relationships. Rebekah also handles requests for shipping merchandise and coordinates all communication with customers for the sales transactions via mail.

Figure CB-5   Brewery tap truck

Oozlefinch Craft Brewery currently has five full-time employees (a brewmaster, an assistant brewer, a taproom/events manager, a marketing/sales manager, and a sales representative for the Hampton Roads market). The brewery also has one part-time cellarman and about a dozen beertenders for the bar, totaling 20 employees.

The brewery started out brewing a consistent, small selection of traditional styled beers (Hefeweizen, Lager, stout, brown ale, porter, and a couple of IPAs), pictured in Figure CB-6. In the first year of being open, Oozlefinch hired a new brewmaster to come in and revamp the brewery's vision for the beers. Russ and Rebekah immediately introduced sour beers and hazy IPAs to the menu, and began making everything on their menu 'one-off' brews (made once and gone). Their new brewmaster had experience from his previous employment overseeing a barrel-aged sour program. So a quick expansion into the existing additional space of the brewery (which doubled their building size) allowed for a collection of barrels to begin to grow, and barrel-aged sours started to appear on the menu as well. This all took place just before the brewery's first anniversary, and the overhaul of beers has been very well received by the firm's customers.

Figure CB-6   Oozlefinch craft beer products

Needless to say, both Russ and Rebekah are very passionate about their new brewery business and their passion is contagious. Russ and Rebekah want to grow their craft brewery business in the local Hampton Roads area, throughout the Commonwealth of Virginia, across the United States, and eventually take it to the global market. They need a strong brand campaign, savvy marketing strategies, dedicated employees, competent, committed distributors, and enthusiastic and loyal customers to help them achieve their desired business development and continued business success. They also need a plan to determine how to prioritize their desired growth and development in the craft beer industry.

CRAFT BEER INDUSTRY

The history of beer dates back to the era of Mesopotamia, but traditional American brewing was built and created from the European tradition of using four simple ingredients (Goldfarb, 2018). In America, they began brewing beer with high-quality oats and grain until Prohibition, which started in 1920 and lasted for 13 years. During the alcohol ban, cheap ingredients, such as corn and rice, were used to brew beer. After Prohibition, it was still illegal to create home-brewed beer higher than 0.5%. In 1978, Congress passed a bill repealing the federal restrictions and excise taxes on home-brewing. President Jimmy Carter signed the bill into law to legalize home-brewing. In the mid-1990s, microbreweries expanded and grew in popularity. This historical event introduced the rise of craft breweries and increased competition in the craft beer industry.

The beer market landscape is changing. High-end products, which include imported and craft beers, are gaining favor with consumers over premium domestic and sub-premium brands. The global beer industry is extremely diverse and industry growth continues to come from craft and imported beers, flavored malt beverages, and cider.

Craft beers are described as those made by small, independent breweries. They typically have a distinct flavor as well as a unique brand name and label. To be considered small, a brewery must have an annual production of no more than six million barrels. Independent means that the brewery has no more than 25 percent ownership by an alcoholic beverage company that produces anything other than craft beers. The traditional aspect of the production assumes that the majority of the brewer's total beverage alcohol volume is in beers made from traditional brewing ingredients, such as water, starch, hops, and yeast (www.brewersassociation.org).

Four distinct segments further define the craft beer industry: brewpubs, microbreweries, regional craft breweries, and contract brewing companies. A brewpub is a combined restaurant and brewery that sells at least 25 percent of its beer production on site. A microbrewery produces less than 15,000 barrels of beer a year, with at least 75 percent of sales taking place off site. A regional craft brewery is an independent, regional brewery that devotes at least 50 percent of its production to malt beer. A contract brewing company is a business that hires another brewery to produce its product but handles its own marketing, sales, and distribution in house.

The growth of small craft breweries in the U.S. began in 1979 when the federal government repealed restrictions on home-brewing beer in small quantities. In 1979, there were only 42 breweries in the U.S. However, by the end of 2014 there were 3,418. Today, there are more than 6,000 craft breweries in the U.S., with 83 percent of Americans living within 10 miles of a brewery (Krommydas, 2018). Over the past decade, craft beer has steadily grown in popularity. In 2017, the craft beer industry controlled 23.4 percent of the overall beer market, representing a $2.5 billion dollar increase from 2016 (Morris, 2018). In addition, 15 percent of all U.S. consumers have visited a brewery within the last three months (Nurin, 2018).

One of the drivers of the craft beer craze is consumers' increasing preference for foods and beverages that are locally sourced. Restaurants are also embracing the craft beer movement by hosting tastings and staffing peer sommeliers to help diners select the right match for their meals. More consumers are now ordering craft beer in restaurants than ever before.

Craft beer brewing is not a recent phenomenon. It first gained popularity in the U.S. in the late 1800s as European immigrants who owned bars often brewed their own beers. These operations quickly ended when Prohibition was enacted in 1920. After its repeal, stringent distribution regulations made it difficult for independent brewers to produce beer that could compete in value with large corporate brewing producers. It was not until the 1970s that microbrewing began to gain popularity among brewers and consumers. In 1976, Jack McAuliffe opened New Albion Brewing in Sonoma, California. He is credited as being America's first craft brewer. McAuliffe formulated the first modern American pale ale, and also produced a porter, stout, and draft ale. Despite selling out quickly, he turned out to be a better brewer than businessman. He spent all of the brewery's cash on an expansion plan, only to discover that no investors would finance a microbrewery. In 1982, New Albion filed for bankruptcy and McAuliffe quit the beer business. His experience caused many aspiring craft brewers to keep their operations small and local.

Today, the craft beer industry is the most crowded it has been since before Prohibition. Many are started by entrepreneurial home-brewers, just as McAuliffe did decades ago. However, since then, a growing number of consumers are now willing to pay more for beer with more taste and alcohol content. The market has evolved.

Craft Beer Trends

Four consumer trends behind the craft beer craze have been identified: premiumization, individualization, communitization, and feminization (Saporito, 2012):

- **Premiumization** is a focus on fewer but better. Enthusiasts would rather purchase two bottles of craft beer over four bottles of domestic premium beer. The social status associated with drinking craft beers often justifies the higher prices paid for these beverages.
- **Individualization** is all about the millennial generation (those born between 1980 and 2001). They represent an intriguing and demanding breed of consumers who possess great—often outlandish—expectations. These young people want to have as many different experiences as possible, including the opportunity to consume diverse brands of craft beer.
- **Communitization** deals with building a sense of belonging. In addition to expressing their own individuality, millennials care about being active community members in areas of interest, including the beer they consume.
- **Feminization** refers to marketing to women. Most traditional beer brands have not done this well. Women have changed their drinking patterns and now are as likely to drink beer or shots as they are a Cosmos or white wine. Women enjoy the variety of tastes represented in craft beers, flavored malt beverages, and hard ciders.

Craft beers feature traditional ingredients, such as malted barley and hops, as well as non-traditional ingredients, including chocolate, raspberries, blueberries, and pumpkin. Craft beer formulas also rely on natural flavors and colors. Many craft breweries capitalize on seasonal tastes, such as pumpkin in the fall, blueberry in the spring, and citrus in the summer. Fullsteam Brewery in Durham, North Carolina, is known for its offbeat flavors, including 'First Frost' winter persimmon ale, 'Paw Paw Belgian-style Golden Ale,' made with the paw paw tree fruit, and 'Fruitcake Beer,' a bourbon-barrel-aged old ale brewed with roasted local chestnuts and grilled figs.

With more than 300 varieties, honey is an extremely versatile ingredient for craft beers. Different floral sources, including alfalfa, wildflower, buckwheat, and tupelo, create distinct flavors in beer (Landi, 2014). The growth in innovative, and sometimes wacky, flavors of beer supports the notion that most craft brewers are creative entrepreneurs who will formulate any recipe to please customers. Some craft brewers are also diversifying their brands with non-beer products. Hard cider is especially popular.

Overall, beer-drinking consumers have become much more adventurous in their craft beer, cocktail, and flavored malt beverage consumption. Enthusiasts perceive craft beer as unique, high quality, and locally focused. It may cost more, but the experience is worth it. According to Nielsen research, women are most interested in beers with crisp, fruity or juicy, hazy flavor profiles (Kendall, 2018).

CRAFT BEER CUSTOMERS

It's a misnomer to think that economic influencers favor inexpensive, mass-marketed beer brands. Price appears to have minimal impact on the purchasing habits of the craft beer enthusiast. Younger consumers are driving the craft beer craze, with consumption led by those who are 30 years old and younger (Carneiro, 2018). Approximately 57 percent of craft beer drinkers are millennials, while 24 percent are considered Generation X (Herz, 2016). However, the composition of the craft beer crowd is important (see Figure CB-7).

Figure CB-7   Oozlefinch busy taproom

The stereotypical 'hipster' image that tends to be used to describe craft beer drinkers is shifting away from an accurate assessment of the consumer demographic profile. According to Nielsen, a weekly craft beer drinker is predominantly male, aged 21–34, and earns approximately $75,000–$99,000 annually. Only 29 percent of women identify themselves as weekly craft beer drinkers; however, 70 percent of women identify as consumers of craft beer (Kendall, 2018).

In the United States, 40 percent of the population aged 21 years or older drink craft beer. In 2018, 68.5 percent of craft beer drinkers were male and 31.5 percent were female. Between 2015 and 2018, the craft beer industry attracted 14.7 million drinkers, and 6.6 million of them were women. In the past three years, 81 percent of new craft beer drinkers were white, and 19 percent were from a minority group. Minority craft beer drinkers are growing but at a slow pace (Watson, 2018).

The surge in the number of microbreweries and demand for craft beer is due, in part, to the millennial generation of consumers who are more affluent than traditional beer drinkers and are not afraid to experiment. This consumer group demands more beer styles than those offered by the big breweries. They want beer with more character and taste. Many young enthusiasts have travelled freely and have tried microbrews that emerged in the Western U.S. in the 1990s (Maier, 2013). Mintel Research reports that craft beer's sweet spot is with 25–34-year-old consumers. Research also found that 43 percent of millennial and Generation X consumers say that craft beer tastes better than domestic beer. In contrast, only 32 percent of Baby Boomers prefer its taste (Riell, 2014).

Consumer Lifestyles and Preferences of Craft Beer Customers

Research shows that most craft beer customers value living a healthy lifestyle and forming healthy habits. Almost 78 percent of monthly craft beer drinkers will read nutritional labels when they purchase food and beverages, 66 percent will go out of their way to eat organic food and beverages because they care about what they are putting in their bodies, while 73 percent are more likely to attend brewery-sponsored exercise and wellness events, especially when a craft beer tasting is included at the event (Furnari and Klineman, 2016). In response to this health focus, many craft breweries hold events that feed into this mindset and lifestyle, including pop-up fitness classes with local fitness centers, featuring yoga, Pilates, kickboxing, cross training, and much more.

The primary motivations for craft beer drinkers to patronize a brewery are to feel an attachment to the local community, to have the brewery experience and overall enjoyment, to socialize, and to drink beer (Taylor and Dipietro, 2017). Most craft brewery owners attempt to make their breweries a warm and friendly community by welcoming families, especially those with children under the legal drinking age, along with pets (see Figure CB-8). The craft beer community is an all-inclusive one that strives to provide a fun experience for customers of all lifestyles.

Figure CB-8   Oozlefinch dog

Approximately 50 percent of craft beer drinkers prefer tasting rooms over bars, mainly because tasting rooms offer flights, while 57 percent of weekly craft beer drinkers prefer their beer to be in cans versus bottles (Kendall, 2018). Millennials enjoy craft beer because they view it as high quality and as an 'affordable luxury' (Herz, 2016). When choosing a craft beer, most millennials claim that flavor is the most important factor, while 61 percent of millennials stated that one of the top reasons for trying craft beers was to 'try something new' (Carnerio, 2018). Craft breweries encourage 'manufacturing tourism', by which consumers travel to different breweries to see how the various craft beers are made and to enjoy samples (Figure CB-9) of the craft beer varieties offered (Krommydas, 2018). Craft beer drinkers like fresh beer, and hometown breweries offer both fresh beer and a sense of community surrounding them that creates a more personal experience for the beer drinker (Conklin, 2019).

Figure CB-9 Oozlefinch tasting

Locality is very important to craft beer drinkers, as are company values. Craft beer customers identify with brands that are local, authentic, sustainable, community-driven, and have strong values (Herz, 2016). Companies supporting causes and those with clear values and beliefs are becoming increasingly important to consumers. Research shows that 73 percent of consumer impressions of a brand are impacted by the causes the respective company supports (Engage for Good, 2019). In addition, 90 percent of consumers would switch to a brand that supports a social or environmental cause and those brands see an 88 percent increase in brand loyalty (Dana, 2018). Savvy craft breweries will tap into cause-related marketing opportunities to form stronger relationships with their customers.

Media and Marketing Preferences of Craft Beer Customers

Social media is a critical platform for marketing to craft beer customers. Approximately 34 percent of millennials like a brand more when it uses social media, and 62 percent reported that they were more likely to become a loyal customer when a brand engages with them on social media (Brewer's Association, 2018).

As most marketers agree, product development should be driven by the customer. In the craft beer industry, that concept is crucial. Craft breweries have a unique opportunity to create close relationships with their customers and use this to their advantage. Many breweries utilize crowd-sourcing as a way to gather input from their customers prior to the development of new craft beer flavors, as well as brew names and label designs.

Special events are another important component for craft breweries to include in their marketing strategies. Event marketing has been known to improve company success and give customers the opportunity to form in-person connections (Rafalson, 2017).

Lastly, cultivating and retaining loyal customers is a critical priority for craft breweries. One way to achieve that is to create hype and excitement regarding new things happening at the local brewery. In addition, creating hype for new experimental beers can be a way to keep that hype trend alive over time.

BUSINESS CUSTOMERS

For craft breweries seeking to mass-distribute their beer, normal business customers include distributors, retailers, bottle shops, and restaurants (Figure CB-10). Current business customers of Oozlefinch Craft Brewery include bars, restaurants, bottle shops, growler-fill stations, specialty wine stores, and two local beer distributors. To effectively market the Oozlefinch Craft Brewery to new business customers, it is critical to analyze the trends of organizational or business purchases. The business consumer purchasing process is more complicated than it is for final consumers. There are many people involved in the organization buying process, meaning that Oozlefinch Craft Brewery salespeople must be able to work with a wide range of people to gain and retain business customers.

Figure CB-10   Oozlefinch barrels

In the ever-changing twenty-first century, business marketing has a heavy focus on digital technology and its capabilities. The average business purchaser conducts approximately 12 online searches before visiting a vendor's website (McLeod, 2019). In addition, with the convenience of Internet searches, business consumers are already 57 percent of the way through the buying process before they correspond with a sales representative (McLeod, 2019).

Finally, business sales rely on derived demand, which means that purchases made by these customers ultimately depend on the final consumer demand for their products. While it is crucial to generate prospective distributor leads and perfect sales presentations for businesses, it is imperative to generate brand awareness with final consumers and stimulate end-user demand.

Therefore, Russ and Rebekah need to use a heavy 'pull strategy' in addition to a 'push strategy' in their marketing activities. A pull strategy aims to generate brand awareness and stimulate consumer demand for Oozlefinch products with final consumers, who then, in turn, influence the demand of business customers. Of course, they need to continue utilizing a push strategy with business customers to create personal relationships and partnerships with restaurants and distributors.

CRAFT BREWERY COMPETITIVE SITUATION

Domestic Market

Russ and Rebekah realize that their direct competitors include any craft brewery located in any of the geographical markets where they intend to sell Oozlefinch Craft Beers. That is stiff competition—which means that Oozlefinch Craft Beers must be consistently branded and uniquely positioned to meet the needs of a specific niche of craft beer drinkers. In the local area, Russ and Rebekah believe that no other craft brewery takes the time to produce live sour ales, live sour lagers, as well as experimental styles of craft beers, in the manner that they do. This is the Oozlefinch competitive edge over the more than 40 craft breweries that operate in its immediate geographical market. Oozlefinch Craft Brewery can expertly craft the 'art in a glass' concept that consumers are not only looking for, but are also willing to pay above-average prices to consume.

Indirect competitors for Oozlefinch Craft Brewery include any other beer or alcoholic beverage that consumers may enjoy instead of Oozlefinch Craft Brewery products. It is well established that consumption of beer tends to be a bit seasonal, higher in the summer months, with a spike in demand in mid-to-late December during the holiday season. An analysis of craft beer sales in the U.S. via Google Trends shows that it is consistent with beer seasonality; however, the peak season for craft beer is during May, with a smaller spike during mid-to-late December. Wineries are considered secondary competitors to craft breweries because they promote and sell the same experience as craft breweries, which includes creating an engaging atmosphere that facilitates comradery.

Russ and Rebekah realize that the dramatic growth of the craft beer industry in the U.S. has brought about heavy competition. Craft breweries have seen exponential growth in recent years; however, this will not last in the long run. Managing growth and determining how to become a recognized and desirable brand are keys to success for small craft breweries. With massive competition for craft breweries in the U.S., many breweries are finding success in foreign markets since the craft beer revolution transcends borders.

Global Market

Just as craft beer has transformed the U.S. beer market, it has also attracted attention and garnered sales around the world. For example, Brooklyn Brewery, founded by Steve Hindy in 1987, has found great success in global markets as approximately 50 percent of its business comes from international sales, with its biggest markets in the U.K., Scandinavia, France, Brazil, Australia, and China (Conick, 2016).

The Brewer's Association reports that craft beer export volume has increased by 3.6 percent, now totaling 482,309 barrels and valued at $125.4 million (Brewer's Association, 2018). Growth was seen in major markets, including in the Asia-Pacific region (not including Japan) which grew by 7.4 percent; Japan, which was up 2.6 percent, and Western Europe, which saw exports increase by 1.3 percent. Canada was again the leading international market for American craft beer, accounting for 51.3 percent of total exports. Other leading importers were the U.K., accounting for 10.5 percent; Sweden, 6.7 percent; Korea, 4.6 percent; Australia, 3.8 percent; and China, with 2.5 percent of exports (Brewer's Association, 2018).

While local and regional craft beers are gaining in popularity in the U.S., they are also earning affection in global markets. Craft beer drinkers are interested in products and cultures different from their own. It has been said that 'A beer from a different country—one which may tell the story of its culture—will have great allure in a foreign market, particularly with Millennials' (Conick, 2016: 43).

How is Oozlefinch positioned and prepared to tackle the global market? Let's explore its SWOT analysis to better understand its current business situation.

OOZLEFINCH CRAFT BREWERY SWOT ANALYSIS

Strengths

- An exclusive brand that quickly moves through distribution channels: Oozlefinch has high-quality and experimental one-off brews; has one of very few live-sour Gose & Berliner programs in the country; has a lab on site that ensures every beer that goes out is high quality; has its own proprietary house bacteria and yeast strains; has successfully harvested a living yeast strain from a civil war era object and uses it in a line of beers.
- Employees: Oozlefinch has excellent employee retention; employees are experienced and knowledgeable brewers and/or friendly and personable beertenders.
- Location: Oozlefinch is set in a historic area; it has a large lawn with stage (which attracts families with kids and dogs); there is a waterfront view, and a barrel room for private events, along with large potential for expansion both of the production space and tasting room space.
- Tasting room: a new point-of-sale system allows for better sales analysis; Mug Club membership has 150 members and room to grow in the future; there is a refurbished historical wood bar from a local Civil War-era drinking establishment; there are permanent discounts for all military, first responders, teachers, and nurses.
- Unique branding: Oozlefinch is tied to the history of Fort Monroe; it has an easily recognizable name and logo.

Weaknesses

- Marketing: there is poor brand recognition outside of the local Hampton Roads area; there is a lack of current marketing activities locally and regionally, and a lack of significant event or festival activities.
- Tasting room: there are very inconsistent 'swag' offerings in the tasting room; there is a lack of seating options; the design and layout of the tasting room could be improved; the outdoor patio area has no shade or rain options; training on Oozlefinch beer offerings and general beer education haven't been a priority.
- Full-time staff: Oozlefinch has an overworked production team; there is a need for more employees as the brewery grows.
- Brewery and production space: there is a need for more tank capacity to meet distribution and tasting room demand.
- Distribution: Oozlefinch has a higher price point than about 85% of other regional breweries; there is a lack of consistency in brand offerings to current distributors.

Opportunities

- National and international distribution: there is a higher demand for sours outside of the local Hampton Roads area; there is high international demand for U.S. craft beers; areas surrounding large cities seem to have less price sensitivity; there is more revenue potential through expansion into new territories—expanding the distribution footprint will allow Oozlefinch to become a more exclusive brand by limiting the amount of beers released to each territory.
- Customers' willingness to pay more for quality beer: this aligns well with the Oozlefinch brand as it has a higher price point, and it allows for the use of better and more expensive ingredients.
- An increase in female craft beer drinkers: Oozlefinch has a female brewer on staff.
- Collaborations with nationally recognized 'exclusive' brands.
- Opportunities to host at least eight festivals each year: state laws allow each craft brewery to apply for eight festival permits a year, while Oozlefinch currently only uses three permits and only one of the three is for a large festival (Annual Oozleversary Party); there is the opportunity to partner with nonprofits who will financially benefit from bigger festivals (cause-related marketing); working with nonprofits will provide a tax benefit if a donation is made to the organization from festival proceeds; there is the ability to promote inclusion through events and attempt to attract a broader audience.

Threats

- A large number of competitors: there are many aggressive competitors, although few are able to craft the types of beer that Oozlefinch does.
- Government regulations: the turnaround time to get labels approved is too long for one-off breweries; Oozlefinch Brewery has to obtain separate licenses for each state in order to distribute and sell its beers, and it has to secure label approval for each state in which it distributes.

PAST OOZLEFINCH MARKETING ACTIVITIES

Russ and Rebekah have primarily used social media to promote Oozlefinch Craft Brewery from the conception of the brewery to mid-2018. Initially, the only social media platforms they used were Facebook and Instagram. Now, they use four different platforms to communicate and engage with consumers.

Facebook has been Oozlefinch's primary source of communication with its consumers by sharing 'weekly line-ups' of its rotating food truck schedules, weekend bands, events, and beer releases. Rebekah has used this for anything informative that she feels it is necessary to share to enhance the customer experience (Figure CB-11).

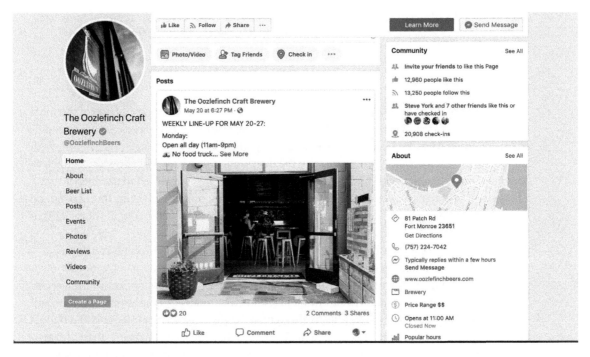

Figure CB-11 Oozlefinch's Facebook screen

Instagram has evolved from just copying posts from Facebook to creating its own focus on the beauty of the liquid that Oozlefinch creates. More artistic shots and beer/brand recognition have become the intent of the posts. Rebekah uses less information and more eye-catching photos on this social media platform. She is still working to improve the use of stories on Instagram as these tend to have a whole other level of followers. Some people prefer just to catch up on followed accounts via their stories versus posts. However, to date, Rebekah has put nearly all her emphasis on posts (Figure CB-12).

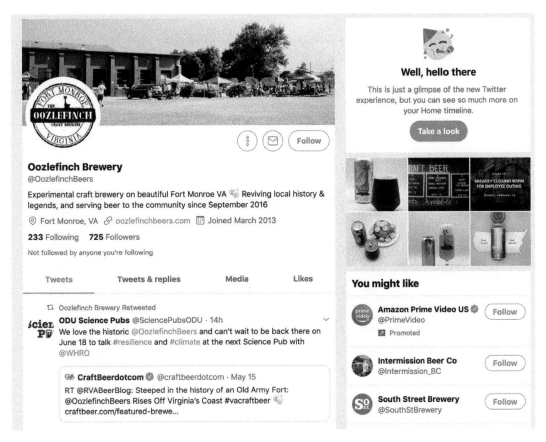

Figure CB-12 Oozlefinch's Twitter screen

Twitter has been used primarily to re-tweet when different retail accounts post that Oozlefinch is now on tap at their establishment. This platform is used to provide consumers a way of finding Oozlefinch out in the community. Russ and Rebekah are constantly being told by customers that they want to know what restaurants have Oozlefinch beers on tap or which bottle shops stock Oozlefinch (Figure CB-13).

An additional social media platform Rebekah has used since the brewery opened is Untappd. On this platform, Rebekah enters all the Oozlefinch beers, and drinkers use it as a social media site for beer where they rate and leave comments about their experiences with the beverages. The platform also shows the locations where consumers are drinking the beer, so Russ and Rebekah can see whether consumers are brewery patrons or just buying Oozlefinch brand beers from other retail accounts (Figure CB-14).

They attended as many local beer festivals as they could to promote their brand of craft beer. Beyond social media and festivals, almost everything they did to promote the brewery was free of charge. However, that changed in 2018 as they began re-evaluating putting money into advertising, setting new goals for growth in 2019, and canning beer and establishing a new branding look for both their craft beer cans and bottles.

Figure CB-13   Oozlefinch's Instagram screen

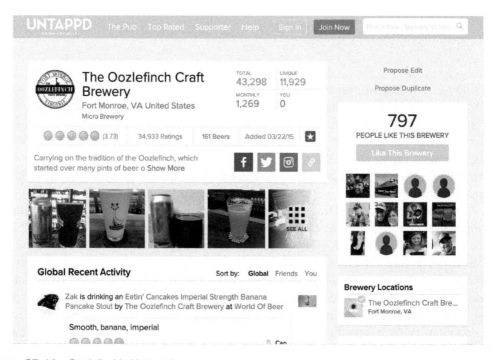

Figure CB-14   Oozlefinch's Untappd screen

They even partnered with a local furniture store and allowed the store to use the Oozlefinch Craft Brewery name for branding a brewery-inspired furniture line in the store. The line has done exceedingly well, and talks are in place to see how this partnership will continue in the future.

Russ and Rebekah began a year-long monthly advertising campaign in a local tourism magazine and agreed to advertise for one year on a local lightrail tram with all the other craft beverage makers in the area. They continued attending as many local festivals as feasible, and sought out new festivals in major cities surrounding their brewery location.

A more proactive marketing approach has recently begun to interact with (and encourage sampling of Oozlefinch beers by) craft beer drinkers who have blogs and Instagram accounts with massive followings. In turn, they will then share their experience with Oozlefinch beverages online and create more buzz around the Oozlefinch brand. Finally, Russ and Rebekah have begun spending more money on fancy glassware with the Tilton Oozlefinch logo, despite the cost of breakage and incredibly high rate of stollen glasses. They figure that having their logo featured in every beer photo that gets posted online from Oozlefinch Brewery customers is worth the extra shrinkage costs (see Figure CB-15).

Figure CB-15   Oozlefinch fancy glasswear

FUTURE BUSINESS MARKETING AND DEVELOPMENT OPPORTUNITIES

Business development opportunities for packaged craft beer products (both in bottles and cans) exist throughout the U.S. and globally. Russ and Rebekah are interested in pursuing new target market areas in the future and would like to begin distributing Oozlefinch promotional teasers (in the form of craft brew samples) to potential business customers and partners in select geographical areas. Initial target markets include all major cities along the Eastern Seaboard, along with select target markets in the Midwest and on the West Coast of the U.S.

Branding Opportunities

The Oozlefinch Craft Brewery has an appealing trademark character named 'Tilton' to help create brand awareness and recognition; however, to date, limited marketing has taken place. Russ and Rebekah feel strongly that their brand position can be strengthened. They are interested in capitalizing on the use of Tilton to enhance overall brand effectiveness and engagement with customers and distributors. How should they feature Tilton? Some of their ideas are:

- having a Tilton mascot costume made
- establishing Tilton hashtags to promote Tilton's brand identity, such as #TipsyTilton and #TravelingTilton
- selling Tilton-branded promotional products, such as magnets, tacker signs, plush Oozlefinch Tilton toys, dog bandanas, and more
- developing 'OozleJuice,' which would be a nonalcoholic beverage for kids
- providing branded pulpboard coasters at bars
- offering a branded decal for the front door of retail establishments that sell Oozlefinch beer.

Consumer Engagement Opportunities

Russ and Rebekah realize that regularly engaging with current and prospective craft beer drinkers is crucial for the long-term success of their brewery. They want to serve the needs and desires of consumers—both in their local area and elsewhere. How to best accomplish this is the question. Here are some of the ideas that Russ and Rebekah are considering:

- holding Oozlefinch 'pop-ups' in cities that are too far away for the average day-trip—his strategy would enable craft beer drinkers to experience 'all things Oozlefinch'; the 'pop-ups' would mean taking a large variety of Oozlefinch beers to a site that would allow for Russ and Rebekah to offer a beer garden or tap-takeover for the day
- establishing a traveling beer festival that Oozlefinch would host in a different city and state every year—once the brewery gains the respective area as a new distribution territory
- making a beer specific to the new markets that Oozlefinch moves into (with ingredients, name, and label graphics) to more closely tie the brewery to that community
- having a new model of a unique beer truck with tap handles through the sides that Oozlefinch could take to festivals and events
- partnering with restaurants to offer Oozlefinch beer and food pairings
- offering brewery/winery collaboration events to target couples who enjoy both beverages
- communicating via regular e-mail blasts to current and prospective Oozlefinch customers
- creating Snapchat filters for events
- developing a mobile app, such as the screens shown in Figures CB-16–CB-20
- identifying and supporting local, national, and global charities or causes on a regular basis.

Figures CB-16–20 Mobile app screens

Business at Oozlefinch Craft Brewery is good, but could be better, especially during the off-season months. Competition is strong for craft breweries in the Hampton Roads area, and clever branding and 'top-of-the-mind' brand awareness are needed to encourage customers to become brand-loyal and patronize Oozlefinch Craft Brewery on a regular basis. Also, loyal customers hold great opportunity for hosting group events and activities at the brewery. In addition, promoting and hosting special events at the brewery can generate strong customer traffic:

- holding various special events, such as a 'How the OozleGrinch Stole Christmas' event; 'Pour Me A Date' event; and a Senior Class Glass (loyalty pint program for college seniors at the brewery)
- offering a 'Flapjacks On Tap' pancake pop-up to coincide with Oozlefinch's pancake beer releases
- renovating the brewery to create a more appealing space
- holding OozleFit fitness pop-ups or fitness classes at the local brewery
- recording some videography footage of the brewery for additional advertising components.

Distributor Opportunities

In attempt to keep the Oozlefinch brand more exclusive, Russ and Rebekah do not want to distribute their product via chain grocery stores. In the past, they have focused on locally owned bottle shops, bars, and restaurants. Creating stronger relationships with Oozlefinch distributors and retailers is critical for business growth and development. Russ and Rebekah have identified many potential activities that may lead to greater affinity:

- developing a loyalty club for distributors and retail accounts where they may win awards from the brewery as they sell Oozlefinch products
- offering onboarding packages for new retail accounts
- giving top-selling bars/restaurants a set of branded yard glasses
- hosting 'thank you' celebrations for distributors and retailers
- distributing an Oozlefinch bobblehead in bars that serve their craft beers.

Global Market Opportunities

Russ and Rebekah realize that they should get involved in some of the valuable programs offered by the Brewers Association Export Development Program (EDP). The EDP is funded by grants from the United States Department of Agriculture and works to inform member breweries about opportunities to sell and promote their products in key international markets. Participating in future EDP craft brewery competitions, promotional events, and educational outreach activities is in the future plans of Oozlefinch Craft Brewery. Here are some of the international ideas that Russ and Rebekah are considering:

- joining the EDP program to have access to a new source of information and a network
- developing a strategy to distribute Oozlefinch in select global markets
- identifying reputable distributors in targeted country markets.

CONCLUSION

The craft beer industry is booming. Russ and Rebekah firmly believe that Oozlefinch Craft Brewery is in a prime position to expand its market both domestically and globally. Now is the time to implement a visionary and strategic marketing plan to tap into bigger markets and achieve even more brewing success.

CASE DISCUSSION QUESTIONS

1. How might Russ and Rebekah fully utilize the Oozlefinch trademark character, Tilton, to generate greater brand awareness and consumer engagement locally, nationally, and internationally?
2. What different strategies should Russ and Rebekah employ in promoting Oozlefinch Craft Brewery to final consumers (B2C) versus business consumers (B2B)?
3. How should Russ and Rebekah prioritize the many different marketing and development opportunities they have identified for Oozlefinch Craft Brewery in the future? Provide justification to support your strategic analysis.
4. What country markets would you recommend Russ and Rebekah investigate in order to expand their craft brewery distribution internationally? How should they begin their global initiatives?
5. How would Oozlefinch Craft Brewery be accepted in your local area? Who would be its primary competitors? How could Oozlefinch gain a competitive advantage?

REFERENCES

Brewer's Association (2018) 'Small and independent American brewers increase international demand and distribution,' April. www.brewersassociation.org/press-releases/american-craft-beer-exports-surpass-125-million, retrieved May 5, 2019.

Carneiro, J. (2018) 'Going for growth in craft brewing? Survival? Here are five U.S. beer drinker stats you need to know,' *Craft Brewing Business*. www.craftbrewingbusiness.com/featured/going-for-growth-in-craft-brewing-survival-here-are-five-u-s-beer-drinker-stats-you-need-to-know, retrieved April 10, 2019.

Conick, H. (2016) 'Local beer, global markets,' *Marketing News*, 50(7), 38–45.

Conklin, M. (2019) 'The 10 beer trends that will dominate 2019,' *Inside Hook*. https://www.insidehook.com/article/food-and-drink/the-beer-trends-that-will-dominate-2019, retrieved March 26, 2019.

Dana, V. (2018) 'Cause marketing for craft brewers (You can do good, but don't let your promotion go bad).' http://beveragelawupdate.com/cause-marketing-for-craft-brewers-you-can-do-good-but-dont-let-your-promotion-go-bad, retrieved May 22, 2019.

Engage for Good (2019) 'Social impact statistics you should know.' https://engageforgood.com/guides/statistics-every-cause-marketer-should-know, retrieved April 10, 2019.

Furnari, C. and Klineman, J. (2016) 'Craft beer drinkers are interested in healthy habits and alcohol abstinence, Nielsen survey finds,' *Brewbound*. www.brewbound.com/news/craft-beer-drinkers-interested-healthy-habits-alcohol-abstinence-nielsen-survey-finds, retrieved May 22, 2019.

Goldfarb, A. (2018) 'An illustrated history of craft beer in America.' https://firstwefeast.com/features/illustrated-history-of-craft-beer-in-america, retrieved May 5, 2019.

Herz, J. (2016) 'Today's craft beer lovers: millennials, women and Hispanics,' *Brewers Association*, August 15. www.brewersassociation.org/communicating-craft/understanding-to-days-craft-beer-lovers-millennials-women-hispanics, retrieved April 10, 2019.

Kendall, J. (2018) 'Power hour: Nielsen shares latest craft beer consumer insights,' *Brewbound*. www.brewbound.com/news/power-hour-nielsen-shares-latest-craft-beer-consumer-insights, retrieved May 22, 2019.

Krommydas, N. (2018) 'Craft brewers predict the biggest beer trends for 2018,' *VinePair*. https://vinepair.com/articles/craft-beer-trends-2018, retrieved March 26, 2019.

Landi, H. (2014) 'The report from the road,' *Beverage World*, 133(3), 39.

McLeod, B. (2019) 'The ultimate B2B marketing strategy guide for 2019,' January 11. www.bluecorona.com/blog/b2b-marketing-strategy-guide, retrieved May 5, 2019.

Maier, T. (2013) 'Selected aspect of the microbreweries boom,' *Agris On-Line Papers in Economics & Informatics*, 5(4), 135–142.

Morris, C. (2018) 'Craft beer's days of explosive growth are over,' *Fortune*. http://fortune.com/2018/03/27/craft-beer-2017-sales, retrieved March 27, 2018.

Nurin, T. (2018) '9 beer and spirits predictions for 2019,' *Forbes*. www.forbes.com/sites/taranurin/2018/12/18/nine-beer-and-spirits-predictions-for-2019/#1eded83b577d, retrieved March 26, 2019.

Porter, E. (2018) 'A history of the Oozlefinch.' http://ed-thelen.org/oozlefinch.html, retrieved April 1, 2019.

Rafalson, B. (2017) '10 jaw-dropping event marketing stats that point to the future of the industry,' https://helloendless.com/event-marketing-stats, retrieved May 22, 2019.

Riell, H. (2014) 'Crafting a winning beer strategy,' *Convenience Store Decisions*, January, 25(1), 50–52.

Saporito, B. (2012) 'Higher spirits,' *Time*, 179(2), 56.

Taylor, S. and Dipietro, R. (2017) 'Segmenting craft beer drinkers: an analysis of motivations, willingness to pay, and repeat patronage intentions,' *International Journal of Hospitality & Tourism Administration*. [Online] https://doi.org/10.1080/15256480.2017.1397585.

Watson, B. (2018) 'Shifting demographics among craft drinkers.' www.brewersassociation.org/insights/shifting-demographics-among-craft-drinker, retrieved March 30, 2019.

Appendix A
THE MARTIN AGENCY: DEVELOPING A DIRECT MARKETING CAMPAIGN

If you think it takes a Madison Avenue address to become a global success in advertising, think again . . . and meet The Martin Agency! The Martin Agency is an award-winning, full-service advertising agency that is becoming well known for creating pop culture icons such as the GEICO gecko and GEICO's cavemen. The Martin Agency was named *Adweek*'s Agency of the Year in 2009. How did this successful company begin, and how does it create award-winning direct marketing campaigns? That's the topic of this appendix. We take a behind-the-scenes look at how The Martin Agency puts together award-winning campaigns for its clients. First, let's meet this famous advertising agency.

THE MARTIN AGENCY

The agency began in 1968 as a small shop doing mostly print work in a southern city far removed from the sophisticated East and West Coast cosmopolitan centers of New York and Los Angeles. It is located in the heart of Richmond, Virginia's Shockoe Slip, a historic area of restored warehouses. The red-brick headquarters is set on a quaint cobblestone square with a circular drive surrounding the water fountain that once was used by dray horses. Historic on the outside? You bet! But, once you step inside the building, it is bursting with energetic, creative minds, high tech, contemporary furnishings, and fine art. This proves that in a wired world, geography doesn't really matter. The external setting of The Martin Agency may be a bit subdued, but its staff of over 600 associates is certainly not.

The Martin Agency was founded by a couple of local ad executives, David Martin and George Woltz. They quickly snagged the bright talent of Harry Jacobs, who, in turn, recruited a young writer, Mike Hughes, to the company. Under this dynamic creative duo, the agency quickly became noticed. Its first national high-visibility campaign was the popular 'Virginia is for Lovers' in 1972. By 1981, the agency was ranked as one of *Advertising Age*'s top ten creative shops. In the 1990s, The Martin Agency moved beyond regional advertising, landing national accounts such as Mercedes-Benz, Wrangler jeans, and Saab. Today, The Martin Agency employs more than 350 people from 23 different countries. The brilliant, visionary, and hard-working individuals serve their clients in such fine, creative and successful fashion.

The agency's client list includes GEICO, Walmart, Discover Card, Pizza Hut, B.F. Goodrich, American Cancer Society, Hanes, Comcast, and many others.

Figure A-1   The Martin Agency. Used with permission of The Martin Agency.[1]

Now let's pretend that we are a new client of The Martin Agency and we have engaged them to plan and develop an award-winning direct marketing campaign for us. What will happen first? Whom will we meet? What's next? What series of stages will the campaign development take? How will we know whether it is a successful campaign? Let's explore the steps involved in planning and developing a direct marketing campaign via The Martin Agency.

CAMPAIGN DEVELOPMENT PROCESS

Initial Consultation

Welcome to The Martin Agency! Your initial meeting is about laying the foundations for a relationship that will produce great work that generates great results. Award-winning direct marketing campaigns aren't stumbled upon—it takes insightful and productive client and agency teams working together to hatch big ideas that motivate actions and elevate brands to a higher status.

Like any personal connection, the best relationships foster a high level of openness, trust, and respect.

Your initial meeting is with your agency ownership team, which is a seasoned group of agency leaders assigned specifically to your account. Ownership team members are from the areas of account management, strategic planning, media, and creative development and provide the vision and direction for the account. A partner in the agency oversees the ownership team, looking over the account and providing you with senior-level accountability and the ability to marshal agency resources on your behalf.

What is covered in the first meeting? The opportunity for the brand. Every brand has an opportunity to extend itself from its current equity and grow, and the first meeting is focused on uncovering that opportunity. A large amount of data and knowledge is presented and discussed to come to a shared understanding of your company's business/category dynamics, current equity, core competencies, and any consumer insights you have. With a solid handle on the business and opportunities for your brand, the next step of campaign planning begins.

Figure A-2　Ownership team meeting at the whiteboard. Used with permission of The Martin Agency.

Campaign Planning Meeting

Campaign development begins with establishing the best agency and client team for the task. The agency ownership team assigns an account director, who is the main contact with your company and oversees the process of campaign development from beginning to end. In a full-service agency, the account director manages all aspects of the relationship, from making sure objectives are established to ensuring the execution will achieve the best results.

At the campaign planning meeting, campaign goals are established, metrics for success are determined, potential target audiences are discussed, budget and timing are outlined, and the protocols for working together are defined. The discussion produces the necessary ingredients for a campaign strategy to be formed. It is exciting, with both agency and client teams embarking on a creative process that can have a monumental impact on your business.

Strategic Development

A direct marketing campaign needs to rise out of solid strategy. At this stage, you'll meet a strategic planner who, alongside key creative, media, account management, and analytics staff, establishes the approach to reaching the campaign objective. Elements of a direct strategy include targeting, offer, and creative methods that are derived from insights about consumers and the category of your company. A test-then-rollout approach may also be considered.

Strategy development is often a collaborative process, so you are encouraged to share past strategies and their effectiveness, competitive strategies and positioning, data from an in-house database (if you have it) to lend support or challenge the strategic approach, and an operational understanding of how a campaign might be deployed and who it might impact, for example a sales force.

Market research is often conducted at this stage. Research helps inform the best strategic approach for the audience you're targeting. Research will reveal the strength of your brand, attitudes and perceptions, key drivers of use for your product, how the audience consumes media, and whether your strategy will likely produce the results you're looking for. Budgets and timing of research vary, so you can expect to talk through options that best fit the campaign strategy.

Also at this stage, since it is likely that there will be digital aspects to the project, 'discovery' related to needs analysis, a definition of requirements, technical specifications, suitable vendors, site map/flow, and information architecture are explored. Budgets for all aspects of the campaign are submitted and the expected return on that investment is projected.

Figure A-3 Strategic development. Used with permission of The Martin Agency.

Figure A-4   The creative development process. Used with permission of The Martin Agency.

Creative Development

Now the fun really begins. Direct marketing creative development is as much of a science as it is an art form. The creative director will work with copywriters and art directors to bring out the strategy in a creative expression that prompts actions from the target audience. The creative director maintains a balance between using proven techniques and challenging old conventions.

The strategic planner and the creative director will produce a document called a creative brief. This succinct document sets up the creative opportunity within the strategic direction and is what the copywriters and art directors use as a touchstone when coming up with great ideas. Brainstormed, then filtered, ideas are refined for a creative presentation to your team.

Creative concepts are presented, complete with the rationale for why they will succeed. Creative directions are discussed and are often put into quantitative or qualitative testing to verify that the work will resonate with the target audience. In many instances, the creative is put into a live-market situation to determine concept effectiveness with the offer and specific audiences the work is intended to reach and create an action from. A creative idea is selected by both the agency and the client team and the process shifts from idea generation to execution.

Campaign Execution

Creative ideas need to be delivered in targeted ways. This is where it all comes together. At this point, the media strategy turns into ideas for media execution that serve as the basis for a completed media plan. A media buyer will join the team along with a production manager to set the wheels in motion for the campaign to be executed.

Figure A-5   The creative development process. Used with permission of The Martin Agency.

This stage is all about the details. Schedules, checklists, specifications, and production all come together to produce a finished campaign. An account manager referees this process between your team and the agency team, making sure everything is taken care of. Multimedia producers, particularly those who know how to bring digital work to life, are key to the process. This is when digital concepts move into the coding phase, the motion designers are called in, it is determined how and which elements should be tracked, engineering is done on sites, beta testing and quality assurance are run, bugs are fixed, and all legal reviews are finalized before creative is deployed to live servers. Any pretesting before roll-out will occur, with results poured back into the communication to refine it for optimization.

Meetings happen all along the way, typically with daily or weekly status get-togethers. Finally, everything has been reviewed, approved, and can be sent to media for distribution. A communications lawyer makes sure there are no trademark or messaging issues, and the public relations department is put into action to generate buzz and excitement about the new work if it is an open-to-the-public campaign.

Tracking and Learning

Campaigns have the benefit of generating tangible results—which are fed back into future strategies, testing, and execution, but are also used to optimize the campaign as it runs. Leading this area will be The Martin Agency's director of analytics, who will not only report on the results of the campaign, but also analyze it for optimization. The maintenance, monitoring, measuring, and

Figure A-6 Polishing the idea. Used with permission of The Martin Agency.

reporting that happen once a campaign launches are as important as the planning and strategic development that happen at the beginning. It allows The Martin Agency to adjust the creative, the media, and the offer 'on the fly' to get the best possible results for your marketing expenditure.

Throughout the campaign and at its conclusion, you'll see a results 'dashboard' with response rates, conversions, and a return on the investment calculation. Results will be analyzed by segment, demographics, and past behavior. When the results are very strong, the campaign may be eligible to win an industry award, such as a Data & Marketing Association ECHO, the Oscar of the direct marketing industry.

CONCLUSION

The process of planning and developing a direct marketing campaign can take as little as four weeks or last as long as eight months, depending on the client objectives and creative challenge. The key to developing a truly successful campaign is that it must meet your company's stated objectives. Is there fun in this process? Sure! But developing creative campaigns also takes a great deal of vision, research, and hard work. As you've seen from the process, it takes many talented people to create a successful direct marketing campaign. If you are thinking of a career with an advertising agency, such as The Martin Agency, please review Appendix B: 'Careers in Direct and Interactive Marketing.' There you will find descriptions of the many different career positions available in direct marketing.

Figure A-7 A patio meeting at The Martin Agency. Used with permission of The Martin Agency.

Note: The information contained in this appendix has been generously provided by The Martin Agency, Richmond, Virginia. The author is grateful for the valuable ongoing contributions of the Martin Agency to higher education. We especially recognize Barbara Joynes, former Partner, Integrated Services, and J. P. LaFors, former Vice-President/ Account Director, for their work on this appendix. All images contained in the appendix have been provided by The Martin Agency and are used with permission.

The Martin Agency is an American advertising agency based in Richmond, Virginia that is part of the Interpublic Group of Companies. It currently has two locations – Richmond and London. Visit https://martinagency.com to check out its awesome creative work!

NOTE

1. All copyright material for figures was supplied to the case authors.

Appendix B
CAREERS IN DIRECT AND INTERACTIVE MARKETING

Select Career Positions in Direct Marketing

Careers in Direct Marketing in Agencies

Careers in a Digital Agency: Marketing Track

Careers in a Digital Agency: Project Track

Careers in a Digital Agency: Account Track

Direct Marketing Career Resources

SELECT CAREER POSITIONS IN DIRECT MARKETING

Account Executive, Advertising Agency

Group Account Director, Advertising Agency

Account Supervisor, Advertising Agency

Market Research Director

Marketing Manager, Business Products/Services

Marketing Manager, Consumer Products/Services

Media Planner/Analyst

Art Director, Catalog Copywriter, Catalog

Catalog Marketing Manager, Consumer

Catalog Marketing Manager, Business-to-Business

Creative Director, Catalog

Catalog Circulation Manager

Catalog Marketing Director, Business-to-Business

Catalog Marketing Director, Consumer

Telemarketing Director, Outbound (B2B)

Telemarketing Director, Outbound (Consumer)

Telemarketing Director, Inbound

Telemarketing Manager, Inbound

Telemarketing Manager, Outbound (B2B)

Telemarketing Manager, Outbound (Consumer)

Circulation Director, Consumer Magazine

Circulation Manager, Consumer Promotion

Circulation Manager, Trade Magazine

Circulation Manager, Newsletter

Marketing Manager, Internet

Website Manager

Search Engine Optimization Manager

In-House SEO Specialist

Blogger

Social Media Specialist

Social Media Marketing Coordinator

Database Analyst

Database Director

Database Manager

List Manager, Corporate

Account Executive, Advertising Agency

The ambassador of an advertising agency in its relationship with clients, the account executive serves a triple role as the liaison officer, consummate marketing advisor, and eyes and ears of the agency's management team.

Duties

Assigned to specific clients, the account executive is responsible for advising the client and for the development and execution of programs designed by the agency, including direct mail, space ads, television, e-marketing, and, in some agencies, catalogs. He or she works with creative directors, art directors and copywriters, media experts, market researchers, and production and traffic professionals to ensure maintenance of the media schedule within budgetary guidelines. He or she is responsible for reflecting client thoughts and for final acceptance of the agency's program.

Group Account Director, Advertising Agency

The last word on the client accounts under his or her direction, the group account director has the final approval of all agency client projects. This person is the primary contact for senior-level marketing professionals on the client side, and must meet client expectations while ensuring the integrity of the agency's beliefs.

Duties

This individual oversees the development of the internal and client business strategy, builds external relationships while maintaining internal ones, develops expertise in a client's product/service and industry, oversees account reviews and analysis, participates in new business development and pitches, provides input for annual and quarterly revenue forecasts, and negotiates contractual agreements between client and agency.

Account Supervisor, Advertising Agency

Account supervisors rely on long days and their depth of knowledge for solving marketing problems for the agency's clients, maintaining a friendly and profitable relationship with them, while also supervising account executives.

Duties

They are responsible for the development of staff, day-to-day supervision and monitoring of agency account executives, and the strategic development and implementation of client programs within budgetary guidelines. They guide marketing, creative, media, and production activities, and participate in securing client approval of cost estimates. As a senior manager, they participate in the acquisition of new clients as a member of the new business team. With a keen understanding of the realities of agency competition, they ensure maximum cost-effectiveness for clients and relentlessly pursue the achievement of client goals.

Market Research Director

Always in demand, even in the ancient epoch of the slide rule, the market research professional has risen in eminence with the development of the computer and analytical tools, and now plays a leading role in all phases of direct marketing.

Duties

This person is responsible for evaluation, analysis, and implementation of research and statistical techniques to develop marketing insights and improve marketing plans, increase response rates, minimize credit risks, and decrease buyer attrition. He or she develops and initiates market segmentation programs using demographic, psychographic, and usage data; conducts front- and back-end analysis and product performance measures; tracks competitor mailing and product programs; prepares reports for departmental needs; presents forecasts to management; and may supervise the staff of managers and analysts.

Marketing Manager, Business Products/Services

All businesses are consumers, but the reverse is not always true. Because there are fewer businesses, business marketers face great challenges in the marketplace, including, for one, continually finding new buyers for their products.

Duties

The business marketing manager is responsible for the maximum penetration of a universe limited by the scope of the product. They must develop promotional direct marketing materials for the generation of profits; supervise all testing and the creation of creative output ranging from, but not exclusive to, direct mail, card decks, bouncebacks, statement stuffers, billing inserts, as well as any e-marketing and response space advertising, generally in trade and business publications; analyze promotions and digest reports from research staff; supervise assistants, decide on internal lists and external list recommendations; and maintain mailing schedules.

Marketing Manager, Consumer Products/Services

Hitting a target that's always shifting, demographically and geographically, is the specialty and challenge of the consumer direct marketer. Lifestyle changes, aging populations, and dual-income families impact all promotions.

Duties

Responsible for the development of the budget, the consumer marketing manager determines marketing position and pricing, directs the creative department in the production of myriad direct marketing promotional vehicles, including, but not limited to, direct mail, space advertisements, e-marketing efforts, freestanding inserts, bouncebacks, billing, package inserts, and even matchbook covers; participates in the selection of products or services sold, credit and collection policies, and list approval; and reviews the results of front- and back-end analysis, sometimes presented by the research department, and uses this information to improve the profit picture.

Media Planner/Analyst

Long after the lights have dimmed in other offices, this professional evaluates the past and ponders the future to ensure that the next direct marketing or telemarketing program achieves its goals, within an established budget.

Duties

For the needs of the client, he or she recommends the size and scope of myriad media options, including, but not restricted to, direct mail, space, TV, broadcast, co-op vehicles, package inserts, and, more recently, cable and Internet promotions; maintains current status reports for the promotion budget, plans media schedules, and proposes new test vehicles and formats; meets with list brokers, space salespeople, and other media vendors; and analyzes front- and back-end results on a timely basis, determines seasonal trends, and maintains an alertness for statistical inferences and variances in response rates.

Art Director, Catalog

Generally under intense time pressure, the art director gives the catalog its direction and aura, also acting as the conciliator between the merchandising and marketing experts, a function that's never written on job specs.

Duties

Responsible, under the leadership of the creative director, for the look and feel of a catalog, the art director constantly struggles with 'square inch' formulas for space allocation made by marketing and merchandising executives. They design with copy and, in the great majority of catalogs, photographic and/or graphic images, to make presentation of a three-dimensional product within the limited confines of a printed page. They are also responsible for revisions and additions to an existing format or other promotional offering and, in some cases, the company website; and they are experienced with paper, type, photography, illustrations, and printing.

Copywriter, Catalog

When consumers read what the catalog copywriter has written, they should feel as if they have found a solution or captured a dream, as well as touched a product or smelled a fragrance. Copywriters know the power of words to create sales.

Duties

Working within the most stringent confines of inches, catalog copywriters bring to life a valve, or a suit, or a book, without deviation from the specifications, quality, essence, or contents of the product, often enhancing it with the benefits; frequently working from a specifications sheet, they write for a printed page, often, but not always, accompanied by a photograph or illustration; they create on paper (or in cyberspace) an image for the consumer at home or a buyer in the office; and they detail the particulars of the product or service offered in the catalog or website, answer questions before they are asked, and, with skill, reduce returns.

Catalog Marketing Manager, Consumer

Working in a universe shifting in taste and lifestyle, the consumer catalog manager is challenged daily to explore new marketing techniques and products. It's a fortuitous day when challenges don't come hourly.

Duties

With profit and loss responsibilities, the consumer catalog marketing manager develops short- and long-range marketing plans and goals, projecting sales, growth, and profit objectives; determines pricing, directs creative output, supervises media (including website and e-marketing efforts), makes list decisions, oversees the telesales department, determines market research requirements, and maintains mailing schedules with the production department; is vigilant for new products at trade shows and maintains contact with customer service for ideas in improving or adding to the product line; and monitors market share and competitive and noncompetitive 'books.'

Catalog Marketing Manager, Business-to-Business

Equivalent to a product manager in a consumer package goods environment, the business-to-business marketing manager for a catalog is responsible for day-to-day marketing, creative, and the operations of one catalog, or often, two or three.

Duties

The business catalog marketing manager carries profit and loss responsibilities for a high-volume catalog or a number of smaller ones, generally under the guidance of the catalog marketing director; develops and executes budget; decides the positioning, theme, pricing, marketing approach, creative thrust, and media selection; supervises production by internal or external facilities to ensure mailing schedules; reviews fulfillment procedures to maintain expeditious delivery of customer orders; confers with the research department and is conversant and knowledgeable in recency/frequency/monetary analysis and its descendants.

Creative Director, Catalog

When dozens of products, in many instances hundreds, must be presented appealingly on a printed page to entice orders, you have an insight into the Herculean task facing the creative director of a catalog.

Duties

Within the limits of a page and budgetary considerations, the catalog creative director directs copywriters, art directors, the traffic department, and often production, in the theme, design, and execution of layouts for catalogs; uses photography and/or illustrations to reflect and achieve marketing objectives; frequently acts in the same function for multiple catalogs targeted at diverse market segments; and is responsible for order forms, direct mail packages, space advertisements, television, websites, cable, packaging, corporate house organs, and ancillary creative materials, particularly if retail operations are involved.

Catalog Circulation Manager

No business has a better understanding of the importance of acquiring new subscribers, and retaining the old, and their lifetime value, than does direct marketing. In this universe, the circulation manager rules.

Duties

With creative insight, the circulation manager develops and tests many media, including direct mail packages, e-marketing efforts, list rentals and exchanges, space ads, statement stuffers, bouncebacks, package and freestanding inserts, and alternative media programs to acquire new customers; has responsibility for the cost and profitability of acquisition efforts; develops greater analysis and utilization of the internal database; establishes inquiry programs to develop circulation; maintains contact and negotiates with list brokerage firms and list managers; and is knowledgeable in merge-purge, enhancement techniques, and segmentation.

Catalog Marketing Director, Business-to-Business

This individual has profit and loss responsibility for catalog sales to businesses, governments, and institutions, generally in a market niche or segment, with a range of proprietary and distributory items; and continually seeks out new markets.

Duties

He or she formulates budget and develops long- and short-term strategic marketing plans and policy; supervises marketing managers and manages teams of creative, merchandising, list, production, research, customer service, and telemarketing professionals; evaluates market share and monitors the competition; continually explores the customer database to develop new products; examines the development of new markets by entry into markets defined by Standard Industrial Codes; explores alternative media for customer acquisition; and monitors sales of ancillary products to broaden the catalog or launch new ones.

Catalog Marketing Director, Consumer

This is the direct marketing executive charged with the profit and loss responsibilities for the company's sale of products and/or services by catalog to consumers at home. He or she enjoys dividing existing catalogs and conquering a new audience.

Duties

The catalog marketing director prepares and executes corporate marketing plans, budgets, and short- and long-term strategies and pricing policy; evaluates, tests, and retests new and old media; assesses, develops, and tests new products to expand market share or introduce new catalogs or programs; supervises department heads responsible for creative, merchandising, marketing, market research, lists and telemarketing, and reviews operations and fulfillment activities; represents the corporation at industry functions; and keeps abreast of legislative and postal regulations as they affect catalogs or telemarketing and e-marketing efforts.

Telemarketing Director, Outbound (B2B)

From an ugly duckling into a beautiful swan, telemarketing has taken on added importance and status as a marketing tool that profitably sells products and services to other businesses. It is a growing discipline with new players.

Duties

The B2B outbound telemarketing director has complete marketing, strategic, and operational responsibility, including profit and loss, for the integration of telemarketing into the corporate marketing mix; coordinates telemarketing with other methods of sales and distribution; monitors the effectiveness of programs; establishes personnel policies, training methodology, and motivation techniques; directs sales activities toward meeting set goals; supervises script and call guide strategies and performance ratios; evaluates and recommends the installation of new equipment; and is responsible for facility planning, systems design, and cost control.

Telemarketing Director, Outbound (Consumer)

Calling consumers at home, at what may be an inconvenient time, is always delicate, but having them enjoy buying your product or service is the unique talent of the telemarketing director whose programs combine poise with sales.

Duties

This director has profit and loss responsibility for an outbound call center; coordinates facility planning, equipment selecting, systems design, and cost control; integrates telemarketing into the total marketing mix and coordinates its function with other avenues of sales and distribution;

establishes personnel policies, incentive or motivational plans, directs training activities, and establishes and maintains performance standards and records; has awareness of stress factors and methods to alleviate them; manages the overall effectiveness of the department and produces progress and productivity reports for upper-level management.

Telemarketing Director, Inbound

The Inbound Department is often the only personal contact a company has with its customer. Everyone relies on this leader to keep customers loyal and happy to buy again, while monitoring productivity and morale.

Duties

This professional has complete strategic and operations responsibility for the inbound division, including the integration of the inbound function with order processing and fulfillment; oversees the development of up-selling and cross-selling techniques and programs; establishes acceptable levels of call handling, including rates for abandonment, busy signals, and time in queue; is responsible for scheduling, setting staff levels, and putting systems in place to measure and control the allowable cost per order; and coordinates the selection of telephone equipment, switches, line configurations, facility planning, and cost control.

Telemarketing Manager, Inbound

In the trenches with the troops, always alert to potential problems, this individual acts as the eyes and ears of the order department to ensure proper staffing, without overstaffing, and maintains a professional atmosphere in a stressful environment.

Duties

The inbound telemarketing manager has supervisory responsibility for a staff of telemarketing sales representatives (TSRs), often headed by supervisor(s), responsible for orders and inquiries; implements and monitors the telemarketing order entry system and develops policies pertaining to the fulfillment of orders; oversees clerical and administrative support staff; is responsible for the instruction of TSRs on product features and pricing; schedules staff for optimum handling of incoming calls; conducts performance reviews; and presents daily, weekly, and monthly reports on activity to management.

Telemarketing Manager, Outbound (B2B)

A three-star general in the sales department, the telemarketing manager works with the troops, ensuring their health, wealth, happiness, and contribution to the profits of the company. No day passes without a new challenge.

Duties

This manager is responsible for planning, implementing, and managing the telemarketing department and its programs. Duties include recruitment, training, and motivating staff in sales, sales techniques, and product awareness. He or she structures incentive and motivation programs to reduce turnover; develops operational procedures; monitors productivity standards and individual quotas; directs list selection and analysis activities; develops direct mail campaigns to support the telemarketing effort and ensures cooperation and synergy between the department and the field sales force.

Telemarketing Manager, Outbound (Consumer)

Under the watchful eye of the telemarketing director, upper management, and the rest of the world, telemarketing managers who sell to the consumer at home watch their team with vigilance while reducing turnover and improving the bottom line.

Duties

Frequently conducted during the afternoon and evening hours, this individual's responsibilities focus on staffing, training, and monitoring the production of a sales force comprised frequently of part-timers. He or she develops recruitment programs beyond 'help-wanted' ads and adds to staff with candidates at shopping malls, college campuses, 'open houses,' and other, nontraditional sources; directs training and motivational sessions to improve productivity; supervises scripts, develops and monitors budget, and recommends lists and direct marketing programs; and monitors calls to ensure quality standards.

Circulation Director, Consumer Magazine

The marketing function in any organization represents one of life's supreme challenges, but when a company's every move is highlighted in the trade, and sometimes in the public press, the job takes on new dimensions. Enter the circulation director.

Duties

Part of a three-legged executive stool with the editor and advertising manager, the circulation director builds the base on which the publication thrives or flounders. A marketing professional with profit and loss responsibilities, he or she determines circulation budget and long- and short-term strategy; usually serves as an advisor and consultant to the editor and publisher; and is responsible for the identification of the target audience, circulation acquisition, marketing policy and pricing adjustments, creative strategy and implementation, renewals, newsstand sales, fulfillment, and audits.

Circulation Manager, Consumer Promotion

The amazing fecundity of the human mind is evident in the activities of the circulation manager, diligently seeking to make substantive inroads into building circulation through the use of every promotional vehicle.

Duties

Involved in acquisition and retention programs, this professional works with the circulation director and/or manager. He or she plans and executes promotions, using all media, including direct mail, insert cards, gift subscriptions, take-ones, blow-in and bind-in cards, newsstand, television and space advertising, as well as e-marketing efforts; tests and analyzes promotions; deals with vendors to develop premiums; is frequently involved in list promotions to develop additional rental activity, including e-mail lists; and works with creative department and list specialists, the computer service bureau, lettershops, and production departments to ensure scheduled mailings.

Circulation Manager, Trade Magazine

Squeezing blood from a stone is an easy task compared to the challenges handed to the circulation manager of trade magazines, competing for the advertising dollar. Of course, they are confined by audit regulations to a limited audience.

Duties

This manager is responsible for yearly budget preparation and the planning and execution of circulation acquisition programs, including creative, list selection, print orders, and production and lettershop activities to ensure scheduled mailings; front- and back-end analysis of promotions; knowledge of audit regulations, generally BPA; qualification and reverification of paid and/or nonpaid subscribers, preparation of audit materials for the publisher's statement, and monitoring of telemarketing; supervision of customer service and the development of research information for the editorial and advertising departments.

Circulation Manager, Newsletter

Each day, the newsletter circulation manager goes home saying, 'Well, at least we don't have to worry about advertisers.' But that's small solace when you worry about renewals and new subscribers.

Duties

This manager has full profit and loss responsibilities for single or multiple newsletters, generally highly specialized; directs artists and copywriters, staff, and/or freelancers in the development of new packages for reader acquisition and renewal and billing series; supervises production and, in some cases, website and Internet marketing efforts as well as lettershop activities to ensure mailing schedules and fulfillment procedures; is heavily involved in the search for affinity lists, compiled or response, for the expansion of markets; is proficient in the analysis of promotion results, the pricing of publication(s), and postal regulations; and supervises telemarketing activities.

Marketing Manager, Internet

The Internet channel is drawing many new recruits to the field of direct marketing. The traditional direct marketing manager's sibling, the Internet marketing manager, has emerged as a very desirable position, managing a source that is growing by leaps and bounds. The opportunities afforded by the Internet channel in terms of cost efficiency, flexibility, and reactivity are just beginning to be fully recognized.

Duties

This individual accesses and uses all relevant research and sales support tools to stay current in the online marketplace; drives sales and customer retention through the website experience; recommends product, content, and marketing programs to support company marketing plans; monitors and reports on online sales and traffic results for the website; builds infrastructures and processes for enabling and executing Web contacts; and works closely with the marketing and IT teams to drive and execute various projects.

Website Manager

The website is the storefront, or at least the corporate brochure, for the organization, and it takes a savvy professional to present it well. An effective website manager keeps customers coming back again and again.

Duties

The website manager is responsible for developing and executing marketing communications focusing on building the company's website customer base; is responsible for growth of page impressions, unique users, Web subscribers, and registered users against target; studies the analysis of site traffic and user surveys to gain understanding of customer purchase patterns; is responsible for the overall 'look and feel' of the site and ensuring consistency with the company's brand image; works closely with advertising technology vendors and partners to ensure advertising is delivered effectively and efficiently; keeps abreast of Web-related developments and evaluates new revenue opportunities.

Search Engine Optimization Manager

Top ten positioning in search engines is the most effective form of online marketing. Mystery shrouds how to accomplish this. Enter the search engine optimization manager.

Duties

With the vast majority of all new visitors to a website originating from major search engines, it is essential that every business implement a search engine optimization marketing campaign that allows customers to find them ahead of the competition. The search engine optimization manager develops and maintains keyword phrases that have a high amount of search traffic, conducts site analysis to ensure the site is user-friendly and optimized, reviews text writing to maximize search engine ranking, and creates a program in which links are utilized. It takes skill and time to ensure that the website is ranked above competitors, while still achieving maximum return on investment.

In-House SEO Specialist

In-house SEO specialists work for a single company in a more niche setting. These professionals have a greater spotlight and ownership of company projects than those working in an agency. As the in-house SEO specialist, you are the only one with SEO knowledge and are tasked to educate the members of your group. Effective communication skills will be essential here. SEO specialists are responsible for improving the company's organic search results.

Duties

The duties of SEO specialists may include writing content for the company website or blog, placing keywords in copy to generate increased search engine traffic, analyzing SEO campaigns and compiling SEO performance reports, and conducting and/or adjusting pay-per-click campaigns.

Blogger

The blogger is part of the rise of social media marketing. Blogging encompasses educating the audience on company stories and new product releases. It can be beneficial in explaining a complicated product. As a mechanism of conversation and brand voice, blogs lead consumers down a path to open exchange and relationship building with brands. The social media platform helps facilitate these conversations in a real-time manner.

Duties

Keeping in mind the goal of customer engagement, a blogger must be adept at identifying information their target market wants to hear, writing compelling headlines that propel customers to a desired action, and using search engine optimization (SEO) best practices to increase viewership and conversion.

Social Media Specialist

Social media use has exploded in recent years, landing itself at the epicenter of many online marketing plans. Social media specialists attract and interact with targeted customers in a real-time manner, and in a way that was not done prior to the rise of social media. The efforts of the social media specialist drive quality traffic to a company's website, establish a customer–brand relationship, and uphold reputation.

Duties

The primary responsibilities of this position include developing brand awareness, spreading brand messaging, promoting leads and sales, and positioning your company and brand strategically to follow search engine optimization best practices. This position requires you to be highly creative, motivated, and knowledgeable on the ways in which consumers interact with brands on social media. The position also requires you to develop a posting schedule that details posting frequency and optimal posting times during the day.

Social Media Marketing Coordinator

A social media marketing coordinator possesses strong social media knowledge and works on media platforms. They work closely with their clients and craft targeted social media messages that advance the interests of their clients.

Duties

A social media marketing coordinator is responsible largely for content development, reporting, and optimization. Their clear priority is developing effective ways to engage customers.

Database Analyst

At the right hand of the database manager, the database analyst knows the inner workings of the database like no other. The ability to manipulate raw data so that diverse audiences can use it is a special skill.

Duties

The database analyst is responsible for interpreting information and reporting results; for compiling and analyzing metrics on customer file; for operational system queries, data cleansing/hygiene, integration, and data quality assurance. He or she recommends lists for internal decisions, pricing, positioning, and marketing; evaluates and reports on data sources and analysis of data, requests sample data, executes the list hygiene plan; ensures merge-purge literacy; reports on and recommends test strategies; has knowledge of SAS or related programs; and is responsible for database integrity issues.

Database Director

Without the talents of this person, the database would be just a mountain of unrelated facts. It takes a professional with a special talent to make the information tell its story.

Duties

The database director oversees the development and implementation of database marketing operation solutions that support marketing and customer relationship management campaigns; establishes the corporate data strategy and strategic focus, including written policies and procedures for database marketing; oversees segmentation and targeting, including list strategy and media plan recommendations, matrix design and cell population, list purchases and merge-purge management, and developing technical specifications; and evaluates data vendors or internal staff capability for database enhancement, modeling, profiling, integrated database creation/management, and data warehousing.

Database Manager

With few ancestors, but beginning a dynasty, the professional database manager has become the toast of all marketers and is wooed for the profits they bring.

Duties

This individual designs and enhances databases, in alliance with the marketing department and research professional, incorporating significant information, including, but not limited to, customer psychographic and demographic attributes, purchasing patterns, and preferences. He or she develops models, including response, predictive, conversion, and Zip, providing insight for marketing decisions to increase sales, market share, and profitability; is an expert on segmentation and list-enhancement techniques; and has the ability to use information to gain meaningful insight into customer purchase motivation.

List Manager, Corporate

Most professionals state that a direct mail promotion is composed of three elements: creative, product, and list. For the list professional, the list comes first, second, and third, and then come creative and product, or product then creative.

Duties

This professional recommends lists for internal marketing decisions; is responsible for pricing, positioning, and marketing the rental of the house file to other firms; liaises with clients and the brokerage community to increase rentals of house lists; directs the execution of list promotions by direct mail, space, and personal visitations; and schedules, selects, and staffs trade shows. In some companies, he or she is also responsible for the list-acquisition function, both response and compiled; analyzes list performance; establishes merge-purge standards; and works with the computer department, service bureau, and lettershops.

Salary Information

Crandall Associates, an executive recruiting firm, provided many of the career position descriptions included in the first section of this appendix. In addition, it can provide salary information for career positions.

Copies of the full salary guide with 52 functions and regional salary variations are available for $75 from Crandall Associates, 6 Litchfield Road, Suite 316, Port Washington, NY 11050; Tel: (516) 767-6800. The guide may be ordered online at www.crandallassociates.com.

Note: Much of the information contained in this section of the appendix has been generously provided by Crandall Associates, Washington, New York. The author is grateful to Wendy Weber, president, Crandall Associates, for her contributions to this appendix section.

CAREERS IN DIRECT MARKETING IN AGENCIES

Whether you are interested in marketing, management, or finance, there is something for you in the direct marketing agency industry. Agencies are businesses, just like any other. Although there are a lot of specialized functions unique to helping agencies create the work that they do, there are also many of the same career opportunities that you might find in any other industry:

- Human resources: staffing, payroll, and benefits
- Accounting: billing, receivables, financial administration
- Facilities management: everything from running the mail room to planning office parties
- Information services: technology infrastructure.

But what makes these jobs a little different in an agency environment is that they require an extra degree of *creativity*. When you are dealing with a very creative staff, the environment needs to be that much more creative (Facilities Management). Hiring and benefits need to have that extra special touch (Human Resources). Connectivity to each other, clients, and what's going on in the world is key (Information Services). Sometimes you even need to figure out how to creatively finance the running of the business (Accounting).

Of course, there are many jobs that are unique to the way agencies work. Each agency may have a different title, but essentially jobs fall into the following categories.

Account Management

Account managers are the liaison between the client and the agency and are responsible for the agency's relationship with the client. Account managers are expected to know their client's business inside-out.

Entry-level positions, such as account coordinators or assistant account executives, are responsible for preparing competitive analyses, monitoring budgets, analyzing data, and developing monthly billing reports. Successful account managers will be strong in three areas as they grow through their careers: organizational skills, strategic thinking, and relationship skills, both with clients and within the agency.

Account managers rely heavily on another function that helps move work through the agency. Project management, or traffic, is a great place to start in an agency if you're not sure what you want to do, but you want to (1) learn how an agency works and (2) become familiar with all of the different departments. You will surely accomplish both of those as an assistant project manager, because this role is responsible for scheduling the jobs an agency has to do, moving the work around the agency, and making sure everything stays on time. This role is vital to every agency, and the people who do it are super-organized and great motivators and negotiators.

Strategic Planning

Strategic planners ensure that all strategic and creative initiatives undertaken by the agency on behalf of a client are strategically sound by incorporating a variety of tools, some qualitative and some quantitative. Planners review secondary research, design and implement primary research, and synthesize their findings. This helps them write sound creative 'briefs,' which guide the creative department in its idea generation.

Assistant account planners or junior planners are responsible for reviewing and synthesizing secondary research sources, drafting research proposals, learning to analyze quantitative data, and writing and editing reports. Planners must have excellent analytical, writing, and verbal skills, as well as the ability to present in a manner that influences and leads others around a great idea.

Increasingly, user experience planners, who use primary research to determine how consumers engage with online media to create the optimal consumer experience, are part of the planning department, as opposed to being in a separate interactive department. This makes a campaign much more holistic when planners are working together to think about all aspects of the work and what a consumer's experience will truly feel like.

Creative

Copywriter and art director are the two creative positions most people are familiar with. To get these positions in an agency, most entry-level hires probably went to a graduate or portfolio school to develop their 'book' (a portfolio of work to demonstrate their creative capability). The copywriter and the art director are those who work on the agency's campaigns, the work that requires 'concepts.'

But there are other opportunities within a creative department where people with excellent technical skills can find entry-level opportunities (especially given the boom in the digital space):

- **studio artist**: this position works with all graphics needs of the agency, especially those in 2D; it requires proficiency in Quark, PhotoShop, and Illustrator and/or Freehand
- **digital designer**: understands how a website comes together; is responsible for art concepts in the production of websites; and has a basic understanding of HTML programming as it relates to design

- **Flash developer**: is responsible for HTML and graphic production as it relates to programming e-mails, landing pages, and microsites; should be conversant in action scripting, the latest version of Flash, click tagging for online banner ads, and file optimization
- **HTML programmer/developer**: converts project specifications and statements into detailed logical charts for coding into computer language
- **interaction designer**: helps ensure that the ideas of the art director are translated into workable ideas online; requires sound fundamentals in information architecture, but must also have a fresh enough design sense to keep all user interfaces and user experiences innovative, while maximizing usability.

Media

As you've learned, the single most important thing in direct marketing is targeting, so the media department is a very important department. Very keen, strategic minds reside here. If you are interested in solving puzzles (Where to find the prospect?), like to play with numbers (How much can I get for the fewest dollars?), and love to analyze and optimize (Did it work? What worked best? How could it work better?), then media might be the right part of the agency for you.

Assistant media planners spend much of their day meeting with representatives of various media and list companies, doing research about those companies' offerings—learning about the demographics of the readers/watchers/listeners/mailing lists of those reps. These assistants are often given the responsibility to pull together the initial recommendation for how a client's budget should be allocated.

Assistant media buyers do the opposite of planning the purchases—they actually do the negotiating and buying! Assistants will be given smaller projects or markets, but they will place the buy, monitor its progress, track spending and results, optimize the buy, prepare reports, and resolve billing issues. (Note: In smaller agencies, the roles of planner and buyer are often combined.)

Analytics

The data analytics group is often closely tied to the media group in a direct agency, because so much of what is done is tied to results. While the senior management in an analytics group often consists of people with doctorate degrees, there are opportunities for entry-level candidates.

An entry-level analyst will compile and analyze data from secondary sources as well as help design and execute primary research. Enhanced computer skills will include knowledge of database software and statistical software.

Production

Last but not least are the terrific people who produce all of the work that has been created. Some of the work can be created digitally by the folks in the creative department. Other assets must be created either with in-house production resources or through outside resources.

The production department maintains a file of directors, photographers, film companies, printers, lettershops, premium companies, box makers—anything and anybody that can help them produce whatever the creative department can dream up.

Assistant producers for video, art, events, branded content, and online create job dockets, prepare bid sheets, manage estimates as they come in, monitor the status of jobs daily, create weekly status reports, coordinate with the talent department on talent releases, and manage billing (to cite a few responsibilities).

Talent payment coordinators maintain all broadcast agreements, prepare talent payment vouchers/authorizations, estimate reuse fees, and prepare talent contracts.

Note: The information contained in this section of the appendix has been generously provided by The Martin Agency, Richmond, Virginia. The author is grateful to Barbara Joynes, former Partner, Integrated Services, at The Martin Agency, for her work on this appendix section.

CAREERS IN A DIGITAL AGENCY: MARKETING TRACK

Digital Marketing Associate

You would assist with the daily production, scheduling, delivery, and reporting of targeted e-mail campaigns on behalf of clients. Responsibilities may include:

- learning and implementing best practice principles for e-mail creative and deployment
- building e-mails using HTML and CSS coding, then testing them to ensure correct rendering
- outlining content for e-mails and occasionally writing e-mail copy
- making creative and content edits using Adobe Creative Suite
- using CMS platforms to create content for landing pages
- reporting on and analyzing e-mail metrics.

Digital Marketing Specialist

You would execute the daily production, scheduling, delivery, and reporting of targeted e-mail campaigns on behalf of clients. You would:

- research and implement best practice principles for e-mail creative and deployment
- communicate directly with clients through a variety of channels
- outline content for e-mails and occasionally write e-mail copy
- coordinate with internal e-mail designers
- build e-mails using HTML and CSS coding, then test them to ensure correct rendering
- plan and perform A/B testing to optimize e-mail performance
- use CMS platforms to create and optimize landing pages
- report on and analyze e-mail metrics, offering actionable recommendations
- plan and execute targeted marketing automation programs.

Digital Marketing Manager

You would manage accounts and execute the daily production, scheduling, delivery, and reporting of targeted e-mail campaigns on behalf of clients. You would:

- research and implement best practice principles for e-mail creative and deployment
- communicate directly with clients through a variety of channels
- manage client relationships
- juggle deadlines and deliverables for multiple clients at once
- outline content for e-mails and occasionally write e-mail copy
- coordinate with internal e-mail designers
- build e-mails using HTML and CSS coding, then test them to ensure correct rendering
- plan and perform A/B testing to optimize e-mail performance
- use CMS platforms to create and optimize landing pages
- report on and analyze e-mail metrics, offering actionable recommendations
- plan and execute targeted marketing automation programs.

Senior Digital Marketing Manager

You would lead the overall strategy, planning, and reporting of targeted e-mail campaigns on behalf of clients. You would:

- mentor digital marketing specialists and digital marketing associates
- ensure best practice principles and act as quality control on your team
- manage client relationships and strategy
- juggle deadlines and deliverables for multiple clients at once
- develop marketing automation strategy for personalized and targeted e-mail campaigns
- create workflow for behavior-based marketing automation campaigns
- create and perform A/B testing to optimize e-mail sends
- use CMS platforms to create and optimize landing pages
- compile and provide recommendations for advanced e-mail and website reporting metrics.

Digital Marketing Strategist

You would manage a team tasked with the overall strategy and daily production, scheduling, delivery, and reporting of targeted e-mail campaigns on behalf of clients. You would:

- manage a team of digital marketing managers, digital marketing specialists and digital marketing associates
- track and manage account hours and profitability
- act as the strategic lead for key accounts
- lead strategy for all team deliverables
- create workflow for behavior-based marketing automation campaigns

- consult with clients on digital strategy and situation analysis
- consult with partners on key initiatives
- analyze e-mail performance and govern execution strategy
- present findings and case studies with other industry professionals at conferences and webinars
- interact with sales to consult on new business opportunities
- lead efforts to expand relationships with existing clients.

CAREERS IN A DIGITAL AGENCY: PROJECT TRACK

Digital Account Coordinator

You would assist with customer support and account management for marketing clients. You would:

- implement best practice principles for e-mail creative and deployment
- communicate directly with clients through a variety of channels
- build content using HTML and CSS coding, then test them to ensure correct rendering
- plan and perform A/B testing to optimize e-mail performance
- make creative and content edits using Adobe Creative Suite
- report on e-mail metrics and provide recommendations based on Web analytic results and A/B testing
- develop lead nurture streams
- build personalized landing pages
- provide expert-level marketing advice and support.

Key Account Manager

You would be responsible for building a strong relationship and ensuring client satisfaction for key accounts. The account manager helps to ensure that both product quality and the client experience are paramount. You would:

- manage client relationships and strategy
- juggle deadlines and deliverables
- develop marketing automation strategy
- decipher HTML code and be able to make edits quickly
- create pivot tables and perform Vlookups in Excel
- understand relational tables and how they interact with a database
- be detail-oriented when it comes to documenting file structures and data governance
- be able to translate technical language into easily understood concepts and ideas
- be able to manage multiple projects simultaneously and be able to adapt to changing requirements

- be self-motivated and able to work autonomously
- report on and analyze e-mail metrics, offering actionable recommendations.

Digital Data Specialist

You would assist with data and integration projects using data management tools and CRM. You would:

- collect customer requirements, determine technical issues, and design solutions to customer needs
- identify new sources of data and methods to improve data collection, cleanliness, analysis, and reporting
- manipulate large data sets
- integrate CRM tools with marketing automation software
- use APIs to pull reporting metrics
- diagnose database sync errors
- manage database cleanup and cleansing projects
- analyze and present complex data sets
- communicate directly with clients through a variety of channels.

Digital Project Associate

You would assist with data and integration projects using marketing automation tools and CRM. You would:

- assist with data cleansing and integration projects
- perform data imports into CRM and marketing automation tools
- learn and implement best practice principles for e-mail creative and deployment
- build e-mails using HTML and CSS coding, then test them to ensure correct rendering
- outline content for e-mails and occasionally write e-mail copy
- make creative and content edits using Adobe Creative Suite
- use marketing automation tools to create content for landing pages
- report on and analyze e-mail metrics.

Digital Project Coordinator

You would assist with strategic data and integration projects using marketing automation tools and CRM. You would:

- assist with data cleansing and integration projects
- use APIs to pull reporting metrics
- diagnose database sync errors

- implement marketing automation scoring models
- communicate directly with clients through a variety of channels
- implement best practice principles for e-mail creative and deployment
- build e-mails using HTML and CSS coding, then test them to ensure correct rendering
- plan and perform A/B testing to optimize e-mail performance
- report on and analyze e-mail metrics, offering actionable recommendations
- plan and execute targeted marketing automation programs.

Digital Project Manager

You would lead strategic data and integration projects using marketing automation tools and CRM. You would:

- mentor project associates and project coordinators
- lead and manage data and integration projects
- develop marketing automation and CRM strategy
- act as CRM manager with knowledge of multiple CRM platforms
- manage client relationships and strategy
- juggle deadlines and deliverables for multiple clients at once
- keep detailed project plans and update clients on a weekly basis
- create workflow for behavior-based marketing automation campaigns
- develop lead scoring models
- create and perform A/B testing to optimize e-mail sends
- use marketing automation tools to create and optimize landing pages
- compile and provide recommendations for advanced e-mail and website reporting metrics.

Digital Project Strategist

You would manage a team tasked with strategic data and integration projects using marketing automation tools and CRM. You would:

- manage a team of project managers, project coordinators, and project associates
- track and manage project hours, billing, and profitability
- act as the strategic lead for key accounts
- lead strategy for all data and integration projects
- develop marketing automation and CRM strategy
- act as CRM strategist with knowledge of multiple CRM platforms
- consult with partners on key initiatives
- present findings and case studies with other industry professionals at conferences and webinars
- interact with sales to consult on new business opportunities.

CAREERS IN A DIGITAL AGENCY: ACCOUNT TRACK

Digital Graphic Designer

You would assist with the daily production and design of websites, mobile apps, and e-mails. You would:

- implement best practice principles
- communicate directly with account managers, coordinators, and associates
- juggle deadlines and deliverables for multiple clients at once
- design content and occasionally write copy
- build content using HTML and CSS coding, then test to ensure correct rendering
- design and build e-mail and landing page content using responsive design
- make creative and content edits using Adobe Creative Suite
- use CMS platforms to create content for landing pages.

Senior Digital Graphic Designer

You would support the daily production and design of websites, mobile apps, and e-mails. You would:

- work with senior digital account managers and digital strategists to lead design strategy
- implement best practice principles
- communicate directly with account managers, coordinators, and associates
- communicate directly with clients
- juggle deadlines and deliverables for multiple clients at once
- design content and occasionally write copy
- build content using HTML and CSS coding, then test to ensure correct rendering
- use JavaScript to enhance Web form functionality
- design and build e-mail and landing page content using responsive design
- make creative and content edits using Adobe Creative Suite
- use CMS platforms to create content for landing pages.

Digital Account Associate

You would assist with the customer support and account management of website, search, analytics, mobile app, and e-mail clients. You would:

- learn and implement best practice principles
- build content using HTML and CSS coding, then test to ensure correct rendering
- outline content and occasionally write copy

- make creative and content edits using Adobe Creative Suite
- use CMS platforms to create content for landing pages
- report on and analyze key performance metrics.

Digital Account Coordinator

You would assist with the customer support and account management of website, search, analytics, mobile app, and e-mail clients. You would:

- receive customer support calls
- implement best practice principles
- communicate directly with clients through a variety of channels
- update data spec documentation
- build content using HTML and CSS coding, then test to ensure correct rendering
- outline content and occasionally write copy
- plan and perform A/B testing to optimize conversion performance
- make creative and content edits using Adobe Creative Suite
- use CMS platforms to create content for landing pages
- report on and analyze key performance metrics, offering actionable recommendations.

Digital Account Manager

You would manage accounts for website, search, analytics, mobile app, and e-mail clients. You would:

- implement best practice principles
- manage client relationships
- communicate directly with clients through a variety of channels
- juggle deadlines and deliverables for multiple clients at once
- outline content and occasionally write copy
- build content using HTML and CSS coding, then test to ensure correct rendering
- create workflow for behavior-based marketing automation campaigns
- plan and perform A/B testing to optimize conversion performance
- make creative and content edits using Adobe Creative Suite
- use CMS platforms to create content for landing pages
- report on and analyze website and e-mail metrics, offering actionable recommendations.

Senior Digital Account Manager

You would lead the account management of website, search, analytics, mobile app, and e-mail clients. You would:

- mentor digital account managers, digital account coordinators, and digital account associates
- ensure best practice principles and act as quality control on your team

- manage client relationships and strategy
- coordinate and manage development team tasks
- juggle deadlines and deliverables for multiple clients at once
- develop omni-channel digital marketing strategy
- update data spec documentation
- create workflow for behavior-based marketing automation campaigns
- plan and perform A/B testing to optimize conversion performance
- make creative and content edits using Adobe Creative Suite
- use CMS platforms to create content for landing pages
- report on and analyze website and e-mail metrics, offering actionable recommendations.

Digital Account Strategist

You would manage a team tasked with the account management of website and e-mail clients. You would:

- manage a team of digital account managers, digital account coordinators, and digital account associates
- track and manage project hours and profitability
- act as the strategic lead for key accounts
- lead strategy for all team deliverables, e-mails, blogs, and social media posts
- develop behavior-based website and marketing automation strategy
- create workflow for behavior-based marketing automation campaigns
- consult with clients on digital strategy and situation analysis
- consult with partners on key initiatives
- analyze e-mail performance and govern execution strategy
- present findings and case studies with other industry professionals at conferences and webinars
- initiate add-on sales opportunities across all client account divisions.

Note: The information contained in the digital agency sections of the appendix has been generously provided by innovative digital agency Whereoware, located in Chantilly, Virginia. The author especially thanks Dan Caro for his assistance in providing the information for this section.

DIRECT MARKETING CAREER RESOURCES

Investigate the following resources to obtain additional information about direct marketing careers:

- Marketing EDGE is a national non-profit that helps college students develop the skills that employers are looking for. Marketing EDGE programs are designed to encourage participation, equip professors with the most up-to-date educational resources, and prepare students for careers in the field. Go to www.findyouredge.org for information on upcoming programs and ongoing resources.

- Some other online sources for internships, jobs, and career support are:
  - Wayup.com
  - LinkedIn.com
  - Indeed.com

Note: The information contained in this final section of the appendix has been generously provided by Marketing EDGE. The author is grateful to Terri Herschlag of Marketing EDGE for her assistance with the appendix, and to Marketing EDGE for its constant support of and commitment to direct marketing education and career placement.

Appendix C
BRANDED DIGITAL MARKETING CERTIFICATION PROGRAMS*

BRANDED DIGITAL MARKETING CERTIFICATION PROGRAM OPTIONS

Table C-1 Certification programs (alphabetically ordered by brand)

Brand	Program
Bing	Bing Ads Accredited Professional
	(see https://advertise.bingads.microsoft.com/en-us/resources/training/get-accredited)
	Bing's program offers one certification path on marketing with Bing ads.
Facebook	Facebook Blueprint
	(see https://www.facebook.com/blueprint/certification/certs)
	There are two certifications: 1) Facebook Certified Planning Professional and 2) Facebook Certified Buying Professional. Both focus on Facebook advertising skills, but the planning program includes analytics and management skills whereas the buying program focuses on technical skills for buying and optimizing Facebook ad campaigns.
Google	Academy of Ads
	(see https://academy.exceedlms.com/)
	Google's Academy for Ads includes courses and learning paths on several digital marketing topics. Google Ads Certification requires completion of the Google Ads Fundamentals course and one advanced course chosen from the following list: Search Advertising, Display Advertising, Mobile Advertising, Video Advertising, and Shopping Advertising. Students may complete multiple advanced courses for certification in each area.
Hootsuite Platform	Hootsuite Academy: Hootsuite Platform
	(see https://hootsuite.com/education)
	Hootsuite Platform is the first program in a series offered as part of the Hootsuite Academy. Marketing educators can register classes for free course access including Hootsuite Platform Certification.

(Continued)

Table C-1 (Continued)

Brand	Program
Hootsuite Social	Hootsuite Academy: Hootsuite Social (see https://hootsuite.com/education) Hootsuite Social is the second program in the Hootsuite Academy series. Course access is free for classes registered by university marketing educators but certification requires a paid fee.
Hubspot	Hubspot Academy (see https://academy.hubspot.com/certification) Hubspot Academy certification programs include email marketing, inbound marketing, social media marketing, content marketing, marketing software, sales enablement, and more. There are also courses (without certification options) on search engine optimization, Facebook advertising, and Facebook marketing.
Twitter	Twitter Flight School (see https://twitterflightschool.com) Twitter offers a marketing leadership and an executive leadership "flight path." Courses focus on Twitter ad campaigns, Twitter content strategy, and integrating Twitter in marketing communications campaigns.

ADVANTAGES AND DISADVANTAGES OF CERTIFICATION PROGRAMS

Table C-2 Advantages and disadvantages

Brand	Overall Value	Advantages	Disadvantages
Bing	Low	• No program/course cost • Lessons designed as series of short videos • Coverage relevant in advertising and digital marketing courses • Appropriate for face-to-face (F2F) and distance education (DE) courses	• Less industry recognition than Google certification • Bing-product specific with little coverage of general digital advertising content
Facebook	Low	• No program/course cost • Lessons use short videos • Coverage relevant for advertising and social media marketing courses • Appropriate for F2F and DE	• Fee ($150) charged for the certification exam • Facebook-specific knowledge for on-site advertising • Exams must be taken in-person at approved proctoring center
Google	High	• No program/course cost • Widely recognized by industry • Popular industry products • Multiple topics including AdWords, search advertising, video advertising, mobile advertising, shopping, and analytics	• Wait period required to repeat failed exams • Specific to Google products • Extensive coverage of tactical content and vocabulary may distract from course emphasis on theory and strategy

Brand	Overall Value	Advantages	Disadvantages
		• Lessons designed as learning paths of short videos with supplemental supporting materials • Well-designed course materials • Relevant advertising and digital marketing courses • Appropriate for F2F and DE	• Addressing student questions and problems with academy interface can be time-consuming
Hootsuite Platform	Low	• No program/course cost • Certification never expires • Popular industry product • Lessons use short videos and supporting materials • Appropriate for F2F and DE	• Primarily platform-specific information not applicable to other vendor products or marketing in general • Social media marketing focus
Hootsuite Social	Moderate	• No program/course cost • Certification never expires • Coverage of social media marketing information valuable for courses in advertising, digital marketing, and social media marketing • Lessons designed as series of short videos with supporting materials • Well-designed materials with high-quality content coverage • Appropriate for F2F and DE	• Fee ($199) for exam required for certification • Lessons may not consistently track to marketing course content • Lesson vocabulary is not always consistent with that in marketing textbooks • Focus on social media marketing but not other digital marketing topics
Hubspot	Moderate	• No program/course cost • Many digital marketing topics • Coverage relevant for courses in digital marketing, advertising, social media marketing, content marketing, selling and sales, and marketing operations • Lessons as series of short videos • Well-designed materials with high-quality content coverage • Appropriate for F2F and DE • Digital badges enhance LinkedIn profiles	• Best when marketing educator matches course topics to specific certification programs in Hubspot Academy (somewhat time intensive)
Twitter	Low	• No program/course cost • Lessons designed around learning paths tied to social media marketing jobs • Utilizes short videos and quizzes • Relevant for advertising and social media marketing courses • Appropriate for F2F and DE	• Focus on use of Twitter for content marketing and/or advertising on Twitter • Little industry awareness of program

Note: This appendix was coauthored by Lisa Spiller and Tracy Tuten and is adapted from: 'Assessing the pedagogical value of branded digital marketing certification programs,' *Journal of Marketing Education,* January, 2019, pp. 1–14.

Appendix D
DIRECT AND DIGITAL MARKETING CAMPAIGN PROPOSAL GUIDE[1]

This guide is designed to help professors and students create direct and digital marketing campaign proposals for class projects and cases for real-world clients. A detailed Campaign Proposal guide, complete with samples and examples, is available to faculty via the online Textbook Supplements.

The fundamental foundation and perhaps the most important detail in successfully developing a direct marketing campaign proposal for any real-world client project is: **Research drives strategy!** This is emphasized in the following theoretical foundations.

THEORETICAL FOUNDATIONS

- The overall campaign's marketing strategy must demonstrate an understanding of the client situation and the project/case challenge.
- Justification of all strategies recommended should flow from detailed market research findings. Strategic recommendations without solid research to support them are not sound.
- The campaign must logically flow from the research that supports its hypotheses, strategies, media choices, offers, response rates, and creative samples.
- The overall campaign development and the projected results must be realistic.
- Often, students want to rush to the creative development portion of the campaign, but quickly realize that they don't have the knowledge needed to craft enticing offers and really alluring creative materials without having deep knowledge about their target market.
- Students/student teams should collect both secondary and primary research information. The more data they can obtain, the better informed they will be to determine their campaign strategies.

ACTIVITIES AND ELEMENTS TO INCLUDE

- While many students today may have a tendency to 'Google' every word to obtain secondary research, they should use other, less obvious sources such as industry-specific journals and publications or corporate materials.

- Each client challenge requires different market research methodology. Students should utilize a variety of primary data collection methods, including surveys, focus group discussions, in-depth interviews, observation methods, and experiments.
- Networking is an effective method to securing market research assistance. Faculty may help connect students with appropriate business professionals, alumni, community leaders, and so on, who are willing to serve as key informants for the research phase of any real-world client project.
- Using Simmons and MRI data, even if dated, about psychographics and media preferences is important.
- Periodical literature research of the business press will define what others have said about the project situation review and will provide additional insights for students about other campaigns that might have an impact on what they are trying to accomplish.
- Review of 10-Ks and other financial data will give insight into the profit structure of competitors and establish ROI threshold objectives for the project.
- Regardless of the research methods employed, students/student teams must learn as much as possible about the company, industry, competitors, and consumers, and really put their arms around the project.
- Empowered with all of this data, students are now in a position to analyze and synthesize the data. This involves answering the following questions: How do we present all this research concisely so that the reader will be engaged and so that our strategies will be understood? How do we use the research to logically build our strategies?
- Students should be encouraged to play with the data and ask probing questions: What can be gleaned from all of this information? What trends are indicated? What have competitors or similar marketing companies in other industries done that could indicate a successful marketing strategy with this challenge? What segmentation strategies should be applied? What offers are most desirable to the target audience? What media preferences do they have? How can we develop a meaningful strategy to spend the budget that has been allocated for the campaign?

CAMPAIGN PROPOSAL ELEMENTS

Research, Analysis and Strategies

- Secondary research overviewed with proper referencing of sources used
- Primary research methodology explained
- Overview of all relevant secondary and primary research findings
- Key research findings provided in a data/strategy table and in graphs and charts.

Consumer and Offer Strategies

- Identification of desired benefits for each market segment/sub-segment (if applicable)
- Consumer analysis summarized to drive strategies for each segment

- Brand strategies (logo, tagline, trademark character usage) integration plan provided (if applicable)
- Effective offer strategies—detailed and logical
- Offer test explained with detailed testing format/process described (optional)
- Detailed/adequate explanation of customer and offer strategies—tied to market research findings.

List Strategies (optional)

- List recommendations (ranked by priority) based on list research
- List explanations and detailed-list selects explained (in list table format)
- Adequate justification of list strategies for each market segment (if applicable)
- List digital data cards/pages included
- Detailed/adequate list strategy explanations—tied to research findings.

Creative Strategies

- Explanation of creative concept
- Creative brief developed and provided
- Creative implementation plan provided
- All creative materials developed and included
- Consistent use of the campaign 'big idea' throughout all creative executions
- Unique creative content recommended for each market segment (if applicable)
- Detailed/adequate creative strategy explanations—tied to research findings.

Media Strategies

- Media strategies explained and tied to research findings
- Logical (given client market objectives and research findings)
- Detailed communication plan and media mix table for consumer segments/prospects
- Detailed/adequate media strategy explanations—tied to research findings.

Budget Allocation and Profit Analysis Strategies

- Marketing campaign overview with all cost estimates explained
- All marketing campaign costs within budget
- Itemized budget table provided
- Detailed/adequate justification for expenditures
- Accurate quantitative methods used for all profit and ROI calculations
- Profit tables included (break-even, cost-per-response, net profit, and ROI projections at multiple response-rate levels).

Executive Summary

The purpose of an executive summary is to summarize the marketing campaign, focusing on market research, marketing strategy, media plan, creative strategy, and budget and ROI metrics. An executive summary:

- foreshadows succinctly what is to follow
- gives a clear understanding, implications, and actions
- is written keeping in mind busy clients at the executive level
- is normally written last once the campaign details have been established
- should be one page or less.

Appendices

Appendixes should provide backup for the executive summary, such as primary research questionnaires, additional research findings, media plan charts, detailed budget/ROI calculations, creative samples, references and citations, and so on. Citations for assumptions made should be provided along with substantiations for industry standards (e.g., costs, response rates). Are substantiations/citations provided that support the market research? Are they valid and clear? Are the appendices indexed/organized well versus a dumping ground?

Layout/Format/Grammar

- Title page
- Detailed table of contents (TOC)
- Executive summary
- Concise writing style
- Headings and subheadings used
- Tabbed dividers and organized binder (if hardcopy is being produced)
- Professional appearance
- Free from typographical, grammatical, and punctuation errors.

Oral Presentation/Client Pitch

- Preparation of slide presentation—format, slide quantity, slide quality
- Delivery—voice, tone, pace, transitions, eye contact, gestures, confidence
- Professionalism—delivery mannerisms, professional dress
- Time limits—multiple rehearsals needed to adhere to length allocations
- Quality of overall 'pitch'—passion, interest, and 'proposed' marketing campaign.

NOTE

1. This guide was created by Lisa Spiller and David Marold (Eastern Michigan University) based on our individual teaching experience and our collective experience advising student teams, both graduate and undergraduate, to participate in the Marketing EDGE Collegiate ECHO Challenge. A number of our respective teams have won Gold, Silver, Bronze and other awards in the Marketing EDGE Collegiate ECHO Challenge over the past 20 years.

    Some of the work in this campaign guide is based on the paper published in the *Journal of Advertising Education* (Volume 14, Number 1, Spring 2010), 'Creating Winners for Life: How to prepare your students to become IDM professionals by using the DMEF's Collegiate ECHO Challenge as a teaching aid,' co-authored by Lisa. D. Spiller, Christopher Newport University; Harvey Markovitz, Pace University; and David W. Marold, Eastern Michigan University.

GLOSSARY

A/B test   designed to compare the effectiveness of two alternatives of marketing activities.

abandonment rule   when visitors start to complete a form and then stall or close the form—at which point a proactive Chat invitation can be issued to help complete the task.

ad fraud   the process of creating fake traffic, clicks, impressions, and other engagements to generate revenue through ads.

ad injections   these operate by replacing ads on a specific website with malicious ads or ads not intended by the publisher.

ad note   a small sticker that is placed on the front page of a newspaper that can be peeled off without damaging the newspaper.

AdWords   keywords used to describe or promote something.

affiliate marketing   a type of marketing that will manage relationships and actually reward people for referring others to a product or service.

aging   the recency of the site.

allowable margin   the amount of money that can be spent to get an order, while still permitting some left over for media costs and the designated profit to be made; also known as advertising allowable.

alternative hypothesis   the hypothesis that is determined when a null hypothesis is proven wrong.

annoyance   in marketing terms, it is the way people feel when they receive too many unsolicited marketing communications.

appeal   the message content of an offer that addresses consumer needs, wants or interests and entices action.

auto responders   e-mails that are automatically sent, when triggered by some variable or some event.

backlinks   the quality of links, number of broken links, the anchor text, and the positioning of the link.

banner advertising   the digital analog to print ads, targeting a broad audience with the goal of creating awareness about the product or service being promoted.

big idea   the idea that becomes the company's logo, slogan or tagline. It is the highlighted unique selling proposition (USP) or creative expression that is the focal point of a whole promotional campaign.

bingo card   an insert or page of a magazine that is created by the publishers to provide a numeric listing of advertisers; also called an information card.

blog   a website that contains continuously updated information that is posted for all viewers to read.

bots   computer programs that are designed to mimic human interaction on a website or an ad.

brand marketing   marketing that boosts knowledge of a company or product's name, logo or slogan.

break even   the point at which the gross profit on a unit sale equals the cost of making that unit sale.

broadcast   television and radio that can be used as methods for direct response advertising.

business-to-business (B2B) marketing   the process of providing goods and services to industrial market intermediaries, as opposed to ultimate consumers.

business-to-government (B2G) marketing   the process of providing goods and services to government agencies and organizations.

button chat   the call-to-action icon resident on a page to enable a visitor to initiate a chat.

call abandonment   in telemarketing, the number of callers that hang up before being serviced by a sales representative.

call center   a dedicated team, supported by various telephone technological resources, that provides a response to customer inquiries.

catalog   a multipage direct mail booklet that displays photographs and/or descriptive details of products/services along with prices and order details.

cause-related marketing   a commercial activity by which businesses and charities or causes form a partnership with each other to market an image, product or service for mutual benefit.

chi-square (χ^2) test   a statistical technique for determining whether an observed difference between the test and the control in an experiment is significant.

chief privacy officer (CPO)   a corporate officer whose responsibility it is to protect the sensitive information the corporation collects, from credit card accounts to health records.

chit   an additional enclosure card or separate slip of paper that highlights a free gift or some other information.

classic format   a direct mail package consisting of an outer envelope, letter, circular, order form, and a reply envelope.

click farm   where people are paid to click on content and engage with an ad in ways that remove the predictability inherent in bot interactions.

click-through rate   the number of times a user clicks on an online ad, often measured as a function of time.

click-to-chat a form of Web-based communication in which a person clicks on an icon to request an immediate connection to another person in real time.

code of ethics a code that generally serves as a guideline for making ethical decisions.

cohort a group of people who have in common a specific experience or characteristic.

cold call a telemarketing term that indicates there is no existing relationship with or recognition of the direct marketer by the customer or potential customer.

collectivist culture a culture in which emphasis is placed on the group as a whole.

compiled lists prospect lists that have been generated by a third party or market research firm via directories, newspapers, public records, and so on. The individuals on these lists do not have a purchase response history.

connecting sites serve as media to connect people for various reasons.

content marketing a strategic marketing approach focused on creating and distributing valuable, relevant, and consistent content to attract and retain a clearly defined audience.

continuity selling offers that are continued on a regular (weekly, monthly, quarterly, annually) basis; also called club offers.

contract manufacturing the process by which a company contracts a local manufacturer to produce goods for the company.

control group a group of subjects on which an experiment is not conducted.

conversion the movement of a prospective customer to a definite buying customer.

conversion rate the rate at which leads are converted into sales.

cookie an electronic tag on the consumer's computer that enables the website to follow consumers as they shop and recognize them on return visits.

cookie stuffing the malicious utilization of the website tracking system by placing cookies from other websites on the original publisher's website without the user being informed.

cooperative mailings provide participants, usually noncompeting direct response advertisers, with opportunities to reduce mailing costs in reaching common prospects.

copy appeal the essential theme, which generally stems from fundamental human needs, of the whole promotion or campaign.

cost of goods sold all costs related to manufacturing or producing a good or service.

cost per click how much the person is willing to bid to show the ad.

cost per inquiry (CPI) promotion costs divided by the number of inquiries (people who responded but did not yet order); also known as cost per lead, or CPL.

cost per response (CPR)   the total promotion budget divided by the total number of orders and/or inquiries received.

cost per viewer (CPV)   the total promotion budget divided by the total number of people in the viewing audience.

coupon   an offer by a manufacturer or retailer that includes an incentive for the purchase of a product or service in the form of a specified price reduction.

cross-selling   an important characteristic of direct marketing where new and related products (or even unrelated products) are offered to existing customers.

crowdfunding   the practice of engaging a group to request financial support.

crowdsourcing   the practice of engaging a group for a common goal — often innovation, problem solving, or efficiency via technology.

customer acquisition   the process of gaining a customer.

customer advocacy   a customer's promotion of a company or brand; positive word of mouth, referrals, product reviews, and blog posts.

customer database   a list of customer names to which additional information has been added in a systematic fashion.

customer journey map   a visual depiction of every interaction and experience a customer has with a company or an organization.

customer lifetime value (CLTV)   the discounted stream of revenue a customer will generate over the lifetime of their relationship or patronage with a company.

customer loyalty program   a program sponsored by the organization or firm that encourages customer repeat purchases through program enrollment processes and the allocation of rewards and/or benefits.

customer relationship management (CRM)   a business strategy to select and manage customers to optimize value.

customer retention   the processes and actions companies put forth to receive continued business and create ongoing relationships with customers.

customer satisfaction   the extent to which a firm fulfills a consumer's needs, desires, and expectations.

data management platform   a centralized computing system that collects, integrates, and manages large sets of data (structured and unstructured) from disparate sources.

data mining   the process of using statistical and mathematical techniques to extract customer information from a customer database to draw inferences about an individual customer's needs and predict future behavior.

data security   the safeguarding and securing of data from unauthorized access or damage.

database analytics   the direct marketer analyzes customer information housed within the customer database to draw inferences about an individual customer's needs.

database enhancement   adding and overlaying information to records to better describe and understand the customer.

degrees of freedom   the number of observations that are allowed to vary.

delivery drones   unmanned aerial vehicles being used to transport lightweight packages to customers in record time.

demographics   identifiable and measurable statistics that describe the consumer population.

dependent variable   a variable in whose outcome or effect the research is interested.

derived demand   demand resulting from demand of something else; for example, demand for industrial goods is ultimately derived from consumer demand.

digital marketing   the process of using technology and its full capabilities to communicate seamlessly with consumers through the Internet and technological devices.

direct investment   the process whereby a company entering a foreign market acquires an existing company or forms a completely new company.

direct mail   the leading print medium that direct marketers use for direct-response advertising.

direct marketing   a database-driven interactive process of directly communicating with targeted customers or prospects, using any medium, to obtain a measurable response or transaction via one or multiple channels.

domain spoofing   where advertisements are created that effectively mimic a trusted domain and generate traffic and engagement to the falsified website.

duty   a tax charged by a government, especially on imports.

e-fulfillment   the integration of people, processes, and technology to ensure customer satisfaction before, during, and after the online buying experience.

e-mail   is a part of the Internet that operates independently from the Web, allowing global communication through the Internet without being indexed on any search engines.

electronic commerce (e-commerce)   the completion of buying and selling transactions online.

electronic data interchange (EDI)   the process by which businesses may exchange information electronically.

emotional appeal   targets consumer wants, desires, and feelings, such as social status, prestige, power, recognition, and acceptance.

ethics   a branch of philosophy; a system of human behavior concerned with morality: the rightness and wrongness of individual actions or deeds.

experiment   a procedure designed to measure the effect of change, often called a 'test' by direct marketers.

experimentation   manipulation of one or more controllable factors.

exporting   where a company sells its products from its home base without any personnel physically located overseas.

fair balance   presenting both the product's benefits and the product's adverse effects in totality and equal weight.

firmographics   descriptive characteristics of individual firms for market segmentation in B2B markets.

fixed costs   costs associated with a business that do not vary with production or number of units sold.

frequency   the number of ad insertions purchased in a specific communication vehicle within a specified time period.

fulfillment   the act of carrying out a customer's expectations by sending the ordered product to the customer or delivering the service agreed upon.

geo-filters   filters or lenses that change based on the customer's geographical location.

geo-tag   a chip of data embedded in a digital media file to provide geographical information about a subject.

geo-tagging   implies that a customer's physical location is registered from their mobile device's GPS or computer's IP address.

Geographic Information System (GIS)   a computer system capable of obtaining, storing, analyzing, and displaying geographically referenced information known according to position.

global market segmentation (GMS)   the practice of identifying particular segments, country groups, or individual consumer groups across countries of potential customers who display similar behaviors in buying.

Global Positioning System (GPS)   a segmentation tool that associates latitude and longitude coordinates with street addresses.

gross domestic product (GDP)   the total market value of all final goods and services produced in a certain year within a nation's borders.

gross rating points (GRPs)   a mathematical value computed by multiplying reach by frequency that measures the number of people exposed to an ad.

gross sales   total sales made.

hashtags   the pound symbol (#) followed by a word or phrase; simplifies users' search of topics.

hotline names   the most recent names acquired by specific list owners, though there is no uniformity as to what chronological period 'recent' describes.

house lists   lists of an organization's own customers (active as well as inactive) and responders.

hypertext markup language (HTML)   a simple coding system used to format documents for viewing by Web clients.

hypothesis   an assertion about the value of the parameter of a variable based on a tentative explanation for a set of facts to be further tested.

hypothesis testing   an assertion about the value of the parameter of a variable (the researcher decides) on the basis of observed facts, such as the relative response to a test of variation in advertising.

inbound calls   a category of telemarketing where customers place calls to an organization to place an order, request more information, or obtain customer service.

independent variable   a controllable factor in an experiment.

individualist culture   a culture in which emphasis and value are in the individual.

industrial demand   market demand that is characterized by being derived from final consumer demand, being inelastic with little price sensitivity, being widely fluctuating, and having well-informed or knowledgeable buyers.

industrial goods   products that are generally used as raw materials or in the fabrication of other goods.

inelastic demand   an economic situation, evident with industrial goods, where the quantity demanded has little impact on price sensitivity.

influencer marketing   a form of content-driven marketing where the content shared is akin to an endorsement or testimonial by a third party or potential consumer.

infomediary   a company that acts as a third party by gathering personal information from a user and providing it to other sites, with the user's approval.

infomercial   a relatively long commercial in the format of a television program that informs viewers about a featured product.

infrastructure   normally a leading indicator of economic development of a country, including the essential services that support business activities.

insert   a popular form of print advertisement commonly used in a magazine or newspaper.

integrated order fulfillment   a term based on the idea that the process of building and delivering products should not begin until after an order has been taken.

intellectual property   products of the mind or ideas.

interactive marketing   two-way communications between the marketer and the prospective customer.

interest-based advertising   the collection of information about consumer online activities and Web viewing behaviors, over time and across non-affiliate websites, to deliver tailored ads.

involvement devices   devices used in direct-response advertising to spur action by involving the reader; examples are tokens, stamps, punch-outs, puzzles, and so on.

Johnson Boxes   boxes in which copy is placed inside text boxes to highlight certain content and to enable the content to stand out in the letter.

joint venture   where two or more investors join forces to conduct a business by sharing ownership and control.

key code   a unique identifier placed on the response device or order form prior to mailing a promotional piece to track and measure results.

keyword density   the number of times that the keyword in a search appears on that website.

layout   the positioning of copy and illustrations in print media to gain attention and direct the reader through the message in an intended sequence.

lead nurturing   connecting and interacting with the customer, where customer engagement is pursued with the communication of relevant information to all leads, all the time.

letter   the principal element of the direct mail package that provides the primary means for communication and personalization.

licensee   a foreign business that enters into an agreement and becomes authorized to manufacture or sell specific brand products in its country on behalf of a licensor.

licensing   similar to franchising, local businesses become authorized to manufacture or sell specific brand products for another company.

licensor   a company located in the home or domestic country that permits overseas manufacturing to occur.

lift   an increase in the average response rate due to making an offer to only those market segments or clusters that are predicted to be most responsive.

list brokers   those who serve as intermediaries to bring list users and list owners together.

list compilers   organizations that develop lists and data about them, often serving as their own list managers and brokers.

list managers   managers who represent the interests of list owners and have the authority and responsibility to be in contact with list brokers and list users on behalf of list owners.

list owners   those who describe and acquire prospects (as market segments) who show the potential of becoming customers.

location-based mobile (LBM)   a program that enables smartphone users to 'check in' to a location, such as a business, and to see other friends' locations.

management contracting   the process whereby a contract is signed with foreign locals or the government to manage the business in that country's market.

market penetration   the proportion of customers to some benchmark.

market segmentation   a marketing strategy devised to attract and meet the needs of a specific submarket where those submarkets are homogeneous.

market segments   placing people (customers or potential customers) into homogeneous groups based on attributes such as age, income, stage in the family life cycle, and so on.

marketing automation   software platforms and technologies designed to effectively carry out marketing activities on multiple online channels, including e-mail, social media, and websites.

marketing funnel   is the progression or stages of the customer or client journey.

match code   abbreviated information about a customer record that is constructed so that each individual record can be matched, pairwise, with every other record.

matchback   the procedure by which an order response is tracked back to the starting place (catalog or offer) from which it was generated.

media efficiency ratio (MER)   a ratio that is calculated by dividing infomercial sales by the media cost.

meme   a self-explanatory symbol, using words, actions, sounds, or pictures, to communicate an entire idea.

merge-purge   a computerized process used to identify and delete duplicate names/addresses within various lists.

micro-targeting   the creation and direct delivery to customers of customized winning messages, proof points, and offers, and accurately predicting their impact.

mobile application   an Internet software program to run on handheld devices such as smartphones.

morals   the judgment of the goodness or badness of human action and character.

motivation   a need that compels a person to take action or behave in a certain way.

multibuyer   an individual whose name/address appears on two or more response lists simultaneously.

multichannel distribution   a marketer using several competing channels of distribution to reach the same target customers.

multimedia messaging service (MMS)   is a method by which messages that include multimedia content can be sent to and from mobile devices.

near field communications (NFC)   location-based communications via short-range wireless technology that makes use of interacting electromagnetic radio fields.

negative option   where the shipment of a product is sent automatically unless the customer specifically requests that it not be.

net profit   the amount of money a company retains after the fixed costs are subtracted from the gross revenues and before taxes; also known as net profit margin.

nixie   mail that has been returned by the U.S. Postal Service because it is undeliverable as addressed.

North American Free Trade Agreement (NAFTA)   an agreement to eliminate tariffs between three North American countries: Canada, Mexico, and the United States.

North American Industry Classification System (NAICS)   an industrial classification system using a six-digit code that focuses on production activities.

null hypothesis   the statistical hypothesis that there is no difference between the means of the groups being compared.

offer   the terms under which a specific product or service is promoted to the customer.

offer box   a text box in which an offer is stated and a call to action or buy button appears.

omni-channel marketing   a concentrated, seamless approach to delivering a consistent brand experience across all available channels and devices a customer uses to interact with a company or an organization and its brands.

online panels   online discussions marketers conduct with people who have agreed to talk about a selected topic over a period of time.

online PR   any type of public relations conducted digitally.

optimization   the process of improving website traffic through the use of search engines.

outbound calls   a category of telemarketing where firms place calls to prospects or customers.

outsourcing   a telemarketing term referring to the process of having all call center activities handled by an outside organization or a service bureau.

overstatement of efficacy   the regulation of superlative interpretations of 'quality of life claims' in pharmaceutical marketing materials.

package inserts   printed offers for products and services included in an order purchased by the recipient.

packing slip   a form or document that identifies the products to be included with an order.

partner relationship management (PRM)   the generation of greater value to customers through companies' cooperation and close work with partners in other companies or departments.

pathing   the sequence in which pages are viewed.

permission marketing   the process of obtaining the consent of a customer before a company sends out online marketing communication to that customer via the Internet.

personalized URL (PURL)   a personalized Web page or microsite that incorporates the prospect's name and is tailored to their interests based on information known about them.

picking list   a list identifying each item on an order list and serving as a routing guide to move the picker efficiently through a warehouse.

platform business model   a model whereby value is created by platforms that connect two or more multi-sided parties, where the parties are dependent on the platform.

political micro-targeting   combining groups of voters based on information about them that is accessible through databases and the Internet, to target them with specific messages.

positioning   a marketing strategy that enables marketers to understand how each consumer perceives a company's product or service based on important attributes; also known as product positioning.

positive option   the process whereby a customer must specifically request shipment of a product for each offer in a series.

PR value   how often Google and other search engines index a site or how often they send their spiders to index it.

preprinted inserts   newspaper advertisements that are usually printed ahead of the newspaper production and are distributed with the newspaper.

prerecorded message   a stored voice message that one may access through various triggers.

price elasticity   the relative change in demand for a product given the change in the price of the product.

price penetration   a pricing strategy used when the objective is to maximize sales volume by charging a low price that will attract and be affordable to nearly all consumers in the given market.

price skimming   a pricing strategy used when the objective of the price is to generate the largest possible return on investment (ROI), where the price must be set at the highest possible level to 'skim the cream' off the top of the market and only target a select number of consumers who can afford to buy the product/service.

privacy   a level of control consumers have over information provided.

Privacy Act of 1974   an act that determined whether limits on what the federal government could do with personal information should be applied to the private sector as well.

privacy fundamentalists   people who believe that they own their name, as well as all the information about themselves, and that no one else may use it without their permission.

privacy pragmatists   people who look at the contact, offer, and the methods of data collection and apply a cost–benefit analysis to make a determination about a marketer's use of information.

privacy unconcerned   those who literally do not care about the issue of privacy at all.

proactive chat   a visitor has triggered a business rule and the chat invitation 'pops in' to the page with a relevant call to action.

proactive telephone marketing   also called 'Outbound calls' are telephone marketing calls where the initiator of the marketing communications is the marketer.

procurement   the procedures or processes by which government organizations buy products and services.

product differentiation   a strategy that uses innovative design, packaging, and positioning to make a clear distinction between products and services serving a market segment.

product positioning   a marketing strategy that enables marketers to understand how each consumer perceives a company's product or service based on important attributes; also called positioning.

promoted tweets   where marketers pay to have their tweets pushed on to people's feeds, regardless of whether those consumers follow the business or not.

psychographics   the study of lifestyles, habits, attitudes, beliefs, and value systems of individuals.

quality score   measures how relevant your keyword is to your ad text and to a user's search query.

quick response codes   two-dimensional barcodes that can be read by barcode scanners on smartphones; also known as QR codes.

random assignment   a component of a valid experiment that refers to the fact that both control and experiment group subjects must be assigned completely arbitrarily so that differences between groups occur by chance alone.

rational appeal   targets a consumer's logical buying motives and presents facts in a logical manner.

reach   the number of people exposed to a particular media vehicle carrying an ad.

reactive telephone marketing   also called 'Inbound calls' are telephone marketing calls where the initiator of the marketing communications is the customer.

recency/frequency/monetary (R/F/M)   a mathematical formula used to evaluate the value or sales potential of customers or prospects.

reference group   a group that influences consumers' opinions, attitudes, and behaviors.

reference individuals   the people a consumer turns to for advice.

referrals   credible recommendations.

response device   a vehicle used by a recipient of a marketing effort to answer the direct marketer's offer.

response lists   lists of those who have responded to another direct marketer's offer.

retargeting   the act of serving previously tagged website visitors display ads when they are recognized in designated online ad networks.

return on investment (ROI)   the net profit divided by the average amount invested in a company in one year; a popular tool of measurement in business.

right to confidentiality   a consumer's right to specify to a given company that information the consumer freely provides should not be shared.

right to information   includes the consumer's right to receive any and all pertinent or requested information.

right to privacy   the ability of an individual to control the access others have to their personal information.

right to safety   a right by the consumer to be protected from physical or psychological harm.

right to selection   a consumer's right to choose or make decisions about their buying behavior.

run-of-paper advertisements (ROP)   small advertisements that appear in the regular section of a newspaper where positioning of the ad is at the will of the newspaper.

salting   the process whereby a direct marketer places decoys, which are either incorrect spellings or fictitious names, on a customer list to track and identify any misuse; also called seeding.

search engine   an index of keywords that enables Web browsers to find what they are looking for.

search engine marketing (SEM)   the whole set of techniques and strategies used to direct more visitors to marketing websites from search engines.

search engine optimization (SEO)   is the process of improving website traffic from search engine results that aims to move a company's link to one of the top links on the results page.

seeding   the process whereby a direct marketer places decoys, which are either incorrect spellings or fictitious names, on a customer list to track and identify any misuse; also called salting.

self-mailer   any direct mail piece mailed without an envelope.

service bureaus   groups that provide data processing, data mining, outsourcing, online analytical processing, and so on, to support the interchange of lists and database information.

SMS text messaging   allows the marketer to track open rates, manage lists, let customers opt in and opt out, and do many of the same functions as e-mail companies.

Snapchat filters (lenses)   stickers, frames, images, and movement-sensitive animations that can be placed over Snapchat images or videos.

social networks   websites used to connect with consumers, gain insights and feedback, conduct online PR, advertise, and drive site traffic.

solo mailer   mail pieces that promote a single product or limited group of related products.

source code   the media, media vehicle, or means by which the person has responded in order to become a customer.

source data   the information contained in a customer database.

spam   unsolicited e-mail messages.

split test   a test where at least two samples are taken from the same list, each considered to be representative of the entire list, and used for package tests or to test the homogeneity of the list.

Standard Industrial Classification (SIC)   a coding system that is a means of industrial market segmentation developed by the federal government many years ago.

stealth marketing   communications secrecy in that direct marketers can communicate with small market segments or individual customers without competitors or other customers having knowledge of it.

storyboard   a series of illustrations that show the visual portion of a TV commercial.

structured data   made up of clearly defined data types whose pattern makes them easily detectable, such as transaction data.

stuffers   printed offers of products and services that are inserted in the envelope with an invoice or statement.

subscription model   a form of a time-limit offer where consumers must pay an up-front subscription price in order to receive regular delivery of or access to products and/or services for a specified period of time.

substantiation of claims   proof or evidence of truth.

Sunday supplements   mass circulation sections that are edited nationally but appear locally in the Sunday editions of many newspapers.

T1   a giant pipeline or conduit through which a user may send multiple voice, data, or video signals.

take-one rack   an alternative method of print distribution where the printed material is placed on a display rack.

telephone script   a call guide used by telemarketers to assist a telephone operator in communicating effectively with the prospect or customer.

test   a term that direct marketers may use for experiment.

til-forbid (TF)   an offer that prearranges continuous shipments on a specified basis, renewed automatically until the customer instructs otherwise.

transactional data   the information contained in a customer database that pertains to the purchases the customer has made.

trending   occurs when a topic is talked about by many users in the form of retweets and hashtags.

Type I error   results when the decision maker rejects the null hypothesis (even though it is true).

Type II error   occurs when the decision maker accepts the null hypothesis (even when it is not true).

unit margin   the amount of money each sale provides to cover fixed costs; also known as unit contribution, unit profit, or trade margin.

unstructured data   comprised of data that is typically not as defined, including formats like audio, video, and social media postings.

up-selling   the promotion of more expensive products or services over the product or service originally discussed or purchased.

variable costs   costs that vary with production and number of units sold.

variable data printing   a form of digital printing in which elements may be changed from one printed piece to the next, without re-setting the printing press or slowing down the printing process. (It is also referred to as variable printing or variable imaging.)

video annotation   a way to add interactive commentary to videos by adding background information about the video and linking related YouTube videos, channels, or search results from within a video.

violation   in marketing terms, the way people feel when they discover too much information about their personal lives is being exchanged between marketers without their knowledge and/ or consent.

viral marketing   a form of electronic word of mouth where e-mail messages are forwarded from one consumer to other consumers.

viral video   an 'infectious' video that individuals want to share, thus promoting the video and its featured products.

viralocity   measures both the number of messages and the rate of speed by which e-mail messages are forwarded by a consumer to other consumers.

virtual enterprise   a company that is primarily a marketing and customer service entity, with actual product development and distribution handled by a broad network of subcontractors.

webinar   is essentially Web conferencing software used for sales presentations.

INDEX

Page numbers in italics indicate illustrations; page numbers in bold indicate tables.